Child Care & Education

SECOND EDITION

Tina Bruce and Carolyn Meggitt

Hodder & Stoughton

A MEMBER OF THE HODDER HEADLINE GROUP

Order: please contact Bookpoint Ltd, 39 Milton Park, Abingdon, Oxon OX14 4TD. Telephone: (44) 01235 400414, Fax: (44) 01235 400454. Lines are open from 9.00–6.00, Monday to Saturday, with a 24 hour message answering service. Email address: orders@bookpoint.co.uk

British Library Cataloguing in Publication Data
A catalogue record for this title is available from The British Library

ISBN 0340 73808 1

First published 1999
Impression number   10 9 8 7 6 5 4
Year   2005   2004   2003   2002   2001   2000

Typeset by Wearset, Boldon, Tyne and Wear.
Printed in Italy for Hodder & Stoughton Educational, a division of Hodder Headline Plc, 338 Euston Road, London NW1 3BH by Printer Trento.

Contents

Acknowledgements

We gratefully acknowledge the help of Sue Grindey, Louise Clunies-Ross, Alun Thomas and Jenny Collis at the RNIB for their constructive criticism on special needs and legal issues; Martin and Alayne Levy for the biography of their daughter Hannah in Chapter 14; Peter Moss for help with the charts in Chapter 12; Jessica Stevens, Child Care Course Co-ordinator, Southfield School for Girls, Kettering, for help with the chapter on children with special needs; Christine Watson, practising midwife, and Sabrina Johnson, student, for contributing information and ideas; Pat Evans, BBC Bristol, for the article about her son, Euan, in Chapter 15; Patricia Juanette for her help with Chapter 1; Alison Mitchell for providing a valuable overview at the draft stage of the book; Trevor Chandler and Margy Whalley for help with Chapter 16 and Alison Hunt and the staff at Pen Green Centre for Under Fives and their families in Corby, Northamptonshire; Helen Tovey, Roehampton Institute; Brenda Swaddle and the staff at Eastwood Nursery School for photographs and staff at James Lee Nursery School for the room chart; the staff at the Pembury Centre for Childhood, Training and Education and Woodlands Park Nursery Centre (the Haringey Early Excellence Network); Margaret Green, Enfield Local Authority; Ruth Forbes, Curriculum Development Manager, Jigsaw Group; Tam Fry, Child Growth Foundation for the growth charts in Chapter 14; Tina would particularly like to thank Elizabeth Bevan Roberts for her wise thoughts, and Wendy Clarke and Elizabeth Rowland for their patient and stalwart support with typing. Also Susan Moxon at NIAS. We also want to thank each other for being such excellent team-mates and for being so enjoyable to work with. We owe a debt of gratitude to our students, past and present, for the insights they provide to our learning.

The authors and publishers would also like to thank the following for permission to photograph, and to reproduce copyright materials and photographs in this book:

Dana Hepburn for resourcing the sections on child development; Pen Green Centre for the Under Fives, Corby; Mrs James, Headteacher, and staff at St James's RC Primary School, Teddington; Carol Pearson, Manager, and Staff at Squirrels Day Nursery, Whitton, Lupe Cunha Picture Agency (pages 80 and 524); Photodisc Ltd (page 92); Annaphie Rogers and Alan Franks; Jane and Richard Bailey; Liz Allen for photos of Jack; Marcus Dennison and Jayne McFarlane; Martin and Alayne Levy for the photo of Hannah; Gigrazyna Lim for photo of Nina; Mike and Lisa Beevers for photo of Emily.

Our special thanks must go to Gerald Sunderland for all his help and patience in producing the specially commissioned photographs for this new edition.

For the quiet but solid support, the feeling of belonging to people
who help and empower, and the team spirit between us –
thank you to Ian, Hannah and Tom

from Tina

This book is dedicated with love and thanks to
Dave, Jonathan, Leo and Laura

from Carolyn

Introduction

The broad aim of this book is to equip readers with a basic knowledge of all aspects of child care and education up to the age of 8 years. Learning does not happen all in one go: it takes both children and adults time to learn new things. It is said that children need to sing a song a thousand times before they know the words, and adults too need time to become familiar with new ideas and words.

This book is designed to help readers understand how children develop and learn. Children, like adults, cannot be rushed in their learning. They need to reflect on what they learn practically, and they do this in their play, talk and representations of all kinds (drawings, models, dances, songs etc.). Adults reflect on and consolidate their learning by reading and writing about their new thinking and knowledge; and as they do this, they organise their ideas, share them and put them into practice.

You will find that this book is unique because whilst it introduces you to different ideas and ways of working with young children and their families, it also has a logical shape. This means that it puts principles of inclusivity and equality first. It looks at children in a holistic way, but never separate from the child's parents or carers, who are placed centrally in the book.

Throughout the book, you will find both *he* and *she* used in a balanced way. This is because both boys and girls need broad roles and relationships, as children and as they become adults. *Early childhood worker* is the term used to describe anyone who works with children from birth to 8 years of age (except parents). It includes nursery nurses, teachers, childminders, nannies, playleaders, etc. The term *early childhood setting* is used to describe the place where the child/children and early childhood worker spend their time together. For the childminder, this will be the childminder's home. For the nursery nurse, it could be a children's centre, family centre, nursery school or class, hospital, etc. Activities can be found at the end of the chapters and there is a comprehensive glossary at the end of the book.

This book will help students and tutors studying on an early childhood course, because it can be used at different levels of understanding and training. It can be used from an introductory level with a tutor's help, e.g. CCE and NVQ1, right though to the newly established Early Childhood Studies degree courses. MA students have reported its use when the chapters cause thoughts which can be followed in more depth through the bibliography. Feedback from the best-selling first edition shows that parents/carers also find a book with this kind of logical shape useful.

This book is particularly recommended for students following the CACHE Diploma in Nursery Nursing and the BTEC National Diploma in Nusery Nursing and a convenient grid at the end of the book shows how the chapters match the course modules and units.

1

Equality of Opportunity

There can be no quality in early childhood services unless there is equality of opportunity

Equality of opportunity means opening up access for every child and family to full participation in early childhood services.

Lack of access brings poor self-esteem, lack of confidence, misunderstandings, lack of respect, stereotyping and discrimination, and lack of inclusion.

It is important for early childhood workers of all kinds to work according to principles of equality and inclusivity. This is at the heart of early childhood work in every kind of setting.

GUIDELINES

Access to full participation in early childhood services

1 Children and their families need to feel part of things, and a sense of belonging.
2 It is a human right to be respected. Children and their families, especially if they belong to a minority group, need to feel valued and respected.
3 When people are narrowly labelled, they are being stereotyped. Instead, children need to build positive images of themselves, helped by those around them.
4 Most discriminating behaviour is not intended. We need to look at what we do and what we take for granted.
5 Every early years setting needs:
   ▶ a policy on equality of opportunity and inclusivity;
   ▶ a code of practice which takes the policy into action;
   ▶ regular meetings to see how it is going.

6 Individuals matter, and each of us can influence a group's efforts towards more equality of opportunity.

Promoting a sense of belonging

Being part of a group

As children grow up, they need to feel that they belong to the group: the family, the culture, the community they live in and experience.

Belonging to a group is the result of either

▶ being allocated to a group defined by someone else, for example being British born; or

▶ deciding to join a group, for example choosing to be a vegetarian, or joining a football club.

Until recently, people tended to be seen as belonging to a particular ethnic group if they shared a culture, language, physical features (e.g. skin colour) or religion. This is no longer thought to be useful. Increasingly, people choose the groups they want to be identified with.

The early childhood setting is often the first experience beyond the family and friendship network that the child joins. It is important in welcoming families that they feel a sense of belonging.

Language and bilingualism

Children are more likely to feel that they belong if their first language or home language is understood and encouraged in other settings as well as their family. It is also important to value dialect or regional accents.

▶ **Dialect** is a variant form of a language. In the Caribbean, for example, Patois is like standard English in some ways, but in other ways it is different. It might seem to a standard English speaker that a dialect speaker is speaking ungrammatical and poor English. Patois is the combination of French language with the local (mainly English) language, as used on the different islands. In Trinidad, it will be a combination of French and the way English is used on that island. The words, phrases and speed of speaking will sound like English, but Patois is not English.

▶ **Accent** is mostly to do with the way the words are pronounced. Some accents, such as Geordie or Glaswegian, can be difficult to understand for those who are not used to hearing them spoken.

Children need to feel that they belong. Being bilingual should not be considered a disadvantage in a group. Learning how to be able to communicate in more than one language helps children to learn in a much broader way. Recent studies in neuroscience give evidence that this is so.

It is very important that early childhood workers of all kinds value a child's first language. It has been known for children to be labelled as having 'no language' when in fact they simply speak a different language from English.

BALANCED BILINGUALISM

Many children are called **bilingual** by staff. Usually this means that their home language is more fluent than English. Very few children are completely balanced across two languages. Most children are unbalanced with one language more developed than the other.

TRANSITIONAL BILINGUALISM

In some early childhood settings the first language has been valued only as a bridge for learning English. It is assumed that the child will no longer need to speak the first language once English begins to take over. For example, a child who speaks Punjabi at home might be expected to speak English at school and gradually to speak English rather than Punjabi at home.

This is called **transitional bilingualism**. In fact children need to use their first language to help them transfer later on to reading and writing in the second language, which is usually English. If the child's first language is not valued as well as the new language that is being learnt, the opportunities for bilingualism and the advantages that bilingualism brings will be wasted.

In order for balanced bilingualism to occur, rather than just transitional bilingualism, children need to be given appropriate help.

- *Comprehensible input*   This phrase, used by Stephen Krashen, means enabling the child to make sense of what is being said. If the adult picks up a cup, points at the jug of orange juice and asks: 'Would you like a drink of orange juice?' the meaning is clear. If the adult just says the words without the actions and props, it is not at all clear to the child. The adult could be saying anything.
- *The period of silence when learning a language*   At first there is often a period of silence on the part of the child, while he or she listens to all the sounds of the new language, and becomes familiar with them. The adult should understand this and be patient.
- *Listening and speaking*   Children need plenty of opportunity to listen to what is being said and make sense of it before they begin to speak in the new language.
  - First there is understanding (comprehension)
  - Then the child speaks (production)
  - and then becomes fluent (performance)
- *Fluent speakers*   When children first begin to speak a new language they will not be fluent. They will make approximate sounds and communicate by intonation (tone of voice) rather than words. They are greatly helped if they can talk with people who are completely fluent and comfortable with the new language. This is why children are no longer separated and taken out of classrooms to be 'taught' English. They learn much more effectively in a real-life setting, which is relaxed and not formal, and with other children and adults who can already speak the language.
- Children need to feel that becoming bilingual is a benefit and not a disadvantage.

THE ADVANTAGES OF BEING BILINGUAL

Some children are fortunate enough to grow up learning more than one language. This helps them to learn in a broader way. When children learn more than one language they are at the same time being introduced to more than one culture in a deeply meaningful way. They are doing several things at once. This helps the brain to think more flexibly.

- They are learning a language.
- They are learning the culture that is linked with this language. In Gujurati, the words 'thank you' are used in special situations. In English they are used often, but usually just as a way of being polite rather than an expression of deep gratitude. And while in English there are two separate words for 'teaching' and 'learning', in Swedish there is only one, which is translated as 'helping children to learn'.
- They can think in different ways about the same thing, for example the Inuit language has seven words for snow compared with the one English word 'snow'. This makes it possible to think about snow in much greater detail.
- They grow up understanding different ways of thinking, and different cultural layers. This helps them to respect and value differences between people.

▶ They understand more easily that names are arbitrarily assigned to objects and that names for things can be changed. This helps them with concept formation.

▶ They find it easier to separate meanings and sounds.

▶ They can think more divergently.

▶ They are more sensitive to the emotional aspects of language, such as intonation, and they can interpret a situation more easily.

SPECIALIST SUPPORT FOR BILINGUAL AND MULTILINGUAL CHILDREN

There is now a variety of workers who support language work in early childhood settings. ESL (English as a Second Language) funding is channelled into schools in local authorities. It is targeted at children of the new Commonwealth, Indian subcontinent and Caribbean, but not the European Union. There are also ESL teachers and bilingual assistants who act as translators working with parents, nursery nurses, etc. They work in various early childhood settings, and with parents at home.

There are also Saturday and community schools, run by religious and community leaders, where, for example, children who are Jewish might learn Hebrew, and children who are Moslems learn about their religion.

A multicultural approach

In the UK we live in a **multicultural society**. This means that it is important to appreciate and understand different cultural and religious ideas, and learn how to respect them.

CULTURAL ARTEFACTS

The whole environment of the early childhood setting needs to reflect a multicultural and multilingual approach. For example, the home area, like every other area of the environment, needs to reflect objects which are familiar to children and link with their homes and culture. These are often called **artefacts of the culture**.

A home area needs to reflect familiar aspects of the child's home. It needs to build on the child's prior experiences. This means that it should have crockery, cutlery and cooking utensils in the West European style. If, for example, there are children from Chinese backgrounds in the group, it would be particularly important also to have chopsticks, bowls, woks, etc. to reflect their home culture. These would need to be available all the time.

But many children will not know about Chinese woks because they do not meet anyone who cooks with one. These children will need extra help in understanding about cultures other than their own. It is very important to include activities which introduce them to the purpose and function of, for example, Chinese ways of cooking. It is important not only that Chinese children will see their own culture reflected, but that other children will also have the opportunity to learn about different cultures in ways which will hold meaning for them, and therefore are not tokenist.

A child who has never seen a wok before will need to do real cookery with it, and be introduced to this by an adult. Remember, children learn through real first-hand experiences. It is no good simply putting a wok in the home area and hoping the children will then know about Chinese cooking. That would be tokenist.

EVERYDAY ACTIVITIES

It is particularly important to introduce children to different cultures through the activities of daily life, such as cooking. This is because they can most easily relate to these events.

For those children who have not met, for example, Chinese people, or experienced

Chinese food, it might be possible to invite someone to the nursery to demonstrate and introduce the children to another culture. It is important to remember that not all children of Chinese background will use chopsticks at home: some families might be using knives and forks. It is important not to stereotype people. (See the section later in this chapter entitled 'Avoiding Stereotypes'.)

Sets of things in the home area should not be mixed up, as this confuses everyone. It also makes it difficult for the children to value the area and take a pride in keeping it looking attractive.

There is also a great deal of opportunity for mathematical learning in sorting out chopsticks from spoons, knives and forks, and Chinese soup spoons, or knowing which sets relate to Chinese life, which to African, Indian or Asian cooking, and which to Europe.

ENCOURAGING CHILDREN TO USE WHAT THEY KNOW

The advantage of playdough, rather than pre-structured plastic food, is that children can bring their own experiences to it. They can make it into roti, pancakes, pasties or pies. This encourages children to use their cultural experience and knowledge.

Giving individual children individual help

There may be children with special educational needs using, for example, the home area, and they may need to have special arrangements in the kitchen area. A child in a wheelchair will need a lower table so that a mixing bowl can be stirred; it might be necessary to make a cooker of an appropriate height. This could be done using a cardboard box. Children love to make their own play props, and allowing them to do so makes for a much more culturally diverse selection because they can say what they need in order to make it like their homes.

Books, stories, poems, songs, action songs and games

These are useful in linking children with their previous experiences. For example, there are stories about children with disabilities or children from different cultures, and stories looking at gender issues. In the last 20 years authors have been recognising the need for children's books to link with the huge range of experiences that different children have.

Religion

Children do not choose their religion. They are born into it. As they grow up they will either accept the belief structure or not. This is also true for children who are born into families who are **atheist**, **agnostic** or **humanist**.

Some children are taught **monotheist** religious beliefs (one god). Others learn **polytheistic** beliefs (more than one god).

Monotheist	**Polytheistic**
Christianity	Pantheism
Islam	Hopi
Buddhist	
Sikh	

Every child needs to feel accepted beyond the home, in other settings. Those working with young children and their families need to learn about belief structures other than their own.

It is also important to remember that being a good person, and leading a good life, has nothing to do with belief in any god or gods. There are many people who lead good lives who are humanists, agnostics or atheists.

Some children are brought up in families which follow more than one religion. For example, there might be a Roman Catholic Christian father and a Jewish mother, or an atheist father and a Quaker Christian mother.

G U I D E L I N E S

Promoting a sense of belonging through equality of opportunity

1 **It is important to be willing to find out about different religions and to respect them. Every religion has a variety within it. For example, there are Orthodox and Reformed Jews; Roman Catholic Christians, Church of England Christians, Methodist Christians, Quaker Christians, Jehovah Witness Christians, and Mormon Christians. Ask religious leaders and parents for information.**

2 **Ask parents and voluntary organisations (e.g. SCOPE, RNIB, RNID) to help you find out about children with disabilities.**

3 **Do not be afraid to say that you don't know and that you want to find out and learn. Remember that minority groups of all kinds are as important as the mainstream groups.**

4 **Respect and value the child's home language. Think how you can make yourself understood using body language, gestures and facial expression; by pointing, by using pictures, by using actions with your words. Try asking children if they would like a drink using one of these strategies. You could use objects as props. It is important to be warm towards children. Remember to smile and enjoy interacting with them. Make sure that you are giving comprehensible language input.**

5 **Create opportunities for children to talk with other children and adults who are already fluent in English. Try to make language accompany a child's actions and describe what is happening. For example, talk with the child, describe what is happening when they cook, use clay etc.**
   (a) **Tell stories using puppets and props, flannel boards, magnet boards etc.**
   (b) **Invite children to act out pictures as you go through the story.**
   (c) **Use facial expressions, eye contact and body language to 'tell' a story and make it meaningful for the children.**

6 **Use books in different languages and tell stories in different languages. Remember that there can be problems with dual-language textbooks because although a language like English reads from left to right, a language like Urdu reads from right to left.**

7 **Invite someone who speaks the child's language to come and tell stories, for example a Hindi speaker to tell a story such as *Where's Spot?* in Hindi, using the book in that language but in a session that is for all the children in a story group. Then tell the story and use the book in English text at the next session, again with all the children in the story group. Remember that**

grandparents are often particularly concerned that children are losing their home language as they become more fluent in English (transitional bilingualism). They may enjoy coming into the group and helping in this way.

Promoting a sense of self-worth

Children need to feel a sense of their own worth. This means:
- ▶ feeling they matter to other people;
- ▶ feeling able to take an active part in things;
- ▶ feeling competent and skilled enough to do so.

Language and culture

A feeling of belonging obviously contributes to a sense of worth, and language is of deep importance in both. In the last section, the importance of recognising things that are familiar from home was stressed. If a child's first language is not reflected in settings beyond the home, a large part of the child's previous experiences is being either ignored or, possibly, actively rejected at school, in the early childhood setting, at clinic, in the local shops, etc. Some linguistic experts argue that 'language is power'. The dominant language of the culture gives those who speak it the power to discriminate against those who do not.

Standard English is the usual way of communicating in English in public, educational, professional or commercial aspects of life.

However, young children need to be confident in talking, reading and writing in their home language and supported in early childhood settings in this. This actually helps children to develop fluency and literacy in English.

It is therefore very important that the child's own language is valued and that efforts are made to develop balanced bilingualism (see p. 2).

Children with disabilities: Principles of inclusivity

It is necessary to make sure that both indoor and outdoor areas of the early childhood setting are arranged so that children with disabilities can take a full part in activities. This might involve providing ramps for wheelchairs, or making sure the light falls on the adult's face, so that a child wearing a hearing aid is able to lip read and a child with a visual impairment can use any residual eyesight to see facial expressions. It might mean having a tray on the table so that objects stay on the table, and a child with a visual impairment does not 'lose' objects that fall off.

It is helpful to some children to learn sign languages, e.g. British Sign Language and Makaton.

Gender roles

It is important to remember that some children will have learnt narrow gender roles. In the traditional home situation mothers usually do housework and fathers mend cars. Children need to see early childhood workers taking on broader gender roles, and so to learn about alternative ways for men and women to behave as men and women.

Sometimes staff think there should be 'girls only' sessions on bicycles or with block play and 'boys only' sessions in the home area, or cooking, or with the dolls' washday. This introduces children to experiences which broaden ideas of gender roles away from traditional stereotypes. It gets rid of the idea that 'boys will be boys' or that girls are born to be mothers. However, such single-sex sessions do not help girls and boys to learn about negotiating with each other, helped and supported by adults. Many researchers and educators now think this is very important, and Dunn says that relationships between boys and girls matter as much as what boys do or what girls do. The way that fathers and mothers work together in bringing up children is an area of great interest for researchers. Children often see their fathers at times when children and parents relax and have fun together, but spend more time with their mothers doing the chores and tasks of daily life. Research is showing that fathers and mothers want to redefine the roles they play in the family, so that both parents are involved in daily life tasks, and therefore both can have time to enjoy with their children. This is the case when families live apart from or with their children. In countries like Sweden, where there is paternity and maternity leave after children are born, these issues are being actively explored.

G U I D E L I N E S

Helping children to have a sense of their own worth in early childhood settings

1 **Provide familiar objects for every child in the different areas of the room. These might be cooking utensils, clothes, fabrics, etc. These are the artefacts of their culture.**
2 **Encourage children to speak to other children and adults within the early childhood setting. Remember that children might feel powerless if they cannot speak to other people.**
3 **Positive images of different children in different cultures are important. Remember that the important thing about the child is not how they look or their learning impairment, but that they are a person. The way you behave and talk will give messages about your mental image of that child.**
4 **Use stories from different cultures to introduce children to myths, legends and folk tales. The same themes crop up over and over again in different stories across the world. Find some of these universal themes in the stories you look at from different cultures, e.g. the wicked stepmother, the greedy rich person, good deeds being rewarded after suffering.**
5 **Make sure you tell stories and make displays and interest tables with positive images of children with disabilities and from different cultures, and that these are also in the book area.**
6 **Make sure the indoor and outdoor areas offer full access to activities for children with disabilities.**
7 **Make sure that children meet adults with broad gender roles in the early childhood setting, to show them that men and women are not restricted respectively to a narrow range of activities.**
8 **Don't forget that you need to have a sense of your own worth too. What did you do today that made you feel that you had a worthwhile day?**

Avoiding stereotypes

Choosing how you want to be described

When adults fill in forms they decide whether to be described as Mr, Ms, Mrs, or Miss, and whether or not they wish to describe themselves according to different ethnic categories. An adult can choose whether to be described as deaf, hearing impaired or aurally challenged. Children need to be given as much choice as possible about these aspects of their lives. If adults describe a child as 'the one with glasses', or comment 'what a pretty dress', or talk about 'the Afro-Caribbean child' they are stereotyping these children and seeing them narrowly rather than as whole people.

Children need positive images of themselves and of other people. Hazareesingh suggests that the cultural identity of a child is 'whatever children hold to be emotionally meaningful and significant, both about themselves and in their lives'.

The restricting effect of stereotypes

The most important thing about working with 'the child with glasses' might be the fact that he loves music. The most important thing about 'the Afro-Caribbean child' might be that she loves mathematics and can remember all the sequences and measurements of cooking even at three years of age. The most important thing about the girl 'in the pretty dress' might be that she is worried about getting it dirty and never plays with blocks in case she knocks over other children's constructions when she passes by. Gender stereotypes are restricting because behaviour is seen as 'what boys do' and 'what girls do'. Through encouraging boys and girls alike to be active, to explore and be gentle and nurturing, all children are enabled to lead fuller lives with broader roles. It equips them much better for their future lives.

Adults working with these children need to empower them rather than narrowly stereotype them. To focus on one feature of the child is much too narrow. It is important not to stereotype children through labels. Children are people, and they have names, not labels!

G U I D E L I N E S

Promoting cultural and gender identity and self labelling

All of the following play their part in cultural identity and the way the child builds on an image of his or her self:
- **disability;**
- **skin colour;**
- **music and songs;**
- **culturally specific home objects (artefacts);**
- **family relationships, occupations;**
- **language (spoken or sign).**
- **gender;**
- **food and dress;**
- **heritage myths and legends;**

It is also important to remember that children are people, and every person in the world is of worth. When we stereotype children, we limit them in our image of what we think they can do. This means that we hold them back in their development.

Inspecting our own thinking, feelings, attitudes and values

In the UK there is now legislation on race, gender and disability discrimination, which helps teams of people working together to have an impact on racism, sexism, and disablist attitudes and work practices, however unconscious these may be.

It is important that each of us inspects what we do so that we become aware of our attitudes and values. Only then can we act on the unwittingly discriminatory behaviour which we will almost inevitably find. Discriminatory behaviour occurs when, usually without meaning it, we are sexist, racist, disablist, etc. For example, the early childhood worker might ask for a strong boy to lift the chair. We need to see if what we say we believe matches what we actually do. It doesn't usually! So then we have to do something about it.

Each of us has to work at this all the time, throughout our lives. It is not useful to feel guilty and dislike yourself when you find you are discriminating against someone. It is useful to do something about it.

Considerable progress has been made in this over the last 30 years, and it is important that this continues as a matter of human rights. Human rights are about respecting other people, and valuing them as individuals (see Chapter 16).

The process of inspecting our basic thinking needs to be done on three levels:

▶ within the legal framework;
▶ in the work setting as part of a team;
▶ and as individuals.

Legislation

This deals with the overt discrimination that results from prejudice, especially when combined with power. Being prejudiced means 'pre-judging' someone. The prejudiced person is unwilling to change their views even when their 'facts' are clearly shown to be wrong. When the prejudiced person has power, they may discriminate against the people towards whom they are prejudiced. This might be in the form of racism or sexism, or being disablist, ageist or homophobic (afraid of and hostile to homosexual people). There are laws which try to deal with all these kinds of discrimination. However, while legal restraints on racism and sexism exist, legal protection against disablism, ageism and sexual prejudice is less well developed.

1976 RACE RELATIONS ACT

This states what is unacceptable racial discriminatory practice. For example, by law black people cannot be excluded admission to an institution on the grounds of their race.

1989 CHILDREN ACT

This requires all early childhood settings to take account of a child's religious persuasion, racial origin, and cultural and linguistic background. The guidance attached to the act (Department of Health 1991) makes it clear what is expected of early childhood services. This includes having a policy of equal opportunities which is regularly reviewed.

For more details of the Race Relations Act and the Children Act, see Chapter 16.

Working as a team

It is important to pause at regular intervals and examine what happens in every work setting. Does what the team members say they believe in match what they do?

Identifying problems in the work setting in the way adults work with children, and looking at how children and adults are relating to each other, is essential before positive action can be taken by the whole team.

It helps to work as a team in doing this because it is hard, if not impossible, for individuals to inspect their own thinking in isolation from other people. It helps to share and discuss things with colleagues. It is then necessary to draw up, as a team, a policy of equality of opportunity and a code of practice, and, as a team, to review them regularly.

- ▶ The policy states the aims and values of the team in its work.
- ▶ The code of practice sets out how the team will put the policy into practice.
- ▶ The review process covers all aspects of the team's work in relation to its policy and code of practice. This means looking at the materials the children are offered. It means seeing how varied the menu is. It means making sure that parents feel involved in the celebration of festivals and are asked about whether staff are being accurate and not tokenist when they do this. It is important that this is meaningful for all the children. It means making sure that every parent understands what behaviour is unacceptable. It means looking to see whether information is given in different languages and whether interpretation is active.

The role of the individual member of staff

Each individual worker needs to be committed and empowered to carry out the policy using the code of practice. In the last two sections of this chapter there are many examples of different ways in which individual staff members can play a very important part in promoting the aims and values of the team in their work. You can make a difference to the lives of the children and families you work with. You can make a difference in your work setting.

Individuals can challenge discriminatory behaviour. It is important to be assertive and not aggressive. Being assertive means talking about how you feel. This is very different from being rude and aggressive. You can say very clearly, politely and firmly that you feel worried about some aspects of the way people are working or the way things are set out. It is best to talk about your feelings clearly but courteously. For example: 'I felt very uncomfortable when you asked me to give a drink to the girl with a hearing aid. I felt I needed to know her name, because I am worried that I might stop seeing her as a person if I just think of her as "the girl with a hearing aid".'

One person can have a great impact. Remember, you matter, and you can have an influence on combating discriminatory behaviour.

It is very important to challenge situations, for example:
- ▶ when a child hits, bites or kicks another;
- ▶ when jokes and insults are made to a child.

Books which are discriminatory can be discussed with the team of early childhood workers, removed and replaced with books (chosen as a team) containing positive images of people with disabilities, or people of different cultures, gender etc.

From time to time you will make mistakes. You will say and do things you regret. For example, someone who lived in Dorset all her life came to London and laughed at the idea of people eating goat meat. She quickly realised how insulting this was to her new friends, and apologised, explaining that it was simply a new idea to her.

It is very important to try to pronounce and spell names correctly and to try to understand the different systems that different cultures use in choosing names for people. It is also very important to learn about the different clothes people wear in different cultures and to try to learn what garments are called.

G U I D E L I N E S

To help you inspect your own feelings and attitudes

1 **Know the legislation on discriminatory behaviour.**
2 **Work within the team to construct a policy on equality of opportunities.**
3 **Use the code of practice drawn up by the staff in the work setting.**
4 **Make sure your team reviews the code of practice together regularly.**
5 **Be assertive (not aggressive) and try to work towards greater equality of opportunity in your work setting.**

Overcoming 'stranger fear' with positive strategies

Humans are not very good at meeting either new situations or new people. They feel more comfortable with the people they know, and situations that are very familiar. Meeting people who are in some way different can sometimes cause a reaction of fear. This often leads to

▶ ignoring or
▶ avoiding.

It is very important that children are helped to meet a wide range of people. Positive images help children towards positive experiences. Ways of helping children to form positive images of people include:

▶ Having storytellers from different ethnic groups, who tell stories in their own languages, as well as in English. This helps children to hear different languages, so that the idea becomes familiar that there are many languages in the world.
▶ Having arts, crafts and artefacts from different cultures (fabrics, interest tables, books, posters, jigsaws, etc.) in the case environment. This helps children to realise, for example, that not everyone uses a knife, fork or spoon when eating: they might use fingers, or chopsticks, instead. Children are helped to learn that there are different ways of eating which might seem strange at first.
▶ Including music and dances from different cultures: listening to them, watching them, perhaps joining in a bit. In every culture children love to stand at the edge while people perform. Children often 'echo dance' on the edge of groups of adults and older children dancing. Watch out the next time you go to a fête. If there are morris dancers or folk dancers you are likely to see children watching them and echo dancing at the sides. Being introduced to different cultures in this way helps children not to reject music with different sounds from those familiar to them. For example, Chinese music has a pentatonic scale; African music sometimes has five beats in a bar, while European music has two, three or four

but not usually five. A child who has never seen ballet before, or a child who has never seen an Indian dance before, might find these strange at first.

▶ Doing cookery from different cultures. You might have cookery books that families can borrow (you might need to make these) using different languages and easy-to-follow pictures and instructions. For example, there could be a copy of a recipe book on how to make roti in English, Urdu and French, or how to make bread in English, Greek and Swahili; the choice of languages would depend on which were used in the early childhood setting.

▶ Making sure that the menu includes food that children will enjoy and which is in some way familiar. One of the things young children worry about when they are away from home is whether they will like the food. Food and eating with others is a very emotional experience.

▶ Making sure that children who look different, because they are from different cultures, or are children with disabilities, feel at ease and part of the group.

Respecting difference

Much can be gained from respecting different ways of bringing up children. For example, the Indian tradition of massaging babies is now widely used in British clinics and family centres; so is the way that African mothers traditionally carry their babies in a sling on their backs. This method is now widely used in the UK, and slings are sold by department stores as part of everyday life.

It is important to respect what the child has been taught to do at home. For example, in Asian cultures it is seen as disrespectful to adults for a child to look at an adult directly in the eye, whereas in Europe, children are considered rude if they do not look at an adult directly.

FIGURE I.I
A Buddhist blessing

Promoting positive strategies to deal with 'stranger fear'

1 **Help children to have positive experiences when they are in new situations, e.g. meeting a child from a different culture, or a child with a disability (e.g. a wheelchair user) for the first time.**
2 **Help children to experience a wide variety of cultures and people, so that they come to expect people to be different. This develops a positive self image. To find people eating, dressing, etc. in a variety of different ways is interesting. Children should be encouraged not to feel anxious about people who are different from themselves.**

How individual people can and do influence groups of people

It is important that every human being is treated with respect. There are some situations which raise large issues, too large for one person to tackle alone. Some things are easier for each and every one of us to do something about. One individual person can have a great impact on the lives of young children and their families.

Children's rights

Working towards children's rights through international cooperation is an important way to make progress towards better quality early childhood services. It sometimes seems that an individual cannot do very much in this respect. However, in every country there are organisations with which you can link up: in the UK, these include the National Children's Bureau, the British Association for Early Childhood Education (BAECE) and the Organisation Mondiale Education Pre-Scholaire (OMEP). It is also important to remember that you can get in touch with your MP and your MEP in local surgeries or by writing to him or her.

There is now an International Charter of Children's Rights. Rights enshrined in such documents are not necessarily protected by laws, but they do provide a useful starting point in looking at the needs of children across the world. The United Nations Charter of Human Rights (1948) and the 54 Articles in the Charter of the 1989 UN Convention of the Rights of the Child are also good reference points for adults who work with children. This is available from the National Children's Bureau.

Poverty

Many children in the world live in poverty. Reports by voluntary organisations in the UK show that from 1979 to 1995 the number of families with children under 5 who are living below the poverty line has greatly increased from a quarter of families to one-third (National Children's Homes 1990; Barnados 1994).

Poverty is in some ways absolute. There are absolute limits to the lack of food, shelter and clothing which humans can bear. These result in starvation, disease and slow death. However, more often poverty is relative. The reports on poverty in the UK show that in relation to most people living in the UK, an increasing number of families are living below an acceptable minimum level. This creates stress when families struggle to make ends meet, especially in a country where most people are financially comfortable. (See Chapter 16.)

In the early childhood setting it is important not to have expensive outings or other activities, and to be sure to invite all parents to take part in the life of the group. No parent or child should be left out because of their economic background. This is an important equality of opportunity issue.

Minority groups

As we have already noted, there are many kinds of minority groups, including disability or ethnic groups. Minority groups have in the main experienced three kinds of treatment from other people: **apartheid**, **assimilation** or **integration**. Recently there has been a move towards principles of **inclusivity**.

APARTHEID

This occurs when, for example, disability, ethnic, gender or age groups live or work separately from others. This almost inevitably means that groups of people become ignorant about each other. For example, children with special needs often used to be placed in residential settings from the age of 2. Consequently, people without disability were often ill at ease and showed stranger fear when meeting them. The practice of apartheid was taken to an extreme in South Africa before 1990 where black Africans lived separately from white Africans. In the UK, children learning English as a second language used to be taken out of the classroom and taught separately, and children who were vegetarians were often made to sit at a separate table during school lunch times.

ASSIMILATION

Assimilation occurs when children are expected to conform to the mainstream culture, e.g. they are expected to learn English rather than use their first language. Having to fit in with the majority with little help or support is very stressful. Blind children are greatly disadvantaged in a building if doors are left half-open and they bump into them and hurt themselves. Children in wheelchairs are greatly disadvantaged in a building with no ramps.

INTEGRATION

There are different kinds of integration. Only a minority of children now need to attend special schools. Many children with disabilities attend different sorts of early childhood provision: nurseries, children's centres, playgroups, family centres and child minders. (See Chapter 15.)

▶ Children in special schools and early years settings of all kinds now spend a great deal of time meeting children in mainstream settings through regular visits to each other, joint projects, etc.

▶ Locational integration involves two schools or early childhood work settings sharing a site so that children meet at different points in the day. They might play together outside or share music together.

▶ A special unit placed in a mainstream school or early childhood setting enables the children within it to join in the mainstream classes when it is good for them and also to go to the unit for specialist help and equipment.

▶ Sometimes all children are in the same early childhood setting, with those who need it given support, sometimes from a peripatetic teacher who visits regularly if they are in an educational setting.

PRINCIPLES OF INCLUSIVITY

This means that all children are seen as having the right to have their needs met in the best way for them. They are seen as already being part of the community. They need perhaps particular help in particular ways. Integration is about bringing people who are different together. Inclusion means they are already there together in a community, but different people need different and appropriate support to be provided within that community. Special schools need, therefore, to be seen as within the community, just as children educated in the mainstream early years settings are not integrated, but are already in the community. This means that special schools are linking with other settings in much deeper ways, through reciprocal visits and projects such as RNIB Northwood School.

ARGUMENTS FOR KEEPING A MINORITY OF CHILDREN IN SPECIAL SCHOOLS

C A S E   S T U D Y

Kuhldeep

Kuhldeep (15 years) was with his friends in the park. They were attacked by a gang and he became completely blind. He went immediately to a special residential school for visually impaired but highly academic pupils. He became a weekly boarder. This was because both he and his family were in shock and devastated by what had happened. His family needed help and support, and were not feeling ready to support him enough in the early stages.

At the school he received expert regular assessment and expert counselling about his feelings, his visual impairment and his state of health. He received individual teaching at the pace he needed while he adjusted to not seeing. He learnt braille and was taught by expert teachers. He learnt mobility using a white cane. He went home at weekends so kept in close contact with his family. His family had the opportunity to learn about his new visual impairment and over time to adjust in a way which was positive and helped him.

He was in the company of other visually impaired people of his own age, who understood how he felt and helped him. He was able to meet his sighted friends at weekends. He took his school exams a year late, and did well.

The key elements in Kuhldeep's experiences were:
▶ expert resources;
▶ expert specialist teaching;
▶ close links with home;
▶ help for his family and help for him while they all adjusted to his new visual impairment.

C A S E   S T U D Y

Winnie

Winnie (6 years) had a range of disabilities, including severe learning difficulties, visual and hearing impairment, and difficulty sitting. Her parents valued joining a parent group run by the staff of the special school. All the parents had similarly disabled children. This gave them support. The equipment in the special school was geared to Winnie's needs. The staff were specialists trained to work with children like Winnie. The children were regularly visited by children from the local primary school, and they would go on outings with them. Winnie lives at home, and goes to school daily.

For Kuhldeep and Winnie, for entirely different reasons, special schools were appropriate and to their advantage. However, the vast majority of children with special educational needs will be integrated into mainstream settings. The Warnock Report (1978) advised keeping a few special schools for children like Kuhldeep and Winnie.

ARGUMENTS FOR INTRODUCING MOST CHILDREN INTO MAINSTREAM SETTINGS FROM AN EARLY AGE

In a special school, staff will need to be careful to concentrate on the child as a whole person and not on disability only. When the latter happens it narrows the experiences that a child has. Concentrating on disability means concentrating on what children find difficult to do rather than being positive and thinking about all the things that the child can do.

The curriculum might become rather rigid and based on exercises instead of equipping the children to make choices and decisions and to become autonomous learners. For example, special schools for hearing-impaired children used to concentrate on language teaching in a narrow curriculum with little art, play, dance, science, etc. All the efforts went into getting the children to talk, read and write. In spite of this emphasis on language and literacy (reading and writing) few children reached a reading age of above 9 years. (A reading age of 9 years is needed to read the tabloid newspapers.)

There is also the difficulty of arranging for the children to meet 'normal' children. This often means that children begin to imitate mannerisms from each other. This can lead to 'double delay' which means that the child not only has the disability that he or she was born with, but the added disadvantage of being in a poor context for learning.

However, there are different problems for children in mainstream schools. If you are working with children with special needs in a mainstream setting you need to consider these. A child might be very lonely if he is the only child in the school with a hearing impairment. It is very important to help children make friends in this setting and not feel that they are different from everyone else.

It is also very easy to underestimate what the child can do. It is therefore essential for adults to have high enough expectations of children with special educational needs in mainstream settings. There might not be any expert teachers who know about the particular disability that the child has. When expert teachers do visit, their visits may be very irregular and not at all frequent, which makes it hard to get as much information as is needed in order to help the child. It is very important to know about the special educational needs code of practice (see Chapter 15). It is also important to bear in mind what most children achieve, and to find ways of helping children with special education needs to move towards this, or to do as much. Children learn to do up coat buttons if encouraged. Sometimes, children with disabilities are over-protected and are not expected to manage things which they could do with a little encouragement.

It is also very important to establish links with voluntary organisations who may be able to put children in touch with each other: for example, there are summer camps where children who are diabetic and attend mainstream schools can come together and enjoy each other's company for a week.

Age

It is ideal if every team of staff has a good spread of ages amongst its members. This would mean that there would be some who have many years of life experience to bring to the team as well as others at the beginning of their work with children and families; those who have done other things before training to work with children and those who will go on to other kinds of work. It is important that young children and their families are with people who learn from each other, who are trained and informed about children, and who are sensitive to the needs and concerns of the parents. It is very important to make parents and children feel welcome in the early childhood setting. It is important that staff learn to make constructive criticisms of each other, to trust each other, respect each other and to build on each other's strengths.

Assertiveness training

Reference needs to be made in the team's code of practice to the cultivation of assertiveness rather than aggression through bullying. Children need to feel protected from aggression and to be able to assert themselves sufficiently to take a full part in their activities. In some early childhood settings children are helped to learn to be assertive. Pen Green Centre in Corby, Northamptonshire, has a 'Learning to be Strong' programme to which children are introduced a few weeks before they leave the nursery to go on to school. This has been made a Centre of Early Years Excellence by the government.

Both the bully and the victim need help to be assertive: one needs help with aggression, and the other with timidity. Visualisation techniques help early childhood workers to use positive images (assertiveness) rather than negative images (bully or victim).

Aggression is not always physical. Being pushed by adults to be highly academic and not take part in childhood pursuits is also a very important issue (see p. 501).

Moore and Klass have identified four categories of 'hurrying' children out of childhood in the USA and UK:

▶ academic hurrying;
▶ over-scheduled lives with no time for the child to have personal space;
▶ expecting children to excel all the time;
▶ expecting children to assume adult responsibilities.

The need for assertiveness rather than aggression or an over-dominant manner in relation to early childhood workers is covered in Chapter 17.

G U I D E L I N E S

To help you as an individual to promote equality of opportunity

1 You cannot be trained to know everything. You cannot be an expert in everything but you can be a good networker. This means linking people together who might be useful to each other. Put people in touch with people who know about
   - welfare rights and social services;
   - health services;
   - voluntarily organisations and self-help groups.

2 Remember that you are part of a multiprofessional team, and that each member has something different to bring to early childhood work.

3 When you meet children who are in a mainstream school or early childhood setting, make sure that your expectations of what each child can do are high enough.

4 Set children tasks which help them to make decisions and exercise choice. It is important to let all children make choices and decisions as much as possible so that they feel a sense of control in their lives. When people feel they have some control over what they do, they learn better. It gives them greater equality of opportunity.

5 Respect yourself and others alike. Try to think why people have different views and customs from yours. Keep thinking about what you do. Think about issues of race, gender, sexual orientation, age, economics, background, disability, assertiveness, culture, special educational needs. Keep changing what you do not like about what you do. Do this without feeling guilt or shame.

6 Value the things you keep learning about equality of opportunity so that you can look forward with positive images about yourself and other people.

7 Remember: equality of opportunity is about giving every child full access to the group.

R E S O U R C E S

A large number of cheap and authentic artefacts can be collected by asking teachers or parents going abroad to bring back specific items for the school i.e. cooking utensils, cleaning utensils, traditional costumes/clothing, postcards, posters, money, dolls, religious artefacts, traditional handicrafts, greetings cards, musical tapes and, of course, photographs.

Minority Group Support Service

Minority Group Support Service
Southfields
South Street
Coventry
CV1 5EJ

Puppets

Ebony Eyes (African puppets)
10 Searson House
Newington Butts
London SE17 3AY

Barnabas (Wooden finger puppets)
28 Gifford Terrace Road
Mutley
Plymouth
Devon PL3 4JE

Jim Gaffney (Turkish shadow puppets)
5 Alexandria Street
Rawtenstall
Lancashire BB4 8HP
(Will give talks and workshops about puppet and Batik making)

Ethnic Dolls

Ebony Eyes (Soft rag dolls)
10 Searson House
Newington Butts
London SE17 3AY

Musical Instruments

Acorn Percussion
Unit 34
Abbey Business Centre
Ingate Place
London SW8 3NS

Knock on Wood
Granary Wharf
Leeds
LS1 4ER

Cultural Artefacts

Muzik Dunyasi (Turkish
materials)
58 Green Lanes
London N16 9NH

The Muslim
Information Centre
233 Seven Sisters Road
London N4 2DA
(Mainly religious artefacts)

**Educational Games and
Toys**

Play Matters
National Toy Libraries
Association
68 Church Way
London NW1 1LT

Positive Choices
10 Hazelbank Road
London SE6 1TL

Asco Educational Supplies
Asco House
19 Rockwood Way
Parkside
Leeds LS11 5TH

Centre for Multi Cultural
Education
Harrison Road
Leicester LE4 6RB

Edu-Play
Vulcan Business Centre Units
H & I
Vulcan Road
Leicester LE5 3EB

Haringey Traveller Support
Team
Educational Support Service
The Lodge
Church Lane
London N17 8BX

Galt Education
Bookfield Road
Cheadle
Cheshire SK8 2PN

Equality Learning Centre
356 Holloway Road
London N7 6PA

Playgear Limited
3 Dennis Parade
Winchmore Hill Road
Southgate N14 6AA

NES/Arnold
Ludlow Hill Road West
Bridgeford
Notts NG2 6HD

Videos

RNIB The World in our
Hands
A series of programmes about
young children with a visual
impairment
1 My Baby is Blind
2 Moving on
3 Sounds Important
4 Clap your Hands,
     Stamp your Feet
5 It's Me!

RNIB and SENSE One of
the Family
A series of programmes about
young children with a
multiplicity of impairments
1 First Sight
2 Going my Way
3 Making Contact
4 That's what it's all about
From RNIB Education
Centre: London
Garrow House
190 Kensal Road
London W10 5BT

The European Commission
COFACE and UNAF
Title: A Certain Idea of the
Father in Europe
From: The European

Commission Equal
Opportunities Unit
(DG V/A/3)
200 rue de la Loi
B-1049 Brussels
Belgium

Title: Coffee-coloured
Children
From: The Albany Video
Distribution
Battersea Studios
Thackeray Road
London SW8 3TW

Title: Let's Play Colour:
Anti-racist Child Care
From: East Birmingham
Health Education
Department
102 Blakesley Road
Yardley
Birmingham B25 8RN

Title: Can you feel a colour?
From: The European
Network on Childcare
Children in Scotland
5 Shandwick Place
Edinburgh EH2 4RG
(The European Network on
Childcare publishes a variety
of videos and books)

Title: A video with Dr Lilli
Nielsen: Lilli Plays with
Natalie; Lilli Plays with
William
(The development of
Children with Visual
Impairment and Multiple
Disabilities)
Produced by: Moray House
College
ETV
Holyrood Road
Edinburgh

Title: Sound Moves. Making
music for Children who have
severe or profound and
multiple learning disabilities.
Available from RNIB
Education Centre: London,
Garrow House,
190 Kempsal Road,
London W10 5DT.

Fathers Handling Small
Children
Video Reportage Productions
Number 3
20 West Parade
Norwich NR2 3DW

**Information about videos
and publications is also
available from:**
The National Children's
Bureau
8 Wakeley Street
London
EC1V 7QE

Posters

Pictorial Wall Charts
Educational Trust (PCET)
27 Kirchen Road
London W13 0UD
Examples:
Festival Friezes (1) Christmas,
Diwali and Hanukah and (2)
Chinese New Year and Eidul
Fitr

In the Oxfam Catalogue of
Resources for Schools, 1995
– Children First
(6 posters of children
from different parts of
the world)

– Africa Map
From: Oxfam
274 Banbury Road
Oxford
Oxon OX2 7DZ

Alexander Galleries
7 Eileen Road
London SE25 5EJ

Books

Bangladesh Resources Centre
First Floor, Hessle Street
London E1 2LR

EYTARN
PO Box 28
Wallasley L45 9NP

Forest Book Shop
8 St Johns Street
Coleford
Gloucestershire GR16 8AR

Books from India (UK)
Limited
45 Museum Street
London WC1A 1LR
(Cheap imported books)

Turkish Language Books
81 Shacklewell Lane
London E8 2EB

Zeno Booksellers & Publishers
6 Denmark Street
London WC2H 8LP
(Greek language books)

Manta Publishing Limited
5 Alexandra Grove
London N12 8NU

Equal from the start (booklet)
BAECE
111 City View House
463 Bethnal Green Road
London E4 9QY

Roy Yates Books
Smallfields Cottage
Cox Green
Rudgwick
Horsham, West Sussex RH12
3DE

Madeleine Lindley Ltd
79 and 90 Acorn Centre
Barry Street
Oldham
OL1 3NE

Community Insight
Pembroke Centre
Cheney Manor
Swindon
SN 2PQ

Eastside Books
178 Whitechapel Road
London
E1 1BJ
(Books, works with schools
and voluntary groups to
increase access to books, shop,
outreach, events, writing
work)

Letterbox (a charity)
Unit 2D Leroy House
36 Essex Road
London N1 3QP

Save the Children
Hazareesingh, S, Simms, K.,
Anderson P. (1989) Educating
the whole child. A Holistic
Approach to Education in the
Early Years. London: Building
Blocks Educational, Save the
Children

Lending Library for children's
books in print and braille
Clear Vision Project
Linden Lodge School
61 Princes Way
London SW19 6JB

A C T I V I T I E S

1 **Plan a multicultural cooking library. Make six cookery books with simple
recipes from a variety of cultures.**

   **Find or draw pictures to illustrate the books. Write the text in English,
and another language if possible. If you write in Urdu or Chinese,
remember you will need two books, as Urdu and Chinese text runs from
right to left.**

   **Use the books with groups of children and run a series of cookery sessions.
Observe the way the children use and respond to the cookery books.**

Evaluate the aim of your plan, the reason for the activity, how the activities were carried out, what you observed in the children's cooking activities.

2   Plan a story which you can tell (rather than read from a book). Find a story you enjoy, and make or find suitable props. You can make puppets out of stuffed socks, finger puppets out of gloves, stick puppets or shadow puppets; or use dolls and dressing-up clothes and various artefacts.

Observe the children listening as you tell the story. Focus on their understanding and their language, especially children whose first language is not English. Evaluate your activity.

3   Plan how you can make the children you work with more aware of religious festivals in a variety of cultures. For example, how would you introduce the children to Diwali in ways which are not tokenist? Remember to offer children meaningful first-hand experiences.

Observe the children and assess how much they understand. Look particularly to see the reactions of children familiar with the festival you choose, and of children for whom this is a new experience. Evaluate your plans and observations.

4   Plan how you would include a child with disabilities in your early childhood setting. Remember your plans will be different according to each child's needs. The child with a hearing impairment will need different help from the child who is a wheelchair user, for example. Carry out and observe your plan in action. Focus on how you meet the child's individual needs through your plan. Evaluate your plan.

5   Draw up a policy on equality of opportunity, and look at actual practices in the daily routine, e.g. mealtimes, books. Does what happens match the policy? Evaluate your observations.

6   Plan a series of music activities which introduce children to the music of a variety of cultures. You will need to help children to listen to music, and make music. Make musical instruments out of cardboard boxes, elastic bands, yoghurt pots, masking tape and other materials.

7   Plan a booklet which would introduce different religious festivals, and help parents to understand different religious perspectives in your early childhood setting.
Make the booklet and use it in your early childhood setting. Evaluate it.

8   Plan and make a display using a multicultural theme. Evaluate it. How did the adults use it? How did the children react?

9   Choose a picture, book, story or poem from each of the five continents: Africa, America (North and South), Asia, Australia and Europe. Make the collection into a book which you can use with children of 3-7 years of age. Evaluate the activity.

10 Plan an area of provision which is multicultural in approach, for example, the home area. Perhaps you can add more ideas to those suggested in this chapter. Implement and evaluate your plan.

2

Holistic Child Development: From Birth to 8 Years

Development

It is important to keep in mind that even a tiny baby is a person. People develop physically, but they are whole human beings from the very start.

The developing child

If different aspects of a child's development are seen as separated strands, each isolated from the others, then the child easily comes to be seen as a collection of bits and pieces instead of a person. On the other hand, it can be useful to look particularly closely at different areas of a child's development, whether to check that all is well, to celebrate progress, to see how to help the child with the next step of development and learning, or to give special help where needed. It is important, however, never to forget that we are looking at a person. A person has a physical body, ideas, feelings and relationships all developing and functioning at the same time.

Is love a feeling?

It is not possible to separate feelings (emotions) from social and physical relationships or thoughts about the people we love. Love is a feeling in yourself. It is also a social relationship with another person. Because of this, people who love each other care about each other's feelings as much as they care about their own feelings. As people share their feelings they use words, a hug or a cuddle. The words contain ideas, and there is a physical and perhaps spiritual experience too. Knowing how the person who is loved thinks about things is an important part of loving someone. For example, to organise a surprise birthday party for someone who would hate it would not be loving. Making breakfast in bed for them, when they love to get up slowly as a treat, would be a loving thing to do.

Why study child development?

Child development is an essential subject of study for everyone who works with young children. Looking after other people's children is not the same as having your own children, and so people who work with other people's children need to be carefully trained. They need to be informed about how children develop and learn.

Parents find it very helpful when bringing up their children to watch television and radio programmes, read magazines and talk to staff in nurseries as they try to understand their children.

Parents are constantly looking for support and help as they bring up their children. It is part of being a parent.

The key to understanding child development is 'wholeness'. Studying child development is a way of seeing children in the round, as whole people.

Child development is a fairly new subject. It is a multidisciplinary subject. This means that it draws on various academic fields, including psychology, neuroscience, sociology, paediatrics, biology and genetics. It has emerged in Western industrialised societies during the last hundred years. Children are brought up in different ways in different parts of the world however, and recently, early childhood workers researching child development have begun to think about how children develop in different cultures and in different sorts of society.

It is very important to find out what different people in different cultures do that is the same when they bring children up. It is also very important to learn about the different ways that children are brought up and yet still turn into stable, successful adults. This means researchers are now asking:

▶ What is the same about all children?
▶ What is different across cultures in the way that children are brought up?

What is a theory of child development?

A theory of child development is someone's idea about how a child might develop. It helps people to predict, for example, that before children talk, they babble, etc. Theories about how children develop are products of the culture in which they arise. So is the research that provides all the evidence for and against various theories of child development. It is very important to remember this, and to realise that there is no such thing as 'the truth' about child development. We always need to stop and ask: who is doing the research? Who is formulating the theory? Two examples illustrate this point:

▶ The child psychologist Vygotsky (1896-1935) grew up in the Soviet Union, where Marxist and Communist ideas dominated. He came from a large family. Is it coincidence that his theory emphasises social relationships and the community?
▶ The psychologist Piaget (1896-1980) grew up in Europe. He was an only child. Is it coincidence that his theory emphasised the child as an individual and as an active learner trying to experiment and solve problems?

Early childhood workers need to look at various different theories and to bring together those ideas that are useful from each so that they can use them in their work. They need to see where theories like those of Vygotsky and Piaget are the same and where they are different. Sometimes the differences between theories are so big that it is not possible to use them together. But sometimes, as with Piaget and Vygotsky, they are very similar in many ways. This means they can be blended into a useful mixture for our work with children. Both theories help us to look at how children learn.

Integrated development

The whole child may be looked at under six headings, that together make up the acronym
P I L E S S:

▶ Physical development;   ▶ Emotional development;
▶ Intellectual development;   ▶ Social development;
▶ Language development;   ▶ Spiritual development.

The advantages of using PILESS in the study of child development are:

▶ it recognises the important contributions of different disciplines – human biology,
  psychology, linguistics, sociology, neuroscience etc.
▶ it provides a useful framework for students to organise their studies;
▶ it provides a focus for the study of children, for example in the use of observation
  techniques, case studies and the planning of activities for work with children

The disadvantages of using PILESS in the study of child development are:

▶ it may make it more difficult to view the child as a whole person;
▶ it may be more difficult to 'contextualise' the child if the categories are rigidly
  prescribed.

THE CONTEXTUALISED CHILD

Researchers in the field of child development now realise that when, for example,
children quarrel, it is almost impossible to say which aspect is emotional (anger), which is
physical (stamping with rage) and which is intellectual or language (what to say or do). It is
also very important to identify who or what made the child angry. It is therefore
important to **contextualise** the child when studying child development. The biological
part of development (physical development, genetic factors) is integrated with the cultural
part of development (social, cultural, intellectual and linguistic factors, as well as
representation, play etc.) Researchers and specialists in child development now prefer to
talk about the contextualised child. This is because development is deeply influenced by
the child's cultural environment and the people she meets. The ideas, language,
communication, feelings, relationships and other cultural elements among which the child
is brought up influence development very deeply.

Measuring development

Normative development

Another aspect of the traditional approach to child development study has been to
emphasise **normative measurement**. This is concerned with milestones in a child's
development. These show what most children can do at a particular age. In reality there is
a wide range of normal development, and this will be influenced by genetic, social and
cultural factors. Children have been labelled as 'backward' or 'forward' in relation to the
so-called 'normal' child. For example, Mark moved around by bottom-shuffling and did
not walk until he was two years old. Most children who crawl in the conventional way on
hands and knees will walk a little earlier.

For example, African children living in rural villages estimate volume and capacity
earlier than European children who live in towns. This is because they practise measuring
out cups of rice into baskets from an early age as part of their daily lives.

Normative measurements can only indicate general trends in development in children across the world. They may vary quite a bit according to the culture in which a child lives. Researchers are beginning to add to our knowledge of how these norms vary with children in different parts of the world or different cultures within a country.

When children do things earlier than the milestones suggest is normal, it does not necessarily mean that they will be outstanding or gifted in any way. Parents sometimes think that because their child speaks early, is potty-trained early or walks early, he is gifted in some way. This is not necessarily so.

Sequences in a child's development

Children across the world seem to pass through similar sequences of development, but in different ways according to the culture and at very different rates. The work of Mary Sheridan has been invaluable, but she suggests that children move through rigidly prescribed stages which are linked to the child's age: the child sits, then crawls, then stands, then walks, etc. In fact, not all children do crawl. Blind children often do not. Some children 'bottom-shuffle', moving along in a sitting position.

Children with special educational needs often seem to 'dance the development ladder': they move through sequences in unusual and very uneven ways. For example, they might walk at the normal age, but they might not talk at the usual age.

As researchers learn more about child development, it is becoming clearer and more useful to think of a child's development as a network which becomes increasingly complex as the child matures and becomes more experienced in the culture. Instead of thinking of child development and learning as a ladder, it is probably more useful to think of the child's development as a web.

Figures 2.1 and 2.2 show the traditional way of giving the milestones of normative development in the areas of PILESS but also in the area of symbolic development which is now recognised as fundamental to human behaviour. For this reason the normative development of play, talk and representation is included.

FIGURE 2.1
Normative development: an updated PILESS framework

P	Physical
I	Intellectual/cognitive, which includes the development of symbolic behaviour
L	(a) Language and communication (b) Representation (drawings and models) (c) Play
E	Emotional
S	Social
S	Spiritual

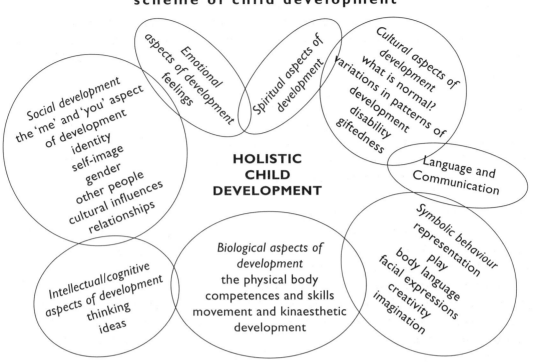

Normative development: a holistic scheme of child development

Normative development: physical, 0–8 years

AGE	GROSS MOTOR	FINE MOTOR
BIRTH TO 4 WEEKS	The baby lies supine (on her back) with head to one side. When placed on her front (the prone position), the baby lies with head turned to one side and by one month can lift the head. If pulled to sitting position, the head will lag, the back curves over and the head falls forward.	The baby turns her head towards the light and stares at bright/shiny objects. The baby is fascinated by human faces and gazes attentively at carer's face when fed or held. The baby's hands are usually tightly closed. The baby reacts to loud sounds but by one month may be soothed by particular music.
4–8 WEEKS	The baby can now turn from side to back. The baby can lift the head briefly from prone position. Arm and leg movements are jerky and uncontrolled. There is head lag if the baby is pulled to sitting position.	The baby turns her head towards the light and stares at bright shiny objects. The baby will show interest and excitement by facial expression and will gaze attentively at carer's face whilst being fed. The baby will grab his/her hand to grasp the carer's finger.

AGE	GROSS MOTOR	FINE MOTOR
8–12 WEEKS	When lying supine, the baby's head is in a central position. The baby can now lift head and chest off bed in prone position, supported on forearms. There is almost no head lag in sitting position. The legs can kick vigorously, both separately and together. The baby can wave her arms and bring hands together over the body.	The baby moves her head to follow adult movements. The baby watches her hands and plays with her fingers. The baby holds a rattle for a brief time before dropping it.
4–5 MONTHS (16–20 WEEKS)	The baby is beginning to use palmar grasp and can transfer objects from hand to hand. The baby is very interested in all activity. Everything is taken to the mouth. The baby moves her head around to follow people and objects.	The baby now has good head control and is beginning to sit with support. The baby rolls over from back to side and is beginning to reach for objects. When supine the baby plays with her own feet. The baby holds the head up when pulled to sitting position.
6–9 MONTHS	The baby can roll from front to back. The baby may attempt to crawl but will often end up sliding backwards. The baby may grasp feet and place in her mouth. The baby can sit without support for longer periods of time. The baby may 'cruise' around furniture and may even stand or walk alone.	The baby is very alert to people and objects. The baby is beginning to use pincer grasp with thumb and index finger. The baby transfers toys from one hand to the other and looks for fallen objects. Everything is explored by putting it in her mouth.
9–12 MONTHS	The baby will now be mobile – may be crawling, bear-walking, bottom-shuffling or even walking. The baby can sit up on her own and lean forward to pick things up. The baby may crawl upstairs and onto low items of furniture. The baby may bounce in rhythm to music.	The baby's pincer grasp is now well developed and she can pick things up and pull them towards her. The baby can poke with one finger and will point to desired objects. The baby can clasp hands and imitate adults' actions. The baby can throw toys deliberately. The baby can manage spoons and finger foods well.
15 MONTHS	The baby probably walks alone, with feet wide apart and arms raised to maintain balance. She is likely to fall over and sit down suddenly a lot.	The baby can build with a few bricks and arrange toys on the floor. She holds crayon in palmar grasp and turns several pages of a book at once.

AGE	GROSS MOTOR	FINE MOTOR
15 MONTHS – *contd.*	The baby can probably manage stairs and steps, but will need supervision. She can get to standing without help from furniture or people and kneels without support.	She can point to desired objects. The baby shows a preference for one hand, but uses either.
18 MONTHS	The child walks confidently and is able to stop without falling. The child can kneel, squat, climb and carry things around with her. The child can climb onto an adult chair forwards and then turn round to sit. The child can come downstairs, usually by creeping backwards on her tummy.	The child can thread large beads. The child uses pincer grasp to pick up small objects. The child can build a tower of several cubes. The child can scribble to and fro on paper.
2 YEARS *(24* MONTHS*)*	The child is very mobile – can run safely. The child can climb up onto the furniture. The child can walk up and down stairs, usually two feet to a step. The child tries to kick a ball with some success – cannot yet catch ball.	The child can draw circles, lines and dots, using preferred hand. She can pick up tiny objects using a fine pincer grasp. She can build tower of six or more blocks (bricks) with longer concentration span. She enjoys picture books and turns pages singly.
3 YEARS	The child can jump from a low step. She can walk backwards and sideways. The child can stand and walk on tiptoe and stand on one foot. She has good spatial awareness. The child rides tricycle using pedals. She can climb stairs with one foot on each step – downwards with two feet per step.	The child can build tall towers of bricks or blocks. She can control a pencil using thumb and first two fingers – dynamic tripod. The child enjoys painting with large brush. She can use scissors to cut paper. She can copy shapes, such as a circle.
4 YEARS	A sense of balance is developing – the child may be able to walk along a line. The child can catch, kick, throw and bounce a ball. She can bend at the waist to pick up objects from the floor. He/she enjoys climbing trees and frames. She can run up and down stairs, one foot per step.	The child can build a tower of bricks and other constructions too. She can draw a recognisable person on request, showing head, legs and trunk. She can thread small beads on a lace.
5 YEARS	The child can use a variety of play equipment – slides, swings, climbing frames.	The child may be able to thread a large-eyed needle and sew large stitches.

AGE	GROSS MOTOR	FINE MOTOR
	She can play ball games. She can hop and run lightly on toes – can move rhythmically to music. The sense of balance is well developed. She can skip.	She can draw a person with head, trunk, legs, nose, mouth and eyes. She has good control over pencils and paintbrushes. She copies shapes, such as a square.
6 AND 7 YEARS	The child has increased agility, muscle co-ordination and balance. The child develops competence in riding a two-wheeled bicycle. She hops easily, with good balance. The child can jump off apparatus at school.	The child can build a tall, straight tower with blocks and other constructions too. The child can draw a person with detail, e.g. clothes and eyebrows. She can write letters of alphabet with similar writing grip to an adult. She can catch a ball thrown from one metre with one hand.

Normative development: language, 0–8 years

NORMATIVE DEVELOPMENT 1: LANGUAGE

0–3 MONTHS	Babies need to share language experiences and co-operate with others from birth onwards. From the start babies need other people.
FROM BIRTH TO 4 WEEKS	The baby responds to sounds, especially familiar voices. She quietens when picked up. She makes eye contact. The baby cries to indicate need. The baby may move the eyes towards the direction of sound.
4 TO 8 WEEKS	The baby recognises carer and familiar objects. She makes non-crying noises such as cooing and gurgling. Her cries become more expressive. She looks for sounds.
8–12 WEEKS	The baby is still distressed by sudden loud noises. She often sucks or licks lips when she hears sound of food preparation. She shows excitement at sound of approaching footsteps or voices.
DURING THE FIRST THREE MONTHS	Babies listen to people's voices. Babies 'call out' for company. When adults close to them talk to them in motherese (a high pitched tone referring to what is around and going on) babies dance, listen, and reply in babble and coo. Babies cry with anger to show they are tired, hungry, and to say they need to be changed. A hearing-impaired baby babbles and cries too. Babies are comforted by the voices of those who are close to them and they will turn especially to the voices of their family.
3–6 MONTHS	Babies become more aware of others so they communicate more and more. As they listen, they imitate sounds they can hear, and they react to the tone of someone's voice. For example, they might become upset by an angry tone, or cheered by a happy tone.

3–6 MONTHS – contd	Babies begin to use vowels, consonants and syllable sounds, e.g. 'ah', 'p', 'ee aw'. Babies begin to laugh and squeal with pleasure. Babies continue to do everything they did in the first three months. Look back at this section to remind yourself about what babies do throughout 0–6 months.
6–9 MONTHS	Babble becomes tuneful like the lilt of the language the baby can hear (except in hearing-impaired babies). Babies begin to understand words like 'up' and 'down' raising their arms to be lifted up, using appropriate gestures. The baby repeats sounds. Babies continue to do everything they did in the first six months. Look back and remind yourself about this.
9–12 MONTHS	Cooperation develops further from the early protoconversations of early motherese. For example, when adults wave bye bye, or say 'show me your shoes' the babies enjoy pointing and waving. Babies can follow simple instructions, e.g. kiss teddy. Word approximations appear, e.g. hee haw = donkey or more typically mumma and dadda and bye bye in English-speaking contexts. The tuneful babble develops into 'jargon' and babies make their voices go up and down just as people do when they talk to each other. Really? Do you? No! The babble is very expressive. Children are already experienced and capable communicators by this time. They are using emergent language/protolanguage. It is nothing short of amazing that all this happens within one year. They know about – facial expressions, combined sounds (hee haw), gestures, shared meanings, persuading, negotiating, co-operating, turn taking, interest in others, their ideas, their feelings, what they do. They know that words stand for people, objects, what they do and what happens. They are taking part in the language of their culture.
1–2 YEARS	Children begin to talk with words or sign language. They add more and more layers to everything they know about language and communication in the first year. Look back and remind yourself of what children can manage at this stage.
BY 18 MONTHS	They enjoy trying to sing as well as to listen to songs and rhymes. Action songs (for example pat-a-cake) are much loved. Books with pictures are of great interest. They point at and often name parts of their body, objects, people and pictures in books. They echo the last part of what others say (echolalia). One word or sign can have several meanings (holophrases). For example, C-A-T = all animals, not just cats. This is sometimes called 'extension'. They begin waving their arms up and down which might mean start again, or I like it, or more. Gestures develop alongside words. Gesture is used in some cultures more than in others.
BY 2 YEARS	Researchers used to say that children are using a vocabulary of 50 or so words but they understand more. Modern researchers do not use vocabulary counts so much and they simply stress that children are rapidly becoming competent speakers of the languages they experience. They over extend the use of a word, e.g. all animals are called 'doggie'. They talk about an absent object when reminded of it, e.g. seeing an empty plate, they say 'biscuit'.

BY 2 YEARS – contd	They use phrases, (telegraphese) doggie-gone, they call themselves by their name, for example Tom. They spend a great deal of energy naming things and what they do. For example, chair, and as they go up a step they might say 'up'. They can follow a simple instruction or request, for example, 'Could you bring me the spoon'. They are wanting to share songs, dance, conversations, finger rhymes, etc. more and more.
2–3 YEARS	During this period, language and the ability to communicate develop so rapidly that it almost seems to explode. The development is stunning. Children begin to use plurals, pronouns, adjectives, possessives, time words, tenses and sentences. They make what are called virtuous errors in the way that they pronounce (articulate) things. It is also true of the way they use grammar (syntax). They might say 'two times' instead of 'twice'. They might say 'I goed there' instead of 'I went there'. They love to converse and chat and ask questions (what, where and who). They enjoy much more complicated stories and ask about their favourite ones over again. It is not unusual for children to stutter because they are trying so hard to tell adults things and to talk. Their thinking goes faster than the pace at which they can say what they want to say. They can quickly become frustrated.
3–4 YEARS	During this time children ask why, when and how questions as they become more and more fascinated with the reasons for things and how things work (cause and effect). They wonder what will happen 'if' (problem solving and hypothesis making). They can think back and they can think forward much more easily than before. They can also think about things from somebody else's point of view, but only fleetingly. Past, present and future tenses are used more often. They can be taught to say their name, address and age. As they become more accurate in the way they pronounce words, and begin to use grammar, they delight in nonsense words which they make up, and jokes using words. This is called metalinguistics. They swear if they hear swearing (see p. 197).
4–8 YEARS	They try to understand the meaning of words. They use adverbs and prepositions. They talk confidently and with more and more fluency. As they become more and more part of their culture they become aware of the roles of the language(s) they speak. They use language creatively. They add vocabulary all the time. Their articulation becomes conventional. They are explorers and communicators – they begin to be able to define objects by their function, e.g. 'What is a ball?' 'You bounce it.' Young children do not learn anything in isolation from other children and adults. They begin to share as they learn. Sharing sharpens and broadens their thinking. This helps them to learn better, e.g. they begin to understand book language, and that stories have characters and a plot (the narrative). They begin to realise that different situations require different ways of talking. They establish a sense of audience (who they are talking to).

Normative Development 2: Intellectual/Cognitive and Symbolic

0–4 weeks *The first month of a baby's life — what a baby perceives through the senses*	Concepts (ideas) are beginning to develop already. Concepts are based in the senses and in what is perceived (i.e. the baby is aware of a sensation). Babies explore through their senses and through their own activity and movement. **Touch and movement (Kinaesthetic)** From the beginning babies feel pain. Their faces, abdomens, hands and the soles of their feet are also very sensitive to touch. They perceive the movements that they themselves make, and the way that other people move them about through their senses. For example, they give a 'startle' response if they are moved suddenly. This is called the 'Moro' response. **Sound** Even a newborn baby will turn to a sound. Babies might become still and listen to a low sound, or quicken their movements when they hear a high sound. A baby often stops crying and listens to a human voice by two weeks of age. **Taste** Babies like sweet tastes, for example breast milk. **Smell** Babies turn to the smell of the breast. **Sight** Babies can focus on objects 20 cm (a few inches) away. Babies are sensitive to light. Babies like to look at human faces — eye contact. They can track the movements of people and objects. They will scan the edges of objects. They will imitate facial expressions (for example, they will put out their tongue if you do). If you know any new-born or very young babies, try it and see! Psychologists think that babies may not see in colour during the early stages of development.
4–16 weeks	They recognise (this is have a concept of) differing speech sounds. By three months they can even imitate low or high pitched sounds. By four months they link objects they know with the sound, for example mother's voice and her face. They know the smell of their mother from that of other mothers.
4–5 months	By 4 months babies reach for objects, which suggests they recognise and judge the distance in relation to the size of the object. This is called depth perception, but it also suggests that the baby is linking the immediate perception with previous ones and predicting the future, which is an early concept. At 4 months babies can know the difference between two- and three-dimensional objects.

5–6 MONTHS	Babies prefer complicated things to look at from 5 to 6 months. They enjoy bright colours. Babies recognise familiar objects, e.g. the feeding bottle. They know that they have one mother. Babies are disturbed if they are shown several images of their mother at the same time. They realise that people are permanent before they realise that objects are. Babies can co-ordinate more, e.g. they can see a rattle, grasp the rattle, put the rattle in their mouths (they co-ordinate tracking, reaching, grasping and sucking). They can develop favourite tastes in food and recognise differences by 5 months.
6–9 MONTHS	The baby understands signs, e.g. the bib means that food is coming. Soon this understanding of signs will lead into symbolic behaviour. From eight to nine months babies show they know objects exist when they have gone out of sight, even under test conditions. This is called the concept of object constancy, or the permanence of the object test (Piaget). They understand that two objects can occupy space. One toy can be covered by a cloth. See also page 177.
9 MONTHS–1 YEAR	Babies are beginning to develop images. Memory develops. They can remember the past. They can anticipate the future. This gives them some understanding of routine daily sequences, e.g. after a feed, changing, and a sleep with teddy. They imitate actions, sounds, gestures and moods after an event is finished, e.g. imitate a temper tantrum they saw a friend have the previous day, wave bye bye remembering Grandma has gone to the shops.
1 YEAR–4 YEARS	Children develop symbolic behaviour. They talk. They pretend play – often talking to themselves as they do so. They take part in simple non-competitive games. They represent events in drawings, models, etc. Personal images dominate, rather than conventions used in the culture, e.g. writing is 'pretend' writing. ~ + o + + + Children tend to focus on one aspect of a situation. It is difficult for them to see things from different points of view. The way people react to what they do helps them to work out what hurts and what helps other people. This is an important time for moral development. They often enjoy music and playing sturdy instruments and join in groups singing and dancing.
4–7 YEARS	Children begin to move into deeper and deeper layers of symbolic behaviour. Language is well established, and opens the way into literacy (talking, listening, writing and reading). Personal symbols still dominate until 6 or 7 years of age. Cultural conventions in writing, drawing, etc begin to influence children increasingly. Where there is a balance in the way children use personal and conventional symbols, children are described as creative. Thinking becomes increasingly co-ordinated as children are able to hold in mind more than one point of view at a time. Concepts of matter – length, measurement, distance, area, time, volume, capacity and weight – develop

4–7 YEARS – contd	steadily. They enjoy chanting and counting (beginning to understand number). They can use their voice in different ways to play different characters in their pretend play. They develop play narratives (stories) which they return to over time. They help younger children into the play. They are interested in their own development – from babies to now. They are beginning to establish differences between what is real and unreal/fantasy. This is not yet always stable, and so they can easily be frightened by supernatural characters. They begin to try and work out right and wrong – e.g. hurting people physically or their feelings as language develops and deeper discussion of issues becomes more possible.

NORMATIVE DEVELOPMENT 3: EMOTIONAL AND SOCIAL

BIRTH TO 4 WEEKS	Baby's first smile in definite response to carer is usually around 5–6 weeks. The baby often imitates certain facial expressions. She uses total body movements to express pleasure at bathtime or when being fed. The baby enjoys feeding and cuddling. In the first month babies are learning where they begin and end, e.g. a hand is part of them but mother's hand is not.
4–8 WEEKS	Baby will smile in response to adult. The baby enjoys sucking. She turns to regard nearby speaker's face. The baby turns to preferred person's voice. She recognises face and hands of preferred adult. The baby may stop crying when she hears, sees or feels her carer.
8–12 WEEKS	The baby shows enjoyment at caring routines such as bathtime. She responds with obvious pleasure to loving attention and cuddles. She fixes the eyes unblinkingly on carer's face when feeding. The baby stays awake for longer periods of time.
4–5 MONTHS (16–20 WEEKS)	The baby enjoys attention and being with others. She shows trust and security. She has recognisable sleep patterns. By 5 months babies have learnt that they only have one mother. They are disturbed when shown several images of their mother at the same time.
6–9 MONTHS	The baby can manage to feed herself with fingers. She is now more wary of strangers, showing stranger fear. She offers toys to others. She shows distress when her mother leaves. Babies begin to crawl and this means they can do more for themselves, reach for objects and get to places and people. Babies are now more aware of other people's feelings. They cry if brother cries, for example. They love an audience to laugh with them. They cry and laugh with others. This is called recognition of an emotion. It does not mean they are really laughing or crying, though.

9–12 MONTHS	The baby enjoys songs and action rhymes. She still likes to be near to a familiar adult. She can drink from a cup with help. She will play alone for long periods. She has and shows definite likes and dislikes at meal and bedtimes. She thoroughly enjoys peek-a-boo games. She likes to look at herself in a mirror (plastic safety mirror). She imitates other people, e.g. clapping hands, waving bye bye, but there is often a time lapse so that she waves after the person has gone. She co-operates when being dressed.
1–2 YEARS	The child begins to have a longer memory. She develops a sense of identity (I am me). She expresses her needs in words and gestures. She enjoys being able to walk, and is eager to try to get dressed 'me do it!'. Toddlers are aware when others are fearful or anxious for them as they climb on and off chairs, etc.
2–3 YEARS	Pretend play develops rapidly when adults foster it. The child begins to be able to say how she is feeling. She can dress herself and go to the lavatory independently, but needs sensitive support in order to feel success rather than frustration.
3–4 YEARS	Pretend play helps children to decentre. (This means they begin to be able to understand how someone else might feel.) They are beginning to develop a gender role as they become aware of being male or female. They make friends and are interested in having friends. They learn to negotiate, give and take through experimenting with feeling powerful, having a sense of control, and through quarrels with other children. Children are easily afraid, for example, of the dark, as they become capable of pretending. They imagine all sorts of things.
4–8 YEARS	Children have developed a stable self concept. They have internalised the rules of their culture. They can hide their feelings once they can begin to control their feelings. They can think of the feelings of others. They can take responsibility, e.g. in helping younger children.

Spiritual aspects of a child's development

0–1 YEAR	Even a tiny baby experiences a sense of awe and wonder, and values people who are loved by them. Worship is about a sense of worthship. People, and loved teddy bears, a daisy on the grass grasped, looked at, (put in the mouth!) are all building the child's spiritual experiences. These have nothing to do with worship of a god or gods. Spirituality is about the developing sense of relating to others ethically, morally and humanely.

1–3 YEARS	Judy Dunn's work suggests that during this period children already have a strongly developed moral sense. They know what hurts and upsets their family (adults and children). They know what delights them and brings warm, pleased responses. Through their pretend play, and the conversations in the family about how people behave, hurt and help each other, they learn how other people feel. They learn to think beyond themselves.
3–7 YEARS	With the help and support of their family, and early childhood workers and the wider community, children develop further concepts like being helpful, forgiving, and fairness.
9 YEARS ONWARDS	These concepts become more abstract – such as justice, right, wrong, good versus evil.

Children with disabilities

Lilli Neilsen, a Danish specialist working with children with multiple disabilities, stressed the importance of carefully assessing the development of the whole child. For example, she observed a child with cerebral palsy. He was lying on his stomach on a mat, with toys around him. He looked at a toy but each time he reached for it, his shoulder jerked involuntarily and he pushed the toy away. She gently weighted down his shoulder. He reached for the toy, and was able to grab it. He smiled and made a contented sound.

It would have been easy to check his physical development, and say 'cannot reach and grasp'. Instead, we have a picture of a boy who:

▶ had an idea (to reach for the toy);
▶ knew what to do (but his body could not manage it);
▶ was given the right help, based on her careful observation and so
▶ experienced success, pleasure and
▶ the motivation to have another go.

Intellectual, physical, emotional and social aspects all merge together.

'Catching up': it's not always too late

Critical periods
Until recently it was thought that there were critical times when children learned to talk, walk, and so on and that if a child has missed out on, for example, bonding with people, or being able to crawl, perhaps through an operation on the feet, or being kept confined in a cot without objects for play, the damage was irreparable. This is rather a pessimistic view.

Recent research suggests that it is not always too late to catch up. This is a much more positive way of thinking about a child's development. Of course, as neuroscience develops we are seeing that this is only possible if the physical mechanisms are there. They may have become latent, buried or weakened through being restrained.

A visually impaired woman, who had been blind throughout her life, had an operation on her eyes. She was delighted to find that every oak tree looked completely different. She had learnt that there were things called oak trees but had not realised how completely different every oak tree's shape is. In the same way, a child who learns to walk after an operation at 3 years of age can 'catch up' on learning about walking and what it involves.

Optimal times or sensitive periods

Rather than critical periods, it seems much more likely that there are optimal times, best times or sensitive times in the child's development for learning to talk, walk, ride a bike, draw, sort out right from wrong, etc.

Children who for any reason are held from development during these sensitive or best times for learning have more difficulty becoming skilled in these areas later on. However, this does not always mean that they cannot catch up after the best time has passed.

These optimal times, or sensitive periods, or best times, last for a number of months, except in the case of the baby's development in utero (in the womb). Once born it is as if nature has designed children so that there is plenty of time to learn things at every stage of their development. This is why it is so important not to rush children in their learning. However, while it is never too late to catch up it does seem to get harder and harder once the sensitive period is missed. It is easier for babies to learn about holding rattles and toys in their hands than it is for a 3- or 4-year-old, and it will take more time to introduce such skills to the older child.

Early is not always best

The existence of 'optimum periods' does not mean that 'early is best' for young children. In fact, neuroscientists think that the windows of most opportunity for an area of development in a child are also periods of great vulnerability for the child's development in that area. The early childhood worker needs to develop the skill of observing children in enough detail to support them at the optimal or best moment for development, whenever this should come. This means not pushing children to do things too early, and it also means not waiting for signs of 'readiness' until it is rather late for children to do things.

▶ Children who are pushed on in advance of optimal times of development usually survive, but can also burn out by 8 or 9 years of age. They can be put off school. A BBC Dispatches programme in 1998 showed the damaging impact of early academic learning when children are hurried over their learning. The children are being pushed to do academic work (reading, writing and number work) too early and too fast. This is sometimes called intellectual abuse (see Chapter 16).

▶ On the other hand, children who are held back during optimal times of development through lack of stimulation usually survive but often suffer low self-esteem because they cannot do things. They lack the competence and skill which they know they need. In an extreme form, this is sometimes called lack of stimulation or intellectual neglect (see Chapter 16).

▶ Children who are helped appropriately, at optimal or best times of development, in a stimulating early childhood environment and home and by people who are sensitive and observant of what an individual child can manage (regardless of norms and average ages for doing things) usually do more than survive. They burgeon and flourish in their own unique way.

Adults working with young children need to know about child development so that they are informed enough to use their observations of children to encourage them into appropriate activity at the appropriate point of development: not too early, not too late, but just right for the particular child. Because development is uneven and each child is a unique person, different from everyone else in the world, each child will need what is 'just right' for them.

What helps one child does not necessarily help another. Different children need different sorts of help in learning, for example to read and write (see Chapter 13 on the early childhood curriculum).

C A S E   S T U D Y

Tom and Hannah

Tom and Hannah, both from the same family, needed completely different help. At 6 years of age, Tom, the second child in the family, liked his parents and older sister to read stories to him at bedtime. He liked quite different stories from his sister, especially the tales of Narnia by C.S. Lewis. He showed no interest in looking at the book. He liked to lie down and listen before he settled down to sleep.

Hannah, when she was 6 years of age, liked to find books that she could read. She would then read these to her parents at bedtime. She liked to read them to her younger brother Tom, who was then 4 years old. She read books like *Spot*. Then she wanted her parents to take a turn at reading and asked the parent to read books that were too difficult for her to read on her own. She liked to sit and follow the text as her parent read to her.

G U I D E L I N E S

Thinking about child development

1 **Children are whole people. It can be useful to focus on one area (e.g. communication and language) but it is not useful to isolate thinking about one aspect of development from thinking about the whole child's development.**
2 **Children seem to go through the same sequences of development but will vary in the exact way they do so.**
3 **Milestones can be very misleading for this reason. Children with disabilities or gifted children (children with a great talent or intellectual gift) may not be 'normal' in the way they go through a sequence.**
4 **Cultural differences mean that norms vary across the world in terms of what young children are expected to do at different points. For example, in some cultures children are expected to speak only one language, while in others they are expected to speak several languages from the moment they can form words.**
5 **Normative development tends to make us compare children with each other. It is also important to compare the child with his or her own development progressed last year. Is this good progress for this particular child?**

Development and learning: what is the difference?

It is important to be clear about the difference between development and learning.

▶ *Development* is about the general way in which a child functions. For example Matthew (2 years old) can run and jump. He cannot yet hop or skip. He runs across spaces. He jumps to music. Matthew's development is spontaneous.

▶ *Learning* is provoked. Learning occurs in a specific situation, at a specific moment, or when a specific problem needs to be tackled. Matthew is taken to the fair, where he learns to jump on an inflatable castle.

Most of the learning children do happens while they develop. We don't even notice that they are learning. It is one of nature's safety mechanisms. It is actually difficult to stop children learning as long as they are with people who encourage their general development – for example, if the adult knows and understands that 2-year-olds need to run and jump.

Children are held back in their learning if they are not allowed to develop in these ways. There have been tragic instances of this in the orphanages of Romania, where children who have been left sitting in a cot all day have become intellectually held back because their general development has not been allowed to move forward fully enough. This example shows that an unstimulating environment can hold back development. It also shows how, if development is held back, a child's learning also suffers.

It is important to take care that children with disabilities are not held back in their learning because their general development is constrained. For example, the child with a hearing impairment needs to communicate, or learning about relating to other people will be held back. Facial expression, gestures, sign language and finger spelling, as well as a hearing aid and help with lip-reading, will all help the child's general development. The child can then, in particular situations, communicate, think and socialise.

Different theories about how children develop and learn

Some theories take the view that learning is closely linked with development. Examples of these are 'leave it to nature' theories and social constructivist theories. Others dismiss the importance of a child's development as the basis of learning. An example is the transmission model theory. When describing how children learn, therefore, it is important to say which theory is being used.

Transmission models of learning

In the seventeenth century the British philosopher John Locke thought that children were like lumps of clay, which adults could mould into the shape they wanted. At the beginning of the twentieth century in the USA two psychologists, Watson and Skinner, and the Russian psychologist Pavlov were developing theories about how people learn. These have had a strong influence and follow in the tradition of Locke's philosophy.

CLASSICAL CONDITIONING

Ivan Petrovich Pavlov (1849–1936) experimented with conditioned responses. He liked to be described as a physiologist, rather than as a psychologist, because he believed that psychological states (e.g. conditioning) are identical with physiological states and processes in the brain. He thought these were the only approaches which could be useful and scientific. In his experiments, there was a neutral conditioned stimulus which was a church bell ringing. This was paired with food which was an unconditioned stimulus. The dog was fed when the church bells rang. This produced an unconditioned response, which was saliva flowing in the dog's mouth when the food appeared. Gradually, the sound of any bell would produce a conditioned response in the dog, who would produce saliva ready for the food which accompanied the ringing of the bell.

CS	+	UCS	→	UCR
bell		food		salivation

gradually turned into

CS	→	CR
bell		salivation

Classical conditioning is the way in which responses come under the control of a new stimulus. In this case, normally food produces salivation. Classical conditioning changes the stimulus, so that the sound of a bell produces salivation. Pavlov would have fed the dogs whether or not they salivated at the sound of the bell. This is very different from operant conditioning.

C A S E   S T U D Y

An example of learning through classical conditioning

Year 2 (children aged 6 and 7) in a primary school were working in groups. One group was painting. Another was writing. Another was involved in a maths game. Another was cooking. The school bell rang. Immediately, the children stopped what they were doing and started to tidy up quickly and go out to play.

CS	+	UCS	→	UCR
bell		playtime		tidy up

CS	→	CR
bell		tidy up

OPERANT CONDITIONING

Burrhus Frederic Skinner (b. 1904) was a behaviourist psychologist who worked in the USA. He did not believe it was useful to theorise about mental states which could not be observed. He thought this was unscientific (although in the 1970s he did not seem able to resist writing about unobservables like dignity and freedom).

Whereas Pavlov fed his dogs when the bell rang whether or not they salivated, Skinner only fed his rats or pigeons if they did as he required. For example, he gave rats a reward of food if they pressed a lever. This was positive reinforcement: the desired behaviour was rewarded. Conversely, undesired behaviour could be negatively reinforced. For example, the rats might receive an electric shock each time they went near one area of a maze. They would then begin to avoid that area. The undesired behaviour was extinguished. The desired behaviour was encouraged.

The 'operant conditioning' is concerned with shaping behaviour. However, the behaviour thus shaped is limited to a specific situation. It does not help the learner to transfer what is learnt to different situations.

This theory met a serious challenge in the 1960s, when Chomsky showed that language development is not a result of operant conditioning.

However, there are still those who talk about shaping a child's behaviour. We still hear remarks such as 'Children will learn what we want them to learn,' 'Children are like absorbent sponges, they soak up the knowledge that we give them.' Children can be reinforced to encourage their 'good' behaviour, that is behaviour that the adult wants to see in a child.

The transmission view of children's learning emphasises:
- the ideas adults want children to have;
- ways of behaving that the adult wants to see;
- getting children to perform as adults want.

C A S E   S T U D Y

An example of learning through operant conditioning

In an early childhood group of children 3–5 years of age, children who were observed to pick up coats that might have fallen off someone's peg in the cloakroom were rewarded with a smiley face badge and given verbal praise. Adults were 'shaping' the children's behaviour to be helpful in the community.

This approach has been challenged by Marion Dowling because it is of short-term success only. It is unlikely to give long-term benefits. This is discussed in more detail on page 202.

ADVANTAGES   DISADVANTAGES

The transmission model of learning

ADVANTAGES	DISADVANTAGES
Adults feel secure. They feel that they know what to teach children about subjects, behaviour, etc.	Adults think they know what they have taught children, when in fact the child might have learnt something quite different.
They can make up ways of testing the children in order to check what the children have learnt.	For example, the child might have stopped hitting a younger child in front of the adult; but they might have learnt that they

They can see if children are doing things properly (i.e. are the children doing what the adult thinks children should do).

This approach produces quick success, which makes adults feel they are good teachers. It makes children who succeed feel they are good learners, who can perform as adults require them to do.

still can hit a younger child, the important thing being not to be seen doing it by an adult.

This approach encourages children to be passive receivers of the learning that adults think is important for them. They are not so likely to have a go at doing things that are new to them or which they are not sure about. They will be less likely to take risks in case they make mistakes.

They only want to do things if they think they can do it successfully and get it right.

The child's learning is controlled by the adult. This quickly leads to a narrow approach to the curriculum. Children are likely to be labelled by adults as poor learners or even as failures if they do not complete adult tests and tasks in the way the adult wants.

Leave it to nature: a laissez-faire model of a child's development and learning

In the eighteenth century the French philosopher Jean Jacques Rousseau thought that children learnt naturally, and that they were biologically programmed to learn particular things at a particular time. He thought that just as a flower unfolds from the bud, so a child's learning unfolds through babbling into language and then on into reading and writing, and from kicking arms and legs to crawling and walking.

In this approach, adults help children to learn by making sure that the environment supports the child's learning as it unfolds. For example, children learn the language that they hear spoken as they grow up. If children hear Chinese, they learn to speak Chinese. If they hear English, they learn to speak English. If children hear more than one language, they are able to learn more than one language and become bilingual or multilingual. This model of learning suggests that children are naturally programmed to learn languages.

This view of learning suggests that children naturally do as they need in order to develop and learn. It sees children as rather active in their learning. Children may be helped by other people or not. It is sometimes called a *laissez-faire* view of how children learn.

ARNOLD GESELL

In the 1930s Arnold Gesell mapped out norms of development (see the section on normative measurement earlier in this chapter). These were used to observe milestones in the child's development as it unfolds. These could be used to check that the pattern of development was 'normal'. This is where the term 'milestones' of development comes from. Gesell's developmental scales looked at motor, adaptive, language and personal-social areas. Later scales, e.g. Bayley Scales, did not emphasise physical aspects as much.

If children reach particular milestones, such as walking, with the normal age range, then their development is making 'normal' progress. This approach is depressing if used with children with special educational needs as they are constantly labelled 'abnormal' in relation to norms of developmental progress.

SIGMUND FREUD (1856–1939)

Freud did not concentrate very much on the development of the youngest children. His daughter Anna Freud did, and so did Melanie Klein who was working at the same time as Anna Freud.

Anna Freud did her work with children in Nazi Germany but had to escape to England with her father. Later on in Hampstead she cared for children who had survived concentration camps in Nazi Germany. There is now a museum in Hampstead which honours her work with children, and the Anna Freud Centre, which works with children and their families.

Sigmund Freud emphasised the unconscious mind (unlike Pavlov or Skinner, who emphasised observable behaviour). He believed that our unconscious minds influence the way we behave. He thought early experiences caused later adult behaviour. He emphasised symbolic behaviour, and tried to interpret dreams.

Freud linked thinking, feeling and social relationships with physical behaviour, such as breastfeeding, toilet training, separation from parents, sexual and aggressive behaviour.

C A S E   S T U D Y

An example of learning through a 'leave it to nature' approach

Because most children of around 3–4 years of age begin to enjoy drawing and painting, the rooms in an early childhood setting were carefully set up to support this. Great care was taken in the way that a variety of colours were put out in pots, with a choice of thick and thin paint brushes. Children could choose paper of different sizes. A drying rack was close to the area and children could choose to paint at a table or on an easel. Adults would be on hand to help if needed, but would be careful not to talk to children while they were painting in case they cut across the children's thinking. Nor would adults 'make' children paint, because not all children will be ready to do so. Readiness is important in this approach to learning.

ADVANTAGES   DISADVANTAGES

The 'leave it to nature' view of development and learning

Adults can learn about how to offer the right physical resources, activities and equipment for each stage of development.	Adults may hold back too much because they are nervous that they might cut across the child's natural development: for example, by not

Children can actively make choices, select, be responsible, explore, try things out and make errors without incurring reproach or feeling a failure.

Adults value observing children and act in the light of their observations. This might mean adding more materials, and having conversations with children to help them learn more.

Adults are able to follow the child's lead and be sensitive to the child.

talking to a child while she is drawing or holding back from playing with children in the home area.

Adults only support children in their learning, rather than extending the learning children do.

Children might be understimulated because adults are waiting for signs of readiness in the child. The signs might never come! Adults wait too long before intervening.

Children might not be shown how to do things in case it is not developmentally the right moment to teach them this.

This means it might not offer enough challenge to children.

Children with special educational needs or from different cultures might be labelled 'abnormal' or 'unready'. In fact they might reach a milestone earlier or later, but still within the normal sequence. They might develop unevenly but in ways which make 'normal' life possible. Milestones in one culture might be different in another culture.

The social constructivist model

In the eighteenth century the German philosopher Kant believed that a child's learning was an interaction between the child and the environment. He believed that children constructed their own understanding and knowledge about things. This approach is now usually called a social constructivist view of how children learn. It is the approach that is most favoured by modern early childhood workers in the 1990s and has the best support from Western theory and research in child development. It draws on both the transmission model and the *laissez-faire* (leave it to nature) model of a child's learning, rearranging elements of both into something that is more helpful to those working with younger children.

JEAN PIAGET (1896-1980)

The important elements of Piaget's theory of how children learn are:
- ▶ that children go through stages and sequences in their learning;
- ▶ that children are active learners;
- ▶ that children use first-hand experiences and prior experiences in order to learn;
- ▶ that children imitate and transform what they learn into symbolic behaviour.

Piaget did not explicitly emphasise the importance of social and emotional aspects of learning. This means he took social and emotional development for granted. He did not write about this in detail. His writing emphasises intellectual/cognitive development and learning. Piaget's theory is called constructivist for this reason. He did not emphasise social relationships as much as the social constructivists.

LEV VYGOTSKY (1896-1935)

Vygotsky stressed the importance of someone who knows more than the child and who can help the child to learn something that would be too difficult for the child to do on his or her own. Vygotsky calls this the zone of potential development. It means that the child can do with help now what it will be possible for him or her to do alone with no help later in life.

Vygotsky emphasised the importance of play for children under 7. This also allows children to do things beyond what they can manage in actual life (such as pretend to drive a car). It is another way through which children reach their zone of potential development.

The zone of potential development is sometimes called the zone of proximal development. The zone of actual development shows what the child can manage without help from anyone.

Vygotsky believed social relationships were at the heart of a child's learning. His theory is called a social constructivist theory.

JEROME BRUNER (1915-   )

The essence of Bruner's theory of how children learn is that children learn through:
- ▶ doing (the enactive mode of learning);
- ▶ imaging things that they have done (the iconic mode of learning);
- ▶ making what they know into symbolic codes, e.g. talking, writing or drawing (the symbolic mode of learning).

Adults can tutor children and help them to learn. They do this by 'scaffolding' what the child is learning in order to make it manageable for the child. This means that children can learn any subject at any age. They simply need to be given the right kind of help. For example, when a baby drops a biscuit over the side of the high chair, the baby can learn about gravity if the adult 'scaffolds' the experience by saying something like: 'It dropped straight down on to the floor, didn't it? Let's both drop a biscuit and see if they get to the floor together.'

Bruner's theory is also called a social constructivist theory.

C A S E   S T U D Y

An example of an interactionist/social constructivist view of development and learning

Through a team approach to record-keeping in an early childhood setting, staff had built up observations of children. They noted that Damian (5 years) kept punching: He punched other children, furniture and other objects. It seemed to be his main way of exploring. The staff introduced activities which allowed punching. They put huge lumps of clay on the table. They made bread with a group (which included Damian) and encouraged energetic kneading. They sang

songs like 'Clap your hands and stamp your feet' and 'Hands knees and bumpsa daisy'. They encouraged hand printing and finger painting. They helped children to choreograph dance fights in acting out a story. Damian told the group about 'baddies' from another planet. He helped to 'beat' the carpet with a beater as part of spring cleaning. He spent a long time at the woodwork bench hammering nails into his model. He soon stopped hitting other children, and began to talk about what he was doing with adults and other children.

Observation led to adults being able to support Damian's learning in educationally worthwhile ways. Adults were also able to extend his learning so that hitting people became learning to hit in a rich variety of ways.

ADVANTAGES   DISADVANTAGES

The social interactionist/constructivist view of learning

This approach is very rewarding and satisfying because adults and children can enjoy working together, struggling at times, concentrating hard, stretching their thinking and ideas, celebrating their learning, and sharing the learning together.

Trusting each other to help each other creates a positive attitude between children, parents and staff. It means taking pride in the way that indoor and outdoor areas of the room are set up, organised, maintained and cared for.

It means teamwork by the adults, which is the way to bring out everyone's strengths in a multiprofessional group of teachers, nursery workers, etc. It means sharing with parents and children all the learning that is going on. It means adults need to go on learning about children's development. When adults continue to develop as people and professionals and learn alongside children, they have more to offer the children.

Adults and children respect and value each other's needs and rights, and help each other to learn.

Although it takes time and experience

It is very hard work compared with the other two approaches to learning that we have looked at in this chapter. This is because there is much more for adults to know about, more to think about, and more to organise and do.

It is much more difficult for those who are not trained to understand how to work in this way.

In Sweden there are now local plazzas where early childhood workers explain the way they work with parents, those working with older children, governing bodies and politicians.

for adults to build up skills in
working this way it is very effective in
helping children to learn during their
early years. Research supporting this
approach is: The Goldsmiths
Principles into Practice (PIP)
Research Project 1993, The Worcester
University College Effective Early
Learning Project (EEL) directed by
Professor Chris Pascal, 1993.
Research reports and projects
supporting this approach such as
Chris Athey's Froebel Nursery
Research Project 1990, the Startright
Report 1995, and the Report of the
National Commission on Education
1994 all suggest that this approach
seems to have a lasting effect
throughout children's lives.

GUIDELINES

The different approaches to development and learning

1 From Figure 2.3 you will see that in a 'leave it to nature' approach to learning, children make a very high contribution to the learning they do, but the adult holds back and takes a very small part.
2 This is very different from the transmission model. In this approach the adult has a very high input into the child's learning, and takes control over the child's learning. The child's contribution is quite low.
3 The 'by-the-book' approach to learning is hardly worth discussing. Here, both the adults and the children have a very low level of participation. This can hardly be called an approach to learning; it is really just a way of keeping children busily occupied. Worksheets, colouring in, tracing, templates, filling in gaps, joining the dots all fall under this heading.
4 In the social constructivist (sometimes called 'interactionist') approach to learning both the adult and the children put an enormous amount of energy into active learning.

FIGURE 2.3
Four approaches to development and learning

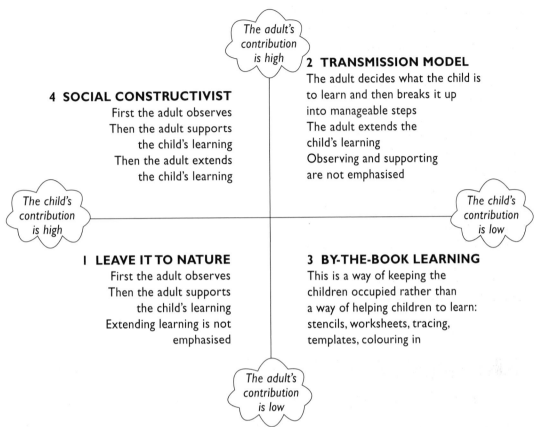

The nature/nurture debate

The nature/nurture debate is concerned with the extent to which development and learning are primarily to do with naturally maturing processes, and the extent to which development and learning progress as a result of experience.

The debate has been very fierce, and it is not over yet. Modern psychologists such as Sir Michael Rutter (1992) believe that the child's learning is probably about 60% nature and 40% nurture. What do you think now that you have read this chapter?

▶ The transmission approach stresses experience and nurture.

▶ The 'leave it to nature' approach stresses maturation and nature.

▶ The social constructivist approach to learning stresses both nature and nurture. A modern way of describing this is to say that both the biological and socio-cultural paths of development are important for learning.

The nature/nurture debate is discussed in more detail in Chapters 6 and 7.

Theories about learning and adult learning

Remember, theories about learning are not just about how children learn. They are about how adults learn too.

Adults who enjoy learning and being with children are much more likely to provide a high-quality early childhood setting for children and their families. When visitors see an early childhood setting which they describe as good practice, or high-quality practice, it is usually that adults and children are both active in their learning.

R E S O U R C E S

Videos

Video Reportage
Productions
Number 3,
20 West Parade
Norwich NR2 3DW

Child Studies One – The
First Year

Child Studies Two – 12 to 18
Months

Child Studies Three – 19
Months to 2+ Years

Child Studies Four – Three
to Five Years

Channel 4 series of videos
Baby it's You
Available in good bookstores.

BBC Education/
National Children's Bureau
Tuning into Children is a
project to develop a range of
video and print resources and
radio broadcasts on child
development. Video and
book by Tina Bruce (1996).
Audio cassette and
pocketbook available from:
Tuning into Children
P.O. Box 20 Tonbridge
TN12 6WU

Books

Konner, M. (1991)
Childhood. Boston/London:
Little, Brown.

Oates, J. (ed.) (1994) *The
Foundations of Child
Development.* Oxford:
Blackwell/Open University.

O'Hagan, M. and Smith, M.
(1993) *Special Issues in Child
Care.* London: Bailliere
Tindall

Carter, R. (1988) *Mapping the
Mind.* London: Wellcome
Trust.

A C T I V I T Y

When you have looked at these milestones of normative development, turn to Figure 2.2
Draw seven circles with the same diameter.
Cut them out.
Write in the aspects of development
Thread the circles on a string.
Bunch them together to remind yourself these are a whole. Spread them out to focus on one aspect of the child, but return them to the whole at the end reminding yourself of each area.

A C T I V I T Y

Think back to your own schooldays. Were any of the lessons based on a transmission model of learning? Evaluate your learning experience.

Make your own scale of normative development, trying to make it as holistic as possible. Apply it in each of the four following ways. In each case, ask yourself: Do I know this child better than I did before, and in what ways?

1 Observe a baby girl and then in a different family, a baby boy of 6–9 months in age. Use the circles activity and Holistic Child Development chart in this chapter and find out everything you can about the child under those headings. (See pages 26 and 27, Figures 2.1 and 2.2).

2 Observe a boy toddler of 15–20 months in age. Repeat the exercise from (1) with him.

3 Observe two 3–4 year olds and repeat the exercise. Choose children from different cultural backgrounds, language backgrounds, or a child with a disability. Remember, it is not useful to do this in the spirit that you are checking to see if children are behind or ahead of 'norms'. Instead, you are using guidelines which help you to build up a complete picture of each child you work with. Then you can see where help is needed, and how to facilitate and extend the child's development and learning.

4 Observe two 5–7 year olds in the same spirit.

Make a chart with these three headings:

▶ Transmission model of learning
▶ *Laissez-faire* or 'leave it to nature' model of learning
▶ Social constructivist or interactionist model of learning

Which sentences go under which heading?
1 Adults should mould the child's learning. After all, adults know more than children.
2 Children know what they need in order to learn.
3 Do you want to have a story first, or tidy up first?
4 We need to tidy up before we go home. We'll have the story after.
5 Children are full of ideas if they are encouraged to have them.
6 Do it because I say so.
7 That child has been 'off task' all morning.
8 Children are born with everything they need in order to learn.
9 Children enjoy conversations with adults.
10 Children must be free to try things out.
11 Children will learn when they are ready and not before.
12 That child performed the task successfully today.
13 Nature knows best.
14 Adults know best.
15 Children must be free to try things out and to learn from the mistakes they make.

Compare your answers with a working partner. Discuss your answers together.

3

Work with Babies: Physical Development and Care

It is essential that those who work with children know how a child grows and develops. Every child is unique – the 'average' child or the 'normal' child does not exist. Learning about child development involves studying patterns of growth and development, and these are taken as guidelines for normality. The early childhood worker is ideally placed to notice when a child is not progressing according to these guidelines.

Defining terms

Growth

Growth refers to an increase in physical size, and can be measured by height (length), weight and head circumference. Growth is determined by:

▶ heredity;
▶ nutrition;
▶ hormones;
▶ emotional influences.

Development

Development is concerned with the possession of skills. Physical development proceeds in a set order, with simple behaviours occurring before more complex skills – for example, a child will sit before he or she stands.

Norm

A norm is a fixed or ideal standard. Developmental norms are sometimes called **'milestones'**, denoting markers in the recognised pattern of physical development which it is expected that children will follow. Each child will develop in a unique way, and using norms helps in understanding the patterns of development while acknowledging the wide variation between individuals.

Preconceptual care

Life does not begin at birth; the individual is already nine months old when born. In China a person's age is determined not by his birth date, but by the date of his conception. A couple planning to start a family will certainly hope for a healthy baby; preconceptual care means both partners reducing known risks before trying to conceive in order to create the best conditions for an **embryo** to grow and develop into a healthy baby. The first twelve weeks of life in the womb (or uterus) are the most crucial as this is the period during which all the essential organs are being formed.

Conception and pregnancy

Conception occurs in the **fallopian tube** when the male sperm meets the female egg (the ovum) and fertilises it. The fertilised ovum now contains genetic material from both mother and father – a total of forty-six **chromosomes** – and a new life begins.

Early days of life

Within about 30 hours of fertilisation the egg divides into two cells, then four, and so on (see Figure 3.1); after five days it has reached the 16-cell stage and has arrived in the **uterus (womb)**. Sometimes a mistake will happen and the ovum implants in the wrong place, such as in the fallopian tube; this is called an **ectopic pregnancy**. By about the tenth day, the blastocyst has embedded itself entirely in the lining of the uterus and the complex process of development and growth begins. The outer cells of the blastocyst go on to form:

 ▶ the **placenta** (called chorionic villi during early development). The placenta (afterbirth) provides the foetus with oxygen and nourishment from the mother via the **umbilical cord** and removes the foetal waste products. The placenta also acts as a barrier to certain micro-organisms, but some may cross this barrier and cause damage to the embryo or foetus.
 ▶ the **membranes** or **amniotic sac**. This sac is filled with amniotic fluid and provides a cushion for the foetus as it grows and becomes more mobile.

FIGURE 3.1
Early days of life

Fertilisation: only one sperm can fertilise the egg   Two-cell stage   Four-cell stage   Blastocyst

Guidelines for Preconceptual Care

Use barrier methods of contraception Use a condom or a diaphragm for three months before trying to conceive. It is advisable to discontinue the Pill so that the woman's natural hormonal pattern can be re-established.	**Stop smoking** Smoking cuts the amount of oxygen supplied to the baby through the placenta and can result in miscarriage or low birth weight. Some men who smoke are less fertile because they produce less sperm.

Eat well

A balanced diet allows a woman to build up reserves of the nutrients vital to the unborn baby in the first three months:

- ▶ *eat something from the four main food groups* every day (potato & cereals, fruit and vegetables, milk & milk products and high protein foods)
- ▶ *cut down on sugary foods* and eat fresh foods where possible
- ▶ *avoid prepacked foods* and any foods which carry the risk of salmonella or listeria
- ▶ *do not go on a slimming diet*; follow your appetite and do not eat more than you need
- ▶ *vegetarian diets* which include milk, fish, cheese and eggs provide the vital protein the baby needs;
- ▶ *vegans* should eat soya products and nuts and pulses to supply protein and Vitamin B12 may need to be taken as a supplement
- ▶ *folic acid tablets and a diet rich in folic acid* taken preconceptually and in pregnancy help the development of the brain and spinal cord

Genetic counselling If there is a fairly high risk that a child may carry a genetic fault, such as cystic fibrosis or sickle cell disease, genetic counselling is offered Tests may be done to try to diagnose any problem prenatally but all carry some element of risk in themselves	**Avoid hazards at work** Some chemicals and gases may increase the risk of miscarriage or birth defects. Women should be aware of the risks and take precautions after discussion with the environmental health officer
Substance misuse and abuse Do not take any drugs unless prescribed by a doctor. Existing conditions such as epilepsy or diabetes will need to be controlled before and during pregnancy Many addictive drugs cross the placental barrier and can damage the unborn baby	**X-rays** X-rays are best avoided in the first three months of pregnancy although the risks to the foetus are thought to be very small
Sexually transmitted diseases (STDs) STDs should be treated – if either partner thinks there is any risk of syphilis, gonorrhoea, genital herpes or HIV infection, then both partners should attend a 'special clinic' for advice and tests. STDs can cause miscarriage, stillbirth or birth defects.	**Cut down on alcohol** The best advice is to cut out alcohol completely; moderate drinking (1–2 glasses of wine or beer a day) increases the risk of miscarriage and babies are born smaller and more vulnerable. Heavy drinking, especially in the first few weeks of pregnancy, can cause **foetal alcohol syndrome** in which the baby is seriously damaged.

FIGURE 3.2
Embryo 4–5 wks

FIGURE 3.3
Embryo 6–7 wks

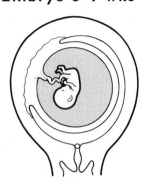
FIGURE 3.4
Embryo 8–9 wks

The inner cell mass goes on to form the embryo proper. Until eight weeks after conception the developing baby is called an embryo; from eight weeks until birth the developing baby is called a foetus. The embryonic cells are divided into three layers:

▶ the **ectoderm**, which forms the outer layer of the baby, the skin, nails and hair; it will soon fold inwards to form the nervous system (brain, spinal cord and nerves) as well;

▶ the **endoderm**, which forms all the organs inside the baby;

▶ the **mesoderm**, which develops into the heart, muscles, blood and bones.

At 4–5 weeks, the embryo is the size of a pea (5 mm) and yet the rudimentary heart has begun to beat and the arms and legs appear as buds growing out of the sides of the body (Figure 3.2).

At 6–7 weeks, the embryo is 8 mm long and the limb buds are beginning to look like real arms and legs; the heart can be seen beating on an ultrasound scan (Figure 3.3).

At 8–9 weeks the unborn baby is called a foetus and measures about 2 cm. Toes and fingers are starting to form and the major internal organs (brain, lungs, kidneys, liver and intestines) are all developing rapidly (Figure 3.4).

At 10–14 weeks the foetus measures about 7 cm and all the organs are complete. By 12 weeks the unborn baby is fully formed and just needs to grow and develop. The top of the uterus (the **fundus**) can usually be felt above the pelvic bones (Figure 3.5).

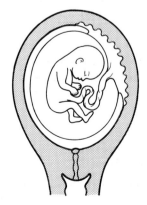
FIGURE 3.5
Foetus at 10–14 wks

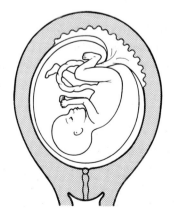
FIGURE 3.6
Foetus at 15–22 wks

FIGURE 3.7
Foetus at 23–30 wks

FIGURE 3.8
Baby at 31–40 wks

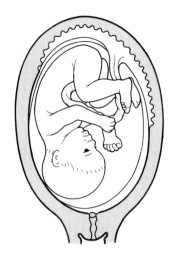

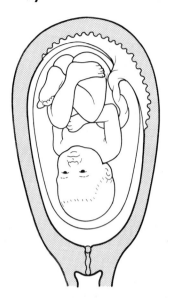

At 15–22 weeks, the foetus is large enough for the mother to feel its movements. A mother who has had a child before may have felt fluttering sensations earlier as she is able to identify them. At 22 weeks the greasy, white protective film called **vernix caseosa** has begun to form and the foetus is covered with a fine, downy hair called **lanugo** (Figure 3.6).

At 23–30 weeks, the foetus is covered in vernix and the lanugo has usually disappeared. From 28 weeks the foetus is said to be **viable** – that is, if born now he has a good chance of surviving, although babies have survived as early as 23 weeks. The mother may be aware of his response to sudden or loud noises and he will be used to the pitch and rhythm of his mother's voice. At 30 weeks the foetus measures 42 cm (Figure 3.7).

At 31–40 weeks, the foetus begins to fill out and become plumper; the vernix and lanugo disappear and the foetus usually settles into the head-down position ready to be born. If his head moves down into the pelvis it is said to be 'engaged', but this may not happen until the onset of labour (Figure 3.8).

Pregnancy

The signs and symptoms of pregnancy occur after the fertilised ovum has implanted in the lining of the uterus. The pregnancy is usually confirmed by a simple urine test – the HCG test, which detects the presence of human chorionic gonadotrophin in the urine.

SIGNS AND SYMPTOMS OF PREGNANCY

AMENHORROEA

Missing a period is a very reliable symptom of pregnancy if the woman has no other reason to experience a change to her menstrual cycle; occasionally periods may be missed because of illness, severe weight loss or emotional upset.

BREAST CHANGES

Sometimes the breasts will tingle and feel heavier or fuller immediately; surface veins become visible and the primary areola, the ring around the nipple, will become darker. This is more noticeable on fair-skinned women. As pregnancy continues (at about 16 weeks) **colostrum** can be expressed from the nipple.

PASSING URINE FREQUENTLY
The effect of hormones and the enlarging uterus result in the women having to pass urine more often than usual.

SICKNESS
Nausea (feeling sick) or vomiting can occur at any time of the day or night, but is usually referred to as 'morning sickness'. Some unlucky women experience nausea throughout pregnancy.

TIREDNESS
This can be noticeable in the first three months of pregnancy but usually lifts as the pregnancy progresses.

The principles of antenatal (or prenatal) care

The main aim of antenatal care is to help the mother successfully deliver a live healthy infant. Women are encouraged to see their family doctor (GP) as soon as they think they may be pregnant. The team of professionals – midwife, doctor, health visitor and obstetrician – will discuss the options of antenatal care, type of delivery and post-natal care with the mother. Antenatal care has the following principles or aims:
- A safe pregnancy and delivery resulting in a healthy mother and baby.
- The identification and management of any deviation from normal.
- Preparation of both parents for labour and parenthood.
- An emotionally satisfying experience.
- Promotion of a healthy lifestyle and breast-feeding.

The management of antenatal care

STATUTORY SERVICES RELATING TO ANTENATAL CARE
The first decision to be made is **where** the birth will take place. Facilities and policies vary a great deal around the UK and some people have more choices than others do. The options are:
- **Home** – some doctors do not agree with home births in any circumstances as they are concerned about the lack of hospital facilities if anything should go wrong during labour; the woman is entitled to register with another doctor if she wishes to have a home birth. Antenatal care is shared between the community midwife, who visits the woman in her own home or at a health centre, and the GP.
- **Hospital** – a full stay in hospital is usually 7 or 8 days, but there are often options to stay only 48 hours or even 6 hours. Antenatal care is shared between the hospital, the GP and the community midwife.
- **GP Units** – These are run by GPs and community midwives, often using beds within a district hospital or in a separate building near the hospital.
- **Midwife Unit** – This unit is run entirely by midwives who undertake all the antenatal care, delivery and postnatal care. The mother and baby usually stay in the unit from six hours after birth to three days. Midwife units are not widely available.
- **Domino schemes** – Domino is an abbreviation of Domiciliary-in-out. Care is shared between the community midwife and the GP. When labour starts, the midwife comes into the hospital or GP unit to deliver the baby. Back-up care can

TABLE 3.2

The Booking Clinic: early pregnancy

Taking a medical and obstetric history

This is usually carried out by the midwife and covers the following areas:

- details of the **menstrual cycle** and the date of the last period; the expected delivery date (EDD) is then calculated.
- details of any **previous pregnancies**, miscarriages, or births
- **medical history** – diabetes, high blood pressure or heart disease can all influence the pregnancy
- **family history** – any serious illness, inherited disorders or history of twins
- **social history** – the need for support at home and the quality of housing will be assessed, especially if the woman has requested a home or Domino delivery

Medical examination

A doctor will need to carry out the following physical examinations:

- **listening to the heart and lungs**
- **examining breasts** for any lumps or for inverted nipples which might cause difficulties with breast feeding
- noting the presence of **varicose veins** in the legs and any swelling of legs or fingers
- **internal examination** to assess the timing of the pregnancy – a cervical smear may be offered

Clinical tests

- **Height** – this can give a guide to the ideal weight; small women (under 1.5 m) will be more carefully monitored in case the pelvis is too narrow for the baby to be delivered vaginally
- **Weight** – this will be recorded at every antenatal appointment; weight gain should be steady (the average gain during pregnancy is 12–15 kg)
- **Blood pressure** – readings are recorded at every antenatal appointment, as **hypertension** or high blood pressure in pregnancy can interfere with the blood supply to the placenta
- **Urine tests** – urine is tested at every antenatal appointment for:
  ▲ **sugar**: occasionally present in the urine during pregnancy, but if it persists may be an early sign of **diabetes**
  ▲ **protein**: traces may indicate an infection or be an early sign of **pre-eclampsia** – a special condition only associated with pregnancy where one of the main signs is high blood pressure
  ▲ **ketones**: these are produced when fats are broken down; the case may be constant vomiting or dieting or there may be some kidney damage
- **Blood tests** – a blood sample will be taken and screenef for:
  ▲ **blood group**: in case transfusion is necessary; everyone belongs to one of four groups: A, AB, B or O
  ▲ **Rhesus factor**: positive or negative (see below)
  ▲ **syphilis**: can damage the baby if left untreated
  ▲ **rubella immunity**: if not immune, the mother should avoid contact with the virus and be offered the vaccination after birth to safeguard future pregnancies
  ▲ **sickle cell disease** – a form of inherited anaemia which affects people of African, West Indian and Asian descent
  ▲ **thalassaemia** – a similar condition which mostly affects people from Mediterranean countries
  ▲ **haemoglobin levels** – the iron content of the blood is checked regularly to exclude **anaemia**

be from the woman's GP or from a hospital doctor. If both mother and baby are well, they can often go home within hours of the birth and the midwife continues to look after them at home.

Professionals involved in antenatal care and childbirth

Midwife

This is a registered nurse who has had further training in the care of women during pregnancy and labour. They can work in hospitals, clinics or in the community. Most routine antenatal care is carried out by midwives and a midwife delivers most babies born in the UK. In the community midwives have a statutory responsibility to care for both mother and baby for 10 days after delivery.

General Practitioner (GP) or family doctor

This is a doctor who has taken further training in general practice. Many GP group practices also have a doctor who has taken further training in obstetrics.

Obstetrician

This is a doctor who has specialised in the care of pregnant women and childbirth. Most of their work is carried out in hospital maternity units and they care for women who have complications in pregnancy or who need a Caesarean section or forceps delivery.

Gynaecologist

This is a doctor who has specialised in the female reproductive system.

Paediatrician

This is a doctor who has specialised in the care of children up to the age of 16. They attend all difficult births in case the baby needs resuscitation.

Health Visitor

This is a qualified nurse who has taken further training for the care of people in the community, including midwifery experience. They work exclusively in the community, and can be approached either directly or via the family doctor. They work primarily with mothers and children up to the age of five years. Their main role is health education and preventive care.

Private services relating to antenatal care

There are many options available to the woman who can afford to pay for private antenatal and postnatal care. She may choose a home birth with a private or independent midwife. The midwife will undertake all antenatal and postnatal care and also deliver the baby. Another option is to have the baby in a private hospital or maternity unit attended by an obstetrician. Many district hospitals also offer private facilities for paying patients.

The significance of the Rhesus factor in pregnancy

Most people are Rhesus positive. If the mother is Rhesus negative (Rh−) and the baby inherits the father's Rhesus positive (Rh+) the baby's blood can enter the mother's bloodstream during delivery. The mother's body reacts to these foreign blood cells by producing antibodies to fight them. These antibody molecules are able to cross the placenta and go back into the baby, resulting in anaemia or more seriously, **haemolytic disease of the newborn**, which may require an exchange blood transfusion. Prevention of this situation is by regular tests to assess the antibodies in the maternal blood and by giving an injection of Anti-D globulin (anti-Rhesus factor) within 72 hours of the first delivery to prevent further formation of antibodies.

Nutrition during pregnancy

A BALANCED DIET

Every pregnant woman hears the advice 'eating for two' but the best information available today suggests that this is not good advice. Research shows that the quality of a baby's nutrition before birth may also lay the foundation for good health in later life. During pregnancy women should eat a well-balanced diet using the following guidelines:

- ▶ high in **carbohydrate** (bread, cereals, rice, pasta, potatoes);
- ▶ low in total **fat**. Reducing fat has the effect of reducing energy intake; therefore it is particularly important that these calories are replaced in the form of carbohydrate. Fat should not be completely avoided, however, as certain types are essential for body functioning as well as containing **fat-soluble vitamins**;
- ▶ **protein** is also important for foetal growth and development; adequate intake is rarely a problem for healthy women in developed countries;
- ▶ eating plenty of **fibre** will prevent constipation, and help to keep the calorie intake down.

Department of Health advice is to eat according to appetite, with only a small increase in energy intake for the last three months of the pregnancy (200 kcal a day).

MICRONUTRIENTS IN PREGNANCY

During pregnancy the foetus gets all its nutrients from the mother. Pregnancy increases the requirements for a range of micronutrients, particularly **folic acid**, **calcium** and **iron**. **Folic acid** is a B vitamin, which is very important throughout pregnancy, but especially in the first twelve weeks when the baby's systems are being formed. Most doctors recommend that pregnant women take a folic acid supplement every day, as more folic acid is required than is available from a normal diet.

WOMEN AT RISK

Some women are at risk from poor nutrition during pregnancy. Any woman who restricts her diet for personal, religious or cultural reasons may have to take care, although well-balanced vegetarian and vegan diets should be safe. The following groups of women are potentially at risk:

▶ Adolescents – who have an increased nutritional requirement for their own growth as well as providing for the foetus	▶ Women with closely spaced pregnancies
	▶ Recent immigrants
▶ Women on low income	▶ Women who are very underweight or overweight
▶ Women with restricted and poorly balanced diets	
▶ Women who have had a previous low birthweight baby	▶ Women with pre-existing medical conditions, such as diabetes mellitus and food allergies.

Antenatal care during the middle months

Visits to the antenatal clinic, GP or community midwife will be monthly, or more often if problems are detected. On each occasion the following checks are made and recorded on the Co-operation Card, which is given to every woman to enable appropriate care to be given wherever she happens to be:

- ▶ weight;
- ▶ urine;
- ▶ blood pressure;
- ▶ fundal height (the size of the uterus);
- ▶ foetal heart (heard through a portable ear trumpet);
- ▶ any oedema or swelling of ankles and/or fingers.

At 28 weeks, the hospital will expect to see the mother booked in for a hospital delivery and visits to the antenatal clinic/GP or midwife are weekly in the final month of pregnancy.

A summary of the tests carried out during pregnancy is shown in Table 3.3.

HEALTH EDUCATION

The midwife, doctor and health visitor are available throughout pregnancy to give advice on diet, rest, exercise or any issue causing concern; they can also offer advice on the current maternity benefits and how to apply for them.

The 'inverse care law' operates in this area of health (see also p. 422): the women most at risk of developing complications during pregnancy are those in poor housing, on a poor diet or whose attendance at antenatal clinics is poor or non-existent. The midwife and health visitor will be aware of the risks such factors pose for both mother and baby and will target such individuals to ensure that preventive health care, such as surveillance and immunisation, reaches them.

PARENTCRAFT CLASSES

Childbirth preparation classes are held in hospitals, health centres, community halls or private homes. They usually welcome couples to attend and aim to cover:

- ▶ all aspects of pregnancy: diet and exercise; sexual activity; how to cope with problems such as nausea, tiredness and heartburn;
- ▶ labour: pain control methods, breathing and relaxation exercises;
- ▶ birth: what happens at each stage and the different methods of delivery.

The classes usually include a tour of the maternity unit at the hospital.

They are also valuable meeting-places for discussion with other parents-to-be about all

TABLE 3.3

Screening tests in pregnancy

NAME	PROCEDURE	WHEN	PROCEDURE PERFORMED TO ASSESS	COMMENTS
CHORIONIC VILLUS SAMPLING (CVS)	A small piece of the placenta is removed via the cervix (neck of the womb) and the cells examined	At about 8–11 weeks	• the risk of Down's syndrome, haemophilia, cystic fibrosis, thalassaemia, sickle-cell disease or other inherited disorders	
AMNIOCENTESIS	After an ultrasound scan a hollow needle is inserted through the abdomen to draw off a sample of amniotic fluid from inside the uterus; the foetal cells are examined under a microscope to detect chromosomal abnormality	At about 16–18 weeks	• the presence of an extra chromosome, i.e. Down's syndrome • any missing or damaged chromosomes	May be offered to any woman with a history of chromosomal abnormalities or sex-linked disorders, or who is over 35 years old
TRIPLE TEST	A blood test which measures levels of the hormones, HCG (Human Chorionic Gonadotrophin) and oestriol and a protein, AFP – alpha-fetoprotein; the levels of the three substances are used in conjunction with the woman's age	At about 16 weeks	• the risk of the baby having Down's syndrome • the risk of the baby having spina bifida	The triple test does not make a diagnosis of these conditions but indicates if further tests such as amniocentesis are necessary
ULTRASOUND SCAN	Ultrasound (sound at higher frequency than can be heard by the human ear) is used to produce pictures of the foetus in the uterus	At any stage, but usually 16–20 weeks	• the size, age and position of the foetus • the position of the placenta • if there is more than one baby • if the foetus is developing normally • if there are fibroids in the womb • if the pregnancy is in the right place or ectopic	

the emotional changes involved in becoming a parent. Classes may also be held for women with special needs – expectant mothers who are schoolgirls, or in one-parent families, or whose first language is not English. Some areas provide classes earlier in pregnancy (from eight to twenty weeks) or aquanatal classes where women can practise special exercises standing in shoulder-high water.

Some organisations e.g. National Childbirth Trust (NCT) also offer parent education classes; these are usually held in small groups in the tutor's home. Fees vary according to circumstances.

MATERNITY RIGHTS AND BENEFITS

All pregnant women are entitled to the following rights and benefits:

- ▶ **free NHS maternity care**
- ▶ **paid time off** for antenatal care; this care includes not only medical examinations but also parentcraft classes;
- ▶ protection against **detrimental treatment** and **unfair dismissal** because of pregnancy;
- ▶ 14 weeks **maternity leave** regardless of service;
- ▶ **free prescriptions** until the baby is one year old;
- ▶ **free dental care** until the baby is one year old;
- ▶ the right to **return to work** up to 29 weeks after the baby is born.

Other maternity benefits, such as Maternity Allowance and Maternity Benefit are administered by the Department of Social Security and are paid only to those who meet certain qualifying conditions or who are on a low income. Free milk and vitamin tokens are available to expectant mothers, and to children under five years, in families receiving Income Support.

Factors affecting physical development of the foetus

Various factors affect growth and development of the foetus. These include:

- ▶ mother's age
- ▶ the use of drugs
- ▶ premature birth
- ▶ number of pregnancies
- ▶ infection
- ▶ diet – see Chapter 11
- ▶ pre-eclampsia

The mother's age

The best age to have a baby from a purely physical point of view is probably between 18 and 30 years. Complications of pregnancy and labour are slightly more likely above and below these ages.

- ▶ **Younger mothers:** Under the age of 16 there is a higher risk of having a small or premature baby, of becoming anaemic and suffering from high blood pressure. Emotionally and socially, very young teenagers are likely to find pregnancy and motherhood much harder to cope with and they will need a great deal of support.

▶ **Older first-time mothers:** First-time mothers over the age of 35 run a risk of having a baby with a chromosomal abnormality. The most common abnormality associated with age is **Down's syndrome**. A woman in her twenties has a chance of only 1 in several thousand of having such a baby, but by forty the risk is about 1 in every 110 births, and at 45 the risk is about 1 in every 30. Aminocentesis can detect the extra chromosome which results in Down's syndrome; it is usually offered routinely to women who are thirty-seven or over.

Number of pregnancies

Some problems occur more frequently in the *first* pregnancy than in later ones, e.g. **breech presentation**, **pre-eclampsia**, **low birth weight** and **neural tube defects**. First babies represent a slightly higher risk than second and third babies do. The risks begin to rise again with a fourth and successive pregnancies; this is partly because the uterine muscles are less efficient, but it also depends to a certain extent on age and social factors associated with larger families.

The use of drugs

Most drugs taken by the mother during pregnancy will cross the placenta and enter the foetal circulation. Some of these may cause harm, particularly during the first three months after conception. Drugs that adversely affect the development of the foetus are known as **teratogenic**.

▶ **Prescription drugs** – Drugs are sometimes prescribed by the woman's doctor to safeguard her health during pregnancy, for example antibiotics or anti-epilepsy treatment; they have to be very carefully monitored to minimise any possible effects on the unborn child.

▶ **Non-prescription drugs** such as aspirin and other painkillers should be checked for safety during pregnancy.

▶ **Alcohol** can harm the foetus if taken in excess. Babies born to mothers who drank large amounts of alcohol throughout the pregnancy may be born with **foetal alcohol syndrome**. These babies have characteristic facial deformities, stunted growth and mental retardation. More moderate drinking may increase the risk of miscarriage, but many women continue to drink small amounts of alcohol throughout their pregnancy with no ill effects.

▶ **Smoking** during pregnancy reduces placental blood flow and therefore the amount of oxygen the foetus receives. Babies born to mothers who smoke are more likely to be born prematurely or to have a low birth weight.

▶ **Illegal drugs** such as cocaine, crack and heroin are **teratogenic** and may cause the foetus to grow more slowly. Babies born to heroin addicts are addicted themselves and suffer painful withdrawal symptoms. They are likely to be underweight and may even die.

Infection

Viruses or small bacteria can cross the placenta from the mother to the foetus and may interfere with normal growth and development. The first three months (the first **trimester**) of a pregnancy are when the foetus is particularly vulnerable. The most common examples are:

▶ **rubella** (German measles). This is a viral infection that is especially harmful to the developing foetus as it can cause congenital defects such as blindness, deafness and mental retardation. All girls in the UK are now immunised against rubella before they reach child-bearing age, and this measure has drastically reduced the incidence of rubella-damaged babies;

▶ **cytomegalovirus (CMV).** This virus causes vague aches and pains and possibly fevers and poses similar risks to the rubella virus, i.e. blindness, deafness and mental retardation, but as yet there is no preventative vaccine. It is thought to infect as many as 1% of unborn babies and of those infected babies, about 10% may suffer permanent damage;

▶ **toxoplasmosis.** Toxoplasmosis is an infection caused by a tiny parasite. It may be caught from eating anything infected with the parasite. This could be:
  ▶ raw or undercooked meat, including raw cured meat such as Parma ham or salami;
  ▶ unwashed, uncooked fruit and vegetables;
  ▶ cat faeces and soil contaminated with cat faeces;
  ▶ unpasteurised goat's milk and dairy products made from it.

In about one-third of cases, toxoplasmosis is transmitted to the foetus and may cause blindness, **hydrocephalus** or mental retardation. Infection in late pregnancy usually has no ill effects.

▶ **Syphilis.** This is a bacterial sexually transmitted disease (STD). It can only be transmitted across the placenta after the 20th week of pregnancy. It will cause the baby to develop congenital syphilis, or can even lead to the death of the foetus. If the woman is diagnosed as having the disease at the beginning of pregnancy (see page 59 Booking etc.) it can be satisfactorily treated before the 20th week.

Pre-eclampsia

Pre-eclampsia is a complication of later pregnancy, which can have serious implications for the well being of both mother and baby as the oxygen supply to the baby may be reduced and early delivery may be necessary. It is characterised by:
  ▶ a rise in blood pressure
  ▶ oedema (swelling) of hands, feet, body or face due to fluid accumulating in the tissues
  ▶ protein in the urine

In severe cases, pre-eclampsia may lead to eclampsia, in which convulsions (seizures) can occur. This can occasionally threaten the life of both mother and baby. If pre-eclampsia is diagnosed, the woman is admitted to hospital for rest and further tests.

Premature birth

Babies who are born before the 37th week of pregnancy are now called **pre-term** babies. Around 4% of babies are born pre-term and most of them weigh less than 2500 g and are therefore also described as **low birth weight babies**. The main problems for pre-term infants are:
  ▶ **temperature control** – heat production is low and heat loss is high, because the surface area is large in proportion to the baby's weight and there is little insulation from subcutaneous fat;
  ▶ **breathing** – the respiratory system is immature and the baby may have difficulty breathing by himself because of **respiratory distress syndrome** (RDS). This is caused by a deficiency in **surfactant**, a fatty substance which coats the baby's lungs and is only produced from about 22 weeks of pregnancy;

▶ **infection** – resistance to infection is poor because they have not had enough time in the uterus to acquire antibodies from the mother to protect them against infection;

▶ **jaundice** – due to immaturity of the liver function.

Birth

The process of birth
STAGE 1: THE NECK OF THE UTERUS OPENS

Towards the end of pregnancy the baby moves down the birth canal and is usually lying head downwards. A woman will recognise the onset of labour (the three-stage process of birth) by the following signs:

▶ 'show' – the discharge of blood-stained mucus from the vagina:

▶ the 'breaking of the waters' or rupture of membranes, when some amniotic fluid escapes via the vagina;

▶ regular muscular contractions, which may start slowly and irregularly, but become stronger and more frequent as labour progresses. They open up the cervix at the neck of the womb.

Stage 1 lasts for up to 24 hours and is usually longer for the first-time mother. Once the membranes have ruptured, which may not occur until late in Stage 1, the woman should contact the midwife or hospital, as there is always a risk of infection entering the uterus if labour is prolonged.

FIGURE 3.9
The first stage of labour

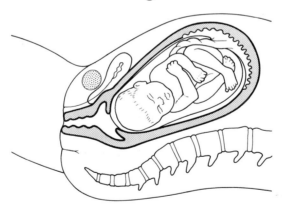

STAGE 2: THE BIRTH OF THE BABY

This begins when the cervix is fully dilated (open) and the baby starts to move down the birth canal, and it ends when the baby is born. The contractions are very strong and the midwife encourages the mother to push with each contraction until the baby's head is ready to be born. When the baby's head stays at the entrance to the vagina, it is said to be 'crowning' and the mother is asked to 'pant' the head out. The baby will then rotate so that the shoulders are turned sideways and the rest of the body is born.

Many mothers prefer to have their baby placed on their abdomen immediately after birth, to feel the closeness and warmth.

FIGURE 3.10
The second stage of labour

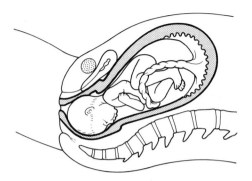 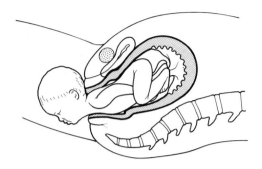

The midwife will clamp and cut the umbilical cord and the baby is labelled with the mother's name on wrist and ankle bands.

STAGE 3: THE DELIVERY OF THE PLACENTA AND MEMBRANES
Normally, the placenta separates from the lining of the uterus within 20 minutes of the birth and is pushed out through the vagina.

Pain relief during labour
Labour is usually painful, but a thorough understanding of what is happening throughout the birth process can help to reduce the fear of the unknown that makes the body tense up and fight the contractions instead of relaxing and working with them. There are various different methods of pain relief:

▶ relaxation and breathing exercises: these are taught at parentcraft classes and the support of a sympathetic partner or friend is invaluable;

▶ gas and air (Entanox): this is a mixture of oxygen and nitrous oxide ('laughing' gas); it is often offered to the mother towards the end of the first stage of labour via a rubber mask or plastic mouthpiece attached to the gas cylinder; it does not affect the baby and the mother is able to control her own intake;

▶ pethidine: this is a strong pain-killing drug given by injection; it relaxes the muscles and makes the mother very drowsy;

▶ epidural anaesthetic: this is injected into the space around the mother's spinal cord; it usually gives total pain relief and leaves the mother fully conscious;

▶ transcutaneous nerve stimulation (TENS): this is delivery of electric pulses via wires from a small control box called a 'pulsar' to rubber pads on either side of the spine; the mother controls the delivery of the pulses which block the sensations of pain before they reach the brain; the technique has no side-effects.

Acupuncture and hypnosis are also used by some women to relieve the pain of labour, but these are not routinely offered within NHS units.

Medical interventions in the birth process
INDUCTION
This means starting labour artificially; it involves rupturing the membranes and/or giving artificial hormones either via a vaginal pessary or by an intravenous infusion or 'drip'. It is necessary when:

▶ the baby is very overdue; *or*

- the placenta is no longer working properly; *or*
- the mother is ill, for example with heart disease, diabetes or pre-eclamptic toxaemia.

EPISIOTOMY

An episiotomy is a small cut made in the **perineum** (the area between the vagina and the rectum) and is used during the second stage of labour:
- to deliver the baby more quickly if there are signs of **foetal distress**;
- to prevent a large, ragged perineal tear which would be difficult to repair;
- to assist with a forceps delivery.

FORCEPS

Forceps are like tongs which fit around the baby's head to form a protective 'cage' and are used during the second stage of labour to help deliver the head. They may be used:
- to protect the head during a breech delivery, that is when the baby presents bottom first;
- if the mother has a condition such as heart disease or high blood pressure and must not over-exert herself;
- if the labour is very prolonged and there are signs of foetal distress;
- if the baby is very small or pre-term (premature).

VACUUM DELIVERY (VENTOUSE)

This is an alternative to forceps, but can be used before the cervix is fully dilated; gentle suction is applied via a rubber cup placed on the baby's head.

CAESARIAN SECTION

A Caesarian section is a surgical operation done under either a general or an epidural anaesthetic; the baby is delivered through a cut in the abdominal wall. The need for a Caesarian section may be identified during pregnancy – an 'elective' or planned operation – or as an emergency:
- when induction of labour has failed;
- when there is severe bleeding;
- when the baby is too large or in too difficult a position to deliver vaginally;
- in placenta praevia – when the placenta is covering the cervix;
- in cases of severe foetal distress;
- if the mother is too ill to withstand labour.

Postnatal care

The postnatal period is the period of six weeks from the time of birth. For the first ten days the mother will receive help and advice from a midwife, either in hospital or at home. From ten days onwards the health visitor visits mother and baby at home. The purpose of these visits is:
- to offer advice on health and safety issues;
- to check that the baby is making expected progress;
- to offer support and advice on any emotional problems, including referring to specialist advice if necessary;
- to advise the parents to attend a baby clinic;
- to discuss a timetable for immunisations;
- to put the parents in touch with other parents locally.

CHILD CARE AND EDUCATION

FIGURE 3.11

Examination of the new-born baby by the paediatrician or family doctor

Skin – vernix and lanugo may still be present, milia may show on the baby's nose; black babies appear lighter in the first week of life as the pigment, malanin, is not yet at full concentration

The spine is checked for any evidence of spina bifida

The face is examined for cleft palate – a gap in the roof of the mouth facial paralysis – temporary paralysis after compression of the facial nerve, usually after forceps delivery

Feet are checked for webbing and talipes (club foot), which needs early treatment

The head is checked for size and shape : any marks from forceps delivery are noted

Genitalia and anus are checked for any malformation

Eyes are checked for cataract a cloudiness of the lens

Hips are tested for congenital dislocation using Barlow' Test

The neck is examined for any obvious injury to the neck muscles after a difficult delivery

The abdomen is checked for any abnormality, e.g. pyloric stenosis, where there may be obstruction of the passage of food from the stomach; the umbilical cord is checked for infection

The heart and lungs are checked using a stethoscope; any abnormal findings will be investigated

Hands are checked for webbing (fingers are joined together at the base) and creases – a single unbroken crease from one side of the palm to the other is a feature of Down's syndrome

FIGURE 3.12

Examination of the new-born baby by the midwife

Eyes are checked for discharge

Labels are applied, usually on the wrist and ankle, soon after delivery and double checked with parents

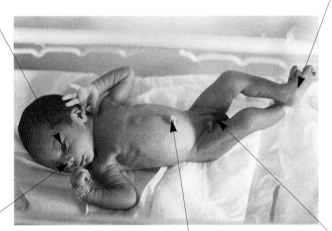

Mucus extraction – any fluid present in the nose and throat when born is sucked out using a soft suction tube

Cord clamp is checked for bleeding

Observation and recording of the first passing of urine and meconium

Giving birth is a momentous event; everyone reacts differently and while many mothers feel an immediate rush of love and excitement, others can feel quite detached and need time to adjust. Early contact with their new-born baby is equally important for fathers as for mothers, and learning how to care for a new-born baby can make couples feel closer.

Many mothers experience the 'baby blues' – a feeling of mild depression caused by hormonal changes, tiredness and reaction to the excitement of the birth. If these feelings persist longer than a few days, then it may be a more serious condition, **postnatal depression**, and the mother will need medical help.

The new-born baby or neonate

Neonatal tests

The first question usually asked by parents is 'Is he/she all right?' The doctor and midwife will observe the new-born baby closely and perform several routine tests which will show whether the baby has any obvious physical problem (Figures 3.11, 3.12).

THE APGAR SCORE

This is a standard method of evaluating the condition of a new-born baby by checking five vital signs (Figure 3.13).

The Apgar Score is assessed at one minute and five minutes after birth; it may be repeated at five-minute intervals if there is cause for concern.

INTERPRETING THE SCORE

10	The baby is in the best possible condition
8–9	The baby is in good condition
5–7	The baby has mild asphyxia and may need treatment
3–4	The baby has moderate asphyxia and will need treatment
0–2	The baby has severe asphyxia and needs urgent resuscitation

FIGURE 3.13

Assessing the condition of the new-born baby: The Apgar Score

SIGNS	0	1	2
HEARTBEAT	absent	slow – below 100	fast – over 100
BREATHING	absent	slow – irregular	good; crying
MUSCLE TONE	limp	some limb movement	active movement
REFLEX RESPONSE (to stimulation of foot or nostril)	absent	grimace	cry, cough, sneeze
COLOUR		body oxygenated, hands and feet blue	well oxygenated

Most healthy babies have an Apgar Score of 9, losing one point for having blue extremities; this often persists for a few hours after birth. A low score at five minutes is more serious than a low score at one minute. In hospital, the paediatrician will be notified if the score is 6 or under at five minutes.

NEONATAL SCREENING TESTS

Three screening tests are carried out on the new-born baby to check for specific disorders that can be treated successfully if detected early enough.

▶ *Barlow's Test:* This is a test for congenital dislocation of the hip and is carried out soon after birth, at six weeks and at all routine developmental testing until the baby is walking. There are varying degrees of severity of this disorder; treatment involves the use of splints positioned to keep the baby's legs in a frog-like position.

▶ *The Guthrie Test:* This is a blood test routinely performed on all babies at 7–11 days old, to detect a rare disorder, phenylketonuria (PKU). A small blood sample is taken from the baby's heel and sent for analysis. Phenylketonuria is very rare, affecting 1 in 10,000 babies; it is a metabolic disorder which leads to brain damage and learning delay. Early diagnosis is vital and treatment involves a special formula protein diet which has to be followed throughout the person's life.

▶ *Thyroid function test:* This is a blood test taken at the same time as the Guthrie test; it checks the baby's thyroid function; if the thyroid gland is not working properly, the baby will require treatment by the hormone thyroxine in order to ensure normal growth and development. The earlier the treatment is started the better the outlook for the child.

Protection against tuberculosis (TB) may be given by an injection of BCG vaccine before the baby leaves hospital in areas with many immigrants from outside Europe, North America or Australasia, or if the baby is known to be in contact with tuberculosis.

Many hospitals routinely give Vitamin K by injection or orally to all new-born infants; this increases the clotting ability of their blood and protects against a serious form of spontaneous bleeding which can occur in new-born babies.

Features of the new-born baby

SIZE

All new-born babies are weighed and their head circumference measured soon after birth; these measurements provide vital information for professionals when charting any abnormality in development.

▶ *Length:* it is difficult to measure accurately the length of a neonate and many hospitals have abandoned this as a routine; the average length of a full-term baby is 50 cm.

▶ *Weight:* the birth weight of full-term babies varies considerably because:
  – first babies tend to weigh less than brothers and sisters born later;
  – boys are usually larger than girls;
  – large parents usually have larger babies and small parents usually have smaller babies.

▶ *Head circumference:* the average head circumference of a full-term baby is about 35 cm.

APPEARANCE

▶ The baby will be wet from the amniotic fluid and she may also have some blood streaks on her head or body, picked up from a tear or an episiotomy.

▶ The *head* is large in proportion to the body, and may be oddly shaped at first, because of:
  – *moulding:* the head may be long and pointed as the skull bones overlap slightly to allow passage through the birth canal;
  – *caput succedaneum:* a swelling on the head, caused by pressure as the head presses on the cervix before birth; it is not dangerous and usually disappears within a few days;
  – *cephalhaematoma:* a localised blood-filled swelling or bruise caused by the rupture of small blood vessels during labour; it is not dangerous but may take several weeks to subside.
▶ *Vernix* (literally, varnish) may be present, especially in the skin folds; it should be left to come off without any harsh rubbing of the skin.
▶ *Lanugo,* or fine downy hair, may be seen all over the body, especially on dark-skinned babies and those who are born pre-term.
▶ *Head hair:* the baby may be born with a lot of hair or be quite bald; often the hair present at birth falls out within weeks and is replaced by hair of a different colour.
▶ *Skin colour:* this varies and depends on the ethnic origin of the baby, at least half of all babies develop **jaundice** on the second or third day after birth which gives the skin a yellow tinge – usually no treatment is necessary.
▶ *Mongolian spot:* this is a smooth bluish-black area of discoloration commonly found at the base of the spine on babies of African or Asian origin; it is caused by an excess of **melanocytes**, the brown pigment cells, and is quite harmless.
▶ *Milia:* sometimes called milk spots, these are small whitish-yellow spots which may be present on the face; they are caused by blocked oil ducts and disappear quite quickly.
▶ *Birth marks:* the most common birth mark is a pinkish mark over the eyelids, often referred to as 'stork marks'; they usually disappear within a few months. Other birth marks, such as strawberry naevus, persist for some years.

MOVEMENTS OF THE NEW-BORN BABY

Babies display a number of automatic movements (known as 'primitive reflexes') which are reflex responses to specific stimuli (Figure 3.14). These movements are inborn and are replaced by voluntary responses as the brain takes control of behaviour; for example, the grasp reflex has to fade before the baby learns to hold objects placed in her hand. The reflexes are important indicators of the health of the nervous system of the baby; if they persist beyond an expected time it may indicate delay in development.

▶ *The swallowing and sucking reflexes:* when anything is put in the mouth, the baby at once sucks and swallows; some babies make their fingers sore by sucking them while still in the womb.
▶ *The rooting reflex:* If one side of the baby's cheek or mouth is gently touched, the baby's head turns towards the touch and the mouth purses as if in search of the nipple (Figure 3.14(a)).
▶ *The grasp reflex:* when an object or finger touches the palm of the baby's hand, it is automatically grasped (Figure 3.14(b)).
▶ *The stepping or walking reflex:* when held upright and tilting slightly forward, with feet placed on a firm surface, the baby will make forward-stepping movements (Figure 3.14(c)).
▶ *The startle reflex:* when the baby is startled by a sudden noise or bright light, she will

FIGURE 3.14
Primitive reflexes in a new-born baby

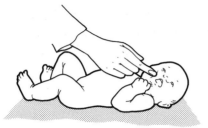

(a) Rooting reflex

(b) Grasp reflex

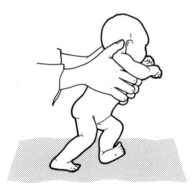

(c) Walking reflex

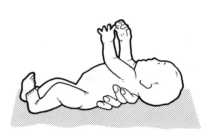

(d) Startle reflex

(e) Asymmetric tonic neck reflex

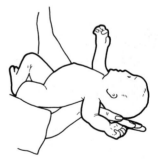

(f) Moro reflex

move her arms outwards with elbows and hands clenched (Figure 3.14(d)).

▶ *The asymmetric tonic neck reflex:* if the baby's head is turned to one side, she will straighten the arm and leg on that side and bend the arm and leg on the opposite side (Figure 3.14(e)).

▶ *The falling reflex (Moro reflex):* Any sudden movement which affects the neck gives the baby the feeling that she may be dropped; she will fling out her arms and open her hands before bringing them back over the chest as if to catch hold of something (Figure 3.14(f)).

The senses of a new-born baby

SIGHT

New-born babies can focus on faces at close range as their range of vision is about 20–25 cm. Research has shown that all young babies prefer to look at a human face above any other object. They can also distinguish colour and are more interested in three-dimensional objects than flat ones.

HEARING

Babies respond to sounds by blinking, drawing in their breath or jerking their limbs. They soon learn to recognise their mothers' voice and may stop feeding if startled by a loud noise.

SMELL AND TASTE

At ten days old, a breast-fed baby can distinguish the smell of her mother's breasts from those of other women who are breast-feeding. At birth, babies show a preference for sweet tastes over salty, sour tastes; this is probably because breast milk has a fair amount of milk sugar (lactose) in it.

TOUCH

Babies explore their world with their mouths as well as with their hands and feet; they will be comforted by being cuddled or held closely. They are sensitive to touch and pain and change of position. As soon as they can, babies put things in their mouths, not to eat them but to find out more about them.

Low-birth-weight babies

Any baby weighing up to 2.5 kg at birth, regardless of the period of gestation, is said to be of low birth weight.

Low-birth-weight babies can be divided into two categories:

▶ *pre-term:* babies born before 37 weeks of pregnancy;
▶ *light-for-dates:* babies who are below the expected weight for their gestational stage (length of pregnancy).

Some babies are both pre-term and light-for-dates.

Low-birth-weight babies are at higher risk of death during the first year of life but, if they survive, most catch up with their full-size peers by school age. Those with birth weights below 1.5 kg, or who are very 'light-for-dates' are more likely to have lasting problems, but the frequency of such problems has declined as neonatal care has improved.

CAUSES

The reasons for low birth weight are often unknown, but common factors are:

▶ multiple births;
▶ toxaemia of pregnancy;
▶ a medical disorder in the mother, e.g. diabetes, heart disease, kidney infection;
▶ drug abuse by the mother, e.g. smoking, drinking or narcotic abuse.

CARE OF THE LOW-BIRTH-WEIGHT BABY

Most low-birth-weight babies will need to be nursed in an **incubator**, which is an enclosed cot with controlled temperature and humidity; the baby is usually nursed naked, sometimes lying on a sheepskin for comfort. Feeding is often via a tube or a dropper until the baby has the strength to suck; extra oxygen is supplied to assist breathing.

Such an environment can seem very frightening for the parents and **Special Care Baby Units (SCBUs)** strive to limit any separation to the minimum. If the baby is too ill or frail to leave the incubator, the hospital will take a photograph of the baby which the parents can have immediately. Staff caring for neonates value the importance of early mother–baby bonding and will encourage parents and close family to talk to and touch the baby after observing the required hygiene precautions. Low-birth-weight babies usually sleep more and may seem less alert than full-term babies and parents will welcome reassurance from the staff that this is normal behaviour.

Post-term babies

When pregnancy is prolonged beyond the expected date of delivery there may be problems for the baby. These result from the placenta declining in function after the 42nd week of pregnancy (NB Full term is 40 weeks). Where the expected delivery date is accurately known, induction of labour is usually undertaken before 42 weeks. The post-term baby has the following characteristics:

▶ being much thinner than normal;
▶ having parchment-like skin which is often cracked and peeling;
▶ having a worried expression; and
▶ being alert, restless and hungry for feeds.

Treatment is similar to that for light-for-dates infants with **hypoglycaemia** presenting an additional problem.

Special Care Baby Units (SCBUs)

Special Care Baby Units are usually situated within the maternity departments of general district hospitals. They employ specially trained midwives and paediatric nurses and are designed to care for the five babies out of every hundred who require extra care that can not be provided within the normal postnatal environment.

Each hospital has its own criteria for deciding which babies need special care; usually these criteria are:

- ▶ babies born before 32 weeks;
- ▶ babies weighing less than 2 kg at birth;
- ▶ babies with breathing difficulties;
- ▶ babies with seizures or blood disorders.

The principles of care in a SCBU are to keep the newborn baby warm and free from infection. This is achieved by expert care of babies in incubators. Babies who are more seriously ill and who require more intensive care will be transferred to a neonatal intensive care unit.

The Neonatal Intensive Care Unit

Neonatal Intensive Care Units are situated in large regional hospitals and care for the smallest and most ill babies, using the most sophisticated technology and specialist skills. SCBUs can ensure that the sick baby receives oxygen via a face mask within the incubator; the intensive care unit can provide a **ventilator** and staff who are trained in such specialist care. Parents whose baby has had to be transferred to an intensive care unit often feel very frightened and helpless. The baby they had so eagerly anticipated is now totally at the mercy of strangers and surrounded by highly technical and noisy machinery. Often the parents feel that there is nothing they can do for their own child and the waiting is very hard to bear.

Multiple births

Multiple pregnancies, where there is more than one baby, always need special care and supervision. Twins are the most common multiple birth, occurring in about one in 87–100 pregnancies.

Twins

IDENTICAL (MONOZYGOTIC) TWINS

Identical twins develop after one sperm has fertilised one egg; the egg splits into two and each half becomes a separate baby. Identical twins are always the same sex and they share the same placenta (Figure 3.15(a)).

NON-IDENTICAL (DIZYGOTIC) TWINS

Non-identical twins develop when two sperms fertilise two different eggs, the mother's ovaries having for some reason produced two eggs at ovulation. They grow together in one womb, with two separate placentas (Figure 3.15(b)). Such twins are sometimes called fraternal twins and can be the same sex or different sexes; they can be as alike or as unlike as any brothers and sisters.

The chances of a woman having non-identical twins increases if she herself is such a twin or if there is a history of twins in her family.

FIGURE 3.15
**Two types of twins:
(a) identical; (b) non-identical**

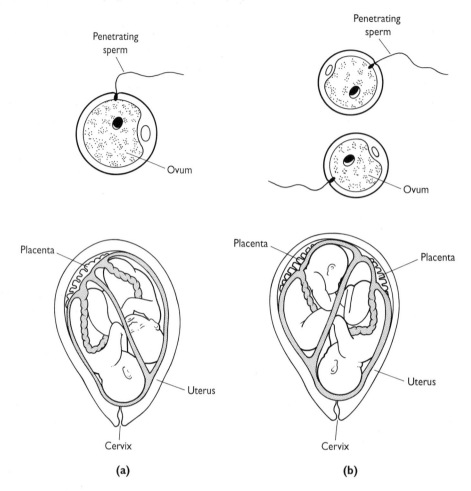

(a)   (b)

Infertility treatments and multiple pregnancies
Fertility drugs work by stimulating follicle ripening and ovulation; sometimes they work too well and result in the ripening of more than one egg at a time. Women who are treated with fertility drugs are therefore more likely to conceive more than one child at a time.

Diagnosing multiple pregnancies
A woman expecting more than one baby is likely to be larger than her dates would suggest and to put on more weight; routine ultrasound scanning can usually diagnose the presence of more than one baby, unless one baby is 'hiding' behind the other.

Caring for twins and triplets
The main risk when there is more than one baby is that they will be born too early and be premature; this risk rises with the number of babies. Usually the woman expecting twins or more babies will be admitted to hospital for the birth; twins may be delivered vaginally provided both babies are in the head-down position, but triplets and quadruplets are usually born by Caesarian section.

FEEDING TWINS

There is no reason why mothers should not totally breast-feed twins and partly breast-feed any number of babies, but this needs great motivation and a lot of extra help and support.

SUPPORT FOR PARENTS WITH TWINS AND MORE BABIES

The community midwife and health visitor will visit more frequently and will put the parents in touch with other parents in the same situation; extra help may be provided for a few weeks and arrangements are made for routine tests and immunisations to be done at home. The La Leche League and the Twins and Multiple Births Association (TAMBA) can offer practical advice and a list of local support groups (see addresses list at the end of this chapter).

If one of the babies dies, either before birth or afterwards, the parents will require specialist bereavement counselling; the Child Bereavement Trust can offer invaluable advice and support.

PRESERVING INDIVIDUALITY

Twins who survive together should each be recognised as an individual in his or her own right. Ways of preserving individual identity are:

- ▶ not using terms such as 'the twins', but always using each child's own name;
- ▶ taking care if dressing twins and triplets alike, which will draw attention to their sameness; some twins insist on wearing identical outfits, but it is important to be aware of the disadvantages of this;
- ▶ ensuring that being 'a twin' is secondary to being 'an individual'; sharing large equipment, such as a pram or buggy, in the early years is inevitable but on birthdays, for example, two cakes could be made;
- ▶ acknowledging that developmental milestones will be reached at different times by each child and that individual attention from parents is worthwhile, even though this may be difficult in practice.

Common neonatal problems and disorders

JAUNDICE

Jaundice is a common condition in newborn infants that usually shows up shortly after birth. In most cases, it goes away on its own; if not, it can be treated easily. A baby has jaundice when **bilirubin**, which is produced naturally by the body, builds up faster than a newborn's liver can break it down and get rid of it in the baby's **stool**. Too much

FIGURE 3.16
A baby in an incubator

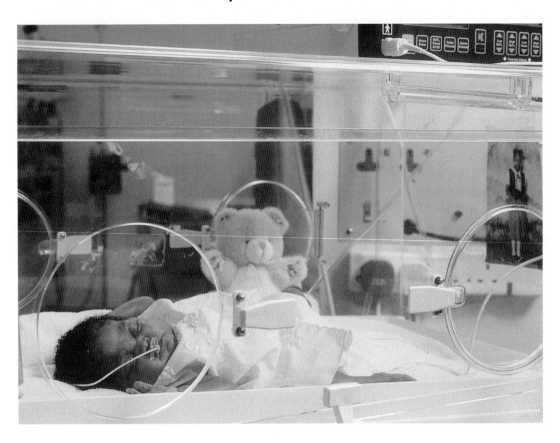

bilirubin makes a jaundiced baby's skin look yellow. This yellow colour will appear first on the face, then on the chest and stomach and finally, on the legs. Older babies, children, and adults get rid of this yellow blood product quickly, usually through bowel movements.

HOW IS JAUNDICE TREATED?

Mild to moderate levels of jaundice do not require any treatment. If high levels of jaundice do not clear up on their own, the baby may be treated with special lights (**phototherapy**) or other treatments. These special lights help get rid of the bilirubin by altering it to make it easier for the baby's liver to excrete it. Another treatment is more frequent feedings of breastmilk or formula to help pass the bilirubin out in the stools. Increasing the amount of water given to a child is not sufficient to pass the bilirubin because it must be passed in the stools.

COMMON SKIN PROBLEMS IN BABIES

A newborn baby's skin has a unique tender quality, as it has not been exposed to the environment and its ultraviolet radiation. There are certain common disorders that may affect the newborn child.

DRY SKIN

Some babies have dry skin that is particularly noticeable in cold weather. It can be treated by using a water-soluble cream (e.g. Unguentum Merck) instead of soap for washing and by applying vaseline to lips, cheeks or noses – the most commonly affected skin areas.

URTICARIA

Neonatal urticaria are red, blotchy spots, often around a small white or yellow blister. They usually appear from around the second day and disappear within a few days. They are harmless to the baby.

SWEAT RASH

Sweat rash is caused by the sweat glands being immature and not allowing heat to evaporate from the skin. A rash of small red spots appears on the face, chest, groin and armpit. The baby should be kept cool and the skin kept dry; calamine lotion will soothe the itch.

MILIA

Milia – often called 'milk spots' – occur in fifty percent of all newborn babies. They are firm, pearly-white pin-head sized spots which are really tiny sebaceous cysts, and are felt and seen mostly around the baby's nose. They will disappear without scarring in three to four weeks.

PEELING

Most newborn babies' skin peels a little in the first few days, especially on the soles of the feet and the palms. Postmature babies may have extra-dry skin, which is prone to peeling. Babies of Asian and Afro-Caribbean descent often have drier skin and hair than babies of European descent. No treatment is necessary.

CRADLE CAP

This is a type of seborrhoeic dermatitis of the scalp and is common in young babies. It is caused by the sebaceous glands on the scalp producing too much sebum or oil. The scalp is covered with white or yellowish brown crusty scales, which although they look unsightly, rarely trouble the baby. It may spread as red, scaly patches over the face, neck, armpits and eyebrows. Sometimes it is caused by inefficient rinsing of shampoo. Treatment is by applying olive oil to the affected area overnight to soften the crusts and by special shampoo.

INFANTILE ECZEMA

Infantile eczema (or atopic dermatitis) presents as an irritating red scaly rash, usually on the baby's cheeks and forehead, though it may spread to the rest of the body. It is thought to be caused by an allergy and appears at 2–3 months. It causes severe itching, made worse by scratching. It should be treated by rehydrating the skin with short, cool baths using an unscented cleanser and frequent application of special moisturisers. If the eczema is severe, the doctor may prescribe special cortisone creams. The baby's finger nails should be kept short and scratch mittens worn. Cotton clothing should be worn and antibiotics may be used to treat any infection. It is not contagious.

Maintaining body temperature

From birth babies have a heat regulating mechanism in the brain which enables them to generate body warmth when they get cold. However they can rapidly become very cold for the following reasons:

- ▶ they are unable to **conserve** that warmth if the surrounding air is at a lower temperature than normal;
- ▶ they have a large surface area compared to body weight;
- ▶ they lack body fat, which is a good insulator.

Maternity units are always kept at a high temperature (usually about 29°C or 80°F) to allow for frequent undressing and bathing of newborn babies. At home the room temperature should not fall below 20°C (or 68°C). A pre-term or light-for-light-for-dates baby is at an even greater risk of **hypothermia**. (see Chapter 14.)

Development of the baby

Normal development is part of a continuous process which begins in the womb. How an individual baby develops depends on two factors:

▶ **maturation of the nervous system:** this tends to occur in the upper body earlier than the lower parts;

▶ response to external stimulation by **environmental factors**, particularly contact with other people.

During the first six months of life, the baby grows at a faster rate than at any other time of her life. This is not just physical growth; her understanding of the world around her and her ability to communicate are growing equally fast. Development is a complex subject and using the integrated approach (see Chapter 2) may help our understanding. The following categories are widely used in the curriculum of child care courses: Physical, Intellectual (or cognitive), Language, Emotional, Social and Spiritual development.

▶ *Physical development* is the way in which the body increases in skill and becomes more complex in its performance. There are two main areas:
  – *gross motor skills*: these use the large muscles in the body and include walking, running, climbing, etc.;
  – *fine motor skills* including *gross manipulative skills* which involve single limb movements, usually the arm, for example throwing, catching and sweeping arm movements; and *fine manipulative skills* which involve precise use of the hands and fingers for drawing, using a knife and fork, writing, doing up shoelaces and buttons, etc.

▶ *Intellectual or cognitive development* is development of the mind – the part of the brain which is used for recognising, reasoning, knowing and understanding.

▶ *Language development* is the development of communication skills through receptive speech (what a child understands), expressive speech (words she produces herself) and articulation (her actual pronunciation of words).

▶ *Emotional development* is the growth of a child's feelings about and awareness of herself; the development of feelings towards other people; and the development of self-identity and self-image.

▶ *Social development* includes the growth of the child's relationships with other people and socialisation, the process of learning the skills and attitudes which enable the child to live easily with other members of the community.

▶ *Spiritual development* is about the developing sense of relating to others ethically, morally and humanely.

All these areas of development are linked, and each affects and is affected by the other areas. For example, once a child has reached the stage of emotional development at which she feels secure when apart from her main carer, she will have access to a much wider range of relationships, experiences and opportunities for learning; similarly, when a child can use language effectively, she will have more opportunities for social interaction.

Stages of development
FROM BIRTH TO 4 WEEKS – AREA OF DEVELOPMENT

Gross motor skills

Baby lies supine (on her back) with head to one side.

When placed on her front (the prone position) she lies with head turned to one side and by one month can lift her head.

If pulled to sitting position, her head will lag, her back curves over and her head falls forward.

Fine motor skills

She will turn her head towards the light and stare at bright shiny objects.

She is fascinated by human faces and gazes attentively at her carer's face when fed or held.

Her hands are usually tightly closed.

She reacts to loud sounds, but by one month may be soothed by particular music.

Cognitive and language

Baby responds to sounds, especially familiar voices.

She quietens when picked up.

She makes eye contact and cries to indicate need.

She may move her eyes towards the direction of sound.

Emotional and social

The first smile in definite response to her carer is usually around 5–6 weeks.

She often imitates certain facial expressions.

She uses total body movements to express pleasure at bathtime or when being fed.

She enjoys feeding and cuddling.

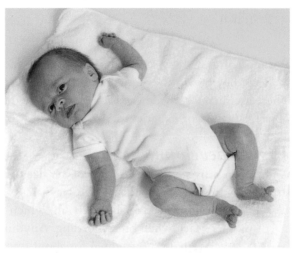

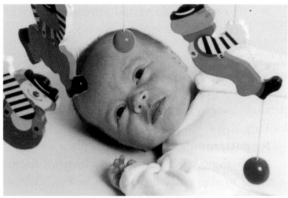

FROM BIRTH TO 4 WEEKS – ROLE OF THE CARER

Stimulating development

Encourage the baby to lie on the floor to kick and experiment safely with movement.

Provide an opportunity for her to feel the freedom of moving without a nappy or clothes on.

Always support the baby's head when playing with her as her neck muscles are not strong enough to control movement.

Use bright colours in furnishings.

Provide a mobile over the cot and/or the nappy-changing area.

Feed on demand and talk and sing to her.

Provide plenty of physical contact and maintain eye contact.

Talk lovingly to her and give her the opportunity to respond.

Introduce her to different household noises.

Provide contact with other adults and children.

Encourage bonding with main carer by enjoying the relationship.

Expect no set routine in the first few weeks.

Pick her up and talk to her face-to-face.

Sensory development

Sensation is the process by which we receive information through the senses:

- vision
- hearing
- smell
- touch
- taste
- proprioception (see below)

Perception is making sense of what we see, hear, touch, smell and taste. Our perception is affected by previous experience and knowledge and by our emotional state at the time. There are therefore wide variations in the way different individuals perceive the same object, situation or experience.

Visual development

A newborn baby's eyes are barely half the size of an adult's, and although they are structurally similar, they differ in two ways:

- their **focus** is fixed at about 20 cm, which is the distance from the baby to her mother's face when breast-feeding. Anything nearer or farther away appears blurred. She will remain shortsighted for about four months.
- the **response to visual stimuli is slower** in babies because the information received by the eye takes longer to reach the brain via the nervous pathway.

A newborn baby is able only poorly to fix her eyes upon objects and follow their movement. Head and eye movement is also poorly co-ordinated; in the first week or two, the eyes lag behind when the baby's head is turned to one side, a feature known by paediatricians as the 'doll's eye phenomenon'. Research has shown that babies prefer looking at:

- **patterned** areas rather than plain ones;
- anything which resembles a **human face**. Babies will actually search out and stare at human faces during their first two months of life;
- **brightly coloured** objects.

By around four months a baby can focus on both near and distant objects and her ability to recognise different objects is improving steadily. By six months the baby will respond visually to movements across the room and will move her head to see what is happening. By one year her eye movements are smoother and she can follow rapidly moving objects with the eyes (a skill known as **tracking**). A squint is normal.

The development of hearing

Newborn babies are able to hear almost as well as adults do. Certain rhythmic sounds seem to have a special soothing effect on babies; the drone of a vacuum cleaner or hairdryer is calming. The sound of a human voice evokes the greatest response and the rhythms of lullabies have been used for centuries in all cultures to help babies to sleep, or to comfort them. Babies can recognise their own mother's voice from the first week and can distinguish its tone and pitch from those of other people.

Sudden changes in noise levels tend to disturb very young babies and make them jump. From about six months, a baby will learn to recognise and distinguish between different sounds; for example, the sound of a spoon in a dish will mean food is on its way. Babies can also discriminate between cheerful and angry voices and respond in kind.

The development of smell, taste and touch

The senses of smell and taste are closely linked. If our sense of smell is defective, for example because of a cold, then our sense of taste is reduced. Babies as young as one week old who are breastfed are able to tell the difference between their own mother's smell and other women's smells. From birth babies are also able to distinguish the four basic tastes – sweet, sour, bitter and salty.

The sense of touch is also well developed in infancy as can be demonstrated by the primitive reflexes (see page 74). Babies seem to be particularly sensitive to touches on the mouth, the face, the hands, the soles of the feet and the abdomen. Research has shown that babies would rather be stroked than fed.

Proprioception is the sense which tells the infant the location of the mobile parts of his body (e.g. his legs) in relation to the rest of him.

Sensory deprivation

A congenitally blind baby (i.e. a baby who is born blind) will develop a more sophisticated sense of touch than a sighted baby will, although they both start life with the same touch potential. As the sense of touch develops, so the area of the brain normally assigned to touch increases in size for the blind baby, and the area of the brain normally assigned to sight decreases.

Similarly, in a congenitally deaf baby, the part of the brain that normally receives auditory stimuli is taken over by the visual input from sign language.

Normative measurements in child development

Each child will develop in a different way; research has shown that although there is a wide variation in the chronological age (i.e. the age in years and months) at which children reach stages of development, there are recognised patterns of these stages. Normative measurements describe averages or 'norms' which provide a framework for assessing development; these norms are the result of observations and research by many professionals in the field of child development. They are useful in helping parents and carers to know what to expect at a certain age, especially when planning a safe, stimulating environment; their use can, however, lead parents to label children as 'slow' or 'bad' if they fall behind the norm. Professionals caring for children need to have a framework of the patterns of expected development to extend their skills in promoting health and stimulating the children's all-round development.

FROM 4 TO 8 WEEKS – AREA OF DEVELOPMENT

Gross motor skills
Baby can now turn from her side to her back.
She can lift her head briefly from the prone position.
Her arm and leg movements are jerky and uncontrolled.
There is head lag if she is pulled to a sitting position.

Fine motor skills
Baby turns her head towards the light and stares at bright shiny objects.
She will show interest and excitement by facial expression and will gaze attentively at her carer's face while being fed.
She will open her hand to grasp your finger.

Cognitive and language
Baby recognises her carer and familiar objects.
She makes non-crying noises such as cooing and gurgling.
Her cries become more expressive.
She looks in the direction of sounds.

Emotional and social
She smiles in response to adult.
She enjoys sucking.
She turns to regard nearby speaker's face.

FROM 4 TO 8 WEEKS – ROLE OF THE CARER

Stimulating development
Use a special supporting infant chair so that the baby can see adult activity.
Let her kick freely, without nappies.
Massage her body and limbs during or after bathing.
Use brightly coloured mobiles and wind chimes over her cot and/or changing mat.
Let her explore different textures.
Light rattles and toys strung over her pram or cot will encourage focusing and coordination.

Talk to and smile with the baby.
Sing while feeding or bathing her – allow her time to respond.
Learn to distinguish her cries and to respond to them differently.
Tickling and teasing her may induce laughter.
Talk to her and hold her close.

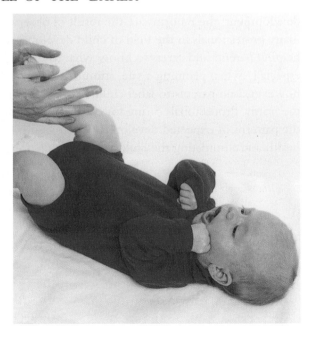

FROM 8 TO 12 WEEKS – AREA OF DEVELOPMENT

Gross motor skills
When lying supine, baby's head is in a central position.
She can now lift her head and chest off the bed in the prone position, supported on forearms.
There is almost no head lag in the sitting position.
Her legs can kick vigorously, both separately and together.
She can wave her arms and brings her hands together over her body.

Fine motor skills
Baby moves her head to follow adult movements.
She watches her hands and plays with her fingers.
She holds a rattle for a brief time before dropping it.

Cognitive and language
Baby is still distressed by sudden loud noises.
She often sucks or licks her lips when she hears sound of food preparation.
She shows excitement at sound of approaching footsteps or voices.

Emotional and social
She shows enjoyment at caring routines such as bathtime.
She responds with obvious pleasure to loving attention and cuddles.
She fixes her eyes unblinkingly on her carer's face when feeding.
She stays awake for longer periods of time.

FROM 8 TO 12 WEEKS – ROLE OF THE CARER

Stimulating development
Place the baby in a supporting infant chair so that she can watch adult activity.
Encourage her to kick without nappies.
Massage and stroke her limbs when bathing or if using massage oil.
Use brightly coloured mobiles and wind chimes to encourage focusing at 20 cm.
Place a rattle in her hand and attach objects which make a noise when struck above the cot.
Enjoys listening to nursery rhymes.
Talk sensibly to her and imitate her sounds to encourage her to repeat them.
Holding her close and talking lovingly will strengthen the bonding process.
Encourage contact with other adults and children.
Respond to her needs and show enjoyment in caring for her.

Caring for babies

The needs of the young baby

Every baby depends completely on an adult to meet all her needs, but the manner of meeting those needs will vary considerably according to the family's circumstances and culture, and the personalities of the baby and caring adult. To achieve and maintain healthy growth and development (physical, intellectual and emotional), certain basic needs must be met. A baby needs:

- ▶ food;
- ▶ shelter, warmth and clothing;
- ▶ cleanliness;
- ▶ fresh air and sunlight;
- ▶ sleep, rest and activity;
- ▶ love and consistent and continuous affection;
- ▶ protection from infection and injury;
- ▶ stimulation;
- ▶ social contacts;
- ▶ security.

It is difficult to separate these basic needs in practical care, as they all contribute to the holistic development of a healthy baby.

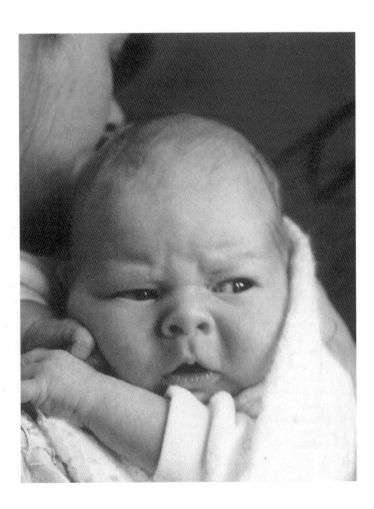

FIGURE 3.16
Mother and baby breast-feeding

Food

The way babies and children are fed involves more than simply providing enough food to meet nutritional requirements; for the new-born baby, sucking milk is a great source of pleasure and is also rewarding and enjoyable for the mother. The ideal food for babies to start life with is breast milk and breast-feeding should always be encouraged as the first choice in infant feeding; however mothers should not be made to feel guilty or inadequate if they choose not to breast-feed their babies.

ADVANTAGES OF BREAST-FEEDING

▶ Human milk provides food constituents in the correct balance for human growth. There is no trial and error to find the right formula to suit the baby.

▶ The milk is sterile and the correct temperature; there is no need for bottles and sterilising equipment.

▶ Breast milk initially provides the infant with maternal antibodies and helps protect the child from infection.

▶ The child is less likely to become overweight as overfeeding by concentrating the formula is not possible and the infant has more freedom of choice as to how much milk she will suckle.

▶ Generally breast milk is considered cheaper despite the extra calorific requirement of the mother.

▶ Sometimes it is easier to promote the mother-infant bonding by breast-feeding, although this is certainly not always the case.

▶ Some babies have an intolerance to the protein in cows' milk.

▶ The uterus returns to its pre-pregnancy state more quickly, by action of oxytocin released when the baby suckles.

FROM 4–5 MONTHS (16–20 WEEKS) – AREA OF DEVELOPMENT

Gross motor skills
Baby has good head control.
She is beginning to sit with support and
can roll over from her back to her side.
She is beginning to reach for objects.
When supine, she plays with her own feet.
She holds her head up when pulled to a
sitting position.

Fine manipulative skills
She is beginning to use palmar grasp.
She can transfer objects from hand to
hand.
She is very interested in all activity.
Everything is taken to her mouth.
She moves her head around to follow
people and objects.

Cognitive and language
The baby recognises her bottle or other
familiar objects.
She laughs and squeals with pleasure.
She reacts to tones of voice; is upset by
angry tone and cheered by happy tone.

Emotional and social
The baby enjoys attention and being with
others.
She shows trust and security.
She has recognisable sleep patterns.

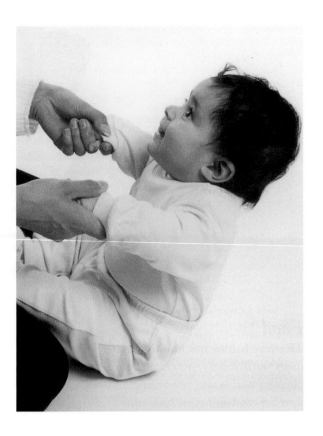

FROM 4–5 MONTHS (16–20 WEEKS) – ROLE OF THE CARER

Stimulating development
Practise sitting with the baby on the
carer's knee.
Play rough and tumble games on the bed.
Play bouncing games on the carer's knee
to songs.
Offer rattles and soft, squashy toys to give
a variety of textures.
Home-made toys e.g. transparent plastic
containers with dried peas inside or empty
cotton reels tied together offer
interest. **NB**: Check lids are secure and
always supervise play.
Continue talking to the baby, particularly
in response to her own sounds.
Provide different toys with a range of
textures and sounds.
Sing nursery rhymes combined with finger
play, e.g. This little piggy . . .
Give her the opportunity to find out
things for herself and begin to choose play
activities.
Encourage playing alone and in the
company of other children.
Waterproof books in the bath give a lot of
pleasure.

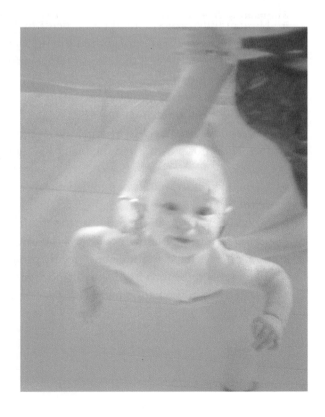

FROM 6–9 MONTHS – AREA OF DEVELOPMENT

Gross motor skills
The baby can roll from front to back.
She may attempt to crawl but will often end up sliding backwards.
She may grasp her feet and place them in her mouth.
She can sit without support for longer periods of time.
She may 'cruise' around furniture and may even stand or walk alone.

Fine manipulative skills
The baby is alert to people and objects.
She is beginning to use pincer grasp with thumb and index finger.
She transfers toys from one hand to the other.
She looks for fallen objects.
Everything is explored by putting it in her mouth.

Cognitive and language
The baby understand signs, e.g. bib means food is coming.
She also understand 'up' and 'down' and makes appropriate gestures, e.g. raising her arms to be picked up.
She babbles tunefully with lots of imitation.
She can imitate, clap and play peek-a-boo.

Emotional and social
The baby can manage to feed herself with her fingers.
She's now more wary of strangers.
She offers toys to others.
She shows distress when her mother leaves.

FROM 6–9 MONTHS – ROLE OF THE CARER

Stimulating development
Encourage confidence and balance by placing toys around the sitting baby. Make sure furniture is stable and has no sharp corners when baby is using it to pull herself up by.
Encourage mobility by placing toys just out of baby's reach.
Encourage visual awareness by providing varied experiences.
Small objects, which must be safe if chewed by the baby, will encourage the pincer grasp (small pieces of biscuit are ideal, but **always** supervise).
Build a tower of bricks with her and watch her delight when they all fall down.
Look at picture books together and encourage her to point at objects with you.
Respond to the baby pointing at objects by naming them.
Talk to her about everyday things.
Widen her experiences by going on outings which include animals.
Imitate animal sounds and encourage her to copy you.
Allow plenty of time for play.
Provide simple 'musical instruments', e.g. xylophone or wooden spoon and saucepan.
Use a safety mirror for the baby to recognise herself.

ADVANTAGES OF BOTTLE-FEEDING

FIGURE 3.17
Father and baby bottle-feeding

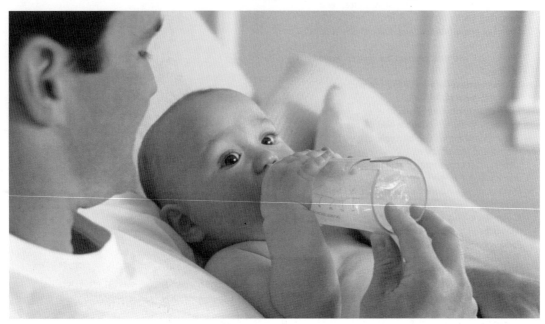

- ▶ The mother knows exactly how much milk the baby has taken.
- ▶ The milk is in no way affected by the mother's state of health, whereas anxiety, tiredness, illness or menstruation may reduce the quantity of breast milk.
- ▶ The infant is unaffected by such factors as maternal medication. Laxatives, antibiotics, alcohol and drugs affecting the central nervous system can affect the quality of breast milk.
- ▶ Other members of the family can feed the infant (Figure 3.17). In this way the father can feel equally involved with the child's care, and during the night could take over one of the feeds so that the mother can get more sleep.
- ▶ There is no fear of embarrassment while feeding.
- ▶ The mother is physically unaffected by feeding the infant, avoiding such problems as sore nipples.

BREAST-FEEDING

The breast is made up of 15–20 segments or lobes, each of which contains alveoli, cells which produce milk (Figure 3.18). Lactiferous ducts drain milk from the alveoli to reservoirs in the area of the areola (the pigmented ring around the nipple). Small glands in the areola called Montgomery's tubercles produce a fluid that keeps the skin of the nipples and the areola soft and supple. The nipple has several openings through which the baby can obtain milk. During pregnancy the breasts produce colostrum, a creamy yellowish fluid, low in fat and sugar, which is uniquely designed to feed the new-born baby. Colostrum also has higher levels of antibodies than mature milk and plays an important part in protecting the baby from infection. Mature milk is present in the breasts around the third day after birth. Hormonal changes in the mother's bloodstream cause the milk to be produced and the sucking of the baby stimulates a steady supply. (Unfortunately, this mechanism also operates in the event of stillbirth or miscarriage and can cause the mother severe distress, especially if she has had no warning.)

FIGURE 3.18
The lactating breast

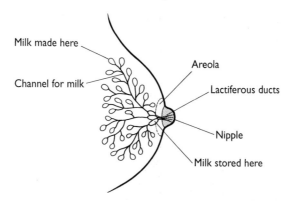

Milk made here

Channel for milk

Areola

Lactiferous ducts

Nipple

Milk stored here

MANAGEMENT OF BREAST-FEEDING

The most difficult part of breast-feeding is usually the beginning and it may take two to three weeks to establish a supply and to settle into some sort of pattern. Even if the mother does not intend to breast-feed her baby, she is encouraged to try for the first few days so that the baby can benefit from the unique properties of colostrum. Many of the problems which cause women to give up breast-feeding could be overcome with the right advice and support. Successful management of breast-feeding involves:

▶ the mother taking a well-balanced diet (see Chapter 11); her diet will affect the composition of the breast milk and some foods may cause colic (vegetarian mothers who drink cows' milk, eat a varied vegetarian diet and take vitamin supplements produce breast milk similar in nutrient value to non-vegetarian mothers; vegan mothers may need to take calcium and vitamin B12 supplements while breast-feeding);

▶ putting the baby to the breast straight after the birth; this has been shown to be a key factor in successful breast-feeding;

▶ feeding on demand, i.e. when the baby is hungry, rather than routinely every four hours;

▶ extra help in the home if possible, at least until breast-feeding is established;

▶ finding the most comfortable position for feeding; if the mother has a sore perineum or Caesarian scar, the midwife or health advisor will be able to advise;

▶ not giving extra (complementary) feeds by bottle;

▶ letting the baby decide when she has had enough milk and allowing her to finish sucking at one breast before offering the other.

Breast milk may be expressed by hand or by breast pump for use when the mother is unavailable; EBM or expressed breast milk can be stored in a sterilised container in a freezer for up to three months.

BOTTLE-FEEDING

Cows' milk is the ideal food for calves but is not suitable for babies as it contains three times as much protein, which is difficult to digest, as breast milk. Commercially modified baby milks (formula milks) *must* be used for bottle-feeding. Soya-based milks can be used if the baby develops an intolerance to modified cows' milks. For the first four to six months the baby will be given infant milk (formula) as a substitute for breast milk; she may then progress to follow-on milk which should be offered until the age of 12 months.

FROM 9–12 MONTHS – AREA OF DEVELOPMENT

Gross motor skills
The baby will now be mobile; she may be crawling, bear-walking, bottom-shuffling or even walking.
She can sit up on her own and lean forwards to pick things up.
She may crawl upstairs and onto low items of furniture.
She may bounce in rhythm to music.

Fine motor skills
Her pincer grasp is now well developed and she can pick things up and pull them towards her.
She can poke with one finger and will point to desired objects.
She can clap her hands and imitate adult actions.
She throws toys deliberately.
She manages spoons and finger foods well.

Cognitive and language
The baby may produce her first words – often 'dada', 'mama' or 'bye-bye'.
She uses more expressive babbling now.
She understands her daily routine and will follow simple instructions, e.g. kiss teddy.

Emotional and social
The baby enjoys songs and action rhymes.
She still likes to be near to a familiar adult.
She can drink from a cup with help.
She will play alone for long periods.
She has and shows definite likes and dislikes at meal and bedtimes.

FROM 9–12 MONTHS – ROLE OF THE CARER

Stimulating development
Provide large-wheeled toys to push around – brick trucks serve the dual purpose of walking and stacking games.
Ensure furniture is safe and stable for climbers.
Swimming, walking, in the park.
Small climbing frames – closely supervised – to increase her balance and coordination.
Stacking and nesting toys.
Roll balls for her to bring back to you.
Sand and water play – **always** supervised.
Cardboard boxes and saucepans to put things into and take things out of.
Partake in plenty of talking to the baby which requires a response that will develop language ability.
Encourage self-feeding – tolerate messes.
Talk constantly to her and use rhymes and action songs.
Offer lots of play opportunities with adult interaction – sharing, taking turns etc.
Encourage her to join in and help with regular chores.
Foster a feeling of self-worth by providing her with her own equipment and utensils, e.g. she will need her own flannel, toothbrush, cup and spoon.

PREPARATION OF FEEDS

A day's supply of bottles may be made and stored in the fridge for up to 24 hours. A rough guide to quantities is: 150 ml of milk per kilogram of body weight per day: thus a baby weighing 4 kg will require approximately

600 ml in 24 hours. This could be given as 6 × 100 ml bottles.

The following equipment will be needed:

▶ a container for sterilising bottles, large enough to submerge everything completely; steam sterilisers are very effective but costly;

▶ eight wide-necked feeding bottles and teats designed for new-born babies;

FIGURE 3.19

Preparing a bottle feed

(a) wash hands and nails thorougly; boil some fresh water and allow it to cool; take bottles from the steriliser; shake but do not rinse because this would desterilise them;

(b) pour the correct amount of boiled water into each bottle (check quantity at eye level on a firm surface);

(c) measure the exact amount of powder into the scoop provided; level with a plastic knife but do not pack down; add powder to each bottle;

(d) take teats from steriliser, taking care to handle by the edges; and fit into the bottles upside down; put caps, rings, and tops on;

(e) shake each bottle vigorously until any lumps have dissolved;

(f) if not using immediately, cool quickly and put bottles in the fridge; if using immediately, test temperature on the inside of your wrist.

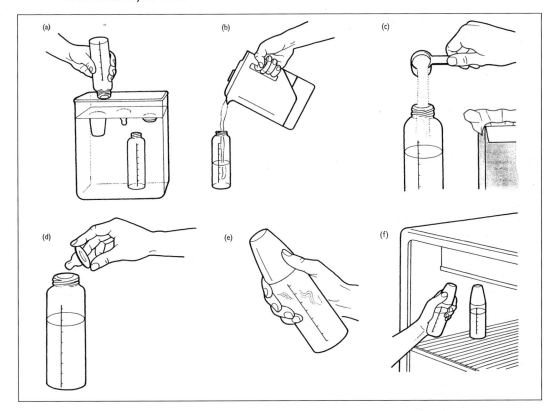

▶ a large plastic or Pyrex measuring jug and a plastic stirrer – or feeds can be made directly in bottles and shaken to mix;

▶ sterilising liquid or tablets – check the manufacturer's instructions for length of time and correct dilution.

It is very important that all bottles and equipment are thoroughly sterilised.
  ▶ After use, scrub all the bottles, caps and covers, using hot soapy water and a special bottle brush. Rinse thoroughly in clean running water.
  ▶ Teats may be cleaned using a special teat cleaner; turn teat inside out to ensure all milk deposits are removed and wash as the bottles.
  ▶ Submerge bottles, teats and all other equipment needed for bottle-feeding in the sterilising solution, checking that no bubbles are trapped inside bottles and that teats are completely immersed.

G U I D E L I N E S

Bottle-feeding

- **Always wash hands thoroughly before preparing feeds for babies.**
- **Never add sugar or salt to the milk, and never make the feed stronger than the instructions state – this could result in too high a salt intake which can lead to severe illness.**
- **Always check the temperature of the milk before giving it to a baby.**
- **Do not use a microwave oven to warm the bottle as it may produce isolated hot spots.**
- **Always check that the teat has a hole the right size and that it is not blocked.**
- **Never prop up a baby with a bottle – choking is a real danger.**
- **Always supervise siblings when feeding small babies.**

GIVING A BOTTLE-FEED
1. Collect all the necessary equipment before picking up the baby. The bottle may be warmed in a jug of hot water; have muslin square/bib and tissues to hand.
2. Check the temperature and flow of the milk by dripping it on to the inside of your wrist (it should feel warm, not hot or cold).
3. Make yourself comfortable with the baby. Do not rush the feed – babies always sense if you are not relaxed and it can make them edgy too.
4. Try to hold the baby in a similar position to that for breast-feeding and maintain eye contact; this is a time for cuddling and talking to the baby.
5. Stimulate the rooting reflex (see p. 74) by placing the teat at the corner of the baby's mouth; then put the teat fully into her mouth and feed by tilting the bottle so that the hole in the teat is always covered with milk.
6. After about ten minutes, the baby may need to be helped to bring up wind; this can be done by leaning her forwards on your lap and gently rubbing her back or by holding her against your shoulder. Unless the baby is showing discomfort, do not insist on trying to produce a 'burp' – the baby may pass it out in the nappy.

The National Children's Bureau state that: 'Babies who are bottle fed should be held and have warm physical contact with an attentive adult whilst being fed. It is strongly recommended that a baby is fed by the same staff member at each feed. Babies should never be left propped up with bottles as it is dangerous and inappropriate to babies' emotional needs.'

FEEDING PROBLEMS IN BABIES

POSSETTING

The baby regularly vomits small amounts of her feed but is generally healthy and has no signs of illness. The cause is weakness of the muscle at the opening of the stomach and eventually the baby will grow out of it; although the condition is messy, there is no cause for alarm!

PYLORIC STENOSIS

This is a condition, commoner in boys than girls, where the muscle surrounding the channel at the end of the stomach (the pylorus) thickens, narrowing the outlet. Symptoms usually appear about three weeks after birth:

▶ the baby will vomit – called **projectile vomiting** – the regurgitated food often shoots several feet away;

▶ the baby becomes constipated;

▶ dehydration may occur and weight gain stops.

Medical advice should be sought; pyloric stenosis is easily diagnosed and usually cured by a simple operation.

COLIC

Colic is an attack of abdominal pain caused by spasms in the intestines as food is being digested; sometimes called 'three-month colic' as it usually disappears by the age of three months, colic causes the baby to draw up her arms and legs and cry inconsolably. Attacks of colic can last anything from a quarter of an hour to several hours and some babies only suffer in the evening. There is no known cause and really no effective cure. The obvious distress of the baby and the helplessness of the carer makes caring for a colicky baby difficult; parents need a lot of support and reassurance that the baby will grow out of it and that there is no lasting damage.

CONSTIPATION

This occurs when stools are hard or infrequent; it can be caused by underfeeding and/or dehydration. The baby's fluid intake should be increased; if weaned, more fruit and vegetables should be included in the diet.

DIARRHOEA

Diarrhoea is caused by food passing through the intestines too quickly, not leaving enough time for it to be digested; the baby will pass frequent, loose, watery stools. It may be caused by poor food hygiene or by viral infection. It should always be taken seriously in a young baby, especially if accompanied by vomiting. Seek medical advice and give cooled, boiled water only; bottle feeding should be stopped, but breast-feeding may continue if the baby wants it.

FOOD INTOLERANCE

Only a small number of reactions to food are true allergic responses, in that they involve an immune reaction in the body. Some babies develop an intolerance to cows' milk protein; the most common symptoms are vomiting, diarrhoea and failure to thrive. After weaning, foods most likely to cause an adverse reaction in babies are:

▶ hen's eggs;

▶ wheat and other cereals;

▶ fish;

▶ pork;
▶ citrus fruits.

Allergies to food additives, such as the colouring agent tartrazine, have been blamed for many different problems, including eczema, asthma and hyperactivity (attention deficit disorder); however, there is no conclusive medical evidence to support this thesis. Sometimes an allergic reaction will be temporary, perhaps following an illness, but the offending food should always be removed from the baby's diet. Dietetic advice should be sought before any changes to a balanced diet are made.

Diets are discussed in more depth in Chapter 11.

WEANING
Weaning is the gradual introduction of solid food to the baby's diet. The reasons for weaning are:

▶ to meet the baby's nutritional needs – from about six months of age, milk alone will not satisfy the baby's increased nutritional requirements, especially for iron;
▶ to develop the chewing mechanism; the muscular movement of the mouth and jaw also aids the development of speech;
▶ to satisfy increasing appetite;
▶ to introduce new tastes and textures; this enables the baby to join in family meals, thus promoting cognitive and social development;
▶ to develop new skills – use of feeding beaker, cup and cutlery.

STAGES OF WEANING
Between three and six months is usually the right time to start feeding solids to a baby; giving solids too early – often in the mistaken belief that the baby might sleep through the night – places a strain on the baby's immature digestive system; it may also make her fat and increases the likelihood of allergy.

▶ **Stage 1 (From 3–6 months)**
  Puréed vegetables, puréed fruit, baby rice, finely puréed dahl or lentils. Milk continues to be the most important food.
▶ **Stage 2: (About 6–8 months)**
  Increase variety; introduce puréed or minced meat, chicken, liver, fish, lentils, beans. Raw eggs should not be used (see Table 11.5) but cooked egg yolk can be introduced from 6 months; wheat-based foods e.g. mashed Weetabix, pieces of bread. Milk feeds decrease as more solids rich in protein are offered.
▶ **Stage 3: (About 9–12 months)**
  Cows' milk can safely be used at about 12 months; lumpier foods such as pasta, pieces of cooked meat, soft cooked beans, pieces of cheese, a variety of breads; additional fluids such as diluted unsweetened fruit juice or water. Three regular meals should be taken as well as drinks.

METHODS OF WEANING
Some babies take very quickly to solid food; others appear not to be interested at all. The baby's demands are a good guide for weaning; mealtimes should never become a battleground. Even babies as young as four months have definite food preferences and should never be forced to eat a particular food, however much thought and effort has gone into the preparation. Table 3.2 gives guidelines on introducing new solids to babies. The best foods to start with are puréed cooked vegetables, fruit, and ground cereals such as rice. Chewing usually starts at around the age of six months, whether the baby has teeth or

TABLE 3.2

Introducing new solids to babies

	4–6 MONTHS	6–8 MONTHS	9–12 MONTHS
YOU CAN GIVE OR ADD	Puréed fruit Puréed vegetables Thin porridge made from oat or rice flakes or cornmeal Finely puréed dhal or lentils	A wider range of puréed fruits and vegetables Purées which include chicken, fish and liver Wheat-based foods, e.g. mashed Weetabix Egg yolk, well cooked Small-sized beans such as aduki beans, cooked soft Pieces of ripe banana Cooked rice Citrus fruits Soft summer fruits Pieces of bread	An increasingly wide range of foods with a variety of textures and flavours Cows' milk Pieces of cheese Fromage frais or yoghurt Pieces of fish Soft cooked beans Pasta A variety of breads Pieces of meat from a casserole Well-cooked egg white Almost anything that is wholesome and that the child can swallow
How	Offer the food on the tip of a clean finger or on the tip of a clean (plastic or horn) teaspoon	On a teaspoon	On a spoon or as finger food
When	A very tiny amount at first, during or after a milk feed	At the end of a milk feed	At established meal times
Why	The start of transition from milk to solids	To introduce other foods when the child is hungry	To encourage full independence
Not yet	Cows' milk – or any except breast or formula milk Citrus fruit Soft summer fruits Wheat (cereals, flour, bread etc.) Spices Spinach, swede, turnip, beetroot Eggs Nuts Salt Sugar Fatty food	Cows' milk, except in small quantities mixed with other food Chillies or chilli powder Egg whites Nuts Salt Sugar Fatty food	Whole nuts Salt Sugar Fatty food

not, and coarser textures can then be offered. The baby should be in a bouncing cradle or high chair – not in the usual feeding position in the carer's arms.

Food can be puréed by:

▶ rubbing through a sieve using a large spoon;
▶ mashing with a fork (for soft foods such as banana or cooked potato);
▶ using a mouli-sieve or hand-blender;
▶ using an electric blender (useful for larger amounts).

G U I D E L I N E S
Weaning

▶ **try to encourage a liking for savoury foods;**
▶ **only introduce one new food at a time;**
▶ **be patient if the baby does not take the food – feed at the baby's pace, not yours;**
▶ **do not add salt or sugar to feeds;**
▶ **make sure that food is the right temperature;**
▶ **avoid giving sweet foods or drinks between meals;**
▶ **never leave a baby when she is eating;**
▶ **limit the use of commercially prepared foods – they are of poorer quality and will not allow the baby to become used to home cooking;**
▶ **select foods approved by the baby's parents.**

Finger foods

Finger foods are any foods which can be given to a baby to manage by themselves. After weaning, encourage the baby to chew, even if there are no teeth, by giving finger foods, or foods which have a few lumps. Examples of finger foods include:

▶ wholemeal toast
▶ chapatti
▶ pitta bread
▶ breadsticks
▶ banana or peeled apple slices
▶ cooked carrot or green bean
▶ cubes of hard cheese, e.g. Cheddar

NB important: Always stay near to the baby during feeding to make sure they don't choke and to give encouragement.

Care for a baby's skin

A baby's skin is soft and delicate, yet forms a tough pliant covering for the body. The skin has many important functions:

▶ protection: it protects underlying organs and, when unbroken, protects against germs entering the body;

▶ sensation: each square centimetre of skin contains up to 250 nerve endings called receptors which detect different feelings such as touch, cold, warmth, pressure, pain and hair movement;

▶ secretion of oil (sebum): this lubricates the skin and gives hair its shine;

▶ manufacture of vitamin D: vitamin D is made when the skin is exposed to sunlight and is essential for healthy bones and teeth; black skin protects against sunburn but is less efficient at making vitamin D, and black children may need a supplement of vitamin D in the winter;

▶ excretion: the skin excretes waste products in sweat;

▶ temperature regulation: the hypothalamus in the brain controls body temperature by releasing sweat, which evaporates from the skin's surface, cooling the body.

A young baby does not have to be bathed every day because only her bottom, face and neck and skin creases get dirty. If a bath is not given daily, the baby should have the important body parts cleansed thoroughly – a process known as 'topping and tailing'. This process limits the amount of undressing. Whatever routine is followed, the newborn baby needs to be handled gently but firmly, and with confidence. Most babies learn to enjoy the sensation of water and are greatly affected by your attitude. The more relaxed and unhurried you are the more enjoyable will be the whole experience.

TOPPING AND TAILING

Babies do not like having their skin exposed to the air, so should be undressed for the shortest possible time. Always ensure the room is warm, not less than 20°C (68°F) and that there are not any draughts. Warm a large, soft towel on a not-too-hot radiator and have it ready to wrap the baby afterwards.

Collect all the equipment you will need:

▶ changing mat;

▶ water that has been boiled and allowed to cool;

▶ cotton-wool swabs;

▶ lidded buckets for soiled nappies, used swabs and clothes;

▶ bowl of warm water;

▶ protective cream e.g. Vaseline;

▶ clean clothes and a nappy.

1. Wash your hands
2. Remove the baby's clothes, leaving on her vest and nappy.
3. Wrap the baby in the towel, keeping her arms inside.
4. Using two separate pieces of cotton wool (one for each eye; this will prevent any infection passing from one eye to the other), squeezed in the boiled water, gently wipe the baby's eyes in one movement from the inner corner outwards.
5. Gently wipe all around the face and behind the ears. Lift the chin and wipe gently under the folds of skin. Dry each area thoroughly by patting with a soft towel or dry cotton wool.
6. Unwrap the towel and take the baby's vest off, raise each arm separately and wipe the armpit carefully as the folds of skin rub together here and can become quite sore – again dry thoroughly and dust with baby powder if used.
7. Until the cord has dropped off, make sure that it is kept clean and dry using special antiseptic powder supplied by the midwife.
8. Wipe and dry the baby's hands.

9. Take the nappy off and place in lidded bucket.
10. Clean the baby's bottom with moist swabs, then wash with soap and water; rinse well with flannel or sponge, pat dry and apply protective cream.
11. Put on clean nappy and clothes.

BATHING THE BABY

When the bath is given will depend on family routines, but it is best not to bath the baby immediately after a feed, as she may be sick. Some babies love being bathed; others dislike even being undressed. Bathtime has several benefits for babies:

Benefits of bath time
▶ **the opportunity to kick and exercise**
▶ **cleaning and refreshing the skin and hair**
▶ **the opportunity for the carer to observe any skin problems – rashes, bruises etc.**
▶ **a valuable time for communication between the baby and the carer**
▶ **a time for relaxation and enjoyment**

FIGURE 3.20
Holding a baby in the bath

Again, ensure the room is warm and draught-free and collect all necessary equipment:

▶ small bowl of boiled water and cotton swabs (as for 'topping and tailing' procedure);
▶ baby bath filled with warm water – test temperature with your elbow, not with hands, which are insensitive to high temperatures; the water should feel warm but not hot;
▶ changing mat;
▶ lidded buckets;
▶ two warmed towels;
▶ clean nappy and clothes;
▶ brush and comb;
▶ toiletries and nail scissors.

1. Undress the baby except for her nappy and wrap her in a towel while you clean her face as for 'topping and tailing'.
2. Wash her hair before putting her in the bath: support her head and neck with one hand, hold her over the bath and wash her head with baby shampoo or soap; rinse head thoroughly and dry with second towel.
3. Unwrap towel, remove nappy and place in bucket.
4. Remove any soiling from the baby's bottom with cotton wool; remember to clean baby girls from front to back to avoid germs from faeces entering the urethra or vagina.

FIGURE 3.21
Methods of folding fabric nappies:
(a) the triple absorbent fold and (b) kite fold

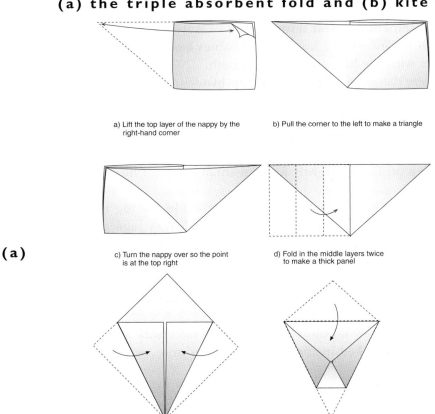

a) Lift the top layer of the nappy by the right-hand corner

b) Pull the corner to the left to make a triangle

c) Turn the nappy over so the point is at the top right

d) Fold in the middle layers twice to make a thick panel

(a)

a) Fold the sides in to the centre to make a kite shape

b) Fold the point at the top down to the centre. Fold the bottom point up to fit the size of the baby.

(b)

5. Lay the baby in the crook of one arm and gently soap her body front and back with baby soap. (If preferred, use baby bath liquid added to the bath beforehand.)

6. Lift the baby off the towel and gently lower her into the water, holding her with one arm around the back of her neck and shoulders and holding the far arm to stop her slipping.

7. Talk to the baby and gently swish the water to rinse off the soap, paying particular attention to all skin creases – under arms, between legs and behind knees. Allow time for the baby to splash and kick but avoid chilling.

8. Lift the baby out and wrap in a warm towel; dry her thoroughly by patting, not rubbing.

9. Baby oil or moisturiser may now be applied to the skin; do not use talcum powder with oils as it will form lumps and cause irritation.

10. Check if fingernails and toenails need cutting. Always use blunt-ended nail scissors and avoid cutting nails too short.

11. Dress the baby in clean nappy and clothes.

G U I D E L I N E S

Bathing babies

▶ Cultural preferences in skin care should be observed; cocoa butter or special moisturisers are usually applied to babies with black skin and their bodies may be massaged with oil after bathing.

▶ Collect equipment and test temperature of water. Always put cold water in the bath before adding hot – many babies have been severely scalded by contact with the hot surface of the bath.

▶ Do not wear dangling earrings or sharp brooches and keep your own nails short and clean.

▶ Never leave a baby or child under ten alone in the bath, even for a few seconds.

▶ Do not top up with hot water while the baby is in the bath; make sure that taps are turned off tightly as even small drops of hot water can cause scalds.

▶ From a few months old, babies may be bathed in the big bath, keeping the water shallow and following the same guidelines regarding temperature and safety. A non-slip mat placed in the bottom of the bath will prevent slipping.

▶ Avoid talcum powder because of the risk of inhalation or allergy; if it *is* used, place on your hands first and then gently smooth it on to completely dry skin.

▶ Do not use cotton-wool buds – they are not necessary and can be dangerous when poked inside a baby's ears or nose, which are self-cleansing anyway.

▶ Nail care should be included in the bathing routine. A young baby's nails should be cut when necessary *after* a bath when they are soft. Some parents use their own teeth to bite them gently off.

▶ Hair should be washed daily in the first few months, but shampoo is not necessary every day. A little bath lotion added to the bath water could be gradually worked into the baby's scalp until a lather forms and may then be rinsed off using a wrung out flannel.

▶ If the baby dislikes having her hair washed, try to keep hair washing separate from bath time so that the two are not associated as unpleasant events.

Excretion

The first 'stool' a new-born baby passes is **meconium** - a greenish-black treacle-like substance which is present in the baby's bowels before birth and is usually passed within 48 hours of birth. Once the baby starts to feed on milk, the stools change:

▶ a breast-fed baby has fluid, yellow mustard-coloured stools which do not smell unpleasant;

▶ a bottle-fed baby has more formed stools which may smell slightly.

Babies pass urine very frequently; bottle-fed babies tend to pass stools less often than breast-fed babies. Constipation can occur in bottle-fed babies but can be relieved by giving extra boiled water to drink.

Nappies

The choice of nappies will depend on several factors: convenience, cost, personal preference and concern for the environment. There are two main types of nappy:

▶ **Fabric nappies:** these are made from terry towelling and come in different qualities and thickness. Two dozen are required for everyday use. Fabric nappies may be squares or shaped to fit. The latest style is similar in shape to the disposable nappy and has popper fastenings. If using fabric squares, you will also need special nappy safety pins and six pairs of plastic pants. Disposable one-way liners may be used with towelling nappies to keep wetness from the baby's skin and to make solid matter easier to dispose of down the toilet.

▶ **Disposable nappies:** these are nappy, liner and plastic pants all in one and are available in a wide range of designs. Some have more padding at the front for boys and there are different absorbencies for day and night time use. Some makes have resealable tapes so that you can check if the nappy is clean.

Changing a nappy

Young babies will need several changes of nappy each day – whenever the nappy is wet or soiled. As with any regular routine, have everything ready before you begin:

▶ a plastic-covered padded changing mat

▶ a bowl of warm water (or baby wipes)

▶ baby lotion

▶ barrier cream e.g. zinc & castor oil

▶ nappy sacks for dirty nappies

▶ cotton wool

▶ baby bath liquid

▶ new, clean nappy

If you are using a special changing table or bed, make sure the baby cannot fall off. Never leave the baby unattended on a high surface. As long as there are no draughts and the room is warm, the changing mat can be placed on the floor.

CLEANING A GIRL

1   First wash your hands and put the baby girl on the changing mat.
2   Undo her clothing and open out the nappy.
3   Clean off as much faeces as possible with the soiled nappy.
4   Use wet cotton wool or baby wipes to clean inside all the skin creases at the top of her legs. Wipe down towards her bottom.
5   Lift her legs using one hand (finger between her ankles) and clean her buttocks and thighs with fresh cotton wool, working inwards towards the anus. Keep clear of her vagina and never clean inside the lips of the vulva.
6   Dry the skin creases and the rest of the nappy area thoroughly. Let her kick freely and then apply barrier cream.

CLEANING A BOY

1   First wash your hands and place the baby boy on the changing mat. It is quite common for baby boys to urinate just as you remove the nappy, so pause for a few seconds with nappy held over the penis.
2   Moisten cotton wool with water or lotion and begin by wiping his tummy across, starting at his navel.
3   Using fresh cotton wool or a wipe, clean the creases at the top of his legs working down towards his anus and back.
4   Wipe all over the testicles holding his penis out of the way. Clean under the penis. Never try to pull back the foreskin.
5   Lift his legs using one hand (finger between his ankles) and wipe away from his anus, to buttocks and to back of thighs.
6   Dry the skin creases and the rest of the nappy area thoroughly. Let him kick freely and then apply barrier cream.

METHODS OF FOLDING FABRIC NAPPIES

There are two main ways of folding fabric nappies:

▶ **the triple absorbent fold** (see page 103): this is the most suitable method for a newborn baby and is a neat shape. It is unsuitable for larger babies. Start with a square nappy folded into four to make a smaller square with the open edges to the top and to the right.

▶ **the kite fold** (see page 103): this is suitable for a larger baby and the depth of the kite can be adjusted to suit the size of the baby.

NAPPY RASH

Almost all babies have occasional bouts of redness and soreness in the nappy area. This may be caused by leaving wet and dirty nappies on too long, poor washing techniques, infections, skin disorders such as **eczema** or **seborrhoeic dermatitis**, or reaction to creams or detergents.

The most common types of nappy rash are:

▶ candidiasis or thrush dermatitis;
▶ ammonia dermatitis.

THRUSH DERMATITIS

This is caused by an organism called *candida albicans*, a yeast fungus which lives naturally in many parts of the body. The rash is pink and pimply and is seen in the folds of the groin and around the anus and genital area; it is sometimes caused in breast-fed babies whose mothers have taken a course of antibiotics, or in bottle-fed babies where the teats have been inadequately cleaned and sterilised.

Treatment:
- ▶ Use a special anti-fungal cream prescribed by the doctor at each nappy change.
- ▶ Do not use zinc and castor oil cream until clear of infection as the thrush organism thrives on it.
- ▶ If oral thrush is present a prescribed ointment may be used.

AMMONIA DERMATITIS

This produces the most severe type of nappy rash and is caused by the ammonia present in the baby's urine and stools reacting with the baby's skin; it is more common in bottle-fed babies because their stools are more alkaline and provide a better medium for the organisms to thrive. The rash is bright red, may be ulcerated and covers the genital area; the ammonia smells very strongly and causes the baby a lot of burning pain.

Treatment:
- ▶ Wash with mild soap and water and dry gently.
- ▶ Expose the baby's bottom to fresh air as much as possible.
- ▶ Only use creams if advised and leave plastic pants off.
- ▶ If using towelling nappies, a solution of 30 ml vinegar to 2.5 litres of warm water should be used as a final rinsing solution to neutralise the ammonia.

CARE OF THE FEET

- ▶ Feet should always be dried thoroughly between the toes and clean socks put on every day.
- ▶ All-in-one baby suits must be large enough not to cramp the baby's growing feet.
- ▶ Toenails should be cut straight across, not down into the corners.

CARE FOR A BABY'S TEETH

Although not yet visible, the teeth of a new-born baby are already developing inside the gums; a baby's first teeth are called deciduous teeth or milk teeth and start to appear at around six months (see Chapter 4). Dental care should begin as soon as the first tooth appears, with visits to the dentist starting in the child's second year. Healthy teeth require:

- ▶ a healthy well-balanced diet by the mother during pregnancy, especially foods rich in protein, calcium and vitamin D;
- ▶ fluoride, which may be given by drops to babies if they live in an area without fluoridated water; fluoride guards against tooth decay but excessive use is dangerous;
- ▶ avoidance of sugary foods, drinks and medicines;
- ▶ routine care of teeth; the baby should have her own toothbrush, kept clean and separate from others.

Teeth need cleaning as soon as they appear, because **plaque** sticks to the teeth and will cause decay if not removed. Caring for the temporary first teeth is important because:

- ▶ it develops a good hygiene habit which will continue throughout life;
- ▶ if milk teeth decay, they may need to be extracted; this could lead to crowding in the mouth as the natural gaps for the second teeth to fill will be too small;
- ▶ painful teeth may prevent chewing and cause eating problems;
- ▶ clean, white shining teeth look good.

CLEANING A BABY'S TEETH

Use a small amount of baby toothpaste on a soft baby toothbrush or a piece of fine cloth (e.g. muslin) to clean the plaque from the teeth. Gently smooth the paste on to her teeth and rub lightly. Rinse the brush in clear water and clean her mouth. Brush twice a day –

after breakfast and before bed. After the first birthday, children can be taught to brush their own teeth – but will need careful supervision. They should be shown when and how to brush, that is, up and down away from the gum; they may need help to clean the back molars.

TEETHING
Some babies cut their teeth with no ill effects; others may experience:
- ▶ general fretfulness and rubbing mouth or ears
- ▶ red or sore patches around the mouth
- ▶ diarrhoea
- ▶ a bright red flush on one or both cheeks and on the chin
- ▶ dribbling

Teething should not be treated as an illness, but babies will need comforting if in pain. Teething rings and hard rusks usually provide relief, but teething powders and gels are not advised, as they are dangerous if given in large quantities. Infant paracetamol may be helpful in relieving pain but is unsuitable for babies under three months unless advised by the doctor.

Fresh air and sunlight
Babies benefit from being outside in the fresh air for a while each day. When air is trapped in a house it becomes stale, the level of humidity rises and there is an increased risk of infections spreading. Carers working in nurseries should ensure that rooms are well ventilated and that there are opportunities for babies to go outside. Sunlight is beneficial too, but care should be taken with babies and young children:
- ▶ Keep children out of the sun when it is at its most dangerous, between 11 a.m. and 3 p.m.; carers of young children should plan outdoor activities to avoid this time unless children are well protected by hats and sun protection cream.
- ▶ Specialists advise keeping babies of six to nine months out of the sun altogether to prevent the risk of developing skin cancer in later life.
- ▶ Use sun hats with a wide brim that will protect face, neck and shoulders on older babies.
- ▶ Use sun protection cream on all sun-exposed areas.
- ▶ Use sun shades or canopies on buggies and prams.

Sleep and rest
Everyone needs sleep, but the amount a baby sleeps varies enormously, and will depend on the maturity of the brain (the pre-term baby may sleep for long periods) and on the need for food. Sleep is divided into two distinct states:
- ▶ rapid eye movement (REM), which is termed active sleep;
- ▶ non-rapid eye movement (NREM), which is termed quiet sleep.

In REM sleep the mind is active and is processing daytime emotional experiences. In NREM sleep the body rests and restoration occurs. In babies under one year, more of the sleep is active (REM). It is important not to wake babies during NREM sleep, as it plays a vital part in restoring energy levels.

Few aspects of parenthood are more stressful than months of broken nights. Carers of babies could try the following strategies to encourage a different sleep pattern between day and night.

▶ Allow the baby time to settle on her own so that she begins to develop her own way of going to sleep. Some babies do cry for a short period as they settle; leave her alone but stay within hearing distance and check after five minutes to see if she is comfortable.

▶ Give the baby plenty of stimulation by talking and playing with her when she is awake during the day.

▶ Try to make night-time feeds as unstimulating as possible; feed, change and settle the baby in her cot.

▶ Make bedtime at night into a routine; by repeating the same process each night, the baby is made to feel secure and comfortable, both good aids to sleep.

ESTABLISHING A BEDTIME ROUTINE

Between three and five months, most babies are ready to settle into a routine:

▶ give the bath or wash and put on a clean nappy and nightwear;

▶ take her to say goodnight to other members of the household;

▶ carry her into her room, telling her in a gentle voice that it is time for bed;

▶ give the last breast- or bottle-feed in the room where the baby sleeps;

▶ sing a song or lullaby to help settle her, while gently rocking her in your arms;

▶ wrap her securely and settle her into the cot or cradle, saying goodnight;

▶ if she likes it, gently 'pat' her to sleep.

The routine can be adapted as the baby grows. In the early weeks, most mothers like to have the cot next to their bed; by about three to four months, the baby can be safely left in her own room.

Exercise

Exercise strengthens and develops muscles. It also helps to promote sleep as the body needs to relax after physical activity. Carers of young babies can provide opportunities for exercise in the following ways:

▶ Give plenty of opportunity for the baby to practise each new aspect of development as she becomes capable of it.

▶ Allow times for wriggling on the floor without being hindered by nappy or clothes.

▶ Allow freedom to look around, to reach and to grasp.

▶ Give opportunities to roll, crawl and eventually walk around the furniture safely.

▶ Provide objects and toys to exercise hand–eye coordination.

▶ After she has had her first triple vaccination, the baby can be taken to special baby sessions at the local swimming pool.

Crying in young babies

Crying is a baby's way of expressing her needs. Finding out why a baby is crying is often a matter of elimination, so it is important that all carers should understand the physical and emotional needs of a baby at each stage of development (see Table 3.4 Causes of crying).

PERSISTENT CRYING

Some babies do cry a great deal more than others and are difficult to soothe and comfort. Parents and carers can feel quite desperate through lack of sleep and personal problems that go with a baby who won't stop crying; they may suffer guilt at not being able to make their baby happy or lack confidence in caring for her. Such feelings of desperation and

exhaustion can result in possible physical violence to the baby – throwing her into the cot, shaking her or even hitting her.

HELP AND ADVICE

Often just talking to others helps the carer to feel less isolated. Self-help groups such as Cry-sis or the National Childbirth Trust Post-natal Support System can help by offering support from someone who has been through the same problem. Talking to the health visitor or GP may help, and some areas run clinics which help to devise a programme to stop the 'spiral' of helplessness.

FAILURE TO THRIVE

Failure to thrive (FTT) can be defined as a failure to gain weight at the expected rate. The first issue to be explored if a baby appears to be under-nourished is feeding; often a newly-weaned baby will fail to thrive (or gain weight) due to intolerance of a newly-introduced feed. Once the food is withdrawn from the diet, the baby will usually thrive. There may be other problems associated with feeding a young baby, such as breathing difficulties or a poor sucking reflex in a premature baby. A baby who is vomiting frequently over a period of time is also unlikely to thrive. Vomiting may be the result of **pyloric stenosis**, **gastro-enteritis** or **whooping cough (pertussis)**.

TABLE 3.4
Causes of crying

Hunger: This is the most common cause of crying. It is quite likely unless the baby has just been fed. Breast-fed and bottle-fed babies should be fed on demand in the early weeks. By the age of four months, the baby will probably need solid foods.

Being undressed: Most new babies hate being undressed and bathed, because they miss the contact between fabric and bare skin. One solution is to place a towel or shawl across the baby's chest and tummy when she is naked.

Discomfort: Until they can turn themselves over, babies rely on an adult to change their position; babies show marked preferences for sleeping positions.

Nappy needs changing: Some babies dislike being in a wet or dirty nappy and there may be nappy rash.

Twitches and jerks: Most new babies make small twitching and jerking movements as they are dropping off to sleep. Some babies are startled awake and find it difficult to settle to sleep because of these twitches. Wrapping a baby up firmly – or swaddling – usually solves the problem.

Over-tired or over-stimulated: Some babies can refuse to settle if there is too much bustle going on around them e.g. loud noises, too much bouncing or bright lights in a shopping centre; take her somewhere quiet and try rhythmical rocking, patting and generally soothing her.

Pain or illness: A baby might have a cold or snuffles and be generally fretful or may have an itchy rash, such as eczema. (For signs and symptoms of illness in babies, see Chapter 14)

Allergy: An intolerance of cow's milk could cause crying; seek medical advice.

Thirst: In particularly hot weather, babies may be thirsty and can be given cool boiled water. Breastfed babies may be offered an extra feed as breast milk is a good thirst-quencher.

Feeling too hot or too cold: Temperature control is not well developed in the young baby; **if too hot**, she will look red in the face, feel very warm and may be sweaty around the neck folds; loosen clothes and wrappings and remove some layers of bedding, but watch for signs of chilling. **If too cold**, she may also have a red face or may be pale; to check, feel the hands, feet, tummy and the back of the neck; cuddle the baby, wrap a blanket around her and try a warm feed.

Boredom/need for physical contact: Babies find being cuddled or carried reassuring; talk to her and provide interesting objects for her to look at and a mobile; put pram under a tree or near a washing line so that she can see movements (NB: remember to fix a cat net to prevent insects and other unwanted visitors).

Colic: If the baby cries after being fed or has long bouts of crying especially in the evening, she may be suffering from colic.

Child abuse: A baby who has been abused in any way may cry and the carer should seek help from appropriate professionals (see Chapter 16).

Sudden infant death syndrome (SIDS)

Sudden infant death syndrome is often called 'cot death'. It is the term applied to the sudden unexplained and unexpected death of an infant. The reasons for cot deaths are complicated and the cause is still unknown. Although cot death is the commonest cause of death in babies up to 1 year old, it is still very rare, occurring in approximately two out of every 1,000 babies. Recent research has identified various risk factors and the Foundation for the Study of Infant Deaths has written the following guidelines:

- ▶ A baby should lie on his back or side, *not* on his tummy.
- ▶ A pillow should never be used for sleeping.
- ▶ The temperature of the baby's room should be kept even and the baby not allowed to get overheated.
- ▶ Avoid exposure to smoke from cigarettes, both before and after birth.
- ▶ Duvets, baby nests and cot bumpers are not recommended for babies under one year old, because of the danger of suffocation.
- ▶ Do not use a sheepskin or a hot-water bottle for the baby, because of the risk of suffocation and over-heating.

GUIDELINES

Avoiding risk of cot death

- ▶ **The room where an infant sleeps should be at a temperature which is comfortable for lightly clothed adults (16–20 °C).**
- ▶ **If the baby is a natural tummy sleeper, keep turning him over and tuck in securely with blankets (as long as the weather is not too hot); a musical mobile may help to keep him happy while lying on his back;**
- ▶ **Always invest in a brand new mattress, if the baby's cot is second-hand.**
- ▶ **If the baby is snuffly or has a blocked nose, place a small pillow *under* the mattress, but make sure he does not slide down to the end of his cot.**
- ▶ **Never allow the baby to come into contact with smoky rooms; ask visitors not to smoke in the house. The risk factor increases with the number of cigarettes smoked.**
- ▶ **Learn to recognise the signs and symptoms of illness and how to respond.**
- ▶ **Use a room thermometer if necessary and check the baby's temperature by feeling his tummy, making sure your hands are warm beforehand.**
- ▶ **Babies over one month of age should never wear hats indoors, as small babies gain and lose heat very quickly through their heads.**
- ▶ **Learn and practise on a special baby resuscitation mannequin how to perform artificial ventilation and cardiac massage. NB This should always be practised under the supervision of a qualified first-aider.**

THE CONI SUPPORT SCHEME

CONI (Care of the Next Infant) is a scheme developed by the Foundation for the Study of Infant Deaths to provide organised support for families who have suffered a loss of a child through cot death. Families who have suffered the loss of a baby in this way experience greater anxiety when expecting their next baby and the programme ensures that their baby will be under increased surveillance during the first few months of life and that extra support will be given if there is a problem. Parents are offered:

- ▶ weekly visits from their health visitor;
- ▶ the loan of an **apnoea monitor**, which records the baby's breathing movements, or electronic scales for daily weighing – whichever they prefer;

> ▶ tuition in resuscitation skills and in the significance of temperature, smoking and positioning the baby on the back or side;
> ▶ a daily diary to record symptoms;
> ▶ additional support from their family doctor (GP) and paediatrician.

CONI is usually offered to parents for a minimum of six months, or two months longer than the age at which their baby died.

Clothing, footwear and equipment

The layette

The layette is the baby's first set of clothes. Many shops specialising in baby goods supply complete layettes, and there is a vast range of clothing available. Baby clothes should be:

> ▶ loose and comfortable to allow for ease of movement; as babies grow rapidly, care should be taken that all-in-one stretch suits do not cramp tiny feet – there should always be growing space at the feet to avoid pressure on the soft bones;
> ▶ easy to wash and dry, as babies need changing often; natural fibres (e.g. cotton and wool mixtures) are more comfortable; any garment for babies up to 3 months old must carry a permanent label showing that it has passed the low flammability test for slow burning;
> ▶ easy to put on and take off – avoid ribbons, bows and lacy-knit fabrics which can trap small fingers and toes;
> ▶ non-irritant – clothes should be lightweight, soft and warm; some synthetic fibres can be too cold in winter as they do not retain body heat, and too hot in the summer as they do not absorb sweat or allow the skin pores to 'breathe'.

Note also that:

> ▶ several layers of clothing are warmer than one thick garment;
> ▶ outside shoes should not be worn until the baby has learned to walk unaided; socks and shoes should be carefully fitted and checked every three months for size;
> ▶ clothing needs will vary according to the season, and the baby will need protective clothes such as pram suits, bonnet or sun hat, mittens and booties.

Equipment for a young baby

Babies will need somewhere to sleep, to be bathed, to feed, to sit, to play and to be transported.

FOR SLEEPING

Cradles and 'Moses baskets' (wicker baskets with carrying handles) can be used as beds for a young baby, but are unsuitable for transporting the baby outside or in a car.

Prams and carry-cots come in a wide variety of designs; safety mattresses are available which are ventilated at the head section to prevent the risk of suffocation. Prams can be bought second-hand or hired for the first year of a baby's life; they must meet the following safety requirements:

> ▶ brakes should be efficient and tested regularly;
> ▶ a shopping basket should be positioned underneath to prevent shopping bags being hung on the handles and causing overbalancing;
> ▶ there must be anchor points for a safety harness;

▶ the vehicle must be stable, easy to steer and the right height for the carer to be able to push easily without stooping.

▶ the mattress must be firm enough to support the baby's back.

COTS

Often a baby will move into a cot for sleeping when he has outgrown his carry-cot, but they are suitable for new-born babies. Cots usually have slatted sides which allow the baby to see out with one side able to be lowered and secured by safety catches. Safety requirements are:

▶ bars must be no more than 7 cm apart;

▶ safety catches must be child-proof;

▶ the mattress should fit snugly with no gaps;

▶ cot bumpers (foam padded screens tied at the head end of the cot) are not recommended;

▶ if the cot has been painted, check that lead-free paint has been used.

TRAVEL COT

This is a folding cot with fabric sides, suitable for temporary use only; it is especially useful if the family travels away from home a lot and can double as a play-pen when the mattress is removed.

BLANKETS AND SHEETS

These should be easy to wash and dry as they will need frequent laundering. The ideal fabric for sheets is brushed cotton, blankets are often made from cellular acrylic fabric, which is lightweight, warm and easily washable.

FOR BATHING

Baby baths are easily transportable (when empty) plastic basins which can be used with the fixed base bought for a carry-cot, or within the adult bath. After a few months, the baby can be bathed in the adult bath; carers should guard against back strain, cover hot taps because of the risk of burns and always use a non-slip rubber mat in the base of the bath.

Safety note: Never leave a baby alone in any bath, even for a few seconds

FOR FEEDING

If the baby is being bottle-fed, eight to ten bottles and teats, sterilising equipment and formula milk will be required. If she is being breast-fed, one bottle and teat is useful to provide extra water or fruit juice. A high chair, with fixed safety harness, is useful for the older baby.

FOR SITTING

BOUNCING CRADLE

This is a soft fabric seat which can be used from birth to about 6 months; it is generally appreciated by babies and their carers as it is easily transported from room to room, encouraging the baby's full involvement in everyday activities. It should *always* be placed on the floor, never on a worktop or bed, as even young babies can 'bounce' themselves off these surfaces and fall.

FOR PLAYING

Babies like to be held where they can see faces, especially the carer's face, clearly; they prefer toys which are brightly coloured and which make a noise. In the first three months, provide:

- mobiles, musical toys and rattles;
- toys to string over cot or pram.
- soft balls and foam bricks;

From about three months, provide:

- cradle gym, bath toys and activity mat;
- saucepans and spoons, building bricks;
- chiming ball and stacking beakers;
- rag books.

FOR TRANSPORT

BABY SLINGS

Baby slings, used on the front of the carer's body, enable close physical contact between carer and baby, but can cause back strain if used with heavy babies; child 'back carriers' which fit on a frame like a rucksack are suitable for larger babies when out walking.

PRAM OR BUGGY

A new-born baby can be transported in a special buggy with a tilting seat which can be used for as long as the baby needs a pushchair; the buggy has the advantage of being easier to handle than a pram, easier to store at home and possible to take on public transport. It is not possible to carry heavy loads of shopping on a buggy and lightweight buggies are not recommended for long periods of sleeping.

CAR SEATS

A baby should never be carried on an adult's lap on the front seat of a car. Small babies can be transported in a sturdy carry-cot with fixed straps on the back seat or in a rearward-facing baby car seat – if the car has a passenger airbag, the baby seat should always be fitted in the back seat; for babies under 10 kg, these seats can be used also as a first seat in the home.

FIGURE 3.22
Baby in front sling

Planning for a baby

Families come under a lot of pressure from friends, from advertising companies and from television programmes to provide the very best clothing and equipment for their new baby. The child-care worker is in an important position to advise on the basic principles when choosing equipment. The idealised picture of happy, smiling parents cuddling their precious bundle of joy is hard to resist; advertisers use these images to bombard the new parents with a dazzling array of objects that are deemed 'essential' to happy parenthood. Parents should prioritise their needs by considering all factors relevant to their circumstances:

▶ *Cost:* How much the parents can afford to spend? What may be available on loan from friends who have children past the baby stage? Can some equipment, e.g. the pram, be bought second-hand or hired cheaply?

▶ *Lifestyle:* Is the family living in a flat where the lifts are often out of action, in bed and breakfast accommodation, or in a house with a large garden? These factors will affect such decisions as pram vs. buggy or where the baby will sleep.

▶ *Single or multiple use:* Will the equipment be used for a subsequent baby – in which case the priority may be to buy a large pram on which a toddler can also be seated? It may be worth buying new, high-quality products if they are to be used again.

▶ *Safety and maintenance:* Does the item of equipment chosen meet all the British Safety Standards? What if it has been bought second-hand? How easy is it to replace worn-out parts?

RESOURCES

Useful addresses

Twins and Multiple Births
Association (TAMBA)
PO Box 30
Little Sutton L66 1TH
Tel: 0151 348 0020

The Multiple Births
Foundation
Queen Charlotte's & Chelsea
Hospital
Goldhawk Road
London W6 0XG
Tel: 020 8740 3519

Association of Breastfeeding
Mothers
26 Holmshaw Close
Sydenham Green
London SE26 4TH
Tel: 020 8778 4769

Cry-sis
BM Crysis
London WC1N 3XX
Tel: 020 7404 5011

La Leche League of Great
Britain
PO Box BM 3424
London WC1N 3XX
Tel: 020 7242 1278

Foundation for the Study of
Infant Deaths
(Cot Death Research and
Support)
15 Belgrave Square
London SW1X 8PS
Tel: 020 7235 0965

Stillbirth and Neonatal Death
Society (SANDS)
28 Portland Place
London W1N 4DE

National Childbirth Trust
Alexandra House
Oldham Terrace
London W3 6NH
Tel: 020 8992 8637

The Child Bereavement
Trust
1 Millside
Riversdale
Bourne End
Buckinghamshire
SL8 5EB

Books

C. Meggitt (1999) *Caring for Babies: A Practical Guide*. London: Hodder & Stoughton

A C T I V I T Y

Antenatal care

1 In groups, discuss the advantages and disadvantages of having a baby
   (a) in hospital;
   (b) at home.
2 (a) Research the effects that smoking when pregnant may have
        on the developing foetus;
   (b) Research the possible effects that alcohol consumption may
        have on the unborn baby.
3 Prepare a weekly menu plan for a pregnant woman:
   (a) who follows a vegan diet;
   (b) who follows a vegetarian diet;
   (c) who is on a limited income.
Note: refer to the principles of nutrition in Chapter 11.

A C T I V I T Y

The skills of the neonate

1 Make a list of all the things a new-born baby is able to do.
2 What is the name given to movements which are automatic and inborn?
   Describe six such movements and explain their importance in the study of
   child development.

A C T I V I T Y

Designing a mobile

1 Think of two or more designs for the mobile.
2 Compare the ideas, considering the following factors:
   ▶ availability of resources and materials;
   ▶ skills and time required;
   ▶ costs of materials;
   ▶ appropriateness of the design for its purpose;
   ▶ safety of the design.

3 Select one of the designs; if possible use a computer graphics program to
   prepare patterns and a word processor to write a set of instructions for
   making the mobile.
4 Follow your written instructions and make the mobile. Evaluate both the
   instructions – were they easy to follow or did you have to modify the plan? –
   and the mobile. If appropriate, offer the mobile as a gift to a baby known to
   you (perhaps in family placement) and conduct a detailed observation on the
   baby's reaction to the mobile and associated behaviour.

A C T I V I T Y

Bottle-feeding

1 Find out the costs involved in bottle-feeding a baby:
   ▶ the initial costs of equipment – sterilising unit, bottles, teats etc.;
   ▶ the costs of formula milk and sterilising tablets for one year.
2 Collect some advertisements for baby milk formulas and analyse their appeal:
   ▶ make a poster using a selection of advertisements and discuss the similarities and differences between them;
   ▶ make a poster which 'sells' the idea of breast milk, using the same methods.
3 Discuss the statement on bottle-feeding by the National Children's Bureau, quoted in the text above. Why is it important that babies are bottle fed in the manner described?
4 Discuss the problems faced by developing countries when large companies promote bottle-feeding by mounting campaigns and distributing free infant milk samples.

A C T I V I T Y

Weaning

1 Prepare a booklet for parents on weaning. Include the following information:
   ▶ when to start weaning a baby;
   ▶ what foods to start with;
   ▶ when and how to offer feeds;
   ▶ a weekly menu plan which includes vegetarian options.

2 Visit a store which stocks a wide variety of commercial baby foods and note their nutritional content e.g. protein, fat, energy, salt, sugar, gluten and additives. Make a chart which shows:
   ▶ the type of food e.g. rusks and cereals, savoury packet food, jars of sweet and savoury food;
   ▶ the average cost in each category;
   ▶ the packaging – note particularly if manufacturers use pictures of babies from different ethnic backgrounds.

3 Ask a parent who has recently used weaning foods what reasons they had for choosing one product over another.

A C T I V I T Y

Research the advantages and disadvantages of terry towelling and disposable nappies, including the following information:

▶ costs – initial outlay and continuing costs of laundry and purchase of nappies, liners, pants, etc.
▶ the effects of each method on the environment – chemicals used in laundering; disposal;
▶ convenience and suitability for the purpose.

A C T I V I T Y

The baby's teeth

1 Prepare a leaflet for parents showing how teeth develop in a young baby and how to ensure their healthy development. Include tips for making caring for the teeth an enjoyable routine activity.

A C T I V I T Y

An unwell baby

1 Imagine you are a nanny looking after a 6-month-old baby in his home. When you pick him up from his morning nap, you notice that he is very hot and sweaty; he refuses his bottle-feed and cries fretfully. What would you do first?
2 Write an essay on the principles of caring for a sick baby.

A C T I V I T Y

SIDS

1 In groups, prepare a display which details the risk factors implicated in sudden infant death syndrome. Using the information provided, make a poster for each risk factor and state clearly the precautions that should be taken to prevent cot death.
2 In pairs, rehearse the procedure to follow if a young baby is found 'apparently lifeless' in his cot, using a baby resuscitation mannequin test each other's skills. NB: Professional supervision will be required.

A C T I V I T Y

Clothing a new baby

You have been asked to advise on the purchase of a layette for a new-born baby.

1   Make a list of the items you consider to be essential, excluding nappies and waterproof pants.
2   Visit several shops and find out the cost of all the items on your list.
3   Evaluate your selection, checking:
    ▶ the ease of washing and drying;
    ▶ the design and colours used – are you reinforcing the stereotypes of pink for girls or blue for boys?
    ▶ the safety aspects – no fancy bows, ties etc;
    ▶ the suitability of the fabrics used;
    ▶ the quantity of clothes needed;
    ▶ the final cost of the layette.

A C T I V I T Y

Toys for babies

1   Visit a toy shop and look at the range of toys for babies under 1 year old. List the toys and activities under two headings:
    ▶ toys that strengthen muscles and improve coordination;
    ▶ toys which will particularly stimulate the sense of touch and sight.

    What safety symbols are shown on the toys?

2   If you are asked to suggest toys and activities for a baby with a visual impairment, what specific toys could you suggest?

4

Children 1–8 Years: Physical Development and Care

Babies and young children follow standard patterns in acquiring physical skills, but there are wide individual variations. A child's range of physical skills or abilities will have a major effect on other areas of development. Once the child has learnt to crawl or shuffle on her bottom, she will be more independent and able to explore things that were previously out of reach.

The responses of other people to the child who has developed new skills will also alter, too: adults will make changes to the child's environment – putting reachable objects out of harm's way – and say 'no' more often.

Common patterns in physical growth and development

The most important factor controlling growth in height are the genes and chromosomes inherited from the parents. Growth in height may be divided into four distinct phases:

> ► *Phase 1:* This is a period of very rapid growth and lasts for about two years; the baby gains 25–30 cm in length and triples her body weight in the first year.
> ► *Phase 2:* This is a slower but steady period of growth which lasts from about 2 years of age through to adolescence; the child gains 5–8 cm in height and about (3 kg) in body weight per year until adolescence.
> ► *Phase 3:* This is a period characterised by a dramatic growth spurt, when the child may add 8–16 cm per year to her height for some years. The biggest weight gain occurs between the ages of 10–14 in girls and 12–16 in boys.
> ► *Phase 4:* This is a period of slow growth with slow increase in height and weight until the final adult size is reached. The age at which the final adult size is reached is variable, but is usually between 18–20 years.

FIGURE 4.I

Height gain in childhood

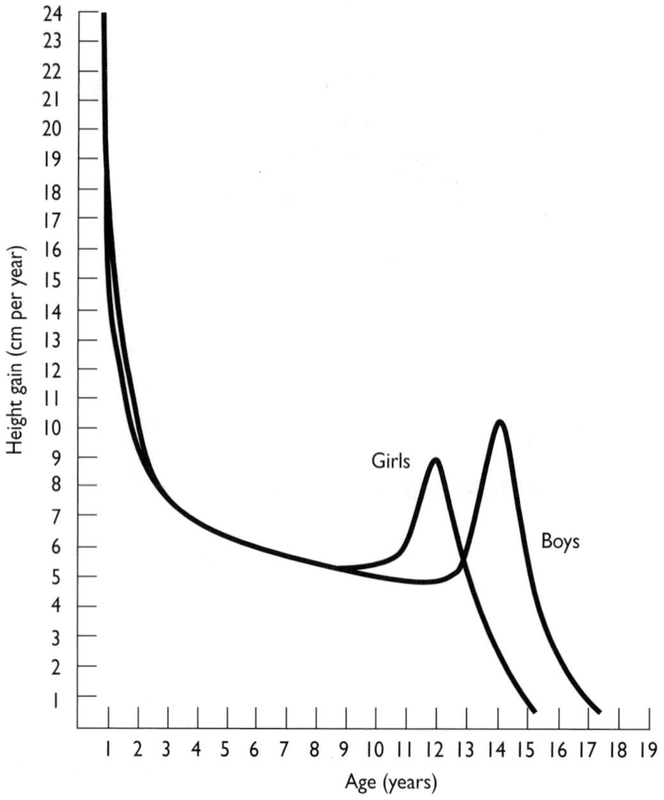

Body proportions

Development is a continuous process from conception to maturity. It depends upon the maturation of the **nervous system**. Variation in the **rate** of development is due to the interaction between the individual's genetic make-up and the environmental experiences encountered during the development process.

As a child grows, the various parts of the body change in shape and proportion as well as increasing in size. The different body parts also grow at different rates, e.g. the feet and hands of a teenager will reach their final adult size before the body does. At birth, a baby's head will account for about one-quarter of the total length of the body, whereas at 7 years old, the head will be about one-sixth of total length.

If a child's height is measured at the age of 2, the final adult height can be estimated by doubling the measurement.

Directions of development

Human development follows a sequence:

▶ from simple to complex, e.g. a child will walk before she can skip or hop;

▶ from head to toe (cephalo-caudal) e.g. head control is acquired before coordination of the spinal muscles, so a child learns to crawl by using upper body movements before he can creep, a movement involving the use of his legs;

▶ from inner to outer (proximodistal), e.g. a child can coordinate her arms to reach

FIGURE 4.2
Directions of development

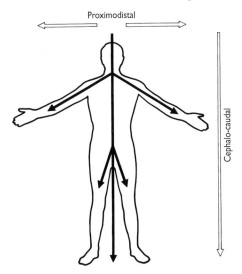

for an object before she has learned the fine manipulative skills necessary to pick it up;

▶ from general to specific, e.g. a young baby shows pleasure by a massive general response (eyes widen, legs and arms move vigorously, etc.); an older child shows pleasure by smiling or using appropriate words and gestures.

AGE 15 MONTHS – AREA OF DEVELOPMENT AND ROLE OF THE CARER

Gross motor skills
The baby probably walks alone with feet wide apart and arms raised to maintain balance.
She is likely to fall over and land suddenly on her bottom.
She can probably manage stairs and steps, but will need supervision.
She can stand without help from furniture or people.
She kneels without support.

Fine manipulative skills
The baby can build with a few bricks and arrange toys on the floor.
She holds crayon in palmar grasp.
She turns several pages of a book at once.
She can point to desired objects.
She shows a preference for one hand, but uses either.

Stimulating development
Provide stacking toys and bricks.
Provide push-and-pull toys for children who are walking.
Read picture books with simple rhymes.
Big empty cardboard boxes are popular.
Provide thick crayons or thick paint-brushes.
Arrange a corner of the kitchen or garden for messy play involving the use of water or paint.
NB: This is a high risk age for accidents – be vigilant at all times.

Promoting physical development

Children do not need lots of expensive toys and play equipment in order to grow and develop physically. The most important factors in healthy development are that the early childhood worker should:

▶ recognise the skills a child has developed and provide plenty of opportunities for him to practise them;

▶ ensure freedom to explore her environment in safety;

▶ be there for the child, to offer reassurance, encouragement and praise;

▶ provide access to a range of facilities and equipment; this need not be expensive – a visit to the local park or toddler's playgroup will provide facilities not available in a small flat.

Promoting physical development in children with special needs

Although the sequence of physical development may remain the same for a child with a special need, the rate at which a 'stage' is passed may be slower. The attitudes and actions of parents and child care workers will have a great influence on the child's behaviour and self-esteem.

▶ All children should be appreciated and encouraged for any *personal* progress made, however small, and *not* compared to the normative measurements.

▶ Adults should recognise and understand that a child who is having difficulty in acquiring a skill may become frustrated and may need more individual attention or specialist help; also that the child may not yet be ready to acquire the particular skill.

▶ Every child must be seen as a child first; activities and equipment should be tailored to the specific needs of that child.

Rest and sleep

Children vary in their need for sleep and in the type of sleep they need (see p. 108). Sleep and rest are needed for:

▶ relaxation of the central nervous system (CNS): the brain does not rest completely during sleep; electrical activity, which can be measured by an electroencephalogram (EEG) continues;

▶ recovery of the muscles and the body's metabolic processes: growth hormone is released during sleep to renew tissues and produce new bone and red blood cells.

Some children prefer to rest quietly in their cots rather than have a sleep during the day; others will continue to have one or two daytime naps even up to the age of 3 or 4 years.

Establishing a routine

All children benefit from a regular routine at bedtime; it helps to establish good habits and makes children feel more secure. A child will only sleep if she is actually tired, so it is vital that enough exercise and activity is provided. The stress on parents of a child who will not sleep at night can be severe (about 10–20% of very young children have some sort of sleep problem); establishing a routine which caters for the child's individual needs may help parents to prevent such problems developing. Principles involved are:

▶ ensuring the child has had enough exercise during the day;

▶ warning the child that bedtime is approaching and then following the set routine;

▶ making sure that the environment is conducive to sleep – a soft nightlight and non-stimulating toys might help, with no activity going on around bedtime;

▶ reducing anxiety and stress – it is quite natural for a small child to fear being left alone or abandoned; the parents should let the child know they are still around by, for example, talking quietly, or having the radio on, rather than creeping around silently;

▶ following the precept 'never let the sun go down on a quarrel' – a child who has been in trouble during the day needs to feel reassured that all is forgiven before bedtime.

A suggested routine

1 Warn the child that bedtime will be at a certain time (e.g. after the bath and story).
2 Take a family meal about one-and-a-half to two hours before bedtime; this should be a relaxing, social occasion.
3 After the meal, the child can play with other members of the family.
4 Make bath-time a relaxing time to unwind and play with the child; this often helps the child to feel drowsy.
5 Give a final bedtime drink followed by teeth cleaning.
6 Read or tell a story: looking at books together or telling a story enables the child to feel close to the carer.
7 Settle the child in bed, with curtain drawn and nightlight on if desired, and then say goodnight and leave.

Any care must take into account cultural preferences, such as later bedtimes, and family circumstances: a family living in bed and breakfast accommodation may have to share bathroom facilities, or bedtime may be delayed to enable a working parent to be involved in the routine.

AGE 18 MONTHS – AREA OF DEVELOPMENT AND ROLE OF THE CARER

Gross motor skills
The baby walks confidently and is able to stop without falling.
She can kneel, squat, climb and carry things around with her.
She can climb onto an adult chair forwards and then turn round to sit.
She comes downstairs, usually by creeping backwards on her tummy.

Fine manipulative skills
The baby can thread large beads.
She uses pincer grasp to pick up small objects.
She builds a tower of three or more cubes.
She scribbles to and fro on paper.

Stimulating development
Push-and-pull toys are still popular.
Teach the baby how to manage stairs safely.
Provide threading toys, and hammer and peg toys.
Encourage and praise early attempts at drawing.

AGE 2 YEARS – AREA OF DEVELOPMENT AND ROLE OF THE CARER

Gross motor skills
The child is very mobile and can run safely.
She can climb up onto the furniture.
She walks up and down stairs, usually two feet to a step.
She tries to kick a ball with some success but cannot yet catch a ball.

Fine manipulative skills
The child can draw circles, lines and dots, using preferred hand.
She can pick up tiny objects using a fine pincer grasp.
She can build a tower of six or seven bricks, with a longer concentration span.
She enjoys picture books and turns pages singly.

Stimulating development
Provide toys to ride and climb on and space to run and play.
Allow trips to parks and opportunities for messy play with water and paints.
Encourage use of safe climbing frames, sandpits, always supervised.
Provide simple models to build (e.g. Duplo) as well as jigsaw puzzles, crayons and paper, picture books and glove puppets.

AGE 3 YEARS – AREA OF DEVELOPMENT AND ROLE OF THE CARER

Gross motor skills
The child can jump from a low step.
She walks backwards and sideways.
She can stand and walk on tiptoe and stand on one foot.
She has good spatial awareness.
She rides tricycle using pedals.
She can climb stairs with one foot on each step – downwards with two feet per step.

Fine manipulative skills
The child can build a tower of nine or ten bricks.
She can control a pencil using her thumb and first two fingers – dynamic tripod.
She enjoys painting with a large brush.
She can copy a circle.

Stimulating development
Provide a wide variety of play things – dough for modelling, sand and safe household utensils.
Encourage play with other children.
Allow swimming, trips to park, maybe even enjoy long walks.
Read to the child and discuss everyday events.
Encourage art and craft activities.
Promote independence by teaching her how to look after and put away her own clothes and toys.
Encourage visits to the library and story times.

AGE 4 YEARS – AREA OF DEVELOPMENT AND ROLE OF THE CARER

Gross motor skills
Sense of balance is developing; she may be able to walk along a line.
She can catch, kick, throw and bounce a ball.
She can bend at the waist to pick up objects from the floor.
She enjoys climbing trees and on frames.
She can run up and down stairs, one foot per step.

Fine manipulative skills
The child can build a tower of ten or more bricks.
She can draw a recognisable person on request, showing head, legs and trunk.
She can thread small beads on a lace.

Stimulating development
Provide plenty of opportunity for exercise.
Play party games – musical statues etc.
Use rope swings and climbing frames.
Obtain access to a bike with stabilisers.
Provide small piece construction toys, jigsaws and board games.
Encourage gluing and sticking activities as well as paint, sand, water and playdough.
Prepare child for school by teaching her how to dress and undress for games and manage going to the toilet by herself.

Care of teeth

During the first year of life, a baby eats her first solid food with the help of her **primary teeth** (or milk teeth). These 20 teeth start to appear at around the age of six months (see Figure 4.4). There are three types of primary teeth:

▶ *incisors:* tough, chisel-shaped teeth with a sharp edge to help in biting food;

▶ *canines:* pointed teeth which help to tear food into manageable chunks;

▶ *molars:* large, strong teeth which grind against each other to crush food.

FIGURE 4.3
Structure of a primary tooth (milk tooth)

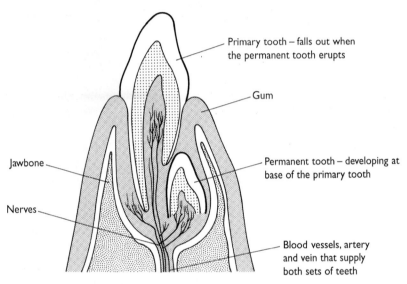

Primary tooth – falls out when the permanent tooth erupts

Gum

Jawbone

Nerves

Permanent tooth – developing at base of the primary tooth

Blood vessels, artery and vein that supply both sets of teeth

Looking after teeth

Teeth need cleaning as soon as they appear, because **plaque** sticks to the teeth and will cause decay if not removed. Caring for the temporary first teeth is important because:

▶ it develops a good hygiene habit which will continue throughout life;

▶ if milk teeth decay, they may need to be extracted; this could lead to crowding in the mouth as the natural gaps for the second teeth to fill will be too small;

▶ painful teeth may prevent chewing and cause eating problems;

▶ clean, white shining teeth look good.

Use a soft baby toothbrush at first to clean the plaque from the teeth; after the first birthday, children can be taught to brush their own teeth, but will need careful supervision. They should be shown when and how to brush, that is, up and away from the gum cleaning the lower teeth, and down and away when cleaning the upper teeth; they may need help to clean the back molars.

FIGURE 4.4

The usual order in which primary teeth appear

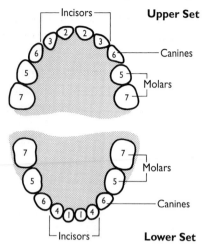

Rarely, a baby is born with the first tooth and it may have to be removed, if it is loose. Most children have 'cut' all 20 primary teeth by the age of 3 years; they usually appear in the order shown in Figure 4.4.

There are 32 **permanent teeth**. These replace the milk teeth, and start to come through at about the age of 6. The milk teeth which were first to appear become loose first and fall out as the permanent teeth begin to push through the gums.

FLUORIDE

Some toothpastes contain fluoride, which is a mineral that can help prevent dental decay. Some water boards in the UK add fluoride to the water supply; in areas where the fluoride level is low, dentists recommend giving fluoride drops daily to children from six months of age until teething is complete (usually by age 12). If water in your area has added fluoride, do not give drops or tablet supplements as an excess of the mineral can cause mottling of the teeth.

DIET

Healthy teeth need calcium, fluoride, vitamins A, C and D, and foods which need chewing, such as apples, carrots and wholemeal bread. Sugar causes decay and can damage teeth even before they have come through – 'dinky feeders' and baby bottles filled with sweet drinks are very harmful. It is better to save sweets and sugary snacks for special occasions only, or at least after meals, and to clean teeth thoroughly afterwards.

Visiting the dentist

The earlier a child is introduced to the family dentist, the less likely she is to feel nervous about dental inspection and treatment. Regular six-monthly visits to a dentist from about the age of 3 will ensure that any necessary advice and treatment is given to combat dental caries (tooth decay). Once the child starts primary school, a visiting dentist will check every child's teeth and refer for treatment if appropriate.

AGE 5 YEARS – AREA OF DEVELOPMENT AND ROLE OF THE CARER

Gross motor skills
The child can use a variety of play equipment – slides, swings, climbing frames.
She can play ball games.
She can hop and run lightly on toes, and move rhythmically to music.
Her sense of balance is well developed.

Fine manipulative skills
The child may be able to thread a large-eyed needle and sew large stitches.
She can draw a person with head, trunk, legs, nose, mouth and eyes.
She has good control over pencils and paintbrushes.
She can copy a square and a triangle.

Stimulating development
Provide plenty of outdoor activities.
Encourage non-stereotypical activities e.g. boys using skipping ropes, girls playing football.
Team sports may be provided at clubs such as Beavers, Rainbows and Woodcraft Folk.
Encourage the use of models, jigsaws sewing kits and craft activities as well as drawing and painting.
Introduce tracing and image patterns.

AGE 6 AND 7 YEARS – AREA OF DEVELOPMENT AND ROLE OF THE CARER

Gross motor skills
The child has increased agility, muscle co-ordination and balance.
She develops competence in riding a two-wheeled bicycle.
She hops easily, with good balance.
She can jump off apparatus at school.

Fine manipulative skills
The child can build a tall, straight tower with bricks.
She can draw a person with detail e.g. clothes and eyebrows.
She writes letters of the alphabet with similar writing hold to an adult.
She can catch a ball thrown from one metre away with one hand.

Stimulating development
Provide opportunity for vigorous exercise.
Team sports, riding a bike, swimming can all be encouraged; give plenty of praise for new skills learnt and *never* force a child to participate.
Provide books and drawing materials, board games and computer games.
Encourage writing skills.
Display the child's work prominently to increase self-esteem.

Physical activity and exercise

Exercise is essential for children's growth and development:

- ▶ it reduces their risk of developing heart disease in later life;
- ▶ it strengthens their muscles;
- ▶ it helps strengthen their joints and promotes good posture;
- ▶ it improves their balance, coordination and flexibility;
- ▶ it increases bone density, so they are less likely to fracture bones.

Apart from these obvious physical benefits, regular exercise develops a child's self-esteem by creating a strong sense of purpose and self-fulfilment; children learn how to interact and cooperate with other children by taking part in team sports and school activities.

Promoting exercise in children

Children need to learn that exercise is fun; the best way to convince them is to show by example. Some team games do not provide all children with the same opportunity for exercise, as they often involve several children standing around for long periods. Child care workers and parents should try to find an activity that the child will enjoy, such as

FIGURE 4.5
Swimming

dancing or roller-skating. Older children could be encouraged to join a local sports or gym club; some areas provide 'gym and movement' classes for toddlers. It is often easier to persuade a child to take up a new activity if she knows she will meet new friends. Family outings could be arranged to include physical activity, such as swimming, walking or boating.

Care of the skin in childhood

As children grow and become involved in more vigorous exercise, especially outside, a daily bath or shower becomes necessary. Most young children love bath-time and adding bubble-bath to the water adds to the fun of getting clean. General rules for skin hygiene are:

- ▶ Wash face and hands in the morning.
- ▶ Always wash hands after using the toilet and before meals; young children will need supervision.
- ▶ After using the toilet, girls should be taught to wipe their bottom from front to back to prevent germs from the anus entering the vagina and urethra.
- ▶ Nails should be scrubbed with a soft nailbrush and trimmed regularly by cutting straight across.
- ▶ Hair usually only needs washing twice a week; children with long or curly hair benefit from the use of a conditioning shampoo which helps to reduce tangles. Hair should always be rinsed thoroughly in clean water and not brushed until it is dry (brushing wet hair damages the hair shafts). A wide-toothed comb is useful for combing wet hair.
- ▶ Afro-Caribbean hair tends to dryness and may need special oil or moisturisers; if the hair is braided (with or without beads), it may be washed with the braids left intact, unless otherwise advised.
- ▶ Rastafarian children with hair styled in dreadlocks may not use either combs or shampoo, preferring to brush the dreadlocks gently and secure them with braid; some will wear scarves or caps in the Rastafarian colours of red, gold, green and black.

▶ Devout Sikhs believe that the hair must never be cut or shaved, and young children usually wear a special head covering.

▶ Each child should have his own flannel, comb and brush, which must be cleaned regularly.

▶ Skin should always be thoroughly dried, taking special care with areas such as between the toes and under the armpits; black skin tends to dryness and may need massaging with special oils or moisturisers.

▶ Observe skin for any defects, such as rashes, dryness or soreness, and act appropriately.

Development and care of children's feet

FIGURE 4.6
The bones of the foot

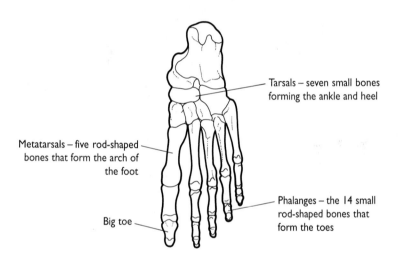

Tarsals – seven small bones forming the ankle and heel

Metatarsals – five rod-shaped bones that form the arch of the foot

Phalanges – the 14 small rod-shaped bones that form the toes

Big toe

While a baby is in its mother's womb, a tough, flexible material called **cartilage** begins to form where harder bones will eventually grow. As the baby grows, cartilage is continually replaced with bone in a process called **ossification**. This takes place in the shafts (or long sections) and heads (or ends) of all bones. There are 26 bones in the foot (see Figure 4.6).

A child's feet are very soft and supple because the bones are not yet rigid and they are spaced widely apart; as the feet grow they change shape, and often one foot tends to be slightly longer or wider than the other.

Care of the feet

Parents and carers should be aware that a child's feet can easily be distorted for life and so foot care must be treated as seriously as dental hygiene. General principles of foot care are:

▶ Ensure that bed covers are not tightly tucked in.

▶ Wash and dry the feet carefully every day and cut toenails straight across; never dig into the sides of the toenails to remove dirt, and take care not to cut the nails too short.

▶ Allow the child to go barefoot as often as possible.

▶ Always check that all-in-one stretch suits have plenty of room for the feet to grow.

► Choose socks with a high cotton content so that moisture from the feet can escape.
► Delay buying proper leather shoes until the child is walking properly and going outdoors regularly; never buy slippers unless they are properly fitted by a reputable shoe fitter.
► Always check that socks fit properly and do not stretch too tightly over the toes or sag and ruck up around the heels.

Foot problems

► *Club foot (talipes)* is fairly common and is caused by the foot being fixed in the same position in the womb for a prolonged time; sometimes the condition rights itself without treatment, but the foot may need gentle manipulation and/or strapping and eventually a surgical operation.
► *Flat feet* are caused by ligaments and muscles that have never developed fully. The condition is very rarely seen in children; parents sometimes misdiagnose flat feet because children's footprints often look completely flat.
► *Pigeon toes* is a minor abnormality in which the leg or foot is rotated, forcing the foot and toes to point inwards. It is fairly common in toddlers and generally requires no treatment, correcting itself by about the age of seven.
► *Chilblains* are red, itchy, swollen areas on toes which can be very painful. They usually heal without treatment, but could be prevented by keeping the feet warm and exercising to improve the circulation.
► *Corns* are small areas of thickened skin on a toe caused by pressure from ill-fitting shoes; they are difficult to remove but easy to prevent.
► *Athlete's foot* and *verrucae* are skin conditions of the feet (see Chapter 14).

Footwear

Parents and carers should always go to a shoe shop where trained children's shoe fitters can help them choose from a wide selection of shoes. Second-hand shoes should never be worn as all shoes take on the shape of the wearer's foot.

Points to check are:

► When shoes are fitted, there should be at least 1 cm between the longest toe and the inside of the shoe.
► *Both* feet should be measured for length, width and girth.
► Shoes must fit snugly around the heel and fasten across the instep to prevent the foot sliding forward.
► The soles of the shoes should be flexible and hard-wearing; non-slip soles are safer,
► Leather is the ideal material for shoes that are to be worn every day as it lets the feet 'breathe' and lets moisture out.
► Padders – soft corduroy shoes – keep a baby's feet warm when crawling or toddling, but should not be worn if the soles become slippery with wear.
► Shoes should never be bought a size too large as they can cause friction and blistering.
► Wellington boots should not be worn routinely because they do not allow the feet to breathe, but they are very useful for outdoor play, with socks worn underneath.

Clothing for children

The same principles that apply to clothing for babies apply to the selection of clothes for children. Parents and carers should *expect* children to become dirty as they explore their surroundings and should not show disapproval when clothes become soiled.

Clothes for children should be hard-wearing, comfortable and easy to put on and take off, especially when going to the toilet.

▶ *Underwear* should be made of cotton, which is comfortable and sweat-absorbent.
▶ *Sleepsuits* – all-in-one pyjamas with hard-wearing socks – are useful for children who kick the bedcovers off at night – (**NB** these must be the correct size to prevent damage to growing feet.)
▶ *Daytime clothes* should be adapted to the stage of mobility and independence of the child: for example, a dress will hinder a young girl trying to crawl; dungarees may prove difficult for a toddler to manage when being toilet-trained. Cotton jersey track-suits, T-shirts and cotton jumpers are all useful garments which are easy to launder.
▶ *Outdoor clothes* must be warm and loose enough to fit over clothing and still allow freedom of movement; a shower-proof anorak with a hood is ideal as it can be easily washed and dried.

The development of bowel and bladder control

New-born babies pass the waste products of digestion automatically; in other words, although they may go red in the face when passing a stool or motion, they have no conscious control over the action. Parents used to boast with pride that all their children were potty trained at 9 months, but the reality is that they were lucky in their timing! Up to the age of 18 months, emptying of the bladder and bowel is still a totally automatic reaction – the child's central nervous system (CNS) is still not sufficiently mature to make the connection between the action and its results.

Toilet training

There is no point in attempting to start toilet training until the toddler shows that he or she is ready, and this rarely occurs before the age of
18 months. The usual signs are:

▶ increased interest when passing urine or a motion – he may pretend play on the potty with his toys;
▶ he may tell the carer when he has passed urine or a bowel motion or look very uncomfortable;
▶ he may start to be more regular with bowel motions or the wet nappies may become rarer.

Toilet training should be approached in a relaxed, unhurried manner. If the potty is introduced too early, or if a child is forced to sit on it for long periods of time, he may rebel and the whole issue of toilet training becomes a battleground.

Toilet training can be over in a few days or may take some months. Becoming dry at night takes longer, but most children manage this before the age of 5.

Toilet training

▶ Before attempting to toilet train a child, make sure he has shown that he is *ready* to be trained, and remember that there is, as with all other developmental milestones, a wide variation in the age range at which children achieve bowel and bladder control.

▶ Be relaxed about toilet training and be prepared for accidents.

▶ Have the potty in the home so that the child becomes familiar with it and can include it in her play.

▶ Some children feel insecure when sitting on a potty with no nappy on – try it first with nappy or pants on if she shows reluctance.

▶ It is easier to attempt toilet training in fine weather when the child can run around without nappies or pants on.

▶ It helps if the child sees other children using the toilet or potty.

▶ If you start training when there is a new baby expected, be prepared for some accidents as many children like to remain babies themselves.

▶ Training pants, similar to ordinary pants but with a waterproof covering, are useful in the early stages of training – and having more than one potty in the house makes life easier.

▶ Always praise the child when she succeeds and do not show anger or disapproval if she doesn't – she may be upset by any accident herself.

▶ Offer the potty regularly so that the child becomes used to the idea of a routine, and get used to the signs that a child needs to use it.

▶ Don't show any disgust for the child's faeces. She will regard using the potty as an achievement and will be proud of them. Children have no natural shame about their bodily functions (unless adults make them ashamed).

▶ Encourage good hygiene right from the start, washing her hands after every visit to the potty.

▶ The child may prefer to try the 'big' toilet seat straight away; a toddler seat fixed onto the normal seat makes this easier. Boys need to learn to stand in front of the toilet and aim at the bowl before passing any urine; you could put a piece of toilet paper in the bowl for him to aim at.

Enuresis (bedwetting)

Enuresis is a common occurrence; about one in ten children wets the bed at the age of 6, and many of these continue to do so until the age of 8 or 9. It is commoner in boys than in girls and the problem tends to run in families. In the majority of children, enuresis is due to slow maturation of the nervous system functions concerned with control of the bladder; very rarely, it occurs because of emotional stress or because of a physical problem, e.g. urinary infection.

MANAGING BEDWETTING

▶ Investigate possible physical causes first by taking the child to the doctor.

▶ Protect the mattress with a plastic sheet.

▶ Do not cut down on the amount a child drinks in a day, although a bedtime drink could be given earlier; never let a child go to bed feeling thirsty.

▶ Encourage the child to pass urine just before going to bed; it sometimes helps to 'lift' the child just before adults go to bed, taking her to the toilet. It is important, however, that the child is thoroughly awake when passing urine; this is because the child will need to recognise the link between passing urine and waking up with a dry bed.

▶ Some parents find a 'star chart' system of rewards for a dry bed encourages the child to become dry sooner, but this should only be used if physical problems have been excluded.

▶ If the child continues to wet the bed after the age of 7 years, a special night-time alarm system can be used: a detector mat is paced under the sheet which triggers a buzzer as soon as it becomes wet; eventually the child will wake *before* she needs to pass urine (this system is said to succeed in over two-thirds of children).

Encopresis (soiling)

Encopresis is a type of soiling in which children who have no physical problems with their bowel motions deliberately pass them in their pants or on the floor. It occurs after the age at which bowel control is usually achieved and in children who know the difference between the right and wrong place to go. It is fortunately a rare condition but one which needs very sensitive treatment. Encopresis may occur because of emotional problems and stress; if it persists, advice should be sought from the health visitor or doctor.

RESOURCES

Books

Mollie Davies, *Helping Children Learn Through a Movement Perspective,* London, Hodder and Stoughton, 1995

Tessa Hilton, *The Great Ormond Street Book of Baby and Child Care,* London, Bodley Head, 1993

K. S. Holt, *Child Development,* Oxford, Butterworth-Heineman, 1991

The Lippincott Manual of Paediatric Nursing, London, Chapman & Hall, 1991

Maureen O'Hagan and Maureen Smith, *Special Issues in Child Care,* London, Bailliere Tindall, 1993

Useful addresses

Child Growth Foundation
2 Mayfield Avenue
Chiswick
London W4 1PW
Tel.: 020 8995 0257

Pre-School Learning Alliance
61-63 King's Cross Road
London WC1X 9LL
Tel.: 020 7833 0991

Child Development Research Unit
University of Nottingham
Psychology Department
University Park
Nottingham NG7 2RD
Tel.: 0115 9515151

Enuresis Resource and Information Centre (ERIC)
65 St Michael's Hill
Bristol BS2 8DZ
Tel.: 01272 264920

ACTIVITY

Physical development in a child with special needs

Either (1) visit a school for children with special needs, *or*
(2) invite a child care worker with experience of working with children with special needs into college.

Prepare the questions you need to ask to find out:

▶ how a child with difficulties in coordination can be helped to develop these skills;

▶ what activities may be used to promote physical development in a child confined to a wheelchair;

▶ what is the role of the early childhood worker in promoting physical development in children with special needs.

ACTIVITY

Bedtime routine

Arrange to visit a family with a young child (ideally, your family placement) to talk about their child's bedtime routine. Devise a questionnaire to find out the following

▶ any problems with settling the child to sleep;

▶ any problems with the child waking in the night;

▶ strategies used to solve the problems.

Using the answers from the questionnaire, devise a bedtime routine for a 3-year-old girl who has just started nursery school and whose mother has 3-month-old twin boys. Points to include are

▶ how to arrange one-to-one care for the 3-year-old;

▶ how to avoid jealousy.

ACTIVITY

A dental hygiene routine

Plan a routine for a toddler which will cover all aspects of dental hygiene:

▶ brushing teeth;

▶ dietary advice;

▶ education about teeth/visits to the dentist.

Include examples of books that could be used to help prepare a child for a visit to the dentist. Remember to give a reason for each part of the routine.

A C T I V I T Y

Personal hygiene

1 What are the benefits of good hygiene for children?
2 How would you encourage children to take responsibility for their own personal hygiene?

A C T I V I T Y

Children's clothing

Plan a wardrobe of clothes suitable for a child aged 3 years throughout a year. For each garment, give:
  ▶ the reason you have chosen it;
  ▶ how it should be laundered or cleaned;
  ▶ how it may promote the child's independence.

A C T I V I T Y

Toilet training

Arrange to interview a parent or carer who has recently toilet-trained a child.
1 Try to find out the methods used and any problems encountered.
2 Write a report of the methods used.
3 In class, discuss the problems which can arise in toilet training and compare the strategies used by different families.
4 In small groups, make a colourful, eye-catching wall display which provides tips for parents and carers on potty training.

5

Working in Partnership with Parents

The variety of family structures

There is no such thing as a standard family. In different parts of the world, different cultures have completely different family structures. Although in some parts of the world one type of family dominates, it is not possible to generalise.

The extended family
In some cultures, the **extended family** is strong. This means that parents, children, grandparents, aunts, uncles and cousins live together in a close-knit community. It might mean, for example, that aunts bring up the children of their brothers and sisters. Or it might mean that grandmothers are the most important people and do most of the child-rearing. There is a huge variety in the way that extended families live.

The nuclear family
In other cultures the **nuclear family** is strong. This means that parents and children live separately from other relatives. This might be at a long distance from the rest of the family. They may meet grandparents, aunts, uncles or cousins much less often.

Disrupting family structures
When a family moves from one cultural setting to another, this can disrupt the family structure. This was shown in the UK in a famous study in the 1960s by Wilmott and Young about families in the East End of London. These families were of the extended family type, living in back-to-back houses. Grandmothers were very important in helping daughters with advice on bringing up children. Some of the families were then rehoused into new high-rise flats some distance away in another part of London. The daughters spent most of their time on the bus, going back to visit their mothers. Family life was seriously disrupted.

It is important that those working with young children are aware of the family structure, and how changes can disrupt it. Moving from one part of the town to another is perhaps not as deep-seated a disruption as moving from one country to another.

The advantage of the extended family

Arguments in favour of the extended family are usually that family members can help and support each other.

The advantages of the nuclear family

Arguments in favour of the nuclear family are usually that families can change and keep up with the times much more rapidly. They are often better off economically because they are much more mobile and seek job opportunities and career development.

The disadvantages of extended families

The disadvantages of extended families are usually that they are often hierarchical. This means that it is difficult for some members of the family (often women) to develop as fully as they might. These families are often much more stable in offering emotional support, but it is argued that they can hold people back in their personal development.

The disadvantages of nuclear families

Arguments against nuclear families are usually that they are mobile, go-getting and fragile because if anything goes wrong between the two parents, they disintegrate. This causes the parents and children a great deal of emotional pain. In the UK, between one-third and one-half of nuclear families are experiencing this, and the divorce rate is rising all the time. It is argued that getting on in life is being put before the emotional well-being of the family.

Researchers are beginning to study these new kinds of family in order to find out more about how children in these families feel and adjust.

Other different kinds of family

Apart from these two main types of family, the nuclear and the extended family, there are other kinds of family.

MONOGAMY

Relationships might be **monogamous** (i.e. two partners stay together unless they decide to part). Partners may be married, and if they part they will divorce. Both marriage and divorce will be legal contracts or they may **co-habit**.

Monogamous relationships might be
- **heterosexual** (a man and a woman);
- **homosexual** (two men or two women in a gay or lesbian relationship).

As yet little is known about children growing up with gay or lesbian parents. It seems likely that the experiences of these families are similar to those of most minorities, such as children growing up with parents of different religions, or children growing up in a family where the parents are wheelchair users. Mixed-race families, and families with people with disabilities are minority groups of a different kind.

POLYGAMY

Relationships might be **polygamous**. It means that one partner will have several partners of the opposite sex – for example, the man may have several wives. In the UK, this is illegal and is called **bigamy**.

FAMILIES IN AGRICULTURAL SOCIETIES

In agricultural societies children often help with chores on the farm.

NOMADIC FAMILIES

These families have no permanent town or village. Children in these families usually help when moving on with all the packing-up and unpacking at each stopping point.

FAMILIES IN INDUSTRIAL SOCIETIES

In industrial societies, children are often either set to work in factories (child labour) or set to work in formal schools. Some researchers argue the latter is really another kind of child labour. Recent studies in neuroscience indicate that the brain develops best in the early years. When children move about and use all their senses they create meaning through them, and this helps the brain to grow. This is called mass action. Children are easily involved in several languages, songs, rhythms and dance like movements during these earliest years. Both types of child labour are concentrating on what society would find it useful for the child to do. Neither approach looks at what the child needs during childhood in order to fulfil their long-term needs as a person who will then be able to contribute much more richly to their society, through a richly developed brain.

In formal schools, children sit at tables and learn reading, writing and number, and are not encouraged to play or move about. This is very different from quality nursery education or care settings, where children can make decisions about the activities they do, and are encouraged to develop their play and learn in ways which respect childhood needs. Children are not hurried through their childhood (see Chapter 1).

Changes in family type

Divorce, co-habitation and remarriage have become more usual in modern life in the UK. Many children now experience changes in their family life, and this might be through the death of the parent, divorce or reordered families.

Children throughout history have always had to adapt to changes, and so there is nothing new in this. However, the kinds of changes that children in the modern United Kingdom are now dealing with in family life are not the same as they were. This is because fewer parents now die when their children are young. The main reason for parents remarrying is now that the parent has been through a divorce.

The UK is a multicultural society, which means that there are many different ideas about and expectations of marriage:

- ► Parents have fewer children than they used to have.
- ► Parents are more likely both to be working, to share home tasks, and to share child care.
- ► Children are more likely to grow up with a lone parent.
- ► They are more likely to grow up with parents who are in a homosexual relationship than in previous times.
- ► They may live in two households, and move across from one to the other during holidays or at weekends.
- ► They may grow up with full brothers and sisters, or half-brothers and half-sisters with parents who co-habit or have remarried after divorce.
- ► They may grow up with parents, step-parents, aunts, etc. And they are more likely to grow up with foster parents or adoptive parents.

Is one type of family structure best? There is probably no 'correct' model for a family structure. There is probably no 'best' way of bringing up children. However, some things do seem to be important for any family.

What all families need to give children

▶ Children need to be fed, clothed and sheltered, and to have sleep. This fulfils their **primary needs**.

▶ Children need to feel loved and to learn to love. This means they need some reliable people in their life to show them affection and warmth, and who enjoy receiving love and warmth from the child.

▶ Families introduce children to their **culture**. This means that through their family children learn what people expect of them. They learn how to get what they need in order to be a fully functioning person. (See Chapter 7). The way this comes about will vary in different parts of the world, and will be different in different families even within one culture. For example, there is no such thing as a typical Christian family, British family, Muslim family, working-class family, First Nation family, or indeed royal family.

Each family is different from every other family. In some families, children sleep in bunks, in others they sleep in hammocks, or beds, on the floor. Some families are vegetarian. Some live in houses on stilts, in a community. Others live in high-rise flats separately. Some live underground. Others live in separate houses set in their own grounds or gardens.

Working with all parents

Early childhood workers need to bear in mind the fact that every family is different and has different needs and traditions. It is also important to remember that the great majority of parents are concerned to do their best for their children, even if they are not always sure what this might be.

Each one of us only really knows what it is like to grow up in our own family. Parents, almost always, like some of the things about their own family and the way they were brought up; but they will just as certainly wish that other aspects of their upbringing had been different. Parents usually welcome help with trying out some alternative ways of doing things. They will not want to change too much, though, and they will not want rapid changes which they feel are forced on them from other people. Early childhood workers need to respect this.

Early childhood workers do their best work when they see themselves as a resource and support that can be used by parents for their children's best interests. Staff can offer ideas but must never insist on, or be judgemental about, the way that parents should bring up their children. If you are not a parent, you will not have experienced some of the things that parents have. If you *are* a parent, you will only know about being a parent of your own children: you will not know what it is like to be a parent of other people's children.

Respecting all parents

The vast majority of parents, including those who abuse their children, love them. It is important not to judge parents, and to respect their good intentions. Almost every parent, even if on the surface they do not seem to be interested or loving, want to do the job well. Staff need to recognise this and to work positively with this as a central focus. Concentrating on the good intentions of parents gives them a **positive image**. Just as children need positive images reflected about themselves, so do parents. The attitude of the staff must therefore involve showing them **respect**. It is hard bringing up a child.

Parents need to feel that the early childhood worker respects their intentions about being a 'good' parent who is trying to do the best for their child.

Showing parents respect and reinforcing their dignity encourages the idea that the child also needs respect and a sense of dignity. One mother of a 3-year-old in a day-care centre said to her family worker, 'When I was little I was always hit when I did wrong. I don't want to do that to Melissa, but I don't know what to do instead.' Almost every person in the world can be helped by seeing alternative ways of doing things. By widening the circle and meeting others, by coming to the early childhood setting, the child and family are meeting other people. This inevitably means that they are meeting other ways of doing things. Melissa's mother can learn about other ways – instead of hitting – of dealing with wrong-doing. She can then decide whether she wants to use some of these other methods, and this will give her more choice about the way she can bring up Melissa.

The relationship between parent, child and staff

The parent is a deeply important person to the child and the relationship between parent and child is always very emotional. Emotional relationships can be very unreasonable at times. Parents and staff will work with children in different ways. It is a bit like hedgehogs. Parents and staff dare not get too close to each other because they might hurt each other with their prickles!

The differences between parents and staff are important. Staff ought not to have such deeply emotional relationships with children. They need to keep a little more distance and yet to work with children in a warm, sensitive way. (Peter Elfer's study at the National Children's Bureau (1995) looked at the effect of early childhood workers withholding emotions.) However, parents and staff have one thing in common which is very important: they all want the best for the child.

The roles involved are not the same, but they *are* complementary:

▶ Staff have knowledge of **general child development**.
▶ Parents know their own child the best.

If the partnership between parents, staff and child is going to develop well, then each needs to trust and respect the other. The Children Act 1989 gives both rights and responsibilities to parents. More is written about this Act in the last chapter of this book.

The **self-esteem** of the parents, the staff members and the child is important when they are working together. Self-esteem is about how we feel about ourselves. This is influenced by how *other* people feel about us (see Chapter 7). Parents may have had bad experiences at school and when their child joins a group setting, this may bring all those past feelings rushing back to the surface. Parents will then be anxious and not feel good about themselves. They might expect this institution to be like the one they went to, and this will make them fear for their child. This is often so when parents are required to bring their child to the early childhood setting under a **child protection order**. Staff will need to be sensitive to the feelings of parents in this sort of situation.

In the 1960s, work with parents concentrated on home–school links. Parents and staff kept respectfully apart, but at least it was acknowledged that links were a good thing. Staff thought links would help them to tell parents about what they expected of families. There was little emphasis on parents telling staff what they expected of the early childhood setting.

In the 1970s, there was an emphasis on what was called 'compensatory education' (see Chapter 6). Some families were thought to lack the ability to help their children in school. Staff talked of 'problem families', 'disadvantaged families' or 'inadequate families'. These negative labels did not respect the parents.

From the 1980s to the present day, there has been a shift towards emphasising *partnership* with parents. Early childhood workers see parents as both the primary carer and the primary educator of the child.

Researchers such as Judy Dunn have found that children have richer conversations at home than at school because their parents or their brothers and sisters understand and help them. In a work setting, children are often in an unfamiliar situation, and it is therefore more difficult for them to talk at a deep level in conversations. Staff may be rather busy and not able to take time for a one-to-one conversation that the child has at home.

Researchers have shown how staff can quickly undermine the confidence of parents by showing off their knowledge and using jargon. Some staff even talk about 'my children'. They are *not* their children: children belong to their families. Staff are there to help, but not to take over.

Early childhood workers are mindful of the balance between the parents' self-esteem, the child's self-esteem and the staff's self-esteem. There are many strategies that help to build everyone's self-esteem. Staff who are well trained are able to use their knowledge sensitively and to appreciate the family background, culture, language, physical surroundings and economic background of each child. They need to be confident enough to be able to build observations together with parents, and to 'share' rather than 'show off' what they know about the child's development and learning. This does not mean that parents must do things the way staff do things. It simply shows other ways of working with children. Exchanging ideas and respecting each other's ideas about children are all important in working with parents.

Beginning the partnership

In some work settings, home visits are set up as soon as the child's name is registered. This means that parents meet staff on their own territory. It is important that parents do not feel forced into accepting a home visit from staff in nurseries or playgroups or from the childminder or nanny. Usually, however, parents *do* welcome them as this is an opportunity to get to know the staff, the childminder or the nanny.

▶ It is important not to go alone, for your safety, especially in the evenings.

▶ It is equally important to make an appointment as the parent may not want to open the door to a stranger.

▶ People usually find that if one family worker (see below) concentrates on the parent(s) and the other worker gets to know the child, then everyone enjoys it. The child has the full attention of one adult with a bag of carefully chosen books and toys. The parents and staff are free to get to know each other, and can fill in basic information records together and without the pressure of being in a busy work setting.

▶ It is important that parents do not feel judged or tested. They need to be sure that their home is not being inspected to see if it is clean, tidy, fashionable or tasteful.

▶ Staff need to make appointments with parents to make sure that a visit is not sprung on them. It should never be assumed that all parents would accept the invitation to be visited. Most parents do, but some will not want to be visited. This should be treated with respect.

A home visit allows an exchange and sharing of ideas and feelings about the child. For the child newly starting in the early childhood setting, the main thing will be to find out:

▶ what the parents are expecting;

▶ what the parents hope for – are they expecting the nursery to be like the schools that *they* went to? Do they want their child to learn reading at 2 or 3 years of age? Do they think that mathematics is another word for numbers? Do they think children should play?

It will also be important to explain to them what to expect and to make sure that the child too is helped to know what to expect. The routines of the day and what equipment the children use will be important information to give here.

It will be necessary too, to explain the family worker system where there is one in place. This is now widely used and recommended in both the Children Act 1989 and the Starting With Quality Report 1990. This kind of information can be shared by going through the 'brochure' together. This is now often a photograph album which shows in a very practical way the philosophy, activities and timetabling of the day. Photographs are enhanced by brief notes. For example, there might be pictures of: children playing with sand, the home area with boys and girls playing, the book area stocking books in different languages and story times with props – all showing the approach to reading, writing, mathematics and science. These brochures can be constantly changed and updated, and can be borrowed by parents at home. Some can also be put out in the early childhood settings for children to browse through in the rooms and entrance hall. A parent library with photograph albums is a very effective way of showing the whole philosophy in action.

Some photograph books can be very general, while others might focus on one aspect of the work with children. For example, one might focus on play, another on meal times, and another on the approach to reading. These photograph albums are usually very popular with children and parents alike, as well as with visitors to the setting.

Parents also appreciate having a booklet of their own, which can be given at the first meeting with the family worker or teacher. This will need to contain:

▶ the address and telephone number of the early childhood setting;
▶ the name of the parents' family worker or teacher;

FIGURE 5.1

Children value and appreciate looking at their own records of achievement

▶ a chart showing the names of the staff, what they do and their qualifications;

▶ information about the opening and closing times;

▶ details of parent–toddler groups, drop-ins, toy library etc.;

▶ information about how the children are admitted, and about fees where needed;

▶ information about what to do if the child is to leave the setting;

▶ information about the age range of the children;

▶ information about what the parent needs to provide – nappies, spare clothes, snacks;

▶ information about the rules and boundaries that are involved in the early childhood setting.

The parent will have to help the family worker or teacher to fill in the basic information record, and will need to be reassured that this record will be treated with confidentiality and stored safely. The record will then be regularly reviewed and kept up to date with the parents' help.

This basic information record will need to include:

▶ the child's name, address and date of birth;

▶ emergency contact addresses and telephone numbers;

▶ the child's doctor's name, address and telephone number;

▶ any medical details which are important – e.g. in relation to diet, allergies, medicine etc.;

▶ information about social workers or other professionals working with the child – e.g. a speech therapist;

▶ the names of people who are allowed to fetch the child, bearing in mind that other children may not fetch the child;

▶ details about the child's fears, interests, favourite toys and comforters and about any special words the child uses.

The family worker or teacher will need to go through all this information by chatting with the parent(s). If the parent(s) speak(s) a different language, it will sometimes be possible to have a translator present. If not, remember that:

▶ eye contact helps;

▶ gesture is a very powerful way of communicating with people;

▶ you can use photographs – the photographs in the brochure will be a great help;

▶ the toys and books that you have taken to use with the child will also be a great help.

This child might be the first child in the family, or an only child, or a middle or youngest child. The parent will probably appreciate as much information and discussion as possible. It will be important to make sure that the parents understand all the admission procedures, and how they need first to stay with the children before leaving them in the nursery.

Sometimes, parents have difficulty taking time off work because of an unsympathetic employer, who does not share a spirit of equal opportunities, in which case the parents will not be able to settle their children in for a full fortnight – which might be the policy of the nursery. The situation will need to be discussed, and an alternative arrangement made. Sometimes, another relative, for example a grandparent, will help to settle a child.

Separation anxiety (see Chapter 7) may need to be dealt with when talking to the parent. If the child is one of several children, the parent might already know about many of the issues involved in starting in an early childhood group setting. Most parents tend to enjoy chatting, so at the beginning of your meeting together it will be important to set a time limit – half an hour to an hour is usual. This is important, or your home-visiting procedures will break down and parents will feel that some are being given much longer visits than others.

It is very important that parents understand, even before their child joins the group, that the staff will not be able to let their child go home with anybody but those adults agreed in the negotiations. Therefore, staff need to know exactly which adults will fetch the child. Furthermore, staff will not be able to let the child go home with any child under 12 years of age.

It will be necessary also to note the *hopes* that parents have – once you know what a parent thinks reading is all about, for example, it will help you to talk about it together.

Building trust

The advantage of home visits is that professionals can ask parents about their views of education and care. By understanding how parents feel, they can use this information as a bridge across what they know and have learnt through their own training. This is especially important when working with families from different cultural backgrounds. The assumptions on both sides about what education is and how it should be carried out are often different. Through respecting each other, trust is established. This brings a deep commitment on both sides to working together for the child.

If the parents hope that their child will learn to read and have taught the alphabet to their 3-year-old, it will be important not to reject their ideas about how children learn to read. Your own point of view might be very different as a result of the influence of your training. You can ask the parent if they would like to know some of the other twelve or so things children need to know in order to read. This does not *reject* the fact that the parent has taught their child the alphabet, but it does open up all sorts of other possibilities for what the parent can do in helping their child to read. This serves to broaden the approach to reading without rejecting the parent's view of how children learn to read. The message to the parent is that the staff too value reading, respect the intentions of the parent and can be a helpful resource for the family in teaching the child to read.

Parents are the child's first educator

Sometimes, staff ask parents to take an observation sheet and keep it at home. They draw or write about interesting things that their child does. Drawing helps parents and staff to have a dialogue without words or writing about what children do. It helps sensitivity towards parents who use a different language, or who are not confident about writing. Until recently, staff have often thought that parents would not want to do this. Chris Athey found that parents, several of whom spoke Urdu but not English, loved to keep observation notes in the Froebel research project: they drew in order that staff and parents could communicate with each other. The first record systems were the parent diaries which were kept by people like Charles Darwin on his son Doddy in the last century. Parents still love to buy baby books and to fill them with the date of the first smile, the first tooth, when the child first walked, the first words, and so on. If drawings and photographs are valued, this helps when parents and staff speak different languages.

Teenage brothers and sisters will often enjoy filling in these observation sheets too. At Pen Green Family Centre, Corby, Northants and the Haringey Early Years Excellence Network, parents regularly fill in observation sheets and meet staff to discuss them.

Visits to the early childhood setting

Not all early childhood staff make home visits. This may be for a variety of reasons. For example, children in a workplace nursery may come from too wide a catchment area for staff to manage.

Where home visits *are* made, staff will need to work together as a team to make a well-thought-through home-visit policy agreed to and understood by the whole team. This will take time, and should never be rushed.

If, however, there is *no* home-visiting policy in your early childhood setting, the same procedures as involved in home visiting can be followed with the family's first visit to the early childhood centre. This visit will usually take place before the child starts to attend regularly. Some settings even encourage families to visit several times beforehand.

First impressions are important:

▶ Do parents feel welcomed by the staff?

▶ Does the building itself feel welcoming?

▶ Notices with arrows to the office help. These might be in different languages. An attractive display in the entrance area also helps, showing some of the recent activities that children have been involved in.

▶ Information showing the names of staff with their photographs helps. Photograph albums (as already mentioned) containing brief notes explaining the setting's philosophy and activities are also helpful.

▶ A menu of the week's meals helps, highlighting a multicultural approach to the early childhood setting.

▶ Something for children to do is helpful. One nursery school has a beautiful rocking horse in the entrance hall and this is very popular with the children. One family centre has an aquarium to look at, with an interest table with baskets full of shells on it which the children are encouraged to touch.

THE PROFESSIONAL RELATIONSHIP

Hopefully, an atmosphere of trust is set up through the first meeting with parents. It is very important to remember that staff are not trying to make friends with parents: this is a professional relationship only. Friendships are about choosing each other. Friendships are based on being interested in the same things, for example the same sort of food, dancing, football. A professional relationship is one where people do not choose each other. They come together because of the work they do together.

Early childhood workers and parents come together because they each spend time with and work with the child. Some people like to use first names, others do not. There will be a policy about this in the work setting. Calling each other by first names does not mean being friends. It means creating a relaxed, warm and inviting atmosphere. It is important either that all staff be called by their first names or that all staff be called by their surnames. It is also important that staff make sure that they address parents correctly and as they would wish. This is particularly important where names are used differently in different cultural traditions.

Parent–toddler groups

These introduce parents and children to group settings in a very informal way. Parents might bring their toddler to the group once a week. There will be drinks and healthy snacks for parents and children, together with activities appropriate for toddlers. Adults can talk and exchange ideas and feelings. Babies can also be brought to the group.

FIGURE 5.2

Preliminary visits

In nursery schools and primary schools with nursery classes, when the time comes for the child (usually at 3 years of age) to begin in the nursery, the family workers can gradually introduce the child to the nursery by visiting. Children settle very happily and quickly in this structure.

Toy libraries

Many early childhood settings now have toy libraries where families can borrow toys:

▶ Families can see if the interest in a particular toy is short lived.

▶ It saves families money.

▶ It broadens the range and play experience for the child.

▶ It helps parents to see how pre-structured toys are less interesting to children than toys which can be used in a variety of ways.

▶ So called educational toys, commercially expensive, are often narrowly pre-structured.

▶ Toy libraries are particularly useful for children with disabilities where it can be much more difficult to predict what the child might enjoy.

Book libraries and activity packs

These also provide a non-cost opportunity for early language and literacy, maths and science experiences in the family home. They encourage parents to enjoy books and educational activities with their children, which is the most important influence on how easily children learn to read. Children can begin to learn mathematics and science in a very natural way. Eastwood Nursery School in London has developed an exciting set of mathematical packs for families to borrow.

Settling in: admissions procedures

Probably the most important thing an early childhood worker does is to successfully settle a child into an early childhood group at any time, in partnership with the parent(s). Many settings have a very clear policy on admissions and on settling in. This helps all adults, staff and parents to have a common approach. For example, the family worker, after the home visit or first meeting, will plan something the child knows and likes, for example if the child has a much-loved teddy bear at home, there might be a basket of different teddies and a picnic set at the setting. If the child loves putting things in and out of boxes, there might be a table with boxes and objects on it – a love of things being put inside and outside is strong in young children (see Schemas, Chapter 6).

It is very important that every child and parent be greeted as they arrive, and that goodbyes be said as they leave – meetings and partings are important to human beings.

The parent will also be encouraged to stay with the child during the settling-in period, which often lasts for the first fortnight. For the sake of the child, there need to be very firm, clear boundaries about this period.

Here, as in Chapter 7, the importance of positive separation from parents and positive reuniting with parents is given great emphasis.

To help the child to settle into an early childhood setting:

▶ prepare the child for what will happen;
▶ prepare the staff for the child;
▶ arrange a home visit by the family worker who will particularly relate to this child and family;
▶ arrange preliminary visit(s) to the early childhood setting;
▶ arrange for the parents and child to look at books or videos about starting at the nursery;
▶ create a doll's-house play about the sort of things that will happen;
▶ make sure that all the staff know about the child's cultural background, diet, health-related issues, and so on;
▶ together with the parents, use the school's policy in such a way as to find the best way of settling the child. The policy needs to cater for the fact that each child will be different.

The way a child settles into a group situation is probably one of the most important factors in a child's life. Parents need to be helped to understand this. Occasionally, they do not realise the importance of this and need to be helped to understand that staff are experienced in knowing that this really is best for the child, and that the settling-in policy needs to be followed. It will be particularly important to be sure of communicating and exchanging ideas, and of negotiating the policy of settling in. Sometimes it is helpful if an interpreter can help with translating in situations where parents come from different cultural backgrounds and speak different languages (British Sign language may be needed if the parent has a hearing impairment).

During the settling-in period, it is best that parents do not join in too actively but sit as a 'safe person' for the child to keep returning to. Staff usually encourage the child to join an activity such as the sand tray. The parents sit next to the sand tray and smile and look encouraging, and staff gradually begin to join in with the child more and more. Eventually, the child turns to the family worker for help as often as the parent.

Children will use **social referencing** (see Chapter 7) as they settle in. If the parent is obviously anxious about leaving, the child will sense this. However, if the family worker is warm and interesting to be with, this helps the child to settle. (See Chapter 8 on communication with children by the early childhood worker.)

It is often said that the worst patients in a hospital are the nurses and doctors! The same can be said for settling children: the worst parents for settling in their children are often early childhood workers! This might be because they are aware of all the things that could go wrong. It is thus important for everyone involved to be very positive and very clear, and to follow the policy laid down.

A typical pattern of admissions procedure

During the first week, the parent will typically stay with the child most of the time. The child and parent will go home after an hour or so, or just before the story time, especially if this is at the end of the morning. Then, the children are in a frame of mind in which they cannot wait to return the next time. Often children leave protesting that they want to stay.

The parent gradually begins to go for 10-minute coffee breaks. However, they might leave a bag with their shopping, but with no money in it, or something else which clearly signals to the child that they are returning.

Parents obviously need to be able to trust the family worker that their child will be number one priority when they make their first trip away from that child. Parents need to tell the child about this trip. Most children like their parents to tell them as they leave, as long as they are with their family worker when the parent goes, and as long as the family worker quickly involves them in something that they will enjoy.

Some children cannot bear 'the parting'. These children are, however, a minority. The policy on parent leaving will need to be talked through with each parent and carefully negotiated and agreed between the parent, the child and the family worker.

If we think about it, throughout our lives it is hard to part from the people we love. Some people like to wave goodbye as the train leaves the platform. Others prefer to say goodbye and leave the platform before the train goes. When children as young as 2 or 3 years old are asked what is best, they are often able to say what they would prefer.

Getting the child involved in something that they enjoy is essential. Distraction will work for a few moments, but unless the child is really involved in what they are doing, feelings about being alone without the parent will rise to the surface. Popular activities for children who are settling are rocking horses and sand play. They can watch what is going on around them while they do these things.

WHEN THE PARENT IS REUNITED WITH THE CHILD

Some parents find it hard to leave, and fear the family worker might compete or even replace them in their child's affections. It is therefore important when the parents are leaving their child, to say things which help them not to worry about this, for example 'The child keeps telling me "My mum does not spread the butter like that. She prefers the way you do it."'

REASSURING THE PARENT/CARER

Parents often worry deep down about whether the staff like their child. When they ask 'Has she been good?' they probably mean 'Do you like my child?' Staff can reassure parents by what they say: 'I had to stop her from hitting Sean today. She wanted the spoon he had. It's a favourite because it has got a bit bent in its handle. I just love the way she is so determined. I really respect it. I told her that she could have a turn with that spoon tomorrow. She seemed to think that was all right.' The parent is receiving the message that this family worker likes the child, respects what she wants and is helping the child to be assertive rather than aggressive.

Parents also worry about how their children behave when they are away from them. Again they need reassurance here. It might be useful to link the bent-spoon situation with some form of mathematical learning. A child who is able to see that one spoon in a set is different from all the others is involved in the mathematical concepts of *sorting* and *seriating* (seeing the differences between things). This will also help the child towards reading: some letters look almost the same but are a little bit different, for example d and b. The parent might then be pleased to think that this is not just naughtiness but mathematics and early reading. This gives a much more positive image of the child.

Once the child is settled – exchanging thoughts between parents and staff

Parents will want to talk as well as listen to you. It is therefore important for staff to develop listening skills. You will need to set a particular time to talk and listen, however, so that parents do not try to take your attention when you are involved with the children. For some parents this can be very difficult to arrange, especially if they are working.

G U I D E L I N E S

Some key points are:
- ▶ **Eye contact helps staff to give full attention to a parent.**
- ▶ **Remember that your body language will show how you really feel.**
- ▶ **Try not to interrupt. Nod and smile instead.**
- ▶ **Never gossip.**
- ▶ **Every so often, summarise the main points of what has been said to the parent.**
- ▶ **If you do not know something, say so, and that you will find the answer for the parent. Do not forget to do this!**
- ▶ **Remember that different cultures have different traditions. Touching and certain gestures might be seen as insulting, so be careful.**
- ▶ **If the parent speaks a different language from you, use photographs and visual aids. Talk slowly and clearly.**
- ▶ **If the parent has a hearing impairment, the above visual aids will also help you if you cannot use sign language.**
- ▶ **When you are talking together, bear in mind whether this is the parent's first child or whether they have had other children already.**
- ▶ **Remember that if the parents have a child with a disability, they may need to talk with you more often in discussing the child's progress. If the parent has a disability, make sure that when you sit together you are at the same level.**
- ▶ **Occasionally, parents might become upset and will shout at you. If this happens, do not shout back. Simply talk quietly and calmly and show that you are listening to them.**

There is usually a policy in the early childhood setting on how a member of staff can get help from a senior colleague if there is an emergency of any kind. Make sure that you know about this and how to keep the children safe.

When parents become upset it is almost always because they are under emotional stress of some kind. Just as you need to 'hold' a child's anger until calm is returned, so you might need to 'hold' a parent's anger in this situation. The paint spilt on the child's clothing may not seem serious to you, but it might be the last straw for a parent after a stressful day.

Your line manager will encourage the parent to move away from public settings, and will help by offering a quiet place to talk.

Confidentiality in the lines of reporting

- ▶ Confidentiality is very important when working in a close partnership with parents.
- ▶ Some information needs to be shared only with your line manager as it will be a matter of strict confidence. If you suspect a child-protection issue, this should be shared only with your line manager and again in strictest confidence, and parents need to be aware of this.
- ▶ Remember, it will be important that right from the beginning of your relationship with parents, there be an understanding between you that although parents may tell you something in confidence, you may have to share the information with your line manager. It is not fair to encourage parents to talk about confidential things with you unless they first understand this.
- ▶ It is important never to gossip about parents or their children.
- ▶ It is important never to discuss one parent with another.
- ▶ It is important not to make value judgements about children or their parents.
- ▶ Some information needs to be shared with the whole staff team, in particular diet, allergy, religious rituals, if the child is being collected by someone else.

Helping parents to understand more about their child's development

Parents often appreciate the support of early childhood workers in seeing what their children are learning. It is depressing for parents to think that their child is disobedient, naughty and aggressive. If parents can understand their children's behaviour, and begin to see some evidence of learning, this is very helpful. There are of course times when it is hard to be positive, but it is always worth a try. It is important to remember that children's self-esteem is deeply affected by how others see them. It also helps when children themselves can see that other children often do not *intend* to be naughty, and that they are often only trying to learn things.

The great pioneer educator Friedrich Froebel (see Chapter 12) believed that behind every bad act is a good intention. He thought that it is the adult's job to find out what the good intention is and to help the child to carry it out in a worthwhile way. It is very reassuring for parents leaving their child with staff that they feel are going to be on the child's side, and are trying to see the best in their child. A positive working partnership makes it easier to tackle together the more challenging aspects of a child's behaviour or difficulty in communicating. This is particularly important when you are developing a partnership with parents whose child is required to attend an early childhood setting.

Often, parents control and manage their child's behaviour in ways which would be illegal for staff in an early childhood setting. The smacking of children by staff in an early childhood setting is illegal. Parents who smack their children were almost always smacked themselves when they were children. They often welcome seeing and trying other ways of managing behaviour and it is easier for them to try a new way of managing a situation when supported by a member of staff they trust. It is important indeed to make it clear that smacking is not allowed in any formal early childhood setting. In Sweden it is illegal even for parents to smack their children. Parents are given support rather than punishment if they find this difficult. Children's rights are paramount in importance. The same is true of discriminatory behaviour: the policy on equality of opportunity needs to be followed by everyone – staff, children and parents.

These boundaries will need to be made clear to parents as part of the admissions procedures. It will be important for staff to report any difficulties in this area to the team leader as quickly as possible.

Consolidating the partnership

There is no one way to have a partnership with parents. There needs to be a whole network of possibilities so that parents can find which is most useful for them. Some parents like to have regular home visits and to collect their child quickly without waiting about for long chats with the family worker at the end of the day. Some parents prefer diaries. In an ideal situation, diaries are kept daily, but more usually they are weekly or even monthly for practical reasons. These are sent home with the child. Parents can add to them and send them back. This is particularly helpful in monitoring children's progress. Some parents like to come to the nursery setting and talk there after work. Staff are often very tired, however, if they have worked a long shift. This can be easier to organise in a nursery school or class. And some parents, finally, like to come to morning or afternoon sessions in the parents/staff room. Many early childhood settings now arrange this. Parents might want to sit with their babies, or they might like a session led by the local health visitor looking at the children's feeding routines, sleep patterns, and other areas of concern.

Workshops

Parents deeply appreciate workshops. These usually take place in the evening. Parents come and experience some of the things their children do, and staff explain what the children are getting out of this. For example, they find out about the mathematics that their children are learning when involved in a cooking activity.

One father said he now understood the link between doing division sums in mathematics and sharing. He had not wanted to share the biscuits he had made when he cooked. He had been shocked by his own feelings, and it made him understand how his child might feel when told that the biscuits must be shared. He had never before seen this as doing a division sum in mathematics. He thought it was a very good way to learn mathematics.

Parents in the early childhood setting

Some parents also enjoy sharing their interests with children. They might spend time in the early childhood setting working alongside the staff. This is very difficult, however, for parents who work. One mother made West Indian patties. She also made pancakes on another day. The staff were very grateful because no-one could toss a pancake as she could. Everyone had such fun. Her commitment was great because she had taken the morning off work to do this on pancake day. Another mother, who was a home-based clothes maker, came into nursery and made costumes for the home area. She sat in the corner with a sewing machine that belonged to one of the staff. The children loved to come and watch and try things on for her. Other parents brought in bits of material that she might be able to use, and they enjoyed chatting to her when they were collecting their children.

Sometimes, parents help on a rota system. However, this can be too formal for some parents. On the other hand, it does help the staff know that a parent is coming to work with them in the early childhood setting, and they can then make sure that the parent is welcome.

At Pen Green Family Centre, Corby, Northants, two children per day are targeted for observation by all the staff. This is part of the record-keeping system. Parents often want to spend a little time hearing what has happened and sharing these observations with their family worker. Sometimes they like to be there and do an activity on that day. Others prefer to come in on a day when their child is not being targeted.

Sharing observations together

It is very important for the partnership between parents and early childhood workers that observations of the child are shared, for as the child settles into the group, the parent will not always be there. Observations can be explained or written down or talked through with parents at home time, on a home visit, on an open evening, or when their child is targeted for observation. There are many ways of meeting parents. A mixture of talking together (oral observations) and written observations is most effective.

Different families have different needs, likes and dislikes. Early childhood settings can respond to this if there is a clear-cut policy on working with parents. Many now use a range of oral and written records, a folder of children's drawings, paintings, photographs, and audio and video tapes. At Pen Green Family Centre, each child has a book called 'A celebration of my achievements'. The children call these their 'special books'. These contain observations and photographs by staff and parents, and drawings, etc. by the children. The children, parents and staff each select some of the things they think are important to include in the book. They do this at regular intervals. Each child also has an edited video of their time in the nursery, which they take with them when they leave as a parent-held record. Parents and staff and children are constantly sharing the life of the centre. Having a chart on the wall which shows some of the activities the children will do helps parents to see that their child is learning mathematics or another subject.

It needs to be remembered that many parents need personal space away from their child for part of the day. This may be while the family adjusts to a new baby or the parent catches up with chores or simply relaxes. It is sometimes thought that all parents want full-time nursery places for their children so that they can work. This is almost certainly not the case. Parents are people, and people vary in what they want. Some parents do want full-time nursery places so that they can work, and because they positively *want* to work. Other parents, however, will want full-time nursery places because they *have* to work, either for economic reasons – i.e. low wages earned by both parents – or because the parent is single. Some parents will be required to bring their child to the nursery as a matter of child protection – they will have no choice in the matter. Other parents will only want part-time nursery places because they will want their children to move in a wider social circle since they think this will help their child, in many ways, to have new

FIGURE 5.3

An example of a wall chart from Eastwood Nursery school

MAKING AND USING THE SENSORY GARDEN

LANGUAGE AND LITERACY
There are many stories, picture books, rhymes, poems and videos to support the focus of making and using the Sensory Garden e.g. stories about gardens and growing
Solomon's Secret   Mr Plum's Paradise
Peter Rabbit   Jasper's Beanstalk
Titch   Worm's Eye View
Links to the senses e.g. Makaton Nursery Rhymes video
Talking about our own gardens at home, window boxes etc
Development of small-world play
Naming parts of plants, trees – link to use of non-fiction books

DESIGN TECHNOLOGY
Miniature gardens – planning
Using the same material in different ways e.g. concrete, clay
Tools for the job
Designing tools e.g. a wheelbarrow
Weather vane

MUSIC AND MOVEMENT
Wind chimes – listening and making
Musical instruments made from natural materials
e.g. bean pod or gourd
Listening to sounds in the garden

ART
Looking at beautiful gardens in paintings and drawings
Dyeing using natural materials e.g. dye from plants
Pressed flowers
Children's drawings and paintings of the environment
Using clay, sand
Rubbings

MORAL AND SPIRITUAL
Appreciating life processes
Awe and wonder
Caring for nature
Creating a joint project – involvement and responsibility
Sense of achievement
Care and maintenance of the garden
Links to the local community
Care of minibeasts and discussion of why they are important to the garden
Sensitive use of the garden – behaviour
Gardens – what people use them for

SCIENCE
The senses – sight, hearing, smell, taste and touch
Using a feely box
Investigating materials – soil, stones, gravel, bark, wooden sleepers, clay, concrete
Effect of light on growth – link to use of the membrane
Soil as food – looking at minibeasts
Making a wormery
Cooking food from other countries
Edible flowers and herbs
Making perfume from petals

I.T.
Using colour magic – drawing and making plans
Using photocopier colour enlargements for a shared display
Use of the camera to record progress and make comparisons
Recording noises made on different surfaces and textures

MATHS
Sundial – telling the time
Measuring, matching, sorting, comparing, estimating, tessellation
Puzzles – growing, sequence etc.
Recording e.g. number of butterflies seen
Shapes of flowers, leaves, stones

HISTORY
Developing the garden – various stages
Sharing ideas
Old songs e.g. Lavender Blue …., Mary, Mary …., I had a little nut tree ….
Posters and paintings which convey a sense of history
Looking at old implements

GEOGRAPHY
Maps and plans
Talking about places where there are different sorts of gardens
Japanese gardens
Weather and its effects
Soil and water
Stones – where they come from
Growing food in other countries

and interesting experiences. Some parents will think it important for their child to have some experiences away from them. Other parents will want to join in with their child – perhaps not every day, but regularly.

Parents joining in with activities in the early childhood setting

One mother was delighted to have the opportunity to try out her English (she spoke Urdu). She had been learning some songs at her English class, and at group time she enjoyed joining in and singing them. She also sang some songs in Urdu.

When parents come into the early childhood setting, although they are giving, they also need to *take* – this is central to volunteer work. People must receive as much as they give when they volunteer to help. The above-mentioned mother also enjoyed being in the nursery at group time, and teaching the children songs she knew.

While understanding that the parent has come into the early childhood setting to help, it is very important not to expect parents to do chores that the staff dislike doing. Most parents will have their own washing-up and cleaning at home. They do not then want to come to the early childhood setting to clean up the paint pots! (Only a *few* will actually enjoy doing this.) Parents much prefer doing something which makes them feel relaxed and secure in what might be a very new situation for them. They might be a bit nervous about the idea of cooking and tossing pancakes, or sewing clothes, or taking a group activity at song time. On the other hand, looking at books with children in the book area or helping children to sweep the garden leaves might be more relaxing and enjoyable for them.

Open days and evenings

These are often popular. They can be purely social, or a mixture of a social occasion and a workshop or talk. Many early childhood settings combine the two. Nursery schools usually present the Annual Report of Governors to parents at a meeting when they explain the philosophy of the school in a practical way and then have a buffet supper, music and dancing. Although it is only in primary schools that this is legally required, most nursery schools think that it is important to follow the same procedures.

Although other early childhood settings do not have Annual Reports, they do have open days and evenings which are greatly appreciated by parents.

At Pen Green Centre the 'working with parents project' is helping staff to develop their work with parents. This is particularly successful with parents who have not in the past come to meetings. The project is encouraging much greater participation by fathers. This is especially so in families where there may have been a divorce.

Recent Government initiatives, such as Sure Start (0–3 years) are aimed at helping families with very young children in areas of need.

There are different approaches to working with parents. It is important to remember that just as there are different theories about how young children learn, there are also different theories about how parents learn!

Some projects are using a transmission model of teaching parents to bring up their children. This means the staff show parents examples of what to do, hoping the parents will copy 'good models'.

Sometimes the approach is very laissez faire. This means that parents are left to get on with it, perhaps being told where local groups are that they might like to join.

However, probably the most effective approach, such as that used at Pen Green Centre, is an interactionist/social constructivist approach to working in a close partnership with parents. In this approach the staff work alongside the parents. They do not try to tell them how to bring up their children. They find out what the parents think and feel, and respect their views. They help parents to build on what they know and want for their children, offering knowledge, information and discussion. In this approach, there is no one way to get things right as a parent, which respects the different ways children can be successfully brought up. The Haringey Early Years Excellence Network uses the same approach

RESOURCES

Books

M. O'Hagan and M. Smith, *Special Issues in Child Care,* London, Bailliere Tindall, 1993

M. Whalley (Ed) *Working with Parents*, London: Hodder & Stoughton, 1997

M. Whalley *Learning to be Strong: Integrating Education and Care in Early Childhood,* London, Hodder & Stoughton, 1994

The Parent Partnership Project
Pen Green Centre
Pen Green Lane
Corby
Northants

Videos

European Commission Network on Childcare *A Certain Idea of the Father in Europe* (see Chapter 1 for the address)

Fathers Handling Small Children
Video Reportage Productions
No. 3, 20 West Parade
Norwich NR2 3DW

Baby Matters Programme 3 – Parentcraft (NCT)
Ironhill Pictures
PO Box 136
Peterborough
PE4 5HA

Pen Green Video
Pen Green Centre, Corby, Northants

Organisations

Exploring Parenthood
41 North Road
London N7 9DP

Gingerbread
35 Wellington Street
London WC2E 7BN

Parent Network
44–46 Caversham Road
London NW5 2DS

New Pin is a national organisation based in Walworth. It works with parents under stress and helps them break the cycle of destructive behaviour through an education and support scheme.
Homestart 0116 2339955

ACTIVITY

Planning brochures

1 **Plan a brochure which will introduce parents to the work setting. Use photographs or drawings and make a booklet with brief notes which show the philosophy of the setting. It will need to show the range of activities, the daily timetable of events, and the rationale behind the organisation.**
2 **Plan further booklets which show particular and specific aspects of the work setting in action, e.g. the importance of the water tray, and what children learn from this mathematically, socially, etc.**
3 **Evaluate this activity.**

ACTIVITY

Planning a display

1 **Plan a display for the entrance hall of the work setting. What is it important to emphasise as a first impression of the setting? If possible, set up the display and observe how the area is used by parents and children.**
2 **Evaluate the activity.**

A C T I V I T Y

Planning, implementing and evaluating a policy

1 Plan a policy for settling a new child into the work setting. Give aims and reasons.
2 Implement your plan, and then evaluate it.

A C T I V I T Y

Researching and debating child punishment

1 Research another country's policy on adults smacking children (for example, Sweden's).
2 Research the history of corporal punishment in the UK.
3 Plan a debate around the topic of parents smacking their children.

A C T I V I T Y

Planning and evaluating a workshop

1 Plan a workshop for parents which will help them to understand how children learn through activities such as cooking, sandpits and painting, for example, Show the materials you would use for demonstration, and use instruction cards and diagrams to help the parents themselves experiment with the materials. Rehearse what you might say in explaining any one of these: the mathematical, scientific, artistic or language learning children might gain from the activities you have targeted.
2 Evaluate how successful this is. (Use Chapter 13 to help you.)

A C T I V I T Y

Planning an achievement book for the child

1 Plan a book which celebrates a child's achievements, which you and the child can share with the child's family/carer. Discuss with the child what should be included.
2 Choose some drawings and photographs yourself. Write notes which will help the parents understand why you and the child want to celebrate the items chosen.
3 Evaluate the activity.

Make a chart with these three headings:
- ▶ Transmission model of parental learning
- ▶ Laissez faire or 'leave it to nature' model of learning
- ▶ Interactionist/social constructivist model of learning

Which sentences go under which heading?

1   Staff in an early needs setting need to educate the parents about how their children learn. Staff need to explain because parents don't know.
2   Parents are their child's first educator. They are the experts on their child and not the staff, and no-one should interfere.
3   Parents are full of interesting knowledge about their children, but they need staff to talk it all over with them so that it begins to make sense.
4   Staff are experts and need to tell parents what to do because they are trained.
5   Parents mean well but they often do all the wrong things and the child behaves better in the nursery than at home. Parents need to be educated.
6   Trained experts know best.
7   Parents never come to meetings, so I need to find out why. I am obviously not getting it right for some parents. I need to get better at including parents because otherwise I can't discuss that child's progress. That means that we will never be able to have a good working relationship together. It's up to me as a trained member of staff to get better at my work.
8   Parents know intuitively how to bring up their children.
9   Staff need to find out how parents think and feel about their children and what they want from them. Otherwise they won't be able to tune into that family and be helpful to them.

6

Intellectual/Cognitive Development: Ideas and Thinking

Intellectual/cognitive development cannot be separated from all the other areas of development. The ideas children have are emotional, physically experienced and shared with other people. Thinking is social, emotional, physical and cultural. Thinking involves the moral and spiritual aspects of development too. Thinking is deeply linked with language and communication and the way symbolic behaviours of all kinds develop, for example art, music, mathematics and dance.

Ideas, intelligence, cognition or thinking

Are children born intelligent or not? This is called the nature–nurture debate. We saw in Chapter 2 that this has been fiercely argued about. The nature–nurture debate continues, and has become a political issue. There are those who believe that people are *born* intelligent (or not). There are others who feel equally strongly that the child's life experiences and the people children meet have a huge influence on how their intelligence develops. The idea that children are born with a fixed amount of intelligence, and that this can be given a score which is measured and which does not change throughout their lives, was not seriously challenged until the 1960s. Neuroscience has further challenged this.

Intelligence tests

Children were often tested in the past to find their IQ (intelligence quotient) using scales such as the Standford–Binet or Merrill–Palmer intelligence tests. Because these tests were developed by white male psychologists with middle-class ways of looking at life they favoured white middle-class male children, who thus scored higher than other groups of children. It became obvious after the 1944 Butler Education Act that mainly white middle-class children went to grammar schools; and there were more places in grammar schools for boys than for girls. Children from other groups went to secondary modern schools and technical schools. This began to worry some researchers.

▶ IQ tests favour children from the culture out of which they emerged. This means they are not as objective as they were first thought to be.

▶ IQ tests measure particular kinds of intelligence, such as memory span and ability with numbers. This means that they only look at intelligence in a narrow way. They do not help us to look at outstanding ability in dancing, music or interpersonal sensitivity. The psychologist Howard Gardner says that there are seven kinds of intelligence. He calls this **multiple intelligence**. The different modes of intelligence proposed by Gardner are linguistic intelligence, musical intelligence, logico-mathematical intelligence, spatial intelligence, bodily kinaesthetic intelligence and personal intelligence (access to personal feelings and relationships with others). Howard Gardner believes these are partly genetic but also open to cultural influences, and can be helped through education. Intelligence tests thus only measure a small part of intelligence.

▶ They often give children labels which are likely to stick, such as 'bright or 'average ability' or 'low ability'.

▶ They do not encourage teachers to have high enough expectations of children ('After all, she's only got an IQ of 80').

Intelligence tests are useful as part of a whole barrage of different ways of making an assessment of a child's needs (especially for children with special educational needs). They are not useful, however, when used in isolation from other forms of assessment.

The **motivation** (the **will to learn**) of a child is very important. Two children might have the same IQ, but the one with the greater will to learn might do better simply because of this **disposition.**

Intelligence can grow

During the 1960s, Piaget's theory made researchers think again about what intelligence is. His theory suggested that intelligence is not fixed and unchangeable – it is not something people are born with or without. His theory suggested that intelligence is *plastic*. This means it can stretch, grow and increase. The idea that intelligence is plastic has been supported by recent studies in neuroscience.

Children can increase their intelligence if:

▶ they mix with adults and other children who help them to develop their intelligence;

▶ they experience a stimulating environment which encourages thinking and ideas.

A group of children with severe learning difficulties were taken from the wards of the Fountain Hospital during the 1960s. They were placed in a stimulating environment of people and first-hand interesting experiences. Their intelligence was found to develop rapidly. This research project was called the Brook Experiment. Research like this led in 1971 to children with special needs in hospitals and day centres being given, by law, education as well as hospital-type care. Until then, such children, and young people with IQs below 50 on the IQ scale, had been considered ineducable.

During the 1960s and 1970s, programmes of compensatory education also developed in the USA and the UK. In the USA, these programmes were called the Head Start

Programmes, and in the UK a series of research projects were set up under the direction of Albert Halsey, a sociologist. Researchers were beginning to realise that intelligence can grow, and so children who were thought to be growing up in unstimulating environments were placed in these education programmes. The idea was that this would compensate for the poverty and social disadvantage of their lives.

However, this view rejected and ignored some important influences on a child's developing intelligence, thinking and understanding:

▶ It did not put enough emphasis on the language and cultural background of children.

▶ It did not emphasise the importance of the child's parents and family life.

By contrast, the Froebel Nursery Research Project directed by Chris Athey in 1972–77 worked in a close partnership with parents. The home language of children was respected and valued, and the children were offered interesting real experiences through a quality curriculum. This involved cooking, a home area, play, modelling with clay, outdoor play etc. The IQs of the children rose, especially the IQs of the younger children who joined the project when they were babies.

This project had a long-lasting effect because:

▶ it worked in a close partnership with parents;

▶ it offered children a stimulating, well-planned environment (i.e. a quality curriculum);

▶ it valued the children's language and culture.

The relationship between having ideas and being creative

Intelligence tests favour people who are **convergent** thinkers – i.e. people who can give 'correct' answers and who are able to solve questions that are set by the testers. Intellectual development is also, however, about having **imaginative** and **creative** ideas.

What is the imagination?

The imagination is about being able to rearrange your past experiences and to put them together to make new ideas. Imaginative people have all sorts of ideas in art (drawing painting, sculpture), architecture, music, dance, drama, scientific research and mathematics. These people are **divergent** or **creative thinkers**. This means they can gather together ideas which can go off in all sorts of directions and organise them into a single interesting idea. Imagination is about having new and fascinating ideas.

What is creativity?

Creative people – children or adults – take an imaginative idea that they have had and turn it into an act of creation. They might make a dance, a cake, a poem or a new scientific theory. Margaret Meek, an expert on the teaching of reading and writing, believes that creativity and the imagination are 'basic' in learning to read and write. Imaginative children read and write with more pleasure and interest. They have imaginative ideas and make (create) stories. Creativity is about using new ideas that have been imagined and *turning them into something* (a creation).

G U I D E L I N E S

Encouraging imagination and creativity

Young children need support and help if their creativity is going to develop well. Imagination and creativity do not arise naturally, although it is true that some children learn about being creative much more easily than others. That is true in every area of learning.

▶ **Children need a wide range of material provisions which they will then be encouraged to use in lots of different ways (see Chapter 13).**

▶ **Children need plenty of time for their play. They must not be over-organised by adult-led tasks all the time (see Chapter 9). Play helps them to have imaginative ideas and to turn these into creative pretend play.**

▶ **Children need plenty of opportunities to *represent* their ideas (see Chapter 8). Having an idea and making it come alive is creative.**

▶ **Children learn about becoming creative thinkers through the people they meet and the materials they are encouraged to use.**

Children need a wide range of material provisions which they will then be encouraged to use in lots of different ways. This is because, as neuroscience shows, children learn through their senses and their movements.

Activities which discourage imagination and creativity are:

▶ templates;

▶ tracing;

▶ the screwed-up-tissue-paper syndrome of filling in a pre-cut outline, colouring in or using stencils.

These activities are all pre-structured by adults and allow almost no opportunities for the children's own ideas and thinking to develop. Such activities are sometimes referred to as 'busy work'. They are low-level ways of keeping children occupied. Children might enjoy doing them, but then children enjoy sweets and all sorts of things that are *not* good for them. Templates are not helpful to a child becoming creative. In the long term, they undermine the child's self-esteem so that children often come to believe they cannot draw or make things without a template or an outline. The children then become very preoccupied with the 'right' or 'correct' ways of doing things. And they often end up learning formulas for drawing which they can quickly produce with only a little effort, especially at 5 or 6 years of age. This cuts across creativity.

A child who has learnt to become creative might be rather frustrated and even miserable when they are undermined in their creativity in this way. For example, Jo was given a card with the outline of a butterfly on it. She was asked to fill in the outline with pieces of screwed-up coloured tissue paper. She cried. She found a piece of paper and made her own picture. She made a path through a wood. This was an imaginative idea and a creative piece of work. The butterfly here would only have been a low-level piece of 'busy' work.

The butterfly cards were going to mothers as Mother's Day cards. The family worker explained to Jo's mother why Jo's card was different. The mother was pleased that her daughter had been so creative, and did not mind the fact that it did not look so good. The imaginative thinking that went into the card and the creative result was far more important than how it looked.

A child who does not know how to think creatively, who has never 'had a go' or taken risks and experimented with different ways of doing things, does not become a confident active thinker. Instead, such children just carry out adult instructions or ideas. They do not become imaginative or creative.

Problem-solving

There is a saying, 'Happiness is not the absence of problems. It is being able to solve them'. Children are natural problem-solvers from the moment they are born. It used to be thought that there was a rigid developmental sequence in the way that children learn to solve problems. It was thought that children tried to solve problems at first through trial and error, and that only later could they develop a **theory** or **hypothesis**.

Researchers have, however, found that even new-born babies will make a hypothesis. This means that they have a theory which they test out to see if it is right. They do not behave in a trial and error way – they do not try, randomly, something until by luck they solve the problem. Every time a new-born baby heard a buzzer and turned towards it, the baby would find a honeyed dummy to suck on. Every time a *bell* rang, the baby would turn to it but would *not* find a honeyed dummy. Soon, the baby only turned for the buzzer. However, once the baby had made the hypothesis that this is what would happen, the baby felt the problem had been solved. The hypothesis the baby had made was correct, but it soon became boring to keep solving the same old problem repeatedly, and so the baby would not do it over and over again. The baby's interest was to solve the problem rather than to get the honey. Once the hypothesis was found to be correct and the problem was solved, there was no reason to carry on with this activity.

New-born babies can hypothesise and make theories to solve such problems even when they are only a few hours old.

Making a false hypothesis
Children of 2 years old and onwards will often make a 'false' hypothesis. Experts think that this is a very important part of learning to problem-solve. Perhaps indeed you too find that children are often rather obstinate about an idea that they have. In order to learn about problem-solving, children need to test out their false or wrong hypothesis as well as the correct and true hypothesis. Experts believe that children *learn* from the mistaken scientific hypothesis being made.

Segun (4 years) saw some paint which glowed in the dark. His mother told him (wrongly) that it was called fluorescent paint. Having painted the stone owl from the garden, Segun put it in his bed so that it would glow in the dark. It did not glow in the dark!

He then painted all sorts of stones from the garden. He put these on his bed each night. They did not glow in the dark either!

He then painted sticks from the garden and put them on his bed each night. They did not glow in the dark either!

His uncle visited him and told him that what he needed was *iridescent* paint. Segun, however, carried on with his idea of making objects glow in the dark using fluorescent paint, until he saw a pot that glowed in the dark. He asked the owner what sort of paint they had used. The answer, again was iridescent. Then he finally agreed to try the new sort of paint. His owl glowed in the dark. So did his stones. So did his sticks.

Segun had worked out, by thoroughly exploring his mistaken hypothesis, that fluorescent paint does not make things glow in the dark. Segun will now know this forever – for the rest of his life. And he also knows that iridescent paint *does* make things glow in the dark. This is real learning which no-one can take away from him.

G U I D E L I N E S

Encouraging children with problem-solving

▶ **Encourage them to make a hypothesis (which is an idea or theory about how to solve a problem): 'What do you think is going to happen?'**
▶ **Help children to use their prior experience – what they already know: 'What happened when you did .... ?'**
▶ **Let them try out their idea, and if it doesn't work, don't argue or dismiss it as wrong. Just point out the bits that did not work and leave it at that.**
▶ **Try to set up situations which help children to go on testing their hypothesis and talking about it: 'Does that give you any ideas for trying again?'**

Concentration and attention

Children concentrate best when they find something is *interesting*. Even children who have an **attention deficit** will concentrate much more when they have:
   ▶ a choice of activities
   ▶ an adult who helps them to do things. In this way, children manage to do things which they could not do alone but can manage if the adult is supporting them.
   ▶ when they enjoy what they do. Laughter and play, according to animal experts, help to develop the brain's ability to work well. One expert even believes that play and laughter fertilises the brain!

Measuring concentration and the child's involvement
The Effective Early Learning Project ('EEL'), directed by Professor Christine Pascal, has two very widely used observation scales which help staff working with young children to see how deeply the children are concentrating in the early childhood setting, namely:
   ▶ the Leuven Involvement Scale;
   ▶ the Adult–Child Engagement Scale.

The Leuven Involvement Scale helps adults to see whether the children are involved in what they are doing in a creative and deep way or whether they are only superficially involved and easily distracted, or whether indeed they are not involved at all.

The Adult–Child Engagement Scale helps adults to look at what they are providing for the children and to see whether they are being helpful to children by being sensitive to their needs or by helping them to be autonomous, independent, self-motivated and self-disciplined in what they are doing. If a child does not concentrate or become involved in anything at any point in the day, there may be a reason:

▶ The child is under stress.

▶ The child is unwell.

▶ The child has learning difficulties or disabilities. The team will need to observe the child carefully at different points of the day, and to note, monitor and assess the child's progress.

▶ The child is tired.

▶ The child is poorly nourished.

It will then be necessary to seek advice and make an action plan to support and help the child's concentration. Often, only minor changes in the way activities are set out, in the way the room is arranged, in the amount of choice given to children or in how much freedom to be outdoors is given can bring about changes in the child's behaviour. Too many adult-led activities and too little freedom of movement is bad for a child's concentration span.

Memory

At first, babies cannot remember things for very long. They can, however, *imitate*. If you put out your tongue at a new-born baby, the baby will, after a time, imitate you. You can see the baby concentrating hard and then managing to imitate the adult.

Gradually, as babies become toddlers, they begin both to imitate *and* remember things after a time delay. One famous example is Piaget's daughter Jacqueline. She saw a friend have a temper tantrum when she was about 18 months old. She was very impressed by this dramatic event! The next day she tried it out herself, i.e. she imitated the temper tantrum.

The influence of having a longer memory

Between 2 and 3 years, children are able to remember more. This means that when they are in unfamiliar situations, they tend to be able to plan things more, so that they do not immediately rush to try new things. Instead they pause, until they have an idea about what they would like to do. In this way, they organise their thinking. They remember what they have done before with similar or different objects and people, and they use this memory to help them plan ideas for this situation. This is called 'inhibition to the unfamiliar', and it means the children can 'think before they do'.

Becoming aware: from sensation to perception

When we say 'He's/she's a very perceptive person', we mean that that person is very aware of things. Children and adults perceive and understand the world through their senses. The senses and movements of the body give people immediate feedback about:

▶ how they are moving;

▶ what is happening to them.

If you sit awkwardly and your leg goes to sleep, it is very difficult to walk. There is not enough sensory feedback! There is not enough immediate sensation to send messages to your brain. You cannot *perceive* your leg! Perceiving something means constructing an idea of that thing that is based on information you have received through your senses. The senses make it possible to perceive and experience life.

For some children with severe learning difficulties, it is quite hard to be sure whether they are aware that they are receiving messages through their senses which tell them they are having an experience. Observing children is always important, but it is extra-important in this situation. For most babies, the senses would help them to perceive experiences even in the first months of their life. Remember: *all* the senses – touch, smell, taste, movement or kinaesthesia, hearing and sight – are important. Look again at Chapter 2 to remind yourself of these aspects of development.

Most people are very aware that babies need love and care, and to feel secure. However, it is also very important to give even new-born babies interesting and new experiences (see Chapter 13 on the curriculum). It is important to choose the right moment to introduce a baby to a new experience. The feedback (perceptions) from their senses will help babies to develop ideas (concepts). Researchers are beginning to realise that concepts develop much earlier than had been thought.

Think again about your leg when it goes to sleep. You know that you have a leg because you have a **concept** of your leg which is based both on your previous experience of your leg and on your ideas about what you therefore expect your leg to be able to do.

Concepts come early

Researchers have shown that concepts develop early in babies. **Concept formation** means that very early on babies move beyond their immediate perceptions (i.e. immediate sensory feedback about things) and begin to link immediate, present feedback with past perceptions. They then use these to think about the future – about what will happen next. When babies think *back* to prior experience and *forward* to the future, they begin to develop early concepts which are ideas about something which are stable thoughts in their mind.

Sensation is about what is being felt now. Perception is about present and immediate feedback. Early concepts then *link* past, present and future around a particular idea. This means that children can predict and plan ahead. They develop their memory. These factors are important for thinking, and for ideas to develop.

Bill is 10 months old. He stands at a coffee table and bangs a biscuit on it. His mother comes in. He perceives his mother (i.e. he is aware that she has come into the room). Bill then links the prior experience he has of his mother with this present one. He also has a concept that she will come and talk to him – she has always done this in the past. This is an early concept of his mother and of the sorts of things she does.

Concepts, in summary, mean that it is possible for children to:

▶ organise their thinking;
▶ have ideas;
▶ organise previous experience and perception – Piaget calls this **assimilation**;
▶ take in new knowledge and understand it – Piaget calls this **accommodation**;
▶ predict things about the future.

For example, if a baby of 5 months of age is beginning to take solids on a spoon and is often offered mashed banana, this is a taste that is known. It fits! (assimilation). But if the baby is given apple purée as a new taste, this will mean taking in a *new* experience. It does not fit! (accommodation). The baby might spit it out.

Life is about keeping a balance. Piaget would say that we are never quite balanced, but that we are always *trying* to keep balanced! Have you ever tried to balance upright on your bike with your feet off the ground while waiting at a traffic light? When you try to balance without putting your feet down from the pedals, it is almost impossible. Balancing, or trying to balance, is what Piaget calls the process of **equilibration**. That is why he saw children as **active learners**. They keep exploring, experimenting and trying to keep balanced. The balancing act between:

▶ assimilation (taking in what is known), and

▶ accommodation (adjusting to what is new)

helps children and adults to organise past experiences into concepts (ideas).

The phenomenon of stranger fear is very interesting in this. The child (usually at about 6–9 months) is exploring and getting to know about faces. One baby, Hannah, cried when her Uncle Dan, who is bald, came to the house. She had never seen a bald person before. She cried. This happened every time Hannah saw her Uncle Dan for a month or so. She had to accommodate and take in this new knowledge about some people not having hair on the tops of their heads. At first her Uncle Dan was very upset, but he was reassured when this was explained. This example also shows how closely linked the child's ideas are with their feelings and relationships with people. Cognitive, emotional and social development are all combined in this story.

Early concepts

Even as young as 1 month of age, babies are organising their perceptions and linking them with previous percepts of people and events. They are using these to work out what will happen next.

Schemas

Piaget calls early concepts **schemas**. Researchers have developed this part of his work. Schemas are patterns of linked behaviours which the child can generalise and use in a whole variety of different situations. It is best to think of schemas as being a cluster of pieces which fit together. For example, children are often fascinated by things that rotate. We see this in toddlers particularly, but older children too (for example, 4-year-olds) might be fascinated by the way the water rotates as it swirls down the plughole, or might try to touch the steering wheel in the car (a dangerous interest). And other examples are the adult mixing the food round and round in the bowl (with the child wanting to join in and stir with a wooden spoon), the wheels going round on the toy car, doing a roly-poly down a grass slope, or joining in with a movement song such as 'Round and round the garden, like a teddy bear'.

Each time the child meets or tries out a situation which involves rotation, either there will be the possibility of fitting the experience to what is known and *assimilating* it, or the child will have to adjust and *change*. Rotating as in the song 'Round and round the garden' means taking turns and not rotating all the time. And it means standing up straight as you rotate. This is very different from the kind of rotation involved in doing a roly-poly down a grassy slope. That involves rotating on your side.

The Different Levels of Schema

1 The senses and actions (**sensori-motor**). At first, schemas occur when babies and toddlers use their senses and movements to link past and immediate perceptions. For example, they might move their arms up and down when shaking a rattle. 'Up' and 'down' are very important schemas which cluster together.

FIGURE 6.1
Schema Focus sheet taken from 'RUMPUS' (formerly Cleveland LEA).

These charts are based on the work of Chris Athey at the Froebel Nursery Research Project 1972–7.

TRANSPORTING

A child may move objects or collections of objects from one place to another, perhaps using a bag, pram or truck.

POSITIONING

A child may be interested in placing objects in particular positions, for example on top of something, around the edge, behind. Paintings and drawings also often show evidence of this.

ORIENTATION

This schema is shown by interest in a different viewpoint as when a child hangs upside down or turns objects upside down.

DAB

A graphic schema used in paintings randomly or systematically to form patterns or to represent, for example, eyes, flowers or buttons.

DYNAMIC VERTICAL (AND HORIZONTAL)

A child may show evidence of particular interest by actions such as climbing, stepping-up and down or lying flat. These schemas may also be seen in constructions, collages or graphically. After schemas of horizontality and verticality have been explored separately the two are often used in conjunction to form crosses or grids. These are very often systematically explored on paper and interest is shown in everyday objects such as a cooling tray, grills or nets.

TRAJECTORY

A fascination with things moving or flying through the air – balls, aeroplanes, rockets, catapults, frisbees – and indeed, anything that can be thrown. When expressed through child's own body movements, this often becomes large arm and leg movements, kicking, or punching, for example.

DIAGONALITY

Usually later than the previous schemas this one emerges via the construction of ramps, slides and sloping walls. Drawings begin to contain diagonal lines forming roofs, hands, triangles, zig-zags.

ENCLOSURE

A child may build enclosures with blocks, Lego or large crates perhaps naming them boats, ponds, beds. The enclosure is sometimes left empty, sometimes carefully filled in. An enclosing line often surrounds paintings and drawings while a child is exploring this schema.

Enveloping
This is often an extension of enclosure. Objects, space or the child herself are completely covered. She may wrap things in paper, enclose them in pots or boxes with covers or lids, wrap herself in a blanket or creep under a rug. Paintings are sometimes covered over with a wash of colour or scrap collages glued over with layers of paper or fabric.

Circles
Circles appear in drawings and paintings as heads, bodies, eyes, ears, hands and feet. They are also used in representing animals, flowers, wheels, the sun and a wide variety of other things.

Semi-circularity
Semi-circles are also used graphically as features, parts of bodies and other objects. Smiles, eyebrows, ears, rainbows and umbrellas are a few of the representational uses for this schema as well as parts of letters of the alphabet.

Radial
Again common in paintings and drawings. Spiders, suns, fingers, eyelashes, hair often appear as a series of radials.

Rotation
A child may become absorbed by things which turn – taps, wheels, cogs and keys. She may roll cylinders along, or roll herself. She may rotate her arms, or construct objects with rotating parts in wood or scrap materials.

Connection
Scrap materials may be glued, sewn and fastened into lines; pieces of wood are nailed into long connecting constructions. Strings, rope or wool are used to tie objects together, often in complex ways. Drawings and paintings sometimes show a series of linked parts. The opposite of this schema may be seen in separation where interest is shown in disconnecting assembled or attached parts.

Ordering
A child may produce paintings and drawings with ordered lines or dabs; collages or constructions with items of scrap carefully glued in sequence. She may place blocks, vehicles or animals in lines and begin to show interest in 'largest' and 'smallest'.

Transforming
A child may become interested in materials which change shape, colour or consistency, for example ice melting, potatoes cooking, clay hardening, paint mixing.

One-to-one Correspondence
There is often evidence of this schema in scrap collages and constructions where a child, for example, glues a button inside each bottle top or places a piece of paper inside each cup of an egg box.

Functional Dependency
Although causal relationships are not fully appreciated, interest may be seen in the dependency of one function upon another. For example, a child may draw a lift with a button beside it and say, 'You have to press this for the lift to come' or pretend to turn an ignition key 'so that the engine will start'.

2 **Symbolic behaviour**. Then, typically during the second year, the child begins to use schemas in a new way. As well as using feedback from actions and senses, the child begins to experiment with symbolic behaviour. For example, the child might be painting at the table and making a line that goes up and down on the paper. The 3-year-old might then say 'Daddy'. The line on paper *stands for* Daddy, and the drawing on the line is therefore an example of symbolic behaviour.

3 **Cause and effect**. A child of 3 might make a line that is thin go up and down on the paper with the paintbrush, and then with a different paintbrush make a wide line and say 'Big one, little one'. The child is interested in the causes and effects involved in using different paintbrushes.

The 'up' and 'down' schemas have thus been used in three different ways:
1 The sensori-motor level was used with the rattle.
2 The symbolic-behaviour level was used in the painting of Daddy.
3 The cause-and-effect level was used with the thick and thin painted lines.

The gradual development of early concepts into operational concepts (2–7 years)

When children become able to combine schemas in a logical way, they start to *link* the different aspects of their experiences: they develop what Piaget calls **operational thinking**. Most children begin to develop operational thinking from middle childhood onwards (from 7 years), but during early childhood (until 7 years) they are already *moving towards* operational thinking. They still find it difficult to think about more than one aspect at a time. Their thinking is rather like a sequence of still photographs, one after the other.

Young children cannot easily go forwards and backwards in quick succession when they are thinking, because every event is a bit like a separate photograph. They need to focus on one thing at a time. Piaget calls this **centration**: they *centre* on something. It is a very good way of making sense of things.

This period when children centrate is still often called the start of **pre-operations**. However, most early childhood workers do not like the idea that children are 'pre' anything because it undervalues what children can do. Indeed, it concentrates too much on what children *cannot* do, and thus conveys a negative image of the young child. It is much more useful to think in terms of *developing* operations, or of the *development into* operational thinking, or of the *move* from early childhood to middle childhood.

As children begin to develop operational concepts during early childhood, they begin to use the following ways of thinking.
- **Seriating**: seeing the *differences* between things. Think of a xylophone. It has many keys, but they are all of different lengths.
- **Classifying**: seeing the *similarities* between things. For example, pigs, dogs, cats and cows are all *animals*.
- **Transformation**: can a process be *reversed*? For example, water freezes into ice, but you can melt it back to water again. However, if you break an egg you cannot put it back together again; if you burn the wood from a tree, you cannot get the wood back again; if you explode a nuclear bomb under water, you cannot bring back the dead shellfish killed by the shock waves running through the water; after cooking a cake, you cannot get the original ingredients back. *Reversibility* is an important concept.

Children gradually begin to link their previous experiences together much more easily: they become more like a video film than a sequence of still photographs. The children also form concepts about the shapes, sizes, colours and classes of objects and animals. The class of animals might be divided into pets and farm animals, while the class of cutlery might be divided into knives, forks and spoons.

This is called **class inclusion**.

FIGURE 6.2
How children might divide the class of animals

Farm animals   **Pets**

FIGURE 6.3
How children might divide the class of cutlery

Later concepts, concrete operations and conservation in middle childhood (7–12 years)

As concept formation elaborates, children begin to understand that things are not always as they seem to be. This typically occurs as children begin to go to junior schools, according to Piaget. They develop thought structures (concepts and ideas) which Piaget calls **operations**. Their thinking at this point becomes more like a video film. It can go forwards and backwards much more easily. It can reverse. Children can also now hold in mind several things at once when they are thinking. Before, as we saw, their thinking was more like a sequence of separate still photographs. Piaget says the child's thinking gradually becomes more *mobile*.

Conservation of mass

Give children two balls of clay, play-doh or plasticine. Check that the child agrees that there is the same amount in each ball. Roll one into a sausage shape while the child is watching. Then ask if there is the same amount of clay in both pieces as before. Children under 7 usually do not **conserve** mass in a formal test situation like this. This means that they will think that either the sausage shape or the ball shape has *more* clay in it. This is because these children can not hold in mind several ideas at once, but can only concentrate on one aspect.

Conservation of number

Show the child two rows of similar buttons. Check that the child agrees that the rows have the same number. Spread one row out to make it longer. Ask the child which row has the most buttons. Children under 7 usually do not conserve number in a formal test situation like this. This means they are likely to think that the spread-out row has *more* buttons. Again, young children usually cannot yet hold in mind more than one thing at a time. Piaget calls this **centration**.

G U I D E L I N E S

Promoting cognitive/intellectual development: schemas, the development of operations and conservation

At each of the different points in the sequence of development from percept to concept development from babyhood onwards, it is important to bear these things in mind:

▶ **See the child as an active learner.**
▶ **Offer a wide range of experiences, and look at Chapter 13 on the curriculum.**
▶ **Adults who are skilled in observation are able to use their observations to inform their planning. They can plan the next step in the child's learning.**

Jean Piaget

Piaget is often talked of as the elder statesman of child development study. He has left us a very rich description of how children develop in their thinking, and he has given us detailed observations which are very sensitively made. He deserves great respect for this. His contribution has helped us to extend, modify and add to his findings. His work has helped people who study child development to move forward in their understanding of how young children think.

The following section – which brings together many of the elements discussed above – outlines the four stages that, according to Piaget, occur in a child's thinking and ideas. The exact ages vary, but the sequences are still thought to be useful.

1 the sensori-motor stage (0–18 months);
2 developing operations (18 months–7 years):
3 concrete operations (7–12 years);
4 formal operations (12 years–adulthood).

Recent research questions whether *all* children go through these stages in the same way. It also questions whether all adults reach the stage of formal operations. Piaget did not believe it possible to 'teach' conservation, and researchers disagreeing with his point of view have not managed to prove conclusively that it *is* possible.

1 The sensori-motor stage, 0–18 months

Babies explore and recognise people and objects through their senses and through their own activity and movements. Schemas are patterns of action which the baby can generalise, and which become increasingly co-ordinated. For example, at $4\frac{1}{2}$ months, the baby can see a rattle, reach out for the rattle, grasp the rattle and put the rattle in their mouth – tracking, reaching, grasping, sucking.

However, toddlers still see things mainly from their own point of view, and cannot **decentre** and look at things from somebody else's point of view. Furthermore, they tend – as already mentioned – to focus on only one aspect of an event (centration). Piaget says they are **intellectually egocentric**.

By the end of their first year, most children have understood that people and objects are permanent and constant, that is they go on existing even when they cannot be seen, for example if they are under a cloth or in another room.

2 Pre-operational period, 18 months to 7 years

Action schemas – for example for rotation, up and down – now become **representational**. This means that children begin to use symbolic behaviour which includes language, representing in drawings and pretend play. Action schemas are internalised in the child, and they become **thinking**. Thinking backwards and forwards with ideas (concepts) is still heavily linked, however, with perception of immediate experiences (i.e. the perception of objects, people and events).

The development of memory – recalling past perceptions and prior experiences – is now important. In their minds, children will form images of a smell, of something they have seen, of something they have heard, of something that moved, of something they tasted, or something they touched. They also now anticipate the future.

Using past and future as well as immediate experiences, children now begin to develop ideas (concepts). This frees them to think more about time and space.

▶ Children begin to refer to things and people who are not present.
▶ They begin to try and share what they know, feel and think with other people.

Because children still only look at one aspect of a situation, it influences the way that they classify or seriate things.

At this stage, children also tend to assume that objects have consciousness (**animism**), for example they get cross with a door for slamming shut. Furthermore, they will base what is right or wrong on *what happens*. For example, if a cup breaks, they think the person who broke it has been naughty. They are not at this stage interested in how the event came about (i.e. the motive). They are likely to think that the child who broke a cup helping to wash up was naughtier than the child who took a valuable cup from the dresser when they had been told not to but did not break it. This is called the stage of **moral realism**.

3 Concrete operations, 7–12 years

Children now begin to understand class inclusion. They begin to understand about the conservation of mass, number, area, quantity, volume, weight and they realise that things are not always as they look. They still, however, need real situations to help them think conceptually, and they have great difficulty thinking in the abstract. For example, they need practical work in understanding number or time concepts in mathematics.

Although the children *can* now see things from somebody else's point of view, they still tend to try to make ideas fit other ways of thinking. They will use symbols in writing, reading, notation in music, drawing, maths, and dance if they are introduced to these.

Children at this stage of development can also take into account several features of an object at the same time when they are classifying and seriating. This means that they no longer centrate, i.e. they no longer concentrate on just one thing at a time. They realise that there might be several correct solutions to a problem: they are able to think about how either this or that could happen.

Children also now enjoy games, and understand about rules.

Formal operations, 12 years old–adulthood

Children can now understand abstract concepts, such as fairness, justice or peace. They also understand that it is possible to create laws and rules which help them to test things out and to have a hypothesis and to solve problems.

They think about time, space and reasons through formal operations, and this means they can speak in an abstract way about subjects – they don't need to do things practically so much. Some adults never reach this stage and continue to rely on concrete situations rather than being able to think in the abstract. Most adults remain concrete-operational for large parts of their lives, for example a car mechanic might use high levels of formal thought to see what is wrong with a car, but not do so when organising a weekly shop for the family. In fact, it is possible to live a fulfilled adult life without using formal thinking at all.

Further developments in Piaget's work

Piaget concentrated on a child's thinking, intellectual development and ideas. This does not mean that he did not think that social, emotional and physical development were also important – he did. It is just that he did not make these the main area of study in his theory. Some people have argued that Piaget ignored social relationships and the cultural aspects of the child's life. In fact, Piaget took these for granted. Social relationships with other people are now thought to be just as central to a child's development as the other kinds of experiences which Piaget emphasised more, such as the way children build up an understanding of objects. Children are not isolated from other people when they learn. Piaget did not emphasise this fact although he did know it. Recent research stresses that children need other people (other adults and other children) in order to learn effectively. People and first-hand experiences of materials and all sorts of provision in indoor and outdoor areas are both of great importance for they help children in the development of their ideas. Neuroscience supports this approach.

Children know that people and objects are permanent much earlier than Piaget realised. His test of **object permanency** (see p. 34) proved difficult for babies at 5 months who did not realise two objects – a cover over a cup, for example – could occupy one space. By the age of 9 months they have worked this out and they remove the cloth to get the object underneath. However, the multiple mother image test demonstrates that at 5 months, babies know they only have one mother.

Piaget – as already pointed out – tended to start with what children *cannot* rather than *can* do. However, we now realise that even very young children *can* decentre and see things from somebody else's point of view, including babies.

Furthermore, when children are in a situation which makes what researchers call 'human sense', they can conserve and they can understand reversibility.

It is just that children find formal test situations rather difficult. This is because it is very hard for a child to understand what it is the questioner is really asking them.

Instead of Piaget's stages of development, researchers now tend to look at networks of **sequences of development**. These give us the basic order, rules and strategies that children develop and learn through. Piaget suggests a linear ladder, which he called **vertical decalage** and **horizontal decalage**. Later researchers have made this instead into a *web* showing a child's development.

The role of the early childhood worker is to observe children and to act on those observations as various points in the sequence are recognised. This means that children are not either rushed along in their learning by adults or held back while adults wait for the correct age or stage of development to appear. It is very important not to underestimate children, just as it is very important not to overestimate them.

Piaget worked with a Western, middle-class, white, industrialised model of society – after all, that is what he knew about – and his stages of development are therefore culturally biased towards this kind of society. In cultures where there is a different lifestyle, the children might appear to be backward according to Piaget's theory. For example, the Swiss children he studied had a much better-developed understanding of the different points of view you would get on different mountain tops than, for example, a child living in the flat Norfolk Broads would have had. It is very important to remember this point when studying Piaget's work. These biases are called **contextual sensitivities**, and they result in variations in the way children think depending on the different places and cultures in which they live. Recent researchers are beginning to look more at this.

▶ Piaget's work was used to focus on intellectual processes in the child until the 1970s.

▶ 1970–1980s **social cognition** was the emphasis. Vygotsky's work was influential. The context, and the people especially, moderated the way a child's thinking developed.

▶ In the 1980s, researchers were beginning to think that both the social and physical contexts, including the physical and biological development of the child, are crucial to the development of thinking. It is important here to look at the *situation* in which a child thinks and learns. This approach is called **situational cognition**.

Piaget has been criticised mostly for what he did not say, and he left lots of gaps which more recent researchers have been trying to fill in. It is a bit like putting more pieces into the jigsaw puzzle. Although Piaget started our thinking in this area of symbolic behaviour, other people have then developed his work. For example, Piaget – as already seen – thought that babies understood that objects had a permanent existence at about 9 months of age. Later researchers gave babies of 5 months of age an object which might be put on either their right-hand or, sometimes, their left-hand side. When they held the babies' hands until a light went out, they found that the babies reached for the object as soon as the light went out. The object could not be seen by the babies but they still reached out, and almost always they reached out in the right direction. The babies seemed to know that the object was still there, even though they could not see it in the dark.

Was Piaget right or are the modern researchers right? They are both right! This often happens when we look at Piaget's work. Piaget is not wrong, but he did not have time in one lifetime to find out all the pieces of the jigsaw puzzle. Modern researchers are helping us to put more pieces into the puzzle so that we can have a fuller picture than the one he gave us. Piaget would cover an object, and the baby had to sit and watch this. By 9 months of age, the baby would reach for the object by uncovering it and picking it up; younger babies did not do this. It is now thought that babies have to realise that two objects (here including the cover on top of the original object) can be in one place in order to complete Piaget's test of the permanence of the object.

Lev Vygotsky

Vygotsky believed that play helped children to make sense of what they learn for the reason that, during play, they are free from all the practical constraints of a real-life situation. He also believed that children can have better ideas and do better thinking when an adult or child who knows more is helping them. For example, an adult can help a child to experience a story like *Spot the Dog* by reading the book for the child. One day, later on, the child will then be able to read the story for themselves. Vygotsky called this the **zone of potential development**. This idea is about what the child will do – potentially. Vygotsky thought that potential development is as important as actual development (what the child can do alone, without any help from anyone else). He said that the zone of actual development shows the results, the fruits of learning, while the zone of potential learning shows the buds, the future of learning.

Jerome Bruner

Bruner believed that children need to move about and be actively having real, first-hand direct experiences. This helps their ideas to develop, and it helps them to think. He agrees with Piaget in this, and he calls the thinking involved here **enactive thinking**.

Bruner's theory has helped us to realise that children need books and interest tables with objects on them displayed to remind them of prior experiences they have had. He calls the thinking involved here **iconic thinking.**

He also believes that 'codes' are important. Languages are very important kinds of code. There are also drawing, painting, dancing, story-time, play, music and mathematical codes. He calls the thinking involved here **symbolic thinking.**

Bruner says that adults can be a great help to children in their thinking, because adults can be like a piece of scaffolding on a building. At first, the building has a great deal of scaffolding (adult support of the child's learning), but gradually, as the children extend their competence and control of the situation, the scaffolding is gradually removed until it is not needed any more. The adult arranges the experience, rather than transmitting what is to be learnt. The child is helped to grow ideas because the adult can see what the child is attempting to learn. This is called 'scaffolding'. For example, a child learning to weave among the Zinacantecon in Southern Mexico goes through six steps of learning scaffolded by the adult. The child learns to set up the loom, and to finish off the piece of weaving. Each time the child weaves a piece of material, the help is reduced. The first time the child weaves, the child is helped most of the time. The next piece the child is only helped half of the time, and so on.

RESOURCES

Videos

Available in good bookstores

Channel 4, *Baby It's You*

Books

C. Athey, *Extending Children's Thinking: A Parent–Teacher Partnership,* London, Paul Chapman Publishing, 1990

L. Bartholomew and T. Bruce, *Getting to Know You: A guide to record-keeping in early childhood education and care,* London, Hodder & Stoughton, 1993

T. Bruce, *Early Childhood Education,* London, Hodder & Stoughton, 1987

V. Lee and P. Das Gupta, *Children's Cognitive and Language Development,* Oxford, Blackwell/Open University, 1995

J. Matthews, *Helping Young Children to Draw and Paint,* London, Hodder & Stoughton, 1995

R. Carter, *Mapping the Mind,* London; Wellcome Trust, 1998

A. Meade with P. Cubey *Thinking Children,* New Zealand Council for Education, 1995 (available from Allstock Book Co. Ltd, Isaac Newton Centre, 108a Lancaster Road, London W11 1QS)

Maureen O'Hagan and Maureen Smith, *Special Issues in Child Care,* London, Bailliere Tindall, 1993

C. Pascal and T. Bertram (Eds), *Effective Early Learning,* London, Hodder & Stoughton, 1997

ACTIVITY

Children at play

1 Set up an area using found materials (see Chapter 13 on the curriculum for ideas to help you in this). Observe what children do. Describe how a child between the age of 3 and 7 years uses the area.

▶ Did you see any imaginative ideas developing?

▶ Did any of the children make anything creative?

▶ Are the children used to being creative, or are they already dependent on adult ideas through outlines or templates?

▶ Did the children feel more secure when they were doing busy work?

How can you help them to have more confidence in their own ideas?

2 Evaluate your observations, relating them to the child's development.

ACTIVITY

Children problem-solving

1 Plan an area using the water tray or sand tray. Observe children (try to have as wide a range of ages as possible) to see if there are examples of problem-solving. Evaluate your observations. What role did you take in helping the child? If possible, repeat the observation of water play, observing a child at bathtime, or in a paddling pool or swimming pool. How do the children problem-solve in these settings?

2 Try to observe children in a sandpit in a park, or using sand on the beach. Focus on the children problem-solving and how you supported them. Evaluate your observations, in whatever settings you made them.

A C T I V I T Y

Encouraging creativity and concentration

1   Plan how you would encourage creativity in the development of young children. Set up an area of the room for this purpose, making sure materials are appropriate and accessible, and that children can use them freely. Evaluate the help you have given in the way you have communicated with the children and through the materials you have offered.

2   Plan ways of encouraging a child's concentration and involvement by finding out about the Leuven Involvement Scale and observing a child in your placement whom you have noticed lacks concentration (use time-sampling or event-sampling observation techniques). (See *How to Make Observations and Assessments* by Jackie Harding and Liz Meldon-Smith.) When does the child concentrate most? Evaluate your observations.

A C T I V I T Y

Interests and schemas of the young child

1   Plan ways of finding out about what fascinates a child between the ages of 2 and 5 years. Observe and note what the child does on a particular day. If possible, observe the child continuously for an hour. You might use video and photographs to enhance your observations. Use the chart on schemas to help you identify and name the areas of interest the child has. Remember, children are interested in a variety of things but might particularly enjoy one activity. Use your observations to add to the materials, for example if the child is particularly interested in rotation, add whisks and spinners or cogs; or if the child is interested in covering things over, there could be finger painting and dressing-up clothes such as cloaks, or burying objects in the sand.
    Evaluate your observations.

2   Look at the basic equipment in the room. How does it support the children's schemas? Either look at a book on the subject or visit a museum of childhood. Look at the toys children had, for example, in the last century. How do traditional toys encourage children to develop their schemas?

Neuroscience and children

1 Neuroscience is showing us that young children need to learn through movement, rhythm, sounds and their senses. Plan a learning experience for a child 0–3 years, or 3–5 years. Use songs with actions. Evaluate your observations.

2 Play short extracts of different kinds of music to a group of children 0–3 or 3–5 years. How do they react in movement or sounds they make? Evaluate your observations.

Testing Piaget's work

1 Plan and carry out Piaget's conservation-of-mass test with a child aged 3 years, 5 years and 7 years. Can the children conserve? Evaluate the activity (see p. 175 for details).

2 Then try the conservation-of-number test devised by Piaget. You can use buttons or other objects, as long as they are all the same. Do children aged 3 years, 5 years and 7 years conserve? Evaluate your findings (see p. 175 for details).

3 Make an experiment based on the work of Martin Hughes in the 1980s. You will need two dolls the size of doll's-house dolls. One will need to be a parent, the other a 'child'. Keep the mother fixed to one point. Ask the child to move the 'child' doll around so that sometimes the mother can see the 'child' and sometimes not. Does the child know when the mother will be able to see the 'child' and when they won't be able to see the 'child'? Margaret Donaldson found that when a situation made 'human sense', children were able to decentre and see things from other people's points of view. However, if it was a rather formal task, which removed them from their real experiences of real life, then they could not manage it. Try also the object-permanency test (see pp. 178–179). Evaluate your observations of a baby of 6 months and 10–18 months. Refer to the cognitive development of the baby.

4 Plan how you can promote a child's cognitive/intellectual development in ways which also value the social relationships and feelings of children. Plan experiences with number, seriation and classification. You might decide to help children choose a recipe, go with them to shop for materials, and then help them to cook the recipe. Evaluate your activity, commenting on the cognitive, social and emotional aspects of the child's development as well as on the way you provided the experiences.

7

Emotional and Social Aspects of Development: Feelings and Relationships

It is important to remember that it is not possible to isolate emotional and social development from any other areas of development. Piaget thought that it was unfortunate that there are two separate words for thinking and feeling. He thought the two were completely inseparable. He said that it was impossible to think without feeling, or to feel without thinking. In the same way, social relationships with other people cannot be separated from intellectual and emotional aspects of development.

We have seen that from the start, children are very aware of other people. When a baby babbles, adults and older children make noises back in a high voice. The baby is using early language and communication. Babies can only make sounds they can physically manage. For example, by 2 months, babies can babble g, b and p sounds. The baby 'calls' people over and enjoys company. This is very emotional. In other words, every aspect of development is involved here, not just social development, and it is important to remember that every aspect of development involves:

▶ the biological part of development, for example, walking, jumping, hopping, skipping as the brain develops;

▶ the cultural part of development, for example, the influence of, and social exchanges with, other people, especially those who are close to and love the child.

Babies have feelings and emotions from the moment they are born. As children become more and more aware of themselves, they can be helped to become more aware of how *other* people feel. Children who feel loved and receive plenty of affection will find it easier both to give love to other people and to like themselves. Neuroscientists call the first years of life the period when children develop an understanding of 'personhood'.

Self-concept, self-image, self-identity, self-esteem

Children develop a **self-concept** and a sense of identity during the first year of life, and this becomes more stable as they develop socially. Developing a sense or concept of your own identity is about:

▶ realising you exist;
▶ who you are;
▶ developing self-esteem;
▶ a positive self-image;
▶ learning to like and respect yourself;
▶ developing skills of caring for and looking after yourself.

Having strong attachments to people and learning about feelings helps babies to develop socially. Being loved and shown affection also helps babies to learn socially. It is now thought that feelings cause chemical reactions which influence the development of the brain.

It used to be thought that once children turned into mature adults, this was the end point of social development. This is not true: we go on developing socially throughout our lives, from birth to death. The psychologist Erikson helped us to begin thinking about this with his eight stages of social and emotional development which go from birth to old age (see p. 209).

It is important for each of us to know ourselves and to be able to respect and value ourselves. The way individual people see themselves is called a self-image or self-concept. The way people value and respect themselves is about:

▶ a positive self-image;
▶ good self-esteem.

Having a good self-image or self-concept is not just about how *we* see ourselves, because the way we see ourselves will be deeply influenced by the way we see that *other* people see us. Principles of equality and inclusivity help early childhood workers to encourage a good self-image in young children. The same is true for very young babies and children. Very young babies, when they begin to move about, will keep looking at the adult who is caring for them. They need to see what their reaction is. This is called **social referencing**. Babies have individual **personalities** which will need to settle in with their particular family and its way of life. In the same way, the family in turn will be learning about this new person who has come to live with them. There will be huge adjustments on all sides. The way children feel about themselves and their bodies is deeply linked with **self-confidence**. This develops in children as they feel unconditionally valued, respected and to be of worth.

Every child needs to know that they matter. From this loving beginning, a child can face and cope with the emotions of life. It is especially important that children who are physically disabled or challenged in any way feel valued and respected. Children who are wheelchair users or children using hearing aids, callipers or wearing glasses all need to receive messages that are positive. It is the same for the child who has been abused, or who is trying to deal with challenging behaviour.

Because young children are very interested in differences in physical appearance, they are also very aware of differences in skin colour. It is very important that every child be given warmth and love regardless not only of personality but also of physical appearance.

Self-esteem

The way we feel about ourselves leads to good or poor **self-esteem**. Our self-esteem is greatly influenced by how other people make us feel. Good self-esteem leads to a good self-image and a strong sense of identity. A strong sense of identity means believing in yourself.

Because of the embarrassment and ignorance of many other people, children with a disability have to come to terms with:

▶ their disability;

▶ the way other people react to it.

It is very important that children who are growing up meet a wide range of people so that this kind of 'stranger fear' (see Chapter 1) gradually disappears from society. This will make it easier for every child to develop good self-esteem.

G U I D E L I N E S

Ways to encourage children to have good self-esteem

▶ **Value children for *who they are*, not what they do or what they look like, or what you want them to be.**

▶ **A child needs love, security and a feeling of trust. There is no one way to give these feelings to children. It will depend on where children live, the family and culture in which the child is growing up. There is no standard family. There is no standard institution. There is no one best way to love children and give them self-esteem.**

▶ **People who give children positive images about themselves (in terms of skin colour, language, gender, disability, principal features, culture, economic background) help children to develop good self-esteem. Look at the book area and displays on the walls with this in mind (see Chapter 1).**

▶ **Even visitors to the nursery are very important in this. The people children meet occasionally or on a daily basis will all have a strong influence on them. If children almost never see men working in early childhood settings or women mending pieces of equipment, they form very narrow ideas about who they might become. Books and pictures and outings and visitors can be very important in offering positive images which extend their ideas of who they might be one day.**

▶ **Adults who are positive role models help a child's self-esteem. Adults need, however, to have a positive self-image of themselves: a depressed, self-doubting adult will not be a really good role model for a child.**

▶ Children need to feel some *success* in what they set out to do. This means that adults must avoid having unrealistic expectations of what children can manage, for example, dressing, eating, going to the lavatory. It is important to appreciate the efforts that children make. They do not have to produce perfect results. The *effort* is more important.

▶ Adults help children's self-esteem if they are *encouraging*. When children make mistakes, don't tell them they are silly or stupid, but instead say something like 'Never mind, let's pick up the pieces and sweep them into the bin. Next time, if you hold it with two hands it will be easier to work with', and so on.

▶ Children need to feel they have some *choices* in their lives. Obviously, safety and consideration for others is important, but it is usually possible to allow children to make some forms of decision.

▶ Children need clear, consistent boundaries, or else they become confused, and when they are confused they begin to test out the boundaries to see what is consistent about them.

▶ Children need consistent care from people they know. Many early childhood settings have now introduced a key-worker or family-worker system which is helpful in this.

▶ Children need to have a feeling of trust that their basic needs for food, rest and shelter will be met. Rigid routines are not helpful, but every day does need a shape. This will give children a predictable environment. It will give children the know-how to help in setting the table, for example, or to go to the lavatory before washing their hands.

▶ Children and their families need first to be given *respect* in order that they can then develop *self-respect*. Children, parents and staff thus need to speak politely and respectfully to each other.

▶ Children have strong and deep feelings. They need help, support and care from adults who feel warmly towards them as they learn to control how they feel.

The different stages of social and emotional development

0–3 months

In the first month, researchers do not think that babies know that they are separate from other people. Babies are only beginning to learn where they begin and end: a toe is part of them; a bed cover is not; neither is the mother's hand.

Babies begin to recognise people they know well very early on. Feelings and relationships develop. They begin to smile. They will turn to their voice. They know their face and hands. When they hear, see, or feel their carer, they may stop crying. Babies who are visually impaired often become very still, as if listening and waiting for more information. Researchers believe that it is almost as if babies are born in order to relate to people.

3–6 months

From the beginning, babies find faces interesting to look at. They turn to their mother's voice in particular, and they like to be held in the arms of someone they love and know. Even very young babies prefer being held by those they are emotionally close to.

By 5 months of age, babies have learnt that they only have one mother. They are very disturbed if several images of their mother are shown to them. They might cry, or they start looking away because they are worried.

Babies begin to enjoy 'peek-a-boo' games. They also show stranger fear (see Chapter 6): they are distressed when separated from the people they know best and love most.

6–12 months

Babies begin moving about, and as they sit, crawl and begin to walk they begin to develop more of a self-image and are able to do things for themselves more and more. They become more aware of other people's feelings. They realise that people and objects are separate from them.

- ▶ They love to play peek-a-boo.
- ▶ They like to look at themselves in the mirror.
- ▶ They know their name, and respond to it.
- ▶ They love to have an audience. They use social referencing to see how other people react to what they do.
- ▶ They are becoming 'affectively tuned' to other people for example, (see p. 215).
- ▶ They imitate other people, for example clapping hands.
- ▶ They are very affectionate when they are shown love.
- ▶ They often show fear of strangers.
- ▶ They recognise how other people feel. They become anxious if someone they love begins to cry. They express their own feelings too. The way they are influenced by the feelings of other people is called **emotional contagion**.
- ▶ They understand the word 'no'. They respond to their own name, and they copy sounds people make. They become full of rage, or very shy with strangers. They cooperate when they are being dressed.

1–2 years

Babies now begin to have a mind of their own. They are developing a sense of identity. They are developing a longer memory for things. They are beginning to express their needs using words and gestures.

They love to do things for themselves – this is called **autonomy**. They are enjoying their new, developing physical skills, such as walking. However, when they try things which are quite new, they quickly sense when others fear for them, for example, when they try to climb onto or off a chair at the meal table (social referencing). They love to be praised for their efforts. It is still easy to distract children and take their attention from one thing to another.

2–3 years

Children imitate what other people do, and begin to become engrossed in **symbolic play**. This means they pretend to be someone else, for example someone pouring out the tea, the person who delivers the post. This is called **role play** because they rehearse adults' roles. They also begin to explain how they are feeling.

They are very anxious to try things for themselves. They quickly become frustrated when something like putting on their shoes does not go easily or well, and they need a great deal of support from adults as they learn to go to the lavatory, to put their clothes on and to feed themselves with forks and spoons or other eating utensils. It is very important during this time that adults help children to experience success as they try to become more and more independent (autonomous). This helps them to deal with problems positively as they face them in their lives. They need clothes which are easy to put on and take off, and easy to do up and undo – straps, laces and small buttons are not helpful, whereas elasticated waist bands do help, and so does velcro on shoes.

3–4 years

Children begin to decentre more as they increasingly try out what it's like to be someone else in their imaginative role play. They are helped if they meet people of multicultural backgrounds and special educational needs. This is a time when it is very important that children meet broad gender roles and do not begin to see what men and women do in narrow ways (**stereotypes**). They will also copy swear words if they hear them.

During this time, children are becoming more influenced by each other. They begin to be interested in having friends. They love to use 'silly talk' and to laugh together. They often have one special friend. They value companionship, but they also value being alone. This means that they need:

- ▶ solitary times;
- ▶ times to do things in parallel;
- ▶ times to be cooperative.

Sometimes they follow the lead of the other child, sometimes they show leadership themselves. Children of this age love to feel power and control over things and people. Sometimes they negotiate at their own level. It is very important that children be encouraged to learn about being cooperative, positive and caring towards each other. During the last 20 years, the work of Judy Dunn has shown how children learn through *quarrels* with other children as well as from situations where everything is going smoothly (see the section on bullying on p. 197). They need a great deal of support from adults when learning in this way. They need to be helped to turn difficult situations into positive ones.

During this time, it is important that children be prepared to have a go at things, to take risks and not be anxious about making errors. Children during this time are beginning to be clear about things which are right and things which are wrong as they develop moral values. They often argue with adults in a dogmatic way, and will not shift at all. It is important that they are helped in such a way that the moral values that they learn, for example, not hurting other people by hitting them – are reflected in the way they behave. Unfortunately, if they are smacked or hit by adults, they will learn to believe that this is acceptable behaviour, especially that adults or bigger people can hit smaller, less powerful people. It is illegal for early childhood workers in institutions to hit or smack children.

Children at this time are easily afraid. For example, they might be afraid of the dark and so might need a night light in their bedroom, or the landing light to be left on with their door ajar. They might need an adult to go with them to open a dark cupboard as reassurance that no monster is in there.

4–8 years

During this period, the child is establishing a stable self-concept and has taken in and internalised the social rules of their culture. They have begun to work out the difference between:

▶ social rules (which will vary from culture to culture, such as the way to greet somebody);

▶ display rules (where they hide their feelings – disappointment that the present given is not what they hoped for);

▶ moral values (which are to do with respect for other people, for example, not hitting people).

Children respond very positively to being given explanations and reasons for things. They are able to follow a series of events from beginning to end, and to be sensitive to the needs of other people as they do so. They are also able to take considerable responsibility, and enjoy helping other younger children. There is a terrific desire to be accepted by other children and adults.

However, it is also important to encourage children to be people in their own right and not simply to conform to what others want. Children with a strong sense of identity learn to be strong people. They learn to be **assertive** without being aggressive.

Personality

Every child has a different **personality**. Recently, researchers have begun to realise that a child's **temperament** in early childhood is the beginning of the later personality. It used to be thought that personality was fixed at birth (just as it used to be thought that intelligence was fixed at birth and unchangeable). As in other areas of development, it seems that a child's temperament *is* partly biological.

Early temperaments are not as stable as the later personality. A child's natural temperament can be changed by all sorts of things, especially by:

▶ the experiences of life;

▶ physical challenges;

▶ the people children meet.

Temperaments

Temperaments are to do with the style of behaviour that is natural to the child. The child's temperament influences the child's personality which emerges later on during late childhood and early adolescence. For example, some babies seem almost prickly when you hold them, while others are full of smiles. Some children are easy to scapegoat because they are always crying and unattractive to the adult. Once children can move about for themselves, it is easier for them to choose the people they want to be with. It is easier for them to do things alone when they do not feel like company.

Some children are accident prone because their temperament is very impulsive and active. They move into less safe situations more readily than a child who has a more cautious temperament.

A child's temperament is about:

▶ **emotionality:** the child's feelings – fearful, anxious, enthusiastic.

▶ **activity:** whether the child does things impulsively or slowly.

▶ **sociability:** whether the child likes company or not;

▶ variations in concentrating on something.

It is very important that adults working with young children do not favour smiling children. It is even more important that they do not scapegoat children with more difficult temperaments. Working professionally with children means being determined to give every child **equality of opportunity** (see Chapter 1).

The way adults help children willingly and with pleasure has a deep influence on the way children develop and learn. The way people react to the child's temperament could lead to low or good self-esteem in the child.

Emotionality and feelings

The moods might be smiles and joy, sad or distressed. Some children are more at ease in unfamiliar situations than others.

Some children can also manage better than others when they are bored (for example, when sitting on the mat for 30 minutes at 3 years old, which is inappropriate at this age); and some children can wait longer than others before they eat when they are hungry.

Activity

Some children are very vigorous and active, and always on the go. Others are able to change and modify what they do more easily than others. Others are very floppy.

Sociability

Some children are easily comforted when they are upset and distressed. Others are not. Some children are easily distracted but others stay involved in what they are doing. Some children positively enjoy meeting new people and going to new places, while others do not. The child's temperamental features will be stable across different times of the day and night, and in different places and with different people. This means that they will have their own style of doing things and of relating to people. Shy, timid children will be more cautious than communicative, sociable children.

Variation in concentration

Some children are easily distracted, while others are not.

Temperament and personality clashes

Sometimes people clash. This might be adults clashing with other adults, or it may be children clashing with other children. Sometimes an adult has a personality clash with a child. This is why it is so helpful to work in a team with other members of staff. It is very important that every early childhood worker tries their best to get on with every child. It is only natural, according to researchers, that there is sometimes a better **'goodness of fit'** between some people than others. Being a professional early childhood worker means that it is important, however, to work at having 'goodness of fit' with *every* child, even though it is easier to do this with some children than with others.

Other people

From the start, it seems as if babies are born to relate to other people. This is called **pro-social behaviour**, and it is important to encourage this by providing opportunities for babies and young children to meet other children and adults. As early as 6 months of age, babies enjoy each other's company. When they sit together, they touch each other's faces. They look at each other, they smile at each other. They enjoy 'peek-a-boo' games with adults and older children. This is cooperative social behaviour. It involves turn-taking. Babies delight in having a shared idea, and they really laugh with delight.

Toddlers' behaviour also shows how very young children cooperate socially. One might pick up a toy, and the other will copy. They laugh together. There is plenty of eye contact. One drops the toy intentionally, and the other copies. They laugh with glee. They have a shared idea which they can enjoy together.

By 2 or 3 years of age, the widening social circle becomes important. Children will need varying amounts of help and support as they meet new and social experiences. These might include joining an early childhood group of some kind.

Settling children positively is probably one of the most important aspects of the role of the early childhood worker. More is written about this in Chapter 5. No two children or adults are the same. No two families are the same. People might be part of the same culture, but they will not think in exactly the same way (see Chapter 1). Children who speak different languages will need to find different ways of being together. Children experiencing a delay in language development or sensory impairment may find it difficult to express what they feel, or indeed to understand other people. These children will need plenty of time without being rushed, and they will need help and support as they find the courage to try to link with other people.

It is important that children are not frightened by other children being aggressive or over-demanding towards them. This can put children off when they are beginning to make social relationships.

Different kinds of social behaviour can show themselves at different times of the day, in different situations and according to the child's mood, personality and previous experiences of relating to people. In the 1930s, Mildred Parten identified the following different kinds of play:

- ▶ **solitary:** children sometimes want to have personal space and do things alone;
- ▶ **spectator:** a child may choose to watch what others do, and not want to join in;
- ▶ **parallel:** there are times when children want companionship but not much interaction, for example, where two children are sitting side by side and drawing together but not looking at each other or talking very much about what they do;
- ▶ **associative:** young children often do things together, but might keep their own ideas separate from each other. For example, in the home area one child might pretend to lay the table for tea, while the other might be cooking a pancake on the same table. They are not concerned that they are *both* using the same table – they are each busy with their own play agenda. They talk to each other about what they are doing, and they do not get in each other's way. This is because their separate agendas do not come into conflict.

As soon as their agendas do conflict, then there will be a problem! For example, the pancake maker wants to make their pancake at the table while the other child wants to lay the table instead. When each child has a separate idea that is not shared by the other, there are likely to be frequent such conflicts. This is partly why young children need help and support in their social play, or in sharing materials together. It is often not appropriate, however, to *force* sharing. Adults might need instead to bring in another table for the pancake maker, or to make space next to the cooker. Separate ideas are *separate*, and if children are not able to share ideas, they cannot share materials! Helping children at moments like this is an important role for the early childhood worker;

▶ **cooperative:** there are times when children can share ideas and materials. These increase as the children grow older, and they increase even more rapidly when children experience being helped and treated positively by adults. The peek-a-boo game enjoyed by babies as young as 6 months of age is an early kind of cooperative behaviour. Gradually, for example, children begin to share and use a set of wooden building blocks together. They decide, together, to make a road. They negotiate and exchange ideas. If this breaks down, adults can help by stating the children's ideas. For example, they can say, 'Sean, you want to build a bridge. Meg, you want to build a row of shops. You both want to use the same blocks. What can we do about this?' The children often find solutions and then return to work together cooperatively again.

It is important to remember that these kinds of social relationship are no longer thought of by child researchers as a simple-to-complex ladder or hierarchy in which a child is first solitary, and then relates to people first in parallel and then associatively and cooperatively. Right from birth, babies interact with other people in a variety of ways. They are sometimes solitary, and sometimes they socialise in parallel, associatively or cooperatively. A better image is to think of a web – which spreads upwards as much as *out*.

Getting on with other children

Children need to feel the warmth of being made to feel that they matter. Then they will know a bit about how to make other people feel the same way. Even a young child, seeing a friend distressed, will quite often spontaneously give them a treasured teddy bear to ease the pain and give comfort. This means that young children are, in their own ways, very *giving*. They are also very *forgiving*. Adults can take great heart from this.

Being giving means that a young child has managed to control their behaviour through thinking of someone else's need. It takes enormous effort for young children to do this, and adults cannot expect children to achieve this all the time. It will come and go depending upon the situation, the people and how tired the children are. Children who become skilled in this way are often leaders, and other children want to be with them. They are popular children because they are friendly and warm, helpful and supportive, and inviting. They are also often physically skilled and able to do things.

Children tend to live according to how they experience life. If they are laughed at or hit, they will be likely to laugh at and hit others, especially children younger and smaller than themselves. This is because children use adults as a model of how to behave. This – as already mentioned - is called social referencing. Some children need a great deal of support in playing with and getting on with other children. Children who know how to 'join in' get on better in this way. This called developing good **access strategies:** first, a child will tend to circle around the edge or outside of an activity, perhaps on a tricycle, and try to work out what is happening; then, once the child knows what to do, they will imitate what the other children are doing, for example, pouring sand in and out of pots and laughing as each pot is upturned. This is called a '**side by side**' strategy: doing the same helps the child to join in with other children. Adults can help children in this by actually showing them how to join in side by side. The adult might say to the child 'Do you want to join in? Let's look at what they are doing, shall we? You do the same as them. Don't ask if you can do the same as them, just do the same as them.' This advice is given because if children ask if they can join in, they are usually told 'No' and rejected. If, on the other hand, children simply copy what the other children are doing, they are very likely to be accepted into the group. This is an important access strategy which adults can help children to develop. It is also useful for adults themselves if they are joining a group.

Friendships

Early friendships are important, and may last throughout life. Or they may be more fleeting. As the children's interests change, they go off in different directions, and the old friendship fades. Early friendships are like adult ones. They are partly based on people sharing the same interests. Of course, as the children become more able to play imaginatively together, the possibilities for sharing and enjoying each other's company become greater. This is because in play, children can rearrange the real world to suit themselves: you can pretend anything when you play.

Sharing

All the same, there will be frequent moments of conflict which will often flare up suddenly, because it is hard for children to share ideas, people, materials and equipment. There will be jealousy, wanting things for themselves or wanting what someone else is currently using and so taking it from them. Possession is a very big issue in capitalist cultures (but it may not, however, be so important in other kinds of society).

Young children can only manage to socialise cooperatively for a small part of their day: it is too much to expect them to do this for large parts of the day. Children who are just settling in might not indeed manage to share at all: all their energy is instead going into adjusting to the new social setting.

Creating an atmosphere which helps children to relate positively to each other and to adults

No-one gets on with people all the time. Children are like adults in this way. All children need:

> ► enough personal space to do things on their own without interruptions or pressure from anyone else;
> ► enough one-to-one individual attention – especially for the younger children – so that they feel they have enough attention and time to talk and share without the pressure of being in a group. For example, they might appreciate a one-to-one story;
> ► to feel nurtured and loved as a person in their own right;
> ► to be able to choose who to be with and what to do for most of the day: always having to do adult-led tasks is a great pressure for young children;
> ► their difficulties to be dealt with sensitively and caringly by adults.

Having too much personal space – the withdrawn or shy child

Although it is important for every child to have their own personal space and to be allowed opportunities to do things alone, some children have difficulty in socialising with other children or with adults in any way. This might be for a variety of reasons.

Some children have not met groups of children of their own age before. When the adults are new to the child, we introduce them: 'Michael, this is Jane. Jane wants to do a painting. Can you help her to get started? Can you tell her how to find the colours she wants?' If a child is shy with adults, it may be helpful just to join the child and be near without exerting any pressure on the child to do or say things. A warm smile, handing the child a lump of clay if they join the clay table, might reassure the child. The child will feel that this adult is good to be with.

It is important that the children like this are noticed by adults, or they can be sad and lonely, even though they are in a group setting. Keeping good observations of all children's social relationships is important. If a child who is normally outgoing and has the full range of social behaviour suddenly becomes quiet, withdrawn and solitary, this should be discussed in the team; and it will be important to include parents in the discussion so that action can be taken. This might mean seeking outside multiprofessional help if the problem cannot be solved within the team.

Every child needs the individual one-to-one attention of an adult

If children do not receive such attention, they begin to demand it. It is important to have a policy between the staff that every child and every parent should be greeted on arrival, and that goodbyes should also be said at the end of the day. This gives the important message, 'You matter to me.'

In some families, bedtime and looking at books or going to the shops give these experiences to the child. Not all children, however, have these opportunities.

When children have the full attention of an adult, they do not need to use attention-seeking behaviour. Rachel Pinney pioneered the idea of giving Children's Hours. Here, the children themselves choose what to do, and the adults do not make judgements about the activities chosen. Children given attention in this way often become less demanding in other situations since they work through what they find difficult during these special times. Children's Hours will not be necessary for most children, but the principle of giving children one-to-one attention from an adult *is* important for every child.

Seeking too much individual attention – the over-demanding child

1   Too much attention often leads to the label 'spoilt' or 'over-demanding child'. This negative image of the child is not helpful. It is best to have a positive image of the child. Some children are the main focus of their family and are given one-to-one attention by adults most of the time. They have not experienced having to wait for things or to take turns. Although such children are often very good conversationalists with adults, they have often not had much experience of being with other children. They might be an only child or a first child (or even a first grandchild) in the family. In China this is called the 4:2:1 factor because *every* child there is the parents' only child. A Chinese lecturer said, as a joke, that this could mean:
    ▶ 4 doting grandparents;
    ▶ 2 doting parents;
    ▶ 1 'spoilt' child!

    Is it the child's fault if he or she seems demanding of adult attention, insecure without it or unpopular or ill at ease with other children? This child needs sensitive help to become involved with parallel, associative and cooperative social behaviour with other children. You might reread p. 191 of this section so that you will be able to work sensitively to help children like this.

2   When a new baby is born, it will be hard-going for a child who is used to having had a lot of attention in the family. **Sibling jealousy** often results in very demanding behaviour for some time, until the family adjusts to new social relationships with each other. Recent research shows that the older child needs to feel that they are being treated in exactly the same way as the new baby.

3   Some children gain attention by being dominant and demanding of other children. These children are so-called 'bossy' children. This is another negative image of the

child. Such children need help in turn-taking, and give-and-take. They are usually afraid of losing control of situations, for example in the play and home area, they control the other children by saying what the storyline is going to be and making the other children do as they say. Just as adults need to show children positive images of themselves in books and displays, so they also need to give children positive images of themselves through the way that they *behave* towards children. These children need an adult to help them to see that the 'story' will be better if other children's ideas are allowed in as well as their own. It takes a bit of courage for the child to dare to let the play 'free flow' along like this. This is because no-one quite knows how the story is going to turn out. Once children know about this kind of free flow play, however, they usually want more of it.

Adults can help them into the give-and-take of play. For example:

'Did you say you had a dog in your story?'

'Yes. I call it to come here.'

'But Jack says it is a horse. You could call the horse over. See what happens.'

'Horsey, come here!'

'Ah, here comes the horse. Shall we stroke it?'

Children who try to make friends by owning status possessions

Children in capitalist societies often have difficulties with possessions. From 2 years of age, they often become eager to own objects. This is a different kind of demanding child. It means the child is demanding attention, and needing to control things, through owning possessions. Children who have not experienced secure social relationships are often especially anxious to possess fashionable objects which hold high status, for example a special commercial toy, or particular clothes or shoes, promoted through advertising.

Adults who help children to see that these are not vital to having a friend and being part of the group are contributing to helping children to develop a deeper quality in their social skills. Friends like you because you are *you*, and not because you own a fashionable hat.

Sometimes, children are so desperate to 'have' that they will steal. If such children cannot return the toy on their own because this is too difficult for them emotionally, they need to be helped by the adult to do so. Many children steal, but when a child does so often and regularly it is usually a sign that the child is under stress. The child needs individual warmth, love and attention from an adult. Sometimes, such children need the help of a specialist such as an educational psychologist.

Angry children

Hitting, kicking, spitting, biting, swearing and disrupting other children's activities are always demanding of the adult's attention. These are all negative labels, and they lead to negative images of a naughty or disruptive child. Again, adults need to clear their heads of images like this. This is called a visualisation technique. If you think of the child positively by trying to see why the child is angry, you can be more helpful to the child. By doing this, moreover, you can create a better atmosphere for all the children in the group.

A more positive approach to the child is to say that anger has erupted, and that the child needs help. The adult needs to find out why the child is so angry, to feel positive about the fact that the child can express such strong feelings, and to help the child deal with these feelings in a way which makes for good relationships with other children and adults.

There may be certain experiences in the child's life which are causing anger and distress. This situation needs to be carefully monitored, reported and acted upon with consultation from the line manager. It may again be necessary to involve a multiprofessional team which will include the parents, the staff in the early childhood setting and possibly a social worker, educational psychologist, health visitor or GP.

Are the children bored and frustrated?

The way the indoor and outdoor areas are set up may be causing boredom and frustration in the child. Thus, it is important to bear in mind:

▶ Children need plenty of choices of activity and interesting people to be with.

▶ They need interesting things to do. Some things need to be exciting. Some need to be new and challenging. Some need to be comfortable and familiar.

Remember, when children get on with each other, they do not need so much adult attention, and so they will not demand it quite so frequently!

Positive images of children are vital

Children need positive images of themselves to be reflected in the social behaviour of the staff in the early childhood setting. Discriminatory practice by children or adults that gives children negative labels of any kind, even if these are conveyed not directly to the child, but in the way that the staff talk about the child, damages social and emotional development, and results in difficult behaviour and poor social skills. This means that expressions of anger and frustration, tiredness or hunger through temper tantrums and aggressive acts by a child need to be dealt with sensitively by staff (see the punishment section on p. 202–204).

TEMPER TANTRUMS

These can be:

▶ *noisy:* the children might hurl themselves about, perhaps hurting themselves – usually in rather a public way;

▶ *quiet:* the children hold their breath, and might even turn blue.

RESTRAINING

It is important not to leave children in this state. Quietly holding them and 'being there' for them supports children through this time until they begin to feel calm. 'Holding' a child's feelings with gentleness and calm physical support helps the child to come round feeling cared about. It also reassures the child that they will not be left to lose control or be abandoned.

It is important to learn how to hold and restrain children from someone who is experienced and knowledgeable about this. It is also important that the child has a good relationship with those who 'hold' their feelings of anger for them in this way. This is called **containment** by psychologists. The adult acts as a 'container' who holds the child's anger in a safe way so that the child does not feel out of control, and who thus helps the child to regain a sense of calm. It is no good trying to discuss what has happened with a child when that child is in the middle of having a temper tantrum or being aggressive. The child needs to become calm.

Aggressive behaviour (hitting or shouting or, say, spoiling another child's painting) can sometimes be prevented if adults put on their 'running shoes': the adult gets there before it happens, saying 'No!' and removes the child so that they cannot damage another child's painting. This can be a very useful strategy. It is particularly useful with children under 3 years of age.

The adult can often also discuss the situation: 'No! Don't spoil the painting! Do you want to use the red paint? Is that the problem? Have you asked Nour for it? Well, let's try that now. I will ask Nour for you. Nour, could you pass the red paint please?' Nour gives the red paint. The adult continues: 'There you are. Just ask. Nour did not realise that you wanted the red paint, you see.'

Eye contact is very important. So is your body language. So are your gestures. These can all often be more important than what you say. But children also need language which explains actions if they are to develop social skills effectively.

In a group situation, disruptive behaviour is best dealt with by not giving the child attention: concentrate instead on all the other children who are not being disruptive. You might say: 'I can see most people are ready for the story. You have all found your cushions and are sitting there looking really interested and ready. I am really looking forward to reading this story because it is one of my favourites.' Being ignored is not what an attention-seeker hopes for. Children are helped if they realise that they will have positive warm attention from you if they are cooperative.

Learning to be assertive – not bullying, and not being a victim

Children who are aggressive are in great difficulty with social relationships. Again, they are often called 'bullies' or 'aggressive' or 'disruptive' children, and this negative image of the child is again not helpful. Try to move from this negative image to a more positive one, using the above-mentioned visualisation technique.

A more positive image might be to think that at least the child is expressing feelings about his/her own self-esteem. Delinquent teenagers always have low self-esteem. They are often bullies.

Name-calling and shouting insults is one kind of bullying. Children pick on weaker children or different children. For example, they tease, or give racial, gender or disability insults. Physical hitting or menacing is another kind of bullying. Pen Green Family Centre (1993) has done pioneer work in helping children:

▶ not to bully
▶ not to *be* bullied (victim).

Children are helped to 'Learn to be Strong' and to be:

▶ assertive without being aggressive
▶ assertive rather than timid.

Try not to use the word 'bully'. Instead, talk about children learning to be assertive through being less timid or less aggressive. This creates a positive image of the child, which in turn will help you to work better with the child.

Swearing can be similar to name-calling. Although it is more often simply the case that swearing is a normal part of the child's life and language experience, it is quite a different thing, however, when children swear in order to shock. Any child who swears needs help:

▶ in learning which are the words they cannot use in the early childhood setting;
▶ in finding new words to replace the swear words, or they will not be able to express their thoughts and feelings;
▶ in building up their vocabulary.

Formal and informal social relationships
FORMAL RELATIONSHIPS – ROLE BEHAVIOUR

There is another aspect to social development, relationships and social behaviour. Children learn about the difference between informal and formal relationships quite naturally. As they experience and understand the culture and society in which they are growing up, they gradually learn how to relate to some people in ways which are not about friendship or companionship or family or the staff in the early childhood setting. These latter kinds of **formal relationships** occur when they are buying something in a shop, going to the Post Office or thanking someone for giving directions in the street. Such relationships do not develop, and they do not last. It is not until adulthood that formal behaviour becomes stable (if then).

Each society has rules which shape formal relationships and create 'role' behaviour. MPs in Parliament have to ask questions, and speak in formal ways. They take on the '**role**' of an MP. Children in turn learn how to answer the telephone and take messages, and this is another kind of formal behaviour – they are taking on the role of 'message-taker'. Other kinds of formal behaviour might be how to thank someone for a present, join a queue at the Post Office, sit quietly on a bus. When parents ask 'Have they been good?', they are expressing a hope that their child is beginning to learn about formal social relationships, and to manage these, as well as the more relaxed **informal relationships**. As children become more able to do this, they are described as becoming **socially skilled**.

Children feel things deeply

Children live life to the full. Living life to the full means that children have powerful and strong feelings. They do not feel by halves, they feel fully. They will need adult help in learning to deal with the strength of their feelings.

Because children feel things deeply, they need a great deal of help in coming to terms with their emotions. Feelings are hard to manage, and even *adults* do not always succeed in dealing with how they feel.

The fears children develop

The fears children have will be very real to them. Some (especially babies and toddlers) are afraid that their parent or carer might leave them. Some are afraid of loud noises, like thunder, or of heights (perhaps they don't like to come down the climbing frame because they are afraid to move), or of sudden movements such as a dog leaping up at them. Going to a strange place like the clinic might bring on feelings of fear for others; and many children are afraid of the dark and need a nightlight or to have the door left open when going to sleep.

Helping children to know and deal with their feelings positively is probably one of the most important things an adult can do if children are to feel that they matter and are valued and respected. Talking about these fearful feelings and showing the child that you understand is important. Later on, children begin to use imaginative play in the home area, dolls' house or toy garage to face and deal with their fears and worries.

Feeling jealous and anxious about the arrival of a new baby at home can be helped by allowing children to take out their aggressive feelings on a soft toy. This channels the aggression and gives the child 'permission to express their feelings'. In addition it can help their emotions to run about outside and be very boisterous; it can help to sit and bash and bang on a huge lump of clay; and it can help to do a splash painting. Children are also helped by knocking down towers of wooden blocks or working at the woodwork bench.

The traditional provision of the early childhood curriculum provides well for children's feelings to be expressed (see Chapter 13).

Body language

Children need to, and will, express their feelings. They do so through physical actions like stamping with rage, screaming with terror, hitting and confusion, jumping with joy or having a cuddle for comfort and calm.

Faces also tell adults how a child feels. A pout tells the adult the child is not happy, compared with eyes that are shining with joy.

The position of the body tells adults more: playing alone with the dolls' house; hovering on the edge of the cooking session to see what happens, or maybe wanting to join in but not knowing how; or playing boats right in the centre of a group of children. A child playing with a dolls' house needs personal space, and perhaps to have this protected from other children. The child who is hovering might need to be left to watch, or might need help to join in – the side-by-side access strategy (see p. 192 above) often helps here. Children, in fact, need different things at different points in a day.

Children who keep twisting their fingers together are not at ease compared with the child who sits in a relaxed way.

How children feel

Feelings during childhood are strong, and can quickly overwhelm the child. This can lead to:

- ▶ sobbing and sadness;
- ▶ temper tantrums that are full of anger and rage;
- ▶ jealousy that makes a child want to hit out;
- ▶ a joy that makes a child literally jump and leap with a wildness that is unnerving to many adults.

PUTTING FEELINGS INTO WORDS

It helps children to manage their feelings if they can put them into words. The child who can say 'Stop hitting me. That hurt. I don't like it' has found a way to deal appropriately with an unpleasant situation.

At first, children often shout a term of abuse rather than using appropriate words. Adults need to decide whether this is a step forward along the way from physical hitting to unacceptable language, to an appropriate expression of feelings in words. It takes time and experience for young children to learn how to express their feelings in words and to negotiate in dialogue with others. It can help here to give them examples of rather staccato-sounding words such as 'Stoppit!'. Children learn the language of feelings through real situations that hold great meaning and that engage their whole attention.

Gradually, the sounds babies make are more like the ones they hear, and they even seem to shout to signal to people that they want to have some attention. Even profoundly hearing-impaired babies will babble, but they will need help, perhaps with learning sign language alongside spoken language.

Children under emotional stress

When children do not experience warm loving relationships, they react according to their personality:

▶ Some children will become aggressive. They are noisy and disrupt other children's play. They always demand the attention of adults by doing things which 'force' the adult to come to them, for example hitting or making a mess which simply cannot be left.

▶ Some children are quite the opposite: they are very quiet and watchful. Their bodies are always rather tense. They are withdrawn and keep themselves to themselves. They are **introverted**.

▶ Some children begin bed-wetting, or begin to soil themselves, having been dry before.

▶ Some children find it difficult to eat. They need to be coaxed with love and care.

▶ Some children return to babyish ways. They want a bottle again, or a comforter. They want to be held and cuddled and carried about. They want to be helped with eating and dressing.

When children are under emotional stress, their behaviour might change quite quickly. It is important, therefore, that early childhood workers be alert to changes of these kinds; and it is very important that they respond sensitively and with understanding. It will be necessary to ask for the advice of parents and professionals. First, it is important to talk with the line manager about your observations, and the discussion will probably then open up for the staff team to look at the child's progress and agree what the next steps are that should be taken. This is so whether the situation is a temporary one for the child or one that is more likely to be long term.

Children's behaviour is a symptom of the feelings underneath. By working as a team, adults can together try to reach the causes of these symptoms. This might involve a multi-professional team including parents, health visitors, child psychologists, educational psychologists, a play therapist, a social worker and doctors, as well as the staff in the early childhood setting. Such a team is a powerful one when everyone working with the child cooperates. The *parents* are the first and most important members of any team that is looking to help the child.

G U I D E L I N E S

The social behaviour of children and the social behaviour of adults who work with them

▶ **Children need to understand, express and deal with their feelings.**

▶ **They need to develop positive relationships with people.**

▶ **Children feel things deeply, and they need a great deal of help in coming to terms with their emotions. Feelings are hard to deal with. It is important to remember that even adults do not succeed all the time in dealing with how they feel.**

▶ **Helping children to express and deal with their feelings constructively and positively is probably one of the most important things an adult can do if children are to feel they matter and are valued and respected.**

▶ **Remember to work as a team and decide together on what is unacceptable behaviour and how to deal with it. Many early childhood settings now have behaviour policies. These should always use positive images of the child as the starting point. Negative images, for example** that of a bully, can be made positive through visualisation techniques. The bully then becomes a child who needs help to become assertive without being aggressive.

▶ It is important that adults working with young children be guided by a child's personality. What helps one child might not help another. Every child is different.

▶ Adults need to remember that all children need:
  – personal space
  – one-to-one attention
  – friends
  – to feel part of the group
  – to feel secure.

Setting clear boundaries

Children need clear, consistent boundaries. They will have to keep testing out boundaries that are not clear or consistent: they will check if the boundary is still there, or see if it can be moved; they will check whether all the adults are keeping this boundary or only one. Boundary checking can become very tedious from the adult's point of view! It is best to have just a few boundaries, agreed to by everyone as a team – including the children, if at all possible. It helps the children feel secure when a boundary is there, strong, clear and comforting. Four-year-olds often say with great satisfaction 'You're not allowed.'

When boundaries are set, however, they need to be explained to the children; and when a child oversteps the boundary, it is important that the child is not made to feel worthless or disliked for what has been done. This can be avoided if the child's *actions* are criticised rather the child themselves:

'Kicking hurts. Jo is very upset because it hurt.'
rather than:

'Don't do that. You are very naughty, and I am cross with you.'

Distractions offering alternatives to children

Sometimes an adult can see trouble looming ahead, and can avoid a confrontation by offering an alternative: kicking a football instead might have saved Jo from being kicked. Alternatives are better than confrontations for young children. This is because temper tantrums and challenging behaviour often result, and are more difficult to deal with positively. No child should feel rejected: it is only what a child *does* – hitting, biting, kicking, stealing, snatching a toy from another child – that might be rejected. The message needs to be 'I am not rejecting *you*. I am rejecting what you *did*.' Children need unconditional warmth and love, no matter who they are or what they do. Don't get 'hooked' into the child's anger and feelings. Try to contain and hold a child's feelings so that the child feels safe. In this way, you will help the children to regain control of their feelings.

Remember that children will be noticing and learning from your feelings, actions and reactions. You are a powerful source of social learning for the child. This process is called **social referencing**.

► Give children a predictable environment – which is different from a rigid routine. Children need to recognise the shape of the day and the order of events (see Chapter 13 on the curriculum).

► Try to avoid confrontations by respecting a child's personality and mood, and knowing what the child can manage without too much struggle.

► If a confrontation becomes unavoidable, you might have to make it clear to the child that there is a real boundary here, a boundary that a child cannot cross.

Managing children's behaviour

Young children often do realise that they are doing something unacceptable. They need help so that they begin to understand when something is inappropriate. Froebel – as already mentioned – believed that behind every bad act is a good intention. He thought that adults should try to find out what this intention was, and help the child by *acknowledging* it. Then, he believed, it is easier to put right the 'bad' the child has done.

There are three main approaches to the management of behaviour. It is very important that you try to use mainly the third type.

1 Using punishment as revenge

This unacceptable approach can be summed up in the statement 'An eye for an eye, a tooth for a tooth.' This means that what you do to me, I will do to you. If you hit me, I will hit you. In many countries such as Sweden it is now illegal to physically smack, beat or 'strap' a child. In the UK, it is illegal in early childhood settings.

Children who are often smacked often then hit other children, usually younger and smaller children. They are imitating the fact that big adults smack small children. This approach thus raises serious ethical questions. In a discussion with their teacher, one child in a group of 10-year-olds in a primary school asked 'How do adults know what age to stop smacking?'. Another replied, 'When the children get bigger than the parents, they might hit back.' Children are very alert to the way adults behave towards them.

2 Behaviour Modification

► punishment

When an adult punishes a child, they introduce something the child doesn't like to put them off doing it. 'If you don't sit still, you won't have any sweets'.

► negative reinforcement

The adult might say to the child, if you will just sit quietly I shall stop being so cross with you and that will be nice for both of us.

The adult changes an unpleasant situation to a pleasant one – if the child sits still.

► positive reinforcement

The adult might say to the child, if you sit quietly, I will give you a sweet.

The adult presents the child with something they like, if they sit still.

Positive reinforcement rewards good behaviour.

Marion Dowling gives this example:

'In one study in a nursery school, a group of children were provided with drawing materials and told that they would receive a prize for drawing which, in due course, they did. Another group were given the same materials but with no mention of prizes. Some time after, drawing was provided as one of a range of optional activities; significantly, the children who chose to spend the least time on drawing were those who had been previously rewarded.'

(Dowling 1995)

Adults can certainly encourage children to do what they want them to do through giving them rewards and positively reinforcing what they do. The problem is that this does not make them think about why they want to do things. In other words, it doesn't have a *long-term effect*.

TIME OUT

The adult might say to the child, 'If you scribble on the books again, you will have to sit on the "Time Out" chair for a few minutes.' This might put the child off scribbling here, but in a *different* situation, for instance when staying at grandma's, it might not put the child off scribbling on the wall of the bedroom. It thus only deters the child from scribbling in the nursery on the books, where the 'Time Out' chair is. Vivian Gussin-Paley has written a book about the limitations of the 'Time Out' chair. The book is called *Wally's Stories*.

Sometimes children are punished some time *after* the event, for example the adult might say, 'You ate two biscuits at snack time. So now you can't go out to play after the story.' This does not help children to make sense either, because they do not connect what they did earlier with what is being done to them *now*.

Always remember, it is not helpful to make children do a drawing or look at a book as a punishment because this will reinforce the message that these are unpleasant activities.

When children do things we don't want them to do, it is easy to feel annoyed and impatient, but it is important not to 'dump' our feelings on the child. Thinking positively and keeping a sense of humour helps the development of a professional way of working with children who challenge the patience and stamina of adults.

Managing behaviour in ways which concentrate on trying to deter children from doing things we do not want them to do may be necessary as emergency action. However, these ways do not produce long-term results because they do not encourage the child to think for themselves or to be *autonomous* in their moral and spiritual development.

3 Managing children's behaviour in ways which focus on reform

The kind of behaviour-management strategies which help children to develop socially, emotionally, intellectually and – most of all – morally are those which focus on reform.

REVENGE DOES NOT WORK

Deterrents do not have lasting effects once they wear off: they only *contain* the situation. They do not move the child on in development and learning.

Jody hits Amandip. The adult says to Jody, 'Amandip is crying because that hurt. He is very upset. How can you make him feel better? What happened? He took your toy? Did you Amandip?' [Amandip nods.] 'Next time, try saying 'It's mine.' Then he will know how you feel about it.'

This approach signals to Amandip that he must not snatch a toy, but it also allows him to find a way out with dignity. Furthermore, it gives Jody the *words* that she needs to use instead of hitting. It rejects what both children did, but it does not reject either child. It helps both children to have some ideas of how they might tackle the situation next time. This is *punishment*

as reform, and it will help the children both to think about moral matters and to develop **self-discipline**. It helps children to look at the result of what they do.

LEARNING SOCIAL BEHAVIOUR THROUGH ADULTS

Research shows that from about 3 years of age, children begin to feel guilt and shame about the things they do. The way adults respond to what they have done will lead to either positive or negative self-esteem. Children *learn* from their relationships with adults and other chidren who are close to them, and gradually they begin to widen the circle of people who can help them to learn *socially*. However, they cannot learn about social behaviour if they cannot make sense of what is done to them. That is why a focus on reform rather than on revenge or deterrent is effective in the long term.

G U I D E L I N E S

Strategies you can use when children become confrontational and personalities clash

▶ **Can you distract the child? If the child keeps grabbing the paint pot from another child, ask the first child to help you mix two more pots of paint. This distracts the child and takes you both out of a negative groove.**

▶ **Does the child need personal space? Sometimes children cannot share or be with other children for too long. They need to 'do their own thing'. Respect this.**

▶ **Does the child need help expressing and talking about how they feel? Opportunities for role play or to bash and bang a lump of clay can be very helpful in this situation.**

▶ **Does the child need help with a side-by-side strategy? This is discussed on p. 192.**

▶ **Should two children be left together? Sometimes children have been together too long, or their personalities are clashing and they find it hard to spend time together. When this happens it is usually best to find a way of separating the children.**

▶ **Can you negotiate together, or is the child too angry and upset to do this?**

▶ **Sometimes children become too angry and upset, and their feelings erupt. They can then be a danger to their own safety, or to that of other children. It is always best if children can be helped before this point is reached, but sometimes the eruption of these feelings is unavoidable. Children are very frightened by the power of these feelings, and overwhelmed at feeling themselves lose control. When this happens, remember that children quickly become very difficult and challenging to be with. They need you to hold their anger and feelings for them.**

▶ **Are the children bored? Is the room and outdoor area an interesting enough place for the child? Are the children free to choose activities for themselves?**

▶ **Check that the child is not hungry.**

▶ **Is the child uncomfortable? If so, try to find out why. (Maybe they have wet themselves.)**

▶ **Check that the child is not tired.**

▶ **Remember, children need safe spaces where they can be noisy and move about freely both indoors and outdoors.**

▶ **Remember, children need calmer periods where they have personal space,** perhaps by making a little den for themselves, or by reading alone in the book area, or by being read a story by an adult while sitting on their lap.

▶ Remember that sometimes you can see that something is building up and you *redirect* the situation by moving in before it happens.

▶ Children are able to tidy up with adult help, but they need their efforts to be recognised and warmly appreciated. Are you appreciating the children's help and telling them this?

▶ Are the children having enough opportunities to play?

▶ It is important to remember that what is positive behaviour in one culture might be interpereted differently in another. For example, owning possessions and learning to respect *other people's* possessions might be valued in one family culture or society more than another.

▶ Remember that showing initiative and negotiating might be valued in some settings, but that conformity might be more important in others, for example in crossing the road.

▶ Remember that behaviour which is valued universally in the world has to do with helping others, feeling for others, sharing and taking turns, and understanding somebody else's feelings and ideas.

Summary

There are various reasons why some children have difficulties getting on with other children or perhaps with adults:

▶ They may look different.

▶ They may be rather young for their age.

▶ They may not be outgoing and warm.

▶ Some children, when they experience anxiety, become aggressive towards smaller or younger children.

Racist, sexist and **disablist** behaviour can begin early. It is important that staff be aware of this fact and act quickly (see Chapter 1) in relation to these kinds of discriminatory behaviour. Many children begin to get on more easily once they are fully settled into the group. Children who are physically, socially or emotionally young, however, may need active help, and plenty of adult support.

Again, it is important that staff always work in a close partnership with parents, and that when it is necessary to involve other professional workers in a multiprofessional team, parents feel that they themselves are part of the decision-making and action plans.

Different theories of feelings (emotional development) and relationships (social development)

The nature–nurture controversy again!

In the past it was thought that personalities are fixed from the moment we are born (this is the nature argument). This is probably too extreme a view, just as the view that intelligence is fixed at birth is extreme. Children who have grown up without other people do not seem to show the kind of social behaviour we think of as human. They do not make human sounds, smile or use eye contact, or even walk about like humans. This suggests that their social behaviour is *not* simply fixed in their genes and inherited. Such children include:

▶ feral children, sometimes known as 'wolf children';
▶ children who are locked away and kept isolated from other people.

But is social behaviour learnt?

The nurture approach includes:

▶ **Behaviourist** theory – Skinner;
▶ **Socialisation** theory;
▶ **Social learning** theory – Bandura.

These theories have been challenged since the 1980s.

The nature approach includes the **psycho-dynamic** theories – Freud, Erikson, Winnicott, Bowlby – which concentrate on the feelings we have inside us, and on how other people can help us to express and deal with these. Our early feelings and experiences never leave us. They are always deep inside us. They are sometimes called 'ghosts from our past'. They affect us throughout our lives.

Theories which involve *both* nature *and* nurture include **social evolution** theory – Dawkins – which concentrates on the whole human race and does not look at individuals at all, and **social constructivist** theory – Trevarthen, Dunn, Vygotsky.

These theories concentrate on the two-way process of feelings and relationships between children and people who are close to them. Children seem to influence adults as much as adults influence children. These theories are the most recent and influential for early childhood workers. According to this approach, children and adults are constantly adjusting to each other and learning from each other.

Behaviourist theory

Until the mid-1980s, this theory had a great influence. It suggested that adults regulated children's behaviour. B. F. Skinner thought that adults shape children's behaviour, so that children conform to the expectations and conventions of the culture in which they grow up. Skinner believed that children could be positively or negatively reinforced so as to behave in the ways adult wanted. (See the examples of negative and positive reinforcement of social behaviour on p. 202.)

Adults who use the behaviourist approach often give children rewards (sweets, badges, stars, smiley faces, verbal praise) for *good* behaviour. Good behaviour here means behaviour that the adult wants to see. It is again important to remember, however, that good behaviour in one culture might be bad behaviour in another. It might be considered rude for a child to look an adult in the eye in one culture when reprimanded, but very rude *not* to do so in another culture.

It is important for adults working with young children to decide whether or not they believe in these kinds of extra intrinsic awards – stars for good behaviour. Marion Dowling (see p. 202) suggests that this approach can quickly bring successful results which might please the adult for a little while. The problem is that children now do things only in order to get a reward, and this novelty soon wears off. It is probably more successful in the long term to help children do something because they realise its benefits, for example sitting quietly ready for a story because they enjoy listening to the story. This is called **intrinsic**

motivation, and it means helping children to become self-disciplined. In a lecture, Judge Tumin said that he found, as Chief Inspector of Prisons, that the teenage delinquents he met there had never learned about intrinsic motivation and self-discipline. He therefore stressed the importance of this in early childhood education.

Socialisation theory

Socialisation is the process by which children learn the expected behaviour for their culture and society. The theory of socialization, which developed out of behaviourist theory, found favour in the 1960s–1980s. According to this theory, children learn the rules of the society they live in. These will vary from society to society and from culture to culture, and the cultural variations involved are fascinating. However, it is important to bear in mind that being socialised in certain cultures could mean denying human rights, for example torturing, as in Nazi Germany, or in South Africa under the regime of apartheid.

1 **Primary socialisation theory**. This is about the way the family and those close to the child help the child's social development. The child learns to behave as *part* of the family. The idea is that the child adapts to the social ways of their family.
2 **Secondary socialisation theory**. The child's social circle then begins to widen to include neighbours, (possibly) an early childhood group and society at large. The influences on social development thus become broader.

Social learning theory

This emphasises that young children learn about social behaviour by:
- watching other people;
- imitating other people.

Albert Bandura found that children tend to imitate people in their lives who they believe hold **status**, especially if those people are warm, powerful personalities. He showed three groups of children a film in which an adult was hitting a bobo doll and shouting at it. The film had three different endings for the three groups respectively:
- First ending: the adult was given a reward for hitting the doll.
- Second ending: the adult was punished for hitting the doll.
- Third ending: nothing was done to the adult for hitting the doll.

Then the children were given a bobo doll like the one in the film. The children who saw the adult rewarded for hitting the doll tended to do the same; they hit the doll. This research study was not a very natural situation for the children, but it does suggest that adults whom children love, or who are powerful **status figures** in their lives, can be very influential on a child's behaviour:
- If children are smacked by adults, they are likely to hit other children.
- If children are shouted at by adults, they are likely to shout at others.
- If children are given explanations, they will try to explain things too.
- If children are comforted when they fall, they will learn to do the same to others.

People who work with young children are very important status figures for the child's social learning.

ROLE PLAY - PART OF THE SOCIAL LEARNING THEORY

Children directly copy what adults do, but they also pretend to be adults (**role play**) when they begin to play imaginatively. The home area is an important area for this, and so is the

FIGURE 7.1
Children directly copy what adults do

outdoor area which can become all sorts of places (shops, markets, streets, building sites). For example, Joe, 4 years, pretended to be the early childhood worker. He told a story to a group of dolls and imitated the way in which the worker talked gently to the children, smiled and held the book.

The problem with this approach is that it does not see children experimenting with *different* ways of doing things: it really only suggests that children merely copy what they see.

Behaviourist theory (the socialisation model) and social learning theory: a summary

▶ At birth, children are born with **reflexes**. They do not inherit social behaviour, according to these approaches: social behaviour is thought to be *learnt*.

▶ Children copy what the *adult* does and thus learn accepted behaviour in their culture from the adults. They will experience:

  – role transition – when they go from nursery to school;

  – role loss – when an only child has a baby brother or sister born into the family;

  – role conflict – when other children want the child to do something that the child knows the adult will disapprove of;

  – the learning of a gender role – what it means to be a boy/male or a girl/female.

▶ Children will be influenced by *other* children: they want to be like their friends – they like to wear the same shoes. This can mean that some children are easily led because they copy others, or that they are easily bullied because of this since they fear losing the approval of other children.

▶ Children rehearse adult life through role play. They learn the correct adult roles for a mother, doctor, receptionist, and these are rehearsed in their play. Children imitate the roles of people who have high status for them.

▶ Positive reinforcement: children are praised and extrinsically rewarded for their good behaviour (behaviour wanted by adults).

▶ Negative reinforcement: children avoid an unpleasant situation (which involves behaviour not wanted by adults). Instead, they do something adults approve of.

▶ Children begin to sort out how adults expect *them* to behave, and they also begin to sort out how they can expect *adults* to behave. Children begin to realise that a carer's role will make that carer behave differently towards them compared with, for example, their parent. Children thus begin to realise that different people have different roles and that people behave according to their own particular role.

Psychodynamic theories
SIGMUND FREUD (1856–1939)

Freud is the founder of **psychoanalytic theory**. He and his daughter fled to England from Nazi Vienna a year before his death.

Freud believed that our **unconscious** feelings direct the way we behave. We are, of course, not aware of these feelings, and this means that we often do not know why we behave as we do in a particular situation.

Freud thought that our earliest childhood experiences deeply influence what we believe and how we feel as adults. He thought people went through **psychosexual** stages of development: **oral, anal, phallic, latency** and **genital**. He tried to help the people he psychoanalysed to understand their behaviour and feelings, and even to change.

Freud thought that people have:

▶ an **id** – which makes 'I want' demands;
▶ an **ego** – which tries to resolve conflicts between the id and the superego;
▶ a **superego** – which is like the demands made by parents or society about how to behave.

When the ego listens to the id more than to the superego, the person is said to be **egocentric** (self-seeking and selfish). When the ego listens to the superego more than to the id, the person is seen as **conformist** and self-denying. When the needs of the id are well balanced with the needs of the superego, the person is seen as a **well-grounded person**.

ERIK H. ERIKSON (1902-1994)

Erikson believed that Sigmund Freud was the rock on which the personality theory that he developed was built. He was the pupil of Anna Freud, Freud's daughter, who worked with children who survived Nazi concentration camps in her clinic in Hampstead. Erikson concentrated on the superego and on the influence of **society** on a child's development. This was very positive thinking because he showed how every time we meet a personal crisis or have to deal with a crisis in the world (for example, living through a war), we are naturally equipped to face difficulties and to deal with them.

Erikson thought that there were eight developmental phases during a person's life (five during childhood and three during adulthood), and that during each phase we have to face and sort out the particular kinds of crisis that occur during that phase:

- *Phase 1: babyhood.* We have to sort out whether we feel a basic sense of trust in life or a basic sense of mistrust. This phase is about being a hopeful person or not.
- *Phase 2: the toddler and nursery years.* We develop either a basic sense of being able to do things (autonomy) or a basic sense of doubt in ourselves and shame. This phase is about our self-identity.
- *Phase 3: the infant school years.* We either take the initiative and 'go for it' or we feel guilty and hold back in case we upset people. This phase is about leading an active life with a sense of purpose, or not.
- *Phase 4: the junior years.* We either begin to be determined to master things, or we do not try hard in case we cannot manage something. This phase is about becoming skilled.
- *Phase 5: adolescence.* We either begin to be at one with ourselves, or we feel uncertain and unsure. We learn to have faith in ourselves and to balance these feelings.
- *Phase 6: young adults.* We begin to have a sense of taking part in our society, and of taking responsibility in it as a shared venture. Or we think only of ourselves, and become isolated.
- *Phase 7: middle age:* We begin to be caring of the next generation and the future of our society. Or we reject the challenge.
- *Phase 8: old age:* We return to our roots and overcome feelings of despair, or of disgust about new lifestyles, or fear of death – or not. This is Erikson's phase of wisdom.

Unfortunately, Erikson called these 'the eight phases of Man'. It is important to bear in mind that theories based on Freud's ideas are based on white middle-class patients in Western Europe. The theories need to be carefully used for that reason. However, they still seem to be useful in many ways.

D. W. WINNICOTT

Winnicott worked with children at the Tavistock Clinic. His work has helped those working with young children to be sensitive to how children feel when they separate from those they live with and love in ways which are positive for the child.

Winnicott taught us to see the importance of the teddy bears and other comforters that children seem to need to carry about with them. He called these **transitional objects**. He believed that children need such objects to help them through the times when they begin to realise that they are a separate person. The teddy stands for, say, the mother, when she leaves the baby in the cot. It is the symbol of the mother who will return. It helps children through a time when they might be alone or feeling sad (or both).

Naturally, the child might enjoy the teddy's company more when the mother is with them. The teddy, as the transitional object, is a link with the mother when she is there, but it also helps the child to be separated from her.

Many adults still have transitional objects when they first leave home, or when their partner goes away for a week or two. It is not only children who have to deal with the feelings of being separated from someone they love.

Until recently, children were not allowed to take teddy bears into hospital in case they were full of germs. In some early childhood settings, transitional toys are still taken away from children when they arrive. This is usually because staff fear they might be lost. The team of adults working in early childhood settings needs to discuss this together and plan a policy which takes care of the deep feelings that children have about their transitional objects.

IMAGINARY FRIENDS

Some children have **imaginary friends**. These are another kind of transitional object, but they are imaginary rather than real. For example, Tracey, 4 years of age, pretended that she had a dog. On holiday in the summer, she led the dog about wherever she went, feeding and stroking it. The dog helped her to get ready in her mind for starting at school after the holiday and for separating from her parents for a whole day instead of just a half day at her nursery.

THUMB-SUCKING, COMFORTERS AND CLOTHS

These are other ways through which children can learn early comfort behaviour such as sucking, stroking or smelling. These do not have an imaginative dimension like a transitional object or imaginary friend. Children usually grow out of this quite naturally, and it is best to leave it this way.

JOHN BOWLBY'S THEORY OF ATTACHMENT, SEPARATION, GRIEF AND LOSS

Bowlby's theory looked at:

▶ how babies become **attached** to the mother figure;
▶ what happens when babies are **separated** from the mother figure;
▶ what happens when babies experience **loss** and **grief** when separated from the people they feel close to.

ATTACHMENT

Babies and those caring for them usually form close **bonds** with each other. Babies and parents who for one reason or another do not make close emotional bonds experience difficulty in stable, warm and loving relationships.

As the baby is fed and held, cuddled and enjoyed, bathed and gently settled to sleep, these emotional loving relationships develop and deepen. Babies who find that adults respond quickly to their cries become trusting of life and well-attached in stable, warm relationships: they know that they will be fed, changed when soiled and wet, comforted when teething and so on.

Mary Ainsworth worked with Bowlby and found that when adults responded quickly to a baby's cries, that child, by 3 years of age, was less demanding than those babies who were usually left to cry. Of course, the individual temperaments of babies will show themselves very early on, and will have an effect on other people. For instance some babies become hysterical very quickly when hungry, while others are of a calmer nature. Bonding is thus partly about adults and babies adjusting to each other and getting to understand each other – learning how to 'read' each other's signals.

John Bowlby (1907–1990) thought that early attachment was very important. He thought that the mother figure and baby together was the most important relationship. This was because mothers tended to be at home with their babies more than other people. He did not say that the most important attachment figure must be the natural mother, but he did say that babies need one central person who is the mother figure.

It is now realised that babies can have deep relationships with several people – mother, father, brothers and sisters, carers, grandparents. Indeed, babies develop in an emotionally and socially healthy way only if they have several people with whom they have bonded. They might enjoy playing with one person and having meals with another; and it is the *quality* of the time the child spends with people which determines whether or not the child becomes attached to them.

Attachment can be more difficult at first for some children in cases where it is hard for the adult and child to communicate:

- if the birth has caused mother and baby to be separated;
- if the child is visually impaired and eye contact is absent;
- if the child is hearing-impaired and does not turn to the parent's voice. Eye contact is harder to establish here because of the non-turning to the face. Introducing sign language early is therefore useful;
- if the child has severe learning difficulties and needs many experiences of the person before bonding can become stable.

Bowlby's work was important because it led to children in institutions being given key workers. This meant that they no longer had a series of different nurses looking after them as each work shift changed. Children were placed in smaller family groups and were looked after by the same team of staff. Furthermore, more children began to be fostered in family homes rather than placed in large institutions. This helped children to form good attachments with people because they were now cared for by only a few people; and people, moreover, who could develop warm, physical loving relationships, and communicate with them.

SEPARATION

By 5 or 6 months, many babies are so closely attached that they show **separation anxiety** when they are taken away from their attachment figures (the people they know and love). When a baby is handed from the parent to a new carer, it is best if:

- the person approaches slowly;
- the person talks gently before picking up and taking the baby from the parent;
- the baby is held looking at the parent during the hand-over (see stranger fear on p. 187) – the baby will want to look at the father or mother.

Researchers have found that toddlers will happily explore toys and play with them if their attachment figure (usually their parent) is present. If, however, the parent goes out of the room, they quickly become anxious and stop exploring or playing. They need the reassurance of someone they know, or they cannot explore and play.

Children who have had to deal with many separations from those they have tried to bond with find it very difficult to understand social situations and relationships. This extract is as reported in *Dagens Nyheter*, a Stockholm newspaper, in 1990.

'The 13th Century Historian Sallimbeni of Parma, Italy, reports that Emperor Fredrik II of the Holy Roman Empire conducted an experiment to find out man's original language. He gathered a number of babies and employed wet nurses to care physically for the children, but they were strictly forbidden to talk, cuddle or sing to the babies.

By not having any human contact, these children were supposed to develop as naturally as possible. The Emperor never found out about man's original language – the children died one after another without any apparent reason.'   *(Dagens Nyheter 1990)*

These babies may have died because they were not able to learn about the important signals that people give to each other when they are together.

When their babyhood and toddler requests and social signals for help and attention are ignored, children become frustrated and do not know how to ask for help or attention, or indeed how to *give* help in the usual ways. They do not understand the things that adults and other children expect and find usual when they get together in a group. It is not helpful to concentrate on what children in this kind of difficulty *cannot* do. It is helpful to begin with what they *can* do.

If they are over-demanding, it means that they want to relate to adults. You can help them to learn to do this positively. Give them the words they need: 'I need some help', or 'Help me'. Adults can help children to understand social rules: 'If you stamp your feet and cry, I can't help you. I need to know the problem. Can you show me the problem? Can you see my face? It is easier for us to listen to each other if I look at your face? You look unhappy. How can I help?'

Help the children to make sense of what you want them to do. Most of all, help the child to see you as someone who *wants* to help, who does not nag, who is warm and encouraging, and who does not keep trying to stop what the child is doing by saying 'no' all the time. Look at what the child is doing, and find things in the room and outdoors that you think make a good fit with the child's interests and mood. Children who are constantly frustrated in what they try to do become angry children. Angry children are very challenging to work with.

BOWLBY'S THEORY OF LOSS AND GRIEF

There was a famous series of films by James and Joyce Robertson which showed Bowlby's theory in action. Children separated from their families in hospital went through various stages in their loss and grief:

1 They protested. They were angry and cried out and tried to resist the change.
2 They despaired about what was happening. They acted as if they were numb to any feelings or interest in life.
3 They became detached in the way they related to people, although they began to join in with their new situation.

We know that children (and adults) move in and out of these stages, which do not occur in any strict order. Bowlby's work has led to important work on how best to deal with the hospitalisation of children. It also helped early childhood workers to settle children into nurseries more positively (see pp. 145-159). And it also led to an organisation being set up to help parents understand why their children are so detached in their relationships after being sent to boarding preparatory schools at 6 or 7 years of age.

Early childhood workers – as already mentioned – can be an important influence in helping children to develop positive, warm and well-attached relationships to others. This is especially important for children who have not yet learnt about these aspects of being with other people. It is never too late for attachments to develop, but the earlier they do, the sooner the quality of the child's life and relationships with other people develop positively.

GRIEF

When someone whom a child loves is no longer with them, it may seem to the child that the person has died. This can happen when a family experiences:

▶ a mother leaving home and going to hospital to have a new baby;
▶ divorce – when one parent no longer sees the child;
▶ a parent being in hospital and unable to see the child, for example after a serious accident;
▶ a loved one who has been sent to prison;
▶ a loved one who goes abroad;
▶ the death of a loved one.

The process of **grieving** then has to be worked through, and this takes time – usually several years.

Grief involves:

▶ feeling disbelief, numbness, shock, panic;

▶ despair and anger and yearning for the lost person;

▶ more interest in life again eventually – but this takes time.

THE CHILD'S CONCEPT OF DEATH

Sometimes, people say different things when someone dies. For example, they tell the child that grandma has gone to heaven, or that grandma has gone to sleep, or has gone away, or has turned into earth. Children can be very confused. They might become frightened that they themselves will be taken away to this place called heaven, or that when they sleep they might not wake up. Children need honest, straightforward explanations of death that make it clear the person will not come back.

G U I D E L I N E S

How you can help the child to grieve

▶ **Explain things – especially if someone is terminally ill, or is divorcing, or is going to prison. Children need to be told of the reality of the situation.**

▶ **Make sure the child does not feel that what has happened is their fault.**

▶ **Don't exclude the child – let the child be part of the family. Let the child go to the funeral, the rituals for which will vary according to the cultural traditions and religious beliefs of the family. Let the child visit the grave and share the sadness.**

▶ **Be especially warm and loving – cuddle the child, be calm and quietly there for them.**

▶ **Give the child reassurance that it is right to feel this way – help the child to know that although these feelings will last for a long time, they are normal, and that the pain will ease over time.**

▶ **Find photographs, and evoke memories.**

▶ **Some children are helped by play therapy.**

▶ **Be prepared for the child to regress – don't demand too much of the child. When the child begins to show an interest in things once more, gently encourage this.**

▶ **Children need to grieve, just as adults do, and if they are not helped to do this, they may experience mental ill health later on in adult life. If they *are* helped, however, they will take up positive relationships with other people and come to terms with their loss in a positive way.**

HOW BOWLBY HAS HELPED EARLY CHILDHOOD WORKERS TO THINK ABOUT ATTACHMENT, SEPARATION AND LOSS

▶ Babies and mothers now usually stay together on maternity wards.

▶ Parents can usually stay in hospital with their children: there are beds for the parent next to their child's bed.

▶ Social workers are more careful about separating children and parents when families experience difficulties.

▶ Most early childhood settings now have policies on how to settle children so as to make it a positive experience (see Chapter 5).

The social constructivist theory of emotional and social development

Modern research is beginning to see how adults and children relate to each other in a two-way process.

From a very early age, babies and children actively:

▶ choose who they want to be with and do things with;

▶ have an influence on the way their family, carers and friends behave towards them – as well as the other way round;

▶ develop social and emotional relationships which involve a two-way process right from the start of their life.

This means that children are not passively 'shaped' or 'regulated' to do what adults want. Some adults find it hard to understand or accept that even a young baby can have preferences for particular people, or can 'call' adults to them and get them to do the things that they want.

In fact, from the start of their lives, young children give and take and contribute in relationships just as adults do:

▶ Sometimes they need other adults or children.

▶ Sometimes they follow what other people do.

▶ Sometimes they negotiate with other people.

JUDY DUNN

Judy Dunn has studied family social life in the Cambridge area for a number of years. She believes that the social and moral development of children is closely linked with their family relationships. In the first year of life, babies begin to notice and be sensitive to the actions of people in their family. She calls this **affective tuning**. It is sometimes also called social referencing.

From 1 to 3 years, children show **self-concern**. They need to:

▶ get the attention of others;

▶ understand what other people feel and say;

▶ comfort someone in distress.

If they do these things, they can get what they want and need for themselves.

Children also begin to work out what is *allowed*. They begin to understand what will meet with disapproval from other people, and how other people will respond either to the way they express their feelings or to what they do.

Young children are curious about other people, and they discover what happens when they try to:

▶ hurt other people;

▶ help other people;

▶ show care for other people.

The concern that children have for themselves leads them to the needs of other people. In order to feel that they are getting fair treatment, children have to find out if they are being treated in the same way as the other children.

Children learn about these things through their family relationships. Before they can talk and discuss these events, they also, however, learn through *situations*. They learn about situations which make them angry, for example. Being angry makes people react to the child; and children also learn what makes other people angry! Through their relationship with people in their families, they also, on the other hand, learn how to care and to be considerate, kind and helpful. These are the basic things needed for moral development.

Unlike the behaviourist, social learning theory or socialisation approach, the social constructivist approach believes that children learn more through experimenting in social situations than just through copying what other people do. Children experiment in social situations:

▶ when they do things that other people don't allow or don't approve of;
▶ when people confront or tease each other;
▶ when people share fun together;
▶ when playing with other children;
▶ through conversations in which people discuss things.

Every culture in every early childhood setting has different relationships in it. Learning how to ask for things means that children are learning how things get done in their particular family, in their particular early childhood setting and in their particular culture.

Social constructivist theory says that it is the way people *interact* together that is important for social development. Children learn as much from confrontation and angry exchanges as they do from having fun with other people. Social development is a two-way process. Adults such as early childhood workers are therefore very important influences in the social constructivist approach. The way children are helped to believe in themselves helps them in turn to develop positive relationships with other people.

It is important that adults help children to *negotiate* with other people rather than to *manipulate* other people.

MANIPULATING

When adults manipulate children through bribes – 'If you do the clearing up quickly, you can have the first go on the swings when we get to the park' – this cuts across the child's developing self-discipline and moral development.

NEGOTIATION

When adults negotiate with children, adults and children *respect* each other, and try to find the best solution together in a spirit of being partners. For example, the adult might say to the child 'I know that you want to go to the shops, but we haven't cleared the toy cars away into the box yet. It will leave a mess behind that won't be very nice for the other children. Some of the toys might get broken. I think we need to clear up before we go. Do you want to do that while I get the coats ready, or shall we clear up together and get the coats afterwards?' Given a choice which is simple and clear, the child usually negotiates a solution that is positive.

Remember, the way that children are helped to negotiate will help both their social and their emotional development and this in turn will affect their moral development.

Social evolution theory and the development of social behaviour in cultures across the world

Throughout this book, it has been stressed that modern researchers think about two different strands in development:

1 the biological path of development;
2 the cultural path of development.

The physical aspects of development are mainly biological. The emotional and social aspects of development, on the other hand, are more influenced by the cultural path of development. The latter is very open to change, and is constantly modified.

Human beings are social animals. This means that when they work together, people can jointly solve all sorts of problems which would be much too hard for one person to manage alone. The same is true of children. For example, moving a truck that is stuck in the mud in the garden is difficult for one 4-year-old on their own, but a group of children aged 4–6 years old working together may well solve the problem.

- The children need to hold in mind others' ideas as well as their own, and this is quite difficult to do.
- The children will have to be able to think in quite an abstract way to manage this (abstract means removed from here and now and all in the mind).
- All this takes much more brain power. It means thinking deeply.
- Each child will have to control their feelings. This is very hard for young children to do, but it is very important that they do so if the group is to work well together.
- The children will be helped if they can use words or signs by which to communicate. New knowledge can then be handed on to other people: 'I know a good way to move a truck,' shouts Lee to Jo who was not there when it was discovered.

Once humans began to walk about on two legs instead of four, their hands became free. They began to make and use tools. They worked together when finding food (foraging and hunting) and defending themselves as a group from enemies. Social cooperation has evolved because it makes people successful in managing new and difficult situations.

All this means that humans have developed larger brains. This is so that social and cultural learning can be handed down to other people. This factor is very important if people are going to survive on this planet. It helps people to deal with things which are uncertain in life, and to cope with lives which are full of changes.

Ever since the Neanderthals used tools, social development has involved the development of cultural tools which help group thinking

Cultural tools and social evolution

Cultural tools help shared thinking. They help the exchange of ideas and information between people, by means of:

- a number system and languages;
- the sharing of plans together;
- social rules, for example about sitting down for a meal together;
- tools which are used in technology and science.

Richard Dawkins, the biologist, calls this the **social evolution approach**. He believes that social learning is a shared process. At first, a baby uses a spoon (which is a cultural tool) in their own way. Once the baby has got used to the spoon, the adult might help to shove some food on it. The baby then tries to do this. The baby's behaviour is partly influenced by being given the spoon in the first place. The baby might use the spoon in a new and interesting way. For example, they might balance a pea on the upturned spoon and take it into the mouth that way. The baby is thus giving an idea about how to use a spoon as well as taking ideas from the way the adult knows how to use the spoon.

Open societies and closed societies

In some cultures new ideas are more acceptable than in others. These societies are called **open societies** rather than **closed societies**. Every culture develops particular ways of doing things. These involve **customs** and **rituals** which are
handed down and give a sense of continuity with the past. The laws of the society and rules of different institutions show both the values themselves and how they are put into practice. Cultures which are rich in ideas about:

▶ the expressive arts – exciting dance groups, music events, drama performances – and

▶ the sciences – with original researchers and ideas in abundance

are usually the result of the culture *valuing* these activities and helping groups by providing the cultural tools they need to help these things blossom.

It is only humans, with their cultural tools, who have achieved these things. People hand ideas on to each other, and they also make new ideas together. People are very influenced by the culture in which they grow up. But each person might also influence that culture. In the same way, each child is influenced by the people and cultural tools in the early childhood setting but just as surely each child also influences the people and cultural tools that they find.

R E S O U R C E S

Books

P. Barnes (ed), *Personal, Social and Emotional Development of Children,* Oxford, Open University/Blackwell, 1995

Judy Dunn, *The Beginnings of Social Understanding,* Oxford, Blackwell, 1988

Maureen O'Hagan and Maureen Smith, *Special Issues in Child Care,* London, Bailliere, Tindall, 1993

Roberts, R., *Self-esteem and Successful Early Learning,* London, Hodder & Stoughton, 1995

Whalley, M. *Learning to be Strong: Integrating Education and Care in Early Childhood.* London: Hodder & Stoughton, 1994

Video

BBC Education/NCB is a project which has developed a video and book, audio cassette and pocket book called *Tuning into Children.* Available from:
Tuning into Children
P.O. Box 20
Tonbridge
Kent
TN12 6WU

A C T I V I T Y

Investigating emotional and social aspects of development

1 **Think about getting up in the morning. Choose a cultural tool – your alarm clock or telephone, or a spoon – and discuss with a friend how you think it has influenced your behaviour in your culture, and how you in turn have influenced the culture you live in through using the cultural tool.**

2 **Plan ways to find out about the friendships young children develop. Observe a group of 3- and 4-year-olds playing together. Who is friends with who? Look again a few weeks later at the same children. Are they still friends? Evaluate your observations.**

3 **Research the role of a key worker or family worker. Make a list of pros and cons. Discuss this with the group.**

4 Find some of the books listed in this chapter which look at children's feelings and help them to express them. Make a book which helps a child to develop a concept of death, or of the birth of a sibling. Evaluate it.

5 What are three important things about theories which support:
   (a) nurture
   (b) nature
   (c) nature and nurture?

6 Observe a child of 3–5 years old. Choose one of the following books and read it to them. Concentrate on the child's feelings. Evaluate your observations and the book you chose.
   ▶ Ruth Brown, *Copycat*, Andersen Press;
   ▶ Marilyn Talbot, *Shy Roland*, Andersen Press;
   ▶ Selina Young, *Whistling in the Woods*, Heinemann;
   ▶ Catherine and Laurence Anholt, *What Makes Me Happy*, Walker Books;
   ▶ Anni Axworthy, *Along Came Toto*, Walker Books;
   ▶ Sue Lewis, *Come Back Grandma*, Red Fox;
   ▶ Susan Varley, *Badgers' Parting Gifts*, Collins Picture Lions;
   ▶ Catherine Robinson, *Leaving Mrs Ellis*, Bodley Head;
   ▶ Sue Cowlishaw, *When My little sister Died*, Merlin Books;
   ▶ Bryan Mellonse and Robert Ingpen, *Lifetimes*, Hill of Content (Australia, 1983)
   ▶ John Burningham, *Granpa*, Jonathan Cape.

8

The Child as a Symbol-User: Representation, Communication and Language Development

Language development as one kind of symbolic behaviour

It is not possible to look at language development without looking at the rich variety of **symbols** that human beings use. It is important before studying the development of language in young children to know a little bit about what symbolic behaviour is.

What are symbols? Symbols are a way of making one thing stand for another, for example a drawing of mother or saying the word 'Mum'. She does not have to be there: these symbols, the drawing or the word, will *stand for her* when she is not there.

Do animals use symbols, or is it only humans who are symbol users? This has been discussed for centuries. Until recently it was argued that humans were superior to other animals. Nowadays, there are many people who prefer to look at similarities and differences between other animals and humans. One similarity, for example, is that animals such as chimpanzees, gorillas and orang-utans do also seem to use symbolic systems. This means that all these animals can make one thing stand for another. There was a famous example in Washoe the chimpanzee in the 1960s. She was taught American sign language by her researchers, the Gardners, and she knew the sign for water and bird. One day, she saw a duck fly over a pond. She did not know the sign for a duck, but without any prompting, she signed 'water bird'.

This is what children do as they learn to share the language of their culture. Washoe was a symbol-user. She was just like human children. However, it does seem that humans can go further and deeper in their ability to make something stand for something else. For a start, humans have a *larynx*, so they can talk. In addition, they can:

- ▶ draw and paint;
- ▶ write;
- ▶ make dances;
- ▶ make music;
- ▶ make sculptures;
- ▶ do scientific thinking;
- ▶ use mathematical notations, such as those for numbers, geometry and algebra.

There is a huge variety in the kinds of symbol that human children begin to use amazingly early, and the symbolic layers involved keep on accumulating throughout life as the culture is actively taken in and used by the child growing up. Indeed, we never finish adding symbolic layers as long as we live.

Layers of symbols

Since Piaget began his pioneering work in the 1930s, researchers have been finding deeper and deeper layers in the symbolic behaviour of people. More is now known about how children begin to become symbol-users. The psychologist Howard Gardner (see Chapter 6) believes that we have multiple intelligences which help us to use a wide range of different kinds of symbol.

Symbolic behaviour is about making one thing stand for another, and it involves beginning to think about:

- ▶ the past
- ▶ the present
- ▶ the future.

Representation

Representation means keeping hold of an experience by bringing it back to the mind and making it into some kind of product. For example, Sharon, 4 years of age, ate an ice-cream on a hot day, and it melted and dripped down her hand. Later she did a painting. She chose white paint, and made it run all over the paper. She then said, 'It's my ice-cream.' Sharon was keeping hold of her experience with a dripping ice-cream by representing it in a painting.

TIME TO CHOOSE

If you do not want to study the different kinds of early representation in the next section, it is not necessary for you to do so. Studying is a kind of travelling. Some people when they travel like to go directly to their destination. Other people like to go down little country lanes and stop off along the way and explore things. This takes longer, but they enjoy the journey just as much. What about you? If you want to go direct, turn to page 223. If you want to explore and find out more about 'representation in young children', then read this next section.

1 KEEPING HOLD OF EXPERIENCES – PROCEDURAL REPRESENTATIONS (TYPICALLY AT 5 MONTHS)

Babies can, researchers believe:

▶ remember
▶ make images;
▶ anticipate;
▶ conceptualise people and objects that are not present.

Babies are beginning to manage to 'keep hold' of experiences, which is what representation is about. The next step will be for the babies to begin to share their highly personal ways of doing this.

2 DECLARING IS SHARING – DECLARATIVE REPRESENTATIONS (TYPICALLY AT 9 MONTHS)

Babies begin to be able to share their representations of things with other people. In fact, they want to share very much. They seem to have a deep need to do things with other people. Shared symbols are only possible with those who are close to the child because they are very unique to each particular child.

Gestures, naming and pointing begin. Naming is likely to be very idiosyncratic – the child might say 'hee haw' when they see a horse. A baby at 9 months will often wave 'bye bye' after a person has gone. When babies do this, it is cause to celebrate, and perhaps to say to the baby 'Yes, you are right, Jill has gone, hasn't she, and we said bye bye to her.' Here the baby is using a gesture to 'represent' saying that Jill has gone. It is very important to notice that these **declarative representations** are about people just as much as they are about objects. People are very important to babies and young children.

Gestures are not the only kind of declarative representation that children use. Gradually, other kinds of representation become possible. A child begins to be able to *draw* or *paint* a person waving bye bye. A child could make a model of someone waving bye bye. A child might do a dance about waving bye bye. A child might make music, singing 'bye bye'. A child might write about saying bye bye to Jill. There are many ways indeed that children begin to keep hold of their experiences and to represent them.

From 1 year to 8 years of age, there is amazing development in the way that children begin to represent their experiences and share symbolic behaviour with other people. The children now begin adding cultural layers to what they know about symbols.

The most important thing to remember about representing experiences is that children cannot represent an experience they have not had! Some other important things to bear in mind are:

▶ Children need real and first-hand experiences.
▶ Children need to *actively* experience things.
▶ Children need to feel ownership of the experiences they have: it is difficult for them to think deeply if their ideas are controlled by other people all the time.
▶ Children need to be encouraged to think back or think forward about experiences they have had or are looking forward to.

A teacher of a class of 5-year-olds asked the children to paint pictures of people skiing. There was a problem: none of the children in the class had been skiing! This meant that they had no experience of skiing and so could neither think back to when they skied nor think forward to when they would ski again. It was not included in their own experience of life. Very young children simply have not enough experiences of their own to be able to:

▶ think what it is like to experience something as if they were someone else;
▶ understand an experience from someone else's point of view. This, as we have seen, is called being able to *decentre*.

Instead, they need help in finding ways of keeping hold of their *own* experiences, not those of other people. This means that tracing someone else's outline, or filling in or colouring in someone else's outline with tissue paper or coloured pencils, or drawing round a template, are low-level activities because they have nothing to do with the children representing their own experience in their *own* way.

In order to help children represent their own experiences and ideas and to share these
▶ with themselves,
▶ with those who are close to them,
▶ with a wider audience,

it is important – as mentioned above – to give children first-hand real experiences in which they can take an active part. Take, for example, a walk to the shops with lots of chatting and lots of stops to look at things. Children might see a dog, or they might help to buy things, to give the money to the shopkeeper, to carry the bags. Then they might go back and help to do cooking. After doing the cooking, the staff might set up an interest table to remind the children about the cooking they have done. Books and some of the utensils might be put on the table. Children might want to do cooking again the following day.

There might also be the possibility for children to represent some of these experiences, but only if they choose to do this. They might want to make a model of the dog. They might want to make a model of the things they have cooked. They might want to act out the way somebody walked down the street. There are many different ways the children might represent the walk to the shops, and there are many different aspects of it that they might particularly have enjoyed and therefore chosen to represent.

MAKING MARKS ON PAPER (GRAPHICS)

Watch out for the marks that children make: they are **cross-cultural**. Children use them quite naturally and without needing to be taught. Remember that children will first use these marks separately, as shown in Figure 8.1. Later on, they will begin to use them in a combination, that is they can *coordinate* them (see Figure 8.2).

Remember, if you ask children to copy these shapes, they will not 'own' them. They will be doing it for you as an adult-led task, but it will not here be their own representation of their own experience which they have chosen to do. It is easy to make children copy. It is not so easy to help children express their own ideas, feelings and relationships with others on paper.

FIGURE 8.1

Elementary cross-cultural marks are made by children

FIGURE 8.2
Combinations of cross-cultural marks

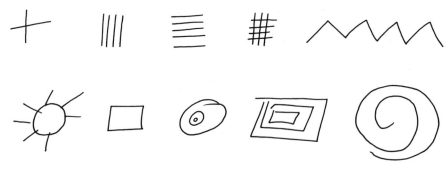

Many children grow up leaving behind these early personal ways of representing their experiences of life. As they grow older, they begin only to use the conventional symbols and ways of representing which are specific to their culture. When this happens, the creative side of the child goes, and learnt formulas take its place. This is why it is very important to keep representation alive, alongside introducing children to the conventions of shared and agreed ways of writing and other ways of representing. Creative, imaginative children *keep* their personal representations and symbols, but can also use the conventional symbols of their culture. Creative children thus have both highly individual and conventional symbols.

Language and communication

From the beginning, babies seem to want to communicate with other people. (Babies with a disability may have difficulty in this, or their parents may find it hard to 'read' the baby's communication signals.) Babies love to share experiences with people, and communication is a huge part of the way that people relate to each other.

Communication involves:

▶ facial expressions (a smile, frown, raised eyebrows) and eye contact;
▶ gesture and body language (hugs, beckoning, clapping hands and applause, a shrug, jumping with surprise, being stiff and ill at ease). This varies according to the culture.
▶ verbal or sign language. This could be a very limited kind of communication, through a personal language that is only understood by those who are very close to the babies, for example always saying 'bubba' for all children and young animals. Babies, toddlers and some children with educational needs, for instance children with severe learning difficulties – will use personal communication systems which are known and understood by those who live with and care for them.

Communicating through a verbal or sign language

Language usually means verbal talking and listening. However, talking and listening can also be done through signs (e.g. British Sign Language) which is now an officially recognised language.

Language of all kinds uses agreed codes which develop according to the cultures in which they arise. They suit that culture, and they are an expression of its important ideas and values.

FIGURE 8.3
The common forms children use universally to make their personal and idiosyncratic representations

Source: *The Crucial Years*, Ed. Daphne Plastow.

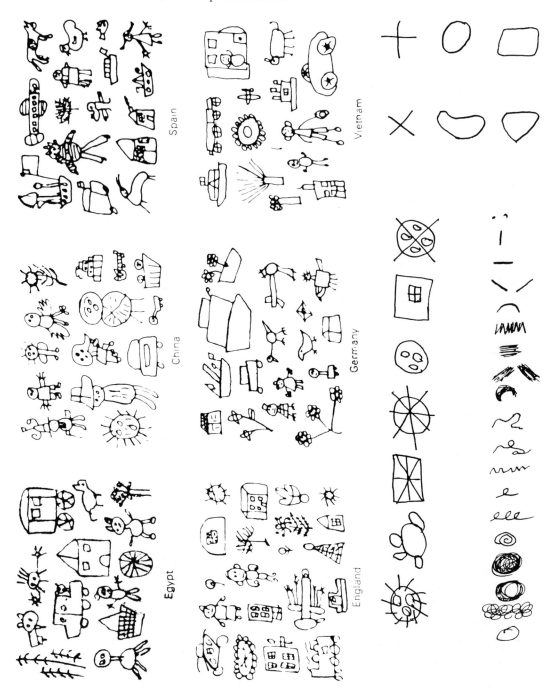

The rhythms, tone and melody of language (its musical aspects) are each of great importance as language develops. So are the gestures and movements, especially of the face and hands, as recent studies in neuroscience show. The brain develops music, movement and language together. If spoken language is not possible (perhaps the child is deaf) the brain develops the movement side more extensively (sign language).

FIGURE 8.4 (a)
Different ways of representing with dance, music, science, maths and writing

Pamela is dancing

by Tarik

FIGURE 8.4 (b)
Different ways of representing with models, drawing and painting

Language adds another layer to communication because:

▶ it helps people to communicate with themselves: children (and adults!) often talk out loud to themselves. Children begin to internalise speech more and more until they can *think* of what they are saying rather than saying it out loud.

▶ it can be spoken or signed;

▶ it helps people to move from here and now into the past or the future;

▶ it helps people to use symbolic behaviour;

▶ it helps people to put into words ideas (concepts) and imaginative thoughts;

▶ it helps people to express feelings.

There are many links here with Chapter 6.

Language involves:

▶ listening or watching and understanding (**reception of language**);

▶ communicating, which involves facial expressions, gestures and verbal or sign speech (**expression of language**).

LANGUAGE AND GRAMMAR

Every language has its own kind of grammar. Some languages put the verb at the end of a sentence, for example British Sign Language, which is rather like Latin in this way. The grammar of a language involves the rules that make it work. To specify the rules of grammar is not to specify that this is how people *ought* to speak. It is simply a way of describing how a language works. The grammar of a language will typically include:

▶ **verbs** (doing words) – 'I am going home';

▶ **nouns**, which might involve either a *subject* – 'The *cat* is asleep in the chair' – or an *object* – 'The cat is asleep in the *chair*';

▶ **adjectives** (words which describe nouns) – 'The baby likes the *red* rattle best';

▶ **adverbs** (words which describe verbs) – 'The baby *quickly* grabs the red rattle';

▶ **pronouns**, such as 'they', 'you', 'he', or 'she', as well as a personal pronoun, 'I' or 'me';

▶ **apostrophes** (indicate possession) – 'the *child's* rattle' (the rattle that belongs to the child).

These are some of the rules which describe how the English language works.

Sometimes, it is very difficult for some children – those who may have a hearing impairment, severe learning difficulties, moderate learning difficulties, or physical challenges such as cerebral palsy – to talk or listen. Not being able to talk or listen easily can often bring frustration, loneliness and a feeling of powerlessness. It is therefore very important that every child be encouraged to find ways of communicating with other people.

Research on the brain is now suggesting that when people speak, they do not use 'rules' of grammar at all. When a sound is heard, it fires certain neurons and *impedes* the firing of others, and gradually, as the sound is heard over and over again, a neural pathway is forged and a language pattern forms. This is part of the **connectionist** theory of how language develops.

The language involved here does not have to be a *verbal* language, and a considerable minority of children are now taught to use sign languages or personal references – perhaps Makaton or British Sign Language – involving:

▶ gestures or touch;

▶ agreed shared signs;

▶ finger spelling, computers and keyboards.

A minority will not use shared signs which are understood by others. They will continue to use personal communication signs which only those close to them will understand. Most children, but not all, will gradually move into the world of shared language, and will learn to speak in a verbal language.

It is important to remember that any child – and adult too – finds it difficult to express their feelings and thoughts when:

▶ they are put under pressure to speak;
▶ they are under stress for any reason (such as a child who has been hit by another child).

Children should not be put in a position where they feel uncomfortable about talking – for example in large groups – or where they are rushed by adults who do not take time to listen to what they are trying to say; children need adults to take time to listen to them.

Language and literacy

Researchers believe that people are capable of more and more complex symbolic layers in what they do. Language is only one kind of symbolic behaviour, and it accumulates more symbolic layers when it moves into writing and reading (there is more about this in Chapter 13 on the curriculum – see pp. 353–360). This is called **literacy**.

WRITING

Writing means that the person has to put language into a **code**.

READING

Reading means that the person then has to **decode** what is written. Young children use *pictures* in books as an extra help when they try to decode what is written.

Reading and writing move along together in the development of language, which involves listening and being listened to, talking and being talked to. Some psychologists think that children are rather like scientists trying to discover things: they seem to try to find out how language systems work in the culture in which they are growing up.

Not being able to read or write (**illiteracy**) is a serious disadvantage in many cultures. However, not all cultures use the written word. The Celtic culture is a very **oral** culture. This is why Celtic songs and dances have lasted so well: they are handed down orally. The same is true with the Celtic story-telling traditions. The Maori culture in New Zealand also has an oral tradition.

In the USA, the UK and Holland, about 15% of adults are illiterate. In Denmark, almost no adults are illiterate. In the USA, the UK and Holland, children are often expected to start using shared conventional ways of writing and to read from 4 years of age, which is exceptionally early compared with most countries in the world. In Denmark, children are read to by adults but they do not begin the formal teaching of reading or writing until the children are 7 years old. What do you think about this? Is earlier best? Are long-term results more important than short-term successes?

What is language?

It is:

▶ **phonology:** the sounds of the language (or visual aspects if a sign language is used);
▶ **intonation:** sounds going up and down;
▶ **vocabulary:** the words;
▶ **grammar:** (sometimes called *syntax*): the word order, and rules which describe how a language works (but not how we ought to speak);

▶ **semantics:** *meanings* of the language;

▶ **communication:** with self and others;

▶ **arbitrary symbols:** which refer to the past, and which help speakers to learn from the past, imagine the future, make jokes, tell lies or have fantasies;

▶ **conversations:** these require a sense of **audience** – i.e. of who you are talking (and listening) to;

▶ **articulation:** how words are spoken in order to be understood.

Different theories about language development

These include:

▶ vocabulary-building (see below);

▶ the normative approach – Gesell in the 1930s–1960s;

▶ behaviourist theory (the nurture approach) – Skinner in the 1920s–1960s;

▶ the theory that language development is innate and genetically predetermined (the nature theory – see Chapter 6) – Chomsky in the 1960s;

▶ social constructivist theory (nature and nurture are both important here – see Chapter 6) – Piaget, Vygotsky and Bruner.

VOCABULARY-BUILDING

Children learn words, then phrases, then sentences, and build up a wide vocabulary. The baby's babble is seized upon by adults and encouraged: 'They're saying "mumma".' This theory suggests that children learn to talk after they are born and through imitating the sounds that they hear. Children are born with a predisposition to learn, talk and listen. This ability, possessed by human beings, is called a **language acquisition device** (LAD). Children learn to talk partly because they are born genetically equipped to do so, and partly through the people they meet and communicate and socialise with.

NORMATIVE ACCOUNTS OF LANGUAGE DEVELOPMENT – WHAT MOST CHILDREN DO

Until the 1960s, experts studied the development of language and young children mainly by using vocabulary counts (e.g. Gessell). They counted the number and types of words that children used. They looked at whether children used single words, phrases and different types of sentence. This tended to stress what children could do at *particular ages*, and could be very misleading. However, it is important that those working with young children know about the general pattern in which all languages develop. The section 'What is language?' on p. 229 above is useful to bear in mind. It helps those working with young children to remember that there is more to language development than mere vocabulary-building.

THE LANGUAGE DEVELOPMENT REVOLUTION OF THE 1960S

An exciting revolution occurred when the behaviourist view that children learn language entirely by imitating was challenged in 1968. Chomsky showed that children can invent new sentences which they had definitely not heard before. He believed children are born ready to learn whatever languages they hear around them. He believed they did this through what he called a language acquisition device (LAD) – as mentioned above.

Researchers studied the mistakes or errors that children make when they talk. They found that these gave important clues about the innate language rules that children all over the world seemed to be born with. This was also true for children using sign languages rather than spoken languages.

THE SOCIAL CONTEXT OF LANGUAGE DEVELOPMENT

It became apparent in the 1960s and 1970s that some children were not as developed in language as others. It was thought then that children from working-class homes were disadvantaged because they used what the researcher Bernstein called a **restricted language code**. He thought this held them back in school. This code contrasted with children from middle-class backgrounds who Bernstein thought used an **elaborated language code**, and he thought that this was why they achieved more in school. As a result, in both the UK and the USA, compensatory educational programmes were launched which tried to enrich the language environment of so-called disadvantaged children in school.

In fact, it is much more likely that because staff in schools often come from different cultures and backgrounds to the children they work with, they do not always understand the child's own particular language and culture. Staff therefore work better with children if:

- they value and respect the child's language and culture, and try to learn about it;
- they have real everyday conversations with children using gestures, eye contact, props and spoken language;
- they encourage children to enjoy and listen to stories and introduce children to what is sometimes called 'book language' – 'Once upon a time, far, far away...'.

This helps children to begin to take a full part in school life, whatever their language or culture.

It is now thought that the positive relationships and communications between people who respect each other is one of the most important factors in language development and in the development of the child's thinking. To be part of a culture is a need human beings are born with, and there is a wide variation in the way that children begin to:

- understand
- communicate
- represent and express things through new language.

This depends on the culture in which the child grows up as much as on the child's biological and genetic development.

Children need a supportive language environment. A child whose first language is not English may need plenty of gestures and actions when learning (action songs, cooking, for example) in order to understand, and to be understood by, those speaking in a different language. Chapter 1 on equality of opportunities gives details about ways of supporting and extending the language development of bilingual and multilingual children, and it also helps us to think about children who do not use verbal ways of communicating. It is essential for anyone working with young children to understand the importance of the child's first language. The chapter on equal opportunities should therefore be read before continuing with this chapter.

Language delay

A child who has, for example, a hearing impairment or Asperger's syndrome or is autistic may be constrained in understanding and using language (i.e. in the *reception* and *expression* of language). (Definition of the term **autistic** can be found on pp. 459.) Speech therapists and specialist teachers and other professional help may be needed in supporting the language development of these children. All children need to mix with other children and adults who speak fluently so that they can hear the patterns of the language they are trying to learn.

If, however, they are always with other people who are also learning a new language, then they do not hear the correct patterns of the language in question, and this means that they then might learn incorrect grammar patterns. It also means that they may have to unlearn some of the things they learn later on. Hearing other people speak fluently means experiencing what is called **comprehensible output**.

Children who do not speak

It does not help if children are *made* to speak. It does help if they are invited to speak but are able to turn down the invitation without being made to feel bad or a failure. It is very important to check that a child can still see and even hear if they never say anything. It is also very important to be sure that the child *understands* what is being said.

It is important to monitor the child through your observations. Children under emotional stress sometimes become withdrawn. Share your observations with your line manager. Other children can also be a great help in explaining things meaningfully to a child. Stories and rhymes need props if they are being told, or pictures if they are read (see again Chapter 1 on equal opportunities).

Language and action

From the beginning, when adults begin to talk to babies, they talk about things that are happening all around them. They use a high-pitched voice and speak slowly, and they use a lot of repetition. This is called 'Motherese' – 'Whose ringing that doorbell then?'. Adults will pause, waiting for the baby to 'reply' using babble. This does not occur in every culture. For example, in some cultures adults do not speak in Motherese to babies, but instead the babies watch their mothers working and talking with other adults.

Language needs to accompany action. For instance, the adult lifts the baby and says 'Up we go. Let's put you in the pram now', and it is important that adults *continue* to describe to their babies what is happening when they become young children – 'You've got to the top of the slide, haven't you! Are you going to come down now?' Children need **comprehensible input** in order to understand what is said to them (see again Chapter 1 on equal opportunities). Actions help children to understand what is being said to them. They give them more clues.

Language and thought/cognition

Remember that all areas of a child's development are interrelated, and language and thought are often considered to be particularly closely linked, Can we think *without* words? Some psychologists have suggested that thinking is not possible without language. Language is important for abstract thinking. This means that it would be difficult to understand the idea, for example, of what is fair or honest unless a child had enough language. However, Piaget emphasised that children learn to think through a variety of different ways of symbolically representing their experiences, ideas, feelings and relationships. Indeed, he thought that language is only one kind of symbolic mode that people use to do this. Piaget's work has been very positive in helping those working with children with language delay or impairment, and with all children who do not begin to use coded or shared language systems, because he stressed personal and individual ways through which children can communicate as well as the later arbitrary symbols used in language:

- ▶ Gestures are one kind of personal communication.
- ▶ Props can be another form of personal communication – the handbag represents mother when she goes for coffee, and the child knows she is coming back because her handbag is there.

► The footprint in the sand tells the child someone was there.
► The child has a teddy bear while the mother is away. This gives the child a link with mother while she is away. The communication is personal between this particular child and this particular mother.

THINKING ABOUT THINKING, AND THINKING ABOUT LANGUAGE

Cognition means thinking and having ideas (concepts). **Metacognition** means children begin to think about their own thinking. They reflect on their own ideas, such as 'that was a good idea', 'that was a bad idea'.

Metalinguisitics means children beginning to think about what they say. By 4 years of age, children usually make jokes and 'play' with words, making nonsense words for fun.

Language and feelings

Children are in difficulty when they are not able to put their feelings into words or express them in any way: this has a damaging impact on the development of self-esteem. If they are full of anger, anxiety, frustration or fear, they need to express this. Talking about feelings is just as important as talking about ideas. Children who cannot express their feelings often have temper tantrums or show other kinds of challenging behaviour. In fact, it is easier to help children to put their ideas into words than it is to help them to express their feelings (emotions) in words.

Language and communication

TALKING TO YOURSELF

Children talk to themselves when they:
► need to think through different ideas;
► are feeling frustrated;
► need to talk about their feelings;
► need to organise their thinking;
► regulate what they do (i.e. tell themselves what to do.)

Textbooks often say that this 'egocentric' speech fades when children begin to internalise their thinking more easily. However, many adults too talk to themselves when they think things over: 'I wish I had that ... .' When looking at language development, egocentric does not mean selfish, it means not being able to imagine how it feels to be someone else. A young child thinks from their own point of view, but this is not selfish.

CONVERSATIONS WITH ANOTHER PERSON

Conversations begin when babies are spoken to by adults close to them in Motherese or Fatherese. Visually impaired babies 'still' and listen intently when they are spoken to. Sighted babies 'dance'.

Researchers, when watching mothers and toddlers together, have noticed that although the toddlers often turn their backs during conversation and say 'No!' to suggestions by their mothers, they do in fact take up and imitate the ideas that are offered to them. It is as if they need to negotiate, create and cooperate and share with other people, even when they can still only say a few words. It is quite possible to have a conversation with sounds but no words.

Children need to be spoken to as individuals. Young children find it hard to put their thoughts and feelings into words, and this takes patience on the part of the listening adult: it's very tempting to keep prompting children and saying things for the child. Try nodding or saying 'Hmm …' instead of saying anything: it gives children time to say what they want.

Some children have an exceptional facility with languages (and often music too). They seek out adults and other children and enjoy a good chat with them. It is important that all children experience unrushed one-to-one conversations with both adults and other children, for example with the latter when sharing a drink together at the snack table, or chatting while using the clay. Research indicates that children are not helped when adults correct their speech by making them pronounce things properly or get the grammar 'right'. Remember, grammar is not about how children 'ought' to speak, but is instead about showing adults that children *understand* things about the language they speak.

It does help children when adults elaborate on what they say and give the correct pattern. For example, Shanaz, at 2 years of age, says 'I falled down', and the adult replies 'Yes you did, didn't you. You fell down. Never mind, I will help you up.'

SMALL GROUP DISCUSSIONS

Children need help when taking part in group discussions through stories, songs and dances. These are best with children of 3–8 years of age in *small* groups. Having to wait for a turn frustrates children rather than helps them to discuss and enjoy things. In fact it is likely to put children off stories, songs and dancing. For children 0–8 years, the time is 'now'. Even children from 5–8 years of age cannot wait too long before being allowed to say their bit in a discussion or a conversation. Chapter 1 on equality of opportunities gives examples of strategies for story-telling with small groups.

ENCOURAGING CONVERSATIONS AND GROUP DISCUSSIONS

Conversations need to:
- be two-way;
- involve a real exchange of ideas and feelings between adults and children;
- involve sharing ideas and feelings;
- involve taking turns;
- involve thinking of each other;
- involve thinking about things of interest to each other as well as about things of interest to oneself.

G U I D E L I N E S

Encouraging conversations

- **It is important to remember that anybody in a group can start or end a conversation.**
- **Two speakers might talk together but using different languages.**
- **In good conversation, there must be comprehensible input (using actions and props which show *meaning*, as well as gestures and facial expressions). The lack of all these extra ways of communicating is probably the reason why many people dislike talking on the telephone.**
- **Children must not be rushed to speak, and they must feel relaxed.**
- **It is better to elaborate on what children say than to correct their errors. This respects children's feelings and helps their self-esteem and confidence in themselves as learners.**

Language and context

Different situations bring about different sorts of language. A formal situation – being introduced to the mayor, or buying a bus ticket – is different from chatting with friends over a cup of coffee or playing in the park. It takes years for children to learn different ways of talking for formal and informal situations. Understanding this difference is important in most cultures.

Children need to be with the same adults each day, so that they learn the subtle signals about how people talk to each other in different situations. Many early childhood settings have now introduced a key-worker system which helps adults to understand what children say, and helps children to 'interpret' situations, what people say and how they say it! In different situations, people comment, describe, give opinions, predict, give commands, use formal phrases, reminisce, etc. 'Go into the hall!' at home might mean a reference to the small area near the front door. In another setting, it might mean a reference to a huge room full of chairs with a platform at one end.

The development of language

0–1 YEARS

The first year is sometimes called 'pre-linguistic'. This is an inaccurate, negative and misleading term. It gives a much more helpful and positive image for a baby if we think of this stage as a stage of early communication before words or signs are used by the baby. It is thus sometimes called the stage of **emerging language**. This is a much more helpful way of describing this stage of early language development.

1–4 YEARS

This is sometimes called the period of language explosion. Look again at the section 'What is language?' on p. 229 above. Every aspect of language seems to move forward rapidly at this time. It is important to remember that language development is part of symbolic behaviour. This is often called the period of **symbolic development**.

4–8 YEARS

This is the time when what has been learnt and understood about language is consolidated and further developments are *enhancements* rather than new developments. For example, children now become better at articulation, conventional grammar patterns, thinking about who they are talking to, the context and situation, and putting ideas and feelings into words. Turn to Chapter 2, which will help you to link language development with the holistic development of the child.

A summary of representation, communication and language development

This chapter has shown that language development is deeply linked with the processes of

▶ representation
▶ communication.

Language makes it easier to represent (to keep hold of experiences) and to communicate (to share these experiences with other people).

Once children can listen and talk, they are well on the way to adding more layers of symbolic behaviour. The **symbolic layers** in language acquisition are:

▶ listening

▶ talking

▶ writing

▶ reading.

There is more about writing and reading in Chapter 13 on the curriculum.

The section 'What is language?' on p. 229 above shows what is involved in learning a language.

R E S O U R C E S

Books

M. Whitehead, *The Development of Language and Literacy in the Early Years*, London, Hodder & Stoughton, 1996

J. Matthews, *Helping Young Children to Draw and Paint*, London, Hodder & Stoughton, 1995

V. Lee and P. Das Gupta, *Children's Cognitive and Language Development*, Oxford, Blackwell/Open University, 1995

Maureen O'Hagan and Maureen Smith, *Special Issues in Child Care*, London, Bailliere Tindall, 1993

Videos

RNIB, *One of the Family, No. 4 Making Contact* (Read also the booklet accompanying the video)

Channel 4, *Baby Monthly*

Baby, Its You Available from good bookstores

BBC Education/NCB 'Tuning Into Children' Project has developed a book and video (1996) and an audiocassette and pocket book by Dorothy Selleck (1999). Available from 'Tuning Into Children' PO Box 20, Tonbridge, Kent, TN12 6WU.

A C T I V I T Y

Investigating representation, communication and language development

1   Make an audio tape of a baby of 6–12 months of age, or of a child of 1–3, 3–5 or 5–7 years of age. Write down the sounds or language that you find. Note any vowels, consonants, syllables, words, holophrases (single-word utterances) or sentences. Make a transcript. Do not use more than 5 minutes' worth of the tape as transcripts take a long time to make. Analyse the transcript. Use the section 'What is language?' p. 229 to help you do this. Write down the child's language. Refer to the child's phonology, vocabulary, syntax, semantics, communications, arbitrary symbols, sense of audience and context, and articulation. Then evaluate the language development of the child.

2   Observe a one-to-one relationship between an adult and a child at 18 months, 3½ years and 5½ years. Note the differences in language in the conversations, and the kinds of non-verbal communication involved. Evaluate the observation.

3   Observe a small group (of three or four children) and then a large group (of six children or more) in a group with an adult. Note examples of turn-taking and any of the things listed on pages 233–234. Note the age of the children involved. Evaluate the activity.

9

The Child as a Symbol-User: Play

Before you read this chapter, think back to your own childhood. Did you make dens in a garden, under the table or with your bedclothes? Did you pretend you were in outer space, on a boat, on a desert island, going shopping or keeping house? Did you feel you had hours and hours to play? Did you enjoy using inexpensive play props, or were your favourite toys very expensive, commercially produced toys? Think back and talk about your childhood memories of play with your friends. It is one of the best ways to find out what is important to children as they grow up.

Children who do not play

It is a myth to say that all children play – they don't. In different parts of the world and according to the culture in which they grow up, play may or may not be encouraged. It is often seen as something children grow out of, and the quicker the better, rather than part of deep learning in the child.

There are various reasons why children might not **play**. A sick, unhappy or over-occupied child will not play. Children who are abused verbally, sexually or physically, or who have experienced an upheaval in their close relationships with people, may have difficulty. Play takes great energy and commitment on the part of the child. Children do not play by halves. They put the whole of themselves into it. A child who has played has concentrated, thought, felt and related to others in deep ways, and will be physically tired. Children who are held back in these ways need great sensitivity to be shown by adults. In some cases, play therapy will help to unlock their play for them. However, usually they will begin to play if given help in any mainstream setting or at home. Once children know how to play, there is usually no stopping them.

Often, children with special educational needs have been underestimated in their ability to play. Even children with severe learning difficulties can play if play is seen as a combination of being allowed to wallow deeply in feelings, ideas and relationships and the physical self together with the application of skills and competencies developed. This gives us a very positive view of play and indeed makes it a possibility for most children.

Some children lead over-occupied lives which leave them little time or energy for personal space and play. They are mainly involved in adult-dictated activities, being encouraged to read and write early, do number work, perhaps learn a musical instrument, learn ballet dancing, do drama sessions, join woodwork and P.E. clubs and play television and computer games, so that they almost never have any time for themselves. Researchers suggest it is likely that many children in the UK could be described as experiencing 'over-occupied' childhoods. These children are often very dependent on adults. They will say things like 'I don't know what to do' or 'I need you to help me.' Such children are very easily bored. This is because they are not developing their inner resources and the energy that is needed in order to play.

Recent research suggests that children, especially boys who do not play, are more likely to bring personal and social tragedy on themselves and their communities, e.g. becoming persistently drunken drivers, or serial murderers. Lack of early childhood play is also becoming linked by some researchers with ADHD Syndrome. The researcher Pellis believes that play and laughter actually 'fertilise' the brain.

TV, computers and stories – second-hand experiences

These are all examples of second-hand experiences. The themes of television programmes, computer games and books are very often taken up by children in their play. When children meet phantasy characters – such as those appearing in cartoon programmes and computer games – whose activities they have not experienced in their own lives, their play is usually at a very low level. When, on the other hand, children can link their own real experiences with what they see on television, in CD-ROM computer programmes – developed, for example, at the Open University – or in story books, their play is likely to be richer. It is therefore best to *limit* the time the children spend on second-hand experiences of any kind, unless these make direct use of real experiences the child has had.

In Sweden, a 6-year-old, when asked the difference between work and play, explained that when she worked she needed adults to help her, but she could not do this for very long, and that when she played it was much more difficult because she had to have her own ideas: in order to play, she said she needed acres of time.

In summary:

- a sick child
- an unhappy child
- an over-occupied child
- a disabled child
- an abused child

may all experience difficulty in playing.

The child's right to play

The Charter of Children's Rights (1989) states that every child in the world should have the right to play. It is important to remember that play is not the same as **recreation** or relaxing. Play is about high levels of learning, while recreation is about relaxing and not thinking very hard. Everyone needs time to relax, of course, but this is very different from having time to play – which takes energy.

Why do we want children to have the right to play? Play is central to a child's learning. It makes a very big contribution to development, and to learning about:

- ideas
- feelings
- relationships
- the physical self
- the moral and spiritual self.

FIGURE 9.1
A child will sometimes enjoy playing alone

FIGURE 9.2
Through play, children try out their skills and competencies

Sometimes people say that play is the only way a child learns. In fact, it is not, and it is important to remember this. Play is, however, a major part of a whole network of learning, and it is important because it brings together, coordinates and makes whole everything that a child learns.

What is play?

Play brings together the ideas, feelings, relationships and physical life of the child. It helps children to use what they know and to understand things about the world and people they meet. When they play, children can: rearrange their lives; rehearse the future; reflect on the past; and get their thoughts, feelings, relationships and physical bodies under their own control. The act of playing gives them a sense of mastery and competence which helps them to face the world and cope with it. This is crucial for the development of good self-esteem and for becoming a rounded personality. Play co-ordinates a child's learning and makes it whole.

Some people believe that children play naturally. In fact, children *learn* to play, although they are also *predisposed* towards it. It's a bit of both: nature *and* nurture. Often, it is older children who teach younger children how to play. In situations where children play in mixed-age groups, younger children easily learn about deep-quality play from those who are experienced and good at it. For example, Maori children traditionally learn in this way.

However, in modern life, in towns where it is often dangerous to play out in the streets, where families are smaller, and where children are at school with classes of children all the same age – e.g. 4-year-olds in reception classes – there is not the same possibility for the younger children (2–5 years) to learn about play from older children (5–8 years or older). This means that many children in modern life, both in towns and in the rural countryside, increasingly depend on adults to help them into deep-quality play.

The prior experience – the childhood experience – of both adults and children is important where play is concerned. Research suggests that it is very important that adults working with young children know and understand what play is. They need to be trained to understand its central contribution to the learning that children experience. Adults need to support and extend children's play with sensitivity and skill.

Defining play

There is no satisfactory definition of play. Play is one of the most complicated concepts to study and understand, with a mass of literature written about it. This may explain why it has become such a political subject. People are often afraid of things they do not know much about and do not understand. There are those who do not think it has a place in a child's education. There are those who believe it must have a central place in a children's education. This debate has continued for 200 years. It is, on the whole, those who work with children on a daily basis, and experts in child development who are constantly in touch with young children all over the word, who argue that play is central to a child's learning.

It is important that the way children develop in their play not be seen as progress through a prescribed sequence or hierarchy. This is because, especially for early childhood workers spending time with children who have disabilities, it is important to emphasise that *any* child can be helped to play. When early childhood workers approach the development of play as if it is a web that the child weaves, this becomes possible.

THE TWELVE FEATURES OF PLAY

1 Children cannot play at a quality level unless they have had previous first-hand experiences of people, objects and materials. Then they can use these experiences in their play. Some of these experiences will have been enjoyable. Some might have been frightening, or painful.

2 When children play, they make up their own rules. These help them to keep control as they play. When the play fades, the rules fade too. Feeling in control is an important part of play.

3 When children represent (keep hold of) their experiences, they might do so by drawing a cat or making a model of a bus. Sometimes what they make becomes a **play prop** which is used in their play.

4 No-one can *make* a child play. A child has to *want* to play.

5 During play, children often rehearse what they will be able to do without any help from adults later on. This is often called **role play**: they pretend to be other people, and they take on adult roles.

6 Children can **pretend** when they play. They can pretend a lump of dough is a cake. They can pretend they are someone else.

7 Children sometimes play alone.

8 Children sometimes play in a pair, in parallel or in a group with other children.

9 Adults who join children in their play need to remember that each person playing has their own play ideas. The adult's play ideas are not more important than the child's play ideas. Play ideas are sometimes called the **play agenda** or **play script**.

10 When children play, they wallow in their feelings, ideas and relationships. They move about and are physically active. They are deeply involved in their play.

11 When children play, they try out what they have been learning. They show their skills and competencies.

12 Play helps children to coordinate what they learn. This means that play brings together all the different aspects of a child's development. The result is that the child is a grounded, centred, together and whole person. Play is thus a *holistic* kind of learning.

WHAT IS PLAY, AND WHAT IS NOT PLAY?

These twelve features are often used as performance indicators or desirable outcomes for **quality play**. If most of these twelve features are present when children are observed in their play, then they *are* probably involved in quality play. However, if only a few are present, it does not necessarily mean that the child is not doing anything of quality.

It probably means that the child is doing something other than play – the child might be **representing** things instead. The child might be involved in a **game** with rules or might be enjoying a **first-hand experience**. It is very useful for staff working with young children in a whole variety of childhood settings to become skilled at knowing what is play and what is not play. However, early childhood workers and parents have always found this difficult. It would be a mistake to call everything that children do play. This is not helpful. Observing which of the twelve features of play are present helps adults working with children to become a little more clear about the kind of learning that the child is involved in.

THE NETWORK FOR LEARNING IN WHICH PLAY HAS A CENTRAL PLACE

Play is central to learning, but it is not the only way that children learn. It is part – as already mentioned – of a whole **network for learning** (see the book *Helping Young Children to Play* (Resources section) for more about this concept).

1   Children need first-hand experiences. Through real, everyday experiences, through the senses, and through their movements, children learn to explore, discover, practise and become competent at doing things. They start as novices and become experts.

2   Children need to understand what games are about. They need to find out the rules that are involved in a game. They need to understand how to *make* and how to *keep to* the rules. They need to understand that rules can be changed. In this way, they begin to understand their culture and to take an active part in it.

3   Children need help in beginning to represent their experiences using symbols. They begin to make something stand for something else. They create a product, which is called a representation, for example a drawing of a house, a model of a spider.

4   Play is important in helping children to learn because – as already mentioned – it coordinates learning and makes it whole. Play is about what a child can do, and about how children *use* what they have been learning.

The stages of play from babyhood to adult life

The stages of play are not like a ladder or hierarchy going from simple baby play to complex adult play. The stages of play are more like a network that becomes increasingly elaborate. A *web* is a better image. Turn to p. 27 which will help you to link play with the holistic development of the child.

The first year
Babies and toddlers are beginning to find out through their senses, movements and relationships with other people what play is – through playing with their own hands.

1–5 years
Children begin to pretend, and this means they are beginning to use symbolic behaviour. This is one of the most important stages of development for human beings.

5–8 years
Play elaborates pretend themes, using more people, props and ideas, sustained characters and stories/narratives, more expression of feeling and more skill. **Free-flow play** is often left out of the school curriculum at this stage in the UK, but in countries like Denmark, Germany and Japan, children still play in school at this age. Unfortunately, this means that just at the stage when play is beginning to flow, it is often cut off in its prime. Without streets to play in safely or friends to play with at home, children cannot easily compensate for the play they cannot do at school. Free-flow play is very important for a child's development and learning at this stage.

8–12 years
Play consolidates and becomes very sophisticated (if it survives). At this stage, play divides into hobbies, games and leisure pursuits, or into creative directions, for example drama, sculpture, making computer programmes, dancing, singing to a guitar.

Adolescence

Play continues to be important for adults who are creative, imaginative and who are innovative, and original thinkers. There is also participation in leisure pursuits, as in the previous stage of development. People who play are less likely to become stressed, depressed, bored or narrow. They are more interested in life, more interesting to be with and more sensitive to other people.

Theories of play

Psychodynamic theories

These were pioneered by Freud, and developed by Erikson in the 1950s and Winnicott in the 1970s. These theories emphasised children's *feelings*:

▶ **positive feelings** – their deepest wishes;
▶ **negative feelings** – their fears.

Children use play to face and cope with their lives. As they play, they try things out as they are, as they were, as they might be and as they *want* them to be. Through play, children begin to gain a sense of control over what happens to them (see Chapter 7 on feelings and relationships). **Play therapists** use psychodynamic theories in their work.

Social constructivist theories about play

These emphasise the child as an **active learner**. Children use objects, props, other people and a variety of different concepts, indoors, outdoors, little dens, dolls' houses, for example, for their play.

PIAGET

Piaget (see Chapter 6, pp. 169–179) saw play as the way in which a child's learning becomes whole. These were his stages of play:

▶ babyhood (0–18 months) – involving sensori-motor behaviour (the senses and movement);
▶ the early years of symbolic play (18 months – 5 years) – making something stand for something else;
▶ the school years (5–8 years) – children move from play to taking part in games with rules. Children are able to play more cooperatively.

In fact, the rules of games are quite different from the rules of play:

▶ in games, the rules are given;
▶ in play, children make up the rules as they go.

VYGOTSKY

Vygotsky particularly emphasised that other people are important to children as they play. He believed that play helps children to do things in advance of what they can manage in real life – to drive a car, for instance.

Piaget and Vygotsky both thought that play led to the enjoyment of games. They did not see play and games as entirely separate forms of learning from the beginning.

The role of the early childhood worker in encouraging play

Time to play

Children need plenty of free choice of activity in order to play. They also need *time* to play. A rigid timetable makes it very difficult for them to develop deep-quality free-flowing play. Play cannot flow under these circumstances, and this means that learning will be held back. If adults truly believe that play is central to learning, play – including free-flow play – needs to be encouraged by flexible timetabling of the day.

Making space for play – indoors and outdoors

Play does not happen to adult order. Both the indoor and outdoor areas need to be made into spaces which encourage the children to develop their *own* play.

Material provision

Children need things to play with – they need play props. These will need to be made, or suitable play clothes and props can be found in the materials provided. Staff will be making plans for the children based on their observations of how the children play. They will choose play props which encourage the children to play more deeply.

CHOOSING PLAY MATERIALS

Children do not need expensive equipment in order to play. Children can play with all sorts of things. They will use whatever they find as play props. By the river, for example, they will be finding twigs and pebbles. In the park, they will be running and using the space. In the garden, they will be climbing. On the sea shore, they will find pebbles, seaweed, rock pools and sand. In a room, likewise, they will use the material provisions that adults put there. It is very important that adults choose materials very carefully and thoroughly plan the physical environment. Then, children can get the most out of opportunities for free-flow play.

  ▶ **Pre-structured materials** more often hold back rather than encourage free-flow play. If there is only one way of doing things, children cannot develop in their imaginative play, dwell on their feelings, or sort out their relationships with each other. And they will probably carry out a very narrow range of physical actions. An example of pre-structured materials is a posting box. So-called educational toys, made by commercial manufacturers and usually very expensive, are often pre-structured in this way.
  ▶ **Open-ended materials** encourage children to think, feel, socialise or concentrate deeply alone, and use a range of fine and gross motor skills. Examples of open-ended materials would be:
    – found materials, used in junk modelling;
    – transforming raw materials like clay and dough, and *self-service* areas in the provision (see Chapter 13);
    – wooden blocks;
    – the home area.

It is important for children to use scissors, for example, for fine motor skills, and for them to learn to put straws in cartons of fruit juice, rather than to do exercises that are split off from life. Learning and exercise split off from the day-to-day context of a child's life can actually stop children from learning very well. When life becomes a drudge, full of boring repetitive exercises, children quickly lose the excitement of learning. It is therefore better to avoid pre-structured toys and encourage open-ended traditional toys such as dolls, peg and rag dolls, a set of wooden blocks etc.

When children play they need:

▶ people who help them to play;

▶ places to play (dens, home area, outdoor areas);

▶ play props which are open-ended and can be used in all sorts of ways.

Think about this when you arrange indoor and outdoor spaces. Chapter 13 on the curriculum will help you to make a good selection of play materials in your provision. It is also probably best, in trying to provide an environment which encourages children to play, if much attention be given to the *maintenance* of the material provision. Such maintenance involves ensuring safety, but it also means keeping the children's interest.

In Chapter 13 on the curriculum, different layouts of work spaces are given which show basic material provision. Chapter 1 on equal opportunities gives a more detailed description of a home area plan that will encourage play.

Structured play – or working towards play

Adult-led tasks are often called 'tutor-led play', 'guided play', or 'structured play'. In this approach, the adult teaches children to play. For example, there is first a visit to a real shop. A play shop is then set up in the room, and the adult shows the child how to 'play shops' guiding them through it. It is very important first to *teach* children what is involved in play so that they can then develop their own play.

In the Oxford Studies in the 1980s, two settings were studied in Miami and Oxford. Children in Miami were involved in adult-led, structured play. The children in this study were less involved in what they were doing than the children in Oxford. In Oxford the children were given more opportunities for free-flow play.

There need to be some adult-led sessions where children are introduced to the materials first through real experience – using them in cooking, for example – and then by using them with the adult in the home area. Children would then gradually use the experiences themselves in their own free-flow play, both safely and creatively.

Having to complete adult-led tasks i.e. 'work' *before* being allowed to play undermines play. But play is also undervalued when adults leave children without *any* help when they play – in these situations, indeed, the play quickly becomes repetitive and superficial. If adults are only found in those areas where children are doing 'work', while children are being sent off to 'play' without any help, this gives children unfortunate messages about the way that adults undervalue their play.

Free-flow play literally occurs when the play begins to flow with quality according to the twelve features described earlier in this chapter. Free-flow play can fade and vanish in a moment. Adults can be a great help to children in keeping it going.

It is important to note that free-flow play, although less directly structured by adults, is in no way inferior to the cookery session, or to the guided session with the adult. In fact, free-flow play shows children using a very high level of knowledge and understanding, as well as a sensitivity to others and their feelings. Children really appreciate adults who sensitively help them to keep their play flowing.

There is widespread misunderstanding about play. Those who are uninformed about its importance tend to see value only when it is structured by adults. These are often the very adults who worry later on when children cannot create their own stories to write. They do not grasp the connection.

Types of play

Different types of play have been described by early childhood workers of all kinds. These different types have been linked with:

▶ particular kinds of material provision – the home area, construction kits, the outdoor area, natural materials, a messy area, a computer, wooden blocks, climbing frames, bats/balls, hoops, clay, paint;

▶ different aspects of the child's development – manipulative play/practice play/repetitive play, symbolic play, superhero play, exploratory play, discovery play, investigative play, pretend play, ludic play, heuristic play, role play, therapeutic play, solitary play, parallel play, cooperative play, epistemic play, imaginative play, physical play, manipulative play, creative play, rough-and-tumble play, boisterous play, fantasy play, socio-dramatic play, phantasy play.

The word play is widely used, often without much thought. In the following breakdown of different kinds of play, you will find play given a high status.

Free-flow play

This is where the child learns at the highest level, using ideas, feelings and relationships that have been experienced, and applies these to what they know and understand with control, mastery and competence. It involves the twelve features of play stated earlier in this chapter (see p. 241).

1 **Symbolic play** (usually from 1 year): this includes pretend play, role play, socio-dramatic play and imaginative play:

   ▶ **Pretend play** or **ludic play:** when an action or object is given a meaning symbolically which is different from real life – a clothes peg becomes a door key.

   ▶ **Role play:** this occurs when 'pretend' symbols are used together – the child pretends to drive to the shops and locks the door with a pretend clothes-peg key, sits on a box (a car) and turns the steering wheel (holds a plate and twists it round), and pretends to be the parent 'doing a shop' for the family.

   ▶ **Socio-dramatic play:** when several children role-play and pretend-play together.

   ▶ **Imaginative play** or **creative play:** children use their own real-life experiences and rearrange them – they make a pretend swimming pool together out of wooden blocks. One of them pretends to be a lifeguard and rescues someone who can't swim. The children already know about learning to swim and rescue.

   • **Fantasy play:** here children role-play situations they do not know about but which might happen to them one day – the experience of getting married, going to the moon in space travel, going to hospital.

   • **Phantasy play:** here children role-play *unreal* events using characters from cartoons on TV – Power Rangers, Superman.
   War play dominates this kind of play. Because it is not rooted in real experience, it is difficult to help children to use this kind of experience for their benefit.

2 **Manipulative play:** when children use and celebrate physical prowess – playing on a skateboard with great competence, riding a two-wheeler bicycle. It is about what they *can* do, not what they are struggling to do (which would not be play).

3 **Play using props:** sometimes children make their own props and use them to

pretend-play – they make a telephone out of boxes and then pretend to book a doctor's appointment by 'phone. This is sometimes called **constructive play**, but it is really a representation, a prop (telephone), that the child uses in order to pretend-play.

4 **Rough-and-tumble play:** this often involves chasing, catching, pretend fights, pillow fights. Unless children are sufficiently coordinated to manage it, it often ends in tears: it requires great sensitivity to other people in order not to hurt them physically. This form of play often occurs before going to sleep (bedtimes). It bonds those playing emotionally and socially. It is difficult to cater for in an early childhood setting, however, as it frightens those not taking part.

Areas of learning which are sometimes called play

These include exploratory, heuristic, discovery and investigative play, as well as epistemic learning. Corrine and John Hutt agree with the authors of this book that when children are exploring materials and finding out about them they are learning but not playing.

Therapeutic play

This kind of play helps children who are in emotional pain to find out more about how they feel, to face their feelings and to deal with them, so that they gain some control over their lives. Helping children through play therapy requires professional training, but every child is helped to be mentally healthy through the feeling of control that play gives. Some children need more help than early childhood workers can give.

Looking at different types of play has become an increasingly unwieldy way of describing play, with more and more categories being added all the time. It is probably better to:

▶ focus on setting up the basic areas of provision with as much quality as possible (see Chapter 13);
▶ focus on how adults can help children to play both alone and together.

Remember that all of these types of play can be catered for through setting up the room with great care. This is why it is very important for staff to work as a team in planning the curriculum for young children. The material provision and the way the space is used are very important in either encouraging, or not, the children to free-flow-play.

It is important to remember that children, when they play, need to be physically active, using fine and gross motor skills; and they need to be actively thinking, actively feeling and actively relating to each other.

G U I D E L I N E S

Helping children to play – a summary

▶ **Think back to your own childhood memories of play. What did you enjoy doing? Remembering back helps you to help children play.**
▶ **Take time to observe children as they play. It will help you to tune into the child's play agenda and to help the play along.**
▶ **Think about equality of opportunity. Some children might be left out of the play when they want to join in. Can you help them to develop access strategies? (See p. 192.)**
▶ **Gender issues need to be given care. Boys and girls need to experience a broad range of play.**

▶ Children with special educational needs might require extra help in developing their play.

▶ Remember that when children play, they can learn at a very high level.

▶ Remember that you cannot *make* children play, because play only happens when the conditions are right for it.

▶ Work at getting the conditions for play as good as you can in your work setting.

▶ People matter. Adults who help children to play are adults who help children to learn. It is important to make play a high priority for this reason.

▶ The provision of play props is important. These should be open-ended and flexible in the ways that children can use them. Don't pre-structure props and equipment so that there is only one way to use it (e.g. a template, cutters in the dough, posting boxes).

▶ Children need places for play, indoors and outdoors – dens, home areas and so on.

▶ Children need uninterrupted time for play.

▶ Allow children freedom of movement indoors and outdoors.

▶ Give children freedom of choice for activities. Some children like doll play, while others prefer to play on climbing frames.

▶ Mixed-age groups encourage play because older children will help younger children and teach them how to play.

▶ Adults can help too by play tutoring. But remember, this is not itself play: it is a way that adults can help children take a step towards play.

▶ Adults can also help children by entering into the spirit of play. You can play with the children as long as you do not try to take over their play and control it.

▶ Know about and provide for the whole network for learning:
(a) Encourage quality first-hand experiences through carefully chosen provision for both indoors and outdoors.
(b) Help children to represent and keep hold of their experiences by using a wide range of materials and activities.
(c) Organise games.

These are all important parts of the network to learning, and they will help children to play – an activity which is also part of the network for learning.

▶ Observe children at play, and add provision that might help their play to make further progress. Extend their play – add shoes to the dressing-up box if children are playing 'shoe shops.'

▶ Do not invade, dominate or change the direction of the children's play. Join the free-flow play, and try to catch what it is about so that you can help it along.

▶ Protect disputes.

▶ Make a safe and healthy environment.

▶ Maintain the environment (stocks, layout, servicing the area). For example, if the block play area has become very messy by 10.00 a.m. ask a group of children to help you tidy it. No-one can play well in a chaotic area.

► Watch out for the twelve features of play (see p. 241) so that you know what the child is doing. Then you can help.
► Help the children to stay in character when they are making a play story.
► Help children to keep in mind the storyline of their play.
► Children need to be free to play indoors or outdoors.

RESOURCES

Books

T. Bruce, *Time to Play*, London, Hodder & Stoughton, 1991

T. Bruce, *Helping Young Children to Play*, London, Hodder & Stoughton, 1996

P. Barnes (ed), *Personal, Social and Emotional Development of Children*, Oxford, Open University/Blackwell, 1995

RNIB, *Play it My Way*, RNIB/HMSO, 1995

L. Neilsen, *Space and Self: Active Learning by Means of the Little Room*, Sikon Press, 1992

J. Moyles (Ed.), *The Excellence of Play*, Milton Keynes, Open University, 1994

Videos

RNIB, *One of the Family, No. 4*, 1995

RNIB, *Play it My Way*, 1995

Froebel Blockplay Project, *Building a Future*, 1991 (available from Community Playthings, Darvill, Robertsbridge, East Sussex)

Video Reportage Productions Number 3 20 West Parade Norwich NR2 3DW *The Many Functions of Children's Play*

ACTIVITY

Making time for play

1 Plan ways of giving children sufficient time to develop rich free-flow play. Plan a flexible routine for children, with a balance between leaving children to 'get on with it' (a leave-it-to-nature approach) and adult-led activities (a transmission model). Observe a child of 3 or 4 years of age. Evaluate your observations.

2 Research how the day is timetabled for children in a reception class and in key stage 1, years 1 and 2, in a primary school. Observe a child of 4–7 years of age for a day: remember to include the mid-morning, afternoon and lunchtime play periods.

3 Plan an outdoor area suitable for children of 3–7 years of age. Remember: it should be possible for a child to do everything that is on offer indoors in the outdoor area also. How will you organise outdoor experiences of paint, water, sand, drawing, home area, clay? In one school there was a clay table indoors and a mud patch to dig in outdoors. In this way, the outdoor provision complemented the indoor provision. Observe a child of 3–7 years of age in the outdoor area. Evaluate their experiences, and compare these with your plan of an outdoor area.

Investigating play

1 Plan how you can assess what kind of learning a child is involved in – is it play, or is the child benefiting from a quality, first-hand experience, for example cooking?

2 Observe a child aged 1 year (if possible), 2–3 years, 3–5 years, 5–7 years. Use the twelve features of play (see p. 241) as observation tools. Evaluate your findings.

3 Observe a child of 1–3 years, 3–5 years and 5–7 years playing in the home area or the small-world area (dolls' house, farm, road). Use the twelve features again to understand (assess) the learning. Plan how you could add to the provision in the light of your observations. Evaluate your activity.

4 Observe a child with special educational needs. Is the child playing according to the twelve features of free-flow play? Evaluate your observations.

5 Observe a child who is sick – at home in bed or in a hospital. Identify which of the twelve features of free-flow play the child is using. Plan how to help the child. Implement your plan, and evaluate the activity.

6 Describe how you could encourage play opportunities through the structured telling of a story.

7 Make a miniature garden using twigs, shells, etc. Make a little pond. Tell a story to a small group, for example *Rosie's Walk* by Pat Hutchins. Leave the garden out on a table with the story props for the children to use after you have finished telling the story. If a child begins to spontaneously play with the garden, observe the play. Write down what the child says and does. Evaluate your activity.

10

Health Education and Child Safety

Models of personal health

The World Health Organization (WHO) defines health as a 'state of complete physical,
mental, and social well-being and not merely the absence of disease or infirmity'.
A person can be described as healthy provided that the three sides of the triangle – social,
mental, physical – remain intact (see Figure 10.1); if the natural equilibrium is damaged

FIGURE 10.1
The three aspects of health

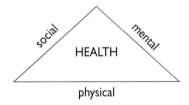

then a state of ill-health – though often only temporary – results. This definition has been
criticised as focusing too much on an ideal state.

Health and social well-being can be categorised thus (see Figure 10.2):

▶ *Physical health:* this is the easiest aspect of health to measure, and is concerned with
  the physical functioning of the body.
▶ *Emotional health:* how we express emotions such as joy, grief, frustration and fear;
  this leads on to coping strategies for anxiety and stress.
▶ *Mental health:* this relates to our ability to organise our thoughts coherently, and is
  closely linked to emotional and social health.
▶ *Social health:* how we relate to others and form relationships.
▶ *Spiritual health:* this includes religious beliefs and practices as well as personal codes
  of conduct and the quest for inner peace.

▶ *Environmental health:* an individual's health depends also on the health of the society in which they live; for example famine areas deny health to their inhabitants, and unemployed people cannot be healthy in a society which only values those who work.

FIGURE 10.2

Six aspects of health

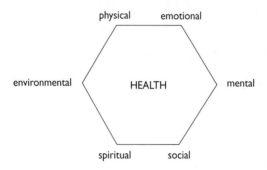

In earlier times, disease or ill-health was seen as punishment from a god or gods, or as a result of bad luck. Now, individuals take more of a personal responsibility for maintaining good health, but rely also on the public sector for provision of sanitation and health-care institutions and services.

Health problems today

Medical advances such as the development of new drugs, improved health services and high technology have not managed to deal with a new generation of diseases: the **chronic degenerative diseases**:

▶ heart disease
▶ cancers
▶ stroke
▶ arthritis.

All these represent the effect of wear and tear on the human body. In addition, new bacteria and viruses have emerged within the last 20 years.

▶ legionnaire's disease
▶ campylobacter enteritis
▶ helicobacter pylori gastritis (duodenal ulcer)
▶ human immuno-deficiency virus (HIV – AIDS)
▶ bovine spongiform encephalopathy (BSE).

Maintenance of health and social well-being

It is now recognised that people's lifestyles and behaviour are contributory factors in most of the diseases mentioned above. Important factors are:

▶ diet
▶ exercise and maintaining mobility
▶ stress

- recreation and or leisure activities
- smoking
- alcohol and substance abuse
- sexual behaviour
- housing and sanitation.

Health promotion

The World Health Organization (WHO) defines health promotion as:

'The process of enabling people to increase control over, and improve their health. To reach a stage of complete physical, mental and social well-being, an individual or group must be able to identify and to realise aspirations, to satisfy needs and to change or cope with the environment. Health is therefore seen as a resource for everyday life, not the object of living. Health is a positive concept emphasising social and personal resources, as well as physical capacities. Therefore, health promotion is not just the responsibility of the health sector but goes beyond lifestyles to well-being. (*WHO, 1986*)

HEALTH FOR ALL 2000

Through its initiative 'Health for All 2000', the World Health Organization has highlighted the need for health promotion as the way forward in reducing the extent – and the cost – of ill-health. The governments of many different countries have now set targets for health improvements – as seen, for example, in the UK government's 1992 White Paper *Health of the Nation*.

WHAT IS HEALTH EDUCATION?

Health education is a method of self-empowerment: it enables people to take more control over their own health, and over the factors which affect their health. Health promotion is a term that includes all aspects of health education, but places greater emphasis on changes in health policy and on positive health as opposed to the rather negative approach of merely preventing ill-health.

PRIMARY, SECONDARY AND TERTIARY HEALTH EDUCATION

Health education may be described in the same way as the concept of primary, secondary and tertiary prevention in community medicine.

Primary health education is directed at healthy people. It is a *prophylactic* (or preventative) measure that aims to prevent ill-health from arising in the first instance. The areas of primary prevention in children are:

- sound nutrition and diet, i.e. healthy eating;
- dental prophylaxis, i.e. the prevention of tooth decay;
- immunisation;
- the prevention of childhood accidents;
- the prevention of emotional and behavioural problems;
- basic hygiene.

Secondary health education is directed at people with a health problem or a reversible condition. It emphasises the importance of the early detection of defects:

- *Screening:* by routinely examining apparently healthy people, screening aims to detect either those who are likely to develop a particular disease or those in whom the disease is already present but has not yet produced symptoms. Screening may detect a problem with hearing, sight, or physical, emotional or behavioural development.

▶ *Reducing behaviours likely to damage health:* overweight people can be encouraged to change their dietary habits, or a smoker to quit smoking.

Tertiary health education is directed at those whose ill-health has not been, or could not be, prevented and who cannot be completely cured. Examples:

▶ Children with brain damage can achieve their own potential through communication and structured play.

▶ Patients dying of cancer can do so with dignity if their pain is kept under control.

Rehabilitation programmes are chiefly concerned with tertiary health education.

REDUCING THE LIKELIHOOD OF DISEASE

The risks to health in society today differ greatly from those of the past. Diseases which were once major threats to life at all stages have been either eradicated or at least controlled:

▶ *Smallpox:* more than half the people of Europe probably had smallpox at some time in their life before Edward Jenner discovered the remedy, vaccination, in 1796.

▶ *Cholera:* the Public Health Acts of the 1870s halted the spread of cholera in the UK by improving water supplies and sewage disposal.

▶ *Tuberculosis:* in 1862 Robert Koch isolated the TB bacillus, leading to the development of a vaccine. (However, this disease is once again increasing in the 1990s, both in the developed and developing countries.)

▶ *Diphtheria:* the anti-toxin was first used in 1890. Before then, death from diphtheria was common (see Figure 10.3).

FIGURE 10.3

The decline in the annual death rate from (a) diphtheria and (b) tuberculosis, England and Wales

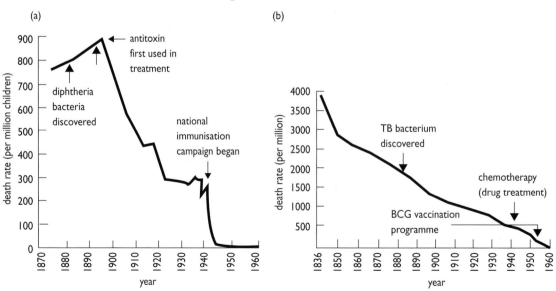

HEALTH EDUCATION CAMPAIGNS

All health promotion programmes require careful planning. The planning process may be broken down into the following stages (see Figure 10.4):

FIGURE 10.4
A flow chart showing the stages involved in planning a health promotion campaign

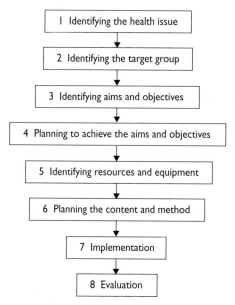

1 Identifying the health issue

2 Identifying the target group

3 Identifying aims and objectives

4 Planning to achieve the aims and objectives

5 Identifying resources and equipment

6 Planning the content and method

7 Implementation

8 Evaluation

STAGE 1: IDENTIFY THE HEALTH ISSUE

For example:

▶ heart disease and the role of stress, exercise, nutrition;
▶ substance abuse – smoking, alcohol, solvents;
▶ accident prevention;
▶ disease prevention by immunisation;
▶ dental care.

STAGE 2: IDENTIFY THE TARGET GROUP

For example:

▶ Middle-aged men are at particular risk from heart disease.
▶ Young people might have just started, or might be tempted to start, smoking.
▶ Parents of babies under 2 years need information on the precautions against the risk of **sudden infant death syndrome (cot death).**
▶ Children are at risk of dental decay.
▶ Parents need information on disease prevention and immunisation.

The age of the target group – i.e. whether they are children, adolescents or adults – will affect the way health-promotion advice is presented to them. It is important to be aware of the different needs of the target audience in order to ensure that the information is presented at an appropriate level and using suitable resources.

STAGE 3: IDENTIFY THE AIMS AND OBJECTIVES OF THE CAMPAIGN

The aims (or goals) are broad statements of what you are trying to achieve from a single session or event, or from the whole campaign. For example:

▶ to examine the issue of sexually transmitted diseases;
▶ to appreciate the role of exercise in preventing coronary heart disease;
▶ to explore the link between drinking and road accidents;
▶ to explore the link between nutrition and tooth decay in young children;
▶ to explore the issue around immunisation against childhood diseases.

The objectives are more *specific* aims; they help you to pinpoint the most realistic method of presenting health advice and information, and to *evaluate* your success in achieving them. For example:

▶ to provide parents with up-to-date information on immunisation, so that they can make an informed decision regarding their own children;
▶ to prepare a display on 'Safer sex' outlining the risks of contracting a sexually transmitted disease.

STAGE 4: PLANNING TO ACHIEVE THE AIMS AND OBJECTIVES

Having identified your objectives, you now need to decide on the method of presentation. This will depend on such factors as cost, the size of the target group, ease of delivery, the availability of material/equipment, and appropriateness for the target group. Suitable presentation methods may include:

▶ a display, perhaps 'tying in' with a national awareness day or week, for example AIDS Awareness Week or National No-Smoking Day;
▶ a video programme;
▶ leaflets;
▶ a group workshop;
▶ a formal lecture with slides or overhead projector (OHP) transparencies.

STAGE 5: IDENTIFY RESOURCES AND EQUIPMENT

The choice of resources and equipment will depend on several factors:

▶ the availability of resources, e.g. the size of the room, video rental, access to display boards and materials;
▶ the cost of equipment;
▶ the time available for promotion activity;
▶ knowing how to operate equipment – e.g. the use of a video recorder;
▶ relevance to the target audience.

STAGE 6: PLANNING THE CONTENT AND METHOD OF THE PROGRAMME

This is where you work out *exactly* how to present the information, using the resources available. The objectives and the target group will guide your choice of method, but it must be one with which you feel confident. The more effort put in at this stage, the greater the chance of success.

STAGE 7: IMPLEMENTATION

Carry out the plan and remember to evaluate the programme as you go along.

STAGE 8: EVALUATION

Evaluation is an important element in any health-education campaign; it allows you to

G U I D E L I N E S

Presentation

▶ **Produce a detailed, timed plan.**

▶ **Allow time to introduce yourselves and the topic.**

▶ **Do a timed test run to ensure that you have enough material.**

▶ **Check the room for seating arrangements and equipment.**

▶ **Rehearse the delivery of the talk – try to use prompt cards which emphasise *key points* even if you have written out the whole talk. Remember to maintain eye contact with your audience.**

▶ ***Sum up* the main points.**

▶ ***Discussion time:* let your audience know that there will be time for any questions or debate at the end. You may need to initiate this phase by asking a question yourself – have a few ideas ready, or split the audience into smaller groups for the discussion of key points and arrange for these smaller groups to give feedback to the whole group.**

▶ ***Empowering the audience:* individuals need to make choices for themselves; your task is to present them with clear, relevant and, above all, *accurate* information. If you don't know the answer to any questions, admit it and apologise!**

assess and review all aspects of the programme. Always refer to the original aims and objectives, and ask if these have been achieved. Before ending your presentation, ask the audience to complete an (anonymous) evaluation form so that you can review the outcome of the session.

GOVERNMENT-RUN CAMPAIGNS

The Health Education Authority runs many different campaigns over a period of years; other campaigns of particular relevance to children include:

▶ **'Sun Know How':** the HEA's program for the prevention of skin cancer. One aspect of the campaign is the availability of sun protective clothing for children through The Sun Know How Catalogue. This is a range of clothing that offers very high sun protection to children playing outdoors (see Figure 10.5 The Sun Safety Code).

▶ **The National Healthy Schools Initiative:** This campaign was set up in 1998 and aims to create a new 'Investors in Health' award for all schools. It will encourage Local Health and Education Authorities to pioneer new ways of working together to raise standards of health among school pupils and staff.

Since 1995, the Health Education Authority (HEA) has undertaken a major **folic acid campaign** funded by the Department of Health. This was in response to the report of a UK Expert Advisory Group which recommended that to reduce the risk of **first-time occurrence** of neural tube defects (NTDs) all women, prior to conception and during the first 12 weeks of pregnancy, should increase their folate and folic acid intake by an extra 400 micrograms (mcg) a day. The term **neural tube defects** includes **anencephaly**, **encephalocoele** and **spina bifida**. These conditions occur if the brain and/or spinal cord, together with its protecting skull and spinal column, fail to develop properly during the 17th to the 30th days of embryonic life. As part of the campaign's overall objective to increase dietary intake of fortified breads and breakfast cereals, the HEA has developed two flashes – **'with extra folic acid'** and **'contains folic acid'**. Food retailers and manufacturers are being encouraged them to adopt this new 'flash' labelling scheme to help consumers identify breads and breakfast cereals foods fortified with folic acid.

FIGURE 10.5

The Sun Safety Code

PRIVATE COMPANIES

Manufacturers of 'healthy' products such as wholemeal bread or high-protein-balanced foods for babies often promote their products both by advertising *and* by using educational leaflets which are offered free in health clinics, postnatal wards and supermarkets. Examples of these methods of health promotion are:

▶ booklets on 'feeding your baby';
▶ child safety on the roads – by manufacturers of child car seats and harnesses;
▶ herbal remedies to encourage a stress-free life.

There are strict controls over the claims that manufacturers can make about the health-giving properties of their product.

Some products have traditionally been associated with promoting healthy lifestyles. Examples are:

▶ the advertising campaign for Guinness ('Guinness is good for you');
▶ 'Lucozade promotes rapid recovery';
▶ 'Go to work on an egg'.

THE VOLUNTARY SECTOR

Voluntary organisations are in a strong position to enhance the health of the population by the following methods:

▶ through self-help – bringing people together to share common problems and to help them to gain more confidence and control over their own health;

▶ by direct service provision – the British Red Cross have a network of shops for the rental of equipment in the home (including walking frames, commodes and chairs);

▶ in community health, where voluntary organisations work with local people to identify and solve problems affecting their health – GASP – Group Against Smoking in Public – is a Bristol-based group which campaigns for an increase in the provision of no-smoking areas in restaurants;

▶ health education and promotion, fund-raising and support for research – The Wellcome Trust is a medical research charity which provides funding for research in the biomedical sciences.

Charities which aim to promote health and inform the public of the risks to health from certain lifestyles also employ advertising methods to get across their message; they often work in conjunction with the Health Education Authority or with private companies, or both. For example, the Child Accident Prevention Trust, with financial support from Start-rite and Volvo, produced a safety leaflet for parents 'First ride, safe ride' aimed at keeping a baby safe in the car.

PREVENTATIVE ACTION

All immunisation programmes are an attempt to prevent disease and therefore to promote health – both in the individual and in the general population. A recent initiative which followed on from research in New Zealand was to reduce the number of babies dying from sudden infant death syndrome (SIDS).

CHILD HEALTH PROMOTION

Child health promotion is a programme of care managed by professionals – family doctors, nurses, health visitors and other members of the primary health-care team. It has four main aims:

▶ to promote good health and development;

▶ to prevent illness, accidents and child abuse;

▶ to recognise and, where possible, eradicate potential problems affecting development, behaviour and education;

▶ to detect abnormality, in order to offer investigation and treatment.

UNDERSTANDING SAFETY ISSUES

Accidents are the most common cause of death in children aged between 1 and 14, accounting for half of all child deaths:

▶ Three children are killed in accidents every day.

▶ 10,000 children are permanently disabled each year.

▶ Each year, 1 in 6 children attend accident and emergency departments.

The pattern of accidents varies with age, in keeping with the child's development and exposure to new hazards.

WHY DO ACCIDENTS HAPPEN?

Babies are vulnerable to accidents because they have no awareness of danger and cannot control their environment; they are totally dependent on their parents or carers to make their world safe. Children are naturally curious and need to investigate their surroundings. As children get older and their memory develops, they start to realise that certain actions have certain consequences (for example, touching a hot oven door hurts), and so they begin to learn a measure of **self-protection**. Carers of young children need to have a sound knowledge of child development in order to anticipate when an accident is likely to happen. Carers also need to be aware of how to make the home, car or care setting a safer place, and where to go for advice and equipment.

WHEN ACCIDENTS ARE MORE LIKELY TO HAPPEN

▶ *Stress:* when adults and children are worried or anxious, they are less alert and less aware of possible dangers.

▶ *Lack of awareness:* parents tend to react to an existing threat of danger, rather than to *anticipate* one; for example, after a fall, parents will report that they had not realised that their child could even climb onto a stool, so had not thought to remove the dangerous object.

▶ *Over-protection:* a child whose parents are overprotective may become over-timid and less likely to be aware of dangers when unsupervised.

▶ *Poor role model:* adults who are always in a hurry may dash across the road instead of crossing in a safe place. Children will imitate their actions, and are less able to judge the speed of traffic.

▶ *Under-protection:* children under 7 should never be left alone in a house, not even when they are apparently safely asleep. Children who are underprotected will not have been made aware of dangers, and their natural curiosity will lead to dangerous play activities.

THE PREVENTION OF ACCIDENTS

Parents and child carers can reduce the risks of childhood accidents by the following means:

▶ *Be a good role model* – set a safe example.

▶ Make the home, garden and nursery as accident-proof as possible.

▶ *Teach children about safety* – make them aware of dangers in their environment.

▶ Never leave children alone in the house.

▶ Always try to buy goods displaying the appropriate safety symbol.

▶ The *kite mark* (see Figure 10.6): this mark on any product means that the British Standards Institution (BSI) has checked the manufacturer's claim that their product meets the specific standards.

▶ The new safety sign (see Figure 10.7): the safety mark means that a product has been checked to ensure that it meets the requirements of the BSI for safety only.

FIGURE 10.6
The kite mark (BSI)

FIGURE 10.7
The safety mark (BSI – found on gas cookers and and other gas appliances)

▶ The *lion mark* (see Figure 10.8): this symbol is only found on British-made toys and means that they have met the safety standards required.

▶ The *age advice safety symbol* (see Figure 10.9): this symbol means 'warning', do not give the toy to children less than 3 years, nor allow them to play with it.

<table>
<tr>
<td align="center">

FIGURE 10.8
The lion mark

</td>
<td align="center">

FIGURE 10.9
The age advice safety symbol

</td>
</tr>
<tr>
<td align="center">

Found only on British made toys;
they will have a CE mark as well

</td>
<td align="center">

</td>
</tr>
</table>

Note: toys and games bought from market stalls, or cheap foreign imports, may be copies of well-known brand-name toys but may *not* meet the safety standards.

Other safety symbols are shown in Figure 10.10.

FIGURE 10.10
Other safety symbols

<table>
<tr>
<td align="center">
Fire resistant furniture</td>
<td align="center">
Corrosive substance</td>
</tr>
<tr>
<td align="center">
BEAB mark (found on electrical goods)</td>
<td align="center">
Highly flammable substances</td>
</tr>
<tr>
<td align="center">
Toxic substance</td>
<td align="center">
Harmful or irritant substances</td>
</tr>
</table>

PREVENTING ACCIDENTS IN THE HOME

1 *Choking and suffocation.* Choking and suffocation is the largest cause of accidental death in babies under 1 year; and older children are also at risk when playing on their own or eating unsupervised.

   ▶ **DO NOT** leave rattles, teething rings or squeeze toys in the baby's cot; they can become wedged in the baby's mouth and cause suffocation.

   ▶ **DO NOT** leave a hose lying in the sun; water in it can get hot enough to scald a baby.

   ▶ **DO NOT** use a pillow for babies under 1 year old. **Baby nests** must meet British Standards No. 6595 and have a flat head area. Baby nests should only be used for carrying a baby – not for leaving a sleeping baby unattended.

► **DO NOT** let a baby or young child get hold of tiny items like coins, marbles, dried peas, buttons or Lego; small children explore with their mouths and can easily choke on small objects.

► **DO NOT** leave babies alone with finger foods such as bananas, carrots, cheese etc. Always supervise eating and drinking.

► **DO NOT** give peanuts to children under 4 years because they can easily choke on them or inhale them into their lungs, causing infection and lung damage.

► **DO NOT** leave a baby alone with a propped-up bottle – always hold the baby whilst feeding.

► **DO** supervise a baby playing with paper, as she may bite off small pieces and choke on them.

► **DO** use a firm mattress that meets British Standard No. 1877. For children over 1 year old, use a pillow that meets the same standard for allowing air to pass through freely whatever position the baby is in.

► **DO** check that there are no hanging cords – for example, from a window blind – which could catch around a child's neck and strangle them if they fall.

► **DO** keep all plastic bags away from babies and children, and teach older children never to put plastic bags on their heads.

► **DO** be aware that dummies on long ribbons, and cardigans with ribbons around the neck can pull tight around a baby's neck if caught on a hook or knob; a dummy must meet safety standards with holes in the flange, in case it is drawn into the back of the throat. Older children have been strangled by lethal tie-cords on anoraks.

► **DO** check that any toys given to babies and young children are safe, with no small loose parts or jagged edges.

2   *Burns and scalds.* As children learn to crawl, climb and walk, the risk of scalds or burns increases.

► **DO NOT** leave burning cigarettes in ashtrays.

► **DO NOT** use tablecloths which young children can pull down on top of themselves.

► **DO NOT** use gas or paraffin heaters in children's bedrooms.

► **DO NOT** ever leave a baby or young child alone in a bath, even for a few moments.

► **DO NOT** leave a hot iron unattended; **DO NOT** iron where children are likely to run past, and try to use a coiled flex.

► **DO** keep the water temperature for the house set at about 60°C (140°F) to prevent scalds and burns.

► **DO** protect fires with a fixed fine-mesh fireguard. Note: It is illegal to leave a child under 12 in a room with an open fire.

► **DO** keep matches and lighters well out of reach.

► **DO** choose night-clothes and dressing gowns that are flame-resistant (BS 3121).

► **DO** install automatic smoke alarms.

► **DO** use fire doors in nurseries and schools; and check you know the location of fire extinguishers and fire blankets.

► **DO** keep children away from bonfires and fireworks except at safe, public displays.

► **DO** keep a young child away from your area while you are cooking; always turn pan handles inwards; cooker guards are not a good idea as they can get very hot.

▶ **DO** keep kettles and hot drinks well out of reach; use a coiled kettle flex, and never pass hot drinks over the heads of children.

▶ **DO** test bath water before putting a child in; always put cold water in first and then add the hot water. A special plastic-strip thermometer can be stuck to the side of the bath to check the temperature.

▶ **DO** teach children the dangers of fire.

FIGURE 10.12
A child coming downstairs backwards on all fours

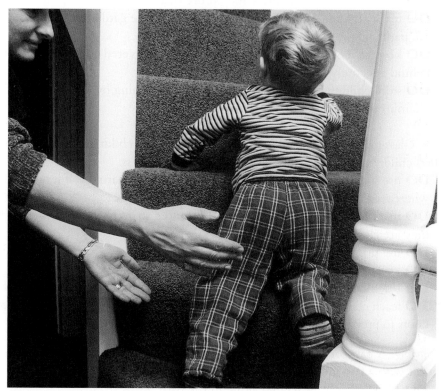

3 *Falls*. All children fall, but there are ways of ensuring that they **DO NOT** fall too far or too hard:

▶ **DO NOT** use baby-walkers. Child-safety experts agree that these are dangerous and cause many accidents as babies steer themselves into dangerous situations.

▶ **DO NOT** place furniture under windows where children may be tempted to climb.

▶ **DO NOT** leave babies unattended on a table, work surface, bed or sofa; lie them on the floor instead.

▶ **DO** use stairgates at the top and the bottom of stairs and at doors which might be left open (BS 4125).

▶ **DO** fit vertical bars to dangerous windows (note: horizontal bars encourage climbing).

▶ **DO** fit child-proof window safety catches on all windows.

▶ **DO** use a harness (BS 6684) in the highchair, pram, pushchair or supermarket trolley.

▶ **DO** teach children how to use the stairs safely; teach them to come down stairs backwards on all fours (see Figure 10.12).

4   *Poisoning:* The peak age for accidents with poisons is 1 to 3 years old, when children are highly mobile and inquisitive.

▶ **DO NOT** store dangerous household chemicals – bleach, disinfectant, white spirit – in the cupboard under the sink. Use a safer, locked cupboard instead.

▶ **DO NOT** transfer chemicals – e.g. weedkiller – into other containers such as a lemonade bottle as a child will not know the difference until it is too late.

▶ **DO** keep all medicines in a locked cupboard.

▶ **DO** use child-proof containers and ensure that they are closed properly.

▶ **DO** teach children not to eat berries or fungi in the garden or in the park.

▶ **DO** keep rubbish and kitchen waste in a tightly covered container, or better still, behind a securely locked door.

▶ **DO** store children's vitamins in a safe place. Poisoning by an overdose of vitamins is very common.

5   *Cuts:* Glass presents the biggest safety hazard to young children; every year, about 7,000 children end up in hospital after being cut by glass.

▶ **DO** use special safety glass in doors; this is relatively harmless if it does break, whereas ordinary glass breaks into lethal, jagged pieces.

▶ **DO** mark large picture windows with coloured strips to make it obvious when they are closed.

▶ **DO** use plastic drinking cups and bottles.

▶ **DO** keep all knives, scissors and razors out of reach.

▶ **DO** teach children never to run with a pencil or lolly stick in their mouth.

▶ **DO** teach children never to play with doors; if possible, fit a device to the top of doors to prevent them from slamming and pinching fingers.

6   *Drowning:* A baby or toddler can drown in a very shallow amount of water – even a bucket with a few inches of water in it presents a risk.

▶ **DO NOT** ever leave a child alone in the bath.

▶ **DO NOT** leave an older child looking after a baby or toddler in the bath.

▶ **DO** use a non-slip mat in the bath.

▶ **DO** always supervise water play.

▶ **DO** guard ponds, water butts and ditches.

▶ **DO** keep the toilet lid down at all times or fit locking device; toddlers are fascinated by the swirling water action and can fall in and drown.

7   Electric shocks. Children may suffer electric shock from poking small objects into sockets or from playing with electric plugs.

▶ **DO** fit safety dummy plugs or socket covers to all electric sockets.

▶ **DO** check that the plugs are correctly wired and safe; when buying Christmas tree lights, check for the British Standard No. 4647.

OTHER FACTORS IN ACCIDENTS IN THE HOME

However careful parents are in making their home a safe place for children, other people's homes may not be so safe. For example, the commonest cause of death in children in the USA and Australia is from children falling into friends' or neighbours' swimming pools. Always be alert to the possible hazards in any environment and keep the children safe.

ROAD SAFETY

Road traffic accidents (RTAs) account for one-half of all accidental deaths. Every year more than 400 children under the age of 15 years are killed, and many more are seriously injured, on the roads of the UK. In the 1970s, Denmark had the highest rate of child deaths from traffic accidents in Western Europe. The Danish government took action by creating a network of traffic-free foot and cycle paths, cutting accidents in those areas by 85%. There are signs that the UK may follow this example.

Educating children about safety on the roads should begin at a very early age, the best method being by example. Children need to learn about road safety in the same way as they learn any new skill: the message needs to be repeated over and over again until the child really has learnt it. The Green Cross Code is a very good method of teaching road safety (see Figure 10.13).

FIGURE 10.13
The Green Cross Code

The Green Cross Code

1. **Find a safe place to cross, then stop. Safe places include zebra and pelican crossings.**

2. **Stand on the pavement near the kerb.**

3. **Look all round for traffic and listen.**

4. **If traffic is coming, let it pass. Look all around again.**

5. **When there is no traffic near, walk straight across the road. Never run.**

6. **Keep looking and listening for traffic while you cross. Repeat and use the code every time.**

Every local authority employs a Road Safety Officer, and the Royal Society for the Prevention of Accidents (ROSPA) runs the Tufty Club for children aged 3 years or over. Children need to wear light-coloured clothes or luminous armbands – or both – when out at dusk or when walking on country roads without pavements.

FIGURE 10.14(a)
An ABC of resuscitation

ABC of resuscitation: babies up to 1-year-old

If a baby appears unconscious and gives no response

A Airway – open the airway

- Place the baby on a firm surface.
- Remove any obstruction from the mouth.
- Put one hand on the forehead and one finger under the chin, and gently tilt the head backwards VERY SLIGHTLY. (If you tilt the head too far back, it will close the airway again.)

B Breathing – check for breathing

- Put your ear close to the baby's mouth.
- Look to see if the chest is rising or falling.
- Listen and feel for the baby's breath on your cheek.
- Do this for five seconds.

If the baby is **not** breathing

1 Start **MOUTH TO MOUTH-AND-NOSE RESUSCITATION**:
   - Seal your lips around the baby's mouth and nose.
   - Blow GENTLY into the lungs until the chest rises.
   - Remove your mouth and allow the chest to fall.
2 Repeat five times at the rate of one breath every three seconds.
3 Check the pulse.

C Circulation – check the pulse

Lightly press your fingers towards the bone on the inside of the upper arm and hold them there for five seconds.

If there is **no** pulse, or the pulse is slower than 60 per minute, and the baby is **not** breathing, start **chest compressions**.

1 Find a position one finger's width below the line joining the baby's nipples, in the centre of the breastbone.
2 Place the tips of two fingers on this point and press to a depth of about 2 cm ($^3/_4$ inch) at a rate of 100 times per minute.

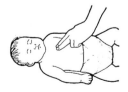

3 After five compressions, blow gently into the lungs once.
4 Continue the cycle for one minute.
5 Carry the baby to a phone and dial 999 for an ambulance.
6 Continue resuscitation, checking the pulse every minute until help arrives.

If the baby is **not** breathing but **does** have a pulse

1 Start **MOUTH TO MOUTH-AND-NOSE RESUSCITATION**, at the rate of one breath every three seconds.
2 Continue for one minute, then carry the baby to a phone and dial 999 for an ambulance.

If the baby **does** have a pulse and **is** breathing

1 Lay the baby on its side, supported by a cushion, pillow, rolled-up blanket or something similar.
2 Dial 999 for an ambulance.
3 Check breathing and pulse every minute, and be prepared to carry out resuscitation.

FIGURE 10.14(b)
An ABC of resuscitation

ABC of resuscitation: children aged 1 to 10

A Airway – open the airway

- Lay the child flat on their back.
- Remove clothing from around the neck.
- Remove any obstruction from the mouth.
- Lift the chin and tilt the head back slightly to open the airway.

If the child is **not** breathing and does **not** have a pulse

1. Begin a cycle of five chest compressions (see chest compression) and one breath (see mouth-to-mouth resuscitation). Continue for one minute.
2. Dial 999 for an ambulance.
3. Continue at the rate of one breath to five compressions until help arrives.

If the child is **not** breathing but **does** have a pulse

1. Give 20 breaths (see mouth-to-mouth resuscitation) in one minute.
2. Dial 999 for an ambulance.
3. Continue mouth-to-mouth resuscitation, rechecking the pulse and breathing after each set of 20 breaths, until help arrives or until the child starts breathing again. When breathing returns, place the child in the recovery position.

B Breathing – check for breathing

- Keep the airway open and place your cheek close to the child's mouth.
- Look to see if their chest is rising and falling.
- Listen and feel for their breath against your cheek.
- Do this for five seconds.
- If the child is not breathing, give five breaths (see mouth-to-mouth resuscitation), then check the pulse.

Mouth-to-mouth resuscitation

1. Open the airway by lifting the chin and tilting back the head. Check the mouth is clear of obstructions.
2. Close the child's nose by pinching the nostrils.
3. Take a deep breath and seal your mouth over the child's.
4. Blow firmly into the mouth for about two seconds, watching the chest rise.
5. Remove your mouth and allow the child's chest to fall.
6. Repeat until help arrives.

C Circulation – check the pulse

- Find the carotid pulse by placing your fingers in the groove between the Adam's apple and the large muscle running down the side of the neck
- Do this for five seconds.

Chest compression

1. Make sure the child is lying on their back on a firm surface (preferably the ground).
2. Find the spot where the bottom of the ribcage joins on to the end of the breastbone, and measure one finger's width up from this point.
3. Using one hand only, press down sharply at a rate of 100 times a minute, to a depth of about 3 cm (1$\frac{1}{4}$ inches). Counting aloud will help you keep at the right speed.
4. Continue until help arrives.

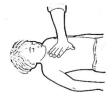

Choking

Check inside the baby's mouth. If the obstruction is visible, try to hook it out with your finger, but don't risk pushing it further down. If this doesn't work, proceed as follows:

* Lay the baby face down along your forearm with your hand supporting her head and neck, and her head lower than her bottom. OR:

* An older baby or toddler may be placed face down across your knee with head and arms hanging down.

* Give five brisk slaps between the shoulder blades.

* Turn the baby over, check the mouth and remove any obstruction.

* Check for breathing.

* If the baby is not breathing, give five breaths (see MOUTH TO MOUTH-AND-NOSE RESUSCITATION page 266).

* If the airway is still obstructed, give five CHEST COMPRESSIONS.

* If the baby is still not breathing, repeat the cycle of back slaps, mouth to mouth-and nose breathing and chest compressions.

* After two cycles, if the baby is not breathing, dial 999 for an ambulance.

NB: Never hold a baby or young child upside down by the ankles and slap their back – you could break their neck.

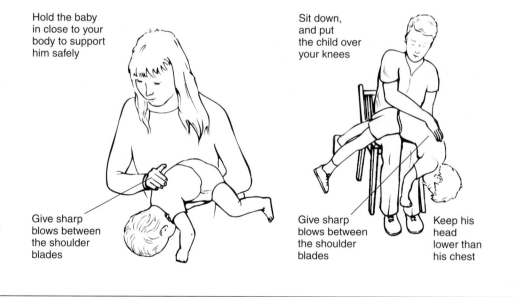

Hold the baby in close to your body to support him safely

Give sharp blows between the shoulder blades

Sit down, and put the child over your knees

Give sharp blows between the shoulder blades

Keep his head lower than his chest

Head Injuries

Babies and young children are particularly prone to injury from falls. Any injury to the head must be investigated carefully. A head injury can damage the scalp, skull or brain.

Symptoms and signs

If the head injury is mild, the only symptom may be a slight headache and this will probably result in a crying baby. More seriously, the baby may:

* lose consciousness even if only for a few minutes;

* vomit;

* seem exceptionally drowsy;

* complain of an ache or pain in the head;

* lose blood from her nose, mouth or ears;

* lose any watery fluid from her nose or ears;

* have an injury to the scalp which might suggest a fracture to the skull bones.

Treatment

If the baby or young child has any of the above symptoms:

Dial 999 for an ambulance or go straight to your nearest A & E department

Meanwhile:

* if the child is unconscious, follow the ABC routine described on pages 266–267;

* stop any bleeding by applying direct pressure, but take care that you are not pressing a broken bone into the delicate tissue underneath; if in doubt, apply pressure around the edge of the wound, using dressings;

* if there is discharge from the ear, position the child so that the affected ear is lower and cover with a clean pad; do not plug the ear.

Burns and Scalds

Burns are injuries to body tissues caused by heat, chemicals or radiations. Scalds are caused by wet heat, such as steam or hot liquids.

Superficial burns involve only the outer layers of the skin, cause redness, swelling, tenderness and usually heal well. Intermediate burns form blisters, can become infected, and need medical aid. Deep burns involve all layers of the skin, which may be pale and charred, may be pain free if the nerves are damaged, and will ALWAYS require medical attention.

Treatment for severe burns and scalds

* Lay the child down and protect burnt area from ground contact

* Check ABC of resuscitation and be ready to resuscitate if necessary

* Gently remove any constricting clothing from the injured area before it begins to swell

* Cover the injured area loosely with a sterile un-medicated dressing or use a clean non-fluffy tea-towel or pillowcase

DO NOT remove anything that is sticking to the burn

DO NOT apply lotions, creams or fat to the injury

DO NOT break blisters

DO NOT use plasters

* If the child is unconscious, lay the child on her side, supported by a cushion, pillow, rolled-up blanket or something similar

* Send for medical attention

Treatment for minor burns and scalds

* Place the injured part under slowly running water, or soak in cold water for 10 minutes

* Gently remove any constricting articles from the injured area before it begins to swell

* Dress with clean, sterile, non-fluffy material

DO NOT use adhesive dressings

DO NOT apply lotions, ointments or fat to burn or scald

DO NOT break blisters or otherwise interfere

* If in doubt, seek medical aid

Treatment for sunburn

* Remove the child to the shade and cool the skin by gently sponging the skin with tepid (lukewarm) water

* Give sips of cold water at frequent intervals

* If the burns are mild, gently apply an after-sun cream

* For extensive blistering, seek medical help

CHILDREN AS PASSENGERS IN CARS

1 *Babies*. Babies not yet sitting are best transported in a rearward-facing restraint which doubles as a baby seat when at home or when visiting friends.

2 *Toddlers and young children*. Once the baby can sit up, the child safety seat is usually suitable for use in the back of the car until the child is 4. The seat must carry the BSI kite mark (see Figure 10.6).

3 *Older children*. When the child is too large for a child safety seat, either a child harness or a special adjustable seat belt may be used – in both cases a rigid booster cushion enables the child to see out of the window.

EMERGENCY FIRST AID

Anyone working in child care settings is advised to attend a first-aid course. St. John's Ambulance has recently introduced a new Lifesaver Award and a Babies and Children Lifesaver Award (see the addresses at the end of the chapter).

THE CHILD ACCIDENT PREVENTION TRUST

The Child Accident Prevention Trust is a voluntary organisation which works closely with health and education professionals to increase public awareness of safety issues. In 1995 it launched the 'Seven steps for safety' initiative:

1 Plan and practise a safer route to school.
2 Use a car seat that fits your child and your car.
3 Fit and check a smoke alarm.
4 Use a harness and reins when out and about with your toddler.
5 Keep household products and medicines locked up or high out of reach.
6 Plan your next safety move – keep one step ahead as your baby grows.
7 Check your safety equipment – does it fit and does it work?

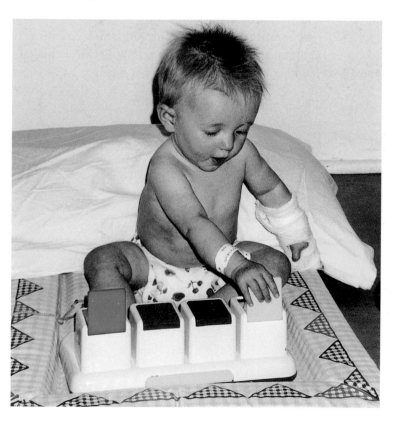

THE SAFETY OF CHILDREN ON OUTINGS

Children derive many benefits from outings: trips to farms, parks, museums and theatres can provide stimulation and a welcome break from normal routine. When taking a group of young children on any outing, awareness of their safety needs must be paramount:

▶ *Planning:* it may be necessary to visit the place beforehand and to discuss any specific requirements, for example lunch arrangements or wet-weather provision.

▶ *Permission:* the manager or head teacher must give permission, and a letter should be sent to all parents/guardians of the children.

▶ Request help from the parents.

▶ Inform parents what the child needs to bring – packed meal, waterproof coat. Emphasise no glass bottles or sweets; spending money if necessary – state the advised maximum sum.

▶ *Supervision:* arrange adequate adult supervision; there should always be trained staff on any outing, however low-key. The adult:child ratio should never exceed 4:1. If the children are under 2 years, or if any of them have special needs, you would expect to have *fewer* children per adult. Swimming trips should only be attempted if the ratio is 1 adult to 1 child for children under 5 years. The younger the children the more adults are required, particularly if the trip involves crossing roads, when an adult must be able to hold the children's hands.

▶ *Transport:* if a coach is being hired, check whether it has seat belts for children. New laws require all *new* minibuses and coaches to have seat belts fitted, and from 1996, all new minibus drivers will have to pass a special test.

SAFETY AT HOME TIMES

Any nursery or school should be secure so that children cannot wander off without anyone realising; there should also be a policy which guards against strangers being able to wander in without reason. Many child care settings now have door entry phones, and staff wear name badges. It is a matter of courtesy and security for all visitors for them to give advance notice of their visit. A balance has to be achieved which ensures that the child is safe (for example, it is important that staff know *who* is to collect the child at the end of the session) but which is welcoming to people who have good reason to be there.

RESOURCES

Books

Linda Ewles and Ina Simnett, *Promoting Health: a Practical Guide to Health Education,* Chichester, John Wiley and Sons Ltd, 1993

First Aid Manual, London, Dorling Kindersley, 1992

Dennis Taylor, *Human Physical Health,* Cambridge, Cambridge University Press, 1989

World Health Organization, *Charter for Health Promotion,* World Health Organization, 1986

Useful addresses

Health Education Authority
Hamilton House
Mabledon Place
London WC1H 9JP
Tel.: 020 7631 0930

Royal Society for the
Promotion of Health
RSH House
38A St George's Drive
London SW1V 4BH
Tel.: 020 7630 0121

British Red Cross
9 Grosvenor Crescent
London SW1X 7EF
Tel.: 020 7235 5454

Child Accident Prevention
Trust
4th Floor, Clerks Court
18–20 Farringdon Lane
London EC1R 3AU
Tel.: 020 7608 3828
Investigates all aspects of
accident prevention and
children's safety

St John's Ambulance
1 Grosvenor Crescent
London SW1X 7EF
Tel.: 020 7235 5231

St Andrew's Ambulance
Association
St Andrew's House
48 Milton Street
Glasgow G4 0HR
Tel.: 0141 332 4031

RoSPA (Royal Society for
the Prevention of Accidents)
Cannon House
The Priory Queensway
Birmingham B4 6BS
Tel.: 0121 200 2461

Royal Life Saving
Society UK
Mountbatten House
Studley
Warwicks B80 7NN
Tel.: 01527 853943

ACTIVITY

Health-product advertising

1 Collect advertisements from magazines and newspapers for any product which claims to promote better health. Discuss their aims and objectives:
   ▶ Which groups are they targeting?
   ▶ Do they give any useful information on healthy living in addition to information on using their product?
2 Find out about the advertising standards which apply to health-product advertising.
3 Which television advertising campaigns for such products are memorable?

ACTIVITY

Health promotion on TV and radio

In small groups, discuss a serial on TV or radio. List all the health-promotion messages you can remember within the storylines:
1 Do you think that radio fiction is a good way of getting a health message across?
2 Does the inclusion of a telephone helpline number detract from or enhance the impact of a health problem?
3 Does the programme mirror real life or is it viewed as escapism?

Fire and safety, and accidents

In a practical work placement, research the following information:
1 *Fire and safety.*
  ▶ What are the instructions in the event of a fire?
  ▶ Where are the fire extinguishers located?
  ▶ Where are the fire exits located?

2 *Accident report book.* Every workplace is required to maintain a record of accidents. Ask for permission to look at the book at your placement:
  ▶ Present the information in the accident book in the form of a pie chart, using the following (and other) categories of accident: falls, cuts, burns and scalds, choking, stings etc.
  ▶ For each category of accident, state how it could have been prevented and what treatment should be given.

Note: remember to preserve confidentiality – DO NOT use names.

First-aid boxes

The contents of a first-aid box in the workplace are determined by the Health and Safety at Work Act (1974).
1 Find out and list the items which should be in the workplace first-aid box.
2 Make a list of all the items that you feel should be in a *home* first-aid box.
3 As a group, compare your lists and discuss the following points:
  ▶ the cost of all the items;
  ▶ possible reasons why the contents of the workplace first-aid box are fairly limited;
  ▶ the contents of the first-aid box in your own workplace;
  ▶ how accessible the first-aid box is;
  ▶ how many members of staff are designated first-aiders, and how they are trained.

1 Design a poster to illustrate the 'Seven steps to safety' (see p. 271).
2 Where would be the best places to display the poster, and why?

A C T I V I T Y

Evaluating the setting

In your work placement, find out the following information:

1 How welcoming is the setting? Describe the factors which help to create a welcoming environment, and list any possible improvements.

2 How safe is the setting? Try to look at the setting from a child's viewpoint and again list any possible improvements.

A C T I V I T Y

Safety Quiz

These questions list some things which children want to do for fun or to help out in the house. Check with the answers on page 276.

How old does a child have to be to do this safely?

1 Cross a quiet street alone.
2 Make a cup of tea.
3 Have a bath without an adult watching.
4 Have a drink without an adult in the room.
5 Play near water without adults around.
6 Ride a bicycle in a back street.
7 Eat peanuts.
8 Play with plastic bags.
9 Walk downstairs without an adult.
10 Climb trees.
11 Play in the playground with other children and without adults around.
12 Use matches.

Answers to the safety quiz on page 275

These answers are guidelines only. Bear in mind how mature the child is.

1 **8 years old.** Children can't judge the speed of cars and cope reliably with traffic until they are 11 or 12. An 8 year old can probably be trusted to wait on the pavement for traffic to clear: they may still dash into the road if they get excited. Children of 2 or 3 don't have any idea that cars are dangerous.

2 **10 years old.** They are strong enough to pick up a kettle and a teapot. They are not clumsy, like a little child, so they can pour the water without getting a scald.

3 **4 years old.** They are old enough not to slip down and go under the water. You can teach them not to fiddle with the taps. There needs to be someone close by to listen out. The bathroom door should be open and never locked.

4 **18 months old.** Babies this age can manage a teacher beaker by themselves. Younger babies can choke on drinks or bottles. Even a toddler can choke on food and needs an adult there when eating.

5 **No age.** Toddlers and babies can drown even in a paddling pool or a puddle. Bigger children can drown outdoors.

6 **11 years old.** Secondary school children are safe to use their bikes for school if they have had some cycle training. They need bright reflective clothing and a cycle helmet.

7 **6 years old.** Peanuts can easily block the lung because they contain a special oil that makes the lining of the lung swell up.

8 **No age.** Plastic bags are not toys. Children will be tempted to use them for dangerous dressing-up games. Six or seven-year-olds may be given plastic bags to keep things in, as long as they know not to use them for games, and there are no little brothers or sisters around.

9 **3 years old.** 2 year olds can be killed falling off stairs. They need stairgates to keep them off the stairs and an adult walking with them.

10 **7 years old.** Climbing trees is always dangerous but you can't stop children having fun. Seven-year-olds can learn to test branches for strength. They can choose trees over grass not concrete. They can climb well unlike little children.

11 **It depends on the playground.** Toddlers won't be happy unless you are there. Some playgrounds are fine for older children and some aren't safe even with an adult around because of broken glass or litter.

12 **7 years old.** They are old enough to hold a match properly and to strike it without getting burnt. They can light their own birthday cake candles but they can't make a bonfire or light a fire in the hearth. Never leave matches where children can reach them.

11

Food, Nutrition and Care of the Environment

Good nutrition, or healthy eating, is one of the most important ways we can help ourselves to feel well and be well. We need food:

▶ to provide **energy** for physical activity and to maintain body temperature;
▶ to provide material for the **growth** of body cells;
▶ for the **repair and replacement** of damaged body tissues.

During childhood we develop food habits that will affect us for life. By the time we are adults most of us will suffer from some disorder which is related to our diet; for example, tooth decay, heart disease or cancer. Establishing healthy eating patterns will help to promote normal growth and development and protect against disease. Those caring for children need to know what constitutes a good diet and how it can be provided (see Table 11.1).

The principles of a healthy diet

Types of food can be arranged into four groups, based on the nutrients they provide. To ensure a balanced, healthy diet, some foods *from each group* should be included in the child's diet *every day* (see Figure 11.1). The easiest way to assess our nutrition is to keep in mind the four food groups; eating a variety of foods from each of these food groups every day will automatically balance our diet.

FIGURE 11.1
The principles of healthy eating

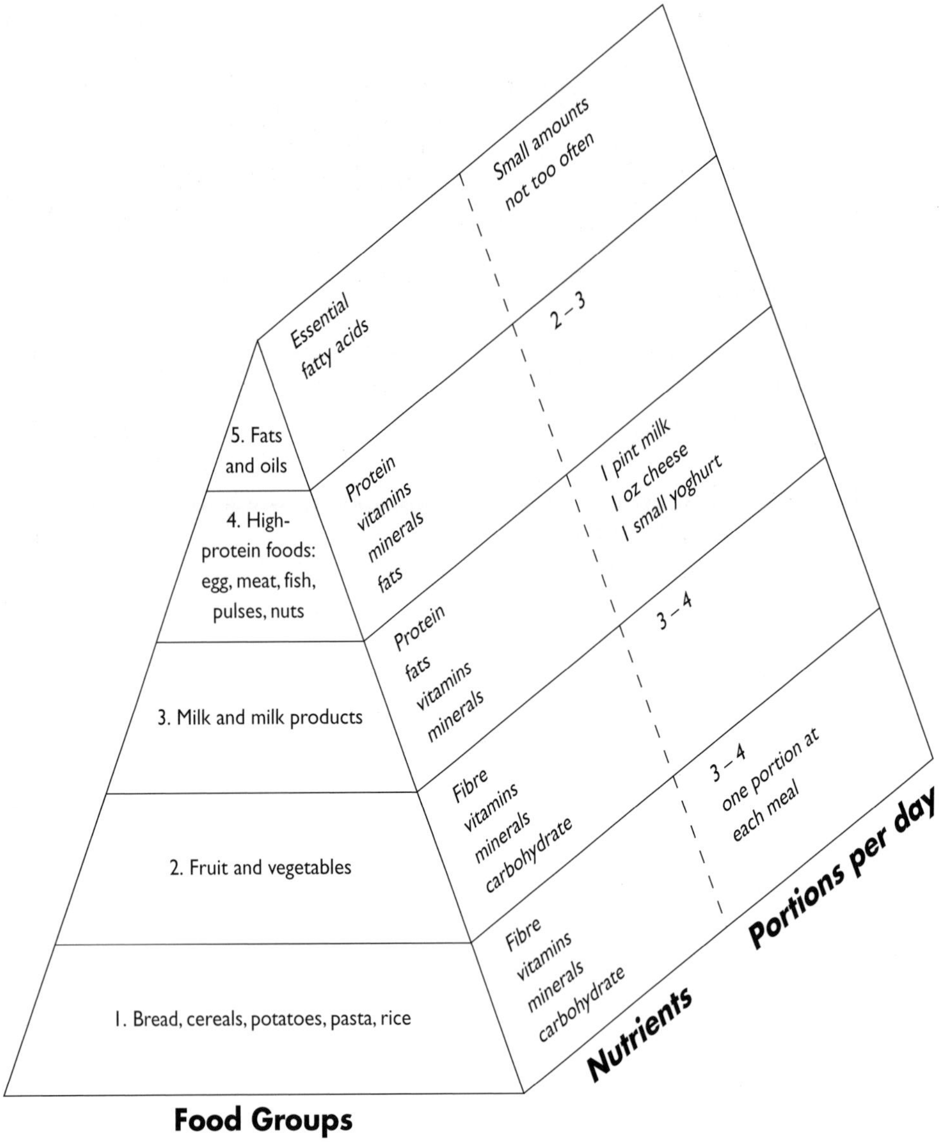

Food groups
FOOD GROUP 1: POTATO AND CEREALS

These are high-energy foods which also contain **vitamins** and **minerals**. Foods in this group include:

▶ rice
▶ potato
▶ bread
▶ pasta
▶ breakfast cereals.

Including wholemeal or whole-grain cereals and potatoes in their skins will increase the fibre content of the diet. Bran should *not* be given to children as an extra source of fibre as

FIGURE 11.2
The balance of good health

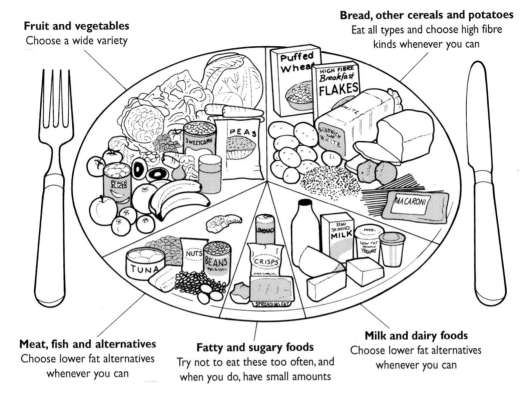

Fruit and vegetables
Choose a wide variety

Bread, other cereals and potatoes
Eat all types and choose high fibre
kinds whenever you can

Meat, fish and alternatives
Choose lower fat alternatives
whenever you can

Fatty and sugary foods
Try not to eat these too often, and
when you do, have small amounts

Milk and dairy foods
Choose lower fat alternatives
whenever you can

it can interfere with the absorption of **calcium** and **iron** and may also cause stomach cramps.

All meals of the day should include foods from this group. For example:

▶ At breakfast: a breakfast cereal or bread;
▶ For cooked meals: pasta/rice/potatoes;
▶ For snack meals: bread/pizza base.

Children require *five serves* from this food group every day. Examples of **one serve** are:

▶ one bowl of breakfast cereal; or
▶ one slice of bread; or
▶ one small potato; or
▶ two tablespoons of rice or pasta.

FOOD GROUP 2: FRUIT AND VEGETABLES

Fruit and vegetables are full of **vitamins, minerals** (see Table 11.2) and fibre which are needed to maintain good health; they are also very low in fat. A fruit or vegetable **high in vitamin C** should be included every day. Examples are:

▶ tomato;
▶ citrus fruit – oranges, grapefruit etc.;
▶ kiwi fruit;
▶ sweet peppers.

Many children will eat slices of raw vegetables or salad in place of cooked vegetables, e.g. carrots, cucumber, tomato or peppers. Children who are reluctant to eat vegetables should be given fruit or fruit juice instead.

TABLE 11.1

Basic food requirements

NUTRIENT/FOOD	USE	SOURCE
CARBOHYDRATES Starches Sugars Cellulose	Major source of energy for growth, body maintenance and activity. Aids the digestion of other foods	Bread, cereals, pasta, plantain, potatoes, pulses rice, grains, sugar, honey, fruit, milk
PROTEINS Consist of building blocks, called *amino acids*, which link together to perform required functions. First-class proteins contain all the *essential* amino acids Second-class proteins contain *some* essential amino acids	Essential for growth and repair of the body. Also produce certain *hormones* and other active chemicals. Only used as energy as last resort in the absence of other sources	First-class proteins: meat, poultry, fish, cheese, milk and milk products. Second-class proteins: nuts and seed, soya, pulses (beans and lentils), cereals (rice, oats and cornmeal) and cereal-based foods e.g. pasta, bread, chapatis
FATS *Saturated fats* – from animal sources. *Unsaturated fats* – from vegetable sources.	Provide energy, contain essential vitamins, conserve body heat	Butter, cheese, meat, lard. Nuts, olive oil, vegetable oils, fish oil
MINERALS Cannot be *manufactured* by the body. Major minerals – calcium, sodium, potassium and magnesium, sulphur, other minerals called *trace elements* or minerals	Needed for building bones, regulating fluid balance, control of muscles and nerves, energy production	Found in nearly all foods in varying amounts. Sodium – in table salt, bread, meat and fish. Fluoride – in water, occurring naturally or added to water supply
VITAMINS Cannot be *manufactured* by the body. Complex chemical substances made by plants and animals. Divided into two groups: *Fat-soluble* (A, D, E and K) *Water-soluble* (C and the B vitamins)	Vitamin A – vision and healthy skin. Vitamin D – growth of bones and teeth. Vitamin E – protects cells from damage. Vitamin K – helps the blood-clotting process. The B Vitamins – blood formation and muscle function Vitamin C – promotes the healing process.	Fat-soluble – in oily fish, cheese, carrots, tomatoes, egg yolk, liver, green vegetables. Water-soluble – fruits, fruit juices, meat, leafy vegetables, beans, eggs
FIBRE Also known as roughage, fibre cannot be broken down and used by the body	Adds bulk to food, helps prevent constipation. Some experts believe that fibre reduces the risk of heart disease, and certain types of cancer	Rolled oats, beans, wholewheat bread, celery, bran, prunes and apples
WATER	Vital component of our diet. Helps in maintaining fluid balance and in elimination of waste products	Present in all foods

TABLE 11.2

Vitamins and minerals – good food sources

VITAMINS AND MINERALS	GOOD FOOD SOURCES	VITAMINS AND MINERALS	GOOD FOOD SOURCES
VITAMIN A	Liver, milk, cheese, green vegetables	FOLIC ACID	Breakfast cereals, green leafy vegetables, offal (mainly liver)
THIAMIN (VITAMIN B1)	Bread, breakfast cereals	COPPER	Found generally in all foods, small amounts
RIBOFLAVIN (VITAMIN B2)	Breakfast cereals, milk and milk products	NIACIN	Meat, potatoes, bread, breakfast cereals
BIOTIN	Eggs, wholewheat breakfast cereals. Also found in small amounts in fish, meat and pulses	MAGNESIUM	Found generally in all foods in small amounts
PANTOTHENIC ACID	Meat, milk, wholewheat breakfast cereals, lentils, beans and pulses	IRON	Read meat, offal, pulses eggs, breakfast cereals, green vegetables
VITAMIN B6	Breakfast cereals mainly, but also found in small amounts in fruit, meat and vegetables	SELENIUM	Seafood, meat, offal, milk, wholewheat breakfast cereals, flour
VITAMIN B12	Eggs, meat, offal (heart, liver, kidney), dairy produce	ZINC	Offal (especially liver), seafood, eggs milk, wholegrain cereals
VITAMIN C	Citrus fruits, berry fruits, potatoes, green vegetables	CALCIUM	Dairy produce, tinned fish, white bread/flour
VITAMIN E	Vegetable oils (especially sunflower oil), eggs, green leafy vegetables	IODINE	Milk and milk products, meat, eggs iodized salt

Children require *four serves* from this group every day. Examples of **one serve** are:
- ▶ one glass of fruit juice; or
- ▶ one piece of fruit; or
- ▶ sliced tomato in a sandwich; or
- ▶ two tablespoons of cooked vegetables; or
- ▶ one tablespoon of dried fruit – e.g. raisins.

Fruit and vegetables are best eaten raw as their vitamin content is easily destroyed by cooking and processing.

Food Group 3: Milk and Milk Products
This group includes:
- ▶ milk
- ▶ yoghurt and fromage frais
- ▶ cheese.

Children require 1 pint of milk each day to ensure an adequate intake of **calcium**. If a child cannot achieve this milk intake, equivalent amounts of calcium can be taken from yoghurt, cheese, fromage frais etc. Reduced-fat milks should not generally be given to children under 5 because of their lower energy and fat-soluble-vitamin content; however, semi-skimmed milk may be introduced from 2 years of age, provided that the child's overall diet is adequate. (Parents on Income Support can get tokens to exchange for 7 pints of milk a week for each child under 5 years of age.)

Children require *three serves* from this food group every day. Examples of **one serve** are:
- ▶ one glass of milk; or
- ▶ one pot of yoghurt or fromage frais; or
- ▶ one tablespoon of grated cheese – e.g. cheese on top of a pizza.

Food Group 4: High-Protein Foods
Foods high in protein include:
- ▶ lean meat
- ▶ poultry
- ▶ fish
- ▶ eggs
- ▶ tofu, quorn
- ▶ pulses – peas, beans (baked beans, kidney beans), lentils, ground nuts and seeds.

Children require *two serves* from this food group every day (see Tables 11.1 and 11.3). Examples of **one serve** are:
- ▶ a portion of fish fingers;
- ▶ a portion of baked beans;
- ▶ chicken nuggets or a small piece of chicken.

The amount of food in each group which makes up one serve will vary according to the age of the individual child; for example a 3-year-old may have two fish fingers, while a 7-year-old may have three or four.

Food Group 5: Fats and Oils
Fats and oils are found in the foods from the four groups. For instance, meat and cheese contain fat and some vegetables contain oil.

TABLE 11.3
Suitable protein combinations

SUITABLE PROTEIN COMBINATIONS	FOUND IN:
FOR VEGETARIANS AND VEGANS: beans + cereal lentils + rice beans + rice	baked beans on toast lentil and rice soup bean casserole with rice
FOR LACTO-VEGETARIANS ONLY: cereal + milk egg + bread pasta + cheese bread + cheese	breakfast cereal with milk scrambled egg on toast macaroni cheese cheese sandwich

OTHER FOODS

Sweets, cakes, chocolate and crisps are all **high-energy foods**, but they have little other nutritional value. If children eat a lot of these foods, they run the risk of putting on too much weight and of suffering tooth decay.

Children may be offered foods with extra fat or sugar – biscuits, cakes, chocolate, crisps and sweet drinks – as long as these items are not *replacing* food from the four food groups.

How to promote healthy eating – guidelines for early childhood workers

Our eating habits, tastes and preferences are shaped very early on – by the example set by parents and other carers and by the food offered in infancy. These early influences often mould our whole attitude towards food and eating throughout school and adult life. Families who lead such busy lives that members prepare their own meal and then eat it while watching television will have a very different perspective on the role of food and mealtimes than families who regularly sit together at an evening meal.

GUIDELINES

Helping carers to organise the dietary needs of young children within a flexible, healthy eating framework

▶ **Offer a *wide variety* of different foods. Give babies and toddlers a chance to try a new food more than once; any refusal on first tasting may be due to dislike of the new rather than of the food itself.**

▶ **Most young children need three small meals and three snacks a day. Teach the child to eat *mainly at mealtimes* and avoid giving them high-**

calorie snacks – e.g. biscuits and sugary drinks – which might take the edge off their appetite for more nutritious food.

▶ *Set an example* – children will imitate both *what* you eat and *how* you eat it. It will be easier to encourage a child to eat sticks of raw celery if *you* eat one too.

▶ *Presentation is important* – manufacturers of food which is mainly bought for children use a variety of techniques to make their products exciting – colours, shapes, themes and characters. Using these tactics can make mealtimes more fun.

▶ *Avoid adding salt* to any food at the table. Too much salt can cause dehydration in babies and may predispose certain people to hypertension (high blood pressure) if taken over a lifetime.

▶ Give healthy foods as *treats*, e.g. raisins and raw carrots rather than sweets or cakes.

▶ Children should be able to *follow their own individual appetites* in deciding how much they want to eat. It is unfair to insist that children clear their plates if they DO NOT want any more food.

▶ When changing the menu in a nursery setting to a more healthy option, introduce the new foods in *stages* – e.g. if switching to wholemeal bread, try a soft-grain white bread first – and always involve the children in choices as far as possible.

Additives

Additives are either natural or **synthetic** (that is, made by a chemical process) substances added to packaged food to preserve it or make it look or taste better. All manufactured foods are required by law to display a label showing the ingredients in the food, listed in order of the amount (by weight) present, starting with the largest. All additives are identified on the content label by an **E number** – a code number recognised within the European Community (EC). Additives are usually grouped according to their purpose.

▶ **Preservatives:** chemicals such as sorbic acid (E200) and sulphur dioxide (E220) are added to food to prevent **microbes** from spoiling the food.

▶ **Antioxidants:** natural substances such as lecithin (E322) and chemicals such as butylated hydroxyanisole (E320) stop fatty foods from becoming rancid and protect vitamins in the food from being destroyed during processing.

▶ **Emulsifiers and stabilisers:** these are substances, such as gum arabic (E414) and locust bean gum (E410), which enable ingredients that would normally separate to be mixed together and to *maintain* that mixed quality.

▶ **Flavouring:** these include all herbs and spices, and monosodium glutamate (621 MSG), which enhance the flavour by making the food taste stronger; these additives are not subject to an E number at present. Artificial sweeteners such as saccharin and sorbitol (E420) are used in low-calorie and in diabetic food.

▶ **Colouring:** substances such as tartrazine (E102), sunset yellow (E110) and caramels (E150) are used to make food look more colourful and attractive.

TABLE 11.4
An example of a balanced diet

MEALS AND SNACKS	NO. OF SERVINGS IN EACH FOOD GROUP				
	POTATO AND CEREALS	FRUIT AND VEGETABLES	MILK AND MILK PRODUCTS	HIGH-PROTEIN FOODS	EXTRA FAT AND SUGAR
BREAKFAST					
I weetabix	I				
+ milk			I		
I slice of toast	I				
MID-MORNING					
I packet raisins		I			
I glass squash					I
LUNCH					
Chicken nuggets				I	
Chips	I				
Peas		I			
Yoghurt			I		
Fruit juice		I			
MID-AFTERNOON					
Bread and jam	I				
I glass of milk			I		
SUPPER					
Baked beans on toast	I			I	
Cucumber slices		I			
Chocolate buttons					I
TOTALS	5	4	3	2	
RECOMMENDED DAILY SERVES	5	4	3	2	

ADDITIVES AND BEHAVIOUR PROBLEMS

Some children may show unacceptable patterns of behaviour, such as hyperactivity, temper tantrums or sleeping problems, which could be caused by a reaction to the additives in their diet. The most commonly cited additives in this context are:

Colourings
▶ tartrazine (E102)
▶ poinceau (E124)

Preservatives
▶ benzoates (E210–E219)

▶ sunset yellow (E110)

▶ erythrosine (E127

▶ anti-oxidants BHA and
BHT (E320 and E321))

There are many further causes for children's behaviour *other* than diet, and a condition such as **hyperactivity** can only be diagnosed by a paediatrician.

Some manufacturers and supermarket chains are now selling additive-free foods.

G U I D E L I N E S

To reduce additives in the diet, parents and carers should:

▶ **always look at the labels on food containers and be wary of a long list of E numbers;**

▶ **use fresh rather than highly processed food;**

▶ **cook their own pies, soups, cakes etc.**

Multicultural provision

The UK is the home of a multicultural and multi-ethnic society. The main ethnic minority groups are situated near large cities; many people came from the West Indies and Asia to the UK in response to labour shortages in the 1950s and 1960s.

The **Asian** community represents the largest ethnic minority in the UK – about 1.25 million people. Asian dietary customs are mainly based on three main religious groups: Muslims (or Moslems), Hindus and Sikhs.

Hindus

Wheat is the main staple food eaten by Hindus in the UK; it is used to make chapattis, puris and parathas. Orthodox Hindus are strict vegetarians as they believe in **Ahimsa** – non-violence towards all living beings – and a minority practise **veganism**. Some will eat dairy products and eggs, whilst others will refuse eggs on the ground that they are a potential source of life. Even non-vegetarians DO NOT eat beef as the cow is considered a sacred animal, and it is unusual for pork to be eaten as the pig is considered unclean. Ghee (clarified butter) and vegetable oil are used in cooking. Three festivals in the Hindu calendar are observed as days of **fasting**, which lasts from dawn to dusk and during which time Hindus only eat 'pure' foods such as fruit and yoghurt:

1 **Mahshivrati** – the birthday of Lord Shiva (March)
2 **Ram Naumi** – the birthday of Lord Rama (April)
3 **Jan Mash Tami** – the birthday of Lord Krishna (late August).

Muslims

Muslims (or Moslems) practise the Islamic religion, and their holy book, The Koran, provides them with their food laws. Unlawful foods (called *haram*) are: pork, all meat which has not been rendered lawful (*halal*), alcohol and fish without scales. Wheat, in the form of chapattis, and rice are the staple foods. The Koran dictates that children should be breast-fed up to the age of 2 years. During the lunar month of **Ramadan**, Muslims fast between sunrise and sunset; fasting involves abstinence from all food and drink, so many Muslims rise early to eat before dawn in order to maintain energy levels. Children under 12 years and the elderly are exempt from fasting.

Sikhs

Most Sikhs will not eat pork or beef or any meat that is killed by the *halal* method. Some Sikhs are vegetarian, but many eat chicken, lamb and fish. Wheat and rice are staple foods. Devout Sikhs will fast once or twice a week, and most will fast on the first day of the **Punjabi** month or when there is a full moon.

Afro-Caribbean diets

The **Afro-Caribbean** community is the second largest ethnic minority group in the UK. Dietary practices here vary widely. Many people include a wide variety of European foods in their diet alongside the traditional foods of cornmeal, coconut, green banana, plantain, okra and yam. Although Afro-Caribbean people are generally Christian, a minority are **Rastafarians**.

Rastafarians

Dietary practices are based on laws, laid down by Moses in the book of Genesis in the Bible, which state that certain types of meat should be avoided. The majority of followers will only eat 'Ital' foods, which are foods considered to be in a whole or natural state. Most Rastafarians are vegetarians and will not consume processed or preserved foods.

Jewish diets

Jewish people observe dietary laws which state that animals and birds must be slaughtered by the Jewish method to render them **kosher** (acceptable). Milk and meat must never be cooked or eaten together, and pork in any form is forbidden. Shellfish are not allowed as they are thought to harbour disease. The most holy day of the Jewish calendar is **Yom Kippur** (the Day of Atonement) when Jewish people fast for 25 hours.

Vegetarian diets

People adopt vegetarian diets for a wide variety of reasons, and they are becoming increasingly popular, especially among young people and women. Reasons may be:
- ▶ concern for animal welfare;
- ▶ ethical beliefs about the use of world resources;
- ▶ religious and cultural beliefs;
- ▶ personal motivations of health and lifestyle.

There are several types of vegetarian diet, which are in contrast to an **omnivorous** diet (one that includes all kinds of animal and plant foods). The most common form is **lacto-ovo-vegetarian**, which excludes all animal flesh but includes milk, milk products and eggs, as well as all plant foods. **Lacto-vegetarians** also exclude eggs. The partial or **semi-vegetarian** diet is not strictly vegetarian and is often adopted for health reasons; it eliminates certain types of animal food, often red meat, while including fish and perhaps poultry.

The vegan diet

A vegan diet completely excludes all foods of animal origin; that is, animal flesh, milk and milk products, eggs, honey and all additives which may be of animal origin. A vegan diet is based on cereals and cereal products, pulses, fruits, vegetables, nuts and seeds. Human breastmilk is acceptable for vegan babies.

Nutritional disorders in children

Nutritional disorders may be caused by an excess or a deficiency of one or more of the elements of nutrition.

Nutritional excess

Obesity (fatness) results from taking in more energy from the diet than is used up by the body. Some children appear to inherit a tendency to put on weight very easily, and some parents and carers offer more high-calorie food than children need. Obesity can lead to emotional problems as well as the physical problem of being more prone to infections: an obese child is often taunted by others, and will be unable to participate in the same vigorous play as their peers.

Nutritional deficiency

When particular items in the diet are absent or in short supply, **deficiency disorders** develop (see Figure 11.5).

FAILURE TO THRIVE

Failure to thrive (FTT) is a term used when a child does not conform to the usual pattern of weight gain and growth. The first issue to be explored if a baby or child appears to be under-nourished is **feeding**; often, a newly weaned baby will fail to thrive (or gain weight) due to intolerance of a newly introduced food. Once the food is withdrawn from the diet, the baby will usually thrive. There may be other problems associated with feeding a young baby, such as breathing difficulties or a poor sucking reflex in a premature baby. A child who is vomiting frequently over a period of time is also unlikely to thrive; vomiting may be the result of **pyloric stenosis** (see p. 97), **gastro–enteritis**, or **whooping cough** (**pertussis**).

MALABSORPTION OF FOOD
▶ **Coeliac disease** is a condition in which the lining of the small intestine is damaged by **gluten**, a protein found in wheat and rye. In babies, it is usually diagnosed about three months after they have been weaned onto solids containing gluten, but some children **DO NOT** show any symptoms until they are older.
▶ **Phenylketonuria** (see p. 72): an affected baby will require a diet which contains limited, measured amounts of **phenylalanine**, an amino acid which is a basic unit of protein.
▶ **Galactosaemia** is a very rare genetic disorder leading to liver disease, eye cataracts and mental handicap; it is caused by an inability to absorb **galactose** (a nutrient found in milk). Treatment is by a **lactose-free diet** for life.

LONG-TERM ILLNESS
Certain *illnesses* may also result in failure to thrive:
▶ congenital heart disease
▶ cystic fibrosis
▶ severe asthma
▶ urinary tract infections
▶ infections.

TABLE 11.5

A summary of deficiency disorders

DISORDER	SHORTAGE	EFFECT
ANAEMIA	Iron or vitamin B12	Fatigue, headaches, weight loss, breathlessness
RICKETS	Calcium or vitamin D	Bones do not form properly, resulting in bow legs
KWASHIORKOR	Protein or calories	Severe malnutrition, swollen tummies, sparse brittle hair
SCURVY	Vitamin C	Wounds are slow to heal; gums loose and bleeding
PELLAGRA	Niacin (a vitamin)	Soreness and cracking of the skin; mental disturbances
NIGHT BLINDNESS	Vitamin A	Inability to see in dim light
BERIBERI	Thiamine (vitamin B1)	Wasting of the muscles: heart failure
MARASMUS	Severe lack of calories and protein	Emaciation, stunted growth and dehydration

Failure to thrive can also result from child abuse: physical abuse, emotional abuse, neglect and sexual abuse. This is a complex subject discussed in Chapter 16.

Poverty and diet

In recent years, many families in the UK have found themselves on a reduced income as a result of the rise in unemployment and the effects of economic recession. Surveys have identified four main problems for the 8 million people who receive Income Support:

1 Healthy food is relatively highly priced. Lean meat costs more than fattier cuts, and wholemeal bread can cost 25% more than white bread.
2 Fuel costs are variable: it is cheaper to cook chips than jacket potatoes.
3 The siting of superstores on the outskirts of towns has meant that shops in inner-city areas are smaller and more expensive, so that healthy foods become less available.
4 Certain facilities and skills are required to prepare healthier foods, so that if the family is living in bed and breakfast accommodation, cooking may be impractical.

Ideas for increasing the nutritional quality of the diet, which may save money as well are:
- Use less meat and more pulses and lentils in stews and casseroles.
- Use as little oil or fat in cooking as possible;
- Cut down on meat and fill up on potatoes, rice and starchy vegetables.

The social and educational role of food and mealtimes

Eating patterns may be influenced by various factors:
- religious beliefs or strong ethical principles;
- cultural background and ethnic origin;
- the availability of different foods;
- time and money constraints;
- preferences and tastes that are shaped during early infancy.

Food is part of every child's culture, and eating rituals vary with different cultures. Mealtimes can provide a valuable opportunity to further the child's social development by:
- promoting listening skills and courtesy towards others;
- providing a social focus in the child's day – a chance to share experiences with adults and peers;
- fostering self-esteem and self-confidence. Each child should be regarded as a unique individual with uniquely individual needs; and children need to see that their family and cultural background are valued.

Educational development can be furthered by:
- promoting hand–eye coordination by the use of cutlery;
- stimulating the senses of taste, touch, sight and smell;
- promoting language development and an increased vocabulary;
- developing the concepts of shape and size, using foods as examples;
- creating opportunities for learning through linked activities – stories about food, origins of food, preparation and cookery etc.

Early childhood workers are ideally placed to ensure that stereotyping is not practised. Mealtimes and the choice of food can be used in a positive sense to affirm a feeling of cultural identity.

Food allergies

A food allergy is an abnormal response (an allergic reaction) of the immune system to otherwise harmless foods. Up to 5 per cent of children have food allergies. Most children outgrow their allergy, although an allergy to peanuts and some other tree nuts is considered life-long.

There are eight foods which cause 90% of all food allergic reactions. These are

▶ peanuts	▶ milk
▶ soy	▶ shellfish
▶ tree nuts (e.g. almonds, walnuts, pecans etc.)	▶ eggs
	▶ wheat
▶ fish	

Milk is the most common cause of food allergies in children, but peanuts, nuts, fish, and shellfish commonly cause the most severe reactions.

What are the symptoms of an allergic reaction?

Symptoms of an allergic response can include:

▶ vomiting	▶ difficulty breathing
▶ hives (or urticaria) – itchy raised rash usually found on the trunk or limbs	▶ cramps
	▶ itching or swelling of the lips, tongue or mouth
▶ itching or tightness in the throat	
▶ diarrhoea	▶ wheezing
▶ eczema	

Allergic symptoms can begin within minutes to one hour after ingesting the food. In some cases, just one bite of food can bring on **anaphylaxis**, a severe reaction that involves various areas of the body simultaneously. In extreme cases, it can cause death.

Anaphylaxis is a sudden severe potentially life-threatening allergic reaction. It can be caused by food allergy, insect stings, or medications. Although any food can potentially cause anaphylaxis, peanuts, nuts, shellfish, fish and eggs are foods that most commonly cause this reaction.

Symptoms of anaphylaxis may include all the above. In addition, the child's breathing is seriously impaired and the pulse rate becomes rapid.

Anaphylaxis is fortunately very rare, but is also very dangerous:
- ▶ Symptoms can occur in as little as 5 to 15 minutes.
- ▶ As little as **1/2 a peanut** can cause a fatal reaction for severely allergic individuals.
- ▶ Some severely allergic children can have a reaction if milk is splashed on their skin.

▶ Being kissed by somebody who has eaten peanuts for example, can cause a reaction in severely allergic individuals.

Emergency treatment

Summon medical help immediately. The child will need oxygen and a life-saving injection of adrenaline. Meanwhile, place the child in a sitting position to help relieve any breathing difficulty and **be prepared to resuscitate** if necessary.

How can food allergies be managed?

The only way to manage food allergies is to strictly avoid the foods to which the child is allergic. It is important to learn how to interpret ingredients on food labels and how to spot high-risk foods. Many children out-grow earlier food-allergic symptoms as they get older, but parents will need professional support and advice to ensure that their child is receiving a safe, balanced diet.

Therapeutic (or special) diets

Most children on special diets are not ill but require a therapeutic diet which replaces or eliminates some particular nutrient to prevent illness.

The diet for diabetes mellitus

Diabetes mellitus occurs in 1 in every 500 children under the age of about 16 years, and results in difficulty in converting carbohydrate into energy due to under-production of **insulin**. Insulin is usually given by daily injection, and a diet sheet is drawn up by the hospital **dietician**. It is important that mealtimes be regular and that some carbohydrate be included. Children with diabetes should be advised to carry glucose sweets whenever they are away from home in case of **hypoglycaemia**.

The diet for cystic fibrosis

The majority of children with **cystic fibrosis** (see p. 447) have difficulty in absorbing fats; they need to eat 20% more protein and calories than children without the disease, and so require a diet high in fats and carbohydrates. They are also given daily vitamin supplements and pancreatic enzymes.

The diet for coeliac disease

Treatment for coeliac disease is by gluten-free diet and is lifelong. All formula milks available in the UK are gluten-free, and many manufactured babyfoods are also gluten-free. Any cakes, bread and biscuits should be made from gluten-free flour, and labels on processed foods should be carefully read to ensure that there is no 'hidden' wheat product in the ingredients list.

    NB: Play-doh is made from 40% ordinary flour, as is the home-made variety used in nurseries and playgroups, so extra vigilance is needed by staff to stop children with coeliac disease putting it in their mouth.

The diet for galactosaemia

The child with galactosaemia cannot digest and use galactose – which together with glucose forms **lactose**, the natural sugar of milk. A list of 'safe foods' with a low galactose content will be issued by the dietician, and food labels should be checked for the presence of milk solids, powdered lactose, etc. which contain large amounts of this sugar.

The diet for obesity

A child who is diagnosed as being overweight will usually be prescribed a diet low in fat and sugar; high-fibre carbohydrates are encouraged e.g. wholemeal bread and other cereals. The child who has to go without crisps, chips and snacks between meals will need a lot of support and encouragement from carers.

The diet for children with difficulties with swallowing and chewing

Children with **cerebral palsy** can experience difficulties with either or both of these problems. Food will have to be liquidised, but should be done in separate batches so that the end result on the plate is not a pool of greyish sludge. Presentation should be imaginative and follow the general principle of making the differences as unobtrusive as possible.

Care of the environment

The physical environment

The surroundings in which we live have an effect on our lifestyle and behaviour. In recent years the UK's inner cities have become less pleasant places to live because of the increase in:

- ▶ **air pollution** – from car exhausts, industrial effluents etc;
- ▶ **poverty** and **unemployment;**
- ▶ **poor living conditions** for those on low incomes;
- ▶ **social isolation** – there are many more one-parent families living in inner-city areas who have no access to the extended family network.
- ▶ **discrimination on the basis of ethnicity or disability** – this is often reinforced by planning decisions; for example, lack of access or mobility for people with physical disabilities.

The rural environment also poses problems for families if there is high unemployment or subsistence on low incomes; transport and housing may be difficult to obtain.

The effects of the environment on children's health

Children and families need:

- ▶ to be safe and to feel safe;
- ▶ access to health- and social-care services;
- ▶ adequate housing;
- ▶ equality of opportunity;
- ▶ education;
- ▶ a nourishing diet;
- ▶ freedom from discrimination;
- ▶ somewhere to play/socialise with peers.

If any of these needs are not met, then the family will be under stress.

Food hygiene

Food hygiene is essential for the prevention of food poisoning; young children are particularly vulnerable to the bacteria which cause **gastro-enteritis** or food poisoning.

How bacteria enter food

Bacteria can enter food without causing the food to look, smell or even taste bad. Bacteria thrive in warm, moist foods, especially those rich in protein, such as meat and poultry (both cooked and raw), seafood, gravy, soup, cooked rice, milk, cream and egg dishes. Harmful bacteria multiply rapidly by dividing into two every 10 to 20 minutes, soon building up a colony of thousands which will cause poisoning.

To live and grow, bacteria must have:

- ▶ *food* – especially the foods mentioned above;
- ▶ *moisture* – fresh foods are more susceptible than dried foods;
- ▶ *warmth* – they thrive most at body temperature (37°C);
- ▶ *time* – bacteria reproduce rapidly in warm, moist food.

The prevention of food poisoning

1 *Safe storage*.
   - ▶ Keep food cold. The fridge should be kept as cold as it will go without actually freezing the food (1–5°C or 34–41°F). To be safe, use a fridge thermometer and open the door as few times as possible.
   - ▶ Cool food quickly before placing in the fridge.
   - ▶ Cover or wrap food with foodwrap or microwave clingfilm.
   - ▶ Store raw foods at the bottom so that juices cannot drip onto cooked food.
   - ▶ Freezers must be at a low enough temperature (-18°C or 0°F maximum).
   - ▶ Never refreeze food which has begun to thaw;
   - ▶ Label each item with the use-by date;
   - ▶ Thaw frozen meat completely before cooking.

2 *Safe preparation and cooking*.
   - ▶ Always wash hands in warm water and soap and dry on a clean towel: before handling food; after using the toilet; after touching raw food; after coughing into your hands; after using a hankie; and after touching your face or hair.
   - ▶ Never cough or sneeze over food.
   - ▶ Always cover any septic cuts or boils with a waterproof dressing.
   - ▶ Never smoke in any room that is used for food – it is illegal anyway.
   - ▶ Keep clean, and wear clean protective clothing which is solely for use in the kitchen.
   - ▶ Cook food thoroughly.
   - ▶ Eggs should be cooked so both the yolk and white are firm.
   - ▶ Chicken must be tested to ensure that it is thoroughly cooked.
   - ▶ Joints of meat and mince dishes must be cooked right through.
   - ▶ Avoid cook-chill foods, which need very careful handling.
   - ▶ Avoid having leftovers – they are a common cause of food poisoning.
   - ▶ DO NOT reheat food – even if it appears wasteful not to.

TABLE 11.6

Food-poisoning bacteria

BACTERIA	TYPICALLY FOUND IN:	SYMPTOMS	TO REDUCE RISK
Salmonella	Meat, poultry, raw eggs, meat pies and pasties, left-over food, unpasteurised milk	Starts suddenly 12 to 14 hours after eating: nausea, vomiting, abdominal pain and headache	Good personal hygiene; cook eggs well; avoid cross-infection from raw to cooked foods; cook food thoroughly
Clostridium Welchii	Meat, poultry, meat dishes, left-over food, gravy	Starts 8 to 18 hours after eating: diarrhoea, abdominal pain, no fever. Lasts 12 to 24 hours	Cook food thoroughly; heat to 100°C
Listeria	Chilled foods, e.g. soft cheeses and meat pâté	Starts 5 to 30 *days* after eating; 1 in 4 cases fatal; miscarriage, blood poisoning, meningitis; babies at risk	Avoid high-risk foods; avoid storing chilled foods for long periods; ensure proper re-heating
Clostridium Botulinum	Canned food not heated properly at time of canning; raw fish	Starts 12 to 36 hours after eating; often fatal; double vision; breathing difficulties	Avoid damaged or 'blown' cans; avoid keeping vacuum-packed fish in warm temperatures
Staphylococcus	Food that needs careful handling; custards and creams, cold desserts, sandwiches, unpasteurised milk	Starts 1 to 6 hours after eating; abdominal cramps, vomiting; lasts up to 24 hours	Good personal hygiene; avoid coughing and sneezing over food; avoid cross-infection from raw to cooked food; heat to 70°C for 15 minutes

> ▶ If using a microwave oven: DO NOT reheat food by this method;
>> – DO NOT use for babies bottles;
>> – always follow instructions and include 'standing' time to avoid burns;
>> – keep the oven clean.

3 *A safe kitchen*
> ▶ Keep the kitchen clean – the floor, work surfaces, sink, utensils, cloths and waste bins should be cleaned regularly.
> ▶ Clean tin-openers, graters and mixers thoroughly after use.
> ▶ Tea towels should be boiled every day and dishcloths boiled or disinfected.
> ▶ Keep flies and other insects away – use a fine mesh over open windows.
> ▶ Keep pets away from the kitchen.
> ▶ Keep all waste bins covered, and empty them regularly.
> ▶ Stay away from the kitchen if you are suffering from diarrhoea or sickness.

Food-poisoning bacteria

Several types of bacteria can cause food poisoning (see Table 11.6), including the following:
> ▶ salmonella
> ▶ clostridium welchii
> ▶ clostridium botulinum
> ▶ listeria
> ▶ staphylococcus.

Food and energy requirements

Food requirements vary according to age, gender, size, occupation or lifestyle and climate. Food energy is traditionally measured in **calories (kcal)** or **kilojoules (kJ)**.

> 1 kcal = 4.2 kJ
> 1000 kJ = 1 MJ (megajoule) = 239 kcal

Different foods contain different amounts of energy per unit of weight; foods which contain a lot of fat and sugar have high energy values. An excess of calories will result in weight gain as the surplus 'energy' is stored as fat; an insufficient intake of calories will result in weight loss as the body has to draw on fat reserves to meet energy requirements. Table 11.6 shows the energy requirements for different age groups. Babies and young children have relatively *high requirements* in relation to their size.

Legal requirements for the safety and hygiene of food

Food safety is dealt with in the **Food Safety Act (1990)**. The main rulings of the Act are:
> ▶ It is an offence to render food injurious to health by any process treatment – it is no longer even necessary for there to be an **intention** that the food be consumed in that state.
> ▶ It is an offence to sell food that does not comply with food requirements.

TABLE 11.7
Dietary reference values

	ENERGY USED IN 1 DAY (KJ)	DIET
BIRTH TO ONE YEAR *0 – 3 MONTHS* *3 – 6 MONTHS* *6 – 9 MONTHS* *9 – 12 MONTHS*	 2,300 3,200 3,800 4,200	At least 2 g of protein are needed per kg of body weight from 0 – 6 months and 1.6 g per kg from 6 – 9 months, gradually reducing to 1 g per kg. Weaning usually begins at about 4 months
8 YEARS (BOTH SEXES, ACTIVE CHILDREN)	8,800	At least 30 g of protein a day but 53 g are recommended
14 – 18 YEARS Males Females *ADULT (LIGHT WORK)* Males Females *ADULT (MODERATE WORK)* Males Females *ADULT (HEAVY WORK)* Males Females	 12,600 9,600 11,550 9,450 12,100 10,500 15,000 – 20,000 12,600	80 – 100 g of protein per day and 60% of this should be first-class protein About 300 g of carbohydrate per day except for those doing heavy work who should eat far more Sugar should not be eaten in large quantities as it increases tooth decay About 100 g of fat should be eaten per day
PREGNANT WOMEN *NURSING MOTHERS*	10,000 11,300	Pregnant women should eat about 85 g of protein per day increasing to 100 g during breast feeding, together with increased amounts of food containing calcium, iron, and all-vitamins

▶ If any part of a batch of food fails to comply with the regulation, the whole batch will be withdrawn until the contrary can be proved;

▶ It is an offence to sell food which is not of the nature, substance or quality demanded by the consumer; it is also an offence to give misleading information about food in an advertisement or label.

The Food Safety Act affords much greater protection to the consumer, and places more responsibility on manufacturers and importers to ensure that their quality-control arrangements are more than adequate.

Enforcement of the Act

Under the Act, local authority staff may, by right:

▶ enter any food premises to investigate possible offences;

▶ take away samples for investigation;

▶ detain suspect food or request that it be destroyed through local court procedures;

▶ require food hygiene to be improved or, in an extreme case, close down a premises if considered to be a health risk.

Trading standards officers deal with:

▶ the labelling of food;

▶ the composition of food;

▶ most cases of chemical contamination.

Environmental health officers deal with:

▶ hygiene;

▶ cases of microbiological (bacterial/viral) contamination of foods;

▶ food which is unfit for human consumption.

Public analysts carry out chemical analysis of food; **food examiners** are responsible for the microbiological examination of food.

REGULATIONS

Two new sets of regulations have been introduced:

1 **Registration.** All premises used for food business must be registered with their local authority; this includes premises, market stalls, vehicles etc. used by charities, and those where catering is provided over several consecutive days (for example, at a sports event).

2 **Training for food handlers.** All those handling food should be trained to an appropriate level in hygiene and be shown to be competent in such practices through independent assessment.

Planning a safe, stimulating environment for children

Young children are usually unaware of the extent of dangers in the environment. They are keen to explore everything that they encounter, and this curiosity involves touching and often tasting objects which may be poisonous or unhygienic. A child attending a nursery class for the first time may find that much of the equipment in daily use is unfamiliar and will require them to learn new skills. Potentially dangerous items are:

▶ climbing frames

▶ hammers and nails at a woodwork bench

▶ large blocks

▶ wheeled toys

▶ scissors

▶ slides.

Added to this list must be the presence of *other* children – collisions in the play area are fairly common, especially involving wheeled toys and slides.

Checking for health and safety hazards

All members of a team in nurseries and schools should monitor the environment to ensure that no hazards have developed. This may involve:

▶ checking equipment regularly for broken parts and sharp edges; ideally there should be a **set routine** for doing this, with one person taking responsibility for each area of monitoring;

▶ checking the outside play area in the early morning – dangerous litter, e.g. broken glass or syringes/needles, may have been thrown into the area;

▶ ensuring that the kitchen area and cupboards containing cleaning equipment are made inaccessible to children uness they are supervised by staff – e.g. during a cookery activity;

▶ checking the toilet and washing facilities regularly;

▶ checking that it is not possible for a child to get out of the building or out of the grounds by themselves;

▶ checking that children always wash their hands after toileting, before eating and after handling pets.

FIGURE 11.4

A stimulating environment

Establishing rules for safety and hygiene

One of the cornerstones of early childhood education is to offer an exciting range of experiences to children which will stimulate them and extend their skills in all areas of development. Ensuring the children's safety at all times means that staff, preferably in collaboration with parents, should:

▶ *identify potential dangers* in both the indoor and outdoor environment;

▶ *develop a strategy* for avoiding these dangers.

This process should result in a **set of safety rules** displayed in relevant areas, for the benefit of parents and relief staff, and given to all staff working with the children.

For more information on safety and accident prevention, see pp. 260–272.

The protection of carers and others

Nursery classes, schools and hospitals must have a policy for dealing with **body fluids** which should be followed at all times. A child may be **HIV positive** or have **hepatitis B** without the carers knowing about it, so the policy should be rigorously adhered to. All local authorities issue guidelines on the safe disposal of body fluids, which specify:

▶ wearing disposable latex gloves when dealing with blood, urine, faeces or vomit;

▶ washing the hands after dealing with spillages – even if gloves have been worn;

▶ using a 1% solution of **hypochlorite** to cover any blood spillages. The area should then be wiped over with a gloved hand using disposable cloths; the cloths must then be discarded into a bag which is sent for **incineration**;

▶ avoiding sharp instruments that could result in injury;

▶ covering any skin abrasion with a waterproof plaster.

NB: extra care must be taken if any body fluid comes into contact with the carer's broken skin, e.g. through a puncture wound. The carer should wash the affected area with soap and water and encourage bleeding to flush out any contamination. An accident form should then be completed and medical advice sought.

Animals in the care and education setting

Small pets can provide a homely atmosphere in nurseries and schools; they can extend children's knowledge and skills as well as giving enjoyment to everyone. Parents choosing a pet for their children should realise that they are totally responsible for its well-being and survival, however keen the children themselves are; a young child cannot judge when the animal has played long enough, whether its diet is suitable or how often its cage needs cleaning.

Guinea pigs

Guinea pigs (or cavies) can be bought from a pet shop at about 6 to 8 weeks old. Guinea pigs are gentle, trusting creatures which are safe for children to handle. It is better to keep two guinea pigs together as they are social animals. They can be kept in a hutch outdoors, but will need to be brought inside if the weather is very cold. About one-third of the hutch should be enclosed as a sleeping area, and this must be raised off the ground out of the way of draughts and rats. Guinea pigs also need space to exercise in, and a wire-covered run should make up the other two-thirds of the cage. They like to eat corn, oats, fruit, vegetables and dandelion leaves; they also drink a lot of water. The cage should be cleaned daily, and any stale food removed.

Hamsters

Hamsters are solitary animals and may fight if more than one is kept in the same cage. They are nocturnal animals – that is, they sleep during the day and are active at night. They make good pets for children at home, but are not so suitable for nurseries and schools because of their sleeping habits.

Gerbils

Gerbils like to live in company. They breed rapidly, so it is better to keep two of the same sex in a glass tank. Children like to observe their habits of burrowing (supply plenty of empty cardboard rolls and jam jars) and gnawing (supply wood blocks). The advantage of keeping gerbils rather than mice or rats is that they are desert animals and so do not pass urine very frequently; they are also easily tamed and appreciate handling.

Dogs and cats

As family pets, dogs and cats are very rewarding animals to keep. They would not, however, be suitable for nurseries and schools.

The RSPCA view

The RSPCA (The Royal Society for the Prevention of Cruelty to Animals) is opposed to the keeping of animals in captivity on school premises **unless** proper provision can be made for their physical and mental wellbeing. The RSPCA believes that ensuring the welfare of animals is extremely difficult in most nursery classrooms or playgroup spaces, for the following reasons:

▶ Animals can be exposed to over-handling by large numbers of enthusiastic children.

▶ Animals may not receive adequate rest periods during the day.

▶ Animals may be left unattended for long periods during weekends and holiday periods.

▶ Animals can also be expensive to keep.

▶ Animals can cause both health and safety problems for children.

The Society believes that animal welfare can be taught **without** keeping animals captive, and has produced two booklets which explore the alternatives to keeping a pet in the nursery, whilst still allowing children valuable first-hand experience of animals and wildlife. The RSPCA suggests the following activities for pre-school children:

▶ **Personal and social development** Ask the children to describe what a pet needs to keep it healthy and contented. They could draw their favourite pet with all the things it needs around it.	▶ **Language and literacy** Involve the children in designing a role-play area with a veterinary surgery, farm or kennel as a theme. Ask the children to role-play the animals, their owners, the veterinary surgeon and the animal carers.
▶ **Mathematics** Design a matching game where children have to match the animal to its home or habitat.	▶ **Physical development** Ask the children to make a model animal hospital using plasticine, clay or waste materials to form the animals and the hospital.
▶ **Creative development** Take the children for a sensory walk to the local park to observe animals in their natural habitat.	

Health and safety hazards posed by animals

A number of infectious or parasitic diseases may be acquired from contact with animals. Young children are most at risk of becoming infected because of their habit of putting objects into their mouths, and crawling babies are nearer the source of infection.

RABIES

Rabies is a serious viral infection transmitted by a bite from a dog. The UK is free of rabies, but travellers to countries where rabies exist should treat any dog bite, especially if the dog is a stray, with suspicion.

DOG BITES

Dog bites can cause serious bleeding and shock and may become infected; fortunately, they are rare but children should be discouraged from patting stray dogs.

TOXOCARIASIS

This disease is caused by the parasite **toxocara** (**roundworm**), found in dog and cat faeces. It is mainly an infection of children who eat dirt or play in areas contaminated by infected dog faeces. It can cause **allergic** symptoms, such as asthma or, rarely, a larva may lodge in the eye and cause **blindness**. Prevention is by:

▶ preventing parasitic infection in dogs and cats – by worming them at three-monthly intervals;

▶ preventing environmental contamination by infective eggs – dog owners should not allow their dogs to foul public places – especially parks and children's play areas;

▶ preventing infection through public education – babies and young children should be discouraged from putting objects from the floor near their mouth; dogs should not be allowed to lick people's faces or be allowed to sleep in children's beds as the dog's hair could harbour infected eggs. Children and adults should be encouraged to wash their hands after playing or working outside, or touching dogs, especially before touching food.

FLEAS

Fleas may transfer from a dog's or cat's fur to humans and can cause irritating bites; the fleas jump onto humans to feed, particularly in the warm weather if the cat or dog is absent.

CAT-SCRATCH FEVER

A rare disease that usually develops after a scratch or bite by a cat, **cat-scratch fever** is thought to be caused by a small bacterium that has not been identified. The main sign of illness is a swollen lymph node near the scratch, fever and headache. It usually clears up completely within two months.

RINGWORM

Ringworm (or **tinea**) is a fungal infection of the skin. The most common type is **tinea pedis (athlete's foot)** (see p. 401) but tinea can also occur on the body or on the scalp. The infection may be passed from animals to people, but more usually is passed from person to person. Treatment is by anti-fungal drugs in the form of **lotions**, **creams**, or **ointments**.

LYME DISEASE

Lyme disease is a disease caused by a bacterium which is transmitted by the bite of a tick that usually lives on deer but can infest dogs. Symptoms are the same as for 'flu but also include some skin changes and joint inflammation. Lyme disease is becoming more common in the UK.

PSITTACOSIS

Psittacosis is a rare illness that is spread from birds to humans. The infection is contracted by inhaling dust contaminated by the droppings of infected birds – usually parrots or pigeons.

LEPTOSPIROSIS

Leptospirosis is also known as **Weil's disease**. It is a rare disease caused by a type of **spirochaete bacterium** harboured by rats and excreted in their urine. It often affects the kidneys and can also cause liver damage.

Health and Safety at Work Acts

Care and education settings are **communities** where people share facilities and concerns. The various Health and Safety at Work Acts cover the conditions in which places of work must be kept:

- ▶ Buildings and services should be well-maintained and designed to ensure safety for users.
- ▶ Cleanliness and sanitation must be observed in food preparation and in the general environment.
- ▶ Equipment must be safely used and safely stored.
- ▶ Working practices must be observed that promote health and safety for clients.
- ▶ A written statement of safety policy should be brought to the attention of all employees.

Health and safety policies

Every employer has a duty to protect employees at work and to keep them informed about health and safety. In general, the employer's duties include:

- ▶ making the workplace safe and without risks to health;
- ▶ keeping dust, fumes and noise under control;
- ▶ ensuring that plant and machinery are safe and that safe systems of work are set and followed;
- ▶ ensuring that articles and substances are moved, stored and used safely;
- ▶ providing adequate welfare facilities;
- ▶ supplying information, training and supervision necessary for the health and safety of employees.

In addition, the employer must:

- ▶ draw up a **health and safety policy** statement if there are more than five employees, and bring it to the attention of employees;
- ▶ provide, free, any protective clothing or equipment specifically required by health and safety law;
- ▶ report certain injuries, diseases and dangerous occurrences to the enforcing authority;
- ▶ provide adequate first-aid facilities;
- ▶ consult a safety representative about issues which affect health and safety in the workplace;
- ▶ set up a committee, if asked in writing by two or more safety representatives.

There are also other more specific duties, for example concerning overcrowding and hygiene; these vary from one workplace to another.

The employee has **legal duties** too, which include:

- ▶ Taking reasonable care of their own health and safety and that of others who may be affected by what is done or not done;
- ▶ cooperating with the employer on health and safety;

▶ not interfering with, or misusing, anything provided for the employee's health, safety or welfare.

Health and safety policies in child care and education settings

In addition to health and safety policies, there are also **standards** and **codes of practice** which give specific guidance for specific types of workplace. Premises in which children are cared for and taught must be large enough, and should provide a separate area for the care of babies and toddlers; and in addition:

▶ Low-level glass (e.g. in doors and cupboards) should be **safety glass** or covered with **boarding** or **guards**.
▶ Sharp corners on low-level furniture should be padded.
▶ Fire exits must be left accessible and unlocked at all times.
▶ Electric sockets should be covered.
▶ Floor surfaces should be clean and free of splinters.
▶ Access should be easy for prams and pushchairs/wheelchairs.
▶ Kitchen facilities must be adequate in terms of hygiene, storage and safety.

All day-care facilities used by children must be registered for that purpose. The Children Act 1989 ensures that the following checks are carried out before registration is accepted:

▶ The applicant must sign an equal-opportunities policy to show commitment to non-discrimination.
▶ A police check is carried out on any people who will be employed to look after the children.
▶ A health check may involve a declaration by the individual members of staff, or a statement from the GP, or both.
▶ Personal references will be taken up on all personnel and a check carried out by the relevant local authority.
▶ Various authorities will be consulted in the early stages of the process: the planning authority; the fire authority; the building inspector, if the building is new or specially adapted; and an environmental health officer.

Answers to the food quiz on p. 307

1 Dental decay – dental services cost the NHS about £450 million every year.
2 The foetus will suffer from the effects of placental insufficiency – the baby may be born prematurely and be light-for-dates, with the following problems:
    ▶ breathing difficulties;
    ▶ feeding difficulties (poor sucking reflex);
    ▶ possible poor temperature regulation.
3 Fat babies and children have less resistance to infection, may have mobility problems and may suffer emotional difficulties. Obesity can be avoided by cutting down on high-calorie foods and snacks such as chips, biscuits, fizzy drinks and cakes.
4 Fibre helps prevent constipation by encouraging the movement of food through the intestine.
5 A **deficiency disorder** is one in which particular nutrients in the diet are absent or in short supply. Examples are: rickets (shortage of vitamin D or calcium); anaemia (shortage of iron or vitamin B12); beriberi (shortage of thiamin or vitamin

B1); pellagra (shortage of niaciri); kwashiorkor (shortage of protein or calories); night blindness (shortage of vitamin A); and marasmus (severe lack of calories and protein.

6   An **E number** is the code which identifies food additives; **colourings** are the additives most often linked to behaviour problems in children.

7   (b)   meat and poultry.

8   (a)   daily.

9   37°C

10   (b)   ham and uncooked mince beef.

R E S O U R C E S

The Nutrition Society,
10 Cambridge Court,
210 Shepherds Bush Road,
London, W6 7NJ, UK
Telephone +44 020 7602 0228
Fax +44 020 7602 1756

Institute of Food Research
Norwich Laboratory
Norwich Research Park
Colney Lane, Norwich
NR4 7UA, UK
Telephone 01603 255000
Fax 01603 507723

The Vegan Society,
Donald Watson House,
7 Battle Road,
St Leonards-on-Sea, East
Sussex. TN37 7AA
Telephone 01424 427393
Fax 01424 717064

Cystic Fibrosis Trust
Alexandra House
5 Blyth Road
Bromley
Kent BR1 3RS
Telephone 0181 464 7211

The Eating Disorders
Association
Sackville Place
44–48 Magdalen Street
Norwich
Norfolk NR3 1JE
Helpline 01603 621414

British Diabetic Association
10 Queen Anne Street
London W1M 0BD
Telephone 020 7323 1531

Action against Allergy
24/26 High Street
Hampton Hill
Middlesex TW12 1PD

Food Safety Advisory Centre
Foodline 0800 282407

The Anaphylaxis Campaign
The Ridges
2 Clockhouse Road
Farnborough
Hampshire
GU14 7QY, UK
Telephone 01252 542029
Fax 01252 377140

RSPCA Education
Causeway
Horsham
West Sussex
RH12 1HG
Telephone 01403 264181
Website
http://www.rspca.org.uk

Eating well for Under 5s in
child care
The Caroline Walker Trust
available from:
PO Box 5
Manchester M60 3GE
Telephone 0870 608 0213

ACTIVITY

The balanced daily diet

1 Look at the following daily diet:
   ▶ *Breakfast:* A glass of milk + boiled egg and toast
   ▶ *Mid-morning:* A packet of crisps + a glass of orange squash.
   ▶ *Lunch:* A cheese and egg flan + chips + baked beans + apple fritters and ice cream + apple juice.
   ▶ *Snack:* Chocolate mini roll + orange squash.
   ▶ *Tea:* Fish fingers + mashed potatoes + peas + strawberry milk shake.

   Arrange the servings in five columns, i.e. the four food groups and one extra column for extra fat and sugar. Count the number of serves from each food group and assess the nutritional adequacy of the diet.
2 How could you improve the menu to ensure a healthy balanced diet?

ACTIVITY

Menu planning

Write up or obtain a copy of an actual weekly menu of a nursery or infant school that you know, and then answer the following questions:
1 Does the menu provide a healthy balance of nutrients?
2 Is there anything that you would change to promote healthy eating? Give reasons for any new foods you may wish to include.

ACTIVITY

Budgeting for a healthy diet

1 Most large supermarkets now label certain foods as 'healthy eating' foods. Plan a menu for one week, for a family of two adults and three children aged 8, 4 and 2 years, which provides a varied and nutritionally balanced diet for the whole family. Cost the items needed and estimate the fuel costs involved.
2 Try to add some practical tips to the ones suggested above for improving diets on a limited budget.

A C T I V I T Y

Cultural needs

The nursery school where you are working has 22 white children and one child from Turkey. The nursery teacher says 'We only offer English food here because we don't have any children from ethnic minorities'. Discuss this statement and decide what your approach would be if you were in charge of the nursery.

A C T I V I T Y

Developmental needs of the one-parent child

1 Think about the problems for a one-parent family living on a very low income in a poorly maintained block of flats, and list them; what particular disadvantages might the children in such a situation have? List these under the headings of the following developmental areas: physical, intellectual, social, emotional and language.
2 How could this young family be helped by:
    (a) the statutory services – e.g. a day care centre
    (b) the voluntary sector – e.g. playgroups, community associations?

A C T I V I T Y

The food quiz

1 Which disease linked to diet is the most widespread in the UK and why?
2 What might be the effect on a baby if the mother has suffered from malnutrition during the last three months of pregnancy?
3 Fat babies and fat children are often unhealthy. Give two reasons for this and suggest how obesity can be prevented in young children.
4 Why is fibre important in a child's diet?
5 What is meant by a deficiency disorder? Give three examples.
6 What is an E number? Which category of E numbers is linked to behaviour problems in children?
7 Which two foods are the most common sources of food poisoning?
    (a) fish and ham
    (b) meat and poultry
    (c) cheese and eggs
    (d) fruit and vegetables.
8 How often should you change a used tea towel for a clean one?
    (a) daily
    (b) once a week
    (c) twice a day.

9 What is the ideal temperature for the growth of food-poisoning bacteria?
   (a) 20°C   (b) 30°C   (c) 37°C

10 Which of the following foods should you never store together?
   (a) raw chicken and uncooked sausages
   (b) ham and uncooked mince beef
   (c) liver pâté and cheese.

Answers on p. 304.

A C T I V I T Y

Safety and hygiene rules

Find out about safety and hygiene rules in the nursery setting, including guidelines for the hygienic disposal of waste and body fluids.
1 For each safety point, state the principle behind it.
2 What can the carer do to prevent infection spreading in the work setting?

A C T I V I T Y

A pet for the nursery

1 You have been asked by your day nursery/nursery school to research the possibility of acquiring a pet for the nursery. Prepare an action plan, to include:
  ▶ how to choose a pet – what criteria you would use;
  ▶ what preparation would be necessary;
  ▶ the routine care of the pet and how it would be carried out;
  ▶ the benefits to the children of having your chosen pet in the nursery.

2 Write a report for the nursery teacher, including all the above material.
3 Write a plan for your nursery, following RSPCA guidelines, where children may enjoy an animal-related experience.

A C T I V I T Y

Evaluating your Health and Safety policy

Ask to see the Health and Safety policy in your workplace.
1 What aspects of care does it cover?
2 Is it reviewed regularly?
3 Is the policy displayed anywhere?
4 Is there anything *you* could add to the policy?

12

Education and Care:
Towards an Integrated Service

Young children need both education and care

Young children are not made up of separate bits and pieces: a child is a *whole* person. It is inappropriate to talk about *either* education *or* caring for young children:

▶ Children need *both*.
▶ They need both *at the same time*.

If you look to the section in Chapter 15 on children's needs, you will see that children need physical and health care as much as they need new, interesting and stimulating experiences.

The child at 0–8 years of age

Children are not 'pre' or 'under' at 0–8 years of age. They are simply in the first phase of their lives. Early childhood is not about being 'under 5' or 'over 5'. Nor is it about being 'under 8' or 'over 8'. It is not about being 'pre-linguistic' or at a 'pre-school', 'pre-reading', 'pre-mathematics', or 'pre-anything'. Being described as 'pre'-something suggests that children are in some way lacking the point where they *are* something. It is much more useful to think of 0–8 years as a *continuum*. Indeed, they will be 'learning for life'. From 0–1 year, from 1–3 years, 3–5 years and from 5–8 years, children will be moving along that continuum. Indeed, they will be moving along the *continuum of life*. Not all children reach the same point on the continuum in the same way or at the same age, but every child *is* nonetheless moving on that continuum, starting life as a baby and then becoming an 8-year-old, a teenager and an adult, and just as life begins at birth, so it ends with death.

0–8 years is called *the first phase of childhood*, and it is internationally recognised – in most countries of the world, at least – as a complete phase in a child's development. Recent government documents are moving towards a greater integration of education, care, health and recreation of young children and their families. This is called 'joined-up thinking'.

In the UK:

▶ provision for this age group has been very patchy and irregular in different parts of the country;

▶ children start school at a much younger age than in most countries;

▶ the kind of education and care offered depends on where the family lives as well as on the economic background of the family.

In order to look at these problems and make major changes, the Government initiatives are that every Local Authority must have an **early years development plan** which involves an **early childhood forum**. This must be made up of people with representatives from statutory, voluntary, private, education, health, social services sectors as well as parents. This group of people have come together in every Local Authority as an **early years development and child care partnership**. Partnerships began by looking at the needs of four-year-olds. The brief was extended to look at how to implement more Government policies. These are:

▶ Sure Start for children aged 0–3 years and their families. This programme targets areas where there is great need.

▶ 0–14 National Childcare Strategy. This involves, for example, after school clubs, wrap around care and holiday clubs.

▶ The involvement of several Government departments on the same issue, e.g. DfEE (Department for Education and Employment), social services department and health ministry are all involved in the Sure Start programme. This is part of **joined-up thinking**.

▶ **Centres of early years excellence** will disseminate group's 'best practice' in education care and health in 25 centres across England (but not Wales, Scotland or Northern Ireland).

Government reports (Wales, Scotland, Northern Ireland and England)

▶ The Hadow Report 1933;

▶ The Plowden Report 1967;

▶ Framework for Expansion 1971:

▶ The Warnock Report on Special Educational Needs 1978;

▶ The Select Committee Report on Educational Provision for Children Under Five 1989;

▶ Starting with Quality 1990.

All the above Government reports have recommended quality education for young children.

Reports by voluntary agencies

These reports use government figures but are funded by charitable trusts:

▶ National Commission for Education 1993;

▶ The Royal Society of Arts (RSA), Start Right Report 1994.

INFLUENTIAL TELEVISION PROGRAMMES:

Channel 4's *Dispatches*, 'Too Much Too Soon' (29 January 1998)

BBC's *Panorama*, Early Education (5 October 1998)

Radio 4 *Tuning Into Children* (January, February and March 1999)

MESSAGES FROM THESE REPORTS AND PROGRAMMES

These reports contain powerful messages based on all the available evidence, and they were written by people representing a wide cross-section of political views. Here is what they say:

▶ Quality childhood education and care helps later learning and behaviour.

▶ It also reduces the need for later remedial work.

▶ It must be of a high quality, or else it could damage children rather than help them.

▶ Work settings need appropriately trained, high-calibre staff.

▶ It is important to positively promote equality of opportunity.

▶ Work settings need to be well-resourced in suitable buildings, with access to indoor and outdoor areas.

▶ Work settings need suitable staff:child ratios.

▶ Children in rural areas, or children in inner cities who live in isolated flats, for example need opportunities to meet a wider circle of children and adults than their homes permit.

▶ Quality education and care supports parents in their role as the child's first educator, through an atmosphere of mutual respect and sharing.

▶ It gives children safe areas for gross activity, with freedom of movement, appropriate equipment and plenty of space.

▶ It can encourage children to meet and value people from other cultures and belief systems, and give them opportunities to learn about different languages and customs.

▶ There have to be opportunities for new experiences which stretch the mind.

▶ Children need to be appreciated and recognised in their efforts and achievements by people beyond their immediate family.

▶ Children need to feel safe and secure and valued beyond their family.

▶ Early childhood settings of various kinds help children to take more and more appropriate responsibility, and be more and more autonomous in what they do.

▶ They also support children in what they know and understand.

▶ Children can be encouraged to have ideas to be creative and imaginative.

▶ Children can be encouraged to become more competent in what they do.

▶ They can be deeply involved in very worthwhile areas of learning.

▶ Early childhood settings can help to lift families from poverty because they provide support for families perhaps while parents are at work.

▶ They give children high-esteem and confidence in themselves.

▶ Children begin to understand that they can get more out of life if they put plenty *into* it.

Since the General Election in 1997, every Local Authority has been required to make an audit of the provision they have for children 0–5 years and their families. This means finding out the number of childminders and children, nursery school places, places in playgroups and pre-schools, private settings etc.

The RSA Report suggested 40% of children attend playgroup or pre-schools for an average of two sessions, and that just under half the children in early childhood provision of one sort or another are in fee-paying places, and that just over half of children are in public provision – which means that they do not pay fees. Most early years experts do not feel that four-year-olds are best placed in reception classes. They would prefer to see children 3–5 years educated in a Foundation Stage together rather than being separated.

Furthermore, 40% of children attend play groups for an average of two sessions – which is less than 10 hours per week. Many of these children are 3-year-olds.

Over 75% of 4-year-olds are admitted to primary school before they are 5. This kind of provision has consistently been criticised in reports on early childhood education and care. A study by Goldsmiths College at the University of London has shown that two-thirds of staff are poorly trained and there are very high child:adult ratios: often, one teacher – who is *not* trained for this age group – will be with a class of *30* 4-year-olds (not in Scotland).

During the 1980s more children were in private provision than ever before. Public provision did not grow at the same rapid pace.

Education and care provision in Europe

In most countries of the world, the education and care of young children are not separated from each other. The first early childhood provision in the UK did not separate childhood education from care either. Since the General Election, the government has made it clear that they intend to bring strands of education, care and health and work in partnership with parents together again. This is a return to traditions of quality education with care. There is therefore a period of great change in the UK at the moment. The nursery schools which were founded by Margaret McMillan at the beginning of the 20th century were as concerned with the care of the child as they were with the child's education. It is also important, however, to remember the great *diversity* of educational provision across different countries.

The RSA Report suggests that New Zealand is the country which has most parallels with the UK in the kinds of diverse provision offered, but children do not start school there until they are 5 years of age.

Many children in the UK are in several types of early childhood provision during a week – e.g. they might be in a nursery class in the morning, have lunch with their childminder and then attend a playgroup two afternoons a week, in which case they are participating in three different types of provision. Table 12.2 shows the number of places in different types of provision in England in 1991. It is important to remember that there are variations *within* each county of the UK, as well as between England, Scotland, Wales and Northern Ireland. As each local authority has been required to undertake an audit of their provision, more recent figures will emerge on the exact situation.

Government initiatives since 1997

▶ Early years development partnerships have expanded into early years development and child care partnerships. These will take forward the child care agenda looking at children 0–14 years.

TABLE 12.1

Early care and education provision in the countries of Europe

NAME OF COUNTRY IN EUROPE	AGE OF COMPULSORY SCHOOLING (IN YEARS)	PERCENTAGE OF CHILDREN ATTENDING PUBLICLY FUNDED EARLY CHILDHOOD PROVISION OF DIVERSE KINDS				
		3 YEARS	4 YEARS	5 YEARS	6 YEARS	7 YEARS
UK	5	60 (by 2002)	100 (but mainly in reception classes in primary schools)	100	100	100
Netherlands	5	67		100	100	100
Luxembourg	5	67		100	100	100
Greece	5½	88		100	100	100
Spain	6	74			100	100
Portugal	6	45			100	100
Italy	6	91			100	100
Ireland	6	51			100	100
Germany	6	77			100	100
France	6	99			100	100
Belgium	6	98			100	100
Sweden	6	68			100	100
Norway	7	53				100
Finland	7	60				100
Denmark	7	79				100

TABLE 12.2
Provision of care and education services in the UK

PROVISION	TIME SPENT	AGE OF CHILD	COST FOR THE FAMILY
Pre-preparatory schools, private nursery and other schools	Usually about 9 am – 3.30 pm Increasingly offer extra hours	$2\frac{1}{2}$–4	The fees vary
Reception classes in primary schools	9 am – 3.30 pm during the school termtime	4	Free
Local education authority nursery schools and classes	Usually morning or afternoon sessions, but some are full time. During the school termtime	3–4	Free
Pre-schools (formerly known as playgroups)	Two or three sessions a week, usually. Sessions are usually $2\frac{1}{2}$ hours. Some are full time	$2\frac{1}{2}$–4	£1.70 or more per session
Local authority day nurseries, children's centres, family centres	Some sessions are part time. Some are all day	0–4 (only a few children are 0–2)	This is means tested
Childminders	Usually all day	0–4	They vary widely, ranging from £50/week
Workplace nurseries, partnership programmes and private day nurseries	Usually all day, but there is variation	0–4	This ranges between £45–£150 each week. Some places are subsidised
Combined nursery centres Centres of Early Years Excellence	part time or all day open all year 8 am–5 pm according to the needs of the family	0–4	Although education places are free, daycare is means tested
Family centres	Part time or all day	Usually 0–4 but there is variation	These vary
Holiday schemes and extended hours schemes, clubs and out of school clubs	During the school holidays. Before and after school	A wide range and increasing because of government initiatives	These vary

TABLE 12.3

TABLE 12.3

A framework for qualifications and training in early years education and childcare

WHO MAKES THE PROVISION?	WHO ARE THE STAFF?	QUALIFICATIONS OF STAFF	ADULT: CHILD RATIOS
Commercial organisations, private individuals	Not specified, but often NNEB, BTEC and NVQ 2/3	Not known	2 1:5 3–4 yrs 1:8 5+ 1:20/30
Local education authority	Primary teachers. Sometimes a teaching assistant or a nursery nurse	Degree and PGCE/ BEd/BA (QTS) NNEB, BTEC, SNNB, SCOTVEC, NVQ	1:30/40 (1:15/20 if a trained nursery nurse is employed)
Local education authority	Nursery teachers Nursery nurses	Degree and PGCE/ BEd/BA/(QTS) NNEB, BTEC, SNNB, SCOTVEC, NVQ	3–4 years 1:10/13
Parents and voluntary groups	Playgroup leader or pre-school leader	Diploma in pre-school practice	3–5 yrs 1:8
Local authority social services	Mostly nursery nurses	NNEB, DPQS, BTEC, SNNB, SCOTVEC, NVQ	0–2 yrs 1:3 2–3 yrs 1:4 3–5 yrs 1:8
Private arrangement	Registered childminder	No national requirements	0–5 yrs 1:3 5–7 yrs 1:6
Private individuals, organisations/employers	Some staff are untrained. Some nursery nurses	50% of the staff must be trained	0–2 yrs 1:3 2–3 yrs 1:4 3–4 yrs 1:8
Local authority education and social services usually, but sometimes voluntary organisations and health authorities	Nursery teachers Nursery nurses	Degree and PGCE/ BEd/BA (QTS) NNEB, BTEC, SNNB, SCOTVEC, NVQ	1:10/13
Local authority social services, health authorities, voluntary organisations	Nursery nurses, Social workers, health visitors, wide range of staff	Very varied	This varies, and depends on the kind of work in the centre
Schools, voluntary organisations, Departments of Leisure	Volunteers, Community workers, Playleaders	Not known	5–7 yrs 1:8

▶ Free places for all four-year-olds if parents want one (but these are mainly in reception classes in primary schools) which early childhood specialists do not regard as quality nursery education on the whole.

▶ Additional resources to extend places to three-year-olds so that participation is doubled to two thirds of three-year-olds over the next few years.

▶ The Sure Start programme (0–3 years) targeted areas of need.

▶ Establishment of early years excellence centres which are models of providing integrated services which will be shared across the sectors and lead to development elsewhere.

▶ The regulation of early years education and day care with an integrated inspection service.

▶ The National Literacy Strategy in primary schools at Key Stages 1 and 2 and the National Numeracy Strategy. These involve direct focus on literacy and numeracy for approximately two hours a day.

▶ A review leading towards the climbing frame of training and qualifications of those working in early childhood care which will integrate with and make links into teaching qualifications so that those working in early years education and child care have more transferability of skills and qualifications to work in different job roles.

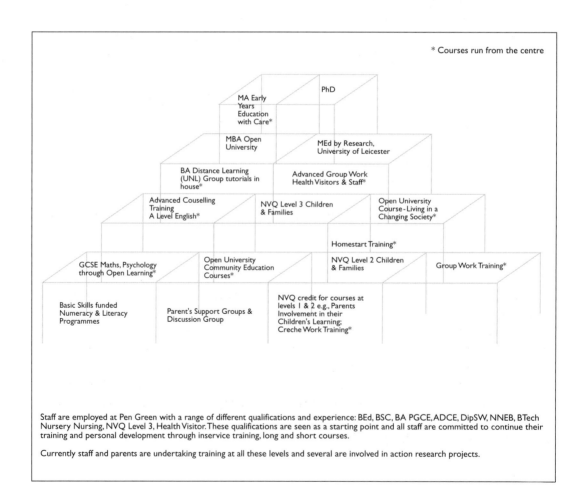

* Courses run from the centre

PhD

MA Early Years Education with Care*

MBA Open University

MEd by Research, University of Leicester

BA Distance Learning (UNL) Group tutorials in house*

Advanced Group Work Health Visitors & Staff*

Advanced Couselling Training A Level English*

NVQ Level 3 Children & Families

Open University Course - Living in a Changing Society*

Homestart Training*

GCSE Maths, Psychology through Open Learning*

Open University Community Education Courses*

NVQ Level 2 Children & Families

Group Work Training*

Basic Skills funded Numeracy & Literacy Programmes

Parent's Support Groups & Discussion Group

NVQ credit for courses at levels 1 & 2 e.g., Parents Involvement in their Children's Learning; Creche Work Training*

Staff are employed at Pen Green with a range of different qualifications and experience: BEd, BSC, BA PGCE, ADCE, DipSW, NNEB, BTech Nursery Nursing, NVQ Level 3, Health Visitor. These qualifications are seen as a starting point and all staff are committed to continue their training and personal development through inservice training, long and short courses.

Currently staff and parents are undertaking training at all these levels and several are involved in action research projects.

0 – 5 YEARS

Different UK early childhood settings are:

- state nursery school;
- family centres;
- nursery classes in primary schools;
- nursery units attached to primary schools;
- day nurseries;
- children's centres;
- community nurseries;
- private day nurseries;
- centres of early years excellence;
- private nursery schools;
- pre-preparatory schools;
- kindergartens;
- extended day sessions after school;
- Pre-School Learning Alliance Groups (formerly known as play groups);
- after-school clubs;
- childminders;
- nannies who look after children in their own home, and may or may not live there themselves.

In England, more than 80% of 4-year-olds are now in reception classes in primary schools. It is not recommended or required for children in these classes to follow key stage 1 of the National Curriculum introduced in England and Wales, from 1988. The content of the Curriculum is completely different in: England, Wales, Scotland and Northern Ireland.

Key stage 1 is a six-term programme which covers Years 1 and 2 (5–7-year-olds). Children can attend:

- one primary school from 5–11 years, or
- an infant school at 5–7 years and a junior school at 7–11 years, or
- a first school at 5–8 years and then a middle school at 9–13 years.

The UK maintained sector

Some provision is from central government or local authority. State nursery schools come under this type of provision, and are run in some parts of the country by **local education authorities**. These offer either full-time or part-time places for children of 3–5 years old. Exceptionally, children may start at $2\frac{1}{2}$ years, but only if there is a recommendation and joint decision with the Education, Health and Social Services Departments. There is a **head teacher** who is trained to specialise in the age group and graduate trained teachers working with qualified **nursery nurses**. Adult:child ratios are 1:10 in England and Wales, but 1:13 in Scotland. These schools are known for offering a quality curriculum for young children as in the Report of the Audit Commission in 1996. Margaret McMillan started the first nursery school in Deptford.

Childcare services in Member States of the European Union

WEST GERMANY	
0–2 YEARS	3% of children in publicly funded services divided between **'Nurseries'** (1.5%); and 2-year-olds in **'Kindergartens'**, 4 hours a day. Also 5,000 children in parent-run nurseries (**Krabbelstuben**), some of which receive some public funds; and some 4,000 children in 'other family care' have fees subsidised from public funds. 'Other family caregivers' and 'nurseries' not publicly funded should be registered and supervised by public authorities.
3–5 YEARS	60%+ of children in **'Kindergarten'** (1.33 million children attend, which is equal to 74% of 3–5-year-olds, but actual proportion of 3–5s attending is lower because some 2- and 6-year-olds included in 1.33 million). 12% of children attend full-time 'kindergartens' open 8 hours a day. Rest attend 4–6 hours a day. In addition, 6% of 5–6-year-olds in **'Pre-primary Schooling'**.
6–10 YEARS	Children attend primary school for 4–5 hours a day, up to 12.00 or 13.00. Starting and finishing hours irregular. 'Centre-based outside school hours care' for 3% of 6–10-year-olds.
FRANCE	
0–2 YEARS	20–25% of children in publicly-funded services . Divided between **'Nurseries'** (4%); **'Organised other family care'** (2%); and places for 17% (half of 2-year-olds) in **'Pre-Primary Schooling'**. In addition, places for 2% in *haltes-garderies,* but these places are used on a part-time basis, so provide for far more children. 'Other family caregivers' and 'nurseries' not publicly funded should be registered and supervised by local authorities.
3–5 YEARS	95% in **'Pre-Primary Schooling'**; available 8 hours a day. **'School-Based Outside School'** care available. Also small number (less than 1%) in **'Kindergartens'**.
6–10 YEARS	Attend primary school for same hours as 'pre-primary schooling', that is 08.30 to 16.30. **'School-based Outside School Hours Care'** available.
	Limited tax relief on childcare costs for children up to 7, plus grant for parent using 'own home' or registered 'other family care' to cover social-security contributions for caregiver.
ITALY	
0–2 YEARS	5% of children in publicly-funded services. All in **'Nurseries'**. 'Nurseries' that are not publicly-funded should be registered, but not 'other family caregivers'.
3–5 YEARS	88% of children in **'Pre-Primary Schooling'**. Most (66%) in schools available over 7 hours a day, and 55% attend over 7 hours a day. Nearly all other children in schools available 4–7 hours a day. Some schools provide **'Outside School Hours'** care.
6–10 YEARS	Most attend primary school for 4 hours a day, up to 12.00 or 12.30, though some schools have a longer day. Some **'School-Based Outside School Hours'** care, but not common.

NETHERLANDS	
0–2 YEARS	1–2% of children in publicly funded services. Nearly all in **'Nurseries'** or **'Pre-School and School Age Centres'**. Although open day, many children attend part-time. Also a few children in **'Other Family Care'** have fees subsidised from public funds. In addition, 8% (a quarter of 2-year-olds) attend **'Playcentres'**, see below. 'Nurseries, 'playcentres' and 'other family caregivers' that are not publicly funded do not have to be registered.
3–4 YEARS	50% of children in publicly funded services. Most (49%) in **'Early Primary Schooling'**, which nearly all 4-year-olds attend, available 5–7 hours a day depending on whether school (or centre) provides lunchtime supervision. A few (1%) in **'Nurseries'** which take children up to 4. **'Centre-Based Outside School Hours Care'** for less than 1% of 4-year-olds. In addition, 25% (a half of 3-year-olds) attend **'Playcentres'**, 5–6 hours a week on average. Over 90% of 'playcentres' are publicly funded, and grants on average cover 45% of costs.
5–10 YEARS	Compulsory School starts at 5 and children must attend for at least 12 hours a week in their first year. Full school day is generally 09.00–16.00 with two-hour lunch break. Supervision during lunch break organised by parents in schools where parents ask for this provision; also provided in centres for a small proportion of children. Increasing number of schools operate 'continuous timetable', with a shorter lunch break and an earlier finish.
	About 1% of age group receive publicly funded **'Outside School Hours Care'** in centres.
	Limited tax relief for childcare costs.
BELGIUM	
0–2 YEARS	20–25% of children in publicly-funded services. Full-time places for 5% of children in **'Nurseries'** but many of these places used on a part-time basis serve more children; and for 3% in **'Organised Other Family Care'**. 9% (a quarter of 2-year-olds) attend **'Pre-Primary Schooling'**. 'Other family caregivers' and 'nurseries' that are not publicly funded should be registered and supervised by local authorities.
3–5 YEARS	95%+ of children in **'Pre-Primary Schooling'** which is available 5–6 hours a day depending on whether schools provided lunchtime supervision. **'Outside School Hours Care'** provided in substantial proportion of schools and **'Organised Other Family Care'** in Flemish Area.
6–10 YEARS	Children attend primary schools from 08.30 to 15.30. Lunchtime supervision and **'Outside School Hours Care'** provided in substantial proportion of schools.

LUXEMBOURG	
0–2 YEARS	Less than 1% of children in publicly funded services, in **'Pre-School and School Age Centres'**. 'Other family caregivers' and 'nurseries' that are not publicly funded are not registered.
3–4 YEARS	48% of children in publicly funded services. Nearly all 4-year-olds in **'Pre-Primary Schooling'**, which is available $3\frac{1}{2}$–6 hours a day (hours vary on different days). Some schools are beginning to provide lunch, which extends school day by 2 hours. Less than 1% of 3-year-olds in **'Pre-School and School Age Centres'**, which also provide lunch and **'Outside School Hours Care'** for less than 1% of 4-year-olds.
5–10 YEARS	The second year of **'Pre-Primary Schooling'** for 5-year-olds, is compulsory. Hours are the same as for 'primary school': 0800 – 16.30 three days a week. Some schools are beginning to provide lunch. A small proportion under 2%, receive **'Outside School Hours Care'**, in **'Pre-School and School Age Centres'**.
	Limited tax relief to parents for childcare costs.
UNITED KINGDOM	
0–2 YEARS	2% of children in publicly-funded services. Divided between **'Nurseries'** and $2\frac{1}{2}$-year-olds in **'Pre-Primary Schooling'**. Also some children (5,600 aged 0–4) in 'other family care' or 'nurseries' have fees subsidised from public funds. In addition, an estimated 5–10% (all 2-year-olds) attend **'Playcentres'**. See below. 'Other family caregivers' and 'nurseries' not publicly funded should be registered and supervised by public authorities: in practice, most are registered.
3–4 YEARS	44% of children in publicly funded services. Divided between **'Pre-Primary Schooling'** which most (19%) attend part-time for $2\frac{1}{2}$ hours a day; **'Early Primary Schooling'** (20%) for 4-year-olds which most (19%) attend full-time for 6–$6\frac{1}{2}$ hours a day; **'Nurseries'** (1%) which take children up to compulsory age. In addition, an estimated 40–45% attend **'Playcentres'**, 5–6 hours a week on average. Only 1 in 4 'playcentres' are publicly funded and grants on average cover less than half of costs.
5–10 YEARS	Children attend primary school from 09.00 to 15.30, with a supervised lunchtime break of $1\frac{1}{2}$ hours. Publicly funded **'Outside School Hours Care'** for less than 1%.
DENMARK	
7–10 years	Children attend primary school for 3–5 hours a day, mostly during the morning. Starting and finishing hours are irregular. Publicly funded **'Outside School Hours Care'** provided for a fifth of children, mostly in centres but some school-based.

GREECE	
0–2 YEARS	2–3% of children in publicly funded services. Divided between **'Nurseries'** (1%); and $2\frac{1}{2}$ year-olds in **'Kindergartens'**. 'Nurseries' and 'kindergartens' that are not publicly funded should be registered.
3–5½ YEARS	62% of children in publicly funded services. Divided between 'Kindergartens' (17%) which are available 8 hours a day mostly for children up to 4, though some take children up to compulsory school age; and **'Pre-Primary Schooling'** (45%) which is available $3\frac{1}{2}$ hours a day for children aged 4–5. Very little **'Outside School Hours Care'**.
5½–10 YEARS	Children attend primary school for 20 hours a week for first 3 years, then for 24–26 hours. Many attend on a shift basis. Virtually no public-funded **'Outside School Hours Care'**.
PORTUGAL	
0–2 YEARS	4% of children in publicly-funded services. Mainly in **'Nurseries'** but some in **'Organised Other Family Care'** which as been recently introduced. 'Nurseries' that are not publicly-funded should be registered; 'other family caregivers' are not registered.
3–5 YEARS	25% of children in publicly funded services. Divided between **'Kindergartens'** (13%) which are available 8 hours or more a day; and **'Pre-Primary Schooling'** (12%) which is available 5–7 hours a day depending on whether school provides lunchtime supervision.
6–10 YEARS	Children attend primary school for 5 hours a day. Most attend on a shift basis. Publicly funded **'Centre-Based Outside School Hours Care'** for 3% of children aged 6–11.
SPAIN	
0–2 YEARS	No information on % of children in publicly funded **'Nurseries'**. 5% of 2-year-olds in **'Pre-Primary Schooling'**. 'Nurseries' and 'other family caregivers' not publicly funded are not registered.
3–5 YEARS	66% of children in **'Pre-Primary Schooling'**, most of which is for 4- and 5-year-olds in which age group 90% attend. Schooling available 3 – 8 hours a day, depending on whether school provides lunchtime supervision. Also an unknown percentage attend publicly funded **'Nurseries'**, some of which take children up to 4, some up to 6.
6–10 YEARS	Children attend primary school for same hours as **'Pre-Primary Schooling'**, that is from 09.00 to 17.00 with a three-hour lunch break, though schools increasingly provide lunch and supervision during this break. No publicly funded **'Outside School Hours Care'** except for some schemes in summer holidays.

Source: Moss, P. 1988 *Child Care and Equality of Opportunity*

CENTRES OF EARLY YEARS EXCELLENCE

These provide integrated provision in education, care and health according to each family's needs. Several centres of early years excellence emerged from being nursery schools and have returned to their Margaret McMillan roots by becoming centres of excellence combining health, education and care for children 0–5 years and their families.

NURSERY CLASSES AND NURSERY UNITS

A **nursery class** is attached to a primary school, and the head teacher of the primary school may or may not be an expert in early years education. The class teacher will be a trained nursery teacher who will work alongside a fully qualified nursery nurse.

Nursery units are usually in a separate building with a separate **coordinator**. They are larger than a nursery class but will have the same adult:child ratio as the nursery class – which is 1:15. Like the nursery class, they come under the management of the head teacher, who again may or may not be trained to work with this age group.

FAMILY CENTRES

These are jointly funded by the Education, Social Services and Health departments. They take a very wide catchment of children, and the provision they offer is as much for the parents as it is for the children. All staff will be qualified and will make up a multiprofessional team including teachers trained for the age group, nursery nurses, social workers, health visitors and so on.

DAY NURSERIES AND CHILDREN'S CENTRES

These offer full-time provision. They are particularly important in working with families who may be facing many challenges. They usually have a staff of trained nursery nurses, and sometimes teachers will work on the staff. They work closely with the Social Services and Health departments and often, although they are not funded by the Education department, make strong links with the nursery schools and classes in their area. There are now often joint training days which are welcomed by everyone working towards a multiprofessional approach.

COMMUNITY NURSERIES

These are often funded by voluntary organisations such as Barnados. They often function in similar ways to family centres. They sometimes offer full-time care but more usually part-time care.

EXTENDED DAY CARE IN SCHOOLS

This is to help parents who are working. Families take up this form of provision under the National Childcare Strategy.

Children will stay on after a session in the nursery school or class, and in a home-like atmosphere, with different staff. They will have tea and recreational activities.

The UK voluntary sector

Some **charitable trusts** offer education and care to children and their families, for instance Barnados, the Royal National Institute for the Blind (RNIB), SENSE and SCOPE (formerly the Spastic Society). These might be home-based or parent/toddler groups, community nurseries, day schools or residential special schools, or groups supporting children in mainstream education.

The Pre-School Learning Alliance was founded by Belle Tutaev in 1961 at a time when there was concern by parents at the lack of nursery education available. Parents ran these **play groups**, and the education and development of both parent and child were emphasised. (Not all play groups, however, are affiliated to the Pre-School Learning Alliance.)

Play groups have now been renamed **pre-schools** (1995). They are usually part-time, and they often offer two or three half-day sessions a week, often in a church hall. Parents pay a small charge – a factor which excludes some families from taking up this form of provision. This type of provision is often the only one available in rural areas.

The UK private sector

Private nursery schools and private day nurseries are only available for those parents who can afford them. There are a few workplace nurseries which may be subsidised in order that staff and students in institutions can take up this form of care.

PRIVATE DAY NURSERIES, PRIVATE NURSERY SCHOOLS, PREPARATORY SCHOOLS, KINDERGARTENS

These may be staffed by qualified people, but not always. There tends to be pressure in the private nursery schools to introduce children early to formal academic learning.

CHILDMINDERS AND NANNIES

Here, children are looked after in their own homes. Nannies may sometimes live in, but not always. Sometimes, nannies will share children from different families.

The integrated provision of education and care

The advantages of such an integrated provision are:
- ▶ It allows flexible provision at times which are useful to the family.
- ▶ It avoids the challenge of placing a predominance of children facing the most stress all into the same kind of provision. It makes for a more balanced mix of families.
- ▶ It can play a part in giving parents opportunities to work where this is wanted or needed.
- ▶ It helps every child to be a whole person.
- ▶ It can combine quality education with quality care.
- ▶ It can offer courses and support for parents in learning about their children's development and learning in the spirit of a working partnership.

Parents

Of course, parents are the most important people in the team working with young children, and this is now recognised in official documents.

Multi-disciplinary work

Children gain when parents, midwives, health visitors, nurses, doctors, nursery teachers, social workers, play therapists, educational psychologists, hospital teachers, experts in special educational needs work (e.g. a teacher of children with hearing impairments) and members of voluntary organisations such as the Pre-School Learning Alliance, the Royal National Institute for the Blind, SENSE and SCOPE all work together.

Mutual respect is also important: on a course for nursery nurses in Enfield in April 1995, 24 out of 28 said they felt deeply valued by the teachers and head teachers they worked with. However, they also said that other teaching staff in their primary and secondary schools did not always understand the depth of training they had received. Nursery nurses make a particularly invaluable contribution because they work across the widest range of settings. Being a good networker can therefore be a great strength in bringing people together in the common cause of getting the best for young children and their families.

COURSES, ORGANISATIONS, SOURCES OF INFORMATION

There are now a variety of courses for those working with young children and parents. These include National Vocational Qualifications (NVQ), certificates, diplomas, degrees, MAs and doctorates for those wishing to move forward in their professional development. There are also some specifically multi-disciplinary courses available (e.g. at Manchester Metropolitan University, University of North London) which are an invaluable way to learn from each other and to value what others do when working with babies, young children and parents.

There are many relevant journals and magazines which are useful to read throughout your working life (see Chapter 17).

What gives children a quality childhood?

Throughout history there have always been people who have been prepared to stand up and fight for what young children need. They are pioneers. Pioneers help everyone working with young children to move forward. Not everyone, however, has the kind of personality which makes a pioneer. The pioneers in this chapter are often called educational pioneers, but each one of them *cared* for children as much as they educated them. Each one of them believed in both education and care settings.

Early childhood education and care in the UK has a long and respected heritage and the greatest influence in the UK in the last century has been that of Friedrich Froebel.

Friedrich Froebel (1782–1852)

Froebel, who founded the first kindergarten in 1840, studied for a time with Pestalozzi in his school in Switzerland. Froebel learnt from him how important it was for children to have real experiences which involved them in being physically active.

Froebel's ideas are now so much part of everyday thinking about the education and care of young children that most people have never heard of the man himself – only his ideas remain. Froebel thought schools should be communities in which the parents are welcome to join their children. He believed that parents were the first educators of the child.

Froebel thought that children learnt outdoors in the garden as well as indoors and he encouraged movement, games and studying natural science in the garden. He invented finger play, songs and rhymes. He encouraged the arts, crafts and a love of literature, as well as mathematical understanding. He thought that children should have freedom of movement, clothes which were easy to move about in, and sensible food which was not too rich.

Froebel deeply valued symbolic behaviour, and he encouraged this even in very young children. He realised how important it is for children to understand that they can make one thing stand for another, for example a daisy can stand for a fried egg, a twig can stand for a knife, a leaf can stand for a plate, a written word can stand for a name. He thought that the best way for children to try out symbolic behaviour was in their *play*. He thought that as they pretend and imagine things, they show their highest levels of learning. He thought that their best *thinking* is done when they are playing.

He also designed various items and activities which would help symbolic behaviour. He encouraged children to draw, make collages and model with clay. He encouraged play with wooden blocks which he called the Gifts. He made up songs, movements and dancing, and the crafts he called his Occupations. He began to allow children to use the Gifts and Occupations without doing set tasks of the kind that adults asked of them, and thus he introduced what is now called free-flow play (see Chapter 9, p. 241). He emphasised the expressive arts, mathematics, literature, the natural sciences, creativity and aesthetic (beautiful) things. He believed that each brought important but different kinds of knowledge and understanding.

He also placed great emphasis on ideas, feelings and relationships. Relationships with *other children*, he believed, were as important as relationships with adults.

Froebel believed that everything links and connects with everything else: he said 'Link only link'. He called this the *principle of unity* that is in all things. But he also believed in what he called the *principle of opposition*. For example, the first Gift is a *soft* ball, but the second Gift is a *hard* wooden ball. He thought that these kinds of contrasts were important in helping children to think.

FIGURE 12.1
Basic block forms

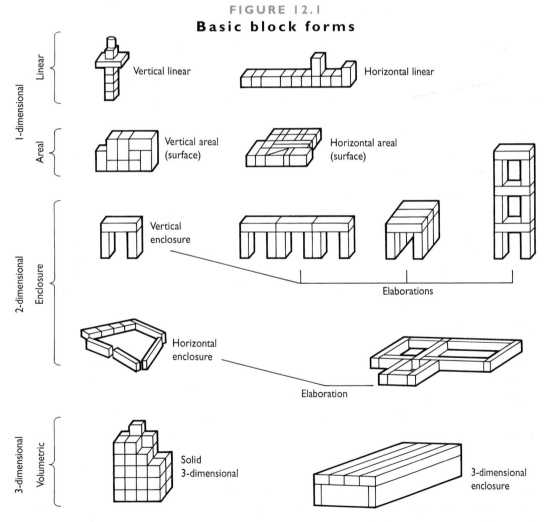

Source: Reprinted with permission from Gura, P. (Ed.) *Exploring Learning: Young Children and Blockplay.* © 1992 London, Paul Chapman Publishing Ltd.

FIGURE 12.2

A set of blocks based on a Community Playthings Design

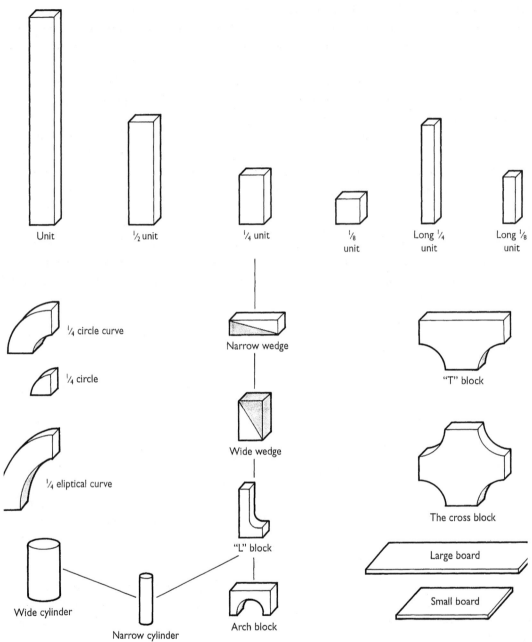

Source: Reprinted with permission from Gura, P. (Ed.) *Exploring Learning: Young Children and Blockplay.* © 1992 London, Paul Chapman Publishing Ltd.

Maria Montessori (1870–1952)

Maria Montessori began her work as a doctor in the poorest areas of Rome at the beginning of the 1900s. She worked with children with learning difficulties. She spent many hours observing children and this is one of the great strengths of her work. She came to the conclusion, supported by modern research, that children pass through sensitive periods of development when they are particularly receptive to particular areas of learning. Like Piaget (and others), she saw children as active learners.

Montessori devised a structured teaching programme which she based on her observations of children who were mentally challenged, and she believed she was making Froebel's work more scientifically rigorous in doing this. She also used the work of Seguin who had given manual-dexterity exercises to children who were handicapped. This he did because he believed that if they could learn to use their hands, they would be able to find work later and so not be a burden to their parents – who were also maybe manual workers.

Montessori designed a set of what she called **didactic** materials which encouraged children to use their hands. Her approach moved children through simple to complex exercises. Here is how she taught a language lesson:

'Then, in order to teach the colours, she says, showing him the red 'this is the red', raising her voice a little and pronouncing the word 'red' slowly and clearly, then showing him the other colour, 'this is blue'. In order to make sure that the child has understood, she says to him 'give me the red, give me the blue'. Let us suppose that the child, following the last direction, made a mistake. The teacher does not repeat and does not insist. She smiles, gives the child a friendly caress, and takes away the colours.'

Whereas Froebel stressed the importance of relationships, feelings and being part of a community, Montessori stressed that children should work alone. She thought that this helped children to become independent learners. For her, the highest moment in a child's learning was what she called 'the polarisation of the attention'. This means that the child is completely silent and absorbed in what they are doing.

Unlike Froebel, she did not see the point in play. She did not encourage children to have their own ideas until they had worked through all her graded learning sequences: she did not believe that they were able to do free drawing or creative work of any kind until they had done this. Montessori has had less influence on the maintained sector of education than she has on private schools.

Rudolf Steiner (1861–1925)

Steiner believed in three phases of childhood. These involved:

1 the *will*, 0–7 years: he believed the spirit fuses with the body at this stage;
2 the *heart*, 7–14 years: he believed that the rhythmic system of the beating heart, the chest and the respiratory system meant that *feelings* were especially important during this time;
3 the *head*, 14 years onwards: this is the period of *thinking*.

Steiner believed in reincarnation. This means that during the first 7 years of their life, the child is like a newcomer finding their way, and the child's reincarnated soul needs protection. The child needs a carefully planned environment. Then the child can develop in an all-round way.

What the child eats is very important (Steiner was a vegetarian). The child also needs proper rest (rest and activity need to be balanced).

The child's temperament is also considered to be very important. A child might be calm (sanguine), easily angered (choleric), sluggish (phlegmatic), or peevish (melancholic). Often children are a combination of these. The golden rule for the adult is never to go against the temperament of the child, and always to go *with* it.

Steiner was like Froebel in that he believed in the importance of the *community*. He believed that maintaining relationships with other people were very important, and for this reason children would keep the same teacher for a number of years.

When children are about to sing and act out a circle game, everyone waits for the last child to be part of the group. It is sung many times so that quicker children learn to help and support slower children. Steiner's curriculum is very powerful for children with special educational needs who can integrate because children are actively helped to care about them. Like Froebel, Steiner thought the symbolic behaviour of the child was important, but in a different way. In the first 7 years of their life, he told special Steinerian fairy tales. He believed children drink these in and absorb them. He gave them dolls without faces, wooden blocks with irregular shapes, silk scarves as dressing-up clothes and particular colour schemes in rooms (pink at first). Baking, gardening, modelling, painting and singing – all of these activities would take place in a carefully designed community.

There are a few schools in the UK called Waldorf schools which use Steiner's methods. These are all in the private sector. Like Montessori, Steiner has had less influence on the statutory public sector than on the private sector.

Margaret McMillan (1860–1931)

Margaret McMillan, like Montessori, began her work using the influence of Seguin. This meant that she emphasised the manual dexterity exercises long before Montessori's ideas reached the UK. However, as time went on, she used Froebel's ideas more and more (she became a member of the Froebel Society in 1903). This meant that she believed first-hand experience and active learning to be important. She emphasised relationships, feelings and ideas as much as the physical aspects of moving and learning. She believed that children become *whole* people through play. She thought play helped them to *apply* what they know and understand.

McMillan pioneered nursery schools, which she saw as an extension of, not a substitute for, home. She believed in very close partnership with parents: she encouraged parents to develop alongside their children, with adult classes and hobbies and language classes available to them. The British Nursery School has been admired and emulated across the world. Nursery schools have gardens, and are communities which welcome both parents and children. Such nursery schools stood out as beacons of light in the poverty-stricken areas of inner cities like Deptford and Bradford in the 1920s.

She said that here families could experience 'fresh air, trees, rock gardens, herbs, vegetables, fruit trees, bushes, opportunities to climb on walls, sand pits, lawns, flowers and flower beds and wildernesses'. She said in 1930, in her book *The Nursery School* (p.80): 'most of the best opportunities for achievement lie in the domain of free play, with access to various material'.

However, perhaps most important of all is the fact that she has been given the honour of being described as the 'godmother' of school meals and the school medical services. She believed that children cannot learn if they are under-nourished, under-clothed or sick and ill with poor teeth, poor eyesight, ear infections, rickets etc. Recent reports emphasise that poor health and poverty are still challenges to be faced for those who work with families in the UK today.

McMillan also placed enormous importance on the training of adults working with children, and on the need for them to be inventive and imaginative in the way they worked.

Susan Isaacs (1885–1948)

Susan Isaacs, like Margaret McMillan, was influenced by Froebel. She was also influenced by the theories of Melanie Klein, the psychoanalyst. She made detailed observations of children in her Malting House School in Cambridge during the 1930s. Isaacs valued play because she believed that it gave children freedom to think, feel and relate to others. She looked at children's fears, their aggression and their anger. She believed that through their play children can move in and out of reality and begin to get a balance in their ideas, feelings and relationships. She said of classrooms where young children had to sit at tables and write that children cannot learn in such places because they need to move about as much as they need to eat and sleep.

Isaacs valued parents as the most important educators in a child's life. She spoke to them on the radio, and she wrote for parents in magazines. On p. 61 of *The Nursery Years*, she wrote: 'If the child had ample opportunity for free play and bodily exercise, if this love of making and doing with his hands is met, if his interest in the world around him is encouraged by sympathy and understanding, if he is left free to make believe or think as his impulses take him, then his advances in skill and interest are but the welcome signs of mental health and vigour.'

Isaacs encouraged people to look at the inner feelings of children. She encouraged children to express the feelings they have which would be very damaging for them to bottle up inside.

She supported both Froebel's and Margaret McMillan's view that nurseries are an extension of the home and not a substitute for it, and she believed that children should be left in a nursery type of education until they are 7 years of age. She kept careful records of her children both for the period they spent in her nursery and for the period after they had left, and she found that many of them *regressed* when they left her nursery and went on to infant school. Modern researchers have found the same.

R E S O U R C E S

Books

Sir Christopher Ball *Start Right: the Importance of Early Learning* (report), The Royal Society of Arts, London, March 1994

E. Bradburn, *Margaret McMillan: Portrait of a Pioneer,* London, Routledge, 1989

M. McMillan, *The Nursery School,* London, J.M. Dent, 1930

T. Bruce, *Early Childhood Education,* London, Hodder & Stoughton, 1997 (2nd edition)

T. Bruce, *Time to Play,* London, Hodder & Stoughton, 1991

DES Starting with Quality Report, HMSO 1990

T. Bruce, A. Findlay, J. Read and M. Scarborough, *Recurring Themes in Education,* London, Paul Chapman Publishing, 1995

D. Gardner, *Susan Isaacs,* London, Methuen, 1969

Gura, P. (Ed.) *Exploring Learning: Young Children and Blockplay,* London, Paul Chapman Publishing, 1992

S. Isaacs, *The Nursery Years,* London, Routledge and Kegan Paul, 1968

M. Montessori, *The Montessori Method,* London, Heinemann, 1912

R. Steiner, *The Essentials of Education,* London, Anthroposophical Publishing Co., 1926

Useful Addresses

Rudolf Steiner House
Baker Street
London W1

Association Montessori
Internationale
Lyndhurst Gardens
Hampstead
London

The Froebel Archive for Childhood Studies
Froebel College
Roehampton Lane
London SW15
j.read@roehampton.ac.uk

A C T I V I T Y

Investigating Froebel's work

1   Research a set of wooden hollow blocks and wooden unit blocks (examples of these are made by Community Play things – see Figures 12.1 and 12.2). Can you find any mathematical relationships between the different blocks? Plan how you could help children to learn about shape using wooden blocks. Implement your plan, and evaluate your observations with children of 3–7 years of age.
2   Try to find twelve examples of finger rhymes. These are songs or rhymes using the fingers for actions. Make a book of them for children to enjoy. Make sure you include a multicultural range and think also about children with disabilities. Share the book with a child of 2–7 years of age. Evaluate your observations.
3   Research what children did in the kindergarten in the last century. For example, each child had their own little garden.
    (a) Plan how *you* will organise a garden activity. What equipment will you need? Where will you do this? How will you clear up?
    (b) Plant some flowers or vegetables with children, and watch them grow.
    (c) Observe a child of 2–7 years of age, and evaluate your garden activity in relation to that particular child's cognitive and language development.
4   Imagine that you are Friedrich Froebel returning today. What do you think he might like or dislike about your early childhood setting?

A C T I V I T Y

Investigating Margaret McMillan's Work

Plan an outdoor area for an early childhood setting. Emphasise the child's need for movement, curiosity about nature, and an area for digging and playing in mud. Evaluate your plan.

A C T I V I T Y

Investigating education and care

1   Research the age at which children start compulsory schooling in six countries, including one country in Africa, Asia, New Zealand, Europe and Australia. You can telephone the relevant embassies, who will help you track down this information.
2   Research the different ways in which Froebel, Montessori and Steiner would introduce children to a set of wooden blocks and help them to use them. Implement each approach with a group of children in three separate sessions. Evaluate your observations, noting the way your role as an early

childhood worked changed according to which approach you used. Note the differences in the way the children responded, especially in relation to creativity (see Chapter 6), language and communication (see Chapter 8) and play (see Chapter 9). Which approaches encouraged the child to be a symbol-user? Evaluate your observations.

A C T I V I T Y

What kind of provision?

Research the Audit of Early Years Provision in your area made by your local authority. What proportion of four-year-olds are in reception classes? What kind of provision are most three-year-olds and their families offered?

13

The Early Childhood Curriculum

About the early childhood curriculum

The early childhood curriculum in the UK is about helping children of 0–8 years of age to develop and learn. It is based on Western educational principles arising from the work of respected pioneers. Researchers are interested to see if these principles are important in other parts of the world.

Principles supporting the early childhood curriculum in the UK

1 The best way to prepare children for their adult life is to give them what they need as children.
2 Children are whole people who have feelings, ideas and relationships with others, and who need to be physically, mentally, morally and spiritually healthy.
3 Subjects such as mathematics and art cannot be separated: young children learn in an integrated way and not in neat, tidy compartments.
4 Children learn best when they are given appropriate responsibility, allowed to make errors, decisions and choices, and respected as autonomous learners.
5 Self-discipline is emphasised. Indeed, this is the only kind of discipline worth having. Reward systems are very short-term and do not work in the long-term. Children need their *efforts* to be *valued*.

6 There are times when children are especially able to learn particular things.
7 What children *can* rather than cannot do is the starting point of the child's education.
8 Imagination, creativity and all kinds of symbolic behaviour (reading, writing, drawing, dancing, music, mathematical numbers, algebra, role play) develop and emerge when conditions are favourable.
9 Relationships with other people (adults and children) are of central importance in a child's life.
10 Quality education is about three things:
   ▶ the child;
   ▶ the context in which learning takes place;
   ▶ the knowledge and understanding which the child develops and learns.

What is the early childhood curriculum

Ask six people what they think the curriculum is. They are likely to say that they think it is to do with children learning maths – especially numbers – or reading or writing. In fact, the curriculum is much more than that, and it is very important that those working with young children look at every aspect of the curriculum and not just one narrow part of it.

The curriculum has three parts. These emphasise:
1 the child's development;
2 the child's access to the curriculum and contextual sensitivities;
3 what the child learns and understands.

These three parts need to be balanced: one is not more important than any of the others.
   ▶ When the three are not in balance, the quality of the curriculum is poor.
   ▶ When the three are in balance, the quality of the curriculum is good.

THE CHILD

The early childhood curriculum begins with the child. Some early childhood workers would say this is what it means to be **child–centred**. It is important that early childhood workers know about how children develop so that they can then help children to learn. Children need adults who are informed about child development. Parents constantly ask for more information in this area. Television programmes, magazines, health visitors and

FIGURE 13.1
The three C's of early childhood curriculum

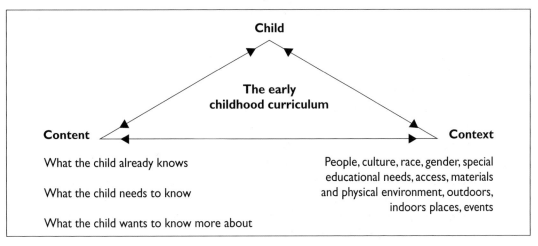

early childhood workers can all support families by helping them to enjoy their children as much as possible. They can help to ease the anxieties that parents experience about their child's behaviour. Parents can then enjoy helping children to learn.

EARLY CHILDHOOD WORKERS NEED TO KNOW ABOUT CHILD DEVELOPMENT

The child's pace and phases of development need to be understood. This means that those working with young children need to learn about the play, language development and communication of children, as well as about: the way they use symbolic behaviour; the way they represent their experiences; their movement; their concepts (ideas); their skills (competency); their attitudes, feelings and relationships; their self-help skills (e.g. going to the toilet, feeding, dressing); and their schemas (patterns of behaviour which the child generalises and uses in different settings and situations). (See Chapter 6.)

In this book, different chapters look at different areas of child development. You will need all of this knowledge in order to offer children a quality early childhood curriculum for three reasons:

1   Knowing about child development helps early childhood workers to:
    ▶ observe and understand a child;
    ▶ support a child's development and learning;
    ▶ extend a child's development and learning.

2   Child-development knowledge helps adults to create a quality curriculum in a very general way. This means that it will be helping most children to learn most of the time. This is sometimes called a **developmentally appropriate curriculum** (NAEYC). It is very important, however to realise that this approach is based only on Western ideas about how children develop. Researchers are now very interested to see whether this approach to child development is also useful in other cultures. The importance of the learning context is now emphasised.

3   Knowing about child development helps early childhood workers to bring about a **differentiated curriculum**. This is a curriculum which caters for the individual child. A quality curriculum cares about the individual child as much as it cares about getting things right in general.

Let's now look at these points in more detail:

1   *Observe, support, extend:*
    ▶ *Observe.* Observations help early childhood workers to plan the curriculum and to see how best to work with a child. It is essential to identify what children are learning by careful observation techniques. Observation is about getting to know the child, and only when adults know the child well can they help that child to learn in any deep sense.
    ▶ *Support.* Children need plenty of opportunities to choose to repeat activities they already know about and ideas they already have, e.g. in the home area, in the graphics area, on the woodwork bench, in the small-world area and with dolls – such activities should always be available. This is how they master skills and become competent. They need to keep returning to the old and familiar. This is why basic provision is essential and should be set out regularly on a daily basis.
    ▶ *Extend.* It is important to extend children in what they already know. Past experiences are central when children are learning new things. If they already

know what a roti is, then it will be easy for them to learn about bread. They can use what they know already and adjust it a little bit. In the same way, if a child knows about bread, then it will be easy to learn in turn about roti. We use what we know as a bridge across to what we don't know. For example, a planned cooking activity might involve making bread rolls. The children might have chosen to do this because they enjoyed making bread before, and some will now be ready to extend the bread-making and follow the cooking sequence with a recipe book. This book will probably have been made by a member of staff and will be full of pictures and simple text showing each step to be taken. Some children will need only a little help in finding their own ingredients and utensils and following the books.

When children learn something new, they try to link it with what they already know, and they might need a considerable amount of adult help in doing this. For example, they might need help to see that their knowledge of banging a spoon on the table can be extended to the use of a hammer at the woodwork bench. Direct teaching on how to use the hammer effectively will extend the child's learning. Woodwork must always be supervised.

2 *A developmentally appropriate curriculum.* The early childhood curriculum needs to offer experiences which are appropriate for most children of this age and stage of development. For example, the 0–1 curriculum will be based on what is known about the development of most children in their 1st year, while the 1–3 and 3–5 curriculum will be based on what is known about most children's development at 1–3 years and between 3 and 5 years of age. The 5–8 curriculum, in turn, should be based on what is known about most children's development at 5 to 8 years of age. In England, Wales, Northern Ireland and Scotland, it is now legally required for children of 5–8 years of age in state schools to follow the key stage 1 curriculum set by central government.

3 *A differentiated curriculum.* A differentiated curriculum helps individual children to learn in their own particular way. It means getting the pace right for each child in their own learning. Some children move through developmental sequences at a faster pace than others. For example, only a *few* children will be able to read at 4 years, while most children will become fluent readers at between 6 and 8 years. It is no advantage, indeed, to be early at doing things; in fact, by the age of 18 years, it is often those who were not particularly early at doing things who go the furthest. (No-one is going to ask job applicants at a job interview whether they were potty trained by 1 year, or if they could read and write at 4 years!)

Most children learn in a rather uneven way: they have bursts of learning and then they have plateaux in their learning when they do not seem to move forward at all. This is why careful observation plus a knowledge of child development are very important. Catching the right point in the sequence of development is a skilled job. So is tuning into the child's pace of learning. Children have their own personalities and moods. They are affected by the weather, the time of day, whether they need food or sleep or the lavatory, the experiences they have, and their degree of self-esteem.

According to Stevenson and Oates at the Open University, some children experience developmental:

1 *delay:* this mean they do things later than most children;
2 *disability:* this means that children are varied in how they can manage to do things;

3 *deviance:* this means that children do not go through the normal sequences of development;

4 *difference:* this means that a child has a varied profile in terms of abilities and skills.

Some children will be **challenged** in their learning, and those working with children with special educational needs will need to be imaginative, determined and resourceful in helping them to learn.

Gifted children

Children who are gifted in music, (e.g. Scott Joplin the composer, Jacqueline Dupré the cellist), dance (e.g. Fred Astaire the film star, Margot Fonteyn the ballet dancer) and mathematics (Richard Feynman and Marie Curie, the physicists) tend to show promise in their subjects very early in life. It is important to remember that being gifted has little to do with a high intelligence quotient (IQ).

Howard Gardner believes in *multiple intelligence* (see p. 163). Being *socially* gifted, for example, means that a child is able to see things from another point of view – leaders such as Nelson Mandela are gifted in their ability to bring people together over difficult issues. Some children show their giftedness early in life, while others show it later in their development.

Children with special educational needs

Many children with special educational needs (see p. 440 for a definition) are under-estimated by the adults working with them. For example, most children of 7 or 8 can run across a field confidently. Visually impaired children in mainstream settings are often not expected to try to do this, and so they don't. No-one suggests it to them, and no-one offers them help to do it. With the right help, however, the child *might* well manage it, and become more confident as a result. However, the experience of running across a field will have to be offered in particular ways, and at a particular time, that depends on that particular child's stage of development, personality and mood. Walking hand in hand together across the field might be important. Talking as you go will help. Then, giving tips about how to pick up feet and trying it out holding hands together; followed by running across the field together holding hands; and finally, standing ahead and talking non stop while the child runs across the field towards the voice. And after this, being positive about tumbles taken: instead of rushing over anxiously and saying 'Are you hurt?', going over quickly and gently touching a child's shoulder, saying 'Can I help you up? I hope your knee is not hurting too much', for example.

Summary

▶ Children need adults who observe, support and extend their development and learning.

▶ Adults need to get the right balance between supporting children in what they already know and understand and using this previous knowledge as a bridge across to new knowledge. Children who are bored or frustrated quickly become rather challenging to be with.

▶ A quality early childhood curriculum means that the curriculum caters for the general development of children at the ages and stages of 0–8 years.

▶ A differentiated curriculum allows the general developmental needs of most children to be linked with the specific needs of an individual child. This means that every child gains access to the generally offered curriculum.

The context of the curriculum – the child-in-context

The context of the curriculum is made up of:
- ▶ people
- ▶ provision.

These give children access to a quality curriculum. Every child needs full access to the curriculum regardless of their ethnic background, culture, language, gender, special educational needs (if they have any), or economic background. No child should be held back in their learning because of not having full access to the curriculum.

People

The context of the curriculum contains many different kinds of people, and they are all important for children.

1 *Parents*. Parents are the first educators of their children. This means that early childhood workers of all kinds need to see themselves as supporting and sharing the education and care of young children in *close partnership* with the parents, which will benefit the child in deep and lasting ways (see Chapter 5). Professional workers sometimes talk of 'my children', but they are not their children: children belong to their parents.

   Research which has been done at Exeter University by Martin Hughes shows that parents want more information about what their children are doing in the curriculum. They do not want to challenge what is there, but they do want to understand more about it. They are interested in what their children are learning (see Chapter 5). They want to help the staff. That is why they often ask quite difficult questions for staff to answer. They might ask 'Why is my child playing so much in nursery and not doing sums or reading and writing.

   Early childhood workers need a good understanding of how children develop and learn. They also need effective ways of exchanging and sharing their learning with parents. When parents and professionals work well together in a spirit of trust and genuine exchange of information and knowledge, then everyone gains: parent, professional, and most of all the child.

2 *Early childhood workers – team work*.

   ▶ A good learning atmosphere (*ethos*) is one where adults helping children to learn have high expectations of children and are positive and warm, supporting and encourage self-esteem. In a quality learning context, adults value each child. They do not make statements which criticise the child's family. It is essential to create a learning context in which children feel appreciated and valued, and where those close to them, usually their families, are also valued.

   ▶ It is through other people that children learn to feel valued, or not. When children feel their efforts are appreciated and see them celebrated, they develop a positive self-image. This helps learning almost more than anything else. On the other hand, if a child spends time with adults who only praise and recognise *results*, most children are bound to fail. If, however, a child spends time with adults who appreciate and value what a child tries to do and the *effort* that the child makes, the child does not feel judged. It means that each child is free from the pressure of having to produce perfect results. It means that a child is free to

FIGURE 13.2
The result is not the important thing!

learn, and to learn from things going badly as well as from things going well. This helps children to be highly motivated and interested in their learning.

▶ Children need adults to provide a safe predictable environment. It is very important for all staff to work as a team so that different messages are not given by different people. For example, if one adult allows children to sit on tables and another doesn't, it leads to boundary testing by children. Children will need to sort out their confusion about what is and is not allowed.

▶ Children need to be safe physically. Then they can explore and enjoy the stimulating context that is provided by the staff. A safe predictable environment does not impose rigid routines or rules on children. However, it does give children clear messages. When children understand why certain things need to be done in certain ways, they find it easier to take responsibility and to be positive and cooperative.

▶ Many settings now have a family-worker system where a worker will link with particular children and families in order to have 'a person' for that family to relate to more deeply. This system was recommended in the Children Act 1989 and the Starting with Quality Report 1990. The team leader will coordinate this, and there will need to be regular meetings of the staff in order to discuss events as they arise. The importance of this is stressed in a study by Peter Elfer at the National Children's Bureau.

Sometimes children need to be directly taught to do something by adults – e.g. how to mix paints. Children appreciate and need:

▶ the right help
▶ at the right time
▶ in the right way.

This means adults need to observe children carefully and this will help them to see if the child:

▶ is struggling;
▶ is avoiding something;
▶ is interested but does not know what to do.

HELPING WHEN A CHILD IS STRUGGLING TO LEARN

The child who is struggling needs direct help in order to avoid a temper tantrum, frustration, anxiety or sadness. The child who is avoiding something difficult perhaps picks up a cloak in the dressing-up area but finds that they cannot tie a bow and so puts it down and chooses a different bit of clothing which fastens with velcro instead. This child really did, however, *want* to use the cloak with strings, and they will need to be helped with this activity.

TEACHING SKILLS IN CONTEXT

A child who picks up the scissors and opens them, then puts them on the paper and looks on, as if expecting the paper to be cut, needs direct teaching on how to use the scissors.

Having reading skills is quite different from having the disposition to read. Having writing skills doesn't mean that the child has the disposition to be a writer.

DISPOSITIONS FOR LEARNING

In New Zealand the Te Whariki Curriculum has tried out five learning dispositions which connect with the strands of the curriculum. The Te Whariki strands are:

▶ Belonging, well being, exploration, communication, contribution.

The dispositions which connect with these strands are:

▶ Courage, trust, perseverance, confidence, responsibility.

ADULTS AND CHILDREN

The Effective Early Learning project based at Worcester University College emphasises three areas in the way adults help children to learn. This is called the Engagement Scale, and it looks at:

▶ the sensitivity of the adult to the child;

▶ the way the adult encourages the child to be autonomous and get on and try things;

▶ the way the adult offers experiences which are stimulating, challenging and interesting.

Direct teaching is most effective for young children when it is linked with a real-life need, as in the above examples of the cloak and scissors. It leads to children feeling they have mastery and control of their learning. This kind of direct teaching leads to effective learning. This is very different from a child being required to stay at a table and thread beads when they really want to move about outside and climb and run – the child here might even feel frustrated or aggressive. A good way to help fine motor skills such as the pincer movement is in fact to encourage *large* motor skills such as those involved in the movement of the shoulder when climbing. The movement of the shoulder affects the movement of the finger and thumb; and adults who cannot move their shoulder find writing difficult.

When children do mostly adult-led tasks such as colouring in, drawing round templates, sticking tissue paper onto outlines, tracing etc., a child will become used to being shown how to do things exactly as the adult wants and this is likely to encourage the child to become a passive learner. It does not bring about a context which gives children good access to deep learning.

LEARNING FROM AND THROUGH OTHER CHILDREN

Children learn through each other as well as through adults, but they can only do this if they are free to choose what they do for large parts of the day. Then they can find friends and children they want to learn with. They need to be free to talk to each other and move about together.

Most of the time, children of 3 to 8 years of age seem to choose to be with one other child in a partnership. Some of the time, they do choose to play in small groups, but these break apart and keep changing. Large group activities, indeed, are difficult for young children. They should therefore be short (10 minutes approximately), move with a good pace and make use of props, songs, dances, finger rhymes, ring games and puppets. This gives a sense of community, but young children might find it hard not to shout out, interrupt or to take turns in discussion, especially if the session lasts too long.

Children under 5 years should not be expected to attend school assemblies.

Provision

It is of central importance to organise a curriculum context which gives children access to the curriculum through the way provision is structured. Provision is structured through:

- ▶ time
- ▶ space
- ▶ materials.

THE CURRICULUM TIMETABLE – PROVIDING CHILDREN WITH ENOUGH TIME

The early childhood curriculum is observation-centred. This means the timetable must be made for the child's needs to be met. Children need plenty of time which is undirected by adults. Then they can develop their play, try things out and have plenty of experiences, pacing their learning to suit themselves. They need time to make relationships and friendships with other children and with adults.

- ▶ Children learn best when they are in a predictable environment. This means that their activities should not be controlled by adults all the time, but that there should be a shape to the day. They also need to feel safe by having some sense of what is coming next and of the rough sequence of the day, with regular mealtimes.
- ▶ The way that the day is organised will need to fit with the natural rhythms of the child. The adults need to keep in mind that it is important not to work with a tight, inflexible routine which is made for the convenience of the adults only. The younger the child (e.g. babies), the more this is so. There are times when children go at a fast pace, and times when they sag, times when they want to be alone, to have a quiet cuddle, and times when they enjoy working with other children or adults (for example with clay).

STRUCTURING THE SPACE IN OFFERING THE CURRICULUM
THE OUTDOOR AREA
The outdoor area needs to be available most of the time. Safety is the only consideration for keeping children *indoors* – e.g. until all the children have arrived at the beginning of the day: this is so that no-one can slip out unnoticed through the door.

Children often love to go out in all weathers provided they are suitably dressed. Adults too need to dress according to the weather so that they can support the children's learning outside as fully as possible.

FIGURE 13.3
Exploring a garden

THE LAYOUT OF THE INDOOR AND OUTDOOR AREA

There is no one way to set out an area. In fact it is best to avoid rigid 'methods' in this. It is important to keep thinking about the way the room is set out. When you go to the supermarket and find it has changed its layout or go down a street and find it has been changed, how do you feel? Is it difficult to find things? Young children are only just finding out where to find things, e.g. scissors, bats, balls, etc. If they have to keep relearning where to go and where things are, it wastes their energy. It is therefore best to keep the areas fixed, but to change what is in them as long as all the basics are there all the time. Then, an area will remain interesting and attractive to use. Donald Hebb, a psychologist, called this 'the difference in the sameness'.

Pembury House Centre for Childhood Training and Education has the Anne Jones Musical Garden, and Woodlands Park Nursery Centre has a hill with scrubs marking dens to hide in. At Rowland's Hill Early Childhood Centre the outdoor area is being planned influenced by the strengths of the New Zealand approach. This means staff think about the flow between, for example the sand area and the climbing frame. Should the areas remain separate, or can they be linked. Pembury House, Woodlands Park and Rowland's Hill form the Haringey Early Excellence Network.

Pen Green Centre has the 'Corby Dome', a covered area including waterfalls which means children can go outside under cover in all weathers.

LAYOUTS OF DIFFERENT ROOMS

The layout of the room also needs to reflect the multi-cultural society of the UK. There may also need to be special equipment for children with special educational needs, for instance a tray on a table to stop objects falling off the table so that a child with a physical disability does not keep losing objects when handling them.

Nothing should be in the room unless it has been put there for a reason. Clutter develops very quickly in early childhood settings. It is a good idea to ask yourself 'Why is this here?'

The layout needs to be carefully planned by the team. It must be safe. If children are to learn how to use to the full the context in which they are learning, they are helped if everything is easy to see and if they can reach all the equipment. This is called *easy access*.

What does a quality curriculum for babies/toddlers look like?

Children learn more in the first 5 years than in the whole of the rest of their lives. It is important when working with young children never to separate education from care, and to make use of evidence about how children learn. Studies in neuroscience (brain studies) give evidence suggesting a curriculum should stress:

Personhood

▶ This involves the babies/toddlers developing a sense of who they are – a sense of identity.

▶ It means relationships with other people are of central importance.

Communication

▶ During this time babies/toddlers do not use verbal language in the conventional sense. Adults with whom they are close often understand their gestures, the way they look at a parent/carer, their movements and the sounds they make. They tune into children. They are affectionate and sensitive to the non-verbal ways in which babies and toddlers 'speak' to us. The rhythm, tone and way babies/toddlers are talked to helps them to develop verbal language with confidence and understanding.

Learning through the senses

▶ Babies need to suck (taste) smell, touch (kick, hold) objects and materials and to look and listen and make sounds. Through the senses babies/toddlers gain feedback which allows them to make sense of experiences. If they are covered in clothes, children cannot feel through their skin.

Learning through movement

▶ Babies/toddlers can't learn much unless they move. Doing several things at once stimulates the brain. This is called mass action.

These examples are from observations by Ruth Forbes, Curriculum Development Manager (Jigsaw Nurseries)

Using everyday events

When Joey is changed (10 months) he dislikes the plastic changing mat. He tries to move off it. His keyworker respects his feelings, and puts a towel on the mat. She talks about this, and sings 'Ten little toes'. He giggles in anticipation of each toe being gently touched.

This everyday event has helped Joey to learn about:
▶ himself and where he ends
▶ affectionate, sensitive communications between people
▶ making sense of what someone says to you
▶ music, with its melody (tune), pitch (loudness)
▶ eye contact when people talk to each other, and facial expressions
▶ having fun together. Babies/toddlers learn better if they are not anxious. Laughing releases chemicals into the brain which open it up to learning (but anxiety closes the brain off from learning

At lunch-time, a group of sitting babies and toddlers were encouraged to choose their pudding. A plate of freshly prepared fruit was placed on the table. A tiny portion was given to babies to try out. Several showed they wanted more through their movements. The key worker passed the plate to the babies, who were allowed to take for themselves.

This encouraged:
▶ mathematics. It's the same.
▶ a feeling of control over what happens to you
▶ independence
▶ decision making

Playing with an adult

The keyworker sat on the floor facing Rebecca (10 months) and did the 'Row the boat' song with her. She sang the song and moved with her twice, and then stopped. Rebecca touched her on her thigh and the carer responded 'again ... you want to sing again'. The singing and moving together was repeated, and Rebecca smiled with pleasure.

In this play:
▶ Rebecca is helped to be imaginative.
▶ her idea to repeat the song is taken up
▶ she is encouraged to use initiative and not be passive
▶ she is learning the basics of drama, music, dance

FIGURE 13.4

FIGURE 13.4
The garden plans for Woodlands Park and Pembury House

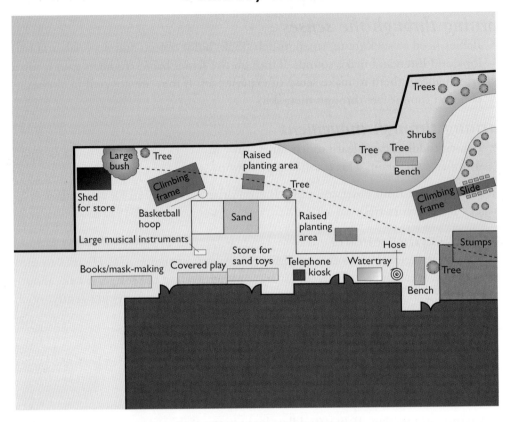

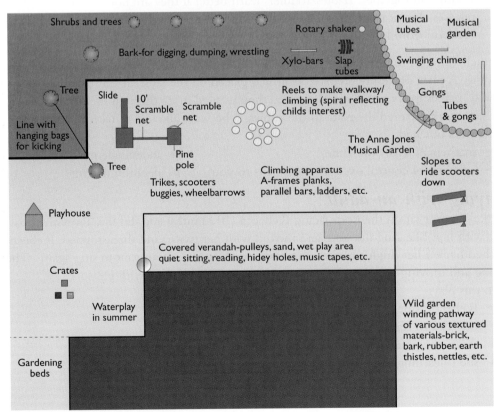

FIGURE 13.5

Room layouts at (a) James Lee Nursery School, (b) Eastwood Nursery School and (c) the garden plan at Eastwood

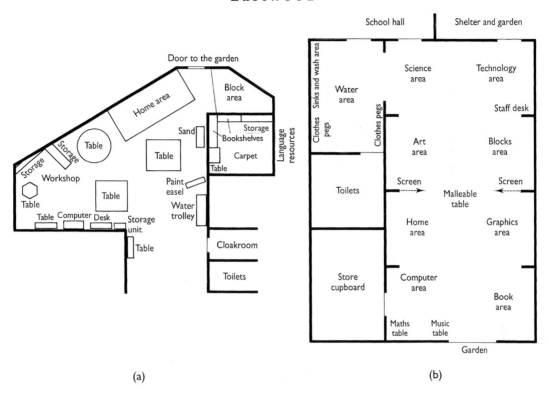

(a)

(b)

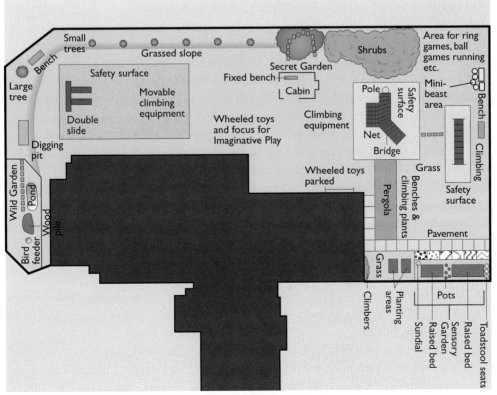

(c)

BASIC CURRICULUM PROVISION FOR *0–1* YEARS

The adults they love are probably the best provision of all!

1   Sing to, talk to and hold the baby. Carry the baby about and show the baby things, objects and people.
>   ▶ You can play games with babies.
>   ▶ Stick your tongue out, and after a delay the baby does the same.
>   ▶ Peek-a-boo games are greatly enjoyed by older babies.

2   Personal space – let the baby quietly lie or sit and watch a mobile. Babies like to look at things under a tree, watching the leaves rustling. Babies need to listen to sounds around them. Having music blaring on a radio all the time stops them from doing this. For example, the sound of someone opening a door, or dropping something in the next room will attract their interest.

3   Babies need places to be propped up safely – e.g. on a mat with cushions on the floor.

4   Objects – find out about Eleanor Goldshmied's 'Treasure Baskets' which are suitable for sitting babies. A video is available from the National Children's Bureau.

5   Have a bag with odds and ends in it which can be changed or thrown away regularly at little or no cost, and check them for safety, for example a bath sponge or paper plate.

6   Toys – these can be home-made or commercial – e.g. a baby mirror (worth buying), a pop-up toy, a wobbling toy, bath toys that float and sink, a teddy bear or soft doll, rattles (which are good for hands to hold and make interesting sounds) and baby books which can be chewed and sucked.

7   Provide comfortable flooring to crawl over, a mixture of carpets and other surfaces to explore and grass to crawl on and fall over on for beginner walkers.

8   Provide stable furniture for babies to pull themselves up on, or cruise between.

BASIC CURRICULUM PROVISION FOR *0–3* YEARS

Keep the same provision as for 0–1 year, but add these:

1   room for vigorous movement and places to run and jump – taking bread to feed the ducks when you go to the park. Offer a soft ball or larger bouncy ball to kick and throw outside;

2   a few wooden blocks which are easy to hold and build small towers with. The Froebel block play project (0–3 years) based at Pen Green Centre of Excellence is researching block play with this age group. The Project Director is Pat Gura;

3 more objects and toys to handle, put in the mouth, squeeze, look at, listen to etc.;

4 finger paint;

5 crayons and fat non-toxic felt pens and paper;

6 silver sand (not builder's sand);

7 play dough. This can be made. Find some good recipes – some recipes involve cooking play dough, which makes it last longer;

8 water play – bath time, paddling pools, bowls of water. Water play should always be carefully supervised.

9 Babies enjoy the treasure baskets devised by Eleanor Goldshmied, and heuristic play bags. Two videos are available from the National Children's Bureau to show you how to set up this kind of basic provision.

10 A tea set or toy cars or other play props which encourage pretend, symbolic play.

11 Turn to the section on schemas (see Chapter 6). Basic curriculum provision should facilitate schemas and their development, for example

▶ small trucks on wheels to transport objects about;

▶ bags and baskets and things that fit in and out of each other;

▶ boxes to put things in (inside and outside);

▶ blankets to cover teddies, dolls etc. (enveloping).

Examples of schemas being supported and extended: transporting and trajectory

12 picture books and simple texts such as *Spot the Dog;*

13 dressing-up clothes. Hats, shoes and belts are best for toddlers;

14 picking flowers. Flowers are for picking as far as toddlers are concerned. Encourage children to pick daisies, dandelions and such like rather than flowers in the flower bed. From time to time, children will enjoy helping you to pick flowers from the flower beds to go in a vase, perhaps on the lunch table;

15 singing action songs, and finger play;

16 listening to music, using real instruments and tapes. From the beginning, these need to be multi-cultural.

LIST OF BASIC MATERIAL PROVISION FOR CHILDREN 3–5 YEARS (INCLUDING RECEPTION CLASSES)
OUTDOORS

A variety of outdoor play equipment is needed:

- small apparatus – bats, balls, hoops, bean bags;
- large apparatus – climbing frame;
- wheeled truck;
- plants and a growing area, a wild area to encourage butterflies etc. Possibly also a pond with a safety fence;
- a grassed area;
- a tarmac area;
- a mud patch for digging.

The following basic curriculum provision should be available both indoors and outdoors. A child should be offered a full range of provision whether they choose to be indoors or outdoors:

- sand – wet and dry, and equipment in boxes on shelves nearby. Boxes should be labelled, with pictures too.
- water – the same applies. It should be possible to have waterfalls, guttering, water wheels etc.
- a small world – dolls' house, train set, garage and cars, farms, zoo, dinosaurs;
- a warm, light and cosy book area indoors. Out-of-doors books might be on a mat with cushions under a shady tree. A range of books is discussed in this chapter, but there should be both home-made and commercially published books;
- mathematical, scientific and technological equipment – a weighing balance, measuring rulers, calibrated jugs, calculators, sieves, colanders, egg whisks;
- a writing/graphics area with a variety of paper and different kinds of pencils and pens. This might be put next to the workshop area which will contain found materials and glue, scissors, masking tape and so on;
- a home area;
- dressing-up clothes;
- a paint area;
- clay;
- a woodwork area;
- small and large construction equipment (e.g. Duplo);
- unit and hollow blocks (e.g. those made by Community Playthings);
- a cookery area with baking materials and equipment;
- growing and living things – growing mustard and cress, hyacinth bowls, fish aquarium, wormery;
- an interest table with interesting objects to handle – a table with different kinds of brushes on it;
- a computer

This list of basic equipment includes material provision which is basic for inspections. It is preferable to use computer programs which encourage children to use imagination rather than responding to computer-led tasks.

BASIC CURRICULUM PROVISION FOR 5–8 YEARS

This will be the same, although unfortunately it is usual that there will be more limited access to the outside area in the UK. This is not so in countries like Denmark or

Germany. Classrooms will also need to provide a computer, word-processing facilities and a printer. The writing and book areas will become bigger. Children will not have such unlimited freedom, but choice and decision making and movement will still be important.

How the Adults Help Children to use the Provision for 3–8 Years (for 0–3 years see pages 343–346)
Anchor provision

It is very important that adults use their time effectively when working with young children. This means that sometimes adults will want to be anchored in one area, doing work 'in depth' with children. At other times they will want to be free to move about. However, it is important to remember that when adults merely flit about, then the children do too! And when adults concentrate, children do too. The Oxford Studies undertaken in the 1980s found that if adults are never *anchored* in an area, they **do not** help the children to reach very much depth in their learning.

The anchored adult needs to sit so that they have an overview of the rest of the room. This adult needs to be free to concentrate on what the children in this area are doing, to be able to have long conversations (one-to-one and in a small group), to be relaxed enough to listen to what children are saying, and to allow them plenty of time.

Another adult will need to be free to help children with their toilet needs, to hang up a painting, to comfort a tearful child, to help a child when asked to do so. If each adult has a clear understanding of their role in the team, it helps everyone to concentrate on the children. It reduces the temptation to chat with other adults rather than to chat with the children.

It will usually only be possible to anchor one adult at any one time. This might be for part of a morning or afternoon. Staff need to discuss and plan so that adults take it in turns to be anchored. And they will need to plan further what the activity will be – e.g. cooking or using clay – and how the activity will be introduced and cleared away.

Double provision

There should always be basic paint materials available to children. However, there might also be *double* provision of paint for a particular reason. It may be that there are several new children in the room who are not yet ready to mix their own paints and are therefore likely to disrupt the other children who know about mixing paint, and so waste the paint. Double provision means that there can be a separate area where paints are ready-made in pots with one brush for each pot, and that children who are new to painting are encouraged to use these paints. This will make it possible for children who are more experienced with paints to mix their own paints, to have palettes for mixing, and to choose from a range of paper and brushes, jugs of water, beakers and tubs of red, blue, yellow, white and black paint. These are the only colours necessary, since children can mix any colour or shade from these basic colours. Through double provision, the curriculum can be differentiated so as to meet the needs of different children.

Staff will need to meet together to discuss and plan which areas will have double provision. There is rarely enough space to have more than a few areas to set up for double provision at any time. Careful planning, based on observations of children, is the key.

Self-servicing areas

Adults cannot be everywhere. It is therefore very important that children **do not** have to depend on adults' help more than is necessary. Waiting for help wastes valuable learning time and also brings about challenging behaviour from bored or frustrated children. It creates a 'don't do' and 'can't do' atmosphere.

Providing children are carefully introduced to self-servicing areas, they can begin to take responsibility for them. Indeed, they take pride in keeping them tidy and attractive places if they are encouraged to do so. The more involved children feel in looking after the room, the more care they are likely to take of it. The older children introduce and help younger children to use the areas. This creates a 'can do' atmosphere. It builds a sense of community, responsibility and good self-esteem for the children. On King Arthur's Round Table were written the words 'When we serve each other, we become free.'

PRESENTATION

It is very important to remember that the *way* material provision is offered is of central importance. Provision should be attractive to children, and carefully thought through in its presentation, bearing in mind also the structuring of the time and space. This also means that there need to be agreements between staff and children about safety policies. For example, what are the boundaries to be set on the children climbing outside? What are the boundaries in the way children use scissors and knives, and should trucks be allowed indoors?

SETTING UP
▶ Each child needs to be greeted at the beginning of the session.
▶ Children need to be helped to get to know the room if any changes have been made.
▶ There needs to be easy access to all the materials.
▶ Some tables will be set up with activities, but some need to be left empty so that children can follow their own initiatives.
▶ Anchor activities might be introduced once most children are in and settled.

PUTTING AWAY AND TIDYING UP
It is equally important that tidy-up time be a valued part of a curriculum.
▶ Enough time is needed so that children are not rushed.
▶ Children need to know that everything in the room has a place. They need to know where to put things, and to take pride in the areas.

DISPLAYS AND INTEREST TABLES
Issues of gender, culture and disability need to be thought through. Positive images and multicultural artefacts need to be discussed and planned by staff as a whole.
▶ Displays should respect children – there should be no cutting-out of a child's painting and turning it into an adult's collage. The paintings children do should be mounted and displayed as they are. How would Van Gogh the painter have felt if the famous painting he did of a chair had been cut out and made into a collage of Goldilocks and the Three Bears?
▶ Adults should not draw or write on children's work without their permission. After all, adults do not allow children to draw or write on their records without permission.
▶ Any writing or notes about a painting should be mounted separately underneath the child's painting or drawing. It should always be discussed with a child, and the child should agree to its being displayed.

> ▶ Any lettering should be carefully done on ruled lines so that it looks attractive and is a good role model for children when they see adults' writing.

MATERIAL PROVISION IN THE CURRICULUM FOR 5–8 YEARS

There will need to be more areas for writing and reading. However, children will still need all the basic provisions which they had in the curriculum for 3-5 years. This is because the first-hand experiences which these provide are needed in order to give children full access to learning. If children do not have these basic materials, they will be held back in their learning.

For example, in the 1980s, in a study of children in the London junior schools, it was found that the children's concepts of volume were late in developing. Most of these schools did not have water trays in their classrooms after the reception class, and this meant the children were not getting the practical experience they needed in order to develop this concept.

The content of the curriculum

The content of the curriculum is about:

> ▶ what the child already knows;
> ▶ what the child wants to know more about;
> ▶ what the child needs to know according to the culture and society in which the child is growing up.

THE CURRICULUM CONTENT FOR 0–3 YEARS

Every culture has different ideas about what young children ought to know. It is only recently in the UK that people have begun to talk about a curriculum for the 0–3-year-olds. It is now realised that babies and toddlers need a quality curriculum as much as do children of 3–8 years of age. In New Zealand, the curriculum Te Whariki is seen as a continuum from 0 to 8 years (see pp. 353 and 359 for more details).

However, it is important to remember that even young babies are learning about the world in which they live and the people they meet. From a very early age, they are beginning to build the cultural layers which will give them knowledge and understanding. When we sing songs to babies, they are learning about the rhymes and rhythms of their culture, the language of their culture, whether people are angry with them or happy about them. They are already beginning to identify shapes and patterns, and to understand about objects moving and staying still.

Holding and rocking the baby in your arms, upright or over your shoulder, singing and talking to the baby as you do so, gives children a number of curriculum content areas.

> ▶ Mathematics – being enclosed and surrounded by your arm, going from side to side and up and down. These are mathematical experiences.
> ▶ Music – listening to singing and talking
> ▶ Action songs and finger play – the songs might be heads, fingers, knees and toes, pat-a-cake. In order to do this, the baby has to begin to judge distances and learn about spatial concepts.
> ▶ Dance – rhythm and patterns as the child is moved about.
> ▶ Language and literacy – learning what language is, and the difference between songs and talking. Dorothy Butler's research in New Zealand suggests that even babies enjoy picture books.
> ▶ Science – when a child is eating and sitting in the high chair, they might drop bread over the side of the high chair, or drop a spoonful of custard on the floor. The child

is learning about gravity and the properties of objects. (Bread bounces, custard goes splat!)

▶ Human and social learning occurs, for example, when children eat a meal with other people, and feel part of it.

The book *Play it My Way* by the RNIB has a wealth of activities suitable for children of 0–3 years, whether or not they have a disability.

Remember, a quality curriculum for 0–3-year-olds is based on what children naturally do, not on what adults wish children could or should do.

THE CURRICULUM CONTENT FOR 3–5 YEARS

The National Curriculum key stage 1 is a programme which lasts for six terms. It is for children in Statutory Schooling in years one and two (key stage 1) in the primary school.

In England, the review of the early childhood curriculum has led to a Foundation Stage for children 3, 4 and 5 years. There are goals expected to be achieved at the end of this stage and these have 6 areas: personal, social, and emotional development, language and literacy, mathematics, knowledge and understanding of the world, physical and creative development. The goals emphasize the 3Rs and have brought criticism from early childhood experts who have condemned this approach as a return to a narrow, nineteenth-century notion of literacy and numeracy.

In Northern Ireland the curriculum framework is less language and literacy dominated. It helps early years workers in a range of settings to offer children a quality curriculum. And in Wales the curriculum relates closely to the heritage principles (see pp. 332–333).

In Wales, the Curriculum and Assessment Authority for Wales (Awdurdod Cwricwlwm AC Asesu Cymru – ACAC) introduced the Welsh version of the Desirable Outcomes document. This relates closely to the heritage of thinking about what makes good practice in the early childhood curriculum. It also links with research evidence, and has a holistic view of young children. It is based on educational principles.

It emphasises the crucial role of observation in planning a curriculum and assessing a child's progress. The areas to be covered are language, literacy and communication skills, personal and social development, mathematics, knowledge and understanding of the world, physical development and creative development. It emphasises the importance of understanding, appreciating and rejoicing in the extraordinary abilities of young children. It makes the importance of play central, together with the principle of appropriateness. It encourages the Welsh language. It emphasises the crucial role of observation in planning a curriculum and assessing a child's progress.

The Scottish curriculum framework emphasises play, emotional, personal and social development, communication and language, knowledge and understanding of the world, expressive and aesthetic development, physical development and movement as well as observation, equality of opportunity and supporting transitions, home and families. It is principled and evidence based.

The curriculum content varies according to the culture

Every culture decides what the children should learn, and this will vary from culture to culture. In India the most important content in the curriculum to learn about is spirituality.

In Laos and Hong Kong, the most important content to learn about in the curriculum is reading, writing and number.

In New Zealand, which is a bicultural country, the Maori people and the Pekara (white people) have made a major contribution to the early years curriculum in the form of Te Whariki (1993), which is based on four principles:

1 empowerment – *Whakamana;*
2 holistic development – *Kotahitanga;*
3 family and community – *Whanau-tangata;*
4 relationships – *Nga Hontanga.*

Whatever the curriculum content that is chosen, children need a broad, balanced and relevant content.

Language and literacy

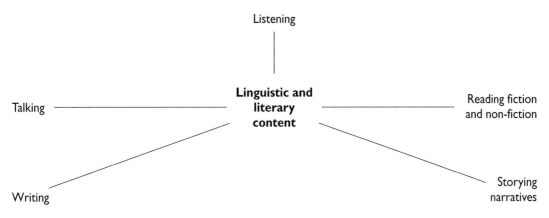

FIGURE 13.8
Elements of the linguistic and literacy content

TALKING AND LISTENING

It is important to share conversations with children. This is helped when adults and children are

▶ talking about the same things
▶ looking at things together
▶ having an experience together.

Children will often point and try to get eye contact as much as possible.

TAKING IT IN TURNS SO THAT I TALK, THEN YOU TALK

This is different from making children reply to questions that have definite answers. These are called *closed questions*. In a real conversation, it is very different. People take it in turns to say things that they are thinking or feeling. One speaker does not decide what the other speaker has to reply.

When questions are asked, they need to be open-ended, and they need to be for a real reason. Children quickly realise when adults are asking questions just for the sake of it, for example when the child asks about something they already know about.

HAVING CONTROL

When children are encouraged to sing songs, tell rhymes to themselves and sing alone or with other people, they do not always want to wait for their turn. Singing songs or saying rhymes together means that no-one has to wait and that everyone can join in. This is very important at large group time. Research also suggests that rhyme and rhythm help children to learn to *read*.

It is very important to encourage children to play with words and to have fun making-up words describing things that are present or not present – e.g.

▶ pot
▶ dot
▶ got.

These words are nearly the same but a little bit different. The sound of p, d and g and the different look of the beginnings of these words is how early phonics and graphic teaching of reading begins in a very natural way. Children love to talk about these things as they share books with adults.

The National Literacy Strategy is not appropriate for the youngest children, especially those in reception classes. This is because it takes control entirely into the adult's hands and removes it from the child who can only react to what the adult introduces. Evidence from neuroscientists suggests that social development and relationships are important in the first five years, and that communication and language develop rapidly at this time. Writing and reading are not priorities for the brain's development during these years.

FIGURE 13.9
Children writing

WRITING

Writing has two aspects: the construction of the writing and what it 'says', and the look of it – the handwriting and letter shapes.

When children begin to write, they construct a **code**. Most languages have a written code.

Writing develops when children begin to use symbols, for example when they try to keep hold of their experiences and represent them in some way. This might be:

▶ in their drawings
▶ in their pretend play
▶ in their early writing.

At first, children write in a very personal way. This will not look like very conventional adult writing. For example, they begin to put 'writing' into their drawings: at first, letter-type shapes appear in the middle of their drawings, and gradually these seem to move to the outer edges of the drawing.

They experiment. At this stage, adults should encourage but not interfere. See how children try different sizes, shapes and numbers. At this stage, children are creating, and are not needing to use conventional print. They need to be free to experiment without criticism. Left-handed children must never be encouraged to write with the right hand.

Let children see print. This will sometimes be in books, but it is also important to talk about it when you go out in the street and see signposts, advertisements etc.

WHEN ARE CHILDREN READY TO BE TAUGHT LETTER SHAPES?

In the UK, children are often rushed into this too early. This may be why many children at junior and secondary school do not enjoy writing and even truant from school. Early childhood experts in most countries are influenced by strong research evidence which suggests that the emphasis should be on communication (gesture, facial expression, etc.) and language in the early years, and not in the formal teaching of writing and reading. Children often ask for help with letter formation.

Children again need plenty of time to experiment without interference before adults introduce formal letter shapes. This may be why many children in junior and secondary school do not enjoy writing, and even truant from school.

Young children find capital letters easier to write than lower casement, and so they tend to write these first. It is not until children are spontaneously beginning to use conventional letters with many curves (a,b,c,d,e) as well as H, A, W, E etc. (which are more linear) that they are ready to form letters correctly and to hold the pencil correctly. Before this:

▶ they need to manipulate and try out different ways of 'writing', using their own personal writing. Tracing letters undermines this process because then it isn't their letter: it's someone else's shape; this holds back the 'have a go' spirit which helps children to be good learners in the long term;
▶ they need to explore what writing is;
▶ they need adults to point out print in books and in the environment, and in notices and street signs.

Then they are ready to start conventional writing.

It is important to value writing from different cultures, e.g. Urdu, Arabic (right to left) and Chinese (up and down on the page).

The age and pace of this sequence of events will greatly vary from child to child, depending on the child's interest, mood and personality, aptitude, and also – and very importantly – prior experience and understanding of what writing is about. It is not possible to miss out these early stages if the child is really to understand and enjoy the writing process for the rest of their life.

Many adults were forced into formal writing lessons too early. This is particularly so in the UK where children are often expected to do this at 4 years old. In most other countries they are not expected to do this until they are 6 or 7 years old. The UK has a relatively high illiteracy rate in relation to other countries. Is there a connection here?

Many adults do not enjoy writing, and this means that their lives have lost something. Recent research (summarised in TV programmes such as Channel 4's Dispatches in 1998) stresses the damage done by too early an introduction to formal writing. Young children are more likely to enjoy writing for the rest of their lives if they are carefully introduced to it without being pressured.

Remember: the first words children write are full of their feelings. Their own name is important to them, and they often write the names of people they love, plus the words 'love from'.

Reading

Reading begins with listening to stories. Listening to stories is very important and helps children to develop the kind of book language which they need later on when they learn to read and write stories.

▶ Stories can be told. Some cultures (Celtic and Maori) stress oral story-telling.
▶ Or they can come from books with both pictures and written text.

Stories have a special way of using language which is called 'book language' – 'Once upon a time...'. Children need a wealth of experiences of book language before they can read well and become enthusiastic readers.

Children need adults to share many different kinds of stories with them. They need one-to-one stories. These are called 'bed-time type' stories. The child can interact with the reader and get deeply involved. The adult and child can chat, pause, carry on and go at their own pace.

Group stories, even small groups of 3 or 4 children, are more difficult for children because the adult needs to keep the story going, and so cannot allow constant interruptions. Skilled adults are able to welcome many of the children's contributions, but it becomes more important for children to 'listen' the larger the group.

Different kinds of stories to tell or read to children

▶ Every day events – these help children to recognise events and feelings. They help children to heighten their awareness of words which describe everyday situations.
▶ Poems – these help rhyming and rhythm, and the chorus gives a predictable element: the repetition helps children. This is also true of many stories, but poems are an enjoyable experience for young children who may not be able to concentrate on a whole story in the early stages.
▶ Folk stories – these introduce children to different cultures. Avoid stories which make animals behave as if they were humans. Also avoid stories which make animals behave in a way which is out of character – e.g. a spider who saves the life of a fly in an act of bravery. These are called *anthropomorphic* stories. They can confuse young children who are trying to sort out what is and is not true.

▶ True stories – these lead to an understanding of non-fiction.

▶ Make-believe stories – these lead to an understanding of fiction. Avoid stories with witches and fairies for very young children: children need to be clear about the distinction between reality and imagination and telling children stories about witches and fairies can cause young children, especially 4-year-olds, to be fearful and to have nightmares. Children do not become clear about the difference between reality and imagination until they are as old as 7. Children in junior school, however, do thoroughly enjoy these stories. It is one thing for a 4-year-old to make up their *own* stories about monsters, witches or ghosts because then the child has control, but if an *adult* introduces these characters, then the adult (not the child) is in control. This is frightening for many 4-year-olds, even in a modern age when they see violence and evil images on television.

▶ Action rhymes and finger rhymes – these help children to predict what is in a text. Predicting is a very large part of learning to read: knowing what comes next is important.

▶ Repeating stories – knowing a story well helps children to read when they begin to learn. Sometimes adults say 'Oh, but he is not reading, he just knows it off by heart,' but knowing what comes next is probably one of the most important parts of learning to read.

▶ Think about issues of gender, ethnicity, culture and disability, and be sure that all children see positive images of themselves in the stories you tell and offer from books.

LISTENING POSTS

You can tape-record stories and let the children listen to them while they also follow the story in a book. They can wear earphones to do this. It is preferable to make tapes out of some of the children's favourite books. If you do this, remember to make a little bell ring when you turn the page. Again, you can use commercial books on tapes, but children appreciate you putting their favourite stories on to tape. It will usually be children from 4 years old and onwards who enjoy this most, although some younger children will too. Evaluate the activity with a focus on concentration, sequencing and storying.

CHILDREN SHARING STORIES WITH EACH OTHER

Encourage children to share stories together whether or not they can read fluently yet. This encourages emergent readers to have warm relationships with each other, and it is very enjoyable for the children. You will often hear children involved in what is called *approximate reading* when they do this. Although they cannot read word for word, and would not be considered as fluent readers, the stage of approximate reading is a very important one. Observe children of 3–7 years of age. Identify which children are emergent, approximate and fluent readers. What are the factors which cause you to decide which? Evaluate the advantages of shared stories.

Gradually, children get better and better at finding the right beginning point and the right ending point as they point to the text. They begin to pick out letters and words that they know. Children need plenty of opportunities to do this in a very relaxed atmosphere. They will not just do this with adults, but will also enjoy doing this with their friends. Often, an older child will enjoy approximate reading for one of their younger friends.

Helping children to read

This means enjoying the stories together (sharing) and cooperating. Beginning to read together should build a child's self-esteem because there is no pressure on the children to join in or not. Looking at books together helps to build the above-mentioned 'book language' and it gives children experience of the way language is used in stories. Language becomes very memorable in this way.

The children see how a book is used by the adult or more experienced reader – perhaps an older child – who acts as a role model for how to read: they demonstrate the way to turn a page, the directions to read the print, pointing at the print.

It is important to have books in different languages, and to ask children who are beginning to be interested in text to look at the different sorts of text. In areas of the UK where only English is spoken – which is becoming increasingly unusual – it is important to invite people who speak different languages to be with the group of children. The direction of the written print will be different if it is Chinese, Urdu or English. The look of the print will be different too. It is important for children to become aware of different sorts of writing.

The adult needs to help children to *predict*: ('What do you think he says then?'). The child sees a pattern, for example of a phrase, repeated regularly, and an adult will talk about what a particular sentence, word or letter is as they go along – e.g. 'What letter does this begin with?' This familiarises children with print.

Sometimes, in a group, everyone speaks together when they tell rhymes. This gives children help with rhythm, intonation and pace. The community experience is very exciting.

Picture cues are very important. These help children to get clues about what the print is saying. It is very important that all of this be fun.

More is written about story time in Chapter 1, and in Chapter 7 where children's feelings and relationships are looked at.

What is important in learning to read?

- ▶ The meaning of the print (the **semantic** aspect);
- ▶ The flow of the print (**syntax** or **grammar**);
- ▶ The look and sound of the print (**grapho-phonic**). 'Grapho' means the look of the text, and 'phonic' means the sound of the text;
- ▶ Having enough 'book language' vocabulary – 'Once upon a time...'

Schools are now encouraged to emphasise all of these elements. Most now have a mixture of real books and reading schemes, and these emphasise the grapho-phonic, grammar and meaning aspects of learning to read. All of these are important in learning to read. This gives children a broad range of strategies which help them to **decode** (make sense of) print in order to read.

It is important to teach the letters and the sounds in the story by pointing them out as you go along. Do not isolate letters and sounds from a story and turn it into exercises. If you lose the meaning, the child will become the sort of child who 'barks at print'. This approach encourages children to 'read' at the level that is appropriate for their stage of development. Remember: the child's own name is the best starting point for learning letters, because children are emotionally attached to their name.

WHY DO WE WANT CHILDREN TO READ?

The aim is to produce fluent, enthusiastic readers. The aim is to produce children who are *bookworms*. The aim is to produce junior school children and secondary school children and adults who do not hear when they are called to come for a meal because they are so deeply involved in reading a book – reading for pleasure.

Children and adults also need to read for information, knowledge and understanding.

ENCOURAGING CHILDREN TO 'HAVE A GO'

Let them approximate read – guess from pictures – and come to know the story almost by heart. Don't point at the text, but encourage the child to do so as they read. This gives the child a feeling of control over their reading.

Point out what letter/sound a word begins with, but don't force this, for example it begins with a 'D' (pronounce it 'Dee') and it sounds like 'D-og' (pronounce it 'Duh').

When children are just beginning to approximate read, sing the alphabet together as a song and introduce alphabet books and friezes. The Reading Recovery Scheme pioneered by Marie Clay in New Zealand in the 1980s has produced excellent results. Here, a trained adult works daily with children at 6½ years who are not yet confident readers. It gives:

- ▶ the right help
- ▶ at the right time
- ▶ daily
- ▶ on an individual basis.

Sadly, this scheme is not available in all infant schools. Six-and-a-half years of age is an ideal age to move towards fluent reading for many children. It is possible to teach children to read earlier, but ask: shouldn't young children be learning other things?

STORYING HELPS CREATIVE WRITING

Learning about different roles and characters and themes is essential if children are going to learn to write stories. Having dressing-up clothes to act out stories helps creative writing. Ask children to act out a story you have told. Encourage children to act out stories that *they* have made up, and which you have written down for them. Vivian Gussin Paley, in her school in Chicago, did this as a daily part of the curriculum.

Acting out stories needs to be done in an atmosphere of *sharing*. It should not involve a performance of the story. The idea is to help children to understand *how* stories are made. This will later help them when they want to write their own stories.

Young children should not be expected to perform stories in school assemblies, or in situations with audiences full of strangers (e.g. the Summer or Christmas show). It is not good practice to encourage children to perform before they have gone through the sequence: make – share – show. They need to be able to make their own stories, and to share these with their friends and adults they know well first.

To perform or 'show' becomes appropriate only in junior school. Any earlier, and some children begin over-acting and playing to the audience rather than becoming involved in the story; and other children are for ever put off because of the stress of being made to perform. Waving at people in the audience during a performance may be very sweet for the adults to see, but it is a clear sign that a child is not involved in what they are doing and therefore not ready to perform in front of an audience of strangers. This means that the exercise is a failure in terms of involving a child in a story. The child needs more experience of making up stories as part of pretend play, and of sharing these stories with children and adults they spent time with.

Research suggests it is likely that when children are encouraged to play, they will be better at creative writing at 7 years of age than children who attend formal reception classes at 4 years of age where letter formation is stressed.

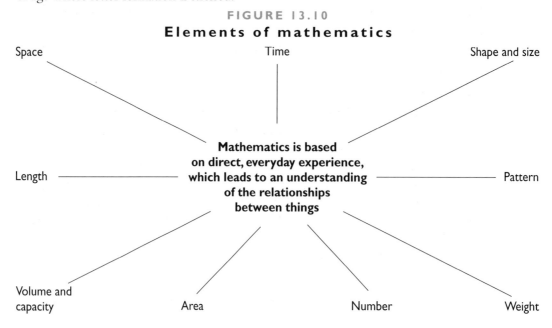

FIGURE 13.10
Elements of mathematics

Mathematics

Mathematics involves problem-solving, finding elegant, logical and beautiful answers, being efficient and drawing and recording solutions. It should have a meaning, function and purpose, so that children can link mathematics with their everyday lives.

SPACE

Children learn about *topological* concepts before they learn about *Euclidean* concepts about space. Examples of topological concepts are:

- on/off
- over/under
- up/down
- in/out
- surrounding
- across.

Use real experiences – commands like 'Put the chair under the desk', plus the use of any of the basic equipment (e.g. cooking equipment) in the room. Reflecting back at children what they are doing by describing it to them will help children to develop topological concepts which they need in learning mathematics. (The above examples of topological concepts are very important for children to understand in their mathematical development. They link with the schemas, the patterns of behaviour in a child's repertoire. They are also part of the 250 most used words in the English language. They are therefore very important when children begin to read.)

It is important to talk to children when they move in space by describing to them what they are doing: 'Oh, you climbed up.'

Examples of Euclidean concepts are:

- circle
- square.

NUMBER

Number has several different aspects:

- ▶ *matching* – 'This looks like this.' Two cups in the home area;
- ▶ *sorting* – 'This looks different from this.' The cups and saucers;
- ▶ *one-to-one correspondence* – 'One biscuit for you, one biscuit for me' etc.;
- ▶ *cardinal number* – the two cups remain two cups however they are arranged (this means the child understands the *twoness* of two);
- ▶ *ordinal number* – 'First I do this, second I do that, third I do that...'. For example, when cooking.

Always remember. Mathematics should not be split off from everyday life. Do not do exercises or tasks with young children which are isolated from their experience. Children learn mathematics through cooking, through tidy-up time, through playing in the home area, through painting and in the garden. Mathematics is everywhere. Numbers are found on rulers, calibrated cooking jugs, the doors of houses, and so on. Counting is only one part of exploring numbers. The same principle applies each time. It is one thing for children to be curious about numbers on calibrated jugs, weights, measures etc., but they need to be free to experiment and explore. This is very different from formally teaching them numbers through an adult led task.

Recent research shows that children understand more about numbers than was previously thought.

Reciting: Children often recite numbers as they go. They love number songs, such as one, two, three, four, five, once I caught a fish alive.

Nominal: Children pick out numbers on cars, doors etc.

Subitize: Children remember simple number patterns (so do chimpanzees) by the way they look. For example the way number dots are on a domino.

Counting backwards: Children love to chant, five, four, three, two, one, blast off. For example when a rocket takes off.

There are three counting principles:
1. A number word is needed for every object that is counted. This is the one to one correspondence principle.
2. The numbers always have the same order, one, two, three, four (not one, three, four, two). This is called the stable order principle.
3. When children count they only have the cardinal number principle if they understand both of these.
   - ▶ that every object must have a number name
   - ▶ that the way the numbers are ordered must always be the same

If they understand these two things they understand that a number is an outcome. In other words when you get to count one, two, three, the answer is three.

Time

This has two aspects:
1. *Personal time:* it feels a long time before a car journey ends. It might only be an hour, but it feels longer.
2. *Universal time:*
   (a) succession – past, present, future
      - ▶ what follows after what
      - ▶ earlier, now, later
      - ▶ Spring, Summer, Autumn, Winter

(b) duration – day, night
- ▶ the length of time
- ▶ month, year
- ▶ hour, minute, second
- ▶ Summer, Winter

Don't be too specific with young children – use general terms. Begin teaching the time with '1 o'clock', '2 o'clock' and 'half past the hour' – introduce more exact time-telling later on. When children look at a watch, and enjoy discussing the numbers and where the hands point, they are learning in an informal way.

SHAPE AND SIZE

In the same way, use general terms to help children learn about these aspects of mathematics. Talk about it while you – or better, the children – do it. They need experience – action, plus language, which means plenty of talking whilst children do things.

Children need adults to describe things that are 'bigger than' and 'smaller than' and these are relative, not absolute sizes. These conversations again need to occur in a real situation: something is 'big' only in relation to something else. So don't use the term 'big' on its own as an absolute. This would be mathematically confusing for children. Always use relative terms, and always compare the size of one object with that of another.

Children learn terms like oblong and circle easily, but children are very three-dimensional in their perception so introduce words like cube and cylinder *first*. Use things like tins of food and everyday objects to do this. Again, use real-life contexts, for example 'A tin of beans is a cylinder', a 'A ball is a sphere'.

LENGTH

Longer than, shorter than – the same sort of thing applies here. Again, use relative terms to describe length. Young children have difficulty with absolute concepts such as a metre.

Children need to be surrounded by rulers and tapes, so that they can become aware that things are measured – this is taller than that, or shorter than that. Which is the tallest plant? Who has the longest feet? They might ask about exact lenghts and you can tell them 'it is 10 cm long' but don't dwell on it. Children will piece together their understanding over a long period of time.

VOLUME AND CAPACITY

'The glass is full to the top. The jug is overspilling with orange juice. This is fuller than that. A bucket is empty, nearly empty'. Listen to yourselves speaking, and you will be surprised at how often you are using mathematical words in everyday situations. This informal approach encourages the dispositions towards learning, such as curiosity, exploring, risk-taking, perseverence, courage.

AREA

Area is about ideas such as a blanket covering the area of the mattress of the bed. Children often explore area in their blockplay (see Figure 13.12).

Another example would be a pancake covered with lemon juice and castor sugar. The lemon and sugar cover the *area* of the pancake.

WEIGHT

Again, it is best to introduce the concept of weight using relative ideas – 'This tin of soup is heavier than that.' Rather than a weighing machine, use a balance.

FIGURE 13.11
Experimenting with volume and capacity

FIGURE 13.12
Children and blockplay – Taller than?

Bear in mind that young children need to physically experience weight. They love to carry heavy things. They love to carry each other sometimes! They are often seen carrying bags. However, it is more usual for them to use their own bodies as a way of exploring weight. For example, Kit, 3 years old, carried a huge piece of ice about in Hampshire one freezing winter. He enjoyed throwing it and watching it skim across an icy stream. He kept saying, 'This is heavy.' His parents helped him to make comparisons: 'Is it heavier than this stone? Is it heavier than this twig?'.

COMPUTERS

There is an urgent need for better computer programs to be developed for the use of young children. Some are nothing more than technological forms of the template colouring in type of activities. This does not encourage children to think at a deep level. They might be fun, but they are certainly not educational.

The most appropriate programmes for young children invite them to be inter-active. Liz and Peter Whalley (Open University) have developed stories revolving around particular children and their activities. The child can interact with the story and change it, or dwell on some parts of the story. There are also stories such as 'Rosie's walk'.

Children also benefit from using a word processor and printer. They often do not need a concept keyboard. They enjoy keying out letters, numbers and punctuation marks. This is exactly the kind of play which will encourage their dispositions to learn to become writers and readers for life.

Art and craft – the aesthetic aspect of the curriculum

Children need experiences which are real, direct and first-hand, for example to use print and clay regularly. Children need opportunities to represent their experiences in different ways. Some children choose solids like dough and clay and wood; others choose to draw and paint on paper. They begin to have a range of skill and competencies with different media – to draw a dog is quite a different experience from making a dog out of clay, or making a dog at the woodwork bench, or dressing up and pretending to be a dog.

FIGURE 13.13
Elements of arts and crafts

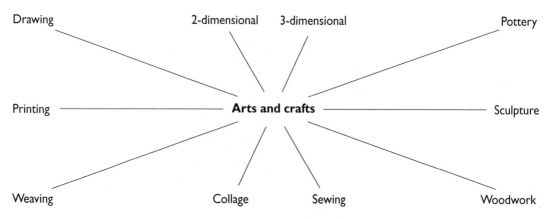

Teach children to use scissors and glue and woodwork bench tools while they are involved in the art and craft work. It is more effective to teach skills in context. Learning a skill just at the time you need it is very helpful.

SCULPTURES

Children need to make three-dimensional models – to use clay, wet sand, wood, junk, carving soap, stocks, dough, wax, rolling pins. They also need glue, sellotape, masking tape, scissors, string wire and bits of material.

POTTERY

Children need clay, and to learn about coil pots etc. These will not be formal lessons. They could be something which the adult shows the children during an anchor activity. There will be clay for the children to use all the time, but this could sometimes be an area of double provision where the adult is anchored to help children make coil pots. Children will come to this area if they would like to make a coil pot.

If a child is known to be fascinated by spirals and has been making them with paper and cutting them out, then it would be appropriate to invite the child to come and make a coil pot. Remember, however, that the child might decline your invitation.

DRAWING AND PAINTING

Paper: plain white is best, of varied sizes, plus pencils, wax crayons, charcoal, felt pens, chalks, slates – a never-ending list of possibilities. There should be powder paints and different thicknesses of brush. Materials should be well stored – easy for children to take what they need. Children should be encouraged to mix their own paints from basic colours (yellow, red, blue with white and black paint to make light and dark shades).

Children love to make books. If they see that you have made books for recipes, stories, poems, they might like to make their own. They will need to learn how to fold paper and, how to cut it. They may need an anchored adult to help them in this.

COLLAGE

This requires glue, found materials and junk bits, and scissors. Materials can be set out in attractive baskets or old shoe boxes which have been covered in old wallpaper. Glue should always be non-toxic.

Remember, the idea is for the child to become involved in these activities. Adults often use children's art lessons as a chance to do art for themselves! do not draw for children. do not use templates. do not ask children to trace. do not ask children to colour in. do not ask children to copy your model step by step.

▶ *Do* give children real first-hand experiences such as looking at plants or mini-beasts in the pond.

▶ *Do* give children opportunities to represent things, and to keep hold of their experiences – e.g. to make a model of the plant out of clay, or perhaps of a cat that they have seen and liked.

▶ *Do* encourage lots of different ideas. It is best when every child in a group has made a different model. This means that children are doing their own thinking and are not dependent on adults for ideas.

▶ *Do* remember that children are creative in lots of different ways. Arts and crafts is only one area in which children are creative. Children can be creative scientists, creative mathematicians, creative writers etc. Creativity is not something that means only art and craft (see Chapter 6).

FIGURE 13.14
Elements of music

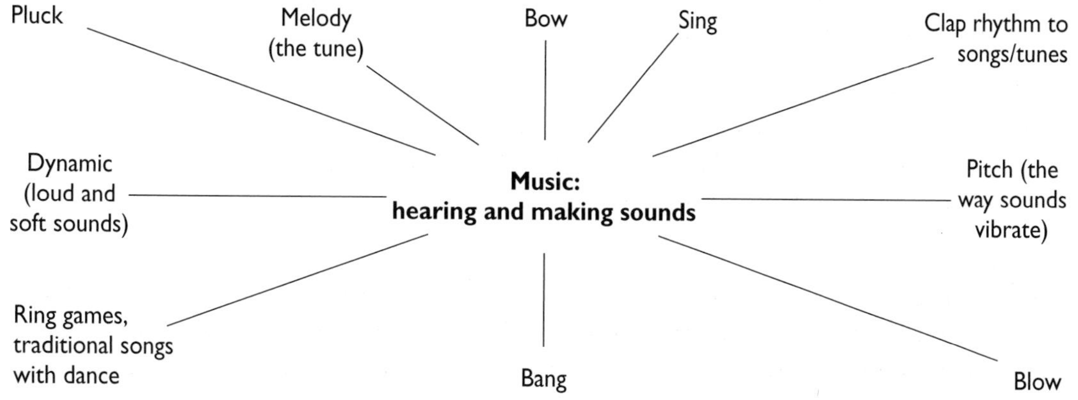

Pluck
Melody (the tune)
Bow
Sing
Clap rhythm to songs/tunes
Dynamic (loud and soft sounds)
Music: hearing and making sounds
Pitch (the way sounds vibrate)
Ring games, traditional songs with dance
Bang
Blow

Music

Listen to sounds that everyday objects make, for example paper – crackle, flap, tear; or keys – shake, drop.

Recent studies on neuroscience show that music is important in helping language and memory to develop. Adults naturally sing 'up we go' when they lift a baby or toddler out of a pram. Music helps children to remember words.

Make home-made instruments with the children. Sing with them.

FIGURE 13.15
Elements of science

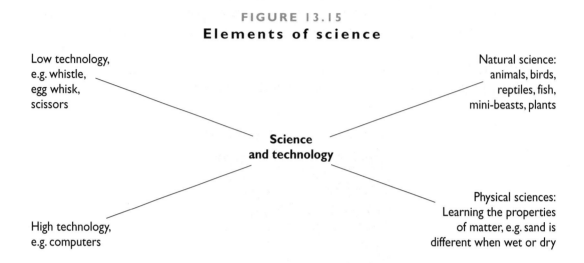

Scientific knowledge and understanding

Use all the basic provision in the indoor and outdoor area – sand, water, clay, wood, painting. Just as mathematics is everywhere, so science is everywhere: Einstein, the famous physicist, said that science is really just the refinement of everyday life.

Use the natural world that is around you. Look at animals, insects, birds, amphibians. Don't just look at these in books: find ways to show children real-life examples. Use books only to follow up and remember the real experiences.

ANIMALS

Think about:

▶ Where do animals live? You can find ants, spiders, birds etc. outside and look at their habitat. Remember, never kill animals, and always return them to their habitat: make a point of explaining this to the children. There are now pots with magnifying glasses in them which makes it easier to look at these creatures without squashing them accidentally.

▶ What do animals eat? Study cats, birds, fish.

▶ How do animals eat? – claws, type of feet, what sort of feet they have. Mouth, beaks, types of teeth, jaws which chew (cows), jaws which gnash – study dogs, cats, humans. A bird that eats nuts needs a beak that's a good nutcracker! A bird that catches fish needs a long beak.

▶ How do animals protect themselves? – camouflage, claws, tusks, fur for warmth, oil on ducks to make them waterproof.

There are reasons why animals, birds, insects have developed as they have done. The above points will give the children an introduction to the evolution of the animal world in ways they can understand.

PLANTS, TREES AND FLOWERS
▶ Why do plants of all kinds have leaves? Do all plants have leaves?
▶ Why is a tree trunk like it is? Do all trees have exactly the same sort of trunk? Make some bark rubbings. Hug trees to see if you can reach all the way round them with your arms.
▶ Why do flowers have colours? Insects are important for plant life.
▶ Why do some flowers have scent and perfume? Again, plants might need to attract insects and birds to visit them, so that they can spread their seeds widely.

THE PHYSICAL SCIENCES
▶ Electricity – electrical circuits are easy to make with young children.

FIGURE 13.16
An electrical circuit

▶ Heat – remember, heat is *not* about temperature. Cookery is one of the best ways to teach children about temperature. Making a jelly or ice-cream means looking at coldness. Making something which needs to be cooked in the oven shows children about high temperatures. Look at the central-heating system and the radiators, and at how the sun makes the playground feel warm on the tarmac. Look at the fridge. What makes things cold? Play with ice cubes in the water tray. Again, talk about *relative* hot and cold. Metal might feel colder than wood, but they might both be at room temperature!
▶ Sound – use the sounds around you, and help children to notice them. Children love to tape-record sounds which they hear. Some sounds are quieter than others. Some are noisier. Young children are not concerned with absolute measures of how many decibels. But they do know that a shout is louder than a whisper.
▶ Light – use torches and lanterns. Make rainbows using prisms, puppet shows, with lighting effects and cellophane paper to make lights of different colours. Children of 5–7 years of age often enjoy making light effects for stories they have made up, or for stories from books.

▶ Levers and pulleys.

FIGURE 13.17
An example of learning about balance

▶ Gravity – use parachutes, or drop objects from heights.

FIGURE 13.18
Gravity in action

▶ Floating and sinking – use water wheels and simple technology.

THE NATURAL SCIENCES

Use *mixtures* to demonstrate transforming things from one state to another – salt and water, sugar and water, flour and water, earth and water, mud and straw bricks, mud pies. All these materials have properties which children can explore. Salt dissolves in water. So does sugar. When the water evaporates the salt and sugar forms again. Steam, liquids and funnels can be very simply introduced to children in these ways.

Looking at activities such as weaving, rug-making (early technology). If you have a frame with string going up and down and from side to side, children love to weave scraps of material and paper in and out. One nursery school had a frame like this by the door, and it was surprising how quickly people added to it from the boxes of ribbons and strips of material. It became a very attractive wall hanging in the office.

FIGURE 13.19
Floating and sinking

FIGURE 13.20
Using a magnifying glass

Use technology which is easy for young children to understand – an egg whisk, tin opener, scissors. Encourage them to use construction kits and wooden unit blocks and hollow blocks.

▶ Low technology – egg whisks, tin openers, water wheels etc.
▶ High technology – computers and word processors and print-outs (CD-ROM), tape recorders for music and stories, telephones for conversations and so on.

Encourage children to ask questions:

▶ What?
▶ Where?
▶ Why?
▶ When?
▶ Who?

FIGURE 13.21

The beginnings of geography and history

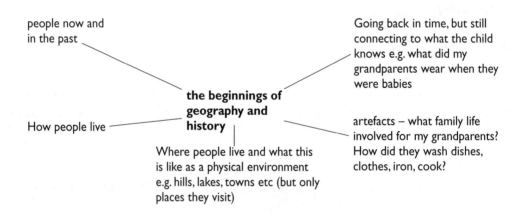

Young children are interested in people, their families and their homes. They like to learn about what people in the community do. They show this in their role play. Through play and visits to workplaces (e.g. an office, shop, clinic, station), they learn about different communities. They develop a sense of geography. They are also interested in old objects, and what things were like when they were babies and when their parents were babies and in their grandparents' experiences. Collecting artefacts of bygone days, and inviting older people to talk about their lives and show their photographs helps children to develop a sense of history.

Physical development

Remember:

▶ Children need to move as much as they need to eat and sleep.
▶ They learn through language with action.
▶ They need to be skilled in a range of movements using both fine and gross motor skills.
▶ They need repetition to consolidate.
▶ Movement needs to be appropriate – stroke a dog gently but throw hard to make a splash with a stone in a puddle.

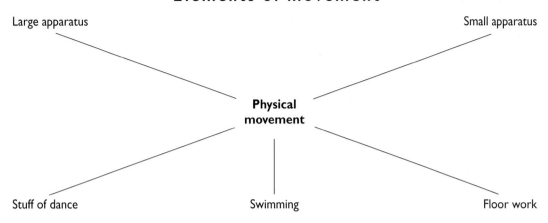

FIGURE 13.22
Elements of movement

LARGE APPARATUS

▶ A climbing frame;
▶ ropes to swing on;
▶ planks to walk across ladders;
▶ things to jump off.

Children need to be encouraged to become generally skilled in movement. do not teach the whole group to climb on for example a rope: give each child opportunities to climb in general.

SMALL APPARATUS

These include bats, balls, hoops, bean bags and ropes. It is very important to encourage cooperation, helping each other and turn-taking.

FLOOR WORK

▶ the importance of weight transfer from one part of the body to another;
▶ travel from one spot to another;
▶ flight – jumps etc.

Give children a general theme, for example starting low and getting higher. Don't make children do just one thing, such as a hand stand. There are lots of ways of changing your balance – a hand stand is only one.

Let children explore weight transfer. Say 'Can you start on your feet and stop with another bit of you touching the floor?' Then, you are helping children to think about their movements. Being aware of the body in this sort of a way increases confidence and builds up self-esteem.

DANCE

Use what children do naturally such as spinning, running, stamping. Make it into a dance with them. 'Singing in the rain' was a dance made up by a group of 5-year-olds helped by their teacher, Dee De Wet, at Ashbourne Primary School, Stoke-on-Trent (Year 1, key stage 1). The children watched a video extract from the film *Singing in the Rain* and they then experimented moving about:

- ► with fancy feet;
- ► by jumping in puddles;
- ► by swishing through puddles;
- ► by dashing about under umbrellas.

They made a dance sequence. Each child had an umbrella and a raincoat, and used the above different sequences in line with the traditional music from the film. Every child made their own dance, and yet they all danced at the same time, and were sensitive to each other's movements and ideas.

Some other ways of helping children to make dances are:
- ► You could take an action phrase, for example shiver and freeze. Let the children move like the words in the phrase.
- ► Take in objects, such as something spiky. Ask them to move in a spiky way and make a dance.
- ► Take an idea from nature and everyday life.
- ► Rush and roar like the wind.
- ► Be a machine (group dance).
- ► A clock.
- ► Shadows moving.
- ► Fish in the aquarium.

Only use experiences which the children have had very recently. For other ideas, see the book by Mollie Davies 1995.

Personal and social development

SENSE OF AWE AND WONDER

Look at nature, plants and insects. Concentrate on the wonder of it all. Introduce poems and songs. Dances are also helpful here.

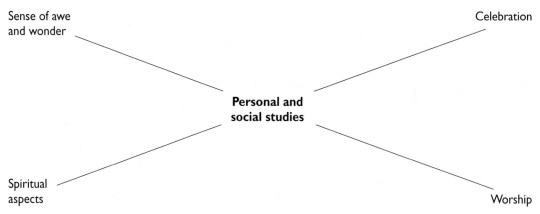

FIGURE 13.23
Elements of personal and social development

CELEBRATION

There are different religious celebrations in different cultures. Children can be introduced to some of the customs of different religions, for example Diwali, Ramadan, Christmas.

WORSHIP

This involves a group or community coming together to consider something of worth ('worthship'), for example being brave, reducing poverty, conserving rare buildings from the past as part of our human heritage, feeding the birds in the winter. It is usually used to mean worship of a god or gods, but this – as is shown – is not the original meaning of the word.

SPIRITUAL ASPECTS

The spiritual needs of the child are about the energy and mental attitude of the child over moral matters – e.g. it is *wrong* to hit. They also involve children in the inner peace that is so necessary to every human being.

Researchers have found that children at 5 years were very clear that it is always wrong to hit, but were quite happy, however, to change the rules about whether or not they had to tidy away the toys. They already had a moral attitude to hitting. They realised that rules about tidying up can change, but that hitting is always wrong.

Spiritual needs which are about children developing morally are basic to all human life and are a very different matter from belonging to a particular religion. Belonging to a religion – being a Christian, Muslim, Buddhist, Sikh, Hindu, Jewish – is not basic to a child's development. Not all children grow up in families that believe in a particular system of faith or worship. Not all families recognise a god or gods. However, this does not mean that such children do not experience spirituality. Spirituality is about the child's relationship with self, others and the universe.

The UK curriculum for 5–8 years – legal requirements

Children in state schools (including special schools) are legally required to follow a government-controlled curriculum at 5–16 years. It is important to remember that the Curriculum is different in England, Wales, Northern Ireland and Scotland (5–14 years).

There is a movement towards inclusion of children with special educational needs. Meeting a child's needs through the SEN Code of Practice has been revised so that practical support can be provided to children with special educational needs in schools. In the USA there are examples of special schools taking mainstream children to make up half the children in the class. Families and staff are finding this successful, for example in schools for visually impaired children.

The English National Curriculum

The English National Curriculum was established by the Education Reform Act 1988 (ERA). It provides a minimum requirement for a curriculum. It requires the curriculum of each school to be 'balanced and broadly based' to promote the 'spiritual, moral, cultural, mental and physical development of pupils...and of society' and to prepare pupils for 'the opportunities, responsibilities and experiences of adult life.'

A few years after its introduction, the National Curriculum was subject to a review chaired by Sir Don Dearing. Changes were made in the Draft Orders in 1995. The aim is to increase the possibilities for teachers to use professional judgement and to give time each week for schools to use as they wish at key stage 1.

In England, there are programmes of study for each subject, plus attainment targets in each subject through which teachers can make rounded assessments of children using eight levels of description. Teachers are encouraged to make observation-based records and plans of work, and not to use checklists in their record-keeping.

There have been no changes made to the National Curriculum in England for five years from August 1995.

The subjects in the English National Curriculum are:
▶ three core subjects: English, maths and science;
▶ foundation subjects: design and technology, information technology, history, geography, art, music, physical education, modern language (from 11 years old).

There is a trend towards allowing schools to use the National Curriculum more flexibly, when schools receive a good Inspection Report.

With the introduction of the National Literacy Strategy and the National Numeracy Strategy, which take up approximately 2 hours of each day in Primary school (for Key Stages 1 and 2), schools are not required to spend so much time on other subjects as they were previously.

The teaching of religious education must also be provided under the heading cultural, moral and spiritual and sex education.

There are four key stages in the English National Curriculum:
▶ Key stage 1 (Years 1 and 2: 5–7 years);
▶ Key stage 2 (7–11 years);
▶ Key stage 3 (11–14 years);
▶ Key stage 4 (14–16 years).

Children are tested through Standard Assessment Tasks (SATS) at the end of each key stage. There has been controversy and debate about whether children should be tested before key stage 1 in order to establish a baseline.

Against the wishes of most early years experts, a baseline assessment is now in place for children entering school. Only the National Scheme or an accredited scheme may be used. Baseline assessments only looks at language and literacy, maths (mainly number) and personal and social development. The Enfield Scheme is an example of an accredited scheme.

It is important to use baseline assessment as positively as possible for the child and family, despite all the difficulties it raises. For example, it has been criticised because it seems to see children with special needs, or children with first-languages other than English, as separate, rather than *included*. All the same, staff in early childhood settings can use baseline assessment to
▶ support and encourage a multi-lingual classroom;
▶ identify children with special educational needs;
▶ encourage a dialogue between home and school, building on the home visit to the child which is made just before the child starts school. In Enfield during the home visit the parents or carers are given the Enfield 'Starting School' booklet.

The Enfield scheme is based on more than one observation of a child in the classroom. All the teachers, NNEB's and classroom assistants have been offered training in this local authority to use the Enfield baseline assessment scheme. They reach agreement together about the level that the child has reached. There are also Helplines during the assessment period.

In Enfield it is recommended that children are assessed within two weeks of starting school and legally the process must be completed by seven weeks.

Baseline assessment focuses on personal and social development, speaking and listening, reading writing and maths (mainly numbers). Children are given an overall numerical score for the baseline assessment, because of government requirements to do this. The assessment is used to inform the staff planning for the child.

Observations take place in normal classroom situations. These include role play in the home corner, family talk in school when collecting children, pictures in public, telephones, playground, maths games, number stories such as the Three Bears, bus numbers, water etc.

It is important that staff observing children who speak English as an additional language avoid false assumptions and inappropriate conclusions. Adults need to be aware of the cultural and linguistic backgrounds of children.

THE LONDON BOROUGH OF ENFIELD: BASELINE ASSESSMENT SCHEME

This is only a sample. The Assessment Scheme also has sections on writing, speaking and listening, and mathematics (number). Only mathematics and language and literacy are given a score

PERSONAL AND SOCIAL DEVELOPMENT

I. RELATIONSHIPS

There are other sections on personal and social development

Date	Observation Comments	Action
16/9/99	Shanaz watches Tariq. He is her friend from home. He is playing with the dough. She imitates what he does. They smile at each other. Next time they both bash the dough at exactly the same time – and laugh – clapping their hands as they finish.	Encourage Shanaz to be with her friend while she settles and gets to know the people and the layout of the room and outdoor area. Smile at her to encourage her to feel comfortable. Remember her first language is Urdu, and support her.

LANGUAGE AND LITERACY DEVELOPMENT

Observe and Comment on:

Reading in English and other languages

4 Reads familiar words in books

3 Recognises print conveys meaning

2 Looks at books from choice

I No observable evidence

Date	Observation Comments	Action
17/9/99	Shanaz chooses a book in the home area. The book has a dual text. She looks at the pictures, but there is no order in this. She often closes the book and then opens it at any page. She points at words and speaks in Urdu to herself.	Invite parents who speak Urdu to look at books with children. Encourage the idea that writing carries meaning as well as pictures.
	Code English 2	
	Code Home Language 3	

Summer-born children are young when tested: 42% of children sitting the 7-year-old SATS are 6 years of age.

Standard Assessment Targets (SATs)

Research shows that summer born children, especially if they are boys, have lower scores than older children. Many early childhood experts interpret this as evidence suggesting an early formal start to education carries long-term disadvantages for a large proportion of children.

The Welsh National Curriculum

There are three or four core subjects depending on whether Welsh is the first language of the child and on whether the child is being educated in a Welsh medium school: English, maths, science and Welsh. Welsh is tested at the end of each key stage where it is a core subject, as are the other core subjects.

Welsh is studied by all children up to key stage 3, but tests are optional if it is the child's second language.

The other subjects are the same as for the English National Curriculum, except:

(a) at key stage 4, when modern language and technology are optional;

(b) in art and music, where there is still a requirement to make and perform dances, music and art. Many educators were saddened and angered to see less emphasis on creativity (i.e. on *making*) in dance, music and art in the English National Curriculum in the new draft orders taking effect in August 1995.

The Scottish Curriculum

The Scottish Curriculum is for 5–14 years. It has been designed largely by practising teachers. Teachers decide when a child is ready to move to the next level. A sample of teacher assessments are monitored as a moderation exercise. This checks that all teachers are using the same criteria correctly. The results of the teacher assessments are shared with parents. 79% of parents voted against SATS being introduced into the Scottish system.

The subject areas are also organised differently, with six different areas of learning. These are: English, mathematics, science, design and technology, creative and expressive studies, and language studies.

The Northern Ireland Curriculum

In some ways, the Northern Ireland Curriculum is more like the Scottish Curriculum, with similar areas of study. (Religious education lies outside these.) In other ways, it is like the English National Curriculum in following similar testing procedures: children are tested at the end of each key stage.

The areas of study are:

▶ English – at key stage 1, this includes drama and media studies;

▶ mathematics;

▶ science;

▶ design and technology – which will probably soon be combined with science;

▶ environment and society – which includes geography and history, and will soon probably include home economics;

▶ creative and expressive studies – which includes PE and dance, art and design, and music;

▶ language studies – only at secondary level. When the Irish language is offered, another modern language must also be offered by the school.

Linking the National Curriculum with good early years practice from 0–8 years

The curriculum for young children should be integrated. This means that in key stage 1 children should do projects, follow themes and use the basic provision in order to link subjects together and make them more meaningful.

Nursery nurses working in key stage 1 settings (Year 1 and Year 2 – children at 5–7-years-old) will work with a teacher who is trained in the details of the National Curriculum subjects. Nursery nurses working in these settings are invaluable because their training helps them to help children learn through an appropriate curriculum. This is a great support, particularly for children with special needs.

In hospital schools where children are sick, nursery nurses and teachers are able, through their training, to help children find their natural rhythms and best times for working at the National Curriculum.

There are different ways of planning the curriculum, and most early childhood workers are anxious about two things:

1 that they might get in a rut with their work with children and families when planning the curriculum;
2 that they might leap into the latest curriculum fashion when planning the curriculum. Neither of these things are likely to happen if staff keep in mind the education and care principles stated at the beginning of this chapter: these have served Western early childhood education for 200 years.

Criticisms of using a specific method or programme are:

▶ It will cause staff to become narrow in the way they think about the curriculum.
▶ It will make them feel they have 'an answer'.
▶ They might get in a rut.
▶ Fashions change quickly, and staff will soon be looking for the next curriculum fashion.

The High-Scope curriculum model

This is a structured programme designed for children in the USA in the 1960s Head Start Programme. The room and equipment is arranged according to the model's requirement. High-Scope has tried to take the traditional British nursery school and make it more organised. Children are required to 'Plan – Do – Review' as an institutional routine: They tell an adult what they have planned, carry out their plan, and then in a small group discuss with an adult, and show how it went.

The Froebel Blockplay Research Project found that children naturally plan at a more complex level when they play with blocks while they talk with adults. However, they might be held back if they have to say in advance what they will do, and indeed they are likely to say anything in order to please the adult.

The long-term effects of the High-Scope model look promising. However it needs to be remembered that other approaches in the UK have not been researched with the same level of funding. Furthermore, the key factor in the High-Scope programme's success in the USA was the close involvement of parents, and the British High-Scope approach has not emphasised this as much.

The Froebel Nursery Research Project directed by Chris Athey suggests that a traditional early childhood approach which closely involves parents and as a quality curriculum has a powerful long-term influence.

The High-Scope Method can quickly be learned and used in adapted form. Most early childhood educators in the UK believe that it is more important for staff to work from basic education and care principles which help them to move on in their thinking and not become settled in any one method. Just as there is no one way to bring up children, so there is unlikely to be one best way to educate them.

Planning the curriculum for young children

When planning the curriculum for young children, it is important to remember that you need to have long-term plans, medium-term and short-term plans. The best planning comes from knowing the children really well – knowing their interests and their needs. This means that planning needs to be informed by the observations that you make of the children. It is important to have a system. Children can be regularly observed and monitored in their progress. Planning can then lead to an outcome which tailors activities to suit the individual child. This helps you to provide a developmentally appropriate curriculum for the group. However – and very importantly – it also helps you to get it right for individual children on a regular basis.

The long-term plans are about the long-term aims that you have for the children. They are about the things which the culture and the society in which the child is growing up believe to be important for that child to know and understand. For children of 5–8 years, there are legal requirements through a National Curriculum. However, it is no good offering children these things if they are unable to make use or sense of them or are not interested in them. The same principles apply whether we are following the National Curriculum or not. It is not just that the context of what is taught is set out by central government from 5 years of age.

When planning the curriculum, it is important to use your training and draw on the things you know about children learning and developing. This involves thinking about the importance of the families and carers, principles of equality and inclusivity, what children already know, what children want to learn more about and what the government curriculum framework requires children to learn.

All the staff should plan the curriculum together.

The best curriculum is one which is based on

- observations made of individual children;
- matches the needs and interests of individual children;
- creates a learning community.

There are three stages of planning

- long term;
- medium term;
- short-term plan.

LONG-TERM PLANNING

This is not something you pluck out of the air!

- It is based on the principles of good early years practice explored in this chapter.
- It turns these principles into practice.

▶ It looks at what children will be offered to learn about and how it will be offered (the resources you will need).

▶ It makes sure a balance of areas of learning is maintained over time in accordance with official requirements.

▶ It meets with the development plan of the early years setting.

▶ It links with the policy documents in the early years setting.

▶ The long-term plans give a general direction to the curriculum (see plan p. 380).

A long-term plan is usually made for a term or a year. This will help you to make sure you are offering a broad, rich and deep curriculum in every area of learning. For example, you may emphasise the personal, social and emotional aspects of learning in the Autumn when many children are settling in to the early years setting. You may emphasise scientific exploration, courage to risk take and persevere in the Summer, especially outdoors.

Long-term planning helps you to be organised in advance. It helps you to think about

▶ events such as outings, festivals, visitors and how to organise these;

▶ organise carefully a child's individual education plan;

▶ keeping a balance across areas of learning and providing experiences which bring this about both indoors and outdoors;

▶ organising materials, resources and equipment linked with the long-term planning.

MEDIUM-TERM PLANNING

This will usually last for three or four weeks.

You will be observing children and getting to know them and their characters. You will need to match your observations with your medium-term plans.

The staff, planning together, will look at how they will create an environment which links the long-term plans with the child as an individual. The medium-term plan will therefore need to gradually grow and will be flexible and open to changes and modifications.

You will need to look at the observation profiles of children.

Many early years settings now target particular children on particular days. This means each child is observed regularly, and the curriculum is regularly planned in a **differentiated** way which caters for the interests and needs of individual children.

In one setting, observations of the target child across a week showed that the 'waterfall' was greatly used. It involved three beakers of graded size. When the beakers were close to each other and the tap was turned on in a lower sink, a series of waterfalls was created which led to much glee and discussion.

The nursery school's development plan showed science as a major area, with money set aside to buy more equipment, and review the indoor and outdoor areas. In observed children, the staff planned to support and extend the learning by introducing cascades of water in many different ways. They developed a project (or medium-term plan) on water for as long as the interest lasted.

The medium-term plan gives Possible Lines of Direction (PLOD) but will need constant fine tuning to keep it relevant to the learning of the children (see page 385).

SHORT-TERM PLANNING

This will be daily. It will focus on the target children for that week. In this way each child is regularly observed. Short-term planning is more specific, but it should not be rigid. Staff will use weekly and daily planning sessions to plan particular learning intentions for particular children. Some will provide opportunities for children to explore and experiment (indirect teaching). Some will be adult led (direct teaching).

EASTWOOD NURSERY SCHOOL LONG-TERM PLANNING AUTUMN TERM

LANGUAGE AND LITERACY

MATHS
Stories and poems linked to maths concepts e.g. number, time, sequence, weight, shape and pattern.
Developing and extending understanding and use of mathematical language e.g. positional language.
Recording e.g. graph of favourite books or poems.
Same story, different sized books — big and small.
Postage stamps — how much?
Links to role play e.g. shopping lists, menus, timetables, prices.

ART
Describing colours.
Response to paintings, drawings and 3-dimensional work.
Own illustrations of stories and poems.
Stories which include famous paintings.
Expressing own ideas through paintings, drawings and 3-D work.
Different forms of illustration, e.g. torn paper, collage, watercolours, oils, pastels etc.

MUSIC AND DANCE
Reading and writing music notation.
Rhymes.
Making up own words to songs.
Listening to songs and dancing to music from a wide range of cultures.
Responding to music.
Using music in story telling.
Musical stories e.g. Opera, Bear Hunt.
Traditional stories linked to music e.g. Peter and the Wolf.
Songs which tell a story e.g. There was a Princess Long Ago.

MORAL AND SPIRITUAL
Describing feelings.
Cards and stories linked to celebrations and festivals.
Development of self esteem.
Being aware of others' feelings.
Using stories as a focus for moral and spiritual development e.g. Alfie Lends a Hand.
Stories and songs with nonsense words — humour.

DRAMA AND STORYING
Imaginative play developing speaking and listening, reading and writing e.g. shops, doctors, vets, firefighters, cafe, home area.
Using Drama Boxes, magnetic board, puppets.
Retelling stories.
Changing stories.
Making up own stories.
Understanding the function of print and handling books appropriately.
Shared reading — use of big books.
Shared writing.
Recall of events.
Poems and rhymes. Different versions of the same story.

SCIENCE
Using language to describe and record.
Written recording.
Naming e.g. parts of the body, types of flowers, materials.
Extending vocabulary e.g. descriptive language.
Using feely box.
Braille.
Describing different tastes and smells.
Recording using audio and video tape.
Using books for information.
Written labels.
Sounds lotto.
Raising questions.
Investigating papers and writing materials.
Making paper.
Using magnetic story props.
Reading and writing recipes, cooking.

INFORMATION AND DESIGN TECHNOLOGY
Using software e.g. Animated Alphabet, Rabbits at Home, DK Dictionary and Word to develop upper and lower case letter awareness and ability to listen and follow instructions.
Story tapes — audio and visual.
Use of photocopier and laminator to change/preserve children's work.
Use of photos as a stimulus for discussion e.g. of other children, activities, places.
Writing own names for peg labels.
Making props to support or retell familiar stories e.g. puppets, masks, buildings.
Book making.
Using a microphone to tell stories.
Using a telephone — conversations.
Describing how things work e.g. wind up toys.

HUMAN AND SOCIAL
Map making.
Symbols and signs.
Developing signs for the garden.
Direction — discussion and signs.
Discussion of different places e.g. through use of a globe or atlas, encyclopaedia.
Stories set in different countries.
Recordings in a range of different languages.
Comparing old forms of writing — style, scripts etc.
Different forms of printing.
Developing vocabulary related to old and new through use of artefacts e.g. telephones, irons, cameras.
Different scripts.
Stories set in the past.
Traditional stories, fairy stories, myths and legends.

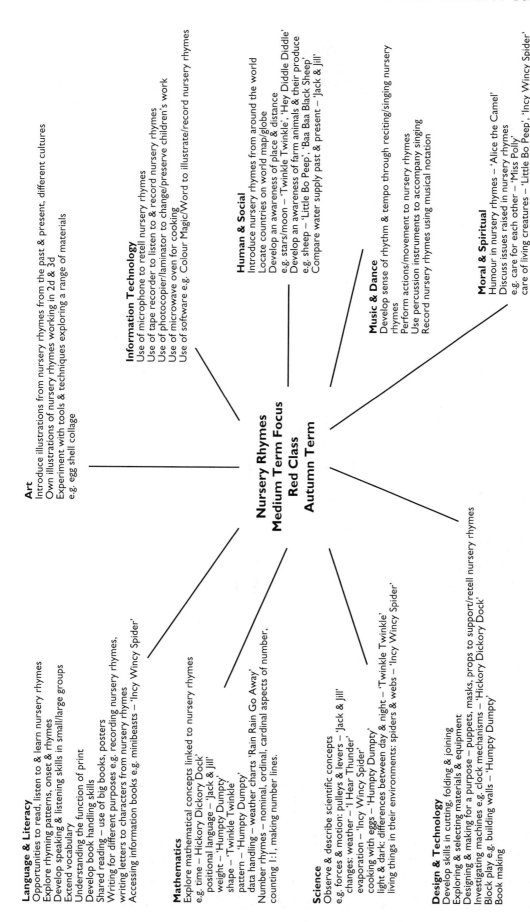

Language & Literacy
Opportunities to read, listen to & learn nursery rhymes
Explore rhyming patterns, onset & rhymes
Develop speaking & listening skills in small/large groups
Extend vocabulary
Understanding the function of print
Develop book handling skills
Shared reading – use of big books, posters
Writing for different purposes e.g. recording nursery rhymes,
writing letters to characters from nursery rhymes
Accessing information books e.g. minibeasts – 'Incy Wincy Spider'

Mathematics
Explore mathematical concepts linked to nursery rhymes
e.g. time – Hickory Dickory Dock'
positional language – 'Jack & Jill'
weight – 'Humpty Dumpty'
shape – 'Twinkle Twinkle'
pattern – 'Humpty Dumpty'
data handling – weather charts 'Rain Rain Go Away'
Number rhymes – nominal, ordinal, cardinal aspects of number,
counting 1:1, making number lines.

Science
Observe & describe scientific concepts
e.g. forces & motion: pulleys & levers – 'Jack & Jill'
changes: weather – 'I Hear Thunder',
evaporation – 'Incy Wincy Spider'
cooking with eggs – 'Humpty Dumpty'
light & dark: differences between day & night – 'Twinkle Twinkle'
living things in their environments: spiders & webs – 'Incy Wincy Spider'

Design & Technology
Develop skills in cutting, folding & joining
Exploring & selecting materials & equipment
Designing & making for a purpose – puppets, masks, props to support/retell nursery rhymes
Investigating machines e.g. clock mechanisms – 'Hickory Dickory Dock'
Block play e.g. building walls – 'Humpty Dumpty'
Book making

EASTWOOD NURSERY SCHOOL

Art
Introduce illustrations from nursery rhymes from the past & present, different cultures
Own illustrations of nursery rhymes working in 2d & 3d
Experiment with tools & techniques exploring a range of materials
e.g. egg shell collage

Information Technology
Use of microphone to retell nursery rhymes
Use of tape recorder to listen to & record nursery rhymes
Use of photocopier/laminator to change/preserve children's work
Use of microwave oven for cooking
Use of software e.g. Colour Magic/Word to illustrate/record nursery rhymes

Nursery Rhymes
Medium Term Focus
Red Class
Autumn Term

Human & Social
Introduce nursery rhymes from around the world
Locate countries on world map/globe
Develop an awareness of place & distance
e.g. stars/moon – 'Twinkle Twinkle'; 'Hey Diddle Diddle'
Develop an awareness of farm animals & their produce
e.g. sheep – 'Little Bo Peep'; 'Baa Baa Black Sheep'
Compare water supply past & present – 'Jack & Jill'

Music & Dance
Develop sense of rhythm & tempo through reciting/singing nursery rhymes
Perform actions/movement to nursery rhymes
Use percussion instruments to accompany singing
Record nursery rhymes using musical notation

Moral & Spiritual
Humour in nursery rhymes – 'Alice the Camel'
Discuss issues raised in nursery rhymes
e.g. care for each other – 'Miss Polly'
care of living creatures – 'Little Bo Peep'; 'Incy Wincy Spider'
emotions – 'Little Miss Muffet'
Consider use of rhymes & lullabies written about/for babies

The staff will prepare by deciding what resources are needed, when in the day and who will be there at particular points. The plan for a child will be based on the staff observations of the child.

The staff have observed Andrew (3 years) who spends 20 minutes with the waterfall beakers. He lines them up next to the tap in the lower sink so that the water falls exactly as he wants. He has a bowl of corks under the waterfall. He aims the water at them one by one to make them bob about.

The Nursery Nurse feeds back this observation of Andrew, who is target child that day, to a group of staff. They decide to put the waterfall out again. They have a bigger version of this in the outside area using buckets and old water trays. They plan how to set up the indoor and outdoor waterfalls. They decide who will be in which areas and what they hope Andrew will learn:

▶ that water flows;
▶ that it flows downwards if it can;
▶ that it splashes;
▶ that it makes a trajectory (which is a moving line);
▶ that it cascades in the outdoor waterfall more than the indoor waterfall;
▶ that it has force to move things in its way.

They plan a visit to the local shopping mall where there is a fountain.

They link the short-term plans for Andrew with the medium-term plan. This means they put a date on the medium-term plan (see chart) and they put his name.

They add that they have done waterfalls, both indoors and outdoors (this is flexible planning). They write down the equipment on the weekly planning sheet for that day (see chart).

EVALUATING

▶ A medium-term plan can be used to check the balance of the long-term plan. Is science being developed so that it reaches every child? Not all children will learn exactly the same science.
▶ How does this science link with the official documents? What science are children supposed to have learned about at this stage in their education? (See the new QCA curriculum framework from Summer 1999).
▶ Are the medium-term planning resources working well for this group of children in their learning? Most experts agree that if there are group plans for individual children, it seems to work well for the whole group.
▶ Are the adults using observation of children to inform their planning?
▶ Are the adults giving support to individual children's learning as well as a group? For example transporting, pouring, sieving.
▶ Are adults able to extend the learning about water to add knowledge that children did not previously have e.g. pumps?
▶ Are children learning about other areas in science? Is there a good balance in this curriculum?

Quality learning comes from matching the child to what is offered in the curriculum. When planning the curriculum make sure you have:

▶ long-term plans – plan a developmentally appropriate curriculum. This helps early curriculum childhood educators to plan a curriculum that is, generally speaking, appropriate for children in this age group.
▶ medium-term plans – sorting out provisions and people with a focus and a purpose.

FIGURE 13.24

A daily plan – Pen Green family centre

AREA	PLAN	CHILDREN	STAFF	OUTINGS
CORRIDOR	Magnets travelling along string Den Stories Self select construction	Kirsten ⎫ Trajectory Jacob ⎬ Keith ⎭ Transporting Leanne ⎫ Clare ⎬ Scatter James ⎭	Cath Cath Jackie	Zoe Laura Natalie Katey Washing windows
WET AREA	Rotary whisks ⎫ Other whisks ⎬ Containers Chocolate powder ⎬ Clear bottles Salt ⎬ Flour shaker Pasta ⎬ Oil ⎭ Powder paint (to add colour) Thursday – mashed Cooked dough potatoes	Robert ⎫ Rotation John ⎭ Kimberly ⎫ Envelopment Jacob ⎭ Natalie ⎫ Zoe ⎬ In + out Craig ⎬ Joely ⎭	Lucy Carmen a.m. Jackie p.m. Carmen	
WORKSHOP	Playing with string Cats cradle Tin can stilts * Add glue and bits	Jacob Connection Robert ⎫ Thomas ⎬ Enclosure	Sarah Linds	
DRAWING	Train set self-service Nice floor – silver + gold * Repeat	Mark Connection Joely Trajectory Daniel Enclosure	Tracy	
CAFÉ	Veg, fruit and toast	Alex Trajectory	Becky a.m. Rie p.m.	
HOME CORNER	Chopping vegetables		Chris	
LOW CEILING	a.m. clear for dentist p.m. large rolls of paper 1/10/92 rolls of paper for wrapping children block jungle. Repeat	Joanne ⎫ Craig ⎬ Envelopment Natalie ⎬ Grant ⎭	Cath	
WRITING	Calculator, envelope Pritt stick, scissors * Repeat	Joely On top Kari Envelopment Jannice B. Dab		
OUTSIDE	Buckets, sponges, brushes Pulleys, buckets, gravel sand & sawdust, paper Bikes with trailers Cornflower on large table Parachute Rolls of paper Different kinds of measures	Kerry Envelopment John M. ⎫ James H. ⎬ Aaron ⎬ Zoe ⎬ Transporting Thomas ⎬ Natalie ⎬ Stephen ⎭ Steven Trajectory Alex ⎫ James ⎬ Rotation Jacob ⎭	Lucy	

FIGURE 13.25

A curriculum planning chart for William Redford House workplace nursery

WILLIAM'S TRANSPORTING & TRAJECTORY SCHEMA JAN/FEB

LITERACY
The POST OFFICE satisfies William in that he can stamp letters and deliver them. Stories offered include *The Hungry Giant* (about a giant who hits) *Mr Gumpy's Outing* and poetry *Noisy Poems*. Whilst involved in these experiences, genuine conversations take place around things which are of great interest to him.
His language has developed dramatically. This is a combination of improved hearing since the adjustment of his grommets and being supported and extended through dialogue with adults whilst involved in activities that fascinate him

MATHEMATICS
SPLASH PAINTING involves mathematics and distance. Post office play with different sized bags and baskets and all the problems associated with getting big boxes into small containers before being able to transport them, offer different experiences (volume, capacity, problem solving).

PHYSICAL
Everything William does indoors and outdoors offers him opportunities for gross and fine motor coordinations. Grommets in his ears help him to experience fully the physical environment.

ENVIRONMENT
Gardening and digging ready for vegetable planting and in particular for William to transport earth to fill garden tubs.

SPIRITUAL
Gardening (free environment) encourages a sense of awe and wonder. Having his constructions valued leads to respect and love. Collaborating with others helps him to appreciate other cultures and diversity amongst human beings.

MORAL
Using pulleys he began to turn-take. (See also constructions and printing and woodwork.)

AESTHETICS/TECHNOLOGY
PRINTING and WOODWORK help William to hit and stab in acceptable ways, without putting him under pressure to cooperate with others before he is ready to do so. His CONSTRUCTIONS with BLOCKS, or rockets using Sellotape and RECYCLED MATERIALS, (up and down, side to side trajectories) were praised and valued by adults, which contributed to his positive self-esteem.

SCIENCE
SPLASH PAINTING (see mathematics)
A PULLEY over the sand tray, using William's trajectory schema, helps him to encounter light/heavy, and forces in physics.

▶ daily plans – a differentiated curriculum that individual children can learn through. See Bartholomew and Bruce for other ways to balance long-term weekly and daily plans.

A quality curriculum

It might be useful to look again at the triangle on p. 333 which gives the main elements in a quality curriculum for children of 0–8 years. It can seem a daunting task to provide a quality curriculum. Remember again that the things that matter the most are:

▶ your relationship with the children, their families and the other staff;

▶ the provision that you offer and the conversations that you have with children as they experience the materials – the learning context is crucial.

Many adults find that they enjoy subjects like maths and science for the first time in their lives when they work with children. If you can help children to enjoy learning, you will have given them a good start which they will take with them through their lives.

Both the adults and the children need to contribute as much as possible if the curriculum is to be of quality.

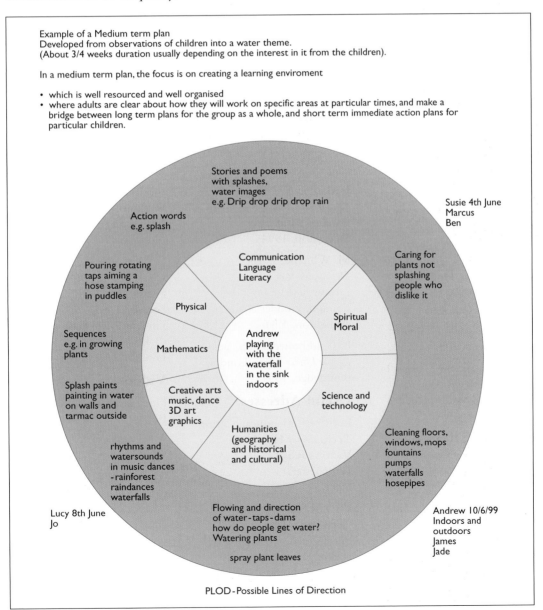

Example of a Medium term plan
Developed from observations of children into a water theme.
(About 3/4 weeks duration usually depending on the interest in it from the children).

In a medium term plan, the focus is on creating a learning enviroment

• which is well resourced and well organised
• where adults are clear about how they will work on specific areas at particular times, and make a bridge between long term plans for the group as a whole, and short term immediate action plans for particular children.

Stories and poems with splashes, water images e.g. Drip drop drip drop rain

Susie 4th June
Marcus
Ben

Action words e.g. splash

Caring for plants not splashing people who dislike it

Pouring rotating taps aiming a hose stamping in puddles

Communication Language Literacy

Physical

Spiritual Moral

Sequences e.g. in growing plants

Mathematics

Andrew playing with the waterfall in the sink indoors

Splash paints painting in water on walls and tarmac outside

Creative arts music, dance 3D art graphics

Science and technology

Cleaning floors, windows, mops fountains pumps waterfalls hosepipes

rhythms and watersounds in music dances -rainforest raindances waterfalls

Humanities (geography and historical and cultural)

Lucy 8th June
Jo

Flowing and direction of water - taps - dams how do people get water? Watering plants

spray plant leaves

Andrew 10/6/99
Indoors and outdoors
James
Jade

PLOD - Possible Lines of Direction

FIGURE 13.26
Children and adults learning together

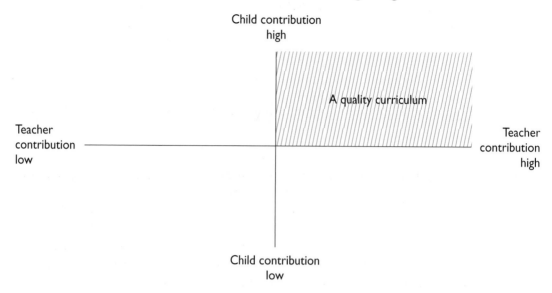

Modified from original source: Child Development 0–5, Roberts, M. and Tamburrini, J. (1981).

The shaded area in Figure 13.26 shows the importance of operating the curriculum in such a way that both the teacher and the child contribute actively as much as possible..

R E S O U R C E S

Books

Bartholomew, L. and Bruce, T. *Getting to Know You: A Guide to Record-Keeping in Early Childhood Education and Care,* London, Hodder & Stoughton, 1999

T. Bruce *Early Childhood Education,* London, Hodder & Stoughton, 1997

M. Davies *Helping Children to Learn through a Movement Perspective,* London, Hodder & Stoughton, 1995

P. Gura (ed)., *Exploring Learning: Young Children and Blockplay,* London, Paul Chapman Publishing, 1990

P. Gura *Resources for Learning,* London, Hodder & Stoughton, 1996

J. Matthews *Helping Young Children to Draw and Paint,* London, Hodder & Stoughton, 1994

M. Whitehead, *The Development of Language and Literacy in the Early Years,* London, Hodder & Stoughton, 1996

L. Goldshmied and S. Jackson *People Under Three,* London, Routledge, 1994

Useful Adresses

Learning to Landscape Trust, Technology House, Victoria Road, Winchester, Hants

Vital (RNIB/VIEW Curriculum Group for Professionals working with multiply disabled visually impaired children),

RNIB Rushton Hall School, Rushton, Nr Keating, Northants NN14 1RR

Clear Vision Project (for Sharing braille and text dual books), Linden Lodge School, 61 Princes Way, London SW19 6JB

Videos

From the National Children's Bureau 8 Wakeley Street London EC1V 7QE

(a) *Treasure Baskets*
(b) *Heuristic Play.*

BAECE
III City View House
463 Bethnal Green Road
London EC 9QY

PCET Wallcharts
27 Kirchen Road
London W13 UD

Life Stories set:
A Bean Story
A Chicken Story
A Frog Story
A Butterfly Story

ACTIVITY

Different ways to share a story

▶ Plan a story you can tell to a group of four 3–4-year-olds. Use puppets or props, and make sounds to illustrate the story:
  (a) For example, make a miniature garden and model hen, and tell the story of Rosie the Hen's walk.
  (b) Use musical instruments as sound effects, perhaps for Mrs Mopple's wash day. The possibilities are endless with different stories. Observe the children (3–7 years) and their participation in relation to concentration, and evaluate your observations.

▶ Plan how you will tell a story about each child in the group, and make each child (3–7 years) a book of their story, or a CD-ROM version. Put the book in the book area, or on the computer, and let them take it home. Perhaps a child found a snail in the garden, or did some cooking, or pretended to be a dog. These events can be turned into the child's story. Evaluate the child's learning in relation to language and literacy.

▶ Plan a story you can read to a large group. Make an enlarged book, and use a pointer. You can rest the book on an easel while you tell the story. There are also commercially made enlarged books, but children appreciate the home-made ones that you make. They often want to make their own books too. This encourages them to write and draw, using you as a role model. Evaluate the activity in relation to the language and literacy aspects of learning.

▶ Make poetry cards. For example:
  'Little robin redbreast, sat upon a wall
  Niddle noddle went his head
  and waggle went his tail.'
  You need a large piece of card to draw the robin on. Cut the outline of the robin out, and write the words all over the robin. Put it in a large box. You can gradually make a collection of these large poetry cards – which are interesting shapes for children to look at – with the words put on them. Evaluate this activity, emphasising what the children have learnt about phonics in an everyday way (i.e. learning in context).

Use pp. 101–106 – giving examples of activity sessions – in the Mollie Davies (1955) book listed in Resources.

Investigating the early childhood curriculum

1   Observe a child in the book area. What interests the child? What do you notice about the child's mathematical development? Make a book specially for this child. Evaluate the activity, emphasizing the learning in relation to mathematics.

2   Observe a child in water play. Try to say what you think the child is learning scientifically, as well as the child's ideas, feelings and relationships while they are involved in the water play. Plan another water activity for this child based on your observations.
    Evaluate your plans and observations.

3   Look at the layouts in the diagrams. Can you find examples of carpet areas to keep down the noise? Is there easy access? Are passageways kept free? Are there dens? Are there quiet spaces? Are they using all the space? Are there dividers to make cosy corners? (Large spaces can be frightening.) Is the indoor equipment acting like a mirror so that children can do the same things indoors and outdoors? Evaluate the provision in terms of the learning context.

4   Look at a room that is set out for children of 3–5 years. Can you find all the basic provision which is on the list of basic equipment? Is anything missing? Are there other things. Evaluate the learning context for a 3–7-year-old based on observing a child in the indoor area.

5   Make a basic set of dressing-up clothes to use with children from 2 years onwards. Remember, hats, shoes, belts and cloaks are important. Plan how you would introduce these. Observe a child dressing up. Evaluate your provision with reference to the twelve principles on p. 241.

6   Make a set of home-made musical instruments to use with a group of children of 3–5 years – e.g. make drums out of tins and boxes, use elastic bands to make stringed instruments, and for shakers, use perhaps yoghurt cartons with uncooked rice in them, using masking tape to join them. Try to make your instruments attractive to look at so that the children will want to use them. Observe a child using them, and evaluate the activity in relation to human and social learning.

7   Write a plan and set up a workshop area to include graphics materials and found materials to encourage aesthetic and artistic education. Observe children of 2–7 years (three children of different ages and at least one of each gender) and evaluate your provision. Observe how the children use the materials that you offer them. What will you change the next time you offer the materials to the children?

8   Write a plan and carry out a painting activity in which children mix their own paints. What science might they learn, and how will it help their fine manipulative skills? Observe two children of 2–7 years of age. Evaluate the activity.

9   Write a plan and make a home area thinking about the mathematics that the children might learn as they use this area. Observe two children, a boy and a girl, of 2–7 years using the area. Evaluate this activity.

14

Baby and Child Health: Care and Surveillance

Infection

Infectious diseases are extremely common in childhood. An infection starts when certain micro-organisms enter the body and start to multiply. The body in turn reacts to this and uses various methods to try to destroy these micro-organisms. The illness which results is partly due to the effects of the multiplying **micro-organisms** and partly due to the body's subsequent reactions. Not all micro-organisms are **pathogenic** (causing disease in humans). Pathogenic micro-organisms are also called **germs** and can only be seen with the aid of a powerful microscope. Germs may be sub-divided into:

▶ bacteria
▶ viruses
▶ protozoa
▶ fungi
▶ animal parasites.

Bacteria

Bacteria are abundant almost everywhere – in the air, soil and water – and most are harmless to humans. Some bacteria indeed are beneficial – e.g. those that live in the intestine and help break down food for digestion. Pathogenic bacteria are classified, on the basis of shape, into four main groups:

▶ **cocci** (spherical). Examples of diseases: pneumonia, tonsillitis, meningitis, bacterial endocarditis, toxic shock syndrome and various skin disorders;
▶ **bacilli** (rod-shaped). Examples of diseases: tuberculosis, pertussis (whooping cough), tetanus, diphtheria, salmonellosis and legionnaire's disease;
▶ **vibrios** (curved shape). Example of disease: cholera;
▶ **spirochaetes** (spiral-shaped). Examples of diseases: syphilis, yaws, Lyme disease and leptospirosis.

Each tiny bacterium consists of a single cell. The bacteria that colonise the human body thrive in warm, moist conditions. They reproduce by dividing into two cells, which in turn divide and so on. Under ideal conditions (i.e. exactly the right temperature and sufficient nutrition for all cells) this division can take place every 20 minutes, resulting in a very rapid rate of reproduction. In a healthy child, such ideal conditions rarely occur, and the body's **immune system** acts quickly to destroy the invading bacteria.

Viruses

Viruses are the smallest known type of pathogenic micro-organism and cannot be seen under an ordinary microscope. **Viral infections** range from the trivial – warts, the common cold and other minor respiratory-tract infections – to mumps, measles and poliomyelitis, and to potentially very serious diseases such as rabies, Lassa fever, AIDS (acquired immuno-deficiency syndrome), and possibly to various cancers.

Protozoa

All types of **protozoa** are simple one-celled animals and are of microscopic size. About 30 different types of protozoa are troublesome parasites of humans. Examples include: **amoebae** which cause diarrhoeal infections, the sexually transmitted infection trichomoniasis, malaria and **toxoplasmosis** (a disease acquired from cats).

Fungi

Fungi are simple, parasitic life-forms including moulds, mildews, mushrooms and yeasts. Some fungi are harmlessly present all the time in areas of the body such as the mouth, skin, intestines and vagina but are prevented from multiplying through competition from bacteria. Other bacteria are dealt with by the body's **immune system**. Examples of fungal infection include thrush (candidiasis), athlete's foot and ringworm.

Animal parasites

Parasites are organisms which live in or on any other living creature. They obtain their food from the host's blood or tissues and are thus able to reproduce. Parasites may remain permanently with their host or may spend only part of their life-cycles in association. Examples include parasites which commonly affect children, such as head lice, scabies mites, fleas and threadworm.

The transmission of infection

Infective micro-organisms cannot survive without their essential needs being met:

▶ warmth
▶ moisture
▶ food
▶ time.

Some also require oxygen, but others do not.

THE CHAIN OF INFECTION

All infection starts with:

1   The **source**. This may be:
   ▶ a person who is already infected with the disease;
   ▶ someone who is unaware of the existence of the disease but may be **incubating** it;

> a **carrier** of the disease, i.e. someone who has either had the disease and is convalescent or who carries the causative organism with no adverse effects on themselves;

> household pets – e.g. cats and dogs may be the source of **streptococcal** infections, as well as of infestation by fleas and roundworms.

2   The **reservoir**. A reservoir of infection may exist which allows organisms to survive and multiply. Examples include:

> dust;

> organic matter – e.g. food;

> secretions – e.g. saliva, sputum and mucus;

> excretions – e.g. urine and faeces;

> discharges – e.g. pus from a wound or a boil;

> sinks, taps, waste pipes and drains.

THE ROUTE OF SPREAD

Organisms may spread from the **reservoir** or **source** in a number of ways:

FIGURE 14.1
The chain of infection

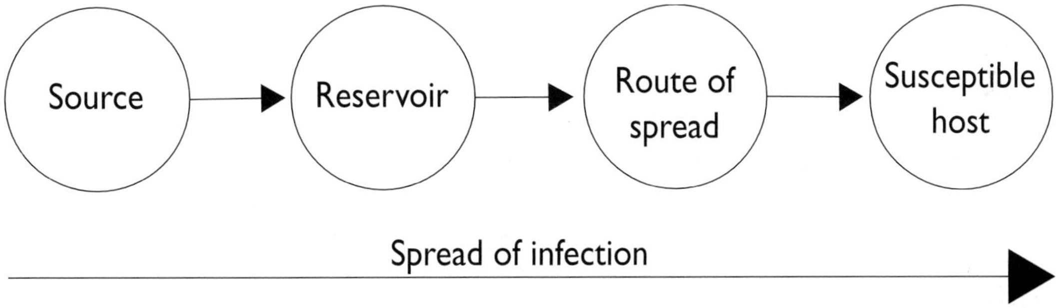

Source → Reservoir → Route of spread → Susceptible host

Spread of infection →

1   **Direct infection.**

> *Touch:* skin which is unbroken (i.e. no cuts or grazes) provides an effective barrier to most organisms, although diseases such as **impetigo** can be transferred onto skin already infected by **eczema**. **Scabies** is also spread by skin contact.

> *Droplet or airborne infection:* if a person coughs or sneezes without covering their nose and mouth, the droplets may be carried several metres and be inhaled by everyone else in the room; similarly, infection may be spread in this way by talking closely with others.

> *Kissing:* organisms are transferred directly from mouth to mouth; **glandular fever (mononucleosis)** is often referred to as the 'kissing disease'.

> *Injection:* the sharing of needles and syringes by drug addicts may cause infection to be transmitted by the blood. HIV infection and hepatitis B may both be transmitted in this way.

> *Sexual contact:* the transmission of diseases such as **syphilis, gonorrhoea,** HIV and **non-specific genital infection (NSGI)** is via sexual intercourse.

2   **Indirect infection.**

> *Water:* the contamination of water used for drinking is a major method of spreading diseases, e.g. **typhoid fever, cholera, viral hepatitis A**. Swimming in polluted water may cause ear infections.

> **Schistosomiasis** is a parasitic disease which afflicts over 200 million people

world-wide; it is acquired by bathing in lakes and rivers infested by the **schistosome fluke**, which enters the human skin. Eating shellfish that live in polluted water may cause food poisoning or tapeworm infestations. Legionnaire's disease is a form of bacterial pneumonia caused by the inhalation of water droplets from contaminated air-conditioning tanks.

▶ *Food:* animals that are kept or caught for food may harbour disease organisms in their tissues. If meat or milk from such an animal is taken without being thoroughly cooked or pasteurised, the organisms may cause illness in the human host, e.g. **food poisoning**.

▶ *Insects:* Many types of **fly** settle first on human or animal excrement and then on food to lay eggs or to feed. Typhoid fever and food poisoning are two diseases spread in this way. Biting insects can spread serious infections through their bites.

  Examples include the mosquito (malaria and filariasis), the **tsetse fly** (African trypanosomiasis), the **rat flea (plague)** and the **sand fly (leishmaniasis)**.

▶ *Rats:* rats may harbour the leptospirosis bacterium which is excreted in their urine and may be transmitted to humans. (Leptospirosis is also known as **Weil's disease**.)

FIGURE 14.2
The spread of infection

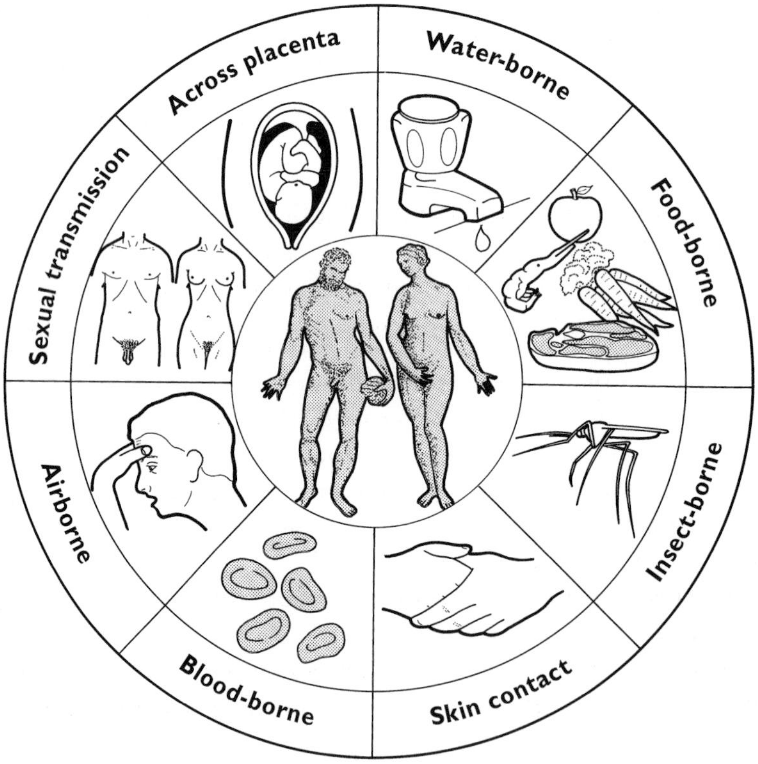

Common childhood infections

Infections may be localised in one part of the body – e.g. **conjunctivitis** – or more widespread with manifestations in many of the body systems (e.g. **measles**).

Incubation period

This is the **time gap** between the entry of the micro-organisms into the body and the first appearance of **symptoms**. This period varies considerably with each infection; during the incubation period, the infected child is likely to pass on the micro-organism to others.

Quarantine period

This refers to the amount of time for which children who have been in contact with the disease are advised to remain at home or otherwise isolated. As some diseases are highly infective even when without symptoms (e.g. **chickenpox**), the quarantine period may have little relevance.

Fomites

Fomites (singular = **fomes**) are inanimate articles – such as clothing, books, toys, towels or a telephone receiver – which are not harmful in themselves but may harbour an infection which can then be passed to another person. They are responsible particularly for the spread of respiratory infections and gastro-enteritis.

Immunity

Immunity is the ability of the body to resist infection. When the body is attacked by bacteria there may be a **localised** reaction in the form of inflammation and a **general** response including fever. There is also a **specific immune response** when the body recognises the bacteria as foreign and produces **antibodies** (proteins with a protective role) which resist the particular bacteria.

The innate immune system

Almost everyone is born with an intact but undeveloped immune system which matures shortly after birth. This innate or **non-specific immunity** cannot guard against *all* disease-causing organisms: the growing child may encounter organisms that overcome these innate barriers and so cause disease. Figure 14.3 shows the external (physical and chemical) barriers to infection.

Breast-feeding

Breastmilk contains antibodies which provide extra immunity until babies can form their own specific antibodies.

There are two types of immunity:

1 **Active immunity** may be **natural** or **artificial**. Natural active immunity is acquired through:

   ▶ an attack of a disease in which the antibodies formed against it confer near-lifelong immunity. Rubella, measles and chickenpox are examples of such diseases;

   ▶ a sub-clinical infection in which the body defences are alerted, but where the attack by the organism is not strong enough to cause an acute attack of the illness.

   Artificial active immunity is acquired through immunisation or inoculation with:

   ▶ living organisms – e.g. vaccination against smallpox;

   ▶ living weakened organisms – e.g. **BCG** (the **Bacillus Calmette-Guerin** vaccine) against tuberculosis;

FIGURE 14.3
Physical and chemical barriers to infection

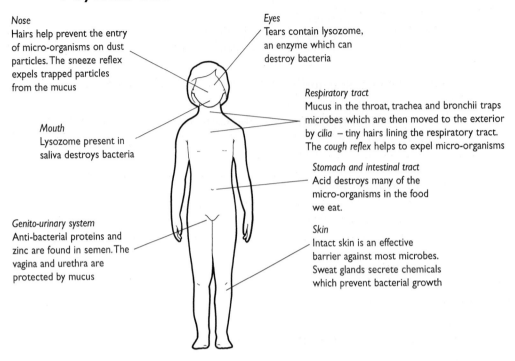

Nose
Hairs help prevent the entry of micro-organisms on dust particles. The sneeze reflex expels trapped particles from the mucus

Eyes
Tears contain lysozome, an enzyme which can destroy bacteria

Respiratory tract
Mucus in the throat, trachea and bronchii traps microbes which are then moved to the exterior by *cilia* – tiny hairs lining the respiratory tract. The *cough reflex* helps to expel micro-organisms

Mouth
Lysozome present in saliva destroys bacteria

Stomach and intestinal tract
Acid destroys many of the micro-organisms in the food we eat.

Genito-urinary system
Anti-bacterial proteins and zinc are found in semen. The vagina and urethra are protected by mucus

Skin
Intact skin is an effective barrier against most microbes. Sweat glands secrete chemicals which prevent bacterial growth

- ▶ dead organisms – e.g. pertussis or whooping-cough vaccine;
- ▶ modified toxins or **toxoids** – e.g. the diphtheria vaccine.

2 **Passive immunity** may also be **natural** or **artificial**. Natural passive immunity is possessed by babies in the first few months of life:

- ▶ in breast milk to the baby after birth; and
- ▶ antibodies are passed from the mother to the foetus via the placenta.

Artificial passive immunity is where a serum containing antibodies produced by a person who is convalescent from the disease is given to a child at risk of developing the disease; it gives immediate but short-lived protection.

Common infectious diseases of childhood

Everyone concerned with the care of babies and young children should be aware of the signs and symptoms of the common infectious diseases, and should know when to summon medical aid (see Table 14.1).

Skin disorders

Up to 3 million micro-organisms exist on each square centimetre of skin. Most of these are **commensals** and are harmless to their host. These commensals (literally 'table companions' from the Latin) have become adapted through evolution to live off human skin scales and the slightly acid secretions produced by the skin. The micro-organisms tend to live in the deeper layers of the **stratum corneum**, near to their food source. Babies are born with no resident **microbial flora** (see Chapter 3). **Pathogens** (the organisms which cause disease) are discouraged by the presence of commensals.

Some important points to note are:

▶ Neonates are particularly prone to skin infection.
▶ Micro-organisms thrive in **moist** conditions, e.g. at the axillae (the armpits) and the groin.
▶ Washing and bathing increase the number of bacteria released from the skin for up to 10 hours.
▶ The skin can never be **sterilised**. Iodine preparations used to prepare skin for surgical operations kill a large percentage of organisms but cannot remove the bacteria which colonise the hair follicles.
▶ To provide a defence against infection, the skin must be *intact*, i.e. *unbroken*.

There are two main reasons why the skin should be kept *clean*.

1 to prevent infection by micro-organisms via the sweat pores;
2 to prevent the accumulation of oil, sweat and micro-organisms which will encourage insect parasites.

Parasitic skin infections

The four most common causes of parasitic skin infection in the Western world are:

1 the **head louse** (Pediculus capitis);
2 the **clothing** or **body louse** (Pediculus humanus);
3 the **crab louse** (Phthirus pubis);
4 the **scabies mite**.

FIGURE 14.4
A head louse and egg case (nit)

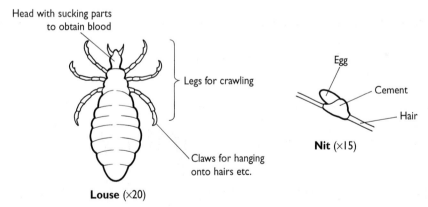

HEAD LICE

Head lice are a common affliction. Anybody can get them but they are particularly prevalent among children. Head lice:

▶ are tiny insects with six legs;
▶ are between 1 and 4 mm in size – slightly larger than a pin head (see Figure 14.4);
▶ only live on human beings; they cannot be caught from animals;
▶ live on, or very close to, the scalp, and they don't wander down the hair shafts for very long;

TABLE 14.1

Childhood infections

DISEASE AND CAUSE	SPREAD	INCU-BATION	SIGNS AND SYMPTOMS	RASH OR SPECIFIC SIGN	TREATMENT	COMPLICATIONS
COMMON COLD (coryza) Virus	Airborne/droplet, hand-to-hand contact	1–3 days	Sneeze, sore throat, running nose, headache, slight fever, irritable, partial deafness		Treat symptoms*. Vaseline to nostrils	Bronchitis, sinusitis, laryngitis
CHICKENPOX (varicella) Virus	Airborne/droplet, direct contact	10–14 days	Slight fever, itchy rash, mild onset, child feels ill, often with severe headache	Red spots with white centre on trunk and limbs at first; blisters and pustuless	Rest, fluids, calamine to rash, cut child's nails to prevent secondary infection	Impetigo, scarring, secondary infection from scratching
DYSENTERY Bacillus or amoeba	Indirect: flies, infected food; poor hygiene	1–7 days	Vomiting, diarrhoea, blood and mucus in stool, abdominal pain, fever, headache		Replace fluids, rest, medical aid, strict hygiene measures	Dehydration from loss of body salts, shock; can be fatal
FOOD POISONING Bacteria or virus	Indirect: infected food or drink	$\frac{1}{2}$ hour to 36 hours	Vomiting, diarrhoea, abdominal pain		Fluids only for 24 hours; medical aid if no better	Dehydration – can be fatal
GASTRO-ENTERITIS Bacteria or virus	Direct contact. Indirect: infected food/drink	Bacterial: 7–14 days Viral: $\frac{1}{2}$ hr –36 hrs	Vomiting, diarrhoea, signs of dehydration		Replace fluids – water or Dioralyte; medical aid urgently	Dehydration, weight loss – death
MEASLES (morbilli) Virus	Airborne/droplet	7–15 days	High fever, fretful, heavy cold – running nose and discharge from eyes; later cough	Day 1: Koplik's spots, white inside mouth. Day 4: blotchy rash starts on face and spreads down to body	Rest, fluids, tepid sponging. Shade room if photophobic	Otitis media, eye infection pneumonia, encephalitis (rare)

Disease (and cause)	How spread	Incubation period	Symptoms	Other signs	Treatment	Complications
MENINGITIS (inflammation of meninges which cover the brain) Bacteria or virus	Airborne/droplet	Variable – usually 2–10 days	Fever, headache, drowsiness, confusion, **photophobia**, (or dislike of bright light) arching of neck	Can have small red spots or bruises	Take to hospital, antibiotics and observation	Deafness, brain damage, death
MUMPS (epidemic parotitis) Virus	Airborne/droplet	14–21 days	Pain, swelling of jaw in front of ears, fever, eating and drinking painful	Swollen face	Fluids: give via straw, hot compresses, oral hygiene*	Meningitis (1 in 400), orchitis (infection of testes) in *young men*
PERTUSSIS (Whooping cough) Bacteria	Airborne/droplet; direct contact	7–21 days	Starts with a snuffly cold, slight cough, mild fever	Spasmodic cough with whoop sound, vomiting	Rest and assurance; feed after coughing attack; support during attack; inhalations	Convulsions, pneumonia, brain damage, hernia, debility
RUBELLA (German measles) Virus	Airborne/droplet; direct contact	14–21 days	Slight cold, sore throat, mild fever, swollen glands behind ears, pain in small joints	Slight pink rash starts behind ears and on forehead. Not itchy	Rest if necessary. Treat symptoms*	Only if contracted by woman in first 3 months of pregnancy – can cause serious defects in unborn baby
SCARLET FEVER (or Scarlatina) Bacteria	Droplet	2–4 days	Sudden fever, loss of appetite, sore throat, pallor around mouth, 'strawberry' tongue	Bright red pinpoint rash over face and body – may peel	Rest, fluids, observe for complications, antibiotics	Kidney infection, otitis media, rheumatic fever (rare)
TONSILLITIS Bacteria or virus	Direct infection, droplet		Very sore throat, fever, headache, pain on swallowing, aches and pains in back and limbs		Rest, fluids, medical aid – antibiotics, iced drinks relieve pain	Quinsy (abscess on tonsils), otitis media, kidney infection, temporary deafness

- ▶ have mouths like small needles which they stick into the scalp and drink the blood;
- ▶ are unable to fly, hop or jump;
- ▶ are caught just by coming into contact with someone who is infested. When heads touch, the lice simply walk from one head to the other;
- ▶ do not discriminate between clean and dirty hair, but tend to live more on smooth, straight hair.
- ▶ are ***not*** the same as nits. Nits are the egg cases laid by lice. Nits may be found 'glued' on to the hair shafts; they are smaller than a pinhead and are pearly white;

The female head louse lays 6–8 eggs a day; these eggs are dull, well camouflaged and glued to the base of hair shafts. Hatching increases in warm, moist atmospheres. Once the eggs have hatched, the empty egg shells (called nits) remain glued to the hair and grow out with it at a rate of 1 cm per month, so distracting attention from the live eggs and lice. The nits are white and shiny and may be found further down the scalp, particularly behind the ears. They may be mistaken for dandruff but unlike dandruff, they are firmly glued to the hair and cannot be shaken off.

If you catch one or two lice, they may breed and increase slowly in number. At this stage, most people have no symptoms. Many people only realise that they have head lice when the itching starts, usually after two to three months. The itching is due to an allergy, not to the louse bites themselves. Sometimes a rash may be seen on the scalp or lice droppings, (a black powder, like fine pepper) may be seen on pillowcases.

PREVENTION
The best way to stop infection is for families to learn how to check their own heads. This way they can find any lice before they have a chance to breed. They can then treat them and stop them being passed around the family. If a living, moving louse is found on one of the family's heads, the others should be checked carefully. Then any of them who have living lice should be treated at the same time.

- ▶ Brush and comb the child's hair daily, but preferably night and morning until the child is old enough to do it alone.
- ▶ Comb thoroughly. Contrary to popular belief, head lice are not easily damaged by ordinary combing. However, regular combing may help to detect lice early and so help to control them.
- ▶ Inspect the child's hair prior to washing it; pay special attention to the areas behind the ears, the top of the head and the neckline.
- ▶ Examine the child's hair closely if he or she complains of an itchy scalp or if there is a reported outbreak of head lice at school or nursery.

How to detect head lice
You will need a plastic detection comb (from the chemist), good lighting and an ordinary comb. Lice are most easily detected by fine tooth-combing wet hair. Some parents find that using a hair conditioner helps to lubricate the hair and ease the combing process; others report that such lubricants make it more difficult to see the eggs.

Treatment
Treatment should only be used if you are sure that you have found a living, moving louse. Special head louse lotions should never be used 'just in case' or as a preventative measure since the lotions may be harmful to young children when used repeatedly. Check the heads of all the people living in your home. Only treat those who have living, moving

lice. Treat them all at the same time, using a special lotion or aromatherapy mixture, **not** a shampoo. There are two main methods of treatment for head lice:

1 Insecticide lotions

Lotions and rinses that are specifically formulated to kill lice and their eggs are available from pharmacists and from some child health clinics. Your school nurse, health visitor or pharmacist will advise you which lotion to use. The lotion is changed frequently, as the lice become resistant to it and it no longer works. If you cannot afford the lotion, you can ask your GP for a prescription. Follow the instruction on the product carefully.

2 Aromatherapy lotions

Aromatherapy lotions have been found to be very effective by parents in treating head lice. They are based on essential oils (containing extracts from plants such as rosemary, lavender, eucalyptus, geranium, teatree etc.). They can either be applied to the hair in the evening, massaging the whole scalp with the oil, to ensure the hair is completely covered in it, left overnight and then in the morning rinsed out. Alternatively, they are thoroughly massaged into the hair at bathtime, left for half an hour, and then rinsed out. Check with the supplier for their advice on the method to use.

The Community Hygiene Concern charity (see Addresses section) has developed the 'bug buster' kit, which can rid a child of head lice without having to subject them to chemical treatments. This method has been approved by the Department of Health.

THE CLOTHING OR BODY LOUSE

Another name for this louse is the **bed bug**. It is similar to the head louse and is distinguished mainly by its different habitat: these lice hide during the day in cracks and crevices, and are often attached to clothing or blankets. They usually feed on people while they sleep at night, visiting their host to suck blood four or five times a night. Transmission is mostly by **contact**, but may also occur through shared bedding and clothing.

TREATMENT

Treatment should be carried out with tact and sympathy in order to preserve self-respect:

▶ The floors and walls of the bedroom should be sprayed with liquid insecticide.
▶ Bedding should be treated with insecticide powder.
▶ Clothing should be exchanged, and the affected clothes treated by **fumigation**, washing in very hot water or dry-cleaning.

THE CRAB LOUSE

The biology of the crab louse is similar to that of the head louse. They are mostly found on adults but also constitute 1% of the lice found in children's hair.

▶ It is 1–2.5 mm in size.
▶ It resembles a crab, with claw-like pincers, and is well camouflaged against the skin.
▶ It is mainly found in coarse, widely-spaced hair – usually in pubic hair, but also in hair under the arms and on the chest and legs.
▶ Transmission is by contact, usually sexual.

TREATMENT

Insecticide is applied. Shaving is not necessary. Crab lice cause much distress to the sufferer and tend to discourage attendance at **STD (sexually transmitted diseases)** clinics.

THE SCABIES MITE

Scabies is largely a disease of families and young children. The scabies mite differs from the louse in that it does not have a recognisable head, thorax and abdomen.

▶ It has a tortoise-like body with four pairs of legs.

▶ It is about 0.3 mm in size.

▶ It lives in burrows in the outer skin which can be mistaken for the tracks made by a hypodermic needle.

▶ It is usually found in the finger webs, wrist, palms and soles.

▶ Transmission is mainly by body contact which must last for at least 20 minutes.

▶ Cleanliness does not prevent infestation.

▶ A widespread itchy rash appears which is most irritating at night.

▶ If untreated, secondary **sepsis** may occur with boils and impetigo.

TREATMENT

Insecticide lotion is applied to the whole body below the neck; treatment is usually repeated after 24 hours. Calamine lotion may be used to soothe the itch which often lasts after treatment.

Allergic skin conditions

ECZEMA

Eczema (from the Greek 'to boil over') is an itchy and sometimes unsightly skin condition which affects millions of people to some degree. The most common type affecting children is **atopic eczema**. About 1 in 8 of all children will show symptoms at some time, ranging from a mild rash lasting a few months to severe symptoms which persist over years.

▶ It is *not* infectious.

▶ It often starts as an irritating red patch in the creases of the elbows or knees or on the face.

▶ It can spread quickly to surrounding skin which becomes cracked, moist and red.

▶ In severe cases it can blister and weep clear fluid if scratched.

▶ Later, the skin becomes thickened and scaly.

▶ Skin damaged by eczema is more likely to become infected, particularly by a bacterium called **staphylococcus aureus** which produces yellow crusts or pus-filled spots.

CAUSES

There is no single known cause, but certain factors predispose a child to suffer from eczema:

▶ an allergy to: certain foods, e.g. cows' milk; airborne substances like pollen, house dust, scales from animal hair or feathers, or fungus spores;

▶ environmental factors, e.g. humidity or cold weather;

▶ a family history of allergy;

▶ emotional or physical stress.

TREATMENT

In mild cases where the child's life is not disrupted, the following measures are usually advised by the child's GP:

▶ *Avoid irritants:* wear cotton and cotton-mix clothing; avoid wool and synthetics; use an aqueous cream (e.g. E45 or Unguentum Merck) instead of soap; avoid extremes of temperature; avoid acid fruits and vegetables, e.g. tomatoes and citrus fruits.

▶ *Keep skin moisturised:* use unperfumed bath oil.
▶ *Apply steroid creams:* prescribed by the GP, these must be used sparingly as over-use can harm the skin.
▶ *Prevent scratching:* cotton mittens should be worn by small children at night; keep child's nails short.

In severe cases, the GP will refer the child to a skin specialist (**dermatologist**).

IMPETIGO

Impetigo is a highly contagious bacterial infection of the skin; the rash commonly appears on the face but can affect the rest of the body and consists of yellowish crusts on top of a reddened area of skin. The child should not mix with others until the condition is treated. Impetigo is easily spread by contact with infected flannels and towels, so scrupulous attention to hygiene is necessary. Treatment is with antibiotic medicines and creams.

WARTS

Warts are the most common **viral** infection of the skin. They appear as raised lumps on the skin and are quite harmless. Most warts occur in children between the ages of 6 and 12 and disappear without treatment. If they become painful the local hospital's out-patient department will arrange for their removal, usually by freezing with liquid nitrogen (a form of **cryosurgery**).

VERRUCAE

Verrucae (or **plantar warts**) are warts on the sole of the foot, and may hurt because of pressure. They are easily picked up in the warm, moist atmosphere of swimming baths. Treatment is by the application of lotions or by freezing. Tincture of thuja is an effective homeopathic remedy.

MOLLUSCUM CONTAGIOSUM

This is a viral infection which consists of clusters of small whitish-yellow, pearl-like spots on any part of the body. No treatment is necessary as they will disappear within a few weeks or months.

PYTIRIASIS ROSEA

This is an unidentified viral infection which affects mainly school-age children. The rash is scaly, consisting of beige-coloured oval patches which appear on the chest, back and limbs. Sometimes the rash will cause irritation and can be controlled by use of a mild steroid cream.

RINGWORM

This is not due to a worm at all: it is a **fungal** infection, often acquired from an animal. On the body it forms a reddish patch with a ring of small pimples at the edge. Usually it affects the scalp, causing the hair to break and sore bald patches to appear. Treatment is by medicine (griseofulvin), and the hair *does* grow again.

ATHLETE'S FOOT

This is the name for **ringworm** which grows on the skin of the feet. It appears as a pink, flaky rash, particularly between the toes, and is intensely irritating. Treatment is by powder or cream; and the child should not walk barefoot around the house as the condition can easily spread to others.

THREADWORMS

Threadworms (enterobius vermicularis) are small white worms that infest the bowel (see Figures 14.5 and 14.6). People of any age can get threadworms, but they are commonest in children between 5 and 12 years old. They cannot be caught from animals.

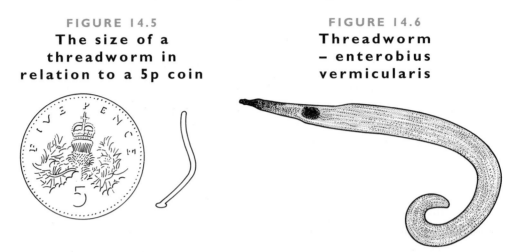

FIGURE 14.5
The size of a threadworm in relation to a 5p coin

FIGURE 14.6
Threadworm – enterobius vermicularis

▶ They are highly contagious, and easily pass from one person to another.
▶ The eggs are usually picked up by the hands and then transferred to the mouth.
▶ The eggs hatch in the small intestine, and the worms migrate downwards to the rectum where they emerge at night.
▶ They cause intense itching: the child will then scratch, eggs will be caught under the nails and the cycle may repeat itself.
▶ Treatment will be prescribed by the doctor, and it is important that the whole family be treated at the same time.
▶ Strict hygiene measures – scrubbing the nails after a bowel movement, the use of separate towels, and daily baths – help to prevent infestation.

TOXOCARIASIS

This is infection from the roundworms which live in the gut of dogs and cats. The eggs of the worm are excreted in the faeces of the animal, and young children may pick them up and transfer them to their mouths. Infection can, occasionally, be serious and lead to epilepsy or blindness. Prevention is through public awareness: all dog and cat owners must regularly worm their pets, and dogs should not be allowed in areas where young children play.

Respiratory disorders

Asthma

Asthma is a condition in which the airways of the lungs become either narrow or completely blocked, impeding normal breathing. However, in asthama, this blockage to the lungs is reversible, either spontaneously or with medication.

What happens to the lungs during an asthma attack
Air reaches the lung by passing through the windpipe (trachea), which divides into large tubes (bronchi), one for each lung. Each bronchus further divides into tubes (bronchioles),

FIGURE 14.7
Using a nebuliser

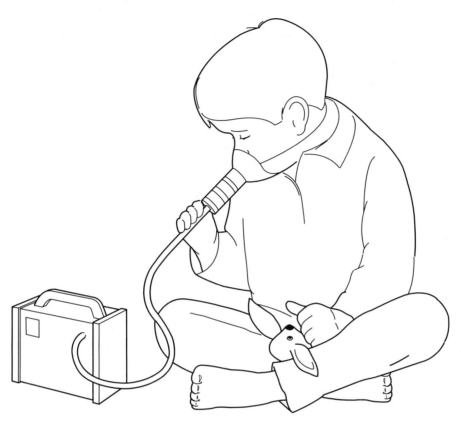

which eventually lead to tiny air sacs (alveoli), from which the air is transferred to the bloodstream, and carbon dioxide from the transferred to the air. Asthma involves only the airways (bronchi and bronchioles not the air sacs. The airways are cleaned by trapping stray particles in a thick mucus which covers the surface of the airways. This mucus is produced by the lung, and is constantly being renewed. The mucus is then either coughed up to the windpipe (trachea) by cilia, tiny hairs on the lining of the airways mucus reaches the throat, it can again be coughed up or, alternatively, swallowed.

Asthma in children

About 1 in 10 children will have an asthma attack (or episode) at some time. In general, children who have mild asthma are more likely to be free of syptoms once they grow up but this is not guaranteed. Some people find that their asthma goes away when they are teenagers but comes back again when they are adults.

Although there is no guarantee that symptoms will go away, they can usually be well controlled. Asthma should never be left untreated in the hope that a child may grow out of it.

Causes of asthma

There is no single cause of asthma, but there are several recognised predisposing factors or **triggers** that can cause an attack. The most common triggers are:

▶ infections, particularly viral respiratory infections, e.g. 'flu, bronchitis and colds	▶ bacterial infections, including sinus infections
▶ allergic rhinitis: inflammation of the lining of the nose, due to an allergic reaction	▶ irritants, such as pollution, cigarette smoke, perfumes, dust, or chemicals
▶ sudden changes in either temperature or humidity, especially exposure to cold air	▶ allergens, for children with allergies, e.g. to house dust mites, animal fur, grass pollen, some foods
▶ emotional upsets, such as stress or excitement, both pleasant and unpleasant	▶ exercise: some children will suffer an attack during moderate or strenuous exercise and will require treatment before sports activities

Generally, the more triggers present, the worse the attack. Typically, a child's first attack will follow one or two days after the onset of a respiratory illness, such as a cold.

Symptoms of asthma

▶ wheezing (some children with asthma do not experience wheezing);
▶ elevated breathing rate (the normal rate is under 25 breaths per minute; over 40 is cause for calling the doctor);
▶ coughing, especially early morning;
▶ longer expiration (breathing out) than inspiration (breathing in);
▶ sweating;
▶ the child may appear very frightened;
▶ the child becomes pale. A darker-skinned child may also appear drained of colour, particularly around the mouth.

Attacks may build over days or occur within seconds. There are two types of asthma:
1 **Acute asthma** (or an asthma attack or episode). This may require medical stabilisation within a hospital setting.
2 **Chronic asthma.** This produces symptoms on a continual basis, and is characterised by persistent, often severe symptoms, requiring regular oral steroid medication.

G U I D E L I N E S

What to do in the event of an acute asthmatic attack

Not all asthma attacks can be prevented. When the child is having an acute attack of wheezing – the difficulty is in breathing out rather than in catching one's breath – he needs a reliever drug (a bronchodilator, usually in a blue inhaler case). Most children will have been shown how to deliver the drug by an aerosol inhaler, a spinhaler or a nebuliser.

- If the attack is the child's first, then call a doctor and the parents.
- Stay calm and reassure the child, who may be very frightened.
- Encourage the child to sit up to increase lung capacity.
- If the child has a reliever inhaler or nebuliser, then supervise him while using the inhaler.
- Never leave the child alone during an attack.
- Try not to let other children crowd around.
- If these measures do not stop the wheezing and the exhaustion caused by the attack, call a doctor. He or she will either give an injection of a broncho-dilator drug or arrange admission to hospital.

FIGURE 14.8

Using an inhaler

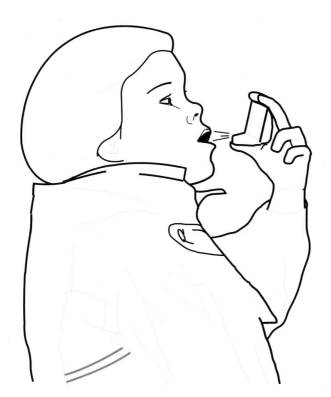

Prevention

- Where possible, avoid likely **triggers** of asthma – see page 404.
- **Preventers:** preventer inhalers are usually brown and contain corticosteroids. They need to be taken regularly every day, even when the child is feeling well; they act by reducing the inflammation and swelling in the airways.

NB Corticosteroid drugs should not be confused with the anabolic steroids taken by athletes to improve their performance.

Croup

This is a condition usually caused by a cold virus. It causes the child's **windpipe** (or **trachea**) to swell, and results in a characteristic barking cough – it sounds like crowing or sea lions barking. The child will feel panic, and may wheeze. Provide a *steamy* atmosphere by:

▶ running a hot bath and directing the steam at the child;

▶ using a **vaporiser** with special vaporizing fluid – available from any chemist.

If the breathing becomes rapidly worse, take the child to hospital for emergency treatment.

Principles of caring for sick babies and children

Small children sometimes cannot explain their symptoms, and display non-specific complaints such as headache, sleeplessness, vomiting or an inability to stand up. Infants have even less certain means of communication, and may simply cry strangely, refuse feeds or become listless and lethargic. In most **infectious** illnesses, there will be **fever**.

Recognising illness in babies

The responsibility of caring for a baby who becomes ill is enormous; it is vital that carers should know the symptoms of illness and when to seek medical aid

Signs and symptoms of illness in babies

Raised temperature: The baby may look flushed or be pale, but will feel hot to the touch (Black babies may look paler than usual and the eyes may lose sparkle); occasionally a high temperature may trigger a seizure (fit) or febrile convulsion.

Diarrhoea: Persistent loose, watery or green stools can quickly dehydrate a baby.

Excessive and persistent crying: If the baby cannot be comforted in the usual way or if the cry is very different from usual cries.

Dry nappies: If his nappies are much drier than usual because he has not passed urine, this may indicate dehydration.

Difficulty with breathing: If breathing becomes laboured or noisy with a cough, the baby may have bronchitis or croup.

Sunken anterior fontanelle: A serious sign of dehydration, possibly after diarrhoea and vomiting.

Loss of appetite: The baby may refuse feeds or take very little; an older baby may only want milk feeds and refuse all solids.

Vomiting: If persistent or projectile in nature and not the more usual possetting (see Chapter 3).

Lethargy or 'floppiness': The baby may appear to lack energy and lack the normal muscle tone.

Persistent coughing: Coughing in spasms lasting more than a few seconds; long spasms often end with vomiting.

Discharge from the ears: Ear infections may not show as a discharge but the baby may pull at his ears and may have a high temperature.

Seizures (also called convulsions or fits): During a seizure a baby either goes stiff or else jerks his arms or legs for a period lasting up to several minutes. His eyes may roll up, he may go blue, may dribble and will be unresponsive to you.

1   Observe the baby carefully and note any changes; record his temperature and take steps
    to reduce a high temperature (see below).
2   Give extra fluids if possible and carry out routine skin care. The baby may want extra
    physical attention or prefer to rest in his cot.

Meningitis

Meningitis is an inflammation of the lining of the brain. It is a very serious illness, but if
it's detected and treated early, most children make a full recovery. The early symptoms of
meningitis such as fever, irritability, restlessness, vomiting and refusing feeds are also
common with colds and 'flu. A baby with meningitis can become seriously ill within
hours. The important signs to look out for in babies are:

▶ fever with cold hands and feet	▶ refusing feeds or being sick
▶ high-pitched, moaning cry or whimpering	▶ being fretful and not liking being picked up
▶ red or purple spots that do not fade under pressure do the 'Glass Test' (see below)	▶ bland and staring expression
	▶ difficult to wake and has no energy
▶ neck retraction with an arched back	

The 'Glass Test': Press the side of a glass firmly against the rash – you will be able to see
if it fades and loses colour under the pressure. If it doesn't change colour, contact a doctor
immediately.

Fever

Known medically as **pyrexia**, a fever is defined as a body temperature above 37°C (see
Table 14.3). The only way to tell if a child has a high fever is to take their temperature
with a **thermometer**. All family first-aid kits should contain a thermometer: either a
plastic strip which is placed on the child's forehead or a clinical thermometer (see
Figure 14.9) which can safely be placed in a child's mouth. Other signs which indicate
fever are:

   ▶ The child may appear 'feverish' – red, hot cheeks, and bright, glittery eyes.
   ▶ The child will usually go off their food.
   ▶ The child will usually appear fretful or restless, or may sleep a lot.

FIGURE 14.9

A clinical thermometer

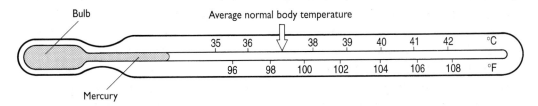

TABLE 14.2
Illness in babies

Condition (and cause)	Signs and symptoms	Role of the carer
Colic	This occurs in the first 12 weeks. It causes sharp, spasmodic pain in the stomach, and is often at its worst in the late evening. Symptoms include inconsolable high-pitched crying, drawing her legs up to her chest, and growing red in the face.	Try to stay calm! Gently massage her abdomen in a clockwise direction, using the tips of your middle fingers. Sucrose solution (3 × 5 ml teaspoons of sugar in a cup of boiling water and left to cool) is said to have a mild pain-killing effect on small babies. Dribble 2 ml of this solution into the corner of the baby's mouth twice a day. If the problem persists, contact the doctor.
Diarrhoea	Frequent loose or watery stools. Can be very serious in young babies, especially when combined with vomiting, as it can lead to severe dehydration.	Give frequent small drinks of cooled, boiled water containing glucose and salt or a made-up sachet of rehydration fluid. If the baby is unable to take the fluid orally, she must be taken to hospital urgently and fed intravenously, by a 'drip'. If anal area becomes sore, treat with a barrier cream.
Gastro-enteritis (virus or bacteria)	The baby may vomit and usually has diarrhoea as well; often has a raised temperature and loss of appetite. May show signs of abdominal pain i.e. drawing up of legs to chest and crying.	Reassure baby. Observe strict hygiene rules. Watch out for signs of dehydration. Offer frequent small amounts of fluid, and possibly rehydration salts.
Neonatal cold injury – or hypothermia	The baby is cold to the touch. Face may be pale or flushed. Lethargic, runny nose, swollen hands and feet. Pre-term infants and babies under 4 months are at particular risk.	Prevention Warm *slowly* by covering with several light layers of blankets and by cuddling. No direct heat. Offer feeds high in sugar and seek medical help urgently.
Reflux	Also known as gastro-intestinal reflux (GIR) or gastro-oesophageal reflux (GOR). The opening to the stomach is not yet efficient enough to allow a large liquid feed through. Symptoms include grizzly crying and excessive **possetting** after feeds.	Try feeding the baby in a more upright position and bring up wind by gently rubbing her back. After feeding leave the baby in a semi-sitting position. Some doctors prescribe a paediatric reflux suppressant or antacid mixture to be given before the feed.
Tonsillitis (virus or bacteria)	Very sore throat, which looks bright red. There is usually fever and the baby will show signs of distress from pain on swallowing and general aches and pains. May vomit.	Encourage plenty of fluids – older babies may have ice lollies to suck. Give pain relief, e.g. paracetamol. Seek medical aid if no improvement and if fever persists.
Cough (usually virus)	Often follows on from a cold; may be a symptom of other illness, e.g. m^easles.	Keep air moist. Check the baby has not inhaled an object. Give medicine if prescribed.

Condition (and cause)	Signs and symptoms	Role of the carer
Croup (virus)	Croup is an infection of the voice box or larynx, which becomes narrowed and inflamed. Barking cough (like sea lions), noisy breathing, distressed; usually occurs at night.	If severe, seek medical help. Reassure her and sit her up. Keep calm and reassure the baby. Inhaling steam may also benefit some babies. You can produce steam by boiling a kettle, running the hot taps in the bathroom, using a room humidifier or putting wet towels over the radiator. If using steam, take care to avoid scalding.
Bronchiolitis (virus)	A harsh dry cough which later becomes wet and chesty; runny nose, raised temperature, wheeze, breathing problems, poor feeding or vomiting. May develop a blue tinge around the lips and on the fingernails (known as cyanosis).	Observe closely. Seek medical help if condition worsens. Increase fluids. Give small regular feeds. Give prescribed medicine. Comfort and reassure.
Febrile convulsions (high temperature)	Convulsions caused by a high temperature (over 39 degrees centigrade, 102 degrees fahrenheit) or fever are called febrile convulsions. Baby will become rigid, then the body may twitch and jerk for one or two minutes.	Try not to panic. Move potentially harmful objects out of the way and place the baby in the recovery position. Loosen clothing. Call doctor. Give tepid sponging. Comfort and reassure.
Otitis media (virus or bacteria)	Will appear unwell; may have raised temperature. May vomit, may cry with pain. May have discharge from ear.	Take to doctor, give antibiotics and analgesics (or painkillers). Increase fluids; comfort and reassure.
Conjunctivitis (virus or bacteria)	Inflammation of the thin, delicate membrane that covers the eyeball and forms the lining of the eyelids. Symptoms include a painful red eye, with watering and sometimes sticky pus.	Take to doctor who may prescribe antibiotic eye drops or ointment. Bathe a sticky eye gently with cool boiled water and clean cotton wool swabs. Always bathe the eye from the inside corner to the outside to avoid spreading infection.
Common cold (coryza) (virus)	Runny nose, sneeze; tiny babies may have breathing problem.	Keep nose clear. Give small frequent feeds. Nasal drops if prescribed.
Meningitis (virus or bacteria)	Raised temperature, may have a blotchy rash. May refuse feeds, have a stiff neck, have a seizure. Bulging fontanelles, may have a shrill, high-pitched cry.	Seek medical help urgently. Reduce temperature. Reassure.

TABLE 14.3
A temperature conversion chart

FAHRENHEIT	CENTIGRADE
95	35.0
96	35.6
97	36.1
98	36.7
98.4	37.0 = normal
99	37.2
100	37.8
101	38.3
102	38.9
103	39.4
104	40.0
105	40.6
106	41.1

Whatever the **cause** of the high temperature, it is important to try to reduce it, as there is always the risk of a fever leading to **convulsions** or **fits**.

Bringing down a high temperature/reducing a fever

▶ Offer cooled boiled water and encourage the child to drink as much water as possible. Avoid fizzy or sweet drinks in case they make him sick.

▶ Sponge him down, using tepid water (see below) – or give him a cool bath.

▶ Give him the correct dose of paracetamol syrup. Follow the instructions on the bottle carefully.★

▶ Try to cool the air in the child's room – use an electric fan or open the window.

▶ Reassure the child who may be very frightened. Remain calm yourself and try to stop the child crying as this will tend to push the temperature higher still.

▶ If the temperature will not come down, then call the doctor.

NB Always consult a doctor if a high fever is accompanied by symptoms such as severe headache with stiff neck, abdominal pain or pain when passing urine.

★Early years workers are advised that medicines should not be given unless the written permission of the parent or next-of-kin is obtained.

G U I D E L I N E S

Tepid sponging to reduce a temperature

▶ **Make sure the air in the room is comfortably warm – not hot, cold or draughty.**

▶ **Lay the child on a towel on your knee or on the bed and gently remove her clothes; reassure her by talking gently.**

▶ **Sponge her body, limbs and face with tepid or lukewarm water – not**

TABLE 14.4
When to call a doctor

If you think the child's life is in danger, dial 999 if you are in the UK, ask for an amublance urgently and explain the situation.

Contact the family doctor (GP) if the child has any of the following symptoms. If the doctor cannot reach you quickly, take the child to accident and emergency department of the nearest hospital:

* Has a temperature of 38.6 deg C (101.4 deg F) which is not lowered by measures to reduce **fever**, or a temperature over 37.8 deg.C (100 deg F) for more than one day.	* Has **convulsions**, or is limp and floppy.
* Has severe or persistent **vomiting** and/or **diarrhoea**, seems dehydrated or has projectile vomiting.	* **Cannon be woken**, is unusually drowsy or may be losing consciousness.
* Has symptoms of **meningitis**.	* Has **croup** symptoms.
* Is pale, listless, and **does not respond** to usual stimulation.	* **Cries or screams** inconsolably and may have severe pain.
* Has bulging **fontanelle** (soft spot on top of head) when not crying.	* Appears to have severe abdominal pain, with symptoms of **shock**.
* **Refuses** two successive feeds.	* Develops **purple-red rash** anywhere on body.
* Passes bowel motions (stools) containing blood.	* Has **jaundice**.
* Has a suspected **ear infection**.	* Has been **injured**, e.g. by a burn which blisters and covers more than 10% of the body surface.
* Has inhaled something, such as a peanut, into the air passages and may be **choking**.	* Has swallowed a **poisonous** substance, or an object, e.g. a safety pin or button.
* Has bright pink cheeks and swollen hands and feet (could be due to **hypothermia**).	* Has difficulty in **breathing**.

cold; as the water evaporates from the skin, it absorbs heat from the blood and so cools the system.

▶ As the child cools down, pat her skin dry with a soft towel and dress her only in a nappy or pants; cover her with a light cotton sheet.

▶ Keep checking her condition to make sure that she does not become cold or shivery; if she does become cold, put more light covers over her.

▶ If the temperature rises again, repeat sponging every 10 minutes.

Acute illness

An **acute illness** is one that occurs *suddenly*, and often without warning, and it is usually of short duration. Examples are:

- ▶ gastro-enteritis
- ▶ otitis media (inflammation of the middle ear)
- ▶ appendicitis
- ▶ tonsillitis
- ▶ an acute asthmatic attack.

SYMPTOMS OF ACUTE ILLNESS IN A CHILD

Signs of such illness in a child include:

- ▶ **anorexia** or loss of appetite;
- ▶ lethargy or listlessness;
- ▶ a lack of interest in play;
- ▶ irritability and fretfulness;
- ▶ unusual crying or screaming bouts;
- ▶ **pallor** – a black child may have a paler area around the lips, and the **conjunctiva** may be pale pink instead of red;
- ▶ diarrhoea and vomiting;
- ▶ pyrexia (fever);
- ▶ abdominal pain – babies with **colic** or abdominal pains will draw their knees up to their chest in an instinctive effort to relieve the pain;
- ▶ **dehydration** – any illness involving fever or loss of fluid through vomiting or diarrhoea may result in dehydration; the mouth and tongue become dry and parched, and cracks may appear on the lips. (The first sign in a baby is a sunken **anterior fontanelle** – see p. 535)

(For specific signs and symptoms of diseases, see Table 14.2 again.)

NB: The darker a child's skin colour, the more that pimples or a rash will show merely as raised areas. Only when the skin is affected by scratching will the spots become noticeably *red*.

Practical hints on nursing sick children at home

Wherever possible, children should stay at home when ill, within the secure environment of their family and surroundings. The child will want their primary carer available at all times. The parents may need advice on how to care for their child, and this is provided by the family GP and primary health-care team – some health authorities have specialist paediatric nursing visiting services.

BEDREST

Children usually dislike being confined to bed and will only stay there if feeling very unwell. Making a bed on a settee in the main living room will save the carer the expense of extra heating and tiring trips up and down stairs; the child will also feel more included in family life and so feel less isolated.

INFECTION

If the illness is infectious, advice may be needed on how it spreads; and visits from friends and relatives may have to be reduced. The most infectious time is during the incubation period, but the dangers of infecting others remain until the main signs and symptoms – e.g. a rash – have disappeared. A child attending nursery or school will usually be kept at home until the GP says that they are clear of infection. If the child has bouts of vomiting, pillows should be protected and a container should be kept close to the bed, emptied and rinsed with an antiseptic/disinfectant – e.g. Savlon – after use. Wet or soiled bed-linen should be changed to prevent discomfort, and paper tissues which can be disposed of either by burning or by sealing in disposal bags are useful for minor accidents. A plastic mattress cover is also useful since an ill child's behaviour may result in bed-wetting (enuresis).

OBSERVATION OF TEMPERATURE AND PULSE
TAKING THE TEMPERATURE

FIGURE 14.10

A poster for the parent with a child who has a temperature

Taking a child's temperature

All family first aid kits should contain a thermometer. This may be:

▶ **a clinical thermometer:** a glass tube with a bulb at one end containing mercury. This tube is marked with gradations of temperature in degrees Centigrade and Fahrenheit. When the bulb end is placed under the child's armpit or in the groin fold, the mercury will expand and so move up the tube until the temperature of the child's body is reached.

1 Check that the silvery column of mercury is shaken down to 35 degrees centigrade.
2 Place the bulb end of the thermometer in the baby's armpit, holding his arm close to his side for two minutes. For an older child, sit him on your lap, show him the thermometer and explain what you are doing.
3 Remove the thermometer, and holding it horizontally and in a good light, read off the

temperature measured by the level of the mercury. Record the time and the temperature reading.

4   After use, wash the thermometer in tepid water, and shake the column of mercury down again to 35 degrees Centigrade. Dry carefully and replace in case.

NB A clinical thermometer should never be placed in a baby's mouth, because of the danger of biting and breaking the glass.

▶ **Digital thermometer:** this is battery-operated and consists of a narrow probe with a tip sensitive to temperature. It is easy to read via a display panel and unbreakable:

1   Place the narrow tip of the thermometer under the child's arm as described above.
2   Read the temperature when it stops rising; some models beep when this point is reached.

▶ **Plastic fever strip:** this is a rectangular strip of thin plastic which contains temperature sensitive crystals that change colour according to the temperature measured. It is not as accurate as the other thermometers but is a useful check.

1   Hold the plastic strip firmly against the child's forehead for about 30 seconds.
2   Record the temperature revealed by the colour change.

TAKING THE PULSE

For a baby: place your middle and third finger over the brachial artery on the inside of the upper arm and record the number of beats for 1 minute.

For an older child:

Place your middle and third finger over the **radial artery** (see Figure 14.11) and record the number of beats for 1 minute.

NB: pulse rates vary with age, physical activity and emotional state. A child's pulse will normally be around 120 beats per minute, decreasing to around 90 at 14 years.

NUTRITION

Children who are ill often have poor **appetites**. A few days without food will not harm the child, but **fluid intake** should be increased as a general rule.

▶ Provide a covered jug of fruit juice or water; any fluid is acceptable according to the child's tastes – e.g. milk, meaty drinks or soups.
NB: if the child has **mumps**, do not give fruit drinks because the acid causes pain to the tender **parotid glands**; if the child has diarrhoea or an upset stomach, do not offer milk.

▶ 'Bendy' straws or feeding beakers are useful.

▶ Drinks should be offered at frequent intervals to prevent dehydration – the child will *not* necessarily *request* drinks.

▶ Try to make *food* as attractive as possible; don't put too much on the plate at once, and remember that weak patients often cope better with foods that do not require too much chewing, e.g. egg custard, milk pudding, thick soups, chicken and ice cream.

HYGIENE

All children benefit from having a **routine**, and this need not be drastically altered during illness.

FIGURE 14.11
Taking the pulse in an older child

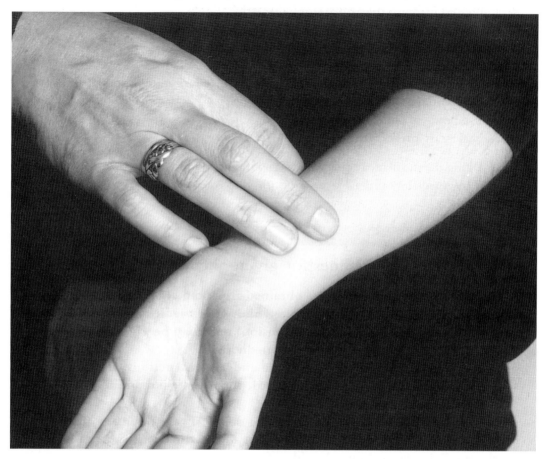

- ▶ The sick room should be well-ventilated and uncluttered. Open a window to prevent stuffiness, but protect the child from draughts.
- ▶ Provide a potty to avoid trips to the lavatory.
- ▶ Protect the mattress with a plastic sheet.
- ▶ A daily bath is important, but during the acute phase, this can be done in the form of an all-over wash in bed.
- ▶ Brush the child's hair daily.
- ▶ Clean teeth after meals – apply Vaseline to sore, cracked lips.
- ▶ Crisp, clean sheets are very soothing – try to change sheets as often as you can.
- ▶ Keep the child's nails short and clean, and prevent the scratching of any spots.
- ▶ Dress the child in cool, cotton clothing.

MEDICINES
Every home should have a properly stocked medicine cabinet, preferably locked and always out of reach of children. The cabinet should contain:
- ▶ a **pain reliever** such as paracetamol syrup. The different doses for children of different ages should be on the bottles.
- ▶ a **hot-water bottle** – when wrapped in a towel it can relieve the pain of an aching abdomen or bruised joint;
- ▶ a **kaolin mixture** for the relief of simple diarrhoea;

- **zinc** and **castor oil** cream – for nappy rashes;
- **calamine** lotion – for itchy spots and rashes;
- a glass and mercury **thermometer**/fever strip;
- a **teething ring** (if appropriate);
- a **measuring spoon** or **glass** for liquid medicines;
- a small packet of **cotton wool**;
- a pack of assorted fabric **plasters**, and one of **hypo-allergenic plasters**;
- **crepe bandages** and **conforming bandages**;
- a small bottle of liquid **antiseptic**;
- any necessary **prescription drugs**.

Before stocking the medicine cabinet, discard all the half-empty, improperly labelled bottles and any medicines that are over 6 months old. Keep down costs by buying non-branded products.

G U I D E L I N E S

Guidelines for giving medicine

Written permission must always be obtained from the child's parent or next-of-kin before you give any medicine to the child. Oral medicine is usually dispensed in liquid form (elixir or suspension) and may be given to a baby by spoon or dropper. When giving a child medicine:

- **Always check the label on the bottle and the instructions. If it has been prescribed by the doctor, check that it is for the child and follow the instructions exactly.**
- **Shake the bottle before measuring the dose. Always pour any medicine bottle with the label uppermost so that the instructions remain legible if the medicine runs down the side of the bottle.**
- **Put a bib on a baby and have some baby wipes or a flannel close at hand to wipe clean. Cradle the baby as if bottle-feeding, with his head tilted back.**
- **Use a 5 ml medicine spoon to measure the dose; if using a dropper, measure the dose in a 5 ml spoon and then suck it up with the dropper.**
- **Spoon or squeeze the dose into the child's mouth.**
- **If tablets or capsules are prescribed, these may be crushed between two spoons and given in fruit juice, jam or honey.**
- **Antibiotics may be prescribed for any infection, or to prevent secondary infections (these sometimes cause diarrhoea). NB: some antibiotics may need to be kept in the fridge.**
- **When a course of antibiotics is prescribed, it is vital that all the tablets/medicines be given, even if the child makes a speedy recovery.**

CONVALESCENCE

After an illness, children will need a period of **convalescence** to recover their strength and readjust to their daily routine. Most children **regress** when unwell, and therefore activities suitable for a younger-aged child should be provided. Some useful activities are:

▶ a favourite jigsaw, placed on a large tray or bed-table;

▶ drawing and painting (protect bedclothes first);

▶ a 'surprise' box containing previously discarded toys, pictures, paper-glue and a scrapbook, books, cut-out kits and scissors;

▶ reading stories aloud;

▶ watching TV;

▶ singing and listening to audio tapes.

PREPARING FOR HOSPITALISATION

Every year 1 in 4 children under 5 years old goes into hospital and over 2 million children are seen in accident and emergency units. How a child reacts to a hospital visit depends on:

▶ their age;

▶ their personality;

▶ the reason for hospitalisation;

▶ their previous experience of hospitals;

▶ the tests and treatment needed;

▶ the attitude and manner of the doctors, nurses and other staff;

▶ the ambience of the ward;

▶ the carer's own anxieties and perceived ability to cope with what is often a very stressful situation.

When a child has to be admitted to hospital either for medical treatment or for a surgical operation, it is best, if at all possible, to prepare them in advance. Often, the experience is just as stressful for the parents too, particularly if they have their own childhood memories of hospitalisation. The majority of children enjoy their hospital stay, but adverse reactions can be avoided in younger children by careful preparation and complete honesty in all information given.

G U I D E L I N E S

Hospitalisation for early childhood workers

▶ **If possible, arrange to visit the ward a few days before admission – most wards welcome such visits and are happy to talk with carers. (Many fears are based on ignorance – fear of the unknown.)**

▶ **Encourage children to talk about their feelings so that you know how to help them.**

▶ **Always be honest – never say that something will not hurt if it might, and only tell them that you will be there all the time if that is your plan.**

▶ **Keep explanations simple – reading a book about a child going to hospital may help allay fears.**

▶ **If they are to have an operation, explain that they will have a 'special hospital sleep' which will stop them from feeling any pain.**

▶ **Do not let the child see your own worry, as this will make him feel frightened.**
▶ **Play hospital games using toys to help the child act out any fears.**
▶ **Try to be involved in the child's care as fully as possible.**
▶ **Take the child's favourite toy or 'comforter' as a link with home – the child could even help to pack their case.**
▶ **Tell the ward staff about the child's eating and sleeping patterns and preferences and any special words that may be used for the toilet etc.**

If the child is of school age, the hospital school will provide educational activities, and play specialists/nursery nurses/teachers will provide play activities for younger children.

ISOLATION
Some conditions – e.g. leukaemia – result in damage to the child's **immune system**, and hospital care here may involve **reverse barrier nursing**. This technique provides the child with protection from those people who have regular contact:
▶ A separate cubicle is used.
▶ Gowns and masks must be worn by any person in contact with the child
▶ Gloves and theatre cups may be worn during certain procedures.
▶ Items – e.g. toys and clothes – cannot be freely taken in or out.

Children in isolation need a parent or carer to stay with them to an even greater extent than do those on an open ward because of the strain of loneliness or boredom; and parents in turn need support from friends and relatives as they are having to cope with many stressful events: the anxiety over their child's illness and treatment, the unnaturalness of being confined with their child, the lack of privacy because of the need for continuous observation by nursing staff. Some hospitals provide a parent's room where they can go and have a cup of tea and share problems with others in similar situations.

Chronic illness
Strauss (1984) states that **chronic illness** has the following characteristics:
▶ It is permanent.
▶ It leaves residual disability.
▶ It is non-reversible.
▶ It requires special training of the patient for rehabilitation.
▶ It is likely to require a long period of supervision, observation and care.

Chronic disorders are usually contrasted with **acute** ones (i.e. those of sudden onset and of short duration). A child with a chronic illness shows little change in symptoms from day to day and may still be able – though possibly with some difficulty – to carry out normal daily activities. The disease process is **continuous** with progressive deterioration, sometimes in spite of treatment. The child may experience an acute **exacerbation** (flare-up) of symptoms.
Some examples of chronic illness in children are:
▶ juvenile rheumatoid arthritis;
▶ chronic renal failure;
▶ **psoriasis** – skin disorder;
▶ atopic eczema;
▶ juvenile diabetes mellitus;

▶ sickle-cell disease (sickle-cell-anaemia);

▶ thalassaemia major (an inherited blood disorder).

Hugh Jolly defined the needs of children with chronic illness as:

▶ *medical* – diagnostic tests, the use of drugs etc.;

▶ *surgical* – treatment by direct physical intervention, organ transplant etc.;

▶ *involving nursing* – having their physical and emotional needs looked after;

▶ *social* – interacting with others;

▶ *emotional* – love, security, belongingness;

▶ *intellectual* – stimulation, play, education.

Long-term illness may mean that the child's ability to exercise freedom of choice in daily activities is curtailed. Frequent periods of hospitalisation disrupt family and social life and impose strain on all members of the family; siblings often resent the extra attention given to the sick child, and the parents themselves may also need financial support. Social workers based at hospitals will give advice on any benefits and can provide a **counselling service**. They may also be able to put parents in touch with an organisation for the parents of children with similar conditions.

Play and the sick child

'Play is essential to the intellectual, social and emotional development of children. It can also help them resolve stressful situations like admission to hospital where they may have to undergo painful procedures and suffer separation from family and friends.'

Department of Health, 1991

Most children's units in hospitals have a separate playroom with trained staff who provide the sick child with an opportunity for a choice of play activities.

GUIDELINES

Play for sick children

▶ **The sick child usually regresses and may prefer to play with toys intended for a younger-age child.**

▶ **The child will tire quickly, so provide a range of activities within the child's capacity from which they can choose.**
Children who are immobile (e.g. in orthopaedic traction) will need playing with; parents will welcome ideas on ways of amusing their child.

▶ **Toys and activities will need to be changed frequently.**

▶ **Big and complicated toys tire a child more quickly than small and simple toys which can be easily changed.**

▶ **Supply a good steady surface, such as a tray, for a child confined to bed or cot.**

▶ **The value of any toys used is quickly lost if they are lying around, neglected or broken. Always tidy away toys, and maintain them regularly.**

▶ **A variety of craft and play materials, including real and miniature medical equipment for the child in hospital, should be available.**

Terminal illness

Children with **cancer** – the most common life-threatening disease – number 1 in 600. **Chemotherapy** (treatment by drugs) and **radiotherapy** (treatment by deep X-rays) have altered the course of the disease and can sometimes effect a complete cure.

WHAT IS CANCER?

Cancer is the term applied to a group of **neoplastic** (literally meaning 'new growth') diseases in which normal body cells are changed into **malignant** ones. (See Table 14.5.) Normally, the cells of tissues are regularly replaced by new growth which stops when the old cells have been replaced. In cancer, this cell growth is **unregulated**: the cells continue to grow even after the repair of damaged tissue is complete. The malignant cells multiply and invade neighbouring tissues, thereby destroying the normal cells and taking their place. If the **lymphatic cells** are invaded, the malignant cells are carried away in the lymph until their progress is halted by the filtering effect of the **lymph glands**. Here, they may be deposited and cause a **secondary** tumour (also called a **metastasis**).

TABLE 14.5
Types of cancer in children

NAME	SITE
Leukaemia	In blood cells
Cancer of the CNS (Central Nervous System)	Brain
Lymphoma	Lymph
Neuroblastoma	Usually in abdomen – in sympathetic nervous system
Rhabdomyosarcoma	Very malignant – found in soft tissue, muscles
Wilm's Tumour	Kidneys
Osteogenic sarcoma	Bone
Retinoblastoma	Congenital – in one or both eyes

Warning signs of cancer in children are:
- a *marked* change in bowel or bladder habits;
- nausea and vomiting for no apparent cause;
- a bloody discharge of any kind, and a failure to stop bleeding in the usual time;
- a swelling, lump or mass anywhere in the body;
- any change in the size or appearance of moles or birthmarks;
- unexplained stumbling;
- a generally run-down condition;
- unexplained pain or persistent crying in an infant or child.

The most common form of childhood cancer is **leukaemia**. In leukaemia, abnormally growing white blood cells are scattered throughout the **bone marrow** rather than grouped into a single tumour. The age of onset is most likely around 5 years. Symptoms include:
- bleeding from the gums – due to an insufficient production of platelet cells needed to stop bleeding;
- headache – due to anaemia;
- epistaxis – nosebleeds;
- enlarged lymph nodes – in the neck, armpit and groin;
- anaemia – causing tiredness, breathlessness on exertion, and pallor;

- bone and joint pain – due to abnormality of the bone marrow;
- frequent bruising – due to reduced platelet production;
- infections – the immature white cells are unable to resist infections, e.g. chest or throat infections, **herpes zoster** or skin infections.

DIAGNOSIS
The diagnosis of acute leukaemia is based on a **bone marrow biopsy** that confirms an abnormal number of immature white blood cells (**blasts**).

TREATMENT
Treatment is by:
- blood and platelet transfusions;
- anti-cancer drugs;
- radiotherapy;
- bone marrow transplantation;
- protective isolation nursing (reverse barrier nursing).

Of those children with the commonest form of leukaemia, 75% are well again five years after diagnosis.

SIDE-EFFECTS OF CANCER TREATMENT
Some anti-cancer treatments have distressing side-effects:
- *Sudden hair loss:* Wigs are provided for children who lose their hair during treatment, but they should not be forced to wear them if it makes them feel uncomfortable.
- *Nausea and vomiting:* the child will need much support to cope with these acute symptoms during treatment.
- *A change in body shape:* some cortico-steroid drugs cause the young patient to develop a characteristic 'moon face' and the build-up of fatty tissue.

It is difficult for parents to understand the benefits of a treatment which causes such distressing side-effects when they are grieving and trying to adjust to the diagnosis of the illness: the treatment can seem more unpleasant than the effects of the illness it is trying to fight.

SUPPORT FOR THE CHILD AND FAMILY
Within the hospital there are many professionals who can offer help and support for the child and family going through the trauma of terminal illness:
- nurses;
- doctors;
- social workers;
- play therapists – they may hold the Diploma in Nursery Nursing, the Hospital Play Specialist Board Certificate, or a psychotherapy qualification or other child-care qualification;
- bereavement counsellors;
- representives of different religious bodies.

In the community can be found:
- Macmillan nurses – trained district nurses who specialise in visiting people with terminal illness;
- the primary health care team – the GP, district nurse, health visitor, practice nurse.

Voluntary support agencies
ACTION FOR SICK CHILDREN

Action for Sick Children (formerly NAWCH – National Association for the Welfare of Children in Hospital) offers:

▶ *family support* – through a national parent advice service and family information booklets;

▶ *information and research* – by publishing and disseminating standard-setting reviews on child health issues such as mental health care, adolescents and the needs of black and minority ethnic children;

▶ *campaigns* – by working at national and local levels to influence policy to improve the standards of health care for all children.

DIAL-A-DREAM

This charity was set up to allow children with life-threatening and debilitating illnesses to fulfil their aspirations by making a dream come true. A dream can help them to regain the will to say 'Let me live another day' – the charity's motto – and give them the strength to face further treatment or hospitalization. Dial-a-dream has organised all sorts of dreams, from meeting the child's favourite celebrity to trips abroad.

THE COMPASSIONATE FRIENDS

This is a nation-wide organisation of bereaved parents who have themselves experienced heartbreak, loneliness and isolation, and who seek to help other bereaved parents.

CRUSE – BEREAVEMENT CARE

This is a national charity which exists to help all who are bereaved. It offers counselling, advice and information on practical matters, and opportunities for contact with others. Cruse has local branches throughout the UK.

THE CHILD BEREAVEMENT TRUST

This Trust was formed in 1994 to promote support and counselling for bereaved families. It focuses particularly on providing training for health-care professional in order that bereaved families can obtain the best possible help from their carers.

Child health surveillance

Surveillance is defined as close supervision or observations, and its primary purpose is to detect any abnormality in development so that the child can be offered treatment. For example, early detection of a hearing impairment gives the young child a better chance of receiving appropriate treatment/specialist education.

THE INVERSE CARE LAW

The families who are most in need of child health surveillance are often those who are *least* likely to make use of the services provided. Although children in the UK today enjoy better health than at any other time, the provisions of a National Health Service have not led to **equality** of health experience. The following might be seen as **priority groups** by health visitors and the primary health-care team when organising caseloads and targeting resources:

▶ very young or unsupported parents, particularly those with their first baby;

▶ parents thought to be at particular risk of abusing their children;

▶ parents who are socially isolated, due to mental-health problems or linguistic or cultural barriers;

- families living in poor housing, including Bed and Breakfast accommodation or housing where there is overcrowding;
- parents with low self-esteem or a lack of confidence;
- parents with unrealistic expectations about the child, or with a poor understanding of the child's needs;
- parents/children suffering significant bereavement (including as a result of a recent divorce);
- previous SIDS (sudden infant death syndrome) in the family.

The health care of such families is difficult and often involves a working partnership with other community services, such as social-service departments or housing departments.

EMPOWERMENT

The aim of health promotion is not to change the parents but to enable them to develop as individuals, to increase their confidence and their own skills in child-rearing, and to enable them to make appropriate decisions about their children's health.

Primary prevention

Good nutrition and the prevention of dental caries are two areas of **primary prevention** which are discussed in Chapter 14 and Chapter 15. The prevention of childhood accidents is discussed in Chapter 9.

Immunisation

In the past 10 years there has been a dramatic reduction in the incidence of common childhood illnesses, due to:

- greater public awareness of the availability of immunisation;
- the introduction of two major new vaccines: MMR and Hib;
- a government policy which has led to national strategies on immunisation and better uptake.

Immunisation schedules vary very slightly between different health districts, but the schedule currently recommended by the Department of Health is shown in Table 14.4.

THE RANGE AND PURPOSE OF IMMUNISATION PROGRAMMES

Immunisations are carried out in child health clinics. The doctor will check that the child has had the relevant immunisations and will discuss any fears the parents may have about particular vaccines. No vaccine is completely risk-free, and parents are asked to sign a **consent form** prior to immunisations being given. Immunisations are only given if the child is well, and may be postponed if the child has had a reaction to any previous immunisation or if the child is taking any medication which might interfere with their ability to fight infection.

The effects of the disease are usually far worse than any side-effects of a vaccine.

THE HIB VACCINE

From 1992 an immunisation against **haemophilus influenzae type b (Hib)** has been offered to all children under 4 years old. Hib is a bacterium which causes a range of illnesses:

- meningitis (inflammation of the **meninges** surrounding the brain;
- epiglottitis – a severe form of croup;

> ▶ septicaemia (blood poisoning);
> ▶ septic arthritis and osteomyelitis (infections in bones and joints);
> ▶ pneumonia.

Children under 4 years are most at risk, with the peak incidence of Hib infection being among babies of 10–11 months. The Hib bacteria normally live in the nose and throat, and are spread in the same way as coughs and colds (i.e. by droplet/airborne).

NB: the Hib vaccine does not protect against other types of meningitis (meningococcal, pneumococcal or viral) or against viral infections such as 'flu.

THE MMR (MEASLES, MUMPS AND RUBELLA) VACCINE

This combined injection replaced the measles vaccine and has reduced the serious complications which often follow an attack of these diseases in childhood. Mumps is often thought to be a mild illness but it is the most common cause of viral meningitis in children, and can cause permanent deafness.

Most children are perfectly well after having the MMR vaccine. However, it is quite common for children to develop a mild fever and a rash, a week to 10 days later, which usually only lasts two to three days. A few children get swollen faces or a mild form of mumps about three weeks after immunisation. Any swelling will gradually go down, however, and none of these reactions are **infectious**. Serious reactions to the MMR vaccine (such as fever or encephalitis) are extremely rare and are far more likely to occur as a result of having the diseases themselves.

Secondary prevention – child health surveillance

All parents are issued with a Personal Child Health Record which enables them to keep a record of their child's development. This is completed by doctors, health visitors and parents, and is a useful source of information if the child is admitted to hospital or is taken ill when the family are away from home.

The importance of early detection

Parents will want to know about their child's problems as soon as possible: it is easier to come to terms with a serious problem in a young baby than in an older child. Health professionals should always take the parent's worries seriously and never assume that parents are fussy, neurotic or over-anxious. Early childhood workers are usually very astute in recognising abnormalities in development because of their experience with a wide variety of children.

Development is usually reviewed under the following headings:

> ▶ *gross motor skills:* sitting, standing, walking, running;
> ▶ *fine motor skills:* handling toys, stacking bricks, doing up buttons and tying shoelaces (gross manipulative and fine manipulative skills).
> ▶ *speech and language* – including hearing;
> ▶ *social behaviour.*

Early detection is important:

> ▶ Early treatment may reduce or even avoid permanent damage in some conditions.
> ▶ An early diagnosis may allow **genetic counselling** and so avoid the birth of another child with a disabling condition.

The immunisation schedules

Birth	BCG	to those in high-risk groups – i.e. likely to be in close contact with a case of tuberculosis
8 weeks	Diphtheria Tetanus Pertussis Hib Polio	Given as a single injection Haemophilus influenza type b Given orally
12 weeks	Diphtheria Tetanus Pertussis Hib Polio	Given as a single injection Given in another site Given orally
16 weeks	Diphtheria Tetanus Pertussis Hib Polio	Given as a single injection Given in another site Given orally
12–18 months	Measles Mumps Rubella	MMR – given as a single injection
4–5 years	Diphtheria Tetanus Polio	Given as a single injection Given orally
10–14 years	Rubella BCG	Given to girls if not already received MMR If tuberculin-negative
15–18 years	Diphtheria Tetanus Polio	Booster, given as a single injection Booster, given orally

Screening
The aim of a screening programme is to examine all children at risk from a certain condition; the term **screening** refers to the examination of apparently healthy children to distinguish those who probably have a condition from those who probably do not. Hearing defects are often detected in this way at one of the **routine** checks carried out at the Child Surveillance Clinic.

NEONATAL EXAMINATION
All babies are examined as soon as possible after birth – see Chapter 2.

THE 6-TO-8 WEEK CHECK

This check usually takes place in the child health clinic. The doctor will enquire about any parental concerns:

- feeding;
- sleeping;
- bowel actions;
- micturition: the act of passing urine.

OBSERVATION

While the parent is undressing the baby for examination, the doctor will look out for:

- the responsiveness of the baby – smiles, eye contact, attentiveness to parent's voice etc.
- any difficulties the parent has with holding the baby – e.g. a depressed mother will lack visual attention and may not give a good supporting hold;
- jaundice, anaemia.

MEASUREMENT

- The baby is weighed naked and the weight plotted on the **growth chart** (see Figure 14.13).
- The head circumference is measured and plotted on the growth chart.

EXAMINATION

This examination follows the lines of the examination at birth (see p. 70):

- The general appearance of the baby will give an indication of whether the child is well nourished.
- The eyes are inspected using a light – the baby will turn their head and follow a small light beam; an **ophthalmoscope** is used to check for a **cataract**.
- The heart is **auscultated**, i.e. listened to with a **stethoscope**, to exclude any **congenital defect**.
- The hips are manipulated, again to exclude the presence of congenital dislocation of the hips.
- The baby is placed prone and will turn her head to one side; hands are held with the thumbs inwards and the fingers wrapped around them.
- The posterior fontanelle is usually closed by now; the anterior fontanelle does not close until around 18 months.

HEARING

There is no specific test at this age; the parent is asked if they think the child can hear. A baby may startle to a sudden noise or freeze for some sounds.

The doctor will discuss health topics, give the first immunization and finally complete the Personal Child Health Record.

HEALTH EDUCATION POINTS AT 0–8 WEEKS

- *Nutrition:* Breast-feeding, preparation of formula feeds, specific feeding difficulties.
- *Immunisation:* Discuss any concerns and initiate a programme of vaccinations.
- *Passive smoking:* babies here are at risk of respiratory infections and **middle ear disease**.
- *Illness in babies:* how to recognise symptoms.
- *Crying:* Coping with frustration and tiredness.
- *Reducing the risk of cot death:* (sudden infant death syndrome).
- *Accident prevention:* see Chapter 10.

THE 6-TO-9 MONTH CHECK

The doctor or health visitor will enquire again about any parental concerns.

OBSERVATION

▶ Socialization and attachment behaviour;

▶ visual behaviour;

▶ communication – sounds, expressions and gestures;

▶ motor development – sitting, balance, use of hands, any abnormal movement patterns.

MEASUREMENT

▶ Head circumference and weight – plotted on the growth chart.

EXAMINATION

▶ Manipulation of the hips is carried out.

▶ The heart is auscultated.

▶ The testes are checked in boys.

▶ The eyes are checked for a **squint** – if this is present, the child is referred to an ophthalmologist (eye specialist); visual behaviour is checked.

▶ Hearing is tested by the **distraction test** – see the next section.

THE DISTRACTION TEST

FIGURE 14.12
The distraction test

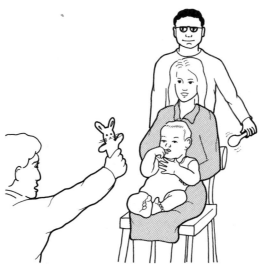

All babies should have a competently performed distraction test for hearing at 7–8 months. It is essential that the test be carried out in a quiet room, and that two trained professionals be involved. The timing of the test is important since by 8 months of age, 95% of babies have acquired the ability to localise a sound correctly, in any position except directly behind or above the head.

The **aim** of the test is to see if the baby can hear sounds of varying pitch. The baby should be alert and well and have adequate head control.

The **baby** is placed on the parent's lap facing the distractor, supported around the waist but held well away from the parent (see figure 14.12). The **distractor** holds the baby's attention with a gently moving toy. When the baby's attention is riveted on the toy, the distractor reduces the stimulation by covering or removing the toy, but does not let the baby handle it.

The **tester** presents sound stimili at a distance of one metre from the baby's ear, on the same horizontal plane and at a sufficient angle so that the baby cannot see the tester. The **test sounds** must be quiet and presented randomly and the object is to demonstrate two high-frequency and two low-frequency responses. High-frequency sounds are usually made using a Nuffield rattle and by saying 'sss' as in 'bus'. Low-frequency sounds are made by saying 'ooooo' as in 'shoe', hummed, not whispered.

If the baby fails the distraction test, the health visitor will usually arrange to repeat the test about one month later, if the test is failed again, the baby will be referred to an **audiologist** (a person trained to assess hearing).

HEALTH EDUCATION POINTS
- *Nutrition:* weaning; control of sugar intake;
- *Immunisations* – check they are up to date.
- *Teeth:* regular brushing once teeth appear; information on fluoride; visit the dentist.
- *The need for play and language stimulation.*
- *Accident prevention* – see Chapter 10.

THE 2-YEAR CHECK
This check is similar to the previous tests. It is often easier for the health visitor to carry out the check on a home visit. The parent is asked about any concerns. A physical examination is not normally carried out at this age.
- The height is measured if the child is cooperative.
- Weight is only checked if there is reason for concern.
- The parent is asked if there are any concerns about vision and hearing, and referred to a specialist if necessary.
- Check that the child is walking and that the gait (manner of walking) is normal.
- Discuss behaviour and any problems here, e.g. tantrums, sleep disturbance, poor appetite or food fads.
- Consider the possibility of **iron deficiency**, which is common at this age and may be a cause of irritability and developmental and behavioural problems, as well as of **anaemia**.

HEALTH EDUCATION POINTS
- *Nutrition and dental care:* refer to the dentist if teeth are obviously decayed.
- *Immunisation:* check it is up to date.
- *Common behavioural difficulties:* such as temper tantrums, sleep disturbance, toilet training.
- *Social behaviour:* learning to play with other children and to share possessions.
- *Accident prevention:* see Chapter 10.

THE 'SCHOOL READINESS CHECK' AT 4–5 YEARS
This check is usually carried out by the GP and the health visitor. The parent is asked if there are any general concerns about the child's progress and development, or any behavioural or emotional problems.

OBSERVATIONS
- *Motor skills:* can the child walk, run and climb stairs? Does the child tire more quickly compared with other children?

- *Fine manipulative skills:* can the child control pencils and paintbrushes?
- *Behaviour:* parents are asked about the child's ability to concentrate, to play with others and to separate from them without distress.
- *Vision, language and hearing:* observation and discussion with the parent will determine any problems which may need specialist assessment.

MEASUREMENT
- Height and weight are measured and plotted on the growth chart.

EXAMINATION
- The **heart** is listened to for any abnormal sounds.
- The **lungs** are listened to for wheezing.
- In a boy, the **testes** will be checked again; if still not descended, he will be referred to a surgeon.
- The **spine** is inspected for signs of **dysraphism** or **spina bifida occulta.**
- **Blood pressure** is usually only measured if the child has a history of **renal disease** or growth problems.

HEALTH EDUCATION POINTS
- *Immunisation:* pre-school booster.
- *Dental care:* diet – danger of sweets and snacks; brushing teeth; dental decay; visits to the dentist.
- *The child's needs for play, conversation and social learning.*
- *The recognition and management of minor ailments.*
- *Accident prevention:* see Chapter 10.

THE 8-YEARS CHECK
This is carried out by the school nurse, and parents are encouraged to attend the sessions at school. It involves the following:
- A general review of progress and development is carried out. The parent may voice concerns such as **bedwetting (enuresis)** or food fads.
- Height and weight are measured.
- Vision is tested, and if a problem is found, the child is referred to an ophthalmologist or optician.

HEALTH EDUCATION POINTS
- *Accident prevention:* particularly safety on the roads and awareness of 'strangers danger';
- *diet;*
- *exercise;*
- *dental health;*

The school nursing service
School nurses are either registered general nurses (RGN) or registered sick children's nurses (RSCN). Most school nurses will also hold the School Nursing Certificate. Their work includes:
- assessing the health needs of children from five years to school leaving age;
- health education;
- counselling;
- child protection; and
- the school immunisation programme.

The school nurse provides a link between health and education and liaises with other agencies such as social services and voluntary organisations. Most school nurses within the primary school sector are **peripatetic**, that is they travel between schools within their health authority. Some school nurses are employed within special schools where they are more involved with day to day nursing care of children.

The use of charts in child health surveillance

Many methods have been devised to record growth and development in a systematic manner; none of them alone provides a **diagnosis**. Their aim is to assist in the detection of those children who need further examination. The early years childhood worker is in an ideal position to be able to notice if a child is not making progress in any area of development. Continuous, structured observation is the most effective tool for assessing development, and any cause for concern should be noted and referred to the health visitor/paediatrician.

1 GROWTH CHARTS

The latest growth charts (published in 1995 – see Figure 14.13) indicate the fact that children in many countries have become taller and heavier at all ages; they also mature earlier and so stop growing at an earlier age. These charts may be used to compare the growth pattern of an individual child with the normal range of growth patterns typical of a large number of children of the same sex; they are used to plot height, weight and head circumference:

▶ The 50th centile (or percentile) is the **median**: it represents the middle of the range of growth patterns.
▶ The 10th centile is close to the bottom of the range; if the height of a child is on the 10th centile, it means that in any typical group of 100 children, 90 would measure more and 9 would measure less than that child.
▶ The 90th centile is close to the top of the range; if the weight of a child is on the 90th centile, then in any typical group of 100 children, 89 would weigh less and 10 would weigh more than that child.

2 DEVELOPMENTAL SCALES

GESELL DEVELOPMENT SCHEDULES (1969)

Most developmental scales are based on the work of American developmental psychologist Arnold Gesell in the 1930s. Gesell's team studied hundreds of children in a fabric observation dome which was brightly lit inside so that the child would be unaware of the students, parents and cameraman observing from outside. A series of tests was carried out using wooden blocks, cups and bells. At 15 months, a child will build a tower of two blocks; at 4 years, a tower of 10 blocks. 'Normal' development is defined in relation to other children rather than to a fixed external standard.

The scales are strongly biased towards **motor** development in the first 2 years, but the overall results are presented in four areas: **motor, adaptive, language** and **personal-social**.

THE DENVER DEVELOPMENTAL SCREENING TEST

The Denver Test is widely used by paediatricians and health visitors to record a child's all-round development in the 1st year; and those recordings the information should be very familiar with child development. The Test provides useful information about the range of ages at which different abilities are usually acquired.

Other tests include:

FIGURE 14.13
Child growth charts:
(a) Boy's weight (kg 0–1 year)
(b) Boy's weight (kg 1–5 years)
(c) Girl's length (cm 0–1 year)
(d) Girl's height (cm 1–5 years)

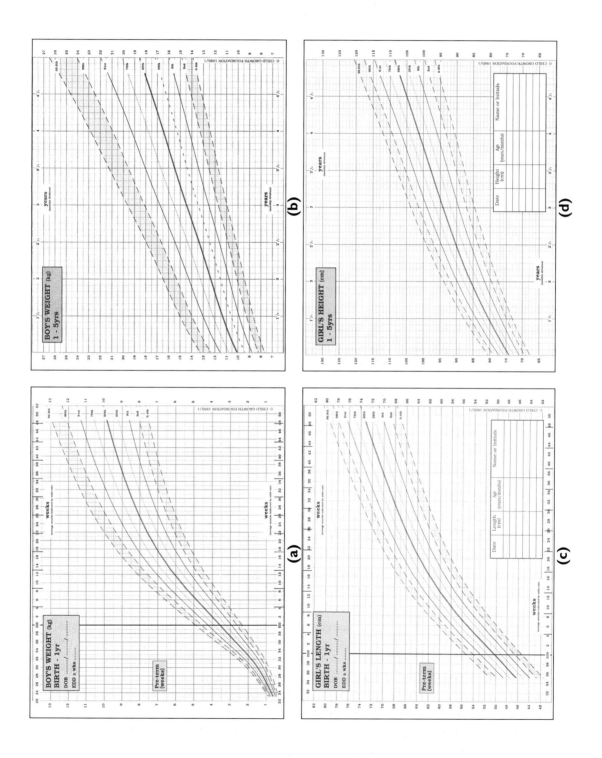

© Child Growth Foundation, UK.

▶ The **Goodenough Draw-a Man Test:** devised by D.B. Harris in 1963, this requires a child aged 3 – 15 years to draw a man; the drawing is analysed and the resulting score is converted into a mental age. It should not be used alone as it tests only part of the range of cognitive skills.

▶ **Bayley Scales of Infant Development:** developed by N. Bayley in 1965, these are widely used for infants of 2 months to 2.5 years. There are three complementary parts: the **mental scale**, the **motor scale** and the **infant behaviour record**.

▶ **The Bus Puzzle Test** developed by D.F. Egan and R. Brown in 1984, is used for children between 2 and 4 years old to test cognitive and language abilities.

There are many other tests, scales and centile charts in use in child health clinics and hospitals.

Notifiable diseases

Some diseases are **notifiable** by law to the Medical Officer for Environmental Health. In England and Wales, they are:

Acute encephalitis	Mumps
Acute meningitis	Ophthalmai neonatorum
Acute poliomyelitis	Paratyphoid fever
Anthrax	Plague
Cholera	Rabies
Diphtheria	Relapsing fever
Dysentery (amoebic and bacillary) Rubella	Scarlet fever
Food poisoning (all sources)	Small pox
Infective jaundice	Tetanus
Lassa fever	Tuberculosis
Leprosy	Typhoid fever
Leptospirosis	Typhus
Malaria	Viral haemorrhagic fever
Marburg disease	(e.g. Ebola fever)
Measles	Whooping cough
Meningococcal septicaemia	Yellow fever

R E S O U R C E S

Books

The BMA Family Health Encyclopedia, London, Dorling Kinderslay, 1990

Jane Coffey, *Health Care for Children,* London, Hodder and Stoughton, 1998

David Hall, Peter Hill, David Elliman, *The Child Surveillance Handbook,* 2nd edition, Oxford, Radcliffe Medical Press, 1994

Pamela Minett, *Child Care and Development,* 3rd edition, London, John Murray, 1994

A. Strauss, *Chronic Illness and the Quality of Life,* Mosby, St. Louis, 1984

Welfare of Children and Young People in Hospital, London, HMSO, Department of Health, 1991

For treatment of head lice:

Community Hygiene Concern charity can be contacted on 020 8341 7167.

Essential oils can be bought from health food shops, from chemists and through the Tisserand Institute on 01273 206640

Useful Addresses

Dial-a-Dream
7 Addison Road
Wanstead
London E11 2RG
Tel.: 020 8530 5589

Action for Sick Children
Argyle House
29–31 Euston Road
London NW1 2SD
Tel.: 020 7833 2041

Asthma Society
300 Upper Street
London N1 2XX
Tel.: 020 7226 2260

Child Growth Foundation
2 Mayfield Avenue
Chiswick
London W4 1PW
Tel: 020 8995 0257

The growth charts
reproduced on p. 460 may be
purchased from
Harlow Printing
Maxwell Street
South Shields
NE33 4PU

The Child Bereavement Trust
1 Millside
Riversdale
Bourne End, Bucks
SL8 5EB

Cruse – Bereavement Centre
126 Sheen Road
Richmond
Surrey TW9 1UR
Tel.: 080 8940 4818

The Compassionate Friends
6 Denmark Street
Bristol BS1 5DQ
Tel.: 01272 292 778

A C T I V I T Y

Awareness of head lice

Prepare a pamphlet for parents whose 5-year-old child has head lice. Include the following information in an easy-to-read format:
- ▶ **what are headlice?**
- ▶ **where to go for treatment;**
- ▶ **how to prevent a recurrence;**
- ▶ **how to treat the condition.**

A C T I V I T Y

Promoting information on asthma

Design a poster, for use in a nursery or primary school, which presents the following information in a lively style:
- ▶ **the main factors known to trigger an asthma attack;**
- ▶ **what to do when a child has an asthma attack;**
- ▶ **how preventers and relievers – via inhalers – work.**

A C T I V I T Y

Learning about hospital play

Invite a play specialist or nursery nurse working in hospital to come and talk about their job. Prepare a list of questions beforehand and collect as much information as you can about the needs of the child in hospital.

ACTIVITY

Information on immunisation

1 Read through the section on common childhood disease and the information on immunisation.
2 Prepare a booklet for parents on those childhood diseases for which there is immunisation. Include the following information:
   ▶ the causes, signs and symptoms of the diseases;
   ▶ possible complications and treatment;
   ▶ the immunisation schedule;
   ▶ contra-indications to immunisation;
   ▶ where to go for further advice and help on immunisation.

Make the booklet as eye-catching as possible, using illustrations.

ACTIVITY

Investigating child health surveillance

Arrange to visit a child health clinic and find out the following information:
   ▶ What surveillance programmes are routinely carried out, and by whom?
   ▶ If further tests are necessary, to whom is the child referred?
   ▶ What records are maintained by health visitors?
   ▶ How do health personnel ensure equality of access to health surveillance?

15

Children with Special Needs and their Families

The term **special needs** evokes an image in many minds of elaborate equipment and technology. Paradoxically, an individual is regarded as having special needs when that individual requires help to satisfy one or more of the **most basic human needs** (see Chapter 3 on the needs of the child).

Defining the terms

Special needs

Obviously there are wide variations in the ways of fulfilling these basic needs, and the term 'special needs' means far more than merely referring to people with well-defined physical or mental disabilities. Children with special needs may be grouped into the following categories, but it should also be noted that a child may only have a *temporary* special need – e.g. when a child's parent or sibling has died, or when they are a victim of **bullying** or **abuse**.

- ▶ *Physical impairment:* problems with mobility or coordination.
- ▶ *Sensory impairment:* i.e. visual or hearing impairment.
- ▶ *Speech or language difficulties:* including delayed language, articulation problems and stuttering.
- ▶ *Moderate to severe learning difficulties.*
- ▶ *Emotional difficulties:* anxiety, fear, depression.
- ▶ *Behavioural difficulties (conduct disorders):* aggression, **hyperactivity, attention deficit disorder (ADD), attention deficit hyperactivity disorder (ADHD)**, anti-social behaviour.
- ▶ *Giftedness:* children who are highly academically or artistically gifted may have special needs.
- ▶ *Specific learning difficulties (SLD):* usually confined to the areas of reading, writing and

FIGURE 15.1
Categories of Special Needs

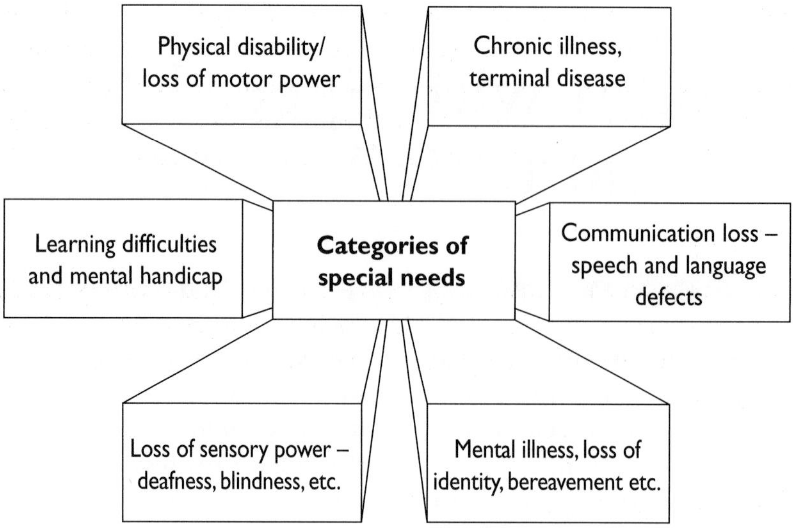

numeracy; **dyslexia** (literally meaning 'non-reading') is a term often applied to difficulty in developing literacy skills.

Disability

The term **disability** is one which persists because of our society's need to 'label' anyone who differs from the normal (in this case, normal = healthy). Throughout history, disabled people have been **marginalised** by society. One example is the way in which 'cripples' were excluded from participating in the creation of social wealth; because industrialised society required able-bodied workers to operate machinery, for example, those classed as 'cripples' or 'mental defectives' were reduced to begging or to relying on charitable hand-outs.

In the late 1950s and early 1960s, there was a growing concern to provide more services for disabled people. Many people are now trying to move away from the term 'disability' and use descriptions such as 'physically challenged' instead. Such phrases emphasise the *positive* side and stress that although people may need help in meeting their basic needs, the challenges they face *can* be met. Before legislation could be formulated, a definition of terms had to be reached.

Handicap

Many people who have a disability reject the term **handicap** as it implies a patronising attitude and dependence on charity. (The term originates from the notion of 'hand in the cap' i.e. begging for money or charity.) However, charities such as Mencap continue to prefer the use of the words 'mentally handicapped' as they feel that the term gives the public a clear understanding of those they are trying to help through their work. Mencap's counterpart charity in Scotland has recently changed its name from The Scottish Society for the Mentally Handicapped to ENABLE.

Advocacy

The movement for **child advocacy** began in the USA in the 1960s. In the UK, the Children Act 1980 makes social-services departments responsible for providing for children with special needs: 'A child is disabled if he is blind, deaf, or dumb or suffers from mental disorder of any kind or is substantially and permanently **handicapped** by illness, injury or congenital deformity or other such disability as may be described. The concept of advocacy is enshrined in the Act. It recognises that children found in the category 'disabled' are the least likely to grow up to be able to speak for themselves, i.e. to perceive their own needs and to know how to achieve them. Therefore, they need an **advocate**. Usually the advocate is an adult care worker who acts as a **spokesperson** for the person 'in need'.

Empowerment

This concept is closely linked to **advocacy**. In the case of children with special needs, the adult should undertake activities with the child which will **empower** (or enable) the child to make his own wishes known by helping with **communication**, giving the child choice and decision-making skills.

Models of special needs

The development of models of special needs (see Figure 15.2) arose from the need to give a structure or framework to the **provision of services** for people with disabilities. Formal models are those which aim to determine the provision in its broadest sense, i.e.:

▶ which organisations will provide services;
▶ how the provision of services is regulated and funded;
▶ which professionals in health, education and social care are involved;
▶ which **groups** of people with special needs are involved, and how they can best be served.

The World Health Organization (WHO) model

A national survey was conducted by the Office of Population Censuses and Surveys (OPCS); published in 1971, it arrived at a threefold classification of disability:

▶ **Impairment:** lacking all or part of a limb, or having a defective limb, organ or mechanism of the body (i.e. a part of the body does not work properly or is missing).
▶ **Disability:** the loss or reduction of functional ability (i.e. you check what people *cannot* do as compared with the majority of other people.)
▶ **Handicap;** the disadvantage or restriction of activity caused by disability (i.e. what an individual can and cannot do in a particular situation and in relationships with other people).

The medical model

This approach has been criticised for having a negative focus: it does not highlight the abilities and requirements that people with *disabilities* have in common with everyone else. The model's usefulness is only apparent where an individual has recently sustained a permanent impairment such that medical intervention and rehabilitation are necessary to establish new skills in body management. The limitations of the medical model become apparent when we turn to examine the service provision for disabled people. By focusing on the **disability** rather than the **ability** of the individual, a climate of **dependency** is fostered where many disabled people are cared for in institutions; and as long as there is no medical cure, disabled people are regarded as inherently 'socially dead' and permanently dependent upon others for their care in the community or in an institution.

FIGURE 15.2
Models of disability

MEDICAL MODEL	WORLD HEALTH ORGANIZATION MODEL	SOCIAL CONSTRUC-TION MODEL
Disability medically diagnosed	Disease leads to: ↓	Disability created by attitudes in society
View of disability as 'tragic event'	Impairment (parts or systems of body that do not work) ↓	Social barriers create disability
Physical explanation to account for disability	Disability (things people cannot do) ↓	Discrimination more a problem than physical impairment
No medical cure, therefore disability seen as 'social death'	Handicap (social and economic disadvantage) ↓	Exclusion and segregation of disabled is main problem
Dependency of disabled person results	Social dimension recognised	Autonomy and independence most important.

The traditional medical model starts by looking at the specific physical impairment and its preceding causes, where these are known. It recognises that physical impairment has two consequences:

▶ **functional limitation:** how the condition affects mobility, communication and bodily functions;

▶ **activity restriction:** what specific activities are difficult or impossible.

It does also, however, recognise:

▶ **social handicap,** which may result from changes in self-perception and the expectations of others – often through **stereotyping** or **stigma**. Social handicap may in its turn affect and exacerbate the underlying physical impairment.

The social model

This model emphasises the need to change society, to remove real barriers to equality of opportunity. The extent of medical intervention should be guided by an analysis of the social and personal barriers to be overcome, rather than by any functional limitations of the individual. The model has the following features:

▶ It sees disability as having a **social dimension**, i.e. the problem of disability is one that is created by the institutions, organisations and processes that make up the whole of society.

▶ It focuses on **attitudes**, i.e. it implies that if the attitudes of the able-bodied change, then the problems disability will be resolved.

▶ It redefines the WHO's definition (impairment, disability) by saying that disability is not the lack of function – e.g. the inability to walk – but is the **social response** to that lack of function – e.g. the lack of ramps for wheelchairs, the exclusion of wheelchair users from public transport.

Disability and discrimination

Having a physical disability means living in society as part of a **minority group** whose particular needs may not be adequately recognised or taken into account, and whose different appearance often leads to being treated differently and less equally. Of course, not all disabilities are readily recognisable as such: – for example, deafness, epilepsy or diabetes.

The following are all **attitudes** commonly encountered by disabled people from able-bodied people:

▶ **Stereotype**: a term used when certain characteristics of any given group are applied to *all* the individuals within that group. The logo denoting access for disabled people is a sign showing a person in a wheelchair, yet less than 5% of the 6 million people with disabilities in the UK use wheelchairs.

▶ **Dependency**: the assumption of dependency on the part of people who have a disability can take the form of trying to be helpful without being asked and thus invading the privacy of the disabled person's life – e.g. the blind person being helped across a road they did not want to cross.

▶ **Hostility:** this may take the form of loud comments being made about the disabled person, or aggression.

▶ **Exclusion:** physical or intellectual differences can make disabled people less than human in the eyes of non-disabled people; they can be excluded from normal human activity because 'they are not normally human'.

▶ **Invasion of privacy:** certain physical characteristics evoke such strong feelings that people often have to express them in some way. The physical difference makes their bodies objects for public comment.

▶ **Patronage:** e.g. the humiliation of people talking to the disabled person's able-bodied companions as if the disabled person himself
would not be able to understand what was being said.

Caring for children with special needs

The term **special needs** is now used to describe children whose development differs from the normal. The aim is to see the **individual child** first and *then* the special need or disability. The basic needs of the child – stability, security and protection – should come before the **special** needs occasioned by the disability.

The self-image of children with disabilities

Any child with a disability may have a problem in developing a **positive self-image**; the problem often results from the reaction of others to the disability. Common reactions include:

▶ *a sense of tragedy:* parents who give birth to a child with a disability experience complex emotions. They may grieve for the loss of a 'normal' child, but to offer **loss counselling** in the same way as one would for a bereavement negates the fact that the child is a **child** first and foremost and that they have a unique personality and identity of their own. Relatives and friends are embarrassed by their own reactions, and their awkward response can leave the parents feeling very isolated at a time which is normally spent in celebrating;

▶ *a fear of making mistakes:* sometimes there is an over-reliance on professional help; the **disability** is seen first, and parents believe that only a medical expert can advise on the care of their child, whereas the reality is that it is the *parent* who will almost always know what is required;

▶ *being over-protective:* this desire to cocoon the child from hidden pitfalls can be counter-productive as the child needs to be equipped for life and can only learn by making mistakes. Siblings may resent the disabled child who is seen as spoilt or never punished;

▶ *exercising control:* this is taking **freedom of choice** away from the child, **disempowering** them; parents and carers often dictate where and with whom the child plays, thus depriving them of an opportunity for valuable social learning.

Unlike parents, a group of children will not make the disabled child the centre of the universe and will reinforce the child's own inadequate sense of identity.

The principles of caring for children with disabilities

An early childhood worker can best promote a child's self-image by regarding them as a child first and the disability second. An awareness is needed of the following issues/skills:

▶ **Self-empowerment:** always encourage independence. Ask how the *child* wants to do things – let *them* make as many choices as possible.

▶ **Empathy:** try to imagine *yourself* in the child's situation – how would *you* like to be helped? (Not to be confused with unwanted sympathy – the 'Does he take sugar?' approach should be avoided!)

▶ **Patience:** always be patient with children, particularly where communication may be difficult or time-consuming.

▶ **Sensitivity:** try to anticipate the child's feelings – e.g. having one's most intimate needs attended to by a stranger can be embarrassing.

▶ **Respect:** show awareness of a child's personal rights, dignity and privacy; never allow other children to poke fun at the child with a disability.

▶ **Communication and interpersonal skills:** develop good listening skills. **Non-verbal communication** (e.g. facial expressions) is just as important as what you *say*.

▶ **Attitude:** an open-minded and non-judgemental attitude is important, as is a warm, friendly manner.

▶ **Be positive:** praise effort rather than achievement and provide activities that are appropriate for the child's ability so that they have a chance of achieving.

▶ **Integration:** make an effort to involve the child with other children.

▶ **Be a good role model:** support the carers/parents to provide a lifestyle that is as normal as possible.

▶ **Set guidelines for behaviour:** these should be the same as for all children: do not make exceptions for the child with a disability.

Special needs and education

Education is obviously a lifelong process, but in formal terms, it involves schooling between the ages of 4 or 5 years old and either 16 or 18, with the option of attending colleges or universities or training schemes with an employer. Until the 1950s in the UK, children born with an obvious disabling condition such as Down's syndrome or cerebral palsy would have been cared for within the family for the first few years of life before being admitted to a large mental handicap hospital where they may have spent the rest of their lives with no contact with mainstream educational institutions.

Various attempts have been made to define **special needs** in the educational sphere:

The Education Act 1921

This act defined five categories of handicap:

- blindness
- deafness
- physical defectiveness
- mental defectiveness
- epilepsy.

Not all children recognised as suffering from one of these disabilities were offered special educational facilities, but many were placed in residential homes for the blind, deaf and dumb.

The Education Act 1944

This act defined 11 categories of handicap:

- blind
- deaf
- physically handicapped
- diabetic
- maladjusted
- speech defective.
- partially sighted
- partially deaf
- delicate
- epileptic
- educationally sub-normal

All local education authorities (LEAs) were legally bound to provide education for children with such disabilities, although this was not necessarily provided within schools but often as an add-on facility within the large institutions mentioned above. As these institutions or hospitals were nearly always situated on the outskirts of large towns, it was not easy for parents and family to visit the child, and as a result the valuable family tie was often broken.

The Education Act 1970

This act further expanded the previous provision to include those children with **severe mental handicap** – such children had hitherto been pronounced 'ineducable'.

The Education Act 1981

Mary Warnock chaired a committee in 1978 which published the Warnock Report. The committee's brief was to 'review the educational provision in England, Scotland and Wales for children and young people handicapped by disabilities of body or mind'. The Report provided the basis of the 1981 Education Act:

- Where possible, children should be **integrated** into mainstream schools.
- Special educational needs were defined as **mild, moderate** or **severe**.
- The assessment of a child's specific needs should be ongoing.
- Reference should be made to a child's **abilities** as well as to his **disabilities**.
- The term **specific learning difficulties** was introduced for those children who may have difficulty in just one area of the school curriculum (e.g. as a result of dyslexia).

Assessment

The assessment of the individual with special needs is not a once-only event but a *continuous* process. Information gained about the person is added to over a period of time so that a clearer picture is formed of the person's particular needs.

Before a statement of need can be drawn up – by a process of negotiation between the education authority and the child's parents – an accurate assessment of the child's functioning and development must be made. Parents are advised to **record** details of the age when key developments – starting to speak, sitting up, crawling, hand-eye coordination – occurred; and a detailed medical history is also valuable, particularly when the assessment applies to a child under 4 years of age.

An assessment must take account of the following factors:

▶ **physical** factors: the person's particular illness or condition;

▶ **psychological** and **emotional** factors: the person's intellectual ability and levels of anxiety or depression will lead to different needs and priorities – e.g. severe anxiety may adversely affect all daily activities, and its alleviation will therefore assume top priority;

▶ **sociocultural** factors: whether or not the person is part of a family, the individual's family of origin and the relationships within the family will all influence needs. Similarly, the individual's wider community and the social class to which they belong are very influential;

▶ **environmental** factors: e.g. a person living in a cold, damp house with an outside toilet will have different needs from someone who is more comfortably housed;

▶ **political/economic** factors: poverty or belonging to a disadvantaged group leads to less choice in day-to-day living.

By considering all these factors, we are acknowledging that a person's needs are likely to **change** according to different circumstances, and any assessment of needs must involve this understanding of the wider context in which we all live. The process of the **assessment** of the specific needs of individual children is known as **statementing**.

THE STATEMENTING PROCESS

Statementing is a formal process of negotiation between the education authority on the one hand and the parents on the other. Its aims: to identify the areas of need and define the treatment/educational requirements for such areas. The **Statement of Special Education Needs** is a legal document which must describe precisely the child's individual needs. The Code of Practice introduced in 1994 gives guidance on the procedures involved. Every school now has to appoint a member of staff who takes responsibility for special education needs.

There are five steps towards statementing, a process which is only expected to be relevant for 2% of children.

1   *Cause for concern:* the family worker or class teacher, through the observations made in the established record-keeping system, might become concerned. This concern should be shared with the **SENCO** (**Special Educational Needs Coordinator**) and preferably also with the parents.

2   *Observation and monitoring:* the child is observed and monitored more closely, and an **Individual Education Plan** is developed with the SENCO and the parents: for example, making sure that a child with a serious stutter has plenty of time to talk and chat without being rushed.

3   *Outside help:* the school asks for outside help, for example from an **educational psychologist**. A new Individual Education Plan is drawn up.

4   *Procedures for statutory assessment begin:* this must take place within 26 weeks.

5   *A statement is drawn up.*

FEATURES OF A STATEMENT

▶ The process may be instigated by the local education authority at any time in a child's school life (i.e. between 4 and 18 years).

▶ If statementing is required before the age of 4, it is undertaken by the health authority. Early education opportunities are usually provided as a result.

▶ A statement *must* be updated regularly – generally once a year.

▶ Extra resources required by children with special needs who attend mainstream schools should be clearly described so that funding is available.

The Statement of Special Educational Needs is in five parts:

1 introduction – details of name, address, religion, date of birth, next of kin etc.;

2 special educational needs as identified by the education authority;

3 special educational provision thought to be appropriate to meet those needs, specifying any facilities, modifications to the National Curriculum or specialist equipment;

4 the type of school or other establishment (e.g. hospital) thought appropriate for the child;

5 any additional non-educational provision required, and which authority should be the provider – e.g. mobility aids may be provided by the health authority.

C A S E   S T U D Y

Problems in statementing

Richard is seven and has muscular dystrophy. The local education authority offered Richard a place at his local mainstream primary school, dependent on the provision of a full-time classroom assistant to help ensure the safety of Richard, who weighs just 3 stone and is partially sighted. To obtain this provision, the LEA required that Richard be statemented. This process took several months; meanwhile Richard's classmates moved up to a classroom on the first floor for many of their regular activities and Richard, who is wheelchair bound, has been – according to his hospital report – 'profoundly affected emotionally by being separated from his peer group.' The head teacher has always been very supportive; Richard is an intelligent boy who needs a full education and could obviously receive one if a lift were installed. His parents are fighting the LEA's refusal to fit a lift at the school; they feel that Richard is being marginalised or punished for having a disability.

1 What can Richard's parents do to ensure that he receives the help he needs?

2 Find out about organisations which fight for the rights of disabled people. Write a report on your findings.

3 Research the range of services available in your own local authority for disabled children and their families.

Causes of disability

There are three main ways in which a person can become disabled:
- **congenital,** when a faulty gene leads to a disabling condition;
- **developmental,** when the foetus is growing in the womb;
- **illness and accident,** affecting individuals who are born with no disability.

We will consider the first two in this chapter.

Hereditary and congenital disorders

Many of the disorders listed below can now be diagnosed **prenatally**, thus enabling parents to decide on a course of action i.e. whether to seek a termination of pregnancy or not. The growth and development of the embryo and foetus are controlled by **genes**. **Abnormal genes** can cause **abnormal growth and development** (see Figure 15.3).

DOMINANT GENE DEFECTS

A parent with a **dominant gene defect** has a 50% chance of passing the defect on to each of their children. Examples of dominant gene defects are:
- tuberous sclerosis (a disorder affecting the skin and nervous system);
- achondroplasia (once called dwarfism);
- Huntington's chorea (a disorder of the central nervous system).

RECESSIVE GENE DEFECTS

These defects are only inherited if *two* recessive genes meet. Therefore, if both parents carry a single **recessive gene defect**, each of their children has a 1 in 4 chance of being affected. Examples of defects transmitted this way are:
- cystic fibrosis (detailed below);
- sickle-cell anaemia (detailed below);
- phenylketonuria (a defective enzyme disorder);
- thalassaemia (a blood disorder);
- Tay-Sachs disease (a disorder of the nervous system);
- Friedreich's ataxia (a disorder of the spinal cord).

CYSTIC FIBROSIS (CF)

This is an inherited disease which is present from birth. Among West Europeans and white Americans, the incidence is 1 per 2,000 live births, and 1 person in 25 is a 'carrier' of the faulty recessive gene. Features of the disease are:
- an inability to absorb fats and other nutrients from food;
- chronic lung infections;
- pancreatitis and gallstones;
- liver problems;
- diabetes;
- infertility in most males and some females;
- heat-stroke and collapse may occur in hot climates due to excessive loss of salt in the sweat.

Recent research has succeeded in locating the gene that causes **cystic fibrois.** It is now possible to detect the carrier state, and also to test for cystic fibrosis before birth. Once cystic fibrosis is suspected in the young baby, simple laboratory tests, including an analysis of sweat content, will confirm or refute the diagnosis.

FIGURE 15.3

A summary of genetic defects and their pattern in inheritance

DOMINANT GENE DEFECTS	RECESSIVE GENE DEFECTS	X-LINKED GENE DEFECTS
Tuberous sclerosis Achondroplasia Huntington's chorea Neurofibromatosis Marfan's syndrome	Cystic fibrosis Friedreich's ataxia Phenylketonuria Sickle cell anaemia Tay-Sachs disease Thalassaemia	Haemophilia Christmas disease Fragile X syndrome Muscular dystrophy (Duchenne type) Colour blindness (most types)

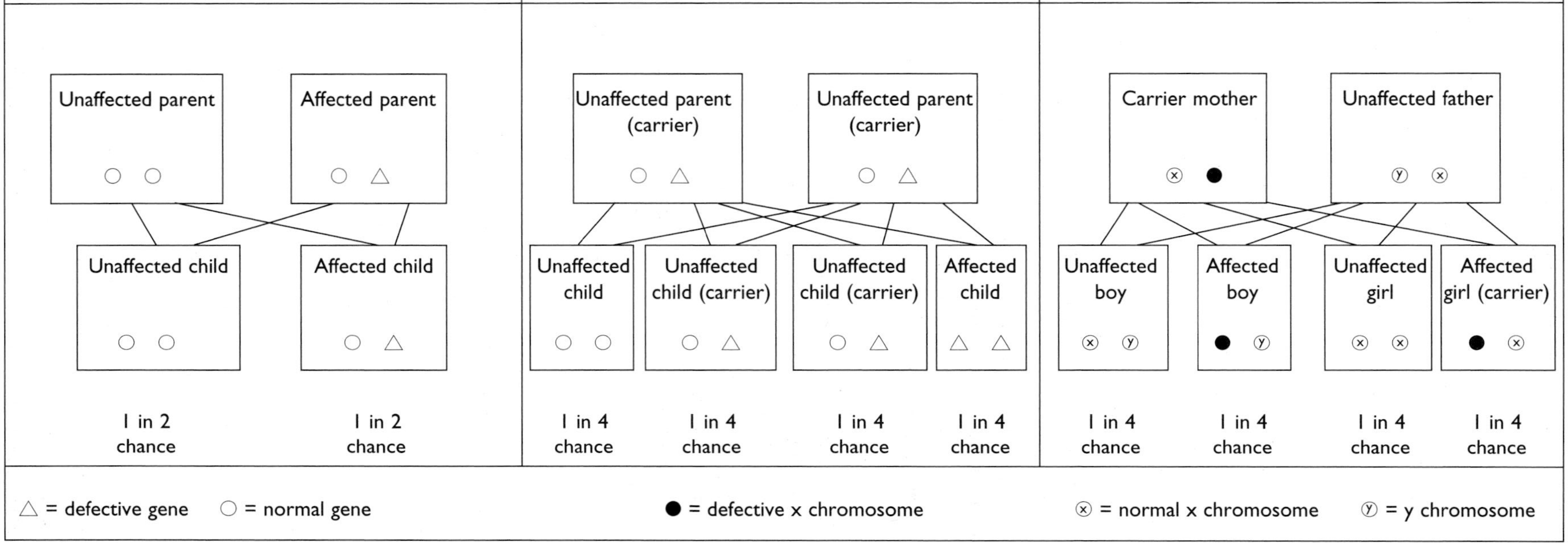

DOMINANT GENE DEFECTS

Unaffected parent

Affected parent

Unaffected child

Affected child

1 in 2 chance

1 in 2 chance

RECESSIVE GENE DEFECTS

Unaffected parent (carrier)

Unaffected parent (carrier)

Unaffected child

Unaffected child (carrier)

Unaffected child (carrier)

Affected child

1 in 4 chance

1 in 4 chance

1 in 4 chance

1 in 4 chance

X-LINKED GENE DEFECTS

Carrier mother

Unaffected father

Unaffected boy

Affected boy

Unaffected girl

Affected girl (carrier)

1 in 4 chance

1 in 4 chance

1 in 4 chance

1 in 4 chance

△ = defective gene   ○ = normal gene

● = defective gene

⊗ = normal x chromosome   Ⓨ = y chromosome

⊗ = normal x chromosome   ● = defective x chromosome

Treatment and care includes:

▶ intensive physiotherapy;

▶ a diet rich in calories and proteins, usually with vitamin supplements;

▶ **pancreatin** (a replacement pancreatic enzyme preparation) given with meals to enable food to be properly digested.

The recurrence of severe respiratory infections often means that cystic fibrosis sufferers have permanent lung damage. Lung transplants are sometimes offered, and can prolong life expectancy.

C A S E   S T U D Y

Karen

Karen is the second child of healthy parents. She appeared to be a healthy baby until she was five months old, when she caught a cold from her brother, Matthew who is three years older. Her cough rapidly worsened, and after bouts of high fever and vomiting every feed, pneumonia was diagnosed and Karen was rushed into hospital. She responded well to antibiotic treatment and intravenous feeding, but X-ray pictures revealed an abnormality of the bronchial tubes. Pancreatic enzyme tests confirmed the diagnosis as cystic fibrosis.

Karen's parents began the daily routine, so familiar to anyone coping with cystic fibrosis, of physiotherapy (postural drainage and coughing to clear the lungs) and antibiotic medicine, vitamin supplements and vital pancreatic enzymes. Recurrent chest infections meant that Karen received the different drugs via a nebuliser worked by a compressor; this delivers mist containing tiny droplets of the drugs which can get right down into the lungs where they are needed (NB: some asthmatic patients too take their drugs via a nebuliser). Karen progressed normally until she was in her first year at infant school; she began to complain of 'colicky' pain and had bouts of vomiting and constipation – this was diagnosed as meconium ileus equivalent, which is a type of intestinal obstruction. Karen was admitted to hospital for intravenous fluids, pain-relieving medicine and special enemas given under X-ray control. Apart from regular visits to the hospital specialist, Karen had not been a hospital patient except for when she had two severe bouts of pneumonia, each caused by a different pathogenic organism.

Karen is now a happy, optimistic 7-year-old who enjoys PE and games; and although small for her age group, she can keep up with her peers, apart from a tendency to wheeze with any strenuous exertion. Karen's parents share the care, and try to ensure that family life is not centred around their daughter's condition.

FIGURE 15.4
A package of care

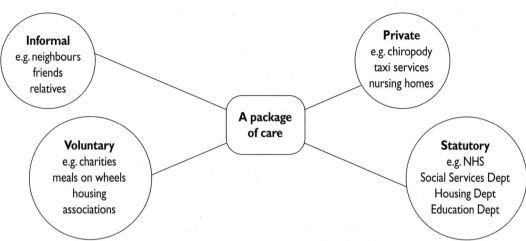

FIGURE 15.4
A package of care

Cystic fibrosis for early childhood workers

▶ **Children with CF can join in with whatever the other children are doing, but they have to remember to carry out their physiotherapy, enzymes and exercise programmes.**

▶ **The lungs of a child with CF must be kept clear to prevent infection; try to learn how to perform the necessary postural drainage and physiotherapy techniques involved (see Figure 15.5).**

▶ **Children with CF can eat a normal diet but also need to take enzyme and vitamin supplements; and they may also need salt tablets if they are undertaking strenuous exercise in hot weather.**

▶ **A child with CF may tire easily but should be encouraged to take lots of exercise to keep healthy. Good exercises are running, swimming, cycling and skipping.**

NB: *always obtain permission from the child's parents or guardians before performing any of the techniques outlined above.*

SICKLE-CELL ANAEMIA

Sickle-cell anaemia is an inherited blood disorder caused by **abnormal haemoglobin**. The red blood cells (normally round) become sickle- or crescent-shaped and clump together and lodge in the smaller blood vessels, preventing normal blood flow and resulting in anaemia (a lack of haemoglobin).

In the UK it is most common in people of African or Caribbean descent, but may also occur in people from India, Pakistan, the Middle East and the East Mediterranean.

THE FEATURES OF SICKLE-CELL ANAEMIA

Children with sickle-cell anaemia can almost always attend a mainstream school but are subject to crises which may involve the following:

FIGURE 15.5

Postural drainage and chest physiotherapy – regular 'chest shaking' is necessary to move secretions from the lungs of children with CF

- ▶ **pain:** often severe, occurring in the arms, legs, back and stomach – due to the blockage to normal blood flow;
- ▶ **infection:** the children are more susceptible to coughs, cold, sore throats, fever and other infectious diseases;
- ▶ **anaemia:** most of the children are anaemic; only if it is severe, however, will they also feel lethargic and ill;
- ▶ **jaundice:** this may show as a yellow staining of the whites of the eyes.

TREATMENT AND CARE

Blood transfusions may be necessary. Infections should be treated promptly, and immunisation against all the normal childhood diseases is recommended.

GUIDELINES

Sickle-cell anaemia for early childhood workers

- ▶ **Know how to recognise a crisis. If the child suddenly becomes unwell or complains of severe abdominal or chest pain, headache, neck stiffness or drowsiness, contact parents without delay: the child needs** urgent hospital treatment.
- ▶ **Make sure the child is always warm and dry. Never let a child with sickle-cell anaemia get chilled after PE or swimming.**
- ▶ **Make sure the child does not become dehydrated – allow them to drink more often and much more than normal.**
- ▶ **Make sure that the child is fully immunised against infectious illnesses and that any prescribed medicines (e.g. vitamins and antibiotics) are given.**

> ► Give support – the child may find it difficult to come to terms with the condition; make allowances when necessary.
> ► Talk to the parents also to find out how the illness is affecting the child.
> ► Help with schoolwork – if badly anaemic, the child may find it difficult to concentrate, and regular visits to the GP or hospital may entail many days off school.

X-LINKED RECESSIVE GENE DEFECTS

In these conditions, the defective gene is on the X-chromosome and usually leads to outward abnormality in males only. Women can be carriers of the defect, and half their sons may be affected. Examples of these defects are:

- ► haemophilia
- ► Christmas disease
- ► 'Fragile X' syndrome
- ► muscular dystrophy (Duchenne type).

CHROMOSOMAL DEFECTS

These vary considerably in the severity of their effect on the individual. About 1 in every 200 babies born alive has a chromosomal abnormality – i.e. the structure or number of chromosomes varies from normal. Among foetuses that have been spontaneously aborted, about 1 in 2 has such an abnormality; and this suggests that most chromosomal abnormalities are incompatible with life, and that those seen in babies born alive are generally the less serious ones.

Examples of defects transmitted this way are:

- ► Down's syndrome: Trisomy 21 is the term used for the chromosomal abnormality which results in Down's syndrome. The extra chromosome is number 21; affected individuals have three, instead of two, number 21 chromosomes This results in short stature as well as mental handicap and an increased susceptibility to infection;
- ► Klinefelter's syndrome: 47xxy is the term used for the chromosomal abnormality which results in Kleinfelter's syndrome. The affected male has one or more extra x chromosomes (normally the pattern is xy). This results in boys who are very tall, with hypogonadism;
- ► Turner's syndrome: 45xo is the term used for the chromosomal abnormality which results in Turner's syndrome. Most affected females have only 45 chromosomes instead of 46; the missing or defective chromosome is the x chromosome. This results in girls with ovarian **dysgenesis**, a webbed neck and a broad chest; they may also have cardiac malfunctions;
- ► Cri du chat syndrome: a very rare condition in which a portion of *one* particular chromosome is missing in each of the affected individual's cells.

Genetic counselling is available for anyone with a child or other member of the family with a chromosomal abnormality, and **chromosome analysis** is offered in **early pregnancy**.

Developmental factors as causes of disability

The first three months (the first **trimester**) of a pregnancy are when the foetus is particularly vulnerable. The lifestyle of the pregnant woman affects the health of the baby in her womb. Important factors are:

- ▶ a healthy diet;
- ▶ the avoidance of alcohol and other drugs;
- ▶ not smoking;
- ▶ regular appropriate exercise.

Rubella ('German measles') is especially harmful to the developing foetus as it can cause deafness, blindness and **mental retardation**. All girls in the UK are now immunised against rubella before they reach child-bearing age, and this measure has drastically reduced the incidence of rubella-damaged babies.

Thalidomide was a drug widely prescribed during the 1960s to alleviate **morning sickness** in pregnant women. Unfortunately, it was found to cause limb deformities in many of the babies born to women who had used the drug, and was withdrawn in 1961.

Toxoplasmosis is an infection caused by the protozoan **toxoplasma gondii**. It may be contracted by pregnant women eating undercooked meat (usually pork) from infected animals, or by poor hygiene after handling cats or their faeces. In about one-third of cases, toxoplasmosis is transmitted to the child and may cause blindness, **hydrocephalus** or mental retardation. Infection in late pregnancy usually has no ill-effects.

Irradiation: if a woman is X-rayed in early pregnancy or receives radiotherapy for the treatment of cancer, the embryo may suffer abnormalities. Radiation damage may also result from atomic radiation or radioactive fall-out (following a nuclear explosion or leak from a nuclear reactor). There is also an increased risk of the child's developing leukaemia in later life after exposure to radiation.

CEREBRAL PALSY

This is the general term for disorders of movement and posture resulting form damage to a child's developing brain in the later months of pregnancy, during birth, in the neonatal period or in early childhood.

INCIDENCE

Cerebral palsy affects 2 to 3 children in every 1,000. In the UK, about 1,500 babies either are born with or develop the condition each year. It can affect boys *and* girls, and people from all races and social backgrounds.

CAUSES

The most common cause is **cerebral hypoxia** (poor oxygen supply to the brain); this may occur during pregnancy or around the time of birth. Other causes include:

- ▶ an infection in the mother during the first weeks of a baby's development in the womb (e.g. rubella or a **cytomegalovirus**);
- ▶ a difficult or **pre-term** birth, perhaps because the baby fails to breathe properly (resulting in cerebral hypoxia);
- ▶ **cerebral bleeding (haematoma)**, which particularly affects pre-term babies;
- ▶ bleeding into cavities inside the brain (**intra-ventricular haemorrhage**), which may occur in pre-term babies;
- ▶ the baby's brain is formed abnormally, for no apparent reason;
- ▶ a genetic disorder which can be inherited even if both parents are completely healthy.

TYPES OF CEREBRAL PALSY

Cerebral palsy jumbles messages between the brain and the muscles. There are three types of cerebral palsy, depending on which messages are affected. Many children with cerebral palsy have a combination of two or more types. In some people, cerebral palsy is barely noticeable, others will be more severely affected. *No two people will be affected in quite the same way*.

The three types of cerebral palsy are:

1   **Spastic:** the muscles of one or more limbs are permanently contracted and stiff, leading to disordered movement. It is usually caused when nerve cells in the outer layer of the brain (the cortex) do not work properly.

About 75% of children with cerebral palsy have this type of disorder. Limbs can be affected as follows:

- ▶ **hemiplegia:** both limbs on one side of the body;
- ▶ **diplegia:** all four limbs, but the legs are more severely affected than the arms;
- ▶ **quadriplegia:** all four limbs are severely affected, but not necessarily symmetrically.

2   **Athetoid:** a condition leading to frequent involuntary movements (i.e. movements over which the child has no control). Children with this kind of cerebral palsy have muscles which change rapidly from floppy to tense; and their speech may be hard to understand because of difficulty in controlling their tongue, breathing and vocal cords.

About 10% of the cerebral-palsy group have this type, which is a result of the middle part of the brain (the **basal ganglia**) not working properly.

3   **Ataxia:** a lack of balance sensation, causing an unsteady way of walking. Those with this form of the disorder are also likely to have shaky hand movements and jerky speech. Ataxic cerebral palsy is a result of the **cerebellum**, at the base of the brain, not working properly.

THE EFFECTS OF CEREBRAL PALSY

A child with cerebral palsy may have some of the following features, in varying degrees of severity:

- ▶ slow, awkward or jerky movements;
- ▶ stiffness;
- ▶ weakness;
- ▶ muscle spasms;
- ▶ floppiness;
- ▶ unwanted (**involuntary**) movements.

OTHER AREAS AFFECTED BY CEREBRAL PALSY

1   *Eyesight:* The most common eye problem is a **squint** which may need correction with glasses or, in severe cases, an operation. Some children may have **cortical vision defect** where the part of the brain that is responsible for understanding the images the child sees is not working properly.

2   *Spatial perception:* Some children with cerebral palsy find it difficult to judge distances or think spatially (e.g. to visualise a three-dimensional building). This is due to an abnormality in a part of the brain and is *not* related to intelligence.

3   *Hearing:* Children with athetoid cerebral palsy are more likely to have severe hearing difficulties than other children, but **glue ear** (see p. 455) is as likely to develop in the child with cerebral palsy as it is in unaffected children.

4   *Speech:* Speech depends on the ability to control tiny muscles in the mouth, tongue,

palate and voice box. Speech difficulties and problems with chewing and swallowing often occur together in children with cerebral palsy.

5 *Epilepsy:* Epilepsy (or abnormal electrical discharge form the brain, causing seisures) affects about 1 in 3 children with cerebral palsy.

6 *Learning ability:* Some children with cerebral palsy do have learning difficulties, but this is by no means always the case. Some have *higher* than average intelligence, and some have average intelligence. Some children have difficulty in learning to do certain tasks – e.g. reading, drawing or arithmetic – because a particular part of the brain is affected, this is then termed a **specific learning difficulty** and should not be confused with the child's general intelligence.

7 *Other difficulties:* Some children with cerebral palsy may experience the following difficulties:
  ▶ a tendency to chest infections;
  ▶ constipation;
  ▶ difficulty in controlling body temperature;
  ▶ not putting on much weight;
  ▶ frustration leading to behavioural difficulties;
  ▶ sleep difficulties.

THE MANAGEMENT OF CHILDREN WITH CEREBRAL PALSY

There is no cure for cerebral palsy. It is a **non-progressive condition**, i.e. it does not become more severe as the child gets older, but some difficulties may become more noticeable. If children are lifted, held and positioned well from an early age, and encouraged to play in a way that helps them to improve their posture and muscle control, they can learn a lot and lead fulfilling lives. **Physiotherapy** is important as it helps with all problems associated with movement; natural methods such as exercise, manipulation, heat and massage are all used to help the child develop good patterns of movement.

Many parents whose children have cerebral palsy seek new ways of improving their progress through education. Three such programmes are:
  ▶ **conductive education:** an intensive learning system designed to help adults and children with certain motor disabilities, including children with cerebral palsy, to become more independent. It has the backing of the charity SCOPE;
  ▶ the **Portage programme:** a home teaching programme for very young children whose development is delayed due to specific disabilities;
  ▶ the **Bobath technique:** specialised physiotherapy for children with cerebral palsy.

SENSORY IMPAIRMENT

This is the general name given to the group of disabilities which involve disorders of the sense: sight, hearing, touch, taste or smell.

BLINDNESS AND PARTIAL SIGHT

The picture of total darkness conjured up by the word 'blindness' is inaccurate: only about 18% of blind people in the UK are affected to this degree; the other 82% all have some remaining sight. In the UK, there are just over 1 million blind and partially sighted people, of whom 40% are blind and 60% are partially sighted.

CAUSES OF VISUAL IMPAIRMENT

The main causes of visual impairment in children are:
  ▶ anomalies of the eyes from birth, such as **cataracts** (cloudiness of the lens);

- ▶ **nystagmus** (involuntary jerkiness of the eyes);
- ▶ **optic atrophy** (damage to the optic nerve);
- ▶ **retinopathy of prematurity** (abnormal development of retinas in premature babies);
- ▶ hereditary factors such as **retinoblastoma**, a tumor of the retina which is often inherited.

Childhood **glaucoma** and **diabetic retinopathy** are quite rare in children, but are common causes of visual impairment in adults.

FIGURE 15.6

The eye and sight

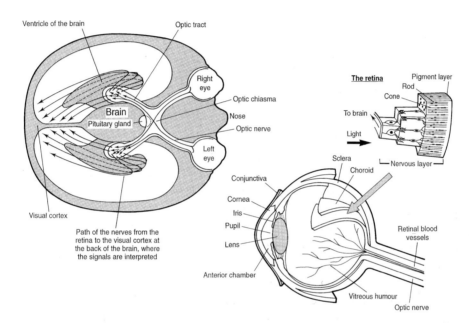

TREATMENT

Some conditions which cause visual impairment are treatable, particularly if detected at an early stage; for example:

- ▶ glaucoma can be halted by medical or surgical means;
- ▶ a cataract may be removed by removal of the lens.

Laser therapy is also now being used to correct various visual defects.

EDUCATION AND TRAINING

More than 55% of visually impaired children in school attend mainstream schools along with sighted children, where most will have a **Statement of Special Education Needs** which details the support and special equipment they need. This is provided by the school, with advice and support from the Local Education Authority Visual Impairment Service and other sources of information, advice and training such as the Royal National Institute for the Blind (RNIB). Many visually impaired children move on to further-education colleges and universities, using special grants to enable them to pay for readers and to buy special tape recorders to help them in their studies.

Specialist counselling and vocational training are available for those of working age and may be accessed through local authorities, the Royal National Institute for the Blind (RNIB) and colleges of further education.

ONE STEP AT A TIME

The Royal Institute for the Blind (RNIB) has produced an excellent booklet 'One step at a time' for parents of visually impaired children. This gives practical advice and tips on such topics as developing the senses, establishing routines and learning to walk. The RNIB and the British Toy and Hobby Association, in addition, have jointly produced a free booklet on popular toys and games for blind and partially sighted children.

DEAFNESS AND PARTIAL HEARING

Deafness is often called 'the hidden disability'. As with total blindness, total deafness is rare and is usually congenital (present from birth). **Partial deafness** is generally the result of an ear disease, injury or degeneration associated with the ageing process.

There are two types of deafness:

▶ **conductive**: when there is faulty transmission of sound from the outer ear to the inner ear;

▶ **sensorineural**: when sounds that do reach the inner ear fail to be transmitted to the brain.

FIGURE 15.7
The ear and hearing

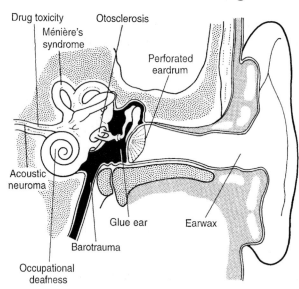

CAUSES OF CONDUCTIVE DEAFNESS

The most common causes of this kind of deafness in children are:

▶ **otitis media:** infection of the middle ear;

▶ **glue ear:** a build-up of sticky fluid in the middle ear (see Figure 15.7) (this condition affects children under 8 years old).

CAUSES OF SENSORINEURAL DEAFNESS

▶ *heredity*: there may be an inherited fault in a chromosome;

▶ *a birth injury;*

FIGURE 15.8
Glue ear

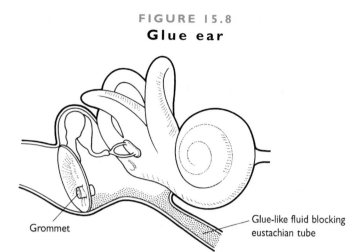

Grommet

Glue-like fluid blocking
eustachian tube

▶ *rubella:* there may be damage to the developing foetus if the mother is infected with
   the rubella (German measles) virus during pregnancy;
▶ *severe jaundice:* in the new-born baby with severe jaundice, there may be damage to
   the inner ear;
▶ *damage to the cochlea or labyrinth, or both:* resulting from e.g. an injury, viral infection
   or prolonged exposure to loud noise;
▶ *Ménière's* syndrome: a rare disorder in which deafness, **vertigo** and **tinnitus** result
   from an accumulation of fluid within the **labyrinth** in the inner ear.

DIAGNOSIS
Hearing tests are performed as part of a routine assessment of child development (see
Chapter 14 on surveillance). The early detection of any hearing defect is vital in order that
the best possible help be offered at the time when development is at its fastest.

TREATMENT
For conductive hearing loss:
▶ surgical correction of the defect;
▶ a **hearing aid.**

For sensorineural hearing loss:
▶ a hearing aid;
▶ special training: language acquisition/speech therapy/perceptual motor training; a
   bilingual approach using British Sign Language (BSL) and verbal speech is not often
   recommended.

HEARING AIDS
Almost all children with sensorineural hearing loss will benefit from a hearing aid; and
they can also be helpful for children with conductive hearing loss – for example, while
they are waiting to be admitted to hospital for corrective surgery.
   There are three types of hearing aid (see Figure 15.9):
▶ *a body-worn hearing aid:* this is often strapped to the child's waist, with a wire
   connecting it to the earpiece; this type is used for **profound hearing loss** as it
   enables greater amplification of sound in the smaller devices;

FIGURE 15.9
Hearing aids:
(a) Body-worn hearing aid,
(b) Post-aural hearing aid
(c) In-the-ear hearing aid

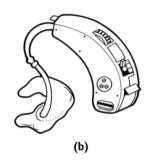

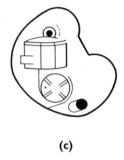

(a)

(b)

(c)

▶ *a post-aural hearing aid:* this fits comfortably behind the ear; it can be used with small babies;
▶ *an in-the-ear hearing aid:* this is generally reserved for use with older children.

The aim of all hearing aids is to **amplify** sounds. In children whose hearing is *not* helped by such aids, a **cochlear implant** may be considered instead.

PROBLEMS ASSOCIATED WITH HEARING IMPAIRMENT

▶ *Communication:* if possible, children should learn to express themselves through a recognisable speech pattern (**language acquisition**). Isolation may result from the deaf child's inability to hear the familiar voices and household noises that the hearing child takes for granted.
▶ *A lack of auditory stimulation:* this may lead to delayed development.
▶ *A potential for injury:* this is related to a failure to detect warning sounds, e.g. traffic, warning shouts.
▶ *Anxiety and coping difficulties:* this is related to reduced social interaction and loneliness.
▶ *Parental anxiety:* this is related to having a child with impaired hearing.

GUIDELINES

Hearing impairment for early childhood workers

▶ **A baby with a hearing impairment may not show the 'startle' reaction to a loud noise; this is evident shortly after birth.**
▶ **A baby of about 4 months will visibly relax and smile at the sound of their mother's voice, even before they can see her; if the baby does not show this response, there may be some hearing loss.**
▶ **If babbling starts and then stops after a few weeks, this is often an indication of hearing loss.**
▶ **Children with hearing loss will be much more observant and *visually* aware than a hearing child – e.g. they may respond to the ringing of**

- doorbells and telephones by reading the body language of those around them and responding appropriately.
- ▶ Toys that make a lot of noise are popular, because children can feel the vibration, even if they cannot hear the sound; dancing to music is also popular for the same reason.
- ▶ A child with a profound hearing loss may still react quite normally and even turn round in response to someone's approach since they may be using their other senses to compensate for the loss of hearing – e.g. they may notice a smell of perfume, or see the reflection of the person in a window or other glass surface.
- ▶ Use your well-developed observational skills to detect hearing loss. If you do think there is a problem, refer it to the parent if you are a nanny, or to your line manager or teacher in a school or nursery.

Early diagnosis and treatment can make a significant difference to the language development and learning potential of a child with a hearing impairment.

CHILDHOOD DEAFNESS AND EDUCATION

The National Deaf Children's Society emphasises the importance of the 'whole child' approach to the care of deaf children, involving family, education, health and social service working together in a balanced, coordinated and supportive way. At present, the quality of schooling and support services a deaf child receives is patchy and depends on *where* the family lives.

Key points for an improved service are:
- ▶ Each health district should have a **District Children's Hearing Assessment Unit** which will accept self-referrals as well as referrals from professionals.
- ▶ Each child should have a key worker to coordinate the various resources.
- ▶ Parents should take a central role in assessment, in the statementing process and in decision-making.
- ▶ Children under school age should be supported by a **peripatetic** teacher for the deaf who will visit families in their own homes, help with common problems and help the child to reach essential levels of development.

Some **Local Education Authorities (LEAs)** have integration schemes which cover the whole of the deaf community from birth to the age of 16. Leeds is one LEA that has an equal-opportunities policy which tailors the method of communication to the individual needs of the child.

Here, each child is given access to sign language (see Figure 15.10) as well as to English and Punjabi; and deaf adults act as **role models** – as teachers, interpreters and helpers in schools.

AUTISM

Autism is a rare developmental disorder which impairs a child's understanding of their environment. It affects about 4 to 5 children in every 10,000, although many more children may exhibit certain features relating to autism.

CAUSES OF AUTISM

There is no known cause, but because about one-quarter of autistic children have neurological symptoms, many specialists now believe there may be a physical/genetic

FIGURE 15.10
The manual spelling alphabet

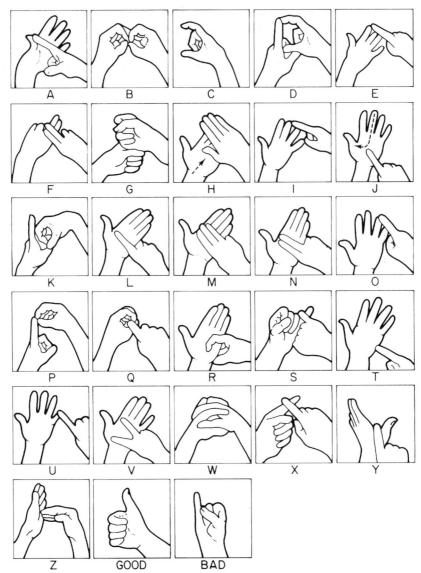

factor. Autism occurs in all parts of the world. Boys are affected more often than girls, in the ratio of 4:1.

FEATURES OF AUTISM

A child with autism may:

- ▶ lack an awareness of other people;
- ▶ avoid eye-to eye contact;
- ▶ prefer to play alone;
- ▶ be over-sensitive to certain sounds;
- ▶ be extremely resistant to change and become obsessed with one particular topic or idea;

► have difficulty in understanding and using normal speech patterns. **Echolalia** – an automatic repetition of what is said to them – is common;

► show abnormal body movements, e.g. arm flapping, flicking their fingers for hours on end, grimacing, rocking and charging in different directions at great speed;

► have sudden screaming fits; and may injure themselves;

► show an isolated special skill – e.g. drawing, music or an outstanding rote memory (See Figure 15.11)

FIGURE 15.11

Characterisitics of a child with autism

DIAGNOSIS

A diagnosis of autism is not usually made until the child is 2 years old, although parents may have noticed a lack of curiosity in their child, with poor sleeping and feeding patterns and general unresponsiveness in the first year.

THE SUPPORT AND MANAGEMENT OF THE CHILD WITH AUTISM

There is no known effective treatment apart from medication to control the associated problems of **epilepsy** and **hyperactivity**. Many therapies are being tried, e.g.:

▶ **holding therapy**, in which parents group together for long periods of time and try to foster emotional responsiveness by firm holding techniques;

▶ **behaviour therapy**, involving reward and discouragement for acceptable and unacceptable behaviour respectively;

▶ **Daily Life Therapy** – developed by Dr Kitahara in the Boston Higashi school in the USA – which offers a programme of physical education and age-appropriate lessons in a residential setting.

The child with autism will need constant one-to-one care requiring considerable patience and skill on the part of all family members. Any changes to the child's routine must be carefully planned.

EDUCATION

Early childhood education, for example at a nursery or playgroup, will help the family integrate into the community. Most children with autism attend local schools for children with severe learning difficulties; others require residential care: the National Autistic Society runs several schools which offer day, weekly or termly facilities.

ASPERGER'S SYNDROME

Most cases of **Asperger's syndrome** represent the other end of the autisitic spectrum. Language delay is not as common, but there are often problems with communication. However, the child with Asperger's syndrome is usually aware of their disability.

Features of the syndrome are:

▶ social naiveté;

▶ good grammatical language, using language only for own interests;

▶ very specialised interest, often highly academic – e.g. the movement of the planets, railway timetables;

▶ a lack of common sense arising from a lack of awareness of their environment.

Children with disabilities and their families

Every parent expecting a baby hopes that the baby will be perfect, and if the baby is disabled in any way, this will have a social, psychological and financial effect on the family and the way it functions. Each family is unique in the way that it will react initially and adjust in the long term. When a mother gives birth to a baby who has a disability, she may experience feelings of guilt – 'It must be because of something I did wrong during pregnancy' – or even of rejection, albeit temporary. Research by Selma Fraiberg (1974–77) showed that blind babies begin to smile at about the same age as sighted babies (about 4 weeks), but that they smile less often: the blind infant's smile is less intense, more fleeting and less frequent than the sighted baby's smile. Blind babies do not enter into a mutual gaze, which is an important factor in the formation of a deep attachment or

bonding between parents and their baby. Fraiberg's research found that most mothers of blind babies in her studies gradually withdrew from their infants and they needed help in being shown how to 'read' the baby's other signals such as body movements and gestures. This help led to an improved interaction between parents and their babies.

The main attachment is generally with the mother and father, but it is possible for other bonds to be formed, e.g. with a nanny, early childhood worker or grandparent. A lack of bonding in early years may lead to a child feeling emotionally insecure.

The following article was written by a mother whose third child has the chromosomal defect **Down's syndrome**. It describes her and her husband's feelings immediately after the birth.

A Mother Celebrates the Birthday of a Very Special Baby

'My third child was born just before Christmas, a beautiful baby boy with squashy fingers and crinkly ears. I was overjoyed – and relieved. I was 37 and the triple test had given me a slightly worrying result. Carried out in pregnancy, it uses a sample of blood to estimate your chances of having a baby with Down's syndrome. Women scoring 1/250 or less are considered high risk and offered an amniocentesis. I scored 1/260, so had no further tests.

I tried to pick the baby up but the umbilical cord was very short. He was reluctant to feed but after much persuasion took the breast. He lay in my arms, a curiously serene little bundle with a dusting of fine hair. I couldn't wait to get him home but the doctor said they would carry out some routine tests because of his initial refusal to feed . . .

The paediatrician arrived just as we decided to call the baby Euan. He let the baby slip through his fingers, stroking the back of his head with a practised hand. Sitting on the bed, he glanced at John, then back at me. 'Here comes the tricky bit,' he said calmly. 'I think your baby's got Down's syndrome.' He went over the telltale signs – the short umbilical cord, stubby fingers, low-set ears, poor muscle tone. We listened numbly, unable to comprehend that the nightmare had come true: there was something wrong with the baby.

As John leant over the cot and kissed the sleeping child, I realised I was crying, great sheets of tears moving slowly down my face. Inside I felt cold, hard, cruel. The paediatrician kept on talking, as if his words were a charm to keep our suffering at bay.

'. . . There's nothing *wrong* with this baby, he's just different. He's not suffering, you are. He'll be in touch with things we aren't.' He made it sound as if anyone in their right mind would have Down's syndrome.

'What about intelligence?' I asked sharply. 'Only intelligent people worry about intelligence.'

He correctly predicted the emotions we would feel: grief for the child we thought we would have, sorrow for the disastrous human being we thought he would be . . .

John went home to see the children and I was left alone with the baby who didn't belong to me but Mr and Mrs Down's syndrome. He didn't bear our features but theirs, his personality arose from their union, not mine and John's.

They offered to take him into the nursery but I refused, terrified that in his absence I would reject him. I had to keep him close, make him mine once more. Waking in the dead of night, I stared into his sleeping face. He almost frightened me, this tiny alien being wearing a mask which separated him from the rest of humanity. He was branded, set apart and now so was I. Stroking his head, I felt an agony of guilt, pity and fear. I had done this to him, I had blighted the flower before it had a chance to bloom. What terrible blackness inside me had afflicted my own child?

Later on they struggled to take blood from a vein in his head and I felt upset in a remote kind of way, the needle made him cry out. He was given a heart scan and I watched, curious about my own reactions. Did I want him to be healthy? Would it be better if he slipped away now? . . . The scan was normal. I took Euan home, just in time for the parties.

Twelve months later, it's nearly Christmas again . . . Euan plays near the foot of the Christmas tree; he has slanted eyes, sticky-out ears and a tongue that pops from his mouth like the label of a collar which refuses to lie flat. He might not go to primary school, let alone university, but every time he smiles – which he does all the time – my heart turns over.

. . . Euan has taught me so many things: that the ability to communicate is more important than IQ and may have nothing to do with it, and that creating love in others is so simple, a child can do it. Try as I might, I can't feel tragic about a baby who shakes with silent laughter as his sister wraps tinsel round his head. Most of all, Euan has made me realise just how much we underestimate our capacity for loving.

Every woman who gives birth to a handicapped child does so in a climate of rejection and fear. Yet even as I struggled to come to terms with Euan's birth, I continued to bond with my baby.

In the end, loving him was easy and – I cannot emphasise this word enough – as natural as falling off a log. Loving Euan, I find I like myself better too . . . When next you see the parents of a handicapped child, don't automatically feel sorry for them, because you have absolutely no idea what they are feeling.'

(Pat Evans in the Guardian, 16 December 1992)

The needs of parents and carers

A recent study by the King's Fund ('Carer's needs – a ten-point plan for carers') suggested the following needs on the part of carers:

1. *Status.* A recognition of their own contribution to society, of their own needs as individuals, and of the fact that they are the people who know their child best is necessary.
2. *Services.* These should be tailored to the carer's individual circumstances and planned in response to the **needs** of the child within the family.
3. *An awareness of cultural diversity.* Every effort should be made to provide services which recognise that people from different backgrounds may well have different requirements. The obvious example is dietary differences, but there are also other issues – e.g. touch by members of the opposite sex.
4. *Leisure.* Carers must have opportunities for a break – both to relax and to have some 'personal space'. Respite care or child-sitting can prove vital.
5. *Practical help.* Domestic help, adaptations to the home, incontinence services and help with transport may provide invaluable help to the carer.
6. *Support.* Carers often want someone to talk to, and with whom they can share their problems and frustrations; and parents in turn may need help in finding pleasure in their child.
7. *Information.* The specific needs of the child being cared for must be detailed, and knowledge of the available benefits and services is vital.
8. *Finance.* An income is needed which covers the costs of caring and which allows the carer to take employment or to share the care with other people. Accommodation may need to be adapted and special equipment purchased.

9   *Planning.* Carers should have the opportunities to explore alternatives to family care, for both the immediate and long-term future.
10 *Consultation.* Services should be designed through consultation with carers at all levels of policy planning. This is particularly important when a child is the subject of a **statement** (see pp. 442 and 443).

Carers may also need training in self-advocacy: putting forward the needs of their child and family effectively.

Special educational needs

A child is defined as having special educational needs if he or she has a learning difficulty which needs special teaching. A learning difficulty means that:

▶ the child has significantly greater difficulty in learning than most children of the same age; or
▶ a child has a disability which needs different educational facilities from those that schools generally provide for children of the same age in the area.

The children who need special educational education are not only those with obvious learning difficulties, such as those who are physically disabled, deaf or blind. They include those whose learning difficulties are less apparent, such as slow learners and emotionally vulnerable children. It is estimated that up to 20% of school children may need special educational help at some stage in their school careers. A child may have learning difficulties caused by:

▶ a physical disability;
▶ a problems with sight, hearing or speech;
▶ a mental disability;
▶ emotional or behavioural problems;
▶ a medical or health problem;
▶ difficulties with reading, writing, speaking or mathematics work;

Speech and language impairments

As many as 250,000 children under 5 – and a similar number of school age – have a speech and language impairment. For some, this is a delay – their language is developing, but more slowly than usual. In some cases, this may be connected with 'glue ear' in early childhood. For others with a language disorder, the difficulty is more complex. These children don't stammer or lisp. They are not autistic. Their general intelligence is often average or above. Their language impairment is specific or primary – not the result of any other disability, it is sometimes referred to as **dysphasia**.

Children with a speech and language impairment have difficulties with:

▶ talking (**expressive** language); this may be due to **dyspraxia,** (difficulty in making the movements which produce speech).
▶ understanding (**receptive** language)
▶ or both of these.

Some children have other difficulties which affect the development of language, including:

▶ difficulties with **listening and attention skills;**

▶ **behaviour difficulties**, due to the frustration of not understanding or being understood;

▶ difficulties with written language (**dyslexia**);

▶ difficulties understanding **abstract ideas** like time, emotions or make-believe; these children have trouble connecting ideas and using language socially.

▶ profound difficulties relating to the outside world; many of these will be described as having 'autistic tendencies'.

Some of these children benefit from learning a 'sign language', such as Makaton or British Sign Language/Signed English.

Makaton

The Makaton Vocabulary is a list of 350 items with corresponding signs and symbols, with an additional resource vocabulary for the national curriculum (approximately 600 items). The signs are based on British Sign Language (BSL), but are used to support spoken English. The Makaton Project publish a book of illustrations of the Makaton vocabulary (see Figure 15.12). Most signs rely on movement as well as position so you can't really learn the signs from the illustrations. Also in many signs facial expression is important.

If a child at school or nursery is learning Makaton, then parents should be invited to learn too. The Makaton Project will support them in this, as they know that everyone involved with the child must use the same signs for this to work.

FIGURE 15.12
Makaton

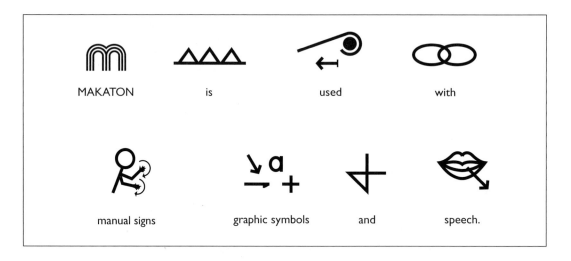

Developmental dyspraxia

Dyspraxia is an immaturity of the brain resulting in messages not being properly transmitted to the body. It affects at least 2% of the population in varying degrees and 70% of those affected are male. Children with dyspraxia can be of average or above intelligence but are often behaviourally immature. They try hard to fit in to the socially accepted behaviour when at school but often throw tantrums when at home. They may find it difficult to understand logic and reason. Dyspraxia is also called Clumsy Child Syndrome, Developmental Coordination Disorder (DCD), or Minimal Brain Dysfunction. Dyspraxia is a disability but, as with autism, those affected do not look disabled. This is both an advantage and a disadvantage. Sometimes children with dyspraxia are labelled as 'clumsy' children.

There are *many early indications* – in the child's first three years – that a child has dyspraxia:

▶ Irritable and difficult to comfort – from birth

▶ Delayed early motor development: sitting unaided, rolling from side to side: do not usually go through the crawling stage

▶ Toilet training may be delayed

▶ Sleeping difficulties: problems establishing routine, requires constant adult reassurance

▶ Continued problems with development of feeding skills

▶ Concentration limited to 2 or 3 minutes on any task

▶ Feeding difficulties: milk allergies, colic, restricted diet

▶ High levels of motor activity: constantly moving arms and legs

▶ Repetitive behaviours: head banging or rolling

▶ Sensitive to high levels of noise

▶ Avoids constructional toys such as jigsaws and Lego

▶ Delayed language development: single words not evident until age 3

▶ Highly emotional: easily distressed, frequent outbursts of uncontrolled behaviour

Later on, a child with dyspraxia may have the following problems;

▶ Very high levels of motor activity
 – feet swinging and tapping when seated
 – hands clapping or twisting
 – unable to stay in one place longer than 5 minutes

▶ Moves awkwardly
 – constantly bumping into objects and falling
 – associated mirror movements, hands flap when running or jumping

▶ Continue to be messy eaters
 – often spill liquid from drinking cups
 – prefer to use fingers to feed

▶ Poor fine motor skills
 – pencil grip
 – use of scissors
 – immature drawings

▶ Isolated in peer group
 – prefers adult company

▶ Sensitive to sensory stimulation
 – high levels of noise
 – dislikes being touched or wearing new clothes

▶ Limited concentration
 – tasks often left unfinished

- ▶ Very excitable
  - voice loud and shrill
  - is easily distressed
  - has temper tantrums

- ▶ Difficulty pedalling tricycle or similar toy
  - poor ground awareness
  - no sense of danger, jumps from inappropriate heights

- ▶ Avoids constructional toys
  - jigsaws
  - building blocks (e.g. Lego)

- ▶ Lack of imaginative play
  - dose not enjoy 'dressing up' or playing appropriately in the home corner or Wendy House. Limited creative play

- ▶ Language difficulties persist
  - children often referred to speech therapist

- ▶ Limited response to verbal instructions
  - slower response time
  - problems with comprehension

Assessment

Assessment involves obtaining a detailed developmental history of the child, and using developmental tests or scales to build up a cognitive profile.

Treatment

There is no cure for dyspraxia but the earlier a child is treated then the greater the chance of improvement. Occupational therapists, physiotherapists and extra help at school can all help a child with dyspraxia to cope or to overcome many difficulties.

Other specific educational needs

1. Giftedness

Some educationalists make a distinction between gifted and talented children:
- ▶ gifted children being those who are of superior ability over a wide range;
- ▶ talented children being those who have a specific area of expertise, e.g. musical aptitude or sporting prowess.

There is much debate about whether children who are gifted **do** have special educational needs. Educational approaches include:
- ▶ **enrichment:** the classroom curriculum is specially adapted to support and extend the child's particular abilities;
- ▶ **segregation:** the child would be placed in a group of other high ability pupils, who would follow a specialised curriculum;
- ▶ **acceleration:** to be moved up a year in school. This is often the obvious choice, but parents and teachers are now much more aware of the social and emotional effects of separation from the peer group

2. Dyslexia

Dyslexia is a specific learning difficulty characterised by difficulty in coping with written symbols. Some problems encountered by the person with dyslexia are:

- Language problems
- Sequencing difficulties
- Viral perception problems
- Poor short-term memory
- A lack of spatial awareness
- Short concentration span
- Directional confusion
- Reversal – of letters and numbers
- Stress and fear of failure

Every child with dyslexia has a different pattern of difficulties. Intelligence is usually unaffected, but the problem may seem more obvious in intelligent children. Dyslexia is a very vague term which tends to be used to cover all kinds of difficulties, ranging from mild problems with spelling to complete literacy (inability to read or write). Recent research has shown that the brains of people with dyslexia are 'wired' differently from other people's. Micro-anatomy carried out on their brains after death shows that whilst there is a lack of efficiency in the left brain hemisphere which relates to language ability, there is *increased* efficiency in the side of the brain which dictates **spatial ability**. Visual spatial skills seem superior in people with dyslexia; their ability to see the world in a more vivid, three-dimensional way points to a link between artistic talent and dyslexia. Dyslexia is often seen as a middle class excuse for academic non-achievement. Early identification of the problem can greatly reduce the difficulties, both for the individual with dyslexia and for their school and family. Teaching strategies include:

- regular praise and rewards. Many children with dyslexia have poor self-esteem and see themselves as failures within the school system;
- keeping records of each lesson plan, so that each lesson builds upon the success of the previous one;
- 'scaffolding' work; structuring the work into a series of small steps which supports the learning;
- the use of specific teaching aids, e.g. Special phonic 'flash' cards for letter recognition;
- the use of concrete and visual ways of explaining, e.g. Presenting instructions in the form of diagrams, or essay plans laid out as patterns.

3. Attention deficit hyperactivity disorder

Attention deficit hyperactivity disorder (ADHD) fits into the category of specific learning difficulty. Children may show some or all of the following characteristics:

- Difficulty remaining seated when asked to do so
- Difficulty playing quietly
- Difficulty in sharing and taking turns in group situations
- Often loses things necessary for tasks or activities at school or at home, e.g. books, pencils etc.
- Often talks excessively
- Difficulty sustaining attention in tasks or play activities
- Easily distracted by extraneous stimuli
- Interrupts others, e.g. Butts into other children's games
- Often appears not to listen when being spoken to
- Often engages in physically dangerous activities without considering possible consequences, e.g. Runs across road without looking
- Appears restless; often fidgets with hands or feet

▶ Inability to focus attention on relevant detail at an age when such control is expected

Attention deficit hyperactivity disorder (ADHD) is sometimes initially diagnosed as an autistic spectrum disorder as many of the features are common to both disorders. It is estimated that about half of children with ADHD also show behavioural (or conduct) disorders.

The cause of ADHD is not known, but there is growing evidence to show that a pattern of hyperactivity is inherited and also that there may be a biological cause, perhaps due to a slower metabolism of glucose by the brain. Treatment is by a stimulant medication (usually Ritalin) which often has an immediate improving effect on the child's behaviour; arriving at the correct dosage for the individual, however, takes time and a high degree of co-operation between school and parents. Daily feedback from the child's class teacher is essential for the treatment to be effective in the long term.

Emotional and behavioural difficulties

Any behaviour that causes a problem to others falls within this category. Such difficulties include:

▶ **conduct disorders**: bullying, aggression, disobedience, delinquency;
▶ **anxiety and withdrawal**: depression and eating disorders;
▶ **socialised aggression**: children who have experienced rejection by their peers and others show a marked tendency to band together, thus supporting and reinforcing their antisocial behaviour.

Assessment of need in this area is difficult and before a child is included in this category, an educational psychologist will look at both the intensity and the frequency of the child's behaviour. Behaviour that is highly inappropriate in one social context may be quite acceptable in another situation.

Children with special needs, and the role of professionals

The role of health-service professionals

FAMILY DOCTORS (GENERAL PRACTITIONERS)

Family doctors are independent professionals who are under contract with the National Health Service but are not employed by it. They are the most available of the medical profession, and are also able to refer carers on to specialist doctors and paramedical services.

HEALTH VISITORS

Health visitors are qualified nurses who have done further training, including midwifery experience. They work exclusively in the community, and can be approached either directly or via the family doctor. They work primarily with children up to the age of 5 years; this obviously includes
all children with disabilities, and they carry out a wide range of developmental checks.

PHYSIOTHERAPISTS

The majority of 'physios' are employed in hospitals, but some work in special schools or residential facilities. **Physiotherapists** assess children's motor development and skills, and provide activities and exercises that parents and carers can use to encourage better mobility and coordination.

OCCUPATIONAL THERAPISTS

Occupational therapists ('OTs') work in hospitals, schools and other residential establishments. Some OTs specialise in working with children (**paediatric occupational therapist**s) and will assess a child's practical abilities and advise on the most appropriate activities and specialist equipment to encourage independent life skills.

COMMUNITY NURSES

Most **community nurses** work closely with family doctors and provide nursing care in the home. They also advise the parent or carer on specialist techniques – e.g. lifting, catheter care etc.

SCHOOL NURSES

School nurses may visit a number of mainstream schools in their health district to monitor child health and development – by checking weight, height, eyesight and hearing, and by giving advice on common problems such as headlice. They may also be employed in special schools to supervise the routine medical care of disabled children.

SPEECH THERAPISTS

Speech therapists may be employed in schools, in hospitals or in the community. They assess a child's speech, tongue and mouth movements and effects of these on eating and swallowing. They further provide exercises and activities both to develop all aspects of children's expressive and receptive communication skills and to encourage language development.

DIETICIANS

Most **dieticians** work in hospitals and can advise on a range of special diets, e.g. for diabetics or those with cystic fibrosis or **coeliac disease**.

PLAY SPECIALISTS

Play specialists are employed in hospitals and are often trained nursery nurses who have additional training and may prepare a child for hospitalisation and provide play opportunities for children confined to bed or in a hospital playroom.

PLAY THERAPISTS

Play therapists also work in hospitals and have undertaken specialist training. They use play to enable children with special needs feel more secure emotionally in potentially threatening situations.

CLINICAL PSYCHOLOGISTS

Clinical psychologists usually work in hospitals. They assess children's emotional, social and intellectual development and advise on appropriate activities to promote development.

The role of social-service professionals

SOCIAL WORKERS

Most **social workers** now work for specialised teams dealing with a specific client group – e.g. a Disability and Learning Difficulties Team. They are employed by social-services departments ('social-work departments' in Scotland) and initially their role is to assess the needs of the child. They offer advice on the availability of all relevant local services, and may refer the family to other departments such as the **Department of Social Security (DSS), the National Health Service (NHS)** or voluntary organisations. A social worker may also act as an **advocate** on behalf of disabled children, ensuring that they receive all the benefits and services to which they are entitled.

TECHNICAL OFFICERS

Technical officers usually work with people with specific disorders: e.g. **audio technicians** or **audiologists** monitor the level of hearing in children as a developmental check; and **sign-language interpreters** translate speech into sign language for deaf and hearing-impaired people.

NURSERY OFFICERS

Nursery officers are trained nursery nurses who work in day nurseries and family centres. Such staff are involved in shift work, and they care for children under 5 when it is not possible for those children to remain at home.

FAMILY AIDS

Family aids used to be called 'home helps'; they provide practical support for families in their own homes – shopping, cooking, looking after children etc.

SOCIAL SECURITY

There is a wide and complex range of benefits and allowances available to disabled children and their families. Advice may be obtained from social workers or from the **Citizen's Advice Bureau**.

The role of education-service professionals

THE SPECIAL EDUCATIONAL NEEDS COORDINATOR (SENCO)

The **special educational needs coordinator** liaises both with colleagues in special schools and the parents of children with special needs. They are responsible for coordinating provision for children with special educational needs, for keeping the school's SEN register and for working with external agencies – e.g. educational-psychology services, social-service departments and voluntary organisations.

EDUCATIONAL PSYCHOLOGISTS

Educational psychologists are involved in the educational assessment of children with special needs, and in preparing the **statement** of special educational needs. They act as advisers to professionals working directly with children with a range of special needs, particularly those with emotional and behavioural difficulties.

SPECIAL NEEDS TEACHERS

Special needs teachers are qualified teachers with additional training and experience in teaching children with special needs. They are supported by:

▶ **special needs support teachers/specialist teachers** who are often **peripatetic** – i.e. they visit disabled children in different mainstream schools – and who may specialise in a particular disorder – e.g. vision or hearing impairment;
▶ **special needs support assistants** who may be qualified nursery nurses and who often work with individual statemented children under the direction of the specialist teacher.

EDUCATIONAL WELFARE OFFICERS

An in mainstream education, **educational welfare officers** will be involved with children whose school attendance is irregular; they may also arrange school transport for disabled children.

Children with disabilities in mainstream settings

Care and education are difficult to separate, especially when children have multiple disabilities. The move towards **inclusive care and education** is therefore one that most parents welcome.

Inclusive care and education

The Children Act 1989 promotes the integration of disabled children in mainstream settings such as nursery schools, day nurseries, schools and family centres.

INTEGRATION

In the UK, **integration** is understood to take place at three levels: locational, social and functional:

▶ **Locational integration** is simply the placement of a child with **special educational needs** in a unit or class for disabled children in a mainstream school, or in a special school that shares the same site as an ordinary school.

▶ **Social integration** occurs when the children in the unit or class mix with mainstream children for a range of non-academic activities.

▶ **Functional integration** occurs when children with special educational needs follow courses, or elements of courses, with their peer group, with any necessary support they require.

FIGURE 15.13
Hannah

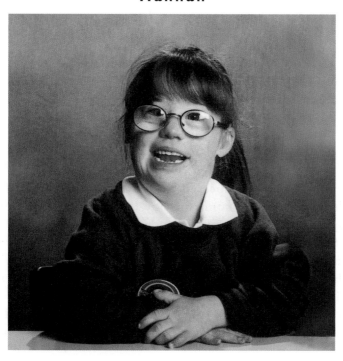

Mainstream schools will need to consider the specific needs of disabled children in order to promote independence and foster learning. These needs are:

1 **Access**
   ▶ Specialised equipment such as ramps and lifts for wheelchairs should provide access for *all* children in the school.
   ▶ Toilet facilities should be large enough to accommodate wheelchairs.
   ▶ Computer equipment must have touch-sensitive controls.
   ▶ Play equipment should be adjustable – e.g. water troughs that can be set on stands at varying levels.
   ▶ Learning materials should also be available in audio, large print or Braille format for visually impaired children.
   ▶ Communication aids such as British Sign Language (see Figure 15.10) have to be available and *taught* – as does any language if a child is to be supported through it in school.

2 **Information**. Staff will need information about specific disorders and disabilities in order to plan learning goals which are realistic for the individual child's needs; such information is available from the various voluntary organisations and self-help groups – e.g. the National Autisitic Society, the National Deaf Children's Society, the Royal Institute for The Blind and SCOPE (see the 'Useful addresses' section at the end of this chapter).

3 **Training**. All staff in schools offering inclusive education must be trained in disability awareness and equal opportunities. Some specialist teachers may be required to work with an individual child; e.g. a partially sighted child may work on a one-to-one basis with a teacher who adapts the learning materials being used during lessons.

4 **Role models**. Children with special needs need **positive role models**. Schools and nurseries can help to improve children's self-image by:
   ▶ involving disabled adults at all levels of care and education;
   ▶ carefully selecting books and activities that promote a positive self-image for disabled children – in the same way that using multicultural resources promotes a positive self-image for minority ethnic groups.

The following case study is a true 'snapshot' biography, written by her parents, of a young girl who has Down's syndrome.

C A S E   S T U D Y

When Hannah was born, we suspected straight away that she had Down's syndrome. Our thoughts were confirmed by the consultant the following morning. Many children with Down's syndrome find it hard to suck, and with Hannah breastfeeding proved very difficult; but with the support of a wonderful nursery nurse at the hospital, we managed it. During this time, a midwife noticed that Hannah appeared to be blue around the face, which suggested that she had a possible heart condition.

At less than a week old, we took Hannah to a London hospital to have a heart scan. She was diagnosed as having an Atrio-Ventricular Septal Defect

(AVSD). Corrective surgery would involve patching up two holes and reconstructing a heart valve. We were informed by a consultant that if surgery were not performed, then Hannah would probably not live beyond her teens. The consultant suggested that we choose not to follow the surgery option, since the quality of life for a teenager with Down's syndrome was poor. At one week old, Hannah was being discriminated against, because she was born with Down's syndrome!

At home we were visited by a Portage worker, a home-based early educational intervention service. Hannah was set different tasks each week for which achievable targets were set. Hannah's babbling and motor skills were developing as one would expect for a child with Down's syndrome. She still had difficulty sucking and eating baby foods. When she was a year old we were visited by a speech therapist and physiotherapist. More tasks were given and Makaton signs were introduced, to aid her communication and eating skills.

Regular visits continued to be made to various hospitals. We decided that Hannah would undergo corrective heart surgery. She was on medication for her heart condition, and her hearing and eyesight were being monitored. Hannah had her open heart surgery at 14 months old at a different London children's hospital. The corrective surgery was successful, but she caught two infections during the recovery phase whilst still in hospital. As a result she became totally floppy again and lost her spontaneous babbling. After five weeks in hospital, Hannah was well enough to return home even though her muscle tone was very poor. Visits to various hospitals continued, and Hannah was gradually weaned off her medicines. With this major hurdle over, we could again begin to concentrate on other areas of her development. For the first time Hannah began to eat real food. Chocolate buttons were an early favourite! We had heard how many children with Down's syndrome tended to be obese, but Hannah was tiny and needed feeding up! We also knew that children with Down's syndrome were 'loving'. Well, Hannah was very affectionate towards some people, but understandably feared any medical staff.

Hannah's verbal and motor skills developed at an extremely slow rate. Her peers who also had Down's syndrome, were beginning to walk and talk, but Hannah was not. It was apparent that her level of understanding was developing much more quickly than her expressive skills.

We were very keen that Hannah should go to an integrated nursery. We eventually found a lovely nursery, but would need to find a volunteer to be with Hannah throughout the sessions she attended. Hannah stayed at nursery for several years. Her volunteers changed although on several occasions I had to go in to support her myself. It was not until her final year that the Local Educational Authority began to fund nursery support for children with Down's syndrome. She then received regular professional support, and for the first time I didn't have to worry if her helper would not turn up.

Hannah was still not walking or talking. She used Makaton to sign her needs, and to read simple books. She was able to count up to five, by pointing to the numbers. She had been allowed to spend an extra year at the nursery, but by the time she was six, the Local Authority were keen to place her in a Special School or a Special Unit. We opposed and fought against this. For the following year, Hannah was educated at home. She developed further many of her basic skills. Finally, after numerous meetings, the Authority finally agreed to allow her to go to our local school. Hannah has settled into school life quickly and easily and has amazed everyone despite all of her difficulties. Although she can be stubborn, Hannah is also very co-operative. She loves the social aspects of school life, as well as the learning activities. The school, children and other parents hold a wonderfully supportive attitude towards her as an individual. Hannah receives the full time support that she is entitled to and, as long as she is progressing and happy at school, then we will continue to fight for an integrated education for her.

It could not be said that Hannah is typical of a child who has Down's syndrome. (In fact, there is no such thing as a typical child who has Down's syndrome). Hannah's physical and verbal difficulties make everyday life harder for her, but her strong personality, charm and determination are helping her get on with life and have earned her the respect of her parents, teachers, helpers and fellow classmates.

Children in residential care

The Children Act 1989 emphasised that the best place for children to be brought up is within their own families, statistics show that the vast majority of disabled children *are* living at home. Some residential special schools offer weekly or termly boarding facilities; children may be in **residential care** for medical reasons or because the family cannot manage the care involved. All homes must be registered and inspected by social-services departments to safeguard the interests of this particularly vulnerable group.

Foster placements

The Foster Placement (Children) Regulations 1991 apply safeguards to any child in foster care (see Chapter 16). Some voluntary organisations provide specialist training programmes for carers **fostering** disabled children, and the carer's active involvement in the child's education is encouraged.

Respite care

This should ideally be renamed 'natural break' or 'short stay' as **respite care** implies the carers need relief from an unwanted burden. The aim of such care is to provide support and encouragement to enable the parents/carers to continue caring for their child within the family. There are four types of respite care:
- care in a foster placement;
- residential care, in a home or sometimes a hospital unit;
- holiday schemes – e.g. diabetic camps etc.;
- care within the child's own home.

The latter is often the best provision of care if the right substitute carer can be found. Provision is patchy and is only worthwhile if the child derives as much benefit from the break as do the carers.

R E S O U R C E S

Books

Christy Brown, *My Left Foot,* London, Secker and Warburg, 1954.

Laura Middleton, *Children First – Working with Children and Disability,* Birmingham, Venture Press, 1992

Stephen Moore, *Social Welfare Alive,* Cheltenham, Stanley Thornes, 1993

O'Grady, *Integration Working,* CSIE Report, 1990

M. Oliver, *Social Work with Disabled People,* London, Macmillan, 1983

Alan Skelt, *Caring for People with Disabilities,* London, Pitman, 1993

John Swain et al. *Disabling Barriers, Enabling Environments,* Sage Publications, 1993

Useful Addresses

Association for Brain-Damaged Children (ABDC)
Clifton House
3 St Paul's Road
Foleshill
Coventry CV6 5DE

Association for Spina Bifida and Hydrocephalus
ASBAH House
42 Park Road
Peterborough
PE1 2UQ
Tel.: 01733 555988

The Bobath Centre
5 Netherhall Gardens
London NW3 5RN
Tel.: 020 7435 3895

British Council of Organisations of Disabled People (BCDOP)
St Mary's Church
Greenlaw Street
London SE18 5AR
Tel.: 020 8316 4184

British Deaf Association
38 Victoria Place
Carlisle CA1 1HU
Tel.: 01228 48844

British Diabetic Association
10 Queen Anne Street
London W1M 0BD
Tel.: 020 7323 1531

British Epilepsy Association
Anstey House
40 Hanover Square
Leeds LS3 1BE
Tel.: 01532 439393

British Polio Fellowship
Bell Close
West End Road
Ruislip
Middlesex HA4 6LP
Tel.: 01895 675515

Brittle Bone Society
112 City Road
Dundee DD2 2PW
Tel.: 01382 817771

Carer's National Association
29 Chilworth Mews
London W2 3RG
Tel.: 020 7724 7776

Cystic Fibrosis Research Trust
5 Blyth Road
Bromley
Kent BR1 3RS
Tel.: 020 8461 7211

Down's Syndrome Association
153–5 Mitcham Road
London SW17 9PG
Tel.: 020 8682 4001

ENABLE (*was* Scottish Society for the Mentally Handicapped)
6th Floor
7 Buchanan Street
Glasgow G1 1JL
Tel.: 0141 226 4541

Epilepsy Association of Scotland
48 Gowan Road
Glasgow G51 3HL
Tel.: 0141 427 4911

Haemophilia Society
123 Westminster Bridge Road
London SE1 7HR
Tel.: 020 7928 2020

John Groome Association for the Disabled
10 Gloucester Drive
London N4 2LP
Tel.: 020 8802 7272

The Kerland Clinic (Doman-Delcato Therapy)
Marsh Lane
Huntworth Gate
Bridgwater
Somerset TA6 6LQ
Tel.: 01278 429089

Makaton Vocabulary Development Project
31 Firwood Drive
Camberley
Surrey
Tel: 01276 61390

Mencap
Mencap National Centre
123 Golden Lane
London EC1Y 0RT
Tel.: 020 7454 0454

Muscular Dystrophy Group
Nattrass House
35 Macauley Road
London SW4 0PQ
Tel.: 020 7720 8055

National Association for Gifted Children
Park Campus
Boughton Green Road
Northampton
Northants NN2 7AL
Tel.: 0604 792300

National Autistic Society
276 Willesden Lane
London NW2 5RB
Tel.: 020 8451 1114

National Deaf Children's Society
45 Hereford Road
London W2 5AH
Tel.: 020 7250 0123

National Portage Association
King Alfred's College
Sparkford Road
Winchester
Hants SO22 4NR
Tel:. 01962 62281

Play Matters/National Toy
Libraries Association
68 Churchway
London NW1 1LT

Tel.: 020 7387 9592

Royal National Institute for
the Blind (RNIB)
224 Great Portland Street
London W1N 6AA
Tel.: 020 7388 1266

SCOPE
12 Park Crescent
London W1N 4EQ
Tel.: 020 7636 5020

Sickle Cell Society
54 Station Road
Harlesden
London NW10 4BO
Tel.: 020 8961 7795

United Kingdom
Thalassaemia Society
107 Nightingale lane
London N8 7QY

A C T I V I T Y

Support for those with cystic fibrosis

The case study on page 446 is an accurate 'snapshot' of a 7-year-old girl with cystic fibrosis, but it tells us little about the impact of cystic fibrosis on the family, or about the network of care-givers which makes life easier for the family.

1 What help is available to Karen's family from:
   ▶ the NHS
   ▶ social services
   ▶ the private care sector
   ▶ voluntary organisations?

2 Find out what educational provision Karen might need if she has to spend more time in hospital.

3 What help do you think the Cystic Fibrosis Research trust can offer Karen and her family?

4 One in 20 of the British population are carriers; the chance of two carriers becoming partners is one in 400. What is the chance of a child of two carriers having cystic fibrosis? Should Matthew, Karen's brother, be worried that he may be a carrier, and can he be genetically tested?

A C T I V I T Y :

1 Choose one of the genetic and chromosomal disorders listed above – a *different* one from those chosen by your fellow students – and research it in preparation for a talk which you will present to the rest of your class. Use the following guidelines to help you structure the talk:
   ▶ what your chosen disorder is;
   ▶ its causes and incidence (use charts);
   ▶ how it is diagnosed/genetic screening availability;
   ▶ its effects;
   ▶ treatment and care needs.

2 The presentation may be recorded on video, assessed on verbal presentation or graded as a written assignment – or two or more of these options – and then be placed in a fact file to be used as a class resource.

NB: the teacher/lecturer could allow three to four weeks for preparation of the talk so that students have time to write off to specialist groups for relevant information (see the 'Useful addresses' section at the end of this chapter).

A C T I V I T Y

Testing/screening methods

1 Find out all you can about (a) amniocentesis; (b) the AFP blood test; (c)chorionic villus sampling; (d) ultrasound. For each, answer the following questions:
   ▶ What is it?
   ▶ What conditions can be detected?
   ▶ What are the risks?

   The Association of Spina Bifida and Hydrocephalus produces an information sheet on antenatal screening. (See also Chapter 3 on babies.)
2 Spina bifida is a congenital defect in which one or more vertebrae fail(s) to develop completely, leaving a portion of the spinal cord exposed.
   ▶ Describe the three forms of spinal bifida.
   ▶ What is hydrocaphalus, and how is it treated?

A C T I V I T Y

Programmes for children with cerebral palsy

1 Find out the principles behind conductive education.
   ▶ Where can parents go to have their child assessed?
   ▶ Which model of disability does it follow?
2 Contact your local Portage group and try to arrange for a speaker to come into college or school to explain its benefits to the disabled child and their family.
3 Find out about the Bobath technique.

A C T I V I T Y

Promoting an awareness of visual impairment

Tutors or students – or both – may wish to send away for copies of the above two booklets (see the RNIB in the 'Useful addresses' section at the end of the chapter) to enable them to carry out the first of the following two activities:

1 A Display. Plan and mount a display on 'Children with visual impairment'. Using the booklets as a guide, each small group should plan and mount a display on each of the following topics:
  ▶ developing the senses;
  ▶ establishing routines;
  ▶ movement games;
  ▶ play and toys.

When the displays are up, each group should evaluate each other's display, using a set of criteria agreed beforehand, e.g.: is the information presented in an easy-to-understand format? Does the material used illustrate the points effectively?

   Try to contact a local group of parents of visually impaired children and invite them to view the display; health visitors/social services departments may be able to make the first contact for you here:

2 An exercise in empathy. The following exercise cannot give a real experience of blindness but may help to promote understanding.
   In pairs:
  ▶ One person ties a blindfold (e.g. a scarf) around their own eyes and the other person then escorts them around the college or neighbourhood. On return, the sighted one offers the 'blind' person a drink and a sandwich.
  ▶ Then, swap roles, and after the exercise, evaluate the activity: how did it feel to be so reliant on someone else? How did it feel to be *responsible* for someone else?
  ▶ Draw up a list of practical points to help others who are offering refreshment and guidance to someone who is blind.

3 Find out about the aids available for those with visual impairment, including the Braille alphabet.

A C T I V I T Y

More on hearing impairment

1 Make a list of toys and games which are especially suitable for children with hearing impairments.
2 What is involved in the operation for glue ear (myringotomy and the insertion of grommets)? How many such operations are carried out in your district health authority each year?

A C T I V I T Y

Finding out about autism

1 Find out if there is any special provision for children with autism in your local area.
2 Find out about the work of the National Autistic Society.
3 List the social skills required to participate fully in daily activities in a reception class. Try to describe the difficulties a child with autism may have in integrating.
4 What help and support is available to the family that has a child with autism? What might the effects be on the siblings of living with a child with autism?

A C T I V I T Y

The parental response to disability

Read the extract 'A mother celebrates the birthday of a very special baby' on page 461.
1 Do you think that the paediatrician showed understanding when he told the parents that their new-born baby had Down's syndrome? Give reasons for your answer.

FIGURE 15.14
Cunningham's model of psychic crisis

SHOCK PHASE:	confusion, denial, irrationality, numbness
REACTION PHASE:	express sorrow, grief, disappointment, anxiety, aggression, feelings of failure
ADAPTION PHASE:	realistic appraisal – what can be done? At this point professionals need to be able to give more information
ORIENTATION PHASE:	begin to organise, seek help and information, and plan for the future

2 Why does the author say that 'every woman who gives birth to a handicapped child does so in a climate of rejection and fear'?
3 Look at Cunningham's model of psychic crisis (Figure 15.14) which outlines the various parental emotions and reactions at the time of finding out about their child's disability. Try to identify the phases which Euan's mother went through.
4 Research the condition Down's syndrome, including the following points:
   ▶ the cause;
   ▶ the incidence in the UK and world-wide;
   ▶ the characteristics of a child with Down's syndrome;
   ▶ the prognosis and help available.

A C T I V I T Y

Research into Integration

Find out about the education and support offered to children with Down's syndrome in your area:

▶ What is available for children with Down's syndrome of nursery school age, or primary school age and of secondary school age?

▶ What are the advantages of inclusive education for children with Down's syndrome, and for their peers?

▶ Find out about Makaton as a method of communication.

A C T I V I T Y

Enabling the child with a disability

1 Look at the layout of your own work placement. What physical changes would be necessary to include (a) a child in a wheelchair; (b) a partially sighted child?

2 Try to write a story in which a child with a disability is the hero/heroine but *not* for bravely enduring or overcoming that disability.

A C T I V I T Y

Access to respite care

Think of ways in which carers of able-bodied children get respite from full-time care. Why can the same avenues not be opened to *all* carers? List the possible problems for parents of disabled children in obtaining respite care, and then list their solutions.

Extension work

1 *Observation: a time sample.* Observe a child in your work placement whom you/the teacher have identified as being shy or withdrawn. Choose a day when you can observe the child at regular intervals, say every 10 or 15 minutes, and display the information obtained on a prepared chart.

Evaluate your observation. Do you think the child has special needs, and if so, what is the nature of those needs and how could you help meet them?

2 *Activity: a talking/listening game.* Plan a talking/listening game which could be adapted to allow full participation by a child with a hearing impairment.

3 *Research activity: communication methods.* Research different methods of communication – in particular:

▶ Makaton – a method of sign language using gross motor movements;

▶ British Sign Language;

▶ the Canon Communicator – a portable communication aid that straps to the wrist; messages are printed onto a paper strip;

▶ Possum Control communication aids – which operate a variety of devices by a simple switching movement.

List the advantages and disadvantages of these different methods of communication.

4 *Discussion topic.* Are televised charity appeals – 'Telethons' – an ethical way of raising money for children's charities?

▶ Is the image of the child 'suffering bravely' a healthy one?

▶ Has not *every* child the right to a fulfilled, comfortable life without having to rely on public generosity?

Organise a debate in class, preferably after watching a recent 'Telethon'.

16

Legal Issues in Child Care Provision

Legal Issues in Child Care Provision

Britain is a **democracy**. There are different types of democracy. For example, in the USA, France and Germany, there are **presidential democracies**. In Sweden, Holland and the UK, the type of democracy is the **constitutional monarchy**.

How laws are made

There are two ways to make a law:

1 **Statute law:** through legislation which is passed by Parliament. A **Bill** goes through both the House of Commons and the House of Lords through different stages:

   ▶ **First reading:** the Bill is formally introduced to Parliament.
   ▶ **Second reading:** the general principles are debated and voted on.
   ▶ A **Committee** debates every clause and votes on it.
   ▶ The Bill is debated in Parliament, and more amendments can be made (**report stage**).
   ▶ **Third reading:** the Bill is again debated, and a final vote is taken.
   ▶ The Monarch gives **Royal Assent**.
   ▶ The Bill becomes law as an **Act of Parliament**.

House of Commons   House of Lords

The UK Parliament

651 Members of Parliament (MPs) are elected in general elections which must occur at least every 5 years. MPs belong to a political party. The main parties in the UK are Conservative, Labour, Liberal Democrat, Unionist, Scottish National and Plaid Cymru.

The party with the most seats forms a government, led by the Prime Minister. The Prime Minister forms a Cabinet of ministers in charge of government departments sometimes called Secretaries of State – to take charge of government departments – e.g. the Department for Education and Employment. Ministers are served in these departments by civil servants.

Bishops and hereditary lords and ladies are found here.

Peerages are given by the government for:
- ▶ service to the party;
- ▶ good deeds done.

There is then secondary legislation which shows how the law is to be applied. This is written in two kinds of document:
- ▶ **Rules of Court**
- ▶ **Regulations.**

2 **Case law:** by rulings in the court. This is sometimes called **common law.** Judgement is made in the:
- ▶ High Court
- ▶ Court of Appeal
- ▶ House of Lords.

Decisions made in these courts are binding on the decisions the lower courts can make.

Laws exist to protect people and to specify the ways in which people must behave – someone who breaks the law acts **illegally**. Almost every aspect of our lives is in some way touched by laws.
- ▶ **Private law** concerns family relationships between children and their families.
- ▶ **Public law** is about the way the *state* provides services, for example, child protection.

RULES OF COURT

These rules show how the law will be applied in the courts. For example, they show how, and for whom, an emergency protection order can be applied for.

There is a checklist which the court must consider when making decisions about children:

1 The wishes and feelings of the child are considered.

2 The physical, emotional and educational needs of the child are considered.

3 The likely effect of changing the child's circumstances are thought through.

4 The child's age, sex, background and anything else that might be relevant is discussed.

5 Whether the child might come to significant harm or is at risk of harm is important.

6 There is discussion on whether the parents are able to meet the child's needs.

7 The court is required to discuss a range of powers that are available in making the decision.

LOCAL GOVERNMENT

No country can be governed entirely by central departments. This is why it is necessary for local government to exist. Local departments are often called **local authorities**. In the UK, these are divided into:

▶ England and Wales: district council; county council; unitary council;

▶ Scotland: district councils;

▶ Northern Ireland: boards.

In every local authority, there will be a **council** and **councillors** who are locally elected every four years.

The power and influence of local government has been reduced since 1976. For example, state schools can now opt out of local authority control and become grant-maintained directly from central government (see Chapter 13 on education).

Every area has, for example, a local Education and Social Services Department. In Scotland, social services are provided through Social Work Departments. In Northern Ireland there are education and library boards and health and social services departments.

How British democracy has developed during 50 years

In the mid-1940s, the major parts of the **welfare state** were introduced. The thinking behind this was that everyone should be entitled to free health care and treatment, free education and a minimum weekly income above the poverty line.

By the 1970s there was anxiety about the ever-increasing financial demands that these entitlements made on the welfare state, and in 1979, the government of the day started to move away from the welfare state approach – Margaret Thatcher, who was then Prime Minister, called it the 'Nanny State'. There was a change towards policies encouraging **market forces**. For example:

▶ Eye tests were no longer free to all.

▶ Dental treatment and check-up charges were significantly increased.

▶ The school meals service was decreased.

▶ Private pensions were encouraged.

The thinking behind this approach was that people should be taxed at a low rate; that public services should provide only a safety net; that people should be given more choice; and that if services were forced to compete in the marketplace, such services would be made more streamlined and more efficient.

These two different approaches – an increased welfare state or an increased free market

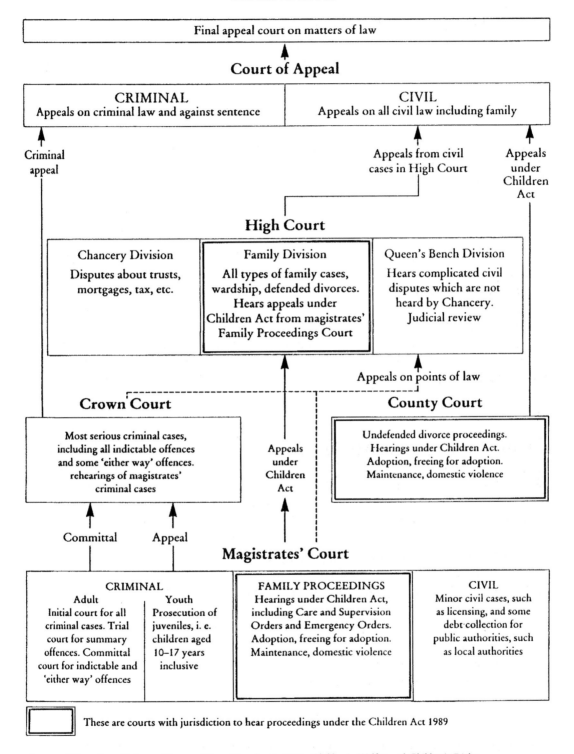

FIGURE 16.1
The UK court system

House of Lords

Final appeal court on matters of law

Court of Appeal

CRIMINAL	CIVIL
Appeals on criminal law and against sentence	Appeals on all civil law including family

Criminal appeal

Appeals from civil cases in High Court

Appeals under Children Act

High Court

Chancery Division	Family Division	Queen's Bench Division
Disputes about trusts, mortgages, tax, etc.	All types of family cases, wardship, defended divorces. Hears appeals under Children Act from magistrates' Family Proceedings Court	Hears complicated civil disputes which are not heard by Chancery. Judicial review

Appeals on points of law

Crown Court

Most serious criminal cases, including all indictable offences and some 'either way' offences. rehearings of magistrates' criminal cases

Appeals under Children Act

County Court

Undefended divorce proceedings. Hearings under Children Act. Adoption, freeing for adoption. Maintenance, domestic violence

Committal   Appeal

Magistrates' Court

CRIMINAL		FAMILY PROCEEDINGS	CIVIL
Adult	Youth	Hearings under Children Act, including Care and Supervision Orders and Emergency Orders. Adoption, freeing for adoption. Maintenance, domestic violence	Minor civil cases, such as licensing, and some debt collection for public authorities, such as local authorities
Initial court for all criminal cases. Trial court for summary offences. Committal court for indictable and 'either way' offences	Prosecution of juveniles, i. e. children aged 10–17 years inclusive		

These are courts with jurisdiction to hear proceedings under the Children Act 1989

Source: Taken from Stainton-Rogers, W and Roche, J. 1994, *Children's Welfare and Children's Rights.*

– demonstrate that there are no simple answers. Depending on someone's political persuasion, one approach would be favoured more than the other.

General elections and local elections

Many women feel that it is very important to vote in both general elections and local elections. This is because it was not until 1918 that women, after many years of struggle, were finally given the right to vote. In order for both men and women to make an informed vote in both general and local elections, it is necessary for them to study the different political views.

G U I D E L I N E S

Three ways to be an informed person:

1 **Read newspapers and watch TV news programmes, and analyse the media.**
2 **Read books about politics, sociology, social sciences and other related subjects which give a background knowledge and understanding.**
3 **Know the laws and the spirit behind the laws which relate to work in early childhood education.**

Let us consider each of the above three points in turn.

1   THE ROLE OF THE MEDIA

It is important to bear in mind that most newspapers reflect the particular political views of their owner. It has even been suggested by political scientists that what people are given to read in the tabloid newspapers wins or loses elections for a political party. There are many advantages to living in a democracy. Freedom of the media (press, radio and television) is one. But it is important to put in a note of caution. It is only freedom of the press in comparison with a **dictatorship**. There are still factors which influence what is printed, what is said and what is broadcast.

2   DEVELOPING BACKGROUND KNOWLEDGE AND UNDERSTANDING

Early childhood workers need to be informed about the statutory, voluntary and private sectors. Examples of services provided by these sectors include:
- social services
- health services
- education provision.

THE CORE STATUTORY SECTOR

This sector comprises:
- central government departments in which policy is led by a Secretary of State (MP), helped by Ministers of State (MPs) and managed by the Permanent Secretary (civil servant);
- executive agencies (e.g. the Benefits Agency issuing social security) contracted to central government departments to deliver services;

- local government departments chaired by an elected Member of the Council and administered by a paid officer, e.g. the Director of Education;
- local health authorities and trusts led by a chairperson and managed by a chief executive.

Statutory services are provided by the government. They are set by laws passed in Parliament.

THE VOLUNTARY SECTOR

This sector is made up of voluntary organisations with a mixture of paid and volunteer workers. Voluntary organisations are often administered by a core of paid staff. Volunteers are then normally trained by them to help the organisation in a variety of ways. There are both national organisations – e.g. BAECE – and local organisations. The local branches of an organisation are not always necessarily closely linked with the national, head branch of the organisation – local groups of the Pre-School Learning Alliance are one such example here.

Voluntary organisations often arise because:
- there is a gap in services – e.g. the Salvation Army and Barnados exist for the *homeless;*
- there is a need for a campaign both to alert awareness of an issue such as homelessness and to push for action to be taken – e.g. Shelter, again for the homeless or CAVE (Campaign Against Vouchers in Education).

Some charities receive government grants, but not all. The National Lottery gives only 4% of its money to voluntary organisations – this is not widely appreciated by the general public. 80% is given in prizes and to the organisers, and taken as a form of tax ($12\frac{1}{2}$%) by central government.

THE PRIVATE SECTOR

This sector comprises businesses making profits. In education, they can involve a chain of private nurseries – e.g. Asquith Court private nurseries – or they might involve one private nursery run by an individual. In social services, they might involve old-peoples' homes run by big chains or by individuals. In health, they might involve private hospitals. Private nurseries, hospitals and schools are legally required to be registered and inspected, and to follow guidelines laid down by laws and local authorities.

It has regularly been argued that there is a strong case for having a Department for Families which would link social service, health and education departments more effectively and would help statutory, voluntary and private sectors to network more easily. Great efforts are being made at grass-roots level to integrate these services through:
- networking amongst professionals
- cooperation amongst professionals
- coordinated services.

POVERTY

During the 19th century, people were labelled as either the *deserving* or the *undeserving* poor, and the Poor Law of 1834 gave relief only to the deserving poor. The focus was on the *relief* of poverty, since it was not thought that poverty could be eradicated; hence the word **charity**.

During the 20th century the emphasis has changed, and the idea that poverty could be eradicated, given the political will, is taken seriously. The introduction of the welfare state aimed to eradicate poverty.

Another development in thinking about poverty is the idea that poverty can be *absolute* or *relative*. **Absolute poverty** exists when people die from starvation and related diseases. **Relative poverty** exists when some people in a country are very rich compared with others. In the UK, a family is said to be living in poverty when its income is less than half the national average weekly wage.

In the UK in the 1990s, there is most poverty amongst families with young children, disabled people and the elderly. A quarter of families with children under 5 now live in poverty. This is three times more than in 1979, according to a DSS Report in 1994, studies by the Child Poverty Action Group (1988) and the National Children's Homes (1990), and the most recent report by Barnardos (1994). The gap between rich and poor is widening. Lack of employment is an important factor, together with the high cost of housing, nutritious food, clothing and transport for families with young children.

THE SOCIAL SECURITY ACT 1986

When someone has too little income to keep themselves, there is a safety net through **social security**. This pays benefits to those on low income. **Contributory benefits** are available to those who have paid National Insurance when employed. **Non-contributory benefits** are either:

► available as of right (Child Benefit, to mothers, and Income Support – provided there is no other source of income), or
► **means tested** – i.e. your income is calculated, and if it is higher than a certain level, no benefit will be paid. Because forms are complicated to fill in, and people feel anxious about the process, these are often not claimed. Examples of the benefits here include help with rent for elderly people, or family credit for families where a parent is working full time but the income falls below a certain level.

Poverty causes a poor quality of life. It brings stress and sometimes also despair, and these can often affect social relationships and health.

HOUSING

The welfare state made cheap, rentable **council housing** a priority. Through the market-forces approach, people have been encouraged to *buy* their council houses, and local authorities have not been permitted to build more. This has meant that:

► government funding has instead supported **housing associations** (these are voluntary organisations) to develop as an alternative to council housing. (Funding for these has, however, been reduced over recent years.)
► There is less cheap rented property available.
► Nearly two-thirds of people have mortgages and are buying their own homes. This has led to increased homelessness through evictions when people cannot keep up rent payments or mortgages.
► Some families live with relatives in over-crowded circumstances.
► Other families have to move into temporary housing, with constant moves and an unstable situation in which to bring up children, for example constantly changing schools and doctors.
► Some families are unsuitably placed in Bed and Breakfast accommodation, with inadequate space for basic cooking and washing facilities.

HEALTH

Free health care and treatment lay at the heart of the welfare state. In 1990, however, the National Health Service and Community Care Act shifted the approach and introduced a more market-forces approach. There are now **purchasers** (e.g. GPs) who buy services for patients from **providers (hospital trusts)**. Once the purchaser has used up all the money in the budget, there is no more.

District health authorities, together with family health services authorities, are now required to:

▶ find out the local health needs;
▶ make plans together;
▶ buy services;
▶ review progress.

There is debate about whether a two-tier system of health care and treatment is developing between private provision and the National Health Service.

RURAL AND URBAN SETTINGS

Different problems exist in rural and urban areas respectively. In the UK, fewer children live in the country, but the children of low-paid casual farm workers often grow up in poverty. They are also often lonely and isolated, and this can have an impact on language development in some cases.

Children in urban settings located in the inner city rather than in the suburbs are more likely to experience poverty, a lack of facilities for play, swimming pools, parks, and poor school buildings. Because of the poorer conditions in many urban areas, teachers, doctors and other professionals do not always stay for long. The trend is indeed for people to leave large inner-city areas and live in the suburbs.

TRAVELLERS

People who are nomads have always been viewed with suspicion by people who are settlers in agricultural or industrial lifestyles. Henry VIII banished travellers in the UK in the 16th century.

Since the Criminal Justice Act 1995 became law, travellers of all kinds (sometimes incorrectly called gypsies) are under threat in the UK, despite the fact that in July 1988 three Appeal Court Judges ruled that gypsies, on their part, are a distinct racial group who have kept their identity within the meaning of the 1976 Race Relations Act. The Criminal Justice Act has drastically reduced stopping places for travellers.

Because, for example, it is difficult for travellers to register with GPs, health care can be inconsistent; and education too can be fragmented. This is because most local authorities do not take account of the needs of travellers when planning services.

Early childhood workers need to implement the equal opportunities policy and code of practice in their work setting. They can incorporate aspects of the traveller's way of life when setting up the home area, for example they can make a caravan. This helps children to focus on the positive aspects of the travelling life.

3 KNOWING THE LAW RELATING TO EARLY CHILDHOOD EDUCATION AND CARE

It is important for early childhood workers to be aware of those laws which relate to their work both in the UK and internationally. Although it is of course illegal not to obey the letter of the law, it is also just as important to understand the spirit and thinking that went into making the law. After all, it is your elected representatives who make the laws.

THE SEX DISCRIMINATION ACT 1975

This Act made it illegal to discriminate against someone because of their sex:

- ▶ when employing someone;
- ▶ when selling or renting a property to them;
- ▶ in their education;
- ▶ when providing them with goods and services.

Men and women are entitled to equal and fair treatment. A job description – e.g. for an early childhood worker – should be the same for a particular job regardless of whether the person is male or female. Moreover, men and women should be paid the same salary for doing the same job. This became law under the Equal Pay Act 1972.

The Equal Opportunities Commission is a watchdog body which can bring action against those who discriminate on the grounds of sex.

The Race Relations Act 1976

This Act makes it illegal to discriminate against someone on the grounds of their colour, race or nationality:

- ▶ **direct discrimination:** this means refusing, for example, to sell something to someone on the grounds of their race – this would be illegal.
- ▶ **indirect discrimination:** this is more difficult to deal with, but just as illegal. It occurs when rules are made which are impossible for someone of a different race to conform with, for example saying that hats may not be worn in school, which would be difficult for a Sikh, Rastafarian, Hutterite girl, or Jewish boy.

This Act was another example of legislation of major importance in moving towards a democracy which offers equality of opportunity for all that live under its laws. However, passing an Act of Parliament is only the first step: enforcing and implementing it is just as important.

In 1976 the Commission for Racial Equality (CRE) was set up. People could now be taken to court by the Commission for either direct or indirect discrimination.

Legislation and disability

In the UK, there has been, until 1995, no legal protection against discriminatory behaviour towards people with disability. Consequently, many people with disabilities are unemployed and therefore poor. Legislation in the form of the Disability Discrimination Act was passed by Parliament in 1995. However, no Commission like those above will be set up to enforce the law against those who discriminate against disabled people.

The Code of Practice for Children With Special Educational Needs, 1994

Parents of children with disabilities have become increasingly concerned about the introduction of the National Curriculum in 1989, when their children seemed to be sidelined. This is in spite of the fact that the curriculum was put forward as an entitlement curriculum for all children.

This was one of the pressures which led to the introduction of the Code of Practice for Children With Special Educational Needs in 1993. This sets out guidelines which must be followed by every local education authority and school; and parents can, if they feel they have grounds for concern, take a complaint to a **court of tribunal**. This tribunal will investigate the situation, but has no legal force to back up its decisions. The Secretary of State for Education will only *recommend* what action a local authority should take.

GOVERNMENT BY CONSENT

Sometimes, laws are of historic importance because they take the first important step towards an *idea*. Laws work best when the spirit behind them is agreed by most people living in a democracy. This is called **government by consent**. By 1975 and 1976, most people agreed that discriminatory behaviour was unacceptable on the grounds of someone's:

▶ sex

▶ race.

Legislation about discriminatory behaviour towards people's disabilities, as we have just seen, has not yet emerged to the same extent.

Sometimes, a law which is passed in Parliament does not carry the consent of the majority of people. This leads to demonstrations and even riots. Take, for example, the controversy concerning the introduction of the poll tax (renamed community charge).

G U I D E L I N E S

Taking an active part in your democracy

▶ **Be informed about the different sectors (see pp. 518–519).**

▶ **Join a local or national voluntary organisation as a volunteer helper. You might offer one day per week, month or year. There are many ways of helping.**

▶ **You might like to help with trade union work in your work setting.**

▶ **Join a political party.**

▶ **Write letters to your MP on matters which concern you, and visit them in your MP's local surgery.**

▶ **Lobby your MP at the House of Commons.**

▶ **Join a legal demonstration about an issue.**

▶ **Make sure you make an informed vote in local and general elections.**

▶ **Check you are on the voting register – especially if you move house.**

The Children Act 1989

In 1944 the welfare state was developed in the UK. To begin with, its services were quite separate from each other. The Seebohm Report (1968) found that some families were being visited by a whole range of professionals – a social worker for the parents, a social worker for the elderly, a speech therapist or a social worker to support the child with a hearing impairment, for example – who often did not know about each other! As a result, the Social Services Act 1970 set up separate government departments for children with *links* between these departments.

The Children Act 1989 has meant that there have been far-reaching changes in the way young children are cared for and protected.

▶ **Private areas** involve parenthood matters and arrangements following parental separation.

▶ **Public areas** involve services provided for children and their families – e.g. child protection care and supervision.

A new approach to parenthood

The Children Act introduced the phrase **parental responsibility**. Instead of rights, parents now have responsibilities.

1 Sometimes, people who are not the natural parents can be given parental responsibility.
2 Parenthood is seen as 'an enduring commitment'. Parents are encouraged to stay involved in bringing up their children, even if the children are not living with them.
3 Parental responsibility can be shared, for example between two divorced parents, or between both parents and foster parents.

In Chapter 3, different sorts of family were looked at. In modern Britain, children now live in a variety of types of family – which include co-habiting parents and reconstituted families (with step-parents) – and may be looked after by other relatives – e.g. grandparents. The Children Act aimed to strengthen all the variety of different kinds of family relationships.

Statutory services under the Children Act

The spirit behind this Act is that families should be respected, and given help in coping with difficulties in bringing up their children. At the same time, the idea is to promote the care and health of the child as paramount. The Act aimed to remove the idea of the professional intervening and taking over through 'enforced intervention'. Like all other landmark legislations before it, the Children Act marks only a beginning.

Under the Children Act, statutory services for children are based on five linked principles:

1 *Children in need.* Services *may* be provided for all children, but they must be provided for all 'children in need'. Parents, in addition, must be helped to show 'parental responsibility'. Children in need are:
   ▶ children with a disability;
   ▶ children whose health or development is:
      – likely to be significantly impaired;
      – likely to be further impaired;
      – unlikely to be maintained;
   ▶ children without the provision of services

   Disability is defined as being blind, deaf or dumb, having a mental disorder, or being handicapped by illness, injury, congenital deformity or any other disease or disorder as may be prescribed. It is very important to know the difference between 'children in need' and 'children with special educational needs'.
   ▶ The Children Act 1989 covers children in need. These include children with disabilities. This Act gives children in need a broader definition than that given above, and children are here given a degree of support that goes beyond that given by the education service.
   ▶ The Education Acts cover children with special educational needs. (See also Chapter 1 on equality of opportunity, and Chapter 4 on children with special needs and their families.)

   By applying the Children Act the various needs of children can be coordinated.
2 *Partnership with parents.* Services must emphasise this by actively seeking

participation, offering real choices and involving parents in decisions. For example, it should be usual for parents to join in on case conferences.

Whenever possible, help should be given by the local authority on a voluntary basis. For example, the parent should be encouraged by the authority to decide when it is best for a child to go into a foster home.

3 *Race, culture, religion and language*. Services must link with children's experiences in relation to these areas. In work settings, staff should not discriminate, and the whole setting should reflect a multi-cultural atmosphere (see Chapter 1). Foster parents, childminders etc. are required to show their support for this principle under the Children Act.

4 *The coordination of services*. Services are required to coordinate with each other in order to support a family. The idea is that families should not be passed from agency to agency. Instead, one agency (e.g. the Education Authority) should request the help of another department.

5 *Meeting the identified needs of an individual family*. Services must be geared to meet the identified needs of a particular family. Local authorities are therefore required to gather information and to plan services which are based on local needs. The aim is thus to produce a needs-led service – i.e. to make the service fit the people, rather than making people fit the service.

The Children (Scotland) Act 1995

The Children (Scotland) Act 1995 has three fundamental child-centred principles which are similar to those of the Children Act 1989. They are:

1 *The welfare of the child is paramount* – the child's interests are always the most important factor, and will always be the deciding factor in any legal decision.

2 *The views of the child must be taken into account* – courts dealing with any matters relating to children's welfare must take account of the child's views. Changes were made to include the child's right to attend their own hearing.

3 *No order principle* – courts and children's hearings need to be convinced that making an order is better than not making one.

The Children (Northern Ireland) Order 1995

The Children (Northern Ireland) Order 1995 came into force in October 1996 and is closely modelled on the Children Act 1989, but contains certain differences:

▶ under the Order those who provide day care and childminding are required to register if they provide services for children under 12

▶ the Order does not provide for fees to be imposed on those providing childminding and day care services

▶ the Order requires all children's homes to be registered irrespective of the number of children being accommodated

▶ the Order removes most of the legal disadvantages of illegitimacy (in England and Wales these had been removed by the Family Law Reform Act 1987)

Child protection and the Children Act

The Children Act was drafted at a time when there was great public and professional concern about children who suffered abuse. It has led to a new approach which believes that children are better off when brought up and cared for in their own family. The emphasis is now on:

▸ prevention: this means supporting and helping the family in situations which involve stress, and which expose children to harm.

▸ intervention on a voluntary basis: when children are at risk, whenever possible it is best for a voluntary agreement to be made with the parents about how to keep their children safe.

▸ intervention only if a situation where 'significant harm' for the child could result – e.g. sexual abuse, physical or emotional abuse, or neglect. Significant harm is prevented by using:
  – a child assessment order
  – an emergency protection order
  – a recovery order
  – a police order.

Protection work is coordinated between professionals. (See the later, more detailed section on child protection for more details.)

How the state has treated the child

The Poor Law (1834) tried to discourage what it saw as 'parental fecklessness' by removing children from the family. It placed them in institutions, believing that it was thus 'rescuing' them from the negligence, immorality and lawlessness of their families. The welfare state (1944) helped parents to care for their children in the family, but the idea of 'rescuing' still continued under the surface. Children were still removed from their families on occasions, and parents were sometimes labelled 'inadequate'. The work of John Bowlby in the 1950s to 1980s (see Chapter 7) showed that institutions were not good places for children to grow up in. Increasingly, children under 7 were now sent to foster parents.

The Children Act has an opposite emphasis to the idea of rescuing children from inadequate families: the aim is that everything possible should be done to keep children *within* their families. This is unless:

▸ the child might be significantly harmed;

▸ the child is 'beyond parental control'.

This is called the **principle of paramountcy**.

The procedures for state intervention are much simpler to understand since the Children Act.

Procedures for state intervention

The courts now decide what is to happen.

▸ The parents are present.

▸ Everyone with parental responsibility is present.

▸ A **guardian ad litem** is appointed who will represent the child's interest in the Court.

There is a 'no delay' policy. The court makes a timetable and sees written information beforehand, so as to avoid delays once the case comes to court.

CARE ORDER

When a child is taken into care, the parents still have parental responsibility, they now share it with the local authority. The parents must still be consulted and encouraged to participate and keep contact with their child. However, their decisions may not be the final ones.

CHILDREN HAVE A VOICE

The wishes and feelings of children must be identified. Children must be involved as active participants in decisions that are made about them. This is especially important when a situation is being *reviewed*.

Complaints and complaints procedures must be set up for children.

Children can be offered the choice of having a resident order and living with a relative or of going into care with a family.

Above all else:

▶ Children should be treated with respect.

▶ Children should be listened to.

▶ Children's ideas should be treated seriously.

▶ Children should play a part in decisions which are made about them.

▶ Children should be protected from harm.

▶ Children should be loved and cared for.

You may find when you are reading the section about the Children Act in this chapter that different bits keep overlapping with other bits. This is exactly what the Children Act itself was designed to do: everything is supposed to link with everything else and make a network which makes possible the care and health of the child.

The main ideas in the Children Act

▶ The welfare of the child is paramount when any decisions are made – this is the principle of paramountcy.

▶ Children are entitled to be protected if they might suffer 'significant harm'. However, decisions to intervene must be challenged.

▶ Children, whenever this is possible, should be brought up and cared for by their own families.

▶ Parents, when their children are in need, should be helped to bring up their children themselves.

▶ Help should be offered as a service to the child and the family. Different agencies should coordinate, including those in the voluntary sector. The services should be provided in partnership with the child's parents. Everyone should work together to meet the child's identified needs, and any provision should take account of the child's race, culture, religion and linguistic background. There must also be an effective complaints procedure.

▶ The state cannot intervene unless there are problems in the care given to children by their parent which indicate that a child might be at risk of 'significant harm'. This situation will require a court order.

▶ When children do not have parents, or where their parents are not able to give adequate care, then high-quality substitute care must be provided.

▶ Children themselves must be consulted about their feelings and wishes. They must be able to take part in the decisions that are made about them.

▶ When a child lives away from home, this must be open to challenge in order to make sure that the best standards of care are maintained.

▶ Parents and the extended family should continue to play a major part in the child's life even when the child is living apart from them. This means that everyone should be encouraged to stay in contact with the child even if they are foster parents.

The ideas for this summary are taken from p. 26 of Stainton-Rogers and Roche 1994 (see the Resources section at the end of this chapter).

Family relationships and the Children Act
MOTHERS
According to the law:
- ▶ the mother is the person who gives birth to the child;
- ▶ someone can be a mother if there is a court order under the Human Fertilisation and Embryology Act 1990;
- ▶ someone can be a mother through adopting a child.

FATHERS
According to the law, someone is a father if:
- ▶ the person is a genetic father;
- ▶ his wife, with his agreement in law, has a child through artificial insemination by a donor.

An unmarried father can apply for parental responsibility. Having parental responsibility involves:
- ▶ being responsible for the physical care and control of the child;
- ▶ being allowed to discipline the child;
- ▶ maintaining the child;
- ▶ arranging a suitable education for the child;
- ▶ giving consent for the child to be medically examined or given treatment;
- ▶ the authority to appoint a **guardian** (although this person will not have parental responsibility);
- ▶ being treated as a parent by the child's school;
- ▶ being eligible to be a **parent governor** at the school.

These responsibilities might be restricted, however, if there is a court order.

WHEN PARENTS SEPARATE
When parents separate, there will be:
- ▶ a divorce petition;
- ▶ a Statement of Arrangements for Children;
- ▶ Maintenance agreements.

If the parents cannot agree, then the court might make a **family assistance order**. This will give a short-term period of help to support parents in making a joint decision about what is best for the children. Usually, a social worker or probation officer will provide the support.

The duties of the local authority in providing for children in need

Children living with their families
In a situation where a child is in need but is living with the family, the local authority must provide advice, information and counselling. In addition,
- ▶ The local authority might also need to provide home help – e.g. help with the laundry.
- ▶ The local authority might need to provide help with travel so that the family can make use of social, cultural or recreational services.

- The local authority might need to help the child have a holiday.
- A child might be required to attend a family centre or day care.
- There may be a need for after-school care or holiday care.

Children who are living with their families

A **Court Order** is necessary if children are not going to be living with their families. There are different kinds of court order. These include a police protection order, an emergency protection order, a child assessment order, a child protection order, a child protection plan and a review.

Regulating and registering services

Anyone who looks after children for more than 2 hours a day, other than in the home, must register with their local authority. The local authority can refuse or cancel registration.

Services which must be registered are:
- day care
- family centres
- childminding
- private fostering.

The number of children in a given setting is always specified. The environment is looked at indoors and outdoors to check it for health and safety. A record must be kept, with the names and addresses of children.

Childminders must also register other people living in the house, or anyone who is likely to be working with the childminder.

Everyone working with the child is subject to a **police check**. A police check makes sure that the person working with the children has no criminal record relating to child abuse.

Child protection

In order to understand the very complex issues surrounding **child protection**, it is necessary to know about children's rights. This situation is not just of great concern in the UK: it is a global issue. In December 1991, the UK government ratified the United Nations Convention on the Rights of the Child. These rights say something about how modern society believes children ought to be treated:
- The views of the child should be listened to and should carry weight. The child has a right to parental care and family life.
- Parents and guardians have the right to appropriate help in carrying out their child-rearing responsibilities.
- Children have the right to protection.

Concerning children's needs:
- Children need to be treated as individuals who have feelings and ideas, and who need to be listened to and respected.
- Children need to be with people who show them love and affection. This is usually their family.
- Their developmental needs should be met and protected. Developmental needs are to do with:

- the physical care they receive;
- the way their ideas and play are encouraged and supported and extended;
- making certain they are shown love and made to feel secure so that their self-image and self-esteem is strong;
- encouraging positive social relationships.

Why do children need protection?

It may be thought unnecessary in the 1990s to need an International Convention on the Rights of the Child, or to make acts of Parliament and laws in the UK which protect children's rights. Nevertheless, for many complex reasons, a minority of children are either neglected or abused, which means that their rights and needs are being violated.

There are many different ways of bringing up children. The aim of legislation and international work towards protecting the rights of children is not to standardise the way children are brought up. There is no one way to bring up a child. (This is discussed in Chapter 5.) However, there are certain aspects of growing up which do seem to be essential for children, and child protection focuses on these crucial elements: if they are missing, the child's development may suffer.

Keeping a sense of proportion

It is easy to imagine that **child abuse** and **child neglect** are present on a vast scale. This is because the media (particularly the tabloid press and regional news programmes) sensationalise and give high focus to these phenomena. It is also important, however, to bear in mind that in the last century, child abuse and neglect were not so frequently recorded or reported. Nowadays, with carefully kept child-protection registers in every local authority, as well as a central register kept by the NSPCC (National Society for the Prevention of Cruelty to Children), recording is more vigorous. It is important to remember that not all children on the register are actually abused or neglected. This is because the modern emphasis on thinking about child protection is on prevention as much as it is on dealing with the aftermath of the detection of abuse or neglect. Public concern has become greater on the subject of child protection, and this is reflected in current legislation – again, the Children Act 1989 is of key importance here. This means that the public is anxious to see local authorities become highly accountable in the child protection work they are required by law to carry out.

Child abuse

There have been various theories about why adults abuse or neglect children.

▶ All sections of society produce adults who abuse or neglect children. It is very dangerous to stereotype:
- the kind of people who might violate a child's rights in these ways; or
- the situations which lead to child abuse or neglect.

▶ As evidence gathers on the subject of child protection, it is becoming apparent that the abusive or neglectful person is almost always known to the child – e.g. a parent, a family member, a friend of the family, or a carer or co-habitee.

▶ Premature babies and children of 0–4 years of age are most likely to be abused or neglected.

▶ Separation for some period of time after birth between the mother and the baby can be associated with child abuse or neglect.

▶ Children who cry a great deal are much more likely to be abused or neglected.

▶ Children who do not enjoy eating are more likely to be abused or neglected.

▶ Step-children are vulnerable.

▶ Children with disabilities are more likely to be abused or neglected.

▶ Children who are boys when parents wanted girls, or girls when parents wanted boys, are likely to be neglected.

What are child abuse and neglect?

There are various types of child abuse and neglect:

▶ physical abuse

▶ physical neglect

▶ emotional abuse

▶ emotional neglect

▶ intellectual abuse

▶ intellectual neglect

▶ sexual abuse

▶ grave concern (failure to thrive).

SPECIFIC INDICATORS FOR CHILD ABUSE (NON-ACCIDENTAL INJURY) NON-ACCIDENTAL INJURY

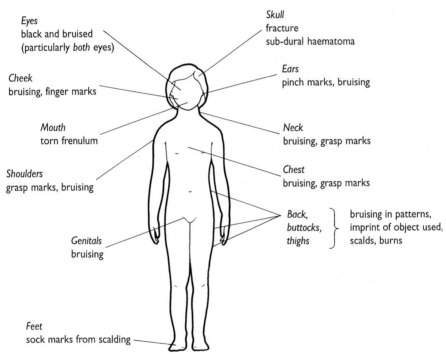

FIGURE 16.2

Non-accidental injury indicators

Eyes
black and bruised
(particularly *both* eyes)

Cheek
bruising, finger marks

Mouth
torn frenulum

Shoulders
grasp marks, bruising

Genitals
bruising

Feet
sock marks from scalding

Skull
fracture
sub-dural haematoma

Ears
pinch marks, bruising

Neck
bruising, grasp marks

Chest
bruising, grasp marks

Back,
buttocks,
thighs
bruising in patterns,
imprint of object used,
scalds, burns

Non-accidental injury (NAI) involves someone deliberately harming a child. This may take the form of:

▶ bruising – from being slapped, shaken, squeezed or punched;

▶ cuts, scratches, bite marks, a torn *frenulum* (the web of skin inside the upper lip);

▶ burns and scalds;

▶ fractures;

▶ poisoning.

It is vital that all people working in child care be aware of the indicators of child abuse (see Table 16.1 and Figure 16.2). Although it is important not to jump to conclusions, any concerns that you may have about the nature of an injury should be dealt with according to the procedures outlined below. Usually, the explanation of the parents or carer of how the

TABLE 16.1
Physical abuse

NON-ACCIDENTAL INJURIES	ACCIDENTAL INJURIES

BRUISES:
Likely to be:
    in a regular pattern
     of various ages
    reflecting the shape of the object used –
    e.g. belt, buckle, teeth marks etc.
    on lips and mouth due to forced feeding
    with a bottle
	BRUISES:
	Likely to be:
	    few but scattered
	    no pattern
	    of the same colour and age
	    N.B. may be confused with *mongolian spot*
	    (smooth bluish-grey patches seen on the
	    buttocks of some children of African or
	    Asian origin in infancy)

CUTS AND ABRASIONS
Suspicious if:
    large, deep scratches
    bite marks and fingernail marks
    torn frenulum web of skin inside upper lip
    incisions e.g. from a razor blade
	CUTS AND ABRASIONS
	Likely to be:
	    minor and superficial
	    easily explained
	    treated

BURNS AND SCALDS
Likely to have:
    a clear outline – splash marks around
    the burn area
    an unusual position – e.g. back of hand,
    palms or buttocks
    immersion scalds – on buttocks or
    socks area
    the shape of the object used –
    e.g. an iron or a cigarette
	BURNS AND SCALDS
	Likely to be:
	    easily explained
	    treated
	    confused with severe nappy rash or
	    impetigo

FRACTURES
Likely to be:
    numerous – in various stages of healing
    to the skull, nose and face
    very rare in very young babies
    a delay in seeking treatment
	FRACTURES
	Likely to be:
	    of arms and legs
	    seldom on ribs except with road traffic
	    accidents
	    due (though rarely) to 'brittle bone
	    syndrome'

injury occurred is inadequate, and their attitude may even be bizarre. The parents may have delayed seeking medical help, or only done so when prompted by others.

PHYSICAL ABUSE
A child who has been physically abused may suffer various symptoms as shown in Figure 16.2.

PHYSICAL NEGLECT
The adult fails to give the child what they need in order to develop physically. They frequently leave children alone and unattended.

Children do not have adequate food, sleep, clothing, clean environments or medical care. This is especially so when a child suddenly changes from thriving to not thriving.

▶ The child may be underweight and show other signs of failure to thrive (see p. 502).

- ▶ Clothing may be inappropriate for the weather, and be smelly and dirty.
- ▶ The child may have poor skin tone and dull matted hair; a baby may have a persistent rash from infrequent nappy changing.
- ▶ The child may be constantly hungry, tired and listless.
- ▶ The child has frequent health problems, and is prone to accidents.
- ▶ The child has low self-esteem and poor social relationships and may show 'frozen watchfulness'. Delay in all developmental areas is likely, due to lack of stimulation.

The causes of child neglect are very complex, but whereas the other categories of child abuse cross all the social and economic groups, most children who are physically neglected are often left unsupervised at home. Children who are neglected in this way are frequently injured in accidents, both in their own homes and on the roads where they play.

EMOTIONAL ABUSE

Children are threatened by the adult. They are insulted and undermined, shouted at and constantly ridiculed. It is not known how common this form of neglect is, because it is not as easy to detect as physical abuse or neglect.

EMOTIONAL NEGLECT

Children do not receive love and affection from the adult. They are often left alone without the support and company of someone who loves them.

PHYSICAL INDICATORS FOR EMOTIONAL ABUSE AND NEGLECT

Physical signs will mainly be in terms of **body language.** There may be withdrawn movements, or signs of frustration, anger and sadness in the form of temper tantrums. Emotional abuse or neglect is therefore less easy to clarify.

BEHAVIOURAL INDICATORS FOR EMOTIONAL ABUSE AND NEGLECT

Some children become withdrawn and cannot play or take an alert, active part in things. Life does not seem to be fun for them. Self-esteem might be low, showing itself in a lack of confidence at 'having a go' at doing things.

Other children react by constantly seeking attention: they seize upon any adult in an attempt to gain their attention. Tantrums might continue later than usual, and speech disorders might emerge. The child might tell lies, and even steal.

INTELLECTUAL ABUSE

Sometimes, adults will 'force' children into so-called academic work for much of their waking lives. This can become rather extreme in some cases: children are pushed to achieving intellectually for most of their waking hours.

INTELLECTUAL NEGLECT

At the opposite extreme of intellectual abuse is intellectual neglect where children are left with little or no intellectual stimulation and cannot develop their own ideas and thinking. Sometimes, children are wrongly thought to have learning difficulties when in fact they are suffering from a severe lack of intellectual stimulation.

SEXUAL ABUSE

The adult uses the child in order to gratify their sexual needs. This could involve sexual intercourse or anal intercourse. It may involve watching pornographic material with the child.

Sexual abuse might mean children being encouraged in sexually explicit behaviour or oral sex, masturbation or the fondling of sexual parts. 10% of sexual abusers are women. Children who are sexually abused can be both boys or girls.

Sexual abuse can continue undetected for some years. It is in the child's interest to recognise it early so that the abuser does not move to greater sexually abusive acts over time.

PHYSICAL INDICATORS FOR SEXUAL ABUSE

Children may have bruises or scratches, as in an accidental injury. There may be itching, or even pain, in the genital area. This might make walking or sitting uncomfortable for the child. It might lead to bed-wetting and poor sleeping and eating patterns. Underclothes might be bloody or torn, and there may be discharges from the penis or vagina.

BEHAVIOURAL INDICATORS FOR SEXUAL ABUSE

The child might have become rather withdrawn from other children or some adults. The child may seem to be lacking in self-confidence and wanting to the 'babied'.

Sexual abuse leads to poor self-esteem and feelings of being dirty or bad on the part of the child. The child may not eat or sleep well.

The child might show an unusual amount of knowledge about sexual behaviour in the things that they say, play with (often in the home area) or draw. The child might seem fascinated about sexual behaviour and flirt with adults as if trying to please.

It is difficult to know how many children are sexually abused, but it is quite likely, on the basis of existing evidence, that about 1 in 5 girls and 1 in 10 boys have had this experience.

CAUSE FOR GRAVE CONCERN (FAILURE TO THRIVE)

When a child does not develop physically, even though there may seem to be no apparent reason for this, it is a matter of grave concern. This needs to be investigated. It will require a multiprofessional team to look into this.

An interesting study in Mexico in the 1960s showed children being taken to hospital, where they put on weight before returning to their families. The failure to thrive then recurred. Instead of readmission to hospital, a team of workers visited the homes and found that the families never came together around a table to share a meal. When the families were encouraged to do this, the children gained weight and began to thrive. Eating is about the *food* that is eaten, but it is also about enjoying good company and conversations during the eating. Eating is thus an emotional and social activity also, an opportunity to share thoughts and ideas.

THE ABUSE OF DISABLED CHILDREN

Children with a physical or learning disability are especially vulnerable to all kinds of abuse; some children are abused by the people who care for them, whilst others are victims of society's view of disabled people as an 'inferior' minority group.

If a child tells you that they have been abused

When a child tells an adult that they have been abused, this has in the past been called a **disclosure interview**. In this situation:

▶ Reassure the child, saying that you are glad they have told you about this.
▶ Believe the child. Tell the child that you will do your best to protect them, but do not *promise* that you can do that.
▶ Remember that the child is not to blame, and that it is important that you make the child understand this.

▶ Do a lot of listening. Don't ask questions.

▶ Report your conversation with the child to your senior designated manager.

Why do adults abuse children?

It is very important not to be judgemental about the person who has abused a child – although it can be very hard not to, especially for people who are committed to children's rights and to their needs being met. It is important to be clear that there are many reasons why an adult might abuse a child.

The modern approach to child protection is to help the child by preventing further abuse or neglect. In the past this was often done by removing the abusing person or the child from the family. However, separating children from their parents is not necessarily best for the child: under the Children Act, this is a principle that is paramount. Separation might result in the child feeling punished for telling about what happened.

There are now programmes whereby families are supported through a family centre, a day nursery or a special **therapeutic centre**. These enable families to stay together but to be supported and supervised by health visitors, educational welfare officers, psychologists, social workers and early childhood workers.

Child abuse is more likely to occur when people (often parents):

▶ have little knowledge about children's needs or how children develop;

▶ find it hard to use the knowledge that they have about the way children develop;

▶ experience a great deal of stress in their lives;

▶ are poor decision-makers;

▶ find it hard to take responsibility for things that they do;

▶ find it difficult to relate to or communicate with other people;

▶ are inconsistent;

▶ find it hard to change their ideas, to change what they have always done, or to change what was done to them when they were a child.

Perhaps these areas are more important than any of the subjects that are studied in the National Curriculum.

C A S E   S T U D Y

Late one Saturday night, the police are called out by neighbours to a flat where it is reported that a child is screaming and no one will answer the door. The police try to gain entrance by the front door but end up forcing their way through a window. In the main living room, a child of about 4 years is strapped to a chair watching television; she appears not to notice her surroundings. The screams have stopped, but slight whimpering sounds are coming from the bedroom. The two police officers enter the bedroom and find a thin baby of about ten months in a filthy nappy, with tobacco and ash over hands and mouth; his eyes look dull and he is moaning softly. The officers notice an open pack of cigarettes and an upturned ashtray on the chair next to the baby's cot. The children are taken to hospital and the baby is kept in overnight for observation; the duty social workers are contacted and the 4-year-old girl is taken to emergency foster parents for the night. The children's parents arrive home at 2 a.m., drunk and high on drugs, having been to a party. The father

finds out from neighbours that the police have been and is furious. He demands the return of his children and claims that they had never left the children on their own before – the mother claimed that a friend had promised to stop by and look after the children at 10 p.m.
(See the Activity on page 508.)

Decision-making, taking responsibility, and being an independent learner are probably some of the most important things that adults (and especially parents) need to be able to do.

Margy Whalley, Pen Green Family Centre (1994), has written about the work of the staff at the Centre in building a close partnership with parents.

THEORIES ABOUT WHY PEOPLE ABUSE CHILDREN
There have been many such theories, including:

▶ The cycle of abuse found in some families was called the 'battered child syndrome' by Kempe and Kempe in 1962. This made it appear that abuse was something predictable, like an illness, which it is not.

▶ Feminist views about the sexual politics of relationships between men and women have been another approach to child protection. Because, however, both men and women abuse both boys and girls, this view has been criticised.

▶ **Dysfunctional** families, where relationships break down, are said to lead to one child being **scapegoated**. This model sees therapy as the way forward, but scapegoating does not *necessarily* come as a result of the family breaking down.

▶ The poverty cycle and health and social factors are thought to predispose some families to abuse. However, rich, poor, healthy and unhealthy people alike all abuse and neglect children – it is found in all sections of society.

None of these theories has been found to be correct. This is because abuse or neglect have been found across a wider range of people than any of these theories suggest. It is always difficult to develop a convincing theory in areas which are very complex and difficult to study. Child protection is one of these areas. The most positive approach, until theory is better developed, is to look at what helps parents to be 'confident parents'.

Procedures for the lines of reporting when there is suspected child abuse or neglect
If child abuse or neglect is suspected, it is very important that
procedures be followed which are regarded as good practice and which fulfil the legal requirements.

▶ Clarify your own thinking. There may be a situation which demands instant action, for example if a child is injured and needs immediate medical attention. Put the child's feelings and physical care first. Be calm, reassuring and warm. This will help the child to have as high a self-esteem as possible.

▶ Usually, evidence about child abuse or neglect emerges in a much less sudden way. Report the indicators which have led you to suspect child abuse or neglect to your designated senior manager. You will need to have written evidence within 24 hours, and it is particularly helpful if you could make observations of the child for that day. If there is already a well-established record-keeping system in the work setting, then this will make it easier to manage.

▶ Your line manager will help you to follow the correct procedures, but you should know them too. They will be written down in every work setting (this is legally required under the Children Act).

▶ You will need to continue to keep carefully written observations. This is because you will be required to make a report, and for this you must have written evidence.

▶ The police, social services and perhaps the National Society for the Prevention of Cruelty to Children (NSPCC) will be involved, and will consult each other in order to:
  – be sure there is evidence;
  – decide whether to issue a police protection order, an emergency protection order or a child assessment order.

The NSPCC and, in Scotland, the RSSPCC (The Royal Scottish Society for the Prevention of Cruelty to Children) are the only voluntary organisations with statutory powers to apply to a court for protection orders for a child.

POLICE PROTECTION ORDER

Specially trained police officers can remove the child into **foster care** for 72 hours. This is to make sure that the child is safe. This officer is then required to inform:

▶ the child
▶ the parent or carer
▶ the local authority.

EMERGENCY PROTECTION ORDER

The concerned adult or teacher can apply, in an emergency, to a court or to an individual Magistrate for an **emergency protection order** for up to 8 days. (This can be extended for another 7 days.) The child can then be taken to a safe place, such as a foster home. After 8 days, if the situation is safe, the emergency protection order can be discharged.

CHILD ASSESSMENT ORDER

Either the local authority or the NSPCC can apply for a **child assessment order**. This gives 7 days during which the child can be assessed. This might be important in a situation where the parents do not cooperate but where there is not an emergency situation.

CHILD PROTECTION CONFERENCE

When it has been established that there is evidence suggesting child abuse or neglect, a **child protection conference** is arranged. Professionals involved with the child or family join together in a multiprofessional discussion of written evidence. The early childhood worker may also be asked to attend. The chairperson decides whether it is further appropriate to invite the parents to attend; and in any case, the parents must be informed that the conference is taking place. It is a requirement that local authorities work towards parents attending at least part of, if not the whole, conference.

An action plan is made.

The child may be placed on the **child protection register**.

THE CHILD PROTECTION PLAN
ASSESSMENT
This will involve setting in motion procedures through which to assess the child and the family situation to see how things are.

PROTECTION OF THE CHILD
This would involve either:
► **a care order** – the child will then be taken into the care of the local authority's social services department (in a foster home or community children's home); or
► A **supervision order** – the local authority will support and supervise the family and the child in the home setting for one year.

REGULAR REVIEW
The child protection plan is reviewed in a **review conference** attended by the multiprofessional team involved with the family, and perhaps also by the parents. This will take place every 6 months, or more often.

The child is **de-registered** if the situation changes and the child no longer requires support or supervised protection.

Child protection and schools
When young children start or are already attending a nursery school, nursery class or primary school, social services are required to notify the head teacher if a child's name is put on the child protection register. This should state:
► whether the child is subject to a care order;
► the name of the key worker on the case;
► what information may be known to the parents.
The child's school must carefully monitor how the child is getting along. This will be particularly important in the area of the child's development.

These observations should be shared with the Social Services Department should any concern arise.

WORKING TOGETHER UNDER THE CHILDREN ACT 1989
This Guidance was published by the Department of Health in 1991.
► Every school is required to appoint a teacher responsible for linking with the Social Service Department.
► Every school is required to have a written policy on child protection procedures and lines of reporting to Social Services and sometimes the NSPCC.
► Registers of named staff taking on this role are kept by the LEA.
Regular training and support are given to these teachers.
► Schools as well as care settings are encouraged to develop curriculum plans which help children to develop skills and practices which protect them from abuse.

Kidscape is a voluntary organisation which encourages children to understand that in some situations it is appropriate to shout and kick in order to keep safe from being harmed. Kidscape works with schools and other early childhood work settings to devise assertiveness training programmes giving young children protection from abuse.

Childline is a voluntary organisation which operates a 24-hour telephone line free of charge for children to call in and discuss with trained counsellors situations which place them under stress for one reason or another.

Pen Green Family Centre (Corby, Northamptonshire) have a leavers programme for the term before the children go to primary school to help them protect themselves from abuse. This is called the Learning to Be Strong Programme.

Helping children and families to deal with the effects of child abuse or neglect

Children are best helped when early childhood workers are not judgemental about the child's family, and in particular, about the person who has abused the child.

BUILDING SELF-ESTEEM

It is important to build the self-esteem of both the child and the family. Low self-esteem is associated with a child who has been abused or neglected, and also with adults who abuse or neglect children. This can be difficult when parents who are required to bring their children, under a child protection order, to a family centre, day nursery or children's centre do not appear responsive or positive to staff or to the child. It takes time to build self-esteem. Staff who give messages of warmth, who respect other people's dignity and who value people, although they may reject what they have done, are more likely to help parents in this way. Feeling valued as an individual, whatever you have done, builds self-esteem.

Children need to be helped to have a positive self-image (see Chapter 7). They need to explore their feelings. Here are some practical strategies.

GUIDELINES

Helping children

▶ Encourage children to play.
▶ Some children will need to be supported by play therapists or psychologists. Where there has been sexual abuse, anatomically correct dolls are sometimes introduced to the child. With help from these professionals, who are highly trained in their use, you might be also be able to use the dolls with the child. These can help children to play and act out their experiences, and so express how they feel and think about what has happened to them.
▶ Be warm and be there for the child. Don't ask questions, and encourage them to try things and enjoy activities with you.
▶ Remember that children who have been abused or neglected are often challenging. Look again at Chapter 7 and remind yourself about ways of helping children who boundary-push and challenge.
▶ Help parents to feel confident in their parenting.
▶ Don't undermine by remarks such as 'He doesn't do that here!' etc. Instead, tackle problems together: 'Shall we try this? Let's both have the same approach. When she does this next time, either at home or in the nursery, shall we both make sure we have the same reaction?'
▶ Remember: the aim is to get parents and children relating well to each other.
▶ Remember that many people working with young children were themselves abused as children. It is important to manage feelings about this subject in a professional way.

One early childhood worker had enjoyed telling stories to John (3 years) who had been referred to the nursery under a child protection order. One day, she went to tell him a story and found that his mother had arrived early. She was in the book area with John, reading him a story. They were completely involved. The early childhood worker felt a pang of disappointment, but it did not last, as she knew it was more important for the parent and child to enjoy stories together than it was for her to do so. She also knew that she had helped to bring about this situation, and she began to realise that it brought a different kind of satisfaction to her work in early childhood education.

R E S O U R C E S

Books

Child Abuse and Neglect: an Introduction, Milton Keynes, Open University Press, 1989

B. Brown, *All Our Children,* London, BBC 1993

Michelle Elliott, *Dealing With Child Abuse,* The Kidscape Training Guide, London, Kidscape, 1989

Allen, N. (1997) Making sense of the Children Act, John Wiley, Chichester.

W. Stainton and J. Roche, *Children's Welfare and Children's Rights: a Practical Guide to the Law,* London, Hodder & Stoughton, 1994

M. Whalley, *Learning to be Strong,* London, Hodder & Stoughton, 1994

Useful Addresses

Childline
Addle Hill Entrance
Faraday Building
Victoria Street
London EC4

Kidscape
World Trade Centre
Europe House
London E1 9AA

NSPCC
67 Saffron Hill
London EC1

Pen Green Centre for Children Under Five and their Families
Pen Green Lane
Corby
Northants

RSSPCC
Melville House
41 Polworth Terrace
Edinburgh EH1

A C T I V I T Y

1 **Divide into groups and list the indicators of neglect/abuse in the case study on page 504.**
2 **What do you think will happen to the children now? Discuss the alternatives.**

A C T I V I T Y

Investigating legal and political issues in child care provision

1 **Write down these three headings:**
   ▶ **statutory sector**
   ▶ **voluntary sector**
   ▶ **private sector.**

How can each help people to find solutions to poor housing?

2 In a group of five, play the game 'balloons'. In this game, each person has to take a different Parliamentary Act and try to argue that all other Parliamentary Acts should be thrown out of the balloon. There is only room for one Parliamentary Act left in the balloon. This means that four people will have to go.

   Research one of the following Acts of Parliament, and write down your reasons for staying in the balloon.
   ▶ the Sex Discrimination Act 1975;
   ▶ the Race Relations Act 1976;
   ▶ the Employment Act 1982;
   ▶ the Health and Safety Act 1982;
   ▶ the Children Act 1989.

3 Day 1: look at news programmes on television. Look at the way the news is reported on the early evening news and on the 9 o'clock news. Then, watch a news analysis programme that is on television late at night (after 10:30 p.m.).
   ▶ How were the programmes different?
   ▶ Did they have the same main headlines?
   ▶ Did they cover the same subjects in the same way?

4 Day 2: listen to the radio. Listen to a radio programme which gives pop music. Listen also to Radio 4 in the early evening, and to the 10 o'clock news.

   Listen also to the World Service at any time of the day or night.
   Is the radio news similar in the way that the news is presented on television?

5 Day 3 (Sunday): read the *Observer*, the *Sunday Times* and a tabloid newspaper. Compare them.
   ▶ Do they choose the same headlines?
   ▶ Do they write about news items in the same way?
   If a group of you do this, make your findings into a chart and put the data onto a computer.

6 Tom is made redundant from work two weeks before Christmas. He has borrowed money at a very high interest from a loan company in order to buy some expensive commercial toys that his children (Karen 4 years and Jason 6 years) have asked for in their letters to Father Christmas. His wife has recently been ill with stress, and is on anti-depressant pills.

   Tom collects his benefit from the DSS each week, but he is not allowed to earn extra or he loses it. He cannot pay back the loan. Who can he go to for advice?

7 Look up the Children Act 1989 in the index of this book. Find all the references to the Act and read them again so that you are thoroughly informed about it. Write down any key messages that you need to know.

8 Try to visit the Houses of Parliament – consult your MP for information on how to do this. If you cannot do this, watch Today in Parliament on television when there is a debate. Summarise the arguments of the different political parties. How are they different from each other?

9   Write down the names of ten voluntary organisations (charities) that come into your mind – this is called 'unprompted awareness'. Research what these organisations do.

   Then turn to the end of each chapter and find ten voluntary organisations that you have not heard of before. Find out what these organisations do. Write down reasons why some of these are better known to the public than others.

10 Plan a scenario which results in a child being taken into the care of the local authority. Who has parental responsibility? What kind of care order is made?

11 Imagine you want to register as a childminder. What must you do? Research this, and make a plan.

12 Plan a debate. Should prisoners or people who are mentally ill be allowed the right to vote in a democracy? Research whether prisoners, the royal family, peers or compulsorily detained psychiatric patients may vote at the current time, before you take part in the debate.

17

Professional Development for Child Carers

The role of the early childhood worker

Having satisfactorily completed a recognised course in Child Care and Education, a professional early childhood worker will be qualified to work in a variety of settings, including nursery, infant or primary schools or classes, family centres, hospitals and the private and voluntary sectors.

What qualities make a good early childhood worker?

Above all else, an early childhood worker needs to like children and enjoy being with them. Caring as a quality is largely *invisible*, difficult to quantify and more noticeable when *absent* than when present. The main individual characteristics involved are:

▶ **Listening:** attentive listening is a vital part of the caring relationship. Sometimes a child's real needs are communicated more by what is left *unsaid* than by what *is* actually said. Facial expressions, posture and other forms of body language all give clues to a child's feelings. A good carer will be aware of these forms of **non-verbal communication.**

▶ **Comforting:** this has a physical and an emotional meaning. Physical comfort may be provided by a cuddle at a time of anxiety, or a social worker may provide a reassuring safe environment to a distressed child. Touching, listening and talking can all provide emotional comfort as well.

▶ **Empathy:** this should not be confused with **sympathy**. Some people find it easy to appreciate how someone else is feeling by imagining themselves in that person's position. A good way of imagining how a strange environment appears to a young child is to kneel on the floor and try to view it from the child's perspective (see Figure 17.1).

▶ **Sensitivity:** this is the ability to be aware of and responsive to the feelings and needs of another person. Being sensitive to others' needs requires the carer to

FIGURE 17.1
Empathising: the child's eye-view of the world

anticipate their feelings, e.g. those of a child whose mother has been admitted to hospital, or whose pet dog has just died.

▶ **Patience:** this involves being patient and tolerant of other people's methods of dealing with problems, even when the carer feels that their own way is better, – e.g. letting a child develop independence by dressing themselves even when you need to hurry;

▶ **Respect:** a carer should have an awareness of a child's personal rights, dignity and privacy, and must show this at all times. Every child is unique, and so the carer's approach will need to be tailored to each individual's needs.

▶ **Interpersonal skills:** a caring relationship is a two-way process. One does not have to *like* the child one is caring for, but warmth and friendliness help to create a positive atmosphere and to break down barriers. **Acceptance** is important: the carer should always look beyond the disability or disruptive behaviour to recognise and accept the **person**.

▶ **Self-awareness:** a carer can be more effective if they are able to perceive what effect their behaviour has on other people. Being part of a team enables us to discover how others perceive us and to modify our behaviour in the caring relationship accordingly.

▶ **Coping with stress:** caring for others effectively in a full-time capacity requires energy, and it is important to be aware of the possibility of **professional burn-out**. In order to help others, we must first help ourselves: the carer who never relaxes or develops any outside interests is more likely to suffer 'burn-out' than the carer who finds his own time and space.

Understanding group dynamics

A **group** is a collection of two or more people who possess a *common purpose*. **Formal groups** are deliberately created by management for particular planned purposes; and it is management who selects group members, leaders and methods of doing work.

Informal groups are formed by people who feel they share a common *interest*. Members organise themselves and develop a sense of affinity both to each other and to a common cause.

Group norms

A **group norm** is a shared perception of how things should be done, or a common attitude, feeling or belief. Norms are closely linked to expectations: as the group norms emerge, individuals will start to behave in ways which they believe other group members **expect** them to behave.

Group cohesion

This means the extent to which group members are prepared to cooperate and to share common goals. **Cohesion** encourages **compliance** to group norms and causes groups to be more stable in their functioning.

Certain factors contribute to the creation of group cohesion:

▶ *the frequency and closeness of interactions:* the more often people meet and the closer the contacts, the more they will perceive themselves as belonging to a distinct group;

▶ *exclusivity of membership:* if membership of the group is selective, members feel a sense of achievement in having been chosen;

▶ *the nature of the external environment:* the environment in which a group operates may offer protection from a hostile external environment – e.g. Neighbourhood Watch groups;

▶ *good interpersonal communication:* if communication is easy, then a collective sense of purpose will readily emerge; and the less contact with outsiders, the greater the internal cohesiveness – e.g. the religious cult group led by David Koresh in the USA probably involved a strict adherence to group norms and a high degree of group cohesion;

▶ *the nature of the task:* if the individuals are all engaged on similar work, then they will more readily perceive themselves as a group;

▶ *homogeneity of membership:* where members are alike in terms of background, education, age, social origin etc., they are likely to share some common attitudes;

▶ *rewards and penalties:* a group that can offer rewards or bonuses or even punish its own members and can exert great pressure on individuals to conform. In such cases, group cohesiveness tends to be very strong.

The value of teamwork

In child-care and education settings, a **team** is a group of people who work together to meet the aims of their establishment – for example, a day nursery providing care for an early-years group. Most early childhood workers are required to work alongside colleagues in a **team**; even the person employed as a nanny in a private home is operating in a team with the family. Some people, furthermore, work in a **multi-disciplinary** team – for example, a doctor, police officer, teacher, social worker and perhaps a parent at a case conference on a child at risk.

To function well as a team, the team members must be:

▶ motivated towards common goals;
▶ provided with the support and encouragement necessary to achieve these goals;
▶ able to communicate effectively.

Management and leadership styles

All organisations have to be **managed**, although the *styles* of management involved can vary considerably. The management of nearly every organisation must:

▶ plan;
▶ establish goals;
▶ control operations;
▶ appraise its employees.

A successful team needs good leadership or management. Leadership is the ability to influence the thoughts and behaviour of others. A leader's position may be formal and result from designated organisational authority – e.g. with a nursery manager – or informal in nature – e.g. depending on the individual's personal ability to exercise power.

There is a **continuum** of possible leadership styles, extending from complete **autocracy** at one extreme to total **democracy** at the other.

Autocratic leadership
The **autocratic** leadership style has the following features:

▶ The leader tells the subordinates exactly what to do, without comment or discussion.
▶ There are rewards for good performance and penalties or threats of sanctions for under-performance.
▶ There is strict control and a highly **formal** network of interpersonal relations between the leader and team members.

ADVANTAGES OF THE AUTOCRATIC STYLES
▶ Everyone knows precisely what is expected of them: tasks, situations and relationships are clearly defined.
▶ Time management is usually good as management sets the standards and coordinates the work.
▶ Decisions are arrived at speedily as there is no consultation with others.
▶ Employees receive direct and immediate help towards achieving their goals.

DISADVANTAGES OF THE AUTOCRATIC STYLE
▶ It stifles the workers' own initiative.
▶ It does not make maximum use of the employee's knowledge, skills and experiences.
▶ Staff cannot reach their true potential.
▶ If the group leader is absent, e.g. ill or on holiday, important work may not be completed.

Autocratic styles of leadership are not often seen in care and education settings.

Democratic styles

At its extreme, this style is the **laissez-faire** approach where a group does not have a leader, but may have a care worker who acts as a **facilitator**.

In the democratic style:

▶ there is much communication and **consultation** between the leader/facilitator and the group, and it is recognised that everyone has a contribution to make;

▶ group members actively participate in the leader's/facilitator's decisions; and if unanimity is impossible, then a vote is taken.

ADVANTAGES OF THE DEMOCRATIC STYLE

▶ The job satisfaction of group members is greater, through widening their responsibilities and making their work more interesting and varied.

▶ The morale of group members is improved as they have a key role in planning and decision-taking.

▶ Specialist knowledge and skills are recognised and used towards achieving goals.

▶ Targets are more likely to be achieved because they have been formulated by group consensus.

DISADVANTAGES OF THE DEMOCRATIC STYLE

▶ Some group members may not want to become involved in the decision-making process.

▶ Time management may be more problematic, because of the extra time necessary for full consultation of the group.

▶ A lack of positive direction may prevent goals from being attained.

▶ Employees may feel resentful because they are only involved in *minor* day-to-day issues and do not have any real say in the major issues.

▶ Subordinates may require closer supervision.

Communication patterns within care organisations

Most business organisations are **hierarchic** in structure. Those at the top of the hierarchy take the most important decisions, and are rewarded by the highest salaries. They communicate their decisions downwards through a **chain of command**. The number of levels within the hierarchy can vary a great deal, but the fewer there are the greater the efficiency.

Information can flow in three directions:

▶ downwards from top to bottom;

▶ upwards from bottom to top;

▶ sideways at various levels.

Whatever system of management is used, a large amount of information must flow down the hierarchy from top management to the shop floor (or ward cleaners). Research has proved that downward communication can be very inefficient, with only 20% of information reaching the bottom of the pyramid.

Communication from the bottom upwards has two important factors:

▶ to feed back information on what action has been taken on messages sent downwards;

▶ to alert the decision-makers to the feelings and attitudes of those lower down the organisation, so that they can devise realistic strategies.

Line managers

Many large organisations with grouped specialities use **line authority**. Line managers are directly responsible for achieving the organisation's objectives, and exert direct authority over their subordinates. In line authority:

▶ authority flows through the **chain of command** from the apex to the base;

▶ the chain of command is illustrated by means of an **organisation chart**;

▶ each position in the line system involves points of contact between manager and subordinates, and shows clearly both the authority of its occupant and to whom that person is responsible.

▶ **vertical** communications proceed only through the line system.

The responsibilities of a professional early childhood worker

The skills required by the professional early childhood worker need to be practised with regard to certain responsibilities:

1 *Respect for the principles of confidentiality.* **Confidentiality** is the preservation of secret (privileged) information, concerning children and their families, which is disclosed in the professional relationship. It is a complex issue which has at its core the principle of **trust**. The giving or receiving of sensitive information should be subject to a careful consideration of the needs of the children and their families; for example, a child who is in need of protection has overriding needs which require that all relevant information be given to *all* the appropriate agencies such as social workers, doctors etc. Within the child-care and education setting, it might be appropriate to discuss sensitive issues, but such information must *never* be disclosed to anyone *outside* the setting.

2 *Commitment to meeting the needs of the children.* The needs and rights of all children should be paramount, and the early childhood worker must seek to meet these needs within the boundaries of the work role. Any personal preferences and prejudices must be put aside; all children should be treated with respect and dignity, irrespective of their ethnic origin, socio-economic group, religion or disability. The equal-opportunities code of practice involved will give detailed guidelines.

3 *Responsibility and accountability in the workplace.* The supervisor, line manager, teacher or parent will have certain expectations about your role, and your responsibilities should be detailed in the job contract. As a professional, you need to carry out all your duties willingly and to be answerable to others for your work. It is vital that all workers know the **lines of reporting** and how to obtain clarification of their own role and responsibility. If you do not feel confident in carrying out a particular task, either because you do not fully understand it or because you have not been adequately trained, then you have a responsibility to state your concerns and ask for guidance.

4 *Respect for parents and other adults.* The training you have received will have emphasised the richness and variety of child-rearing practices in the UK. It is an important part of your professional role that you respect the wishes and views of parents and other carers, even when you may disagree with them. You should also recognise that parents are usually the people who know their children best; and in all your dealings with parents and other adults, you must show that you respect their cultural values and religious beliefs.

5 *Communicate effectively with team members and other professionals.* The training you have received will have emphasised the importance of effective communication in the workplace. You will also be aware of the need to plan in advance for your work with young children: a knowledge of children's needs in all developmental areas will enable you to fulfil these within your own structured role. Good practice as a team member will depend on liaising with others, to report on and review your activities. Conflicts between team members often arise from *poor* communication: for example, a child-care worker who fails to report, verbally or in writing, that a parent will be late that day in collecting their child may cause conflict when a colleague challenges their conduct.

Stress and conflict in the workplace

There are a number of reasons why conflicts arise in the workplace – the nature of the caring relationship imposes particular stress which can lead to conflict between team members. There may be:

▶ low morale – if individuals feel unsupported and undervalued in their role;
▶ confusions over **individual roles** in the hierarchy of the organisation;
▶ responsibility and accountability for providing care for children who are ill or disadvantaged;
▶ a lack of communication with superiors and colleagues;
▶ ambiguity over which tasks should take priority during the working day;
▶ an excessive workload in both *quantitative* – i.e. having too much to do – and *qualitative* i.e. finding work too difficult – terms;
▶ feelings of personal inadequacy and insecurity, often following destructive criticism of one's work.

C A S E   S T U D Y

The stressful situation

Tom recently obtained a qualification in child care and has been employed as a nursery nurse at Meadlands Day Nursery for two weeks. He has just been called in to see his supervisor as his colleagues have reported that he is frequently tearful and unable to contribute to activities in the nursery. Carol, his supervisor, asks why he is unhappy, and Tom says that he 'doesn't like the atmosphere in the nursery, that there is a lot of bickering between the staff, and he feels that one particular child is constantly being ridiculed by his colleagues'. Carol asks him to give more information about the complaints, but Tom bursts into tears and asks if he can go home as he can't cope anymore.

1 **Identify and write down the stressors (the factors producing stress) which Tom mentions.**

2 **How should Carol deal with this situation?**

3 **Find out about the Type A and Type B personalities from psychology textbooks. Are some personalities more suited to child care work?**

Anxiety

Unresolved anxiety will lead to **stress**. The physical effects of anxiety developed originally as aids to survival, triggered off by dangerous situations (the 'fight or flight' responses).

There are two types of anxiety:

▶ **objective** anxiety – caused by stressful events;

▶ **neurotic** anxiety – subjective, often unconscious feelings which arise within the individual. Although they have different sources, each instance of this type of anxiety is experienced as the same painful emotional state.

Objective anxiety can be coped with by changing the circumstances of the environment in which a person functions; e.g. a social worker who is worried about their own ability to cope with a difficult client can enlist help from their colleagues, or even transfer their responsibilities if necessary.

Neurotic anxiety cannot be removed by external events. Consequently, the **ego** develops additional ways to protect itself from internal threats, which are called the **ego defences**:

▶ **Repression:** unpleasant memories and thoughts are banished from consciousness and forced into the unconscious mind; this process of repression requires much mental energy, and can quickly lead to abnormal behaviour.

▶ **Regression:** the individual behaves as they did in an earlier phase of their life; **immature behaviour** is thus characteristic of those experiencing this event.

▶ **Displacement**: displacement occurs when an individual diverts their energies away from the area of work which they are finding difficult and instead devotes themselves completely to other things – e.g. a nursery manager whose record-keeping skills are inadequate might channel all their energies into staff training issues, thereby replacing the need to deal with essential administration with an unnecessary concern for trivial matters.

▶ **Projection**: simple projection occurs when a person unconsciously attributes to another person a characteristic that is in fact their own. Personal feelings of dislike, hatred or envy that one person feels towards another and which give rise to internal feelings of neurotic anxiety are projected onto that person. What was originally an **internal** threat is now experienced as an **external** threat. Instead of feeling 'I hate you', projection changes this to 'You hate me'. The extreme case is that of the **paranoid** individual who feels continually threatened by everyone with whom they come into contact.

Contribution to team meetings

Team meetings are usually held regularly, and are conducted according to an agreed agenda. Ideally, the written agenda should be given to *all* team members and should include a space for anyone to add their own item for discussion.

Certain factors may detract from the value of team meetings:

▶ *distractions:* constant interruptions, from either telephone calls or visitors;

▶ *irrelevant topics:* some meetings become a forum for gossip or other topics irrelevant to the task in hand.

▶ *a dominating member:* one person may be aggressive and outspoken, with the effect of blocking other people's contributions.

Assertiveness makes communication at team meetings more effective; and it should not be confused with loudness or aggressive behaviour. Assertiveness may be defined in this context as standing up for your own basic rights and beliefs, without isolating those of others, and as making your behaviour 'match' your feelings. If you are assertive in your behaviour, you:

▶ are expressive with your feelings, without being unpleasant;

▶ are able to state your views and wishes directly, spontaneously and honestly;

▶ respect the feelings and rights of other people;

▶ feel good about yourself and others too;

▶ can evaluate a situation, decide how to act and then act without reservation;

▶ are true to yourself;

▶ value self-expression and the freedom to choose;

▶ may not always achieve your goals, but that is not as important as the actual process of asserting yourself;

▶ are *able* to say what you have to say, whether it is positive or negative, while also leaving the other person's dignity intact.

FIGURE 17.2
Working together as a team – written agendas and assertiveness on the part of all staff make meetings more effective

Non-verbal methods of assertiveness at meetings include:

▶ good eye contact;

▶ a confident posture – standing or sitting comfortably;

▶ talking in a strong, steady voice;

▶ not clenching one's fist or pointing with a finger.

Verbal methods of assertiveness include:

▶ avoiding qualifying words (e.g. 'maybe', 'only' or 'just');

▶ avoiding disqualifying attacking phrases (e.g. 'I'm sure this isn't important, but . . . ');

▶ avoiding attacking phrases (e.g. those that begin with 'you'; use assertive phrases such as 'I feel').

Staff appraisal

People need to have feedback on their performance and to know that they are doing well. Appraisal of staff is a means of working with staff to identify their strengths within their work role. It should be viewed by staff as a positive action – even when there are criticisms of performance – which helps to promote good practice within the work setting. Most appraisals are carried out annually and by interview.

Appraisals are also useful in identifying staff-development needs; for example, an early childhood care worker who is lacking in assertiveness may be sent on an assertiveness training course.

Codes and policies in the workplace

A code of practice is not a legal document, but it does give direction and cohesion to the organisation for which it has been designed. Codes of practice and policy documents cover areas of ethical concern and good practice, such as:

▶ equal opportunities

▶ confidentiality

▶ safety aspects

▶ partnerships with parents

▶ first-aid responsibilities

▶ staff:children ratios

▶ child protection

▶ record-keeping

▶ food service

▶ staff training.

All workplace policies and codes of practice must be drawn up within the framework of current legislation; and the laws which are most relevant to child-care and education services are:

▶ the Children Act (1989);

▶ the Education Reform Act (1988);

▶ the Race Relations Act (1976);

▶ the Sex Discrimination Act (1975).

Equal opportunities policy

An **equal opportunities policy** represents a commitment by an organisation to ensuring that its activities do not lead to any individual receiving less favourable treatment on the grounds of:

- sex
- religious belief
- disability
- ethnic or national origins.

- marital status
- race
- skin colour

It does *not* mean reverse discrimination in favour of black people. An effective policy will establish a fairer system in relation to:

- recruitment
- training
- promotion opportunities

POLICY STATEMENT

Each employing organisation should set out a clear policy statement which can be made available to employees and service-users. The statement should include:

- a recognition of past discrimination;
- a commitment to redressing inequalities;
- a commitment to positive action.

Training should be provided to explain to all staff the implications and practical consequences of the policy. The organisation must also provide information about the law on **direct** and **indirect discrimination.**

Any policy which attempts to promote equality is only effective if the individuals working in the organisation incorporate its principles into their individual practice. Some suggestions for implementation are:

- Ethnic-minority staff should be kept informed about, and encouraged to apply for, training programmes and promotion.
- Encourage all staff to accept that racial and ethnic variations should not be ignored but rather recognised **positively** in the context of care.
- All staff should be aware that attitudes or actions based on racial prejudice are unprofessional and unacceptable in the workplace.
- Take up the interests of ethnic-minority staff and find out whether there are special needs for canteen, social or cultural facilities, religious holidays etc.
- Try to ensure a higher level of participation of ethnic-minority staff in team meetings and case conferences – e.g. include on the agenda 'Multiracial and multicultural aspects of care'.

Health and safety policies
See pp 303–304.

Trade unions and professional organisations

Trade unions and **professional organisations** exist to represent and protect their own members' interests. Their main functions are to:

- negotiate for better pay and conditions of service;
- provide legal protection and support;
- represent members at grievance and disciplinary hearings.

Two such organisations which child care workers can join are:

- UNISON – a union for health workers;
- the Professional Association of Nursery Nurses (PANN).

In addition to representing their members' interests, most trade unions and professional organisations publish newsletters and hold regular local meetings to discuss workplace issues.

Working with children

- the family home, as a nanny;
- maternity units in hospitals;
- workplace creches
- special schools or special units within mainstream schools;
- babysitting;
- jobs within the holiday and leisure industry – e.g. abroad as a ski or summer resort nanny or as a nanny in a special children's hotel.

- local authority day nurseries;
- private nurseries;
- nursery schools;
- primary and preparatory schools
- child minding;

There are many opportunities for employment for people with child care qualifications to work with children, for example in:

Working as a nanny

A nanny is someone who is making a career out of caring for children. Responsibilities vary widely from post to post. Most jobs involve the nanny having full responsibility for all aspects of childcare, including:

- the children's health and welfare while they are under your supervision;
- their social, emotional and educational development while caring for them as their nanny;
- ensuring that the children always play in safety in an environment free from danger and minor hazards;
- some light domestic duties, closely related to the care of the children.

Some employers place greater emphasis on experience and personality than on professional qualifications. Other parents will only employ someone with a recognised childcare qualification.

There are many nanny employment agencies which usually offer qualified nannies:

- contact with a wide range of suitable employers within your chosen area of work;
- advice on matters of pay, tax and contractual obligations, such as hours of pay and specific duties;
- a formal contract between a nanny and the employer (see page 528);
- a free follow-up service after the start of employment, with the aim of sorting out any teething problems that may arise.

THE INTERVIEW

Nanny agencies offer advice to parents on what to ask at interview to ensure that the person they employ suits their particular family's needs. Typical questions include:

WHY DO YOU WISH TO BE A NANNY?

Employers are looking for someone whose answers show a love of children. Taking care of children involves a very big commitment and is not a suitable career for anyone who is not enthusiastic or who is unsure about being a nanny.

WHAT ARE YOUR CHILDCARE EXPERIENCES?

You should be prepared to give a brief account of your past jobs, your formal college training and other relevant experience, such as regular babysitting jobs, playgroup experience etc. Most employers will also ask for at least three references from people who can verify your experience and your suitability for childcare work.

WHAT ARE YOUR CHILD-REARING PHILOSOPHIES?

Employers may ask how you would react in a specific situation; for example, if a child refuses to put on her coat when you need to take her to nursery school and 'throws a tantrum'. Always answer truthfully and try to expand on how you feel about dealing with difficult behaviour and any experiences and examples you can relate.

WHY DOES THIS PARTICULAR POST INTEREST YOU?

You should already be aware of the details of the post or job specification, i.e. the hours, responsibilities, days off, salary etc. The employer will want to know if there is any particular reason why you have chosen the post; this might be the ages of the children or it might be the location.

What do you feel are your personal qualities that suit you for this job?

Many nannies feel uncomfortable when asked to list their personal strengths; they feel that they are boasting. However, an employer may have several candidates to interview and will need to know where you feel your special qualities lie, so try to speak honestly without being embarrassed.

WHAT DOMESTIC DUTIES WOULD YOU EXPECT TO BE INCLUDED IN THE JOB?

This area of work is one that is most often the subject of disagreement between a nanny and the family. Some nannies are willing to do all the family's ironing in addition to caring for the children's laundry; others may resent being asked to do any tasks that are not directly related to care of the children. Issues such as extra babysitting duties in the evenings also need to be discussed.

WHAT ARE YOUR HOBBIES AND INTERESTS?

Most employers are trying to find out what sort of person you are, to see whether or not you will fit in with the family. For instance, some families will be looking for a nanny that wants to travel, or one who will encourage children's sporting interests.

Other typical questions if you are applying for a live-in-nanny post are:

WHAT QUALITIES ARE YOU LOOKING FOR IN A FAMILY?

It is very important to you and to the family that the 'chemistry' is right. Employers want a nanny whose personality meshes with their own. Some live-in nannies expect to be part of the family, while others view the relationship as strictly that of employer/employee. Ask relevant questions if they are not answered already, e.g.: Are you expected to eat with the family, and will you be expected to travel on holidays with the family?

FIGURE 17.3
An interview

CAN YOU DRIVE?

If you drive you will be asked if you have a clean driving licence. You may need to find out whether there is a car available for your day off and what your duties are in respect of driving the children to school etc.

DO YOU SMOKE?

The employer will probably describe the house rules about smoking. You should know if any members of the household smoke and exactly what the rules are concerning smoking in your time off in the house.

DO YOU HAVE ANY SPECIAL DIETARY NEEDS OR ANY MEDICAL PROBLEMS?

If you have any allergies or special dietary needs or preferences, you should mention them at the interview. Some employers ask for a letter from your GP.

PREPARATION FOR THE INTERVIEW

First impressions are very important. Dress smartly and avoid lots of make-up and jewellery. Non-verbal communication is also important:

Facial expression: you may be very nervous, but make an effort to smile and to appear cheerful and relaxed;

> ▶ Try to maintain **eye-contact** when the interviewer is speaking to you and when you reply;

▶ **Shake hands** firmly with the interviewer, and try not to fidget; clasp your hands loosely in your lap; never sit with your arms folded.

▶ **Eat before the interview,** so that your stomach does not rumble.

▶ **Don't smoke** even if the interviewer does. It is not acceptable to smoke during your working hours even if the household has no objections.

▶ **Be realistic:** there may be many other applicants for the post; if you are not successful it does not reflect on you personally.

Caring for children outside the family home

I. LOCAL AUTHORITY DAY NURSERIES

Local Authority day nurseries are funded by social services and offer full-time provision for children under school age. They are particularly important in working with families, who may be facing many challenges. Staffing levels are high, the usual ratio being one staff member for every four children. Some local authority day nurseries also operate as family centres, providing advice, guidance and counselling to the families with difficulties. They usually have a staff of trained nursery nurses and sometimes trained teachers or social workers will work on the staff. Most day nurseries operate a system of key workers.

Key workers

A key worker is usually a trained early childhood worker who takes on responsibility for one or more particular children each day. By ensuring continuity of care, the difficulty of separation for the child from his parent is minimised. Parents appreciate having a familiar worker with whom they can talk in confidence about any concerns they may have relating to their child's wellbeing. Responsibilities of a key worker will include:

▶ assessing the child's needs, often by visiting the family before admission to the nursery;

▶ sharing information with the parents on all aspects of their child's care;

▶ planning the child's daily routine;

▶ meeting all the child's needs when in the nursery, involving:
  – physical needs: nappy changing, skin care and bottle feeding;
  – emotional needs: settling the child on arrival each session and comforting her when distressed;
  – intellectual needs: planning a learning programmes to promote development and to stimulate the child;
  – observing and recording the child's development;
  – returning the child to the care of his parents at the end of each session with a report.

II. PRIVATE DAY NURSERIES AND WORKPLACE CRECHES

The increase in numbers of working mothers has led to the setting up of more private day nurseries and workplace creches which care for babies and pre-school children during the normal working week. Such organisations are required by law to register with social services and are subject to regular inspections of facilities, safety and staff.

III. CHILDMINDING

Childminders usually use their own home to care for babies and pre-school children. Similar registration and inspection duties apply to childminding as to day care. The local authority must:

- ► specify the maximum number of children;
- ► require the premises and equipment used to be adequately maintained and kept safe;
- ► require a record to be kept of the name and address of:
- —   any children looked after,
- —   any person who assists in looking after such a child, and
- —   any person living or likely to be living on those premises;
- ► require that they be notified by the childminder, in writing, of any change in the circumstances above.

Childminders are allowed to fix their own charges and many nursery nurses choose this career option when they have children of their own.

Working with children in schools

There are some opportunities for qualified childcare staff to work alongside teachers in primary schools and special schools. There are recognised courses to take after completion of the basic child care qualification (see page 531 on post-basic courses).

Caring for children in hospitals

Some health authorities employ trained early years workers to care for babies on maternity units and in Special Care Baby Units, but the opportunities are decreasing as the care of sick babies becomes more technically demanding. The Hospital Play Specialist scheme provides training and career opportunities for nursery nurses wishing to work with children in a hospital environment.

Babysitting and childsitting

When parents trust you to babysit, they are placing their child's safety in your hands. Babysitting is one of the biggest responsibilities you will ever accept. It is wise to take some precautions when accepting a new babysitting job:

- ► Know your employer; only accept jobs from people you already know or for whom you have reliable, personal references.
- ► Make sure that your parent (or someone you live with) knows where *you* are babysitting. Leave them the name, address and telephone number of the people you are sitting for, and let them know what time to expect you home.
- ► Find out what time the parents expect to be home. Let them know if you have a curfew. Ask them to call if they are running late.
- ► Compile a checklist and make sure you fill it in before the parents leave:

Safety tips for nannies and babysitters

Before the parents leave, ask for the information on the checklist above. Keep the list near the phone at all times:

- ► If the house has an electronic security system, learn how to use it.
- ► Do not open the door to strangers. Don't let anyone at the door or on the phone know that you're there alone. If asked, respond by saying that you're visiting, the children's parents cannot come to the door and that you'll deliver a message.
- ► If you plan to take the children out, make sure that you have a key to lock and unlock doors; don't forget window locks.
- ► When you get back to the house, don't go inside if anything seems unusual, – broken window, door open etc. Go to a neighbour and call the police.
- ► Make sure that you have an escort home if babysitting at night.

Babysitter's checklist

1 Address of the house ....

2 Phone number at the house..

3 Name and phone no. of GP ....

4 Nearest hospital and number ....

5 Where the parents will be ....

6 Phone number where the parents can be reached ....

7 What time the parents are expected home ....

8 Name and phone number of neighbours ....

9 Other contacts e.g. grandparents..

10 Any allergies or special medical info. for children ....

NB This checklist is also useful to keep next to the phone if you are employed as a nanny.

In an emergency:

▶ If there is a fire, get the children and yourself OUT! Go to a neighbour's and call the fire department – dial 999. If you can, call the parents and let them know where you and the children are, and what is happening.

▶ Try not to panic during an emergency. It will not only prevent you from thinking clearly, but will frighten the children.

▶ If you suspect that a child has swallowed a poisonous substance, call 999 immediately. Be able to identify the poison and the amount taken.

Conditions of employment

The Employment Protection Act 1978 and the Employment Acts 1980 and 1982 require that any employee who works for more than 16 hours a week should have a **contract of employment**. This document must contain the following information:

▶ the name of the employer and employee;
▶ the title of the job;
▶ the date when employment commenced;
▶ the scale of pay;
▶ the hours of work;
▶ entitlement to holidays;
▶ sick-pay provision;
▶ pensions and pension schemes;

Specimen Nanny Contract of Employment

Date of issue: ....

This is a contract between (Employer's names) and (your name). (Your name) is contracted to work as a nanny by (Employer's name) at (Employer's address), starting on (Starting Date).

General information

The employers are solely responsible for accounting for the employer's and employees National Insurance and Income Tax contributions. Employers should ensure that they have employer's public liability insurance to cover them should the nanny be injured in the course of work.

Remuneration

The salary is .... per *week/month *before/after deduction of Income Tax and national Insurance payable on .... The employers will ensure that the employee is given a payslip on the day of payment, detailing gross payment, National Insurance and Income Tax deductions and net payment. Overtime will be paid at £ .... net per hour or part thereof. The salary will be reviewed *once/twice a year/on the date of ....

Hours of work

The employee will be required to work (hours) .... (days of the week) .... and may be called upon for baby-sitting up to (nights per week) .... In addition, the employee may be required to work overtime provided that .... days' notice have been given and agreed in advance. Overtime will be paid in accordance with the overtime detailed in the paragraph above. In addition, the employee will be entitled to .... *days/weeks paid holiday per year. In the first or final year of service, the employee will be entitled to holidays on a pro rata basis. Holidays may only be carried into next year with the express permission of the employers. Paid compensation is not normally given for holidays not actually taken. The employee will be free on all Bank Holidays or will receive a day off in lieu by agreement.

Duties (please specify)

....

The employee shall be entitled to:

a) Accommodation ☐
b) Bathroom *sole use/shared ☐
c) Meals (please specify) ☐
d) Use of car *on duty/off duty ☐
e) Other benefits:

Sickness

The employer will pay Statutory Sick Pay (SSP) in accordance with current legislation. Any additional sick pay will be at the employer's discretion.

Termination

In the first four weeks of employment, one week's notice is required on either side. After four weeks continuous service, either the employer or the employee may terminate the contract by giving .... weeks notice.

Confidentiality

The employee shall keep all affairs and concerns of the employers, their household and business confidential, unless otherwise required by law.

Discipline

Reasons which might give rise to the need for disciplinary action include the following:

a) Causing a disruptive influence in the household.
b) Job incompetence.
c) Unsatisfactory standard of dress or appearance.
d) Conduct during or outside working hours prejudicial to the interest or reputation of the employers.
e) Unreliability in time keeping or attendance.
f) Failure to comply with instructions and procedures.
g) Breach of confidentiality clause.

In the event of the need for disciplinary action, the procedure will be firstly, an oral warning; secondly, a written warning, and thirdly, dismissal. Reasons which might give rise to summary dismissal include drunkenness, theft, illegal drug-taking, child abuse.

Signed by the employer ....

Date ....

Signed by the employee ....

Date ....

*delete as necessary

- the length of notice required from employer and employee;
- the procedures for disciplinary action or grievances.

Responsibility for paying income tax and national-insurance contributions will need to be decided; such payments are usually deducted from your gross pay. Those applying for jobs within the private sector may want to consider using a reputable nanny agency; such agencies are used to negotiating contracts designed to suit both employer and employee.

Preparing a CV

It is always useful to compile a curriculum vitae (CV) and to keep it up to date. The purposes of a CV are to:
- provide a brief outline of your life history;
- to set out basic factual information in a concise manner; and
- to help in filling out application forms

Many word processing packages have a useful format for preparing a CV or resume. The main headings to include are:

Curriculum Vitae	First name and family name
Personal details: date of birth, full postal address, and telephone number	**Education and qualifications:** Include names of schools and colleges attended with dates and qualifications obtained.
Employment history: If you have not worked before, include babysitting experience, college work experience and Saturday and holiday jobs.	**Other experience:** Include any voluntary work, involvement in local organisations or groups, sport and leisure interests.
Referees: Give the names, positions and address of two people who are willing to provide references for you. Always ask them first.	

CVs should be neatly typed and presented and free from any mistakes.

Grievance and complaints procedures

If a **dispute** arises in the workplace, either among employees or between employees and employers, it *must* be settled. Usually, this is achieved at an early stage through discussion between colleagues or between the aggrieved person and his immediate superior. If, however, the grievance is not easily settled, then an official procedure is needed:
- All employees have a right to seek redress for grievances relating to their employment, and every employee must be told how to proceed on this matter.
- Except in very small establishments, there must be a **formal** procedure for settling grievances.
- The procedure should be in writing and should be simple and rapid in operation.
- The grievance should normally be discussed first between the employee and their immediate supervisor.

▶ The employee should be accompanied, at the next stage of the discussion with management, by their employee representative if they so wish.

▶ There should be a right of appeal.

Managers should always try to settle the grievance 'as near as possible to the point of origin', in the words of the Industrial Relations Code of Practice.

C A S E   S T U D Y

Problem-solving

Helen is a manager in a day nursery in an inner city area. There are six full-time members of staff at the nursery, caring for 34 children. Two newly qualified nursery nurses have recently been employed, and Helen has noticed new tensions within the nursery. One of the new workers, Sarah, has asked for three weeks' annual leave at Christmas so that she can visit her family in Australia. Darren, who has worked there for eight years, always takes two weeks off at that time to visit Ireland. The other new staff member, Dianne, has suggested a more positive approach to equal opportunities, with more emphasis on multicultural provision, the observance of festivals and more variety in the daily menu etc. One of the more experienced members of staff claims that the nursery already offers equal opportunities and that any changes are both unnecessary and expensive; she also claims that parents are not in agreement with such plans.

In addition, another staff member, Pat, has had a great deal of time off work because her father has recently died; the rest of the staff feel that her absences have gone on for an unreasonable length of time, and they are tired of having to take on extra work.

Divide into groups and discuss the following questions:

1 How should Helen deal with these issues?

2 Do you think they are all equally important, or should any one issue be addressed *before* the others?

3 Which management style works best in this care setting?

Feed back each group's answers into the whole group and summarise the strategies for solving the problems.

The professional development of the early childhood worker

Working in the field of child care and education can be physically and emotionally exhausting, and professionals will need to consolidate their skills and to develop the ability to be reflective in their practice. It is important to keep abreast of all the changes in child care practices by reading the relevant journals such as *Nursery World*, *Infant Education*, and by being willing to attend in-service courses when available.

The need for qualified early childhood workers is increasing, and more courses are being developed. National Vocational Qualifications (NVQs) in Child Care and

Education are offered at some colleges, and these enable child carers to achieve competencies in the workplace. Other courses/bodies which offer professional development are:

- ▶ the Advanced Diploma in Child Care and Education;
- ▶ Specialist Teacher Assistant (STA) course;
- ▶ the Certificate in Social Work (CSS);
- ▶ the Certificate for Qualified Social Workers (CQSW);
- ▶ the Hospital Play Specialist Examination Board.

R E S O U R C E S

Books

Charles Handy, *Understanding Organisations,* Harmondsworth, Penguin, 1976

Robert Maddux, *Team Building*, London, Kogan Page, 1988

Maureen O'Hagan and Maureen Smith, *Special Issues in Child Care,* London, Bailliere Tindall, 1993

Thomson et al, *Health and Social Care,* London, Hodder and Stoughton, 1994

Useful addresses

CACHE – Council for Awards in Children's Care and Education
8 Chequer Street
St Albans
Hertfordshire AL1 3XZ
Tel: 01727 847636

CCETSW – Central Council for Education and training of Social Workers
Derbyshire House
St Chad Street
London WC1H 8AD
Tel: 020 7278 2455

National Council for Vocational Qualifications (NCVQ)
222 Euston Road
London NW1 2BZ
Tel: 020 7387 9898

Hospital Play Staff Examination Trust,
12 Broadwood Close
Disley, Stockport, Cheshire
SK12 2NJ
Tel: 01663 766064

A C T I V I T Y

Evaluating your caring qualities

1 **Think about the qualities outlined above. Do you feel you already possess these qualities? Do you think that academic knowledge is important for someone working in care organisations?**
2 **Evaluate your own interpersonal skills. Can you empathise – i.e. put yourself in someone else's situation? Think of someone you know who has a problem, and focus on viewing the world as that person sees it. Write a description of a 'day in the life' of the person you have chosen, told from their viewpoint.**

Assertiveness and communication

1 Construct an assertiveness self-assessment table.
2 In your work placement, analyse group communication: prepare a record
   sheet, a sociogram and an analysis grid, and record who communicates with
   whom and how often. (A sociogram is a representation in graphic form of
   the network of relationships between different individuals. It is a useful
   technique for observing children's behaviour in group settings.)

FIGURE 17.4
A sociogram

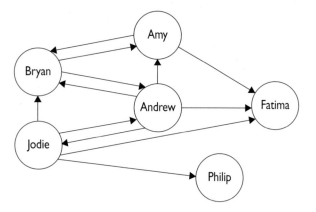

Appendix: Relating modules/units of courses in child care and education to chapters in text

CHAPTER NUMBER AND TITLE	CACHE (DCE) Units	BTEC National Units	CACHE CCE Units	NVQ Level 2 Early Years Care and Education	NVQ Level 3 Early Years Care and Education
1. Equality of opportunity	10	1	All units		C17, C18
2. Holistic child development (0–8 years)	4 & 10	6	1 & 3	C1, C4, C8, C9	C3, C5, C10, C11
3. Working with babies (0–1 year)	7	6, 8	Option A	C12, C13	C14
4. Physical care and development (1–8 years)	4	6, 8	1 & 3	C1	C2, C3
5. Working in partnership with parents	11		4, option B	P1, P9	P2, P4, P5, P7
6. Intellectual/cognitive development: ideas and thinking	4	7, 12	1 & 2	C8, C9	C10, C11
7. Emotional and social aspects of development: feelings and relationships	4	8, 11	3	C4	C5
8. The child as a symbol-user: representation, communication and language development	4 & 6	8	2	C9	C11
9. The child as a symbol-user: play	6	9	2	C8, C9	C10, C11
10. Health education and child safety	3 & 5	10	1 & 2	E2	C2, E3
11. Food, nutrition and care of the environment	3 & 5	5	1	C1, E1	C2, E3
12. Education and care: towards an integrated service	9	13, 21	4	E1, E2	E3, M7
13. The early childhood curriculum	2 & 6	23	2	C4, C9	C10, C11, C24, C25
14. Baby and child health: care and surveillance	5	4	1	E2	C2
15. Children with special needs and their families	4 & 10	22	2		C17, C18
16. Legal issues in child care provision	9	13	2, 4	E2, M3	C15
17. Professional development and early childhood workers	8 & 10	2 & 3	Option B	M3, CU10	M6

Glossary

Adult-led activities: the adult decides what the child should do

Ageism: discriminatory behaviour relating to someone's age

Allergy: a hypersensitivity to certain antigens called allergens

Ambience: the general atmosphere of a place

Amenorrhoea: the absence of menstrual periods

Anaemia: a condition in which the concentration of the oxygen-carrying pigment, haemoglobin, in the blood is below normal

Anencephaly: a condition in which most of the brain and skull are absent. Stillbirth or death shortly after delivery is inevitable

Anorexia nervosa: A recognised eating disorder, characterised by severe weight loss, wilful avoidance of food, and intense fear of being fat

Anterior fontanelle: a diamond-shaped soft area at the front of the head, just above the brow. It is covered by a tough membrane; you can often see the baby's pulse beating there under the skin. The fontanelle closes between 12 and 18 months of age

Articulation: the ability to speak clearly

Attention deficit disorder: a disorder of childhood characterised by marked failure of attention, impulsiveness and increased motor activity

Bias: a predisposition or likelihood that you will favour a particular idea or approach.

Bilingual: speaking two languages

Biological path of development: physical, genetic aspects of development

Blood pressure: the pressure exerted by the flow of blood through the main arteries

Blood transfusion: the infusion of large volumes of blood or blood components directly into the bloodstream

Bone marrow: the soft fatty tissue found in bone cavities

Bone marrow biopsy: a procedure to obtain a sample of cells from the bone marrow; it is usually taken from the sternum (breastbone) or the iliac crests (upper part of the hip-bones)

Book language: the formal language that is found in books – 'And they lived happily ever after'

Bovine spongiform encephalopathy (BSE): A disorder contracted by cows from infected sheep or cattle tissue in their feed. BSE causes degeneration of the infected cow's brain and is fatal

Brochure: a book giving information about the aims and philosophy in action of the early childhood work setting

Campylobacter enteritis: An acute infection of the stomach and intestines caused by the Campylobacter bacterium

Care orders: these are issued when intervention is necessary if there is a situation where 'significant harm' to the child could result

Case law (common law): legislation by rulings in the highest courts

Cataract: loss of transparency of the cystalline lens of the eye

Central nervous system: the brain and spinal cord – the control centres of the body

Cervical smear test: a test to detect abnormal changes in the cervix (the neck of the womb) and so prevent the development of cervical cancer

Children in need: children whose health or development is likely to be significantly impaired without the provision of services, and children with disabilities

Cholera: An infection of the small intestine caused by swallowing food or water contaminated with the bacterium vibrio cholerae. It is a notifiable disease.

Christmas disease: a rare type of bleeding disorder caused by a defect in the blood–clotting system

Chromosome: a threadlike structure in the cell nucleus that carries genetic information in the form of genes

Chromosome analysis: the study of the chromosomal material in an adult's, child's or unborn baby's cells to discover whether a chromosomal abnormality is present, or to establish its nature

Cochlear implant: a device for treating severe deafness that consists of one or more electrodes surgically implanted inside or outside the cochlea in the inner ear

Code of practice for equal opportunities: document stating how the equal opportunities policy is to be put into practice

Communication: facial expressions, body language, gestures and verbal or sign languages – language involves *reception* (understanding) and *expression*. Talking about feelings, ideas and relationships through signs or words

Comprehensible input: using actions and gestures to make what is said understandable

Concept: being able to link past, present and future ideas which share some properties or attributes. A child may sit on a variety of chairs, but a concept of a chair is an idea the child has in the mind

Conforming bandage: a fabric bandage used to secure dressings and to provide light support to injuries

Conservation: linking past, present and future ideas (concepts) but being able to hold in mind aspects of an idea at the same time (decentrating)

Content: what the child knows and understands, wants to know more about and needs to know according to the culture and society in which the child grows up

Context: this is made up of people and provision. It creates both the access to learning and the ethos in which the child learns

Contextual sensitivities: the child is not seen in isolation from the people, culture and experiences which influence development and learning

Creativity: making something of the idea you imagined, for example a dance, model, poem, mathematical equation – i.e. making something through an act of creativity

Cultural artefacts: the objects which are familiar to the child because they relate the child's culture

Cultural identity: feeling part of a culture

Cultural path of development: social, cultural, intellectual, linguistics, representational and play aspects of development

Curriculum: this is a balance between the knowledge and understanding of the child's development, contextual sensitivities and what the child learns and understands

Development: the general sequence in the way that the child functions in terms of movement, language, thinking, feelings, etc. Development continues from birth to death

Developmentally appropriate curriculum: this is a curriculum appropriate for most children at the particular age and stage of development for which the curriculum is designed. The term was developed in the USA by the National Association for the Education of Young Children (NAEYC)

Diabetes mellitus: a disorder caused by insufficient production of the hormone insulin by the pancreas

Diagnosis: the determination by a doctor of the nature and cause of a person's problem

Differentiated curriculum: this helps individual children to learn in ways which are suitable for their stage of development, personality, linguistic needs, cultural background etc.

Diphtheria: An acute bacterial illness that causes a sore throat and fever; it was responsible for many childhood deaths until mass immunisation against the bacillus was introduced

Disability: see Chapter 15

Display rules: culturally acquired patterns of behaviour which hide how the child feels from other people

Divorce: a legal contract separating husband and wife

Dysgenesis: defective development or malformation

Dyslexia: a specific reading disability characterised by difficulty in coping with written symbols

Dysraphism: Abnormal appearance or curvature of the spine

Ectopic pregnancy: a pregnancy that develops outside the uterus, most usually in the fallopian tube

Empowerment: helping people to believe in themselves, so that they feel able to attempt something they might not previously have thought they could do

Encephalocoele: a rare condition with the brain protruding through a defect in the skull

Encopresis: incontinence of faeces (soiling) not due to any physical defect or illness

Enuresis: the medical term for bed-wetting

Epistaxis: the medical term for a nosebleed

Equal opportunities policy: a statement of non-discriminatory aims and values

Ethnic group: a traditional way to describe a group of people who share the same culture, language, physical features or religion

Ethos: the characteristic spirit of a group of people or community, e.g. a happy ethos or a caring ethos.

Exacerbation: a worsening of the condition as shown by the signs and symptoms

Family: a group of people living together or apart who have strong emotional relationships and who are significant to each other through blood or other links

Fatherese: when men (often fathers) talk to babies in a high-pitched tone about what is happening

First Nation Family: e.g. a Hopi family living in Arizona, USA. The Hopi Indians were settled in Arizona long before the white settlers arrived. They were the First Nation in this part of the USA. The Aborigines in Australia and the Maori people in New Zealand are other examples

Fragile X syndrome: an inherited defect in the X-chromosome that causes mental retardation

Gastro-enteritis: inflammation of the stomach and intestines, often causing sudden and violent upsets – diarrhoea, cramps, nausea and vomiting are common symptoms

Gender role: the way that boys learn to be male and girls learn to be female in the culture they grow up in. The gender role might be narrow or broad according to the culture.

Genetic counselling: guidance given (usually by a doctor with experience in genetics) to individuals who are considering having a child but who are concerned because there is a blood relative with an inherited disorder

Goodness of fit: the match between a child's temperament and a parent's way of bringing up the child. This influences the child's social development

Graphic representation: making marks on paper which relate to prior or future experiences

Haemophilia: an inherited bleeding disorder caused by a deficiency of a particular blood protein

Helicobacter pylori gastritis (duodenal ulcer): A raw area in the wall of the duodenum (first part of the small intestine) caused by erosion of its inner surface lining

Hepatitis B: inflammation of the liver, caused by a virus. A mother can unknowingly pass the infection to the child she carries in her womb

Heritage, myths and legends: stories, poems, dances, songs which have been handed down across time; many contain a shred of original truth which has since been embroidered out of recognition

Holistic: seeing a child in the round as a whole person, emotionally, intellectually, socially, physically, morally, culturally and spiritually

Homophobic: fear of gay or lesbian homosexual people

Human immuno-deficiency virus (HIV): A virus which causes AIDS

Hydrocephalus: an excessive accumulation of cerebrospinal fluid under increased pressure within the skull. Commonly known as 'water on the brain', hydrocephalus occurs in more than 80% of babies born with spina bifida

Hyperactivity: abnormally increased activity

Hypoglycaemia: an abnormally low level of glucose (sugar) in the blood

Hypogonadism: underactivity of the gonads (testes or ovaries)

Hypothesis: making a prediction that if you do one thing, something else will happen as a result

Illiteracy: when someone cannot write or read

Imagination: having a new idea which has emerged from your first-hand experiences of life

Immunisation: The process of inducing immunity as a preventative measure against certain infectious diseases

Intellectual/cognitive: these words both refer to the ideas and thinking of the child. Cognition emphasises that children are aware, active learners, and that understanding is an important part of intellectual life. Intelligence is about the ability to profit from experience

IQ: a measurement of some aspects of intelligence, through an intelligence quotient which gives a score. An IQ of 100 is the average

Jaundice: yellowing of the skin and the whites of the eyes caused by an accumulation of the pigment bilirubin in the blood

Laissez-faire: leaving learning to nature: the idea is that if the environment and relationships are good, the child will learn naturally (nature)

Learning skills in context: children learn to master things and become competent when they are doing something that really needs doing, rather than an exercise that is removed from meaningful situations

Legionnaire's disease: A form of pneumonia (infection of the lungs) caused by a bacterium often found in contaminated water systems

Lines of reporting: procedures for ensuring child protection

Listeria: A bacterial infection resulting from eating chilled foods, particularly soft cheeses, meat pâté. It causes a 'flu-like' illness, can also cause miscarriages, and is sometimes fatal in babies and elderly people

Literacy: when spoken language is put into code, it is *written*. When written codes are decoded, they are *read*

Marriage: a legal contract between husband and wife

Material provisions: play dough, paint, paper, pencils, home area, etc

Membranes: tough membranes which surround the amniotic fluid in which the baby floats in the womb.

Meninges: the covering of the brain and spinal cord. In meningitis, they become inflamed because of infection by bacteria or a virus

Micturition: a term for passing urine

Motherese: when adults (often mothers) talk to babies in a high-pitched tone about what is happening

Multicultural: drawing on the rich variety of cultural influences

Multilingual: speaking many languages

Muscular dystrophy: an inherited muscle disorder of unknown cause in which there is slow but progressive degeneration of muscle fibres

Myalgic Encephalomyelitis (ME): Often known as post-viral fatigue, ME is a disorder of unknown origin that causes severe muscle fatigue on exertion

Neonate: a newly born infant (under the age of one month)

The network for learning: this involves children in first-hand experiences, games, representation and play

Neural tube defects: The term neural tube defects includes **anencephaly, encephalocoele** and **Spina bifida**. These conditions occur if the brain and/or spinal cord, together with its protecting skull and spinal column, fail to develop properly during the first month of embryonic life

Neuroscience: studies of the brain which are providing evidence which helps early childhood specialists to work with young children.

Nutrient: essential dietary factors, such as carbohydrates, proteins, certain fats, vitamins and minerals

Oedema: an abnormal accumulation of fluid in the body tissues; in pregnancy, oedema is often shown as swollen ankles and fingers

Open-ended materials: there are many possible ways to use the material, for example clay, wooden blocks

Operations: linking past, present and future ideas (concepts) but concentrating on *one* aspect of an idea at a time (centrating)

Ophthalmologist: a doctor who specialises in care of the eyes

Optimum period: the best time for the child to learn something

Optometry: the practice of assessing vision and deciding whether glasses are needed to correct any visual defect

Orthopaedic traction: a procedure in which part of the body is placed under tension to correct the alignment of two adjoining structures or to hold them in position

Parental responsibility: parents should have responsibility to bring up their own children but may need support in order to do so

Perception: making sense, understanding and getting feedback through the senses and movements of your own body

Peripatetic: travelling about

Personality: the experiences children have of life and of other people influence this, as well as the child's own natural temperament. It thus involves both nature and nurture

Placenta: the organ that develops in the uterus during pregnancy and links the blood supplies of mother and baby; often referred to as the 'afterbirth'

Plaque: a rough, sticky coating on the teeth that consists of saliva, bacteria and food debris

Play-tutoring: the adult teaches the child what is involved in play

Possetting: the regurgitation (or bringing back) of small amounts of milk by infants after they have been fed

Posterior fontanelle: a small triangular-shaped soft area near the crown of the head; it is much smaller and less noticeable than the anterior fontanelle

Pre-eclampsia: a serious condition in which hypertension, oedema and protein in the urine develop in the latter part of the pregnancy

Prescription drugs: medicines that are only available on the authorization of a doctor because they may dangerous, habit-forming, or used to treat a disease that needs to be monitored

Pre-structured materials: where there are only a few narrow ways to use the material 'correctly', for example stacking toys

Principle of paramountcy: the welfare of the child is paramount

Private sector: profit-making services – e.g. a private nursery

Prognosis: a medical assessment of the probable course and outcome of a disease

Provision: the way in which time, space and materials are structured in the curriculum

Psoriasis: A common skin disease characterized by thickened patches of inflamed, red skin, often covered by silvery scales

Racism: discriminatory behaviour relating to someone's race

Repetitive strain injury (RSI): A term for any injury that has been caused by repetitive movement of part of the body; the strain is felt in the joints and muscles, e.g. tennis elbow

Representation: ways of keeping hold of first-hand experiences – drawing or models, dances, music, etc.

Rules of court: how the law is to be applied

Salmonellosis: An infection caused by the Salmonella group of bacteria, generally by ingesting infected food; the organisms can be found in raw meats, raw poultry, eggs and dairy products

Schemas: patterns of linked actions and behaviours which the child can generalise and use in a whole variety of different situations, for example up and down, in and out, round and round

Self-esteem: the way you feel about yourself – good or bad – leads to high or low self-esteem

Self-identification or self-labelling: choosing how you would like to be described

Self-identity: a sense of who you are; liking yourself, respecting yourself and developing the skills and care to look after yourself

Self-image/self-concept: how you see yourself and how you think others see you

Sensation: being aware that you are having an experience through seeing, smelling, hearing, touching, tasting, moving (kinaesthetic)

Sensori–motor: using the senses and your own movement/actions

Sexual orientation: whether someone is heterosexual, bisexual, transsexual or homosexual

Social constructivist: using nature and nurture to help the child learn through people and provision offered

Social referencing: babies and young children look at adults to see how they react, as a guide to how they should react to a situation themselves

Special educational needs: It has been estimated that, nationally, twenty per cent of children will have special educational needs at some point during their time at school. These range from a temporary need to a more permanent need. Special educational needs is covered in more detail in Chapter 15.

Spina bifida: this occurs when the spinal canal in the vertebral columns is not closed (although it may be covered with skin). Individuals with spina bifida can have a wide range of physical disabilities. In the more severe forms the spinal cord bulges out of the back, the legs and bladder may be paralysed, and obstruction to the fluid surrounding the brain causes **hydrocephalus**

Statute law: legislation which is passed by an Act of Parliament

Statutory service: any service provided and managed by the state or government – e.g. the NHS or a local authority day nursery

Statutory services: central government services and local government services – e.g. social services

STD or Sexually Transmitted Disease: infection transmitted primarily, but not exclusively, by sexual intercourse

Stereotype: a limited image of someone and what they can do or be

Structured/guided play: the adult decides what the play is to be about and helps the child to carry this out, for example stacking toys, building a tower of wooden blocks, acting out a scene such as going shopping

Sudden Infant Death Syndrome (SIDS): Often termed 'cot death', Sudden Infant Death Syndrome is the sudden and unexpected death of a baby for no obvious reason

Symbolic behaviour: making something stand for something else

Temperament: this is the style of behaviour which comes naturally to you, for example relaxed

Teratogen: an agent or influence (e.g. a drug) that causes physical defects in the developing embryo

Tetanus (lockjaw): a bacterial infection in which the muscles of the jaw and neck go into spasm. Rarely seen in the UK now because of the effective immunisation campaign

Theory: a prediction about how something will be. This can then be tested out

Tinnitus: a ringing, buzzing, whistling, hissing or other kind of noise heard in the ear in the absence of a noise in the environment

Tokenist: a stereotyped symbol which is like a short-hand code for a culture. It gives a superficial and often inaccurate introduction to a culture, people with disabilities or of different genders

Transitional bilingualism: using the first language in order to learn English (or the main language)

Transmission: shaping the child's behaviour so that the child has the knowledge the adult wants to transmit (or send) to him or her (nurture)

Tuberculosis (TB): An infectious disease, caused by the tubercle bacillus, which commonly affects the lungs. It used to be a major killer in childhood and early adult life

Uterus: another name for the womb

Vaccination: A type of immunisation in which killed or weakened micro-organisms are introduced into the body, usually by injection

Varicose veins: enlarged or twisted superficial veins, usually in the legs (varicose veins of the anus are called haemorrhoids or piles)

Vertigo: an illusion that one's surroundings are spinning, either horizontally or vertically

Visualisation technique: thinking positive images about how you would like things to be

Voluntary organisation: an association or society which has been created by its members rather than being created by the state, for example a charity

Bibliography, References and Videos

Abbott, L. and Moylett, H. (1997) *Working with the Under-3s: Responding to Children's Needs*. Buckingham: Open University Press.

Abbott, L. and Pugh, G. (eds) (1998) *Training to Work in the Early Years – Developing the Climbing Frame*. Buckingham: Open University Press.

Abbott, L. and Rodgers, R. (eds.) (1994) *Quality Education in the Early Years*. Buckingham/Philadelphia: Open University.

Aitchinson, J. (1994) *Words in the Mind: An Introduction to the Mental Lexicon*. Oxford: Blackwell.

Arnold, C. (1990) *Children Who Play Together have Similar Schemas*. (Available from Pen Green Centre for Families and Children Under Five, Corby, Northants).

Arnold, C. (1999) *Child Development and Learning 2–5 Years: Georgia's Story*. London: Hodder & Stoughton.

Athey, C. (1990) *Extending Thought in Young Children: A parent-teacher partnership*. London: Paul Chapman Publishing.

Athey, C. (1998) 'Graphic Representation' (Article referring to Teletubbies) *Early Education* no. 24, Spring 1998.

Audit Commission (1996) *National Report: Counting to Five: Education of Children Under Five*. London: HMSO.

BAECE Booklets (circa 1995) *Equal from the Start; Living and Learning with a Toddler; Let's Go Outside; Maths is Everywhere; Stories and Rhymes; Beginning with Scribbles*.

Ball, C. (1994) *Start Right*. London: Royal Society of Arts.

Bancroft, D. and Carr, R. (1995) *Influencing Children's Development*. Oxford: Open University, Blackwell.

Bandura, A. (1993) *Aggression: A Social Learning Analysis*. Prentice Hall, NJ: Englewood Cliffs.

Barber, P. (ed.) (1996) *BEAM Mathematics in the Early Years*. Available Institute of Education, University of London.

Barnes, P. (ed.) (1995) *Personal Social and Emotional Development of Children*. Oxford: Open University, Blackwell.

Barnet Local Education Authority (1997) *The Barnet Early Years Record:* A Framework *for Planning.*

Barnet Local Education Authority Booklets (circa 1998). Available from Barnet Inspection and Advisory Service, Professional Development Centre, 451 High Road, Finchley, London N12 OAS: *Imaginative Play* (Role Areas, The Home Corner, Small World); *Outdoor Play* (Physical, Imaginative, Investigative); *Natural Materials* (Sand, Water, Clay and Dough, Miscellaneous); *Early Literacy* (Speaking and Listening, Early Reading, Early Writing); *Construction* (Blocks, Kits, Junk, Outdoor).

Bartholomew, L. and Bruce, T. (1999 2nd Edition) *Getting to Know You: A Guide to Record-Keeping in Early Childhood Education and Care*. London: Hodder & Stoughton.

Bayley, N. (1965) in Francis-Williams, J. and Yule, W. (1967) *The Bayley Infant Scales of Mental and Motor Development*. Development of Medical Child Neurology, **9**, 31.

Bedford Local Education Authority (1989) *Schema Ahead Booklet*.

Bekoff, M. and Byers, J.A. (eds) (1998) *Animal Play: Evolutionary, Comparative and Ecological Perspectives*. Cambridge: Cambridge University Press.

Bee, H. (1992) *The Developing Child*. New York; HarperCollins.

Blakemore, C. (1993) *The Mind Machine*. London: BBC Books.

Blakemore, C. (1998) 'What makes a developmentally appropriate early childhood curriculum?' Unpublished talk to the Pen Green Conference, November 1998. Available from the Pen Green Centre.

Blenkin, G. and Kelly, V. (1996) Second ed. *Early Childhood Education: A Developmental Curriculum*. London: Paul Chapman Publishing.

The BMA Family Health Encyclopaedia (1990) London; Dorling Kindersley.

Bowlby, J. (1975) *Attachment and Loss, volume 1: Attachment*. Harmondsworth: Pelican.

Bowlby, J. (1979) *The Making and Breaking of Affectionate Bonds*. London: Tavistock.

Bower, T. (1974) *Development in Infancy*. Oxford: Freeman.

Bradburn, E. (1989) *Margaret McMillan: Portrait of a Pioneer*. London: Routledge.

Bray, M. (1989) *Children's Hour: A Special Listen*. London: Nightingale Books.

Bredekamp, S. (ed.) (Expanded Edition) (1987) (1992). *Developmentally Appropriate Practice in Early Childhood Programs. Serving Children from Birth Through 8*. National Association for the Education of Young Children, 1834 Connecticut Avenue, NW Washington DC.

Brice-Heath, S. (1983) *Ways with Words*. Cambridge: Cambridge University Press.

Brown, B. (1993) *All Our Children: A Guide for Those Who Care*. BBC.

Brown, B. (1998) *Unlearning Discrimination in the Early Years*. Stoke on Trent: Trentham Books.

Brown, C. (1954) *My Left Foot*. Martin, Secker and Warburg.

Brown, N. and France, P. (1986) *Untying the Apron Strings*. Milton Keynes: Open University.

Bruce, T. (1987) (Second ed. 1997) *Early Childhood Education*. London: Hodder & Stoughton.

Bruce, T. (1991) *Time to Play in Early Childhood Education and Care*. London: Hodder & Stoughton.

Bruce, T. (1998) 'What makes a developmentally appropriate early childhood curriculum? Unpublished talk at the Pen Green Conference, November 1998. Available from the Pen Green Centre.

Bruce, T. (1998) 'Deepening our understanding of schemas.' Unpublished talk at Pen Green Conference, June 1998. Available from the Pen Green Centre, Corby, Northants.

Bruce, T., Findlay, A., Read, J., Scarborough, M. (1995) *Recurring Themes in Education*. London: Paul Chapman Publishing.

Bruce, T. (1996) *Helping Young Children to Play*. London: Hodder & Stoughton.

Bruce, T. 'Tuning Into Children'. Booklet to accompany videos. *A Child's World*. (1997) BBC/NCB (National Children's Bureau).

Bruner, J., Wood, D., and Ross, G. 'The Role of Tutoring in Problem-Solving.' *Journal of Child Psychology and Psychiatry*. 1976, **17**, pp. 89–100.

Bruner, J. (1980) *Under Five in Britain: The Oxford Pre-School Project*. Oxford: Grant McIntyre/Blackwell.

Bruner, J. (1990). *Acts of Meaning*, Cambridge M.A: Harvard University Press.

Buss, A.H. and Plomin, R. (1984) *Temperament. Early Developing Personality Traits.* Hillsdale, N.J: Lawrence Erlbaum.

Butler, D. (1987) *Cushla and Her Books: The Fascinating Story of the Role of Books in the Life of a Handicapped Child.* Harmondsworth: Penguin Ltd.

Calvin, W. (1997) *How Brains Think.* London: Weidenfeld and Nicholson.

Carlsson-Paige, N. and Levin, D.E. (1990) *Who's Calling the Shots? How to Respond Effectively to Children's Fascination with War Play and War Toys.* Philadelphia P.A., Gabriola Island BC: New Society Publishers.

Carter, R. (1988) *Mapping the Mind.* London: Weidenfeld and Nicholson.

Clements, P. and Spinks, T. (1996) *The Equal Opportunities Guide.* London: Kogan Page.

Coffey, J. (1998) *Health Care for Children.* London: Hodder & Stoughton.

Connolly, Y. (1983) *Keynote Speech: A Multi-Cultural Approach.* London: OMEP Conference.

Cowley, L. (1991) *Young Children In Group Day Care.* London: National Children's Bureau.

Childs, C.P. and Greenfield, P.M. (1982) 'Informal Modes of Learning and Teaching: The Case of Zinacenteco Learning.' In Warren, N. (ed.). *Advances in Cross-Cultural Psychology.* London: Academic Press.

Chomsky, N. (1968) *Language and Mind.* N.Y: Harcourt, Brace and World.

Clay, M.M. (1992) *The Detection of Reading Difficulties.* Newcastle-Upon-Tyne. Heinemann.

Corsaro, W. 'We're Friends Right? Children's use of access rituals in a Nursery School.' *Language in Society* 1979, **8**, pp. 315–316.

Dahlberg, G. and Asén, G. (1995) 'Towards an Inclusional Approach in Defining Quality.' In Moss, P. and Pence, A. (eds.) *Valuing Quality in Early Childhood Services,* (1995) London: Paul Chapman Publishing.

Dare, A. and O'Donovan, M. (1994) *A Practical Guide to Working with Babies.* Cheltenham: Stanley Thornes.

Davies, A. (ed.) Mason, M. (1993) Inclusion: The Way Forward. *Starting Points,* 13 March 1994, VOLCUF.

Davies, M. (1995) *Helping Children to Learn Through a Movement Perspective.* London: Hodder & Stoughton.

David, T. (1990) *Under Five – Under Educated?* Milton Keynes: Open University.

David, T. (ed.) (1993) *Educational Provision for Our Youngest Children. European Perspectives.* London: Paul Chapman Publishing.

Dawkins, R. (1993) *The Extended Phenotype.* Oxford: Oxford University Press.

Department of Health (1991) *Welfare of Children and Young People in Hospital.* London: HMSO.

Derman-Sparks and the ABC Task Force (1989) *Anti-Bias Curriculum: Tools for Empowering Young Children.* Washington DC: NAEYC/London: VOLCUF.

DES Haddow Report 1933. *The Report of the Consultative Committee on Infant and Nursery Schools.* London: HMSO.

DES Plowden Report 1967. *Children and Their Primary Schools: A Report of the Central Advisory Council for Education.* Volume 1, London: HMSO.

DES 1991. *The Children Act. Family Support. Day Care and Educational Provision for Young Children.* Volume 2, London: HMSO.

DES 1990. *Starting with Quality: The Report of Inquiry into the Quality of the Educational Experience Offered to 3 and 4 Year Olds.* London: HMSO.

Department of Health 1991. *Working Together Under the Children Act 1989.* London: HMSO.

DFE 1994. *Code of Practice on the Identification and Assessment of Special Educational Needs.* London: HMSO.

DFEE 1998. *Nursery Education: Review of the Desirable Outcomes for Children's Learning on Entering Compulsory Education.* SCAA.

DfEE (1997) *Excellence in Schools.* London: HMSO.

DfEE (1998) *Meeting Special Educational Needs - A Programme of Action.* Ref: MSENPAS.

De'ath, E. 'Changing Families: A Guide for Early Years Workers'. *Starting Points* Number 10. VOLCUF. October 1991.

Donaldson, M. (1978) Children's Minds. London: Fortuna/Collins.

Donaldson, M., Grieve, R. and Pratt, C. (1983) *Early Childhood Development and Education: Readings in Psychology.* Oxford: Blackwell.

Douglas, J.W.B (1964) *The Home and the School.* London: MacGibbon and Kee.

Dowling, M. (1995) *Starting School at Four: A Joint Endeavour.* London: Paul Chapman Publishing.

Drummond, M.J. (1993) *Assessing Children's Learning.* London: David Fulton.

Dunn, J. (1988) *The Beginnings of Social Understanding.* Oxford: Blackwell.

Dunn, J. (1991) 'Young children's understanding of other people: evidence from observations within the family' in Fye, K. and Moore, C. (eds.) *Theories of Mind.* Hillsdale, N.J: Lawrence Erlbaum.

Edgington, M. (1991) *The Nursery Teacher in Action.* London: Paul Chapman Publishing.

Egan, D.F. and Brown, R. (1984) *Developmental Assessment: eighteen months to 4.5 years. The Bus Puzzle Test.* Child Care Health and Development **10**, 381–390.

Elfer, P. 'Building intimacy in relationships with young children in nurseries'. *Early Years TACTYC Journal.* Spring 1996.

Entwhistle, I. and Bryan, B. (1993) *Health Education in the Early Years.* London: BAECE.

Erikson, E. (1963) *Childhood and Society.* London: Routledge and Kegan Paul.

Ewles, L. and Simnett, I. (1993) *Promoting Health: A Practical Guide to Health Education.* Chichester: John Wiley and Sons Ltd.

European Commission (Brussels) Equal Opportunities Unit (1996). Review of Services for Young Children in the European Union.

Fein, G. (1984) 'The self-building potential of pretend play or "I got a fish, all by myself".' In Yawkey, T.D. and Pellegrini, A.D. (eds.) *Child's Play: Developmental and Applied.* Hillsdale, N.J.: Lawrence Erlbaum Associates.

Ferreiro, E. and Teberosky, A. (1983) *Literacy Before Schooling.* (Translation Karen Goodman Castro). London: Heinemann.

First Aid Manual (1992) London: Dorling Kindersley.

Froebel, F.W. (1887) *The Education of Man.* New York: Appleton.

Gardner, D. (1969) *Susan Isaacs.* London: Methuen.

Gardner, H. (1983) *Frames of Mind. The Theory of Multiple Intelligence.* New York Basic Books.

Gardner, H. (1983) *The Unschooled Mind.* London: Fontana.

Ghedini, P. with Chandler, T., Whalley, M. and Moss, P. (1995) *Fathers, Nurseries and Childcare.* European Commission Network.

Gifford, S. (1994) 'Number in Early Childhood.' *Early Childhood Development and Care.* 1995, **109**, pp. 95–119. Amsterdam: Gordon & Breach.

Goldschmied, E. (1989) 'Play and Learning in the Nursery' in Williams, V. (ed.) *Babies in Day Care,* London: Day Care Trust.

Goldschmied, E. and Jackson, S. (1994) *People Under Three*. London: Routledge.

Goldsmith's College. Quality in Diversity Project. Department of Educational Studies, Lewisham Way, London SE14.

Goswami, U. and Bryant, P. (1990) *Phonological Skills and Learning to Read*. Hove: Laurence Erlbaum Associates Ltd.

Gura, P. (ed.). (1992) *Exploring Learning: Young Children and Blockplay*. Paul Chapman Publishing, London.

Gura, P. (1997) *Resources for Early Learning:* Children, Adults and Stuff. London: Hodder & Stoughton.

Gussin-Paley, V. (1981) *Wally's Stories*. Cambridge M.A. London: Harvard University Press.

Gussin-Paley, V. (1986) *Mollie is Three*. Chicago, London: University of Chicago.

Gussin-Paley, V. (1990) *The Boy Who Would be a Helicopter*. Cambridge M.A. London: Harvard University Press.

Hall, D. (ed.) (1994) *The Child Surveillance Handbook,* (Second ed.) Oxford: Radcliffe Medical Press.

Handy, C. (1976) *Understanding Organisations*. Harmondsworth: Penguin.

Harlen, W. (1993) *Teaching and Learning Primary Science* (Second ed.). London: Paul Chapman Publishing.

Harris, D.B. (1963) *Children's Drawings as Measures of Intellectual Maturity*. New York: Harcourt, Brace and Would.

Hartup, W. (1983) 'Peer Relations' in Hetherington, E.M. (ed.) *The Handbook of Child Psychology: Social Development*. New York: Wiley.

Hay, S. (1997) *Essential Nursery Management*. London: Bailliere Tindall.

Hazareesingh, S., Simms, K. Anderson, P. (1989) *Educating the Whole Child. Holistic Approach to Education in the Early Years*. London: Building Blocks Education, Save The Children.

Hennessy, E., Martin, S., Moss, P., Meluish, E. (1992) *Children and Day Care*. London: Paul Chapman Publishing.

Hilton, T. (1993) *The Great Ormond Street Book of Baby and Child Care*. London: The Bodley Head.

Hohmann, M., Barnet, B. and Weikart, D., (1979) *Young Children in Action*. Ypsilanti Michigan: High Scope Press.

Holdaway, D. (1979) *The Foundations of Literacy*. Gosford, NSW, Australia: Ashton Skelastic.

Holland, P. (1999) 'Warplay - some gender issues'. *Early Childhood Practice: the Journal for Multiprofessional Partnerships.*

Holmes, J. (1993) *John Bowlby and Attachment Theory*. London: Routledge.

Holt, K.S. (1991) *Child Development*. Oxford: Butterworth-Heinemann.

Hughes, M., Wikeley, F. and Nash, T. (1994) *Parents and their Children's Schools*. Oxford: Blackwell.

Hurst, V. (1991) *Planning for Early Learning: Education in the First Five Years*. London: Paul Chapman Publishing.

Hutt, J.F. and Tyler, S., Hutt, C., Christopherson, H. (1988) *Play, Exploration and Learning: A Natural History of the Pre-School*. London: Routledge.

James, C. (1993) *Play: The Key to Young Children's Learning*. London: BAECE.

Jolly, J. (1981) *The Other Side of Paediatrics: A Guide to the Everyday Care of Sick Children*. London: Macmillan.

Jones, J. (1993) *Chimp Talk*. BBC Horizon Booklet.

Kagan, J. (1988) 'Temperamental contributions to social behaviour.' *American Psychologist* 1988, **44**, pp. 668–74.

Karrby, G. (1989) *Children's Concepts of their Own Play in The Voice of the Child*. Conference Proceedings, London: OMEP 1989.

Katz, L. (1983) Talks with Parents. ERIC Clearing House on Elementary and Early Childhood Education. Urbana, Illinois.

Kempe, R. and Kempe, H. (1978) *Child Abuse*. London: Fontana.

King, P.M. (1985) 'Formal reasoning in adults: A review and critique'. In Mines, R.A., and Kitchener, K.S. (eds.) *Adult Cognitive Development*. New York: Praeger.

Konner, M. (1991) *Childhood*. Canada, USA: Little Brown & Co.

Krashen, S. (1981) *First Language Acquisition and Second Language Learning*. London: Pergamon.

Lee, V. and Das Gupta, P. (1995) *Children's Cognitive and Language Development*. Oxford: Blackwell – Open University.

Lindon, J. (1986) (Third ed.) *Working with Young Children*. London: Hodder & Stoughton.

The Lippincott Manual of Paediatric Nursing (1991) London: Chapman & Hall.

London Borough on Enfield (1997) *Baseline Assessment Scheme: Teacher's Handbook*.

Maddux, R. (1988) *Team Building*. London: Kogan Page.

Manolson, A. (1992) *It Takes Two to Talk: A Parent's Guide to Helping Children Communicate*. The Hanen Centre, 252 Blor Street West, Suite 3-390, Toronto, Ontario, Canada M55 1U5.

Matthews, J. (1994) *Helping Children to Draw and Paint In Early Childhood: Children and Visual Representation*. London: Hodder & Stoughton.

Matterson, E. (1989) *Play with a Purpose for Under Sevens*. Harmondsworth: Penguin.

McKellar, P. (1957) *Imagination and Thinking*. London: Cohen and West.

Meade, A. with Cubey, P. (1995) *Thinking Children*. New Zealand Council for Educational Research, PO Box 3237, Wellington, New Zealand.

Meek, M. (1985) 'Play and Paradoxes. Some Considerations for Imagination and Language. In Wells, G. and Nicholls, J. (eds.) *Language and Learning: An Interactional Perspective*. London: Falmer Press.

Middleton, L. (1992) *Children First – Working with Children and Disability*. Birmingham: Venture Press.

Miller, J. (1983) *Many Voices, Bilingualism, Culture and Education*. London, Boston, Melbourne, Henley: Routledge and Kegan Paul.

Minett, P. (1994) *Child Care and Development*. London: John Murray.

Montessori, M. (1912) *The Montessori Method*. London: Heinemann.

Moore, M.K. and Klauss, P.H. *Understanding Parents' Expectations on Hurrying Children*. United States and England. *OMEP*, **27**, no. 2, 1995.

Moore, S. (1993) *Social Welfare Alive*. Cheltenham: Stanley Thornes.

Moss, P. and Pence, A. (ed.) (1994) *Valuing Quality in Early Childhood Services: New Approaches to Defining Quality*. London: Paul Chapman Publishing.

Moss, P.A. A series of articles (monthly) about education and care in the European Union in *Nursery World,* from August 1996.

Moyles, J. (ed.) (1994) *The Excellence of Play*. Buckingham, Philadelphia: Open University.

'My Belief' Series (1993) Hong Kong: Watts Books.

National Association for the Education of Young Children. 1834 Connecticut Avenue, NW Washington DC, 20009–5786.

National Children's Bureau. Highlights Papers, available to update on topics from the National Children's Bureau, 8 Wakeley Street, London EC4.

National Children's Homes (1990) *Children in Danger*. London: NCH.

The National Commission on Education: A Report. (1993) *Learning to Succeed*. London: Heineman.

Nelson, K. (1986) *Event Knowledge: Structure and Function in Development.* Hillsdale, N.J: Lawrence Erlbaum Associates.

Newell, P. (1991) *The UN Convention and Children's Rights in the UK.* London: National Children's Bureau.

New Zealand Ministry of Education, 1993 (Final draft 1997). *Te Whaariki: Draft Guidelines for Developmentally Appropriate Programmes in Early Childhood Services.* Wellington: Ministry of Education.

Nicholls, R. (ed.) (1986) Rumpus Schema Extra. Cleveland Teachers, Nursery Nurses and Parents. Based on lectures by Chris Athey.

Nielsen, L. (1992) *Space and Self: Active Learning by Means of the Little Room.* Sikon (available from RNIB).

Nutbrown, C. (1994) *Threads of Learning.* London: Paul Chapman Publishing.

Nutbrown, C. (ed.) (1996) *Respectful Educators – Capable Learners. Children's Rights and Early Education.* London: Paul Chapman Publishing.

Oates, J. (ed.) (1995) *The Foundations of Child Development.* Oxford: Open University Blackwell.

Ockelford, A. (1996) *Objects of Reference.* London: RNIB.

OFSTED Handbook: Guidance on the Inspection of Nursery and Primary Schools 1995. London: OFSTED/HMSO.

O'Grady (1990) *Integration Working* (CSIE Report).

O'Hagan, M. and Smith, M. (1993) *Special Issues in Childcare.* London: Bailliere Tindall.

Oliver, M. (1983) *Social Work with Disabled People.* London: Macmillan.

Omotayo, L. (1995) Nigeria Yoruba Culture. Southwark Education Resource Centre, Cator Street, London SE15.

Opie, I. and Opie, P. (1988) *The Singing Game.* Oxford: Oxford University Press.

Oxfam, posters and map, Support Services, 274 Ambury Road, Oxford.

Panter-Brick, C. (1998) *Biosocial Perspectives on Children.* Cambridge: Cambridge University Press.

Pascal, C. and Bertram, T. (eds.) (1997) *Effective Early Learning.* London: Hodder & Stoughton.

Parker Jenkins, M. (1995) *Children of Islam.* Stoke on Trent: Trentham Books.

Parten, M. 'Social Participation among pre-school children.' *Journal of Abnormal and Social Psychology.* 1932–1933, **27**, pp. 243–69.

Pen Green Staff (1995) *A Schema Booklet for Parents and Carers.* Pen Green Centre for Under Fives and Their Families, Corby, Northamptonshire.

Phillips, A. (1993) *The Trouble with Boys.* London: Pandora.

Piaget, J. (1962) *Play, Dreams and Imitation in Childhood.* London: Routledge and Kegan Paul.

Piaget, J. (1968) *Six Psychological Studies.* London: University of London Press.

Pictorial Wall Charts Educational Trust (PCET). Festival Friezes One and Two, Life Stories One to Four, 27 Kirchen Road, London W1.

Pinker, S. (1994) *The Language Instinct.* Harmondsworth: Penguin Books.

Pugh, G. (ed.) (1996) (Second ed.). *Contemporary Issues in the Early Years: Working Collaboratively for the Children.* London: Paul Chapman Publishing.

QCA (1998) *An Introduction to Curriculum Planning for Under Fives.*

Redfern, A. (circa 1995) *Helping Your Child with Reading.* Reading and Language Information Centre, University of Reading/Early Learning Centre.

RNIB (1995) *Play it My Way.* London: HMSO.

RNIB. Welsh Braille Project. RNIB Education Centre: Wales, 14 Neville Street, Cardiff, CF1 8UX.

Roberts, R. (1995) *Self-esteem and Successful Early Learning*. London: Hodder & Stoughton.

Rosenthal, R. and Jacobson, L. (1968) *Pygmalion in the Classroom*. New York: Holt, Rinehart & Winston.

Rouse-Selleck, D. (1991) *Babies and Toddlers, Carers and Educators. Quality for the Under Threes*. London: National Children's Bureau.

Rutter, M. and Rutter, M. (1992) *Developing Minds*. Harmondsworth: Penguin Books.

Saarni, C. 'An observational study of children's attempts to monitor their expressive behaviour'. *Child Development,* 1984, **55**, pp. 1504–13.

Selleck, D. and Purvis, L. (1999) *Tuning Into Children*. Pocket booklet. London: BBC Books.

Scottish Consultative Council on the Curriculum (1998). Compiled by Aline-Wendy Dunlop, Early Years Education Resource Guide.

The Scottish Office (1997) *Curriculum Framework for Children in their Pre-School Years.*

Sharp, C. (1998) 'Age of starting school and the early years curriculum'. Paper prepared for the NFER Annual Conference, 6 October 1998. NFER.

Shaw and Lawson (1994) *Clinical Paediatric Dietetics*. Oxford: Blackwell.

Singer, D.G. and Singer, J.L. (1990) *The House of Make Believe*. London: Harvard University Press.

Siraj-Blachford, I. (1994) *The Early Years: Laying the Foundations for Racial Equality*. Stoke on Trent: Trentham Books.

Skelt, Alan (1993) *Caring for People with Disabilities*. London: Pitman.

Stainton Rogers, W. and Roche, J. (1994) *Children's Welfare and Children's Rights: A Practical Guide to the Law*. London: Hodder & Stoughton.

Steiner, R. (1926) *The Essentials of Education*. London: Anthroposophical Publishing Co.

Strauss, A. (1984) Chronic Illness and the Quality of Life. Mosby: St. Louis.

Swain, J. (ed.) (1993) *Disabling Barriers, Enabling Environments*. Sage Publications.

Sylva, K. and Moss, P. (1992) *Learning Before School*. National Commission for Education Briefing Paper no. 8.

Thomas, B. (ed.) (1994) *Manual of Dietetic Practice,* (Second ed.) Oxford: Blackwell Scientific Publications.

Thomas, S. (1998) *Teletubbies playback*. London: BBC Educational Publishing.

Thomson *et al.* (1994) *Health and Social Care*. London: Hodder & Stoughton.

Trevarthen, C. (1993) 'The function of emotions on early infant communication and development.' In Nadel, J. and Camaioni, L. (eds.) *New Perspectives in Early Communicative Development*. London: Routledge.

Trevarthen, C. 'The child's need to learn a culture' in Woodhead, M., Faulkner, D. and Littlejohn, K. (eds) (1998) *Cultural Worlds of Early Childhood*. London: Routledge.

Tumin, S. (July 1994) *Inspecting Prisons*. One of a series of lectures by distinguished speakers sponsored by *The Sunday Times Newspaper* at the Royal Geographical Society, Kensington, London.

Vygotsky, L. (1978) *Mind in Society*. Cambridge, M.A: Harvard University Press.

Ward, I. (ed) (1998) *The Psychology of Nursery Education*. Anna Freud Museum.

Wells, G (1987) *The Meaning Makers*. London: Hodder & Stoughton.

Wells, R. (1988) *Helping Children Cope with Grief. Facing A Death in the Family*. London: Sheldon Press.

Whalley, E. 'Patterns in Play: The use of schemas theory by teachers and parents'. In *Primary Life,* **3**, 2, Autumn 1994, published for the National Primary Centre by Oxford: Blackwell.

Whalley, M. (1994) *Learning to be Strong: Integrating Education and Care in Early Childhood.* London: Hodder & Stoughton.

Whalley, M. (ed.) *Working with Parents.* London: Hodder & Stoughton.

Whalley, M. (1997) *Working with Parents as Partners in Education and Care.* London: Hodder & Stoughton.

Whitehead, M (1996) *The Development of Language and Literacy in the Early Years.* London: Hodder & Stoughton.

Whiting, B. and Edwards, C.P. (1992) *Children in Different Worlds: The Formation of Social Behaviour.* Cambridge M.A.: Harvard University Press.

Whiting, M. and Lobstein, T. (1992) *The Nursery Food Book.* London: Edward Arnold.

Wilkinson, R.G. (1994) *Unfair Shares.* London: Barnados Publishing.

Williams, K. and Gardner, R. (1993) *Caring for Children.* Boston: Pitman.

Winnicott, D.W. (1974) *Playing and Reality.* Harmondsworth: Penguin.

Wylie, C. (1994) *What Research on Early Childhood Education/Care Outcomes Can and Can't Tell Policy Makers.* New Zealand Council for Educational Research.

List of videos

BAECE, 1994. *Our Present, Their Future.* Available from 111 City View House, 463 Bethnal Green Road, London E2 9QY.

BBC/National Children's Bureau. *The Tuning into Children* project to develop a range of video and print resources and broadcasts on child development from 1996 onwards. BBC Education. Available from Tuning Into Children, PO Box 20, Tonbridge, TN12 6WU

BBC, *Panorama*, 'Early Education' 5/10/1998.

Carr, Margaret (1998) *Assessing Children's Learning in Early Childhood Settings.* Available from NZCER, P.O. Box 3237, Wellington, New Zealand (3 videos, book and OHPs).

Channel 4, *Dispatches*, 'Too Much Too Soon' 29/1/1998.

Channel 4, 1995. *Baby It's You.* Available from good book shops.

Video Reportage Productions, 20 West Parade, Norwich, NR2 2DW. From 1993: *Child Studies One: 0–1 Years; Child Studies Two: 12–18 months; Child Studies Three: 19 months to 2+ years; Child Studies Four: 3–5 years; Child Minders; Fathers Handling Small Children; Feeding Techniques with Toddlers; Imaginative Supervised Play at Home; Restraining Small Children; Supervised Learning and Playing at Home.*

Available from Community Play Things, Darvell, Robertsbridge, East Sussex. Froebel Block Play Research Project 1992, *Building a Future.*

Available from National Children's Bureau, 8 Whakeley Street, London EC4 7QE: E. Goldschmeid, *Infants at Work*; E Goldschmeid; *Heuristic Play.*

Available from the European Commission Network on Child Care. Thomas Coram Reasearch Unit, 27/28 Woburn Square, London WC1H 0AA. *Can You Feel a Colour?*

Available from the European Commission Network on Child Care. Thomas Coram Reasearch Unit, 27/28 Woburn Square, London WC1H 0AA. *A Certain View of the Father.*

Lilli Nielsen Plays with, Lilli Plays with William Videos. The development of children with visual impairment and multi-disabilities. Moray House College ETV, Holyrood Road, Edinburgh.

Pen Green video. *Working with Parents*. Available from Pen Green Centre, Corby, Northants.

Robertson, J. and J. (1969) *Young Children in Brief Separation*. Ipswich: Concorde Films.

Available from RNIB *One of the family*. A series of five videos about children with multiple disabilities. National Education Centre, Garrow House, 190 Kensal Road, London W10 5BT. RNIB.

RNIB. *The World in Our Hands*. A series of five videos about children who are blind. Available from RNIB National Education Centre, Garrow House, 190 Kensal Road, London W10 5BT.

RNIB. *Sound Moves*. Making music for children who have severe or profound and multiple learning disabilities. Available from RNIB above.

RNIB and SENSE. A series of five videos about children with multi-disabilities. Available from RNIB.

Index

learning (*cont.*)
  compared to development 40
  difficulties and dispositions 339–40
  and disabled children 40
  laissez-faire models 43–5
  and play 242, 247
  social constructivist models 45–8
  transmission models 40–3
legislation
  applied in the courts 483–4
  Butler Education Act (1944) 163
  Children Acts 10, 304, 471, 474, 491–6
  court system 485
  Criminal Justice Act (1995) 489
  and disability 490
  Education Acts 373, 441
  Employment Acts 527
  Equal Pay Act (1972) 490
  Food Safety Act (1990) 296–8
  Foster Placement (Children) Regulations
    (1991) 474
  Health and Safety at Work Acts 303–4
  making laws 482–3
  National Curriculum 373–7
  National Health Service and Community
    Care Act (1990) 488–9
  Poor Law (1834) 494
  Race Relations Act (1976) 10, 489, 490
  Sex Discrimination Act 489–90
  Social Security Act (1986) 488
  Social Services Act (1970) 491
  and special educational needs 490
leptospirosis (Weil's disease) 303, 392
leukaemia 420–1
Leuven Involvement Scale 167
libraries 150–1
lifestyle and health 252–3, 449–50
light, learning about 367
line managers 516
lion mark 261
listening posts 357
listening skills 353, 511
literacy 229, 353–60, 380
local elections 486
local government 484, 496–7
  service provision 310–12, 314–15, 320, 322,
    486–7, 492–3
loss and grief 213–14
love 23
low-birth-weight babies 76
Luxembourg 313, 320
Lyme disease 302

McMillan, Margaret 328

Makaton Vocabulary 464
malabsorption of food 288
management style 514–15
manipulating children 216
manipulative skills
  birth to 12 months 82–3, 86–7, 90–1, 94
  normative development 27–30
  1 to 8 years 123, 126–7, 130
Maori culture 229
material provision 244–5
  see also curriculum provision
maternity rights and benefits 64
mathematics 360–4
  area 362
  computers 364
  length 362
  numbers 360–1
  shape and size 362
  space 360
  time 361–2
  volume and capacity 362
  weight 362–3
mealtimes 290–1
measles 396, 424
media 238, 311, 486
medical model of special needs 437–8
medicine cabinet 415–16
Meek, Margaret 164
memory 168
Ménière's syndrome 455
meningitis 397, 407, 409, 423–4
mesoderm 56
micronutrients 61
midwives 58, 60
milestones (norms) 53–4
milia 73, 81
milk and milk products 282
milk spots 73, 81
minerals and vitamins 281
Minimal Brain Dysfunction 465
minority groups 15–16
  ethnic diets 286–7
MMR (measles, mumps and rubella) vaccine
  424
molluscum contagiosum 401
Mongolian spot 73
monogamous relationships 141
mononucleosis (glandular fever) 391
Montessori, Maria 326–7
moral realism 176
Moses baskets 113
mothers *see* parents
motivation 206–7
motor skills